# THE FESTIVAL HOPPER'S GUIDE TO CALIFORNIA & NEVADA

Phil -
Hope you enjoy
the book! Thanks
for the tip.
We'll try to
work in
your request
Enjoy
Darrin

Darrin and Julie Craig

CREATIVE CHAOS ✦ SAN JOSE, CALIFORNIA
PRINTED IN THE UNITED STATES OF AMERICA

*The Festival Hopper's Guide™ to California & Nevada*

ISBN number 0-9624538-2-X



This book has been entirely desktop-published with Macintosh® II and Macintosh IIfx computers manufactured by Apple Computer, Inc.



Mention of restaurants, hotels, and RV, boating, and campground facilities is informational and does not constitute an endorsement by Creative Chaos. All festival dates, parade times, entrance, and parking fees are subject to change.

**Back cover photography credits:** Santa Cruz Chamber of Commerce (Garfield and grapes); Kathleen and Gary McLoughlin (John at Pumpkin Festival).

**Published by:**
**Creative Chaos**
**3108 Acorn Court**
**San Jose, California 95117**
**(408) 249-0657**

*To our mothers, Karen and Patty,*
*whose wisdom, strength and tenacity—each in her own way—*
*motivates us to believe in ourselves*

# *Preface*

Well, here you have it...the ***third*** edition! And with that, you get three major enhancements:

- You'll notice that the book is no longer dated. You see, we encouraged the Chambers to commit to a generic date (i.e., the third weekend in May, the Saturday following summer soltice, etc.) so that this book would not outdate itself in one year. (Hard-Core Festival Hoppers: Don't worry, we'll still come out with new editions frequently!)
- Due to popular demand, the back of the book now offers names and addresses for artists and craft vendors. The list is not as complete as we would have liked, but we figured *any* information might be helpful!
- Welcome NEVADA! She's an awfully big state with some exciting festivals. Check 'em out!

As two working people, we cherish our weekends and like to go, see, or do *something*! So, we wrote this book for others like us—the ones who look forward to Friday and dread Monday; the ones who like to get up and go on weekend jaunts.

**BEWARE!** Try as we might, *The Festival Hopper's Guide to California & Nevada* is not a complete book! We rely heavily on the local Chambers to help us out. If we have missed one of your favorites, or an obscure one you stumbled upon...jot it down on the form we've provided in the back of the book. We'll even give you a discount on your next Creative Chaos book purchase if you contribute!

Please **BE PREPARED!** Festival dates, times and locations have a funny way of changing at the last minute, so we ***strongly*** urge you to consult the phone number we've provided before packing the kids and the car! Please note: the maps we provide are *nearly* drawn to scale!

Enjoy your *Festival Hopper's Guide to California & Nevada!* And if your're ready to see more of America's Western states, *The Festival Hopper's Guide to the Great Northwest* (Alaska, Idaho, Montana, Oregon, and Washington) and *The Festival Hopper's Guide to the Rocky West* (Arizona, Colorado, New Mexico, Utah, and Wyoming) are available at a bookstore near you! If they aren't, order them directly from Creative Chaos (information at the back of the book).

# *Acknowledgements and Appreciations*

***Big*** thanks to Dennis Marshall, Product Manager for Claris Corporation's FileMaker Pro®—it's brilliant; to Ben Bauermeister, President of Elsewhere™ Corporation and creator of an incredibly ***hot*** new database publishing product called DataShaper™.

Without assistance from California and Nevada's Chamber offices, this book would not be possible! Thanks a million for *your* help in making these states so great!

A *warm* thank you to all of our good friends who have encouraged us: Jacqui, Eileen, Pam, Betsey, Greg (and *ditto* for your technical assistance!) and Sue, Kathleen and Gary, Traci and Mike, and Jeff.

Special thanks goes to Independent Publishers Group—especially Mark! We're grateful for your support and appreciate your answers to the zillions of questions we've asked!

Jacqui and David deserve a warmhearted thank you for proofing and doing just about anything we asked—on little-to-no notice! *You're both terrific!*

Apple Computer, we continue to find the power to be our best with your outstanding products! *BRAVO!*

We're grateful...thanks to you all!

# *How-to Use This Book*

## BOOK LAYOUT

*The Festival Hopper's Guide to California & Nevada* is organized by Northern, Central, and Southern California, and Nevada; within each section the book is compiled chronologically by calendar-year.

At the beginning of each section you will find a map indicating the boundaries of that California territory.

The back of the book provides you with a few things:

- Index by town within each state;
- Index by festival within each state;
- A listing of the festival coordinators for potential vendors;
- 1991 and 1992 calendars for quick reference;
- Triva on California & Nevada; and
- Information on how to order other Festival Hoppers Guides!

## STUFF

Generally, "N/A" in our book means that the information was not available at press time. If you require this information for your planning, please do not hesitate to call the number we provide.

Sometimes space got tight in the Entrance Fee area. So that you can decipher our codes: S=Seniors; A=Adults; and K=Kids. *Easy, huh?*

PRCA stands for Professional Rodeo Cowboys Association.

**Creative Chaos**
**3108 Acorn Court**
**San Jose, California 95117**
**(408) 249-0657**

# *Northern California*

# *Central California*

# *Southern California*

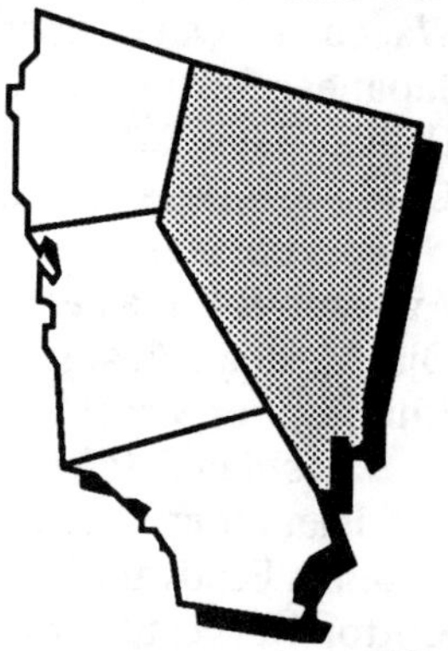

# *Nevada*

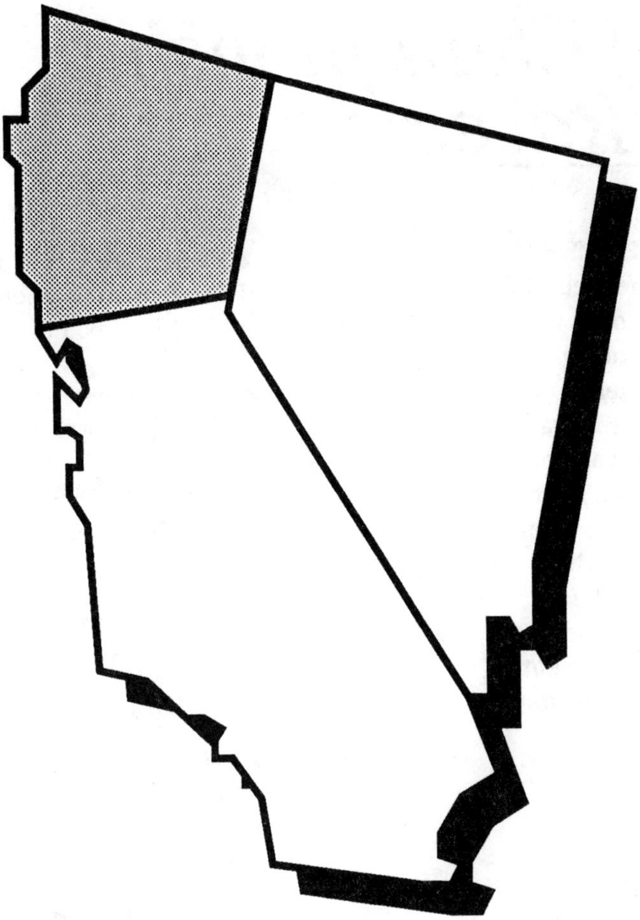

# Northern California

# *World Championship Crab Races*

**WORLD CHAMPIONSHIP Crab** Races? Where else but "where the redwoods meet the sea"—in charming Crescent City. Onlookers root for 9-11-inch Dungeness crabs as they scamper down 4-foot raceways, urged on by their coaches. But I hafta warn you...the *real* highlight of the day is the huge crab feed, which takes place after the races, where you'll be entertained by a band of bagpipes during the feed.

## Crescent City, California

Third Sunday in February
10:00 AM - 4:00 PM

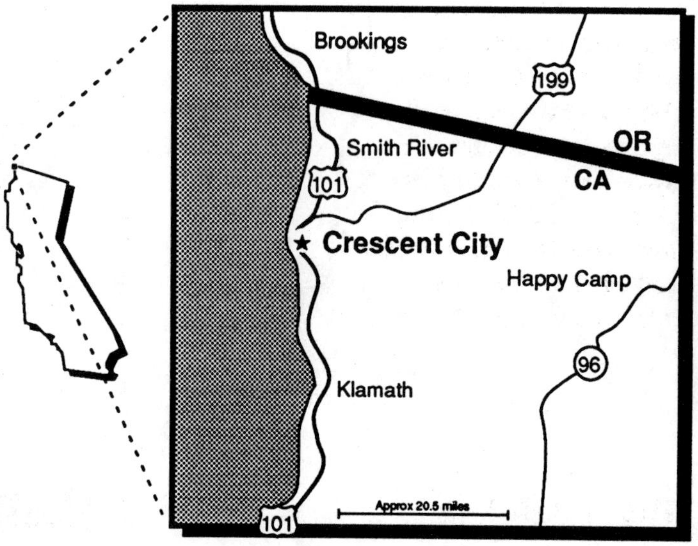


*Up-to-date festival information is available from:*
*Crescent City Chamber of Commerce*
*(707) 464-3174*

## What's goin' on...

Town population: **4,100**
Last year's attendance: **2,000**
Average outdoor temperature: **55°**
Festival location: **Fairgrounds**

| | |
|---|---|
| X | Wine tasting/beer for sale |
| | Food booths |
| | Arts/crafts for sale |
| X | Live music |
| | Clowns |
| | Face painters |
| | Childrens games |
| | Animal exhibits/petting zoo |
| | Dogs allowed on leash |
| | Lost and found |
| X | Bicycle racks |
| | First aid area available |
| | Self-brought picnics allowed |
| | Self-brought alcohol allowed |
| | Stroller/wheelchair rentals available |

| | |
|---|---|
| | Parade |
| | Parking fee |
| X | Entrance fee: Adults $1.50; Kids 50¢ |
| X | Camping facilities: 1 mile |
| X | Boating facilities: harbor |
| X | RV facilities w/ hookups: 1 mile |
| X | Accomodations in town: Breakers Motel, Camp Marigold, Harbor Motel, El Patio, Curly Redwood Lodge, B&Bs |
| X | Restaurants in town: Alias Jones, Harbor View Grotto, China Hut, Rowland's, Ship Ashore, Wakefields |

# *President's Doll Show*

HUNDREDS OF DOLLS ARE dressed in their fanciest garb for the **President's Doll Show** in Tehama. Clean and quiet, Tehama is surrounded by fields and orchards and has a special charm of it's own. A relic from the old steamboat days, except for cars and power lines, it could be right out of the 1870's! The railroad bridge was built in 1870 and planked solid for wagon traffic—and it still is!

## Tehama, California

Weekend closest to Washington's birthday
Daily 10:00 AM - 4:00 PM

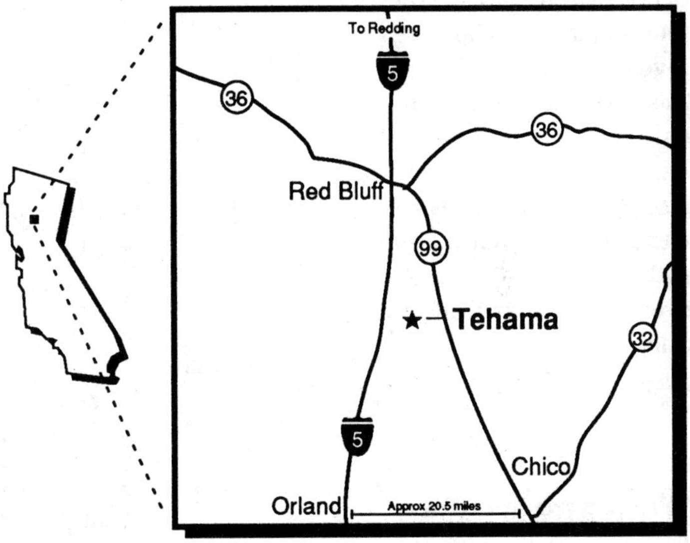


## What's goin' on...

Town population: **350**
Last year's attendance: **500**
Average outdoor temperature: **N/A-inside**
Festival location: **Tehama Co. Museum**

*Up-to-date festival information is available from:*
*Tehama Chamber of Commerce*
*(916) 384-2251*

| | |
|---|---|
| | Wine tasting/beer for sale |
| | Food booths |
| X | Arts/crafts for sale |
| X | Live music |
| | Clowns |
| | Face painters |
| | Childrens games |
| | Animal exhibits/petting zoo |
| | Dogs allowed on leash |
| X | Lost and found |
| | Bicycle racks |
| X | First aid area available |
| | Self-brought picnics allowed |
| | Self-brought alcohol allowed |
| | Stroller/wheelchair rentals available |

| | |
|---|---|
| | Parade |
| | Parking fee |
| | Entrance fee |
| X | Camping facilities: 1 mile |
| X | Boating facilities: Sacramento River |
| X | RV facilities w/ hookups: 1 mile |
| X | Accomodations in town<br>Garden Valley Motel, Los Molinos |
| X | Restaurants in town<br>Berry's, N & B |

# *Boi Kai Festival*

MARYSVILLE (HOME OF California's *sweetest* peaches!) annually holds its **Bok Kai Festival** downtown. In honor of the United States' only temple that worships the River God of Good Fortune, this celebration lasts an entire weekend! The temple, located at the foot of D Street, was erected before levees were built. Bok Kai is credited with preventing floods and averting famines in ancient China.

## Marysville, California

March (call Chamber for exact date)
Sat. 9:00 AM - 5:00 PM; Sun. noon - 5:00 PM

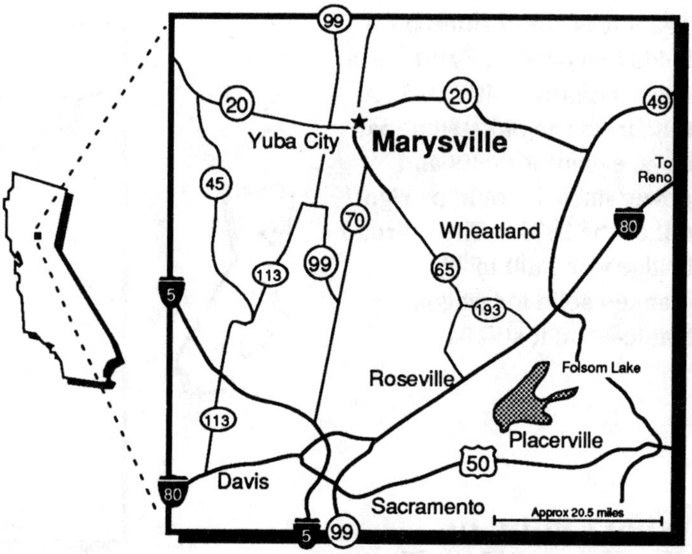


*Up-to-date festival information is available from:*
*Marysville Chamber of Commerce*
*(916) 743-6501*

## What's goin' on...

Town population: **12,000**
Last year's attendance: **20,000**
Average outdoor temperature: **62°**
Festival location: **Downtown**

| | |
|---|---|
| | Wine tasting/beer for sale |
| X | Food booths |
| X | Arts/crafts for sale |
| X | Live music |
| X | Clowns |
| X | Face painters |
| X | Childrens games |
| | Animal exhibits/petting zoo |
| | Dogs allowed on leash |
| | Lost and found |
| | Bicycle racks |
| | First aid area available |
| X | Self-brought picnics allowed |
| | Self-brought alcohol allowed |
| | Stroller/wheelchair rentals available |

| | |
|---|---|
| X | Parade: Sat. 11:00 AM on "D" St. |
| | Parking fee |
| | Entrance fee |
| X | Camping facilities: 1 mile |
| X | Boating facilities: Collins Lake |
| X | RV facilities w/ hookups: 1 mile |
| X | Accomodations in town<br>Bonanza Inn, Marysville Motor Lodge, The Oxbow |
| X | Restaurants in town<br>Daikoku, Cannery, The Eagle's Nest, China Moon |

# *Whale Festival*

MENDOCINO OVERLOOKS the scenic Pacific, and hosts the **Whale Festival**! Due to the large cliffs, you'll have an excellent view of the large mammals lunging through the chilly waters as they head north. Whale-watch tours, both walking and aquatic, are available in this marvelous little town. Purchase a commemorative wine glass and tour the local art galleries—you'll be as enchanted as we were!

## Mendocino, California

Second weekend in March
Daily 11:00 AM - 5:00 PM

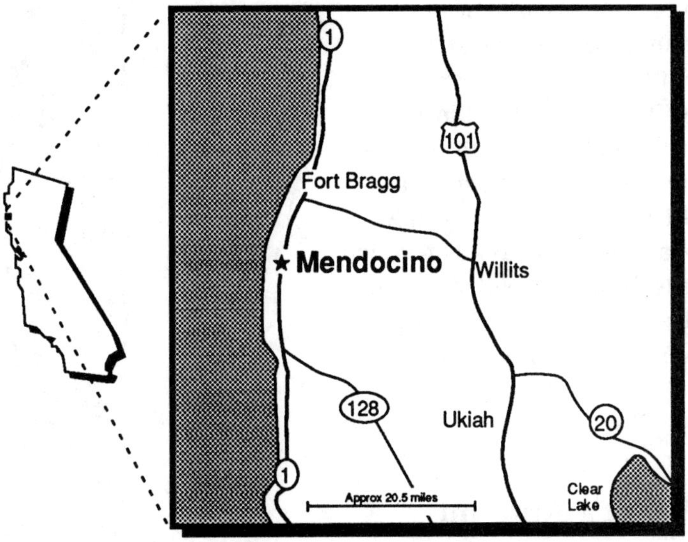


*Up-to-date festival information is available from:*
*Mendocino Chamber of Commerce*
*(800)-7-COAST-0*

## What's goin' on...

Town population: **1,100**
Last year's attendance: **2,000**
Average outdoor temperature: **60°**
Festival location: **Ocean & citywide**

| | |
|---|---|
| X | Wine tasting/beer for sale |
| X | Food booths |
| X | Arts/crafts for sale |
| | Live music |
| | Clowns |
| | Face painters |
| | Childrens games |
| | Animal exhibits/petting zoo |
| X | Dogs allowed on leash |
| | Lost and found |
| X | Bicycle racks |
| | First aid area available |
| X | Self-brought picnics allowed |
| | Self-brought alcohol allowed |
| | Stroller/wheelchair rentals available |

| | |
|---|---|
| | Parade |
| | Parking fee |
| | Entrance fee |
| X | Camping facilities: 1 mile |
| X | Boating facilities: River |
| X | RV facilities w/ hookups: 8 miles |
| X | Accomodations in town: Whitegate Inn, Mendocino Village Inn, Blair House, The Blue Heron Inn, Mendocino Hotel |
| X | Restaurants in town: Chocolate Moosse, MacCallum House, Cafe Beaujolais, Restaurant, Grey Whale Bar, 955 Ukiah |

# *Fort Bragg Whaler Beer Fest*

FOR A WHALE OF A GOOD time, check out the **Fort Bragg Whaler Beer Fest**! Microbrewers from all over the state bring their best to sample! Purchasing the commemorative beer mug will keep the suds flowing while you sample the chowder and seafood—superb! Besides doing some whale watching, take a walk through the boutiques and art galleries for the true flavor of a charming California town!

## Fort Bragg, California

Fourth Saturday in March
10:00 AM - 5:00 PM

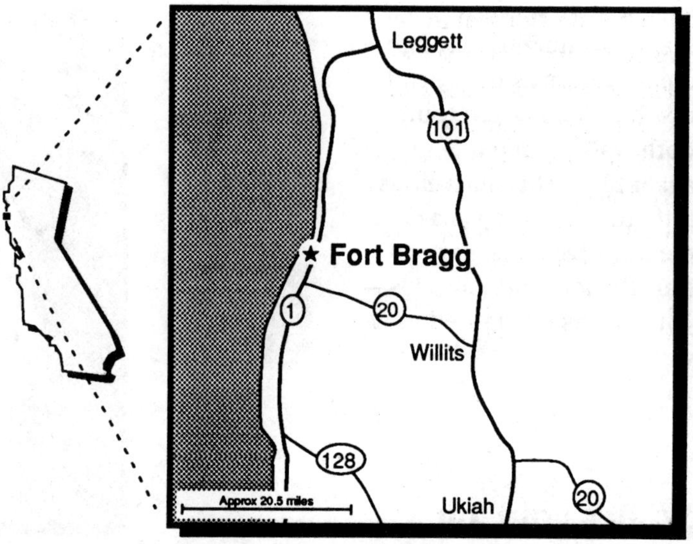


*Up-to-date festival information is available from:*
*Fort Bragg Chamber of Commerce*
*(800)-7-COAST-0*

## What's goin' on...

Town population: **5,900**
Last year's attendance: **1,500**
Average outdoor temperature: **60°**
Festival location: **N/A**

| | |
|---|---|
| ✗ | Wine tasting/beer for sale |
| ✗ | Food booths |
| ✗ | Arts/crafts for sale |
| ✗ | Live music |
| ✗ | Clowns |
| ✗ | Face painters |
| | Childrens games |
| | Animal exhibits/petting zoo |
| ✗ | Dogs allowed on leash |
| | Lost and found |
| ✗ | Bicycle racks |
| | First aid area available |
| | Self-brought picnics allowed |
| | Self-brought alcohol allowed |
| | Stroller/wheelchair rentals available |

| | |
|---|---|
| | Parade |
| | Parking fee |
| | Entrance fee |
| ✗ | Camping facilities: 2 miles |
| ✗ | Boating facilities: Pacific Ocean |
| ✗ | RV facilities w/ hookups: 2 miles |
| ✗ | Accomodations in town: Noyo River Lodge, Surf Motel, Country Inn B&B, Beachcomber Motel, Quality Inn Seabird |
| ✗ | Restaurants in town: Cap'n Flints Sea Food, Coast Hotel, Redwood Cookhouse, Wharf Restaurant, D'Aurelio & Sons |

# *Fiddle Contest*

TOP FIDDLERS FROM THE western states rival for cash prizes in six divisions of competition at the Redwood Open **Fiddle Contest** in Crescent City. This two-day event shows residents and visitors a good time with music of all sorts during the day. A big barbecue dinner and western dance top off Saturday evening!

## Crescent City, California

First weekend in April

Daily 11:00 AM - 10:00 PM

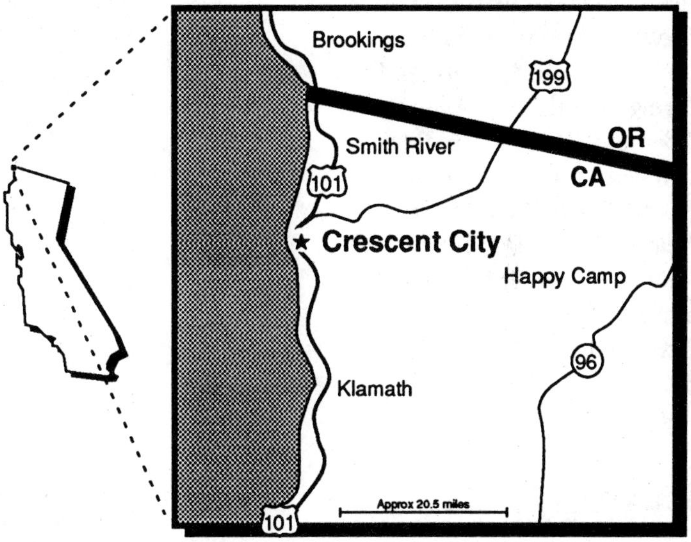


☞ *Up-to-date festival information is available from:*
*Crescent City Chamber of Commerce*
*(707) 464-3174*

## What's goin' on...

Town population: **4,100**
Last year's attendance: **1,200**
Average outdoor temperature: **55°**
Festival location: **Fairgrounds**

| | |
|---|---|
| | Wine tasting/beer for sale |
| ✗ | Food booths |
| | Arts/crafts for sale |
| ✗ | Live music |
| | Clowns |
| | Face painters |
| | Childrens games |
| | Animal exhibits/petting zoo |
| | Dogs allowed on leash |
| | Lost and found |
| ✗ | Bicycle racks |
| | First aid area available |
| | Self-brought picnics allowed |
| | Self-brought alcohol allowed |
| | Stroller/wheelchair rentals available |

| | |
|---|---|
| | Parade |
| | Parking fee |
| ✗ | Entrance fee: S $10; A $12; K free |
| ✗ | Camping facilities: 1 mile |
| ✗ | Boating facilities: harbor |
| ✗ | RV facilities w/ hookups: 1 mile |
| ✗ | Accomodations in town<br>Breakers Motel, Camp Marigold, Harbor Motel, El Patio, Curly Redwood Lodge, B&Bs |
| ✗ | Restaurants in town<br>Alias Jones, Harbor View Grotto, China Hut, Rowland's, Ship Ashore, Wakefields |

# *Shasta Dixieland Jazz Festival*

COME SEE THE GREATEST Jazz Show on Earth—the **Shasta Dixieland Jazz Festival** is one hot number! A few of the concerts to look forward to: traditional jazz, dance, big-band, youth and foreign bands. The Asphalt Cowboys Pancake Breakfast will wake you up on Saturday morning then head out to hear over 15 bands! Advanced tickets ($35.00) available from Shasta Dixieland Jazz Festival, P.O.B. 520, Redding, CA 96099.

## Redding, California

First weekend in April (beginning Friday)
Hours vary

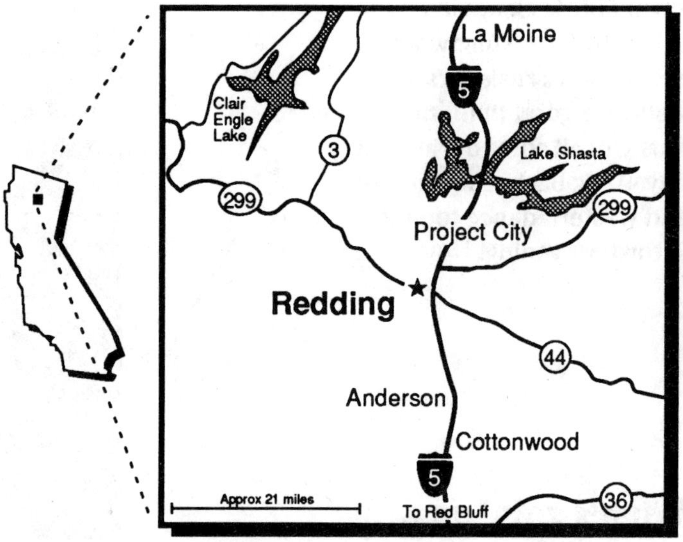


*Up-to-date festival information is available from:*
*Redding Shasta Dixieland Jazz Festival*
*(916) 244-5870*

## What's goin' on...

Town population: **65,000**
Last year's attendance: **15,000**
Average outdoor temperature: **75°**
Festival location: **Citywide**

| | |
|---|---|
| X | Wine tasting/beer for sale |
| | Food booths |
| | Arts/crafts for sale |
| X | Live music |
| | Clowns |
| | Face painters |
| | Childrens games |
| | Animal exhibits/petting zoo |
| | Dogs allowed on leash |
| | Lost and found |
| | Bicycle racks |
| | First aid area available |
| | Self-brought picnics allowed |
| | Self-brought alcohol allowed |
| | Stroller/wheelchair rentals available |

| | |
|---|---|
| | Parade |
| | Parking fee |
| X | Entrance fee: $40 |
| X | Camping facilities: 15 miles |
| X | Boating facilities: Lake Shasta |
| X | RV facilities w/ hookups: In town |
| X | Accomodations in town<br>Budget Lodge, Super 8, Vagabond Motor Lodge, Motel Orleans, Motel 6, River Inn |
| X | Restaurants in town<br>Golden Dragon, River City Bar & Grill, New Orleans Cafe, Post Office, Tortilla Flats |

NORTHERN

# *Apple Blossom Festival*

IN THE HEART OF CALIFORNIA's apple orchards of is Sebastopol, with its **Apple Blossom Festival**. This April event finds the apple trees in all of their magnificent glory—covered with delicate blossoms. The parade down Main Street happens on Saturday, and on Sunday stretch out for the Apple Juice Run. Jest in Time Theatrics provides the live entertainment all weekend in this quaint California town.

## Sebastopol, California

First Weekend in April
Daily 10:00 AM - 6:00 PM

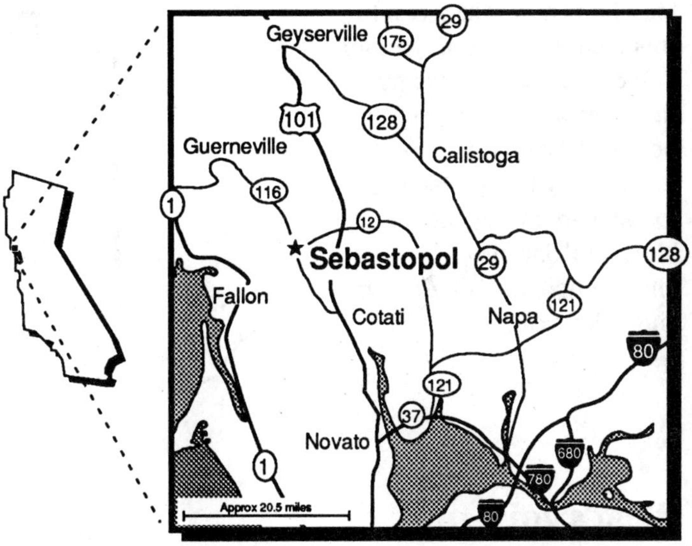


## What's goin' on...

Town population: **3,600**
Last year's attendance: **20,000**
Average outdoor temperature: **75°**
Festival location: **Downtown**

*Up-to-date festival information is available from:*
*Sebastopol Chamber of Commerce*
*(707) 823-3032*

| | |
|---|---|
| ✗ | Wine tasting/beer for sale |
| ✗ | Food booths |
| ✗ | Arts/crafts for sale |
| ✗ | Live music |
| ✗ | Clowns |
| ✗ | Face painters |
| ✗ | Childrens games |
| | Animal exhibits/petting zoo |
| ✗ | Dogs allowed on leash |
| ✗ | Lost and found |
| ✗ | Bicycle racks |
| | First aid area available |
| ✗ | Self-brought picnics allowed |
| | Self-brought alcohol allowed |
| | Stroller/wheelchair rentals available |

| | |
|---|---|
| ✗ | Parade: Saturday 10:00 AM on Main St. |
| | Parking fee |
| | Entrance fee |
| ✗ | Camping facilities: 10 miles |
| ✗ | Boating facilities: River, Lake, Bay |
| ✗ | RV facilities w/ hookups: 10 miles |
| ✗ | Accomodations in town |
| ✗ | Restaurants in town<br>Maestro's, Truffles, Chez Peyo |

# *Rough & Ready Chili Cook-Off*

SHORTLY AFTER APRIL Fool's Day comes the **Rough & Ready Chili Cook-Off!** Yessiree, folks, freshen your tastebuds and take a trip to this beautiful part of Northern California! Local cooks put on their aprons and buy all the beans and cayenne pepper the grocery stores can supply to make this weekend a real blow- out! Sample one...sample all, but do come and enjoy yourself!

## Rough & Ready, California

First Sunday in April
9:00 AM - 4:00 PM

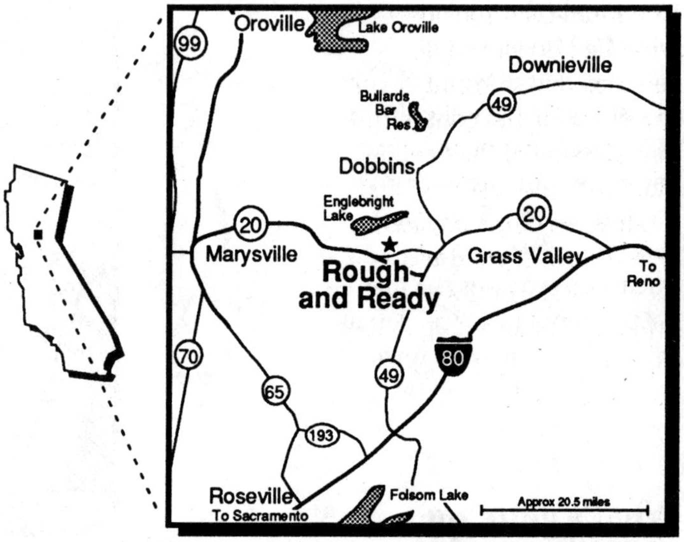


*Up-to-date festival information is available from:*
*Rough & Ready Chamber of Commerce*
*(916) 273-9774*

## What's goin' on...

Town population: **1,508**
Last year's attendance: **3,000**
Average outdoor temperature: **75°**
Festival location: **Downtown**

| | |
|---|---|
| ✗ | Wine tasting/beer for sale |
| ✗ | Food booths |
| ✗ | Arts/crafts for sale |
| ✗ | Live music |
| ✗ | Clowns |
| | Face painters |
| ✗ | Childrens games |
| | Animal exhibits/petting zoo |
| ✗ | Dogs allowed on leash |
| | Lost and found |
| | Bicycle racks |
| | First aid area available |
| | Self-brought picnics allowed |
| | Self-brought alcohol allowed |
| | Stroller/wheelchair rentals available |

| | |
|---|---|
| ✗ | Parade: (time & date not avbl.) |
| | Parking fee |
| | Entrance fee |
| ✗ | Camping facilities: 4 miles |
| ✗ | Boating facilities: Lake Wildwood |
| ✗ | RV facilities w/ hookups: 4 miles |
| ✗ | Accomodations in town |
| ✗ | Restaurants in town<br>Midget Kitchen, Mexican Villa |

# *Fishermen's Festival & Kite Fly*

THIS HERE AIN'T JUS' NO ordinary festival, nosireeeee; this here's the **Fishermen's Festival & Kite Fly** of Bodega Bay! More than 100 boats are scrubbed down and decorated up one side and down the other for the boat parade and blessing of the fleet on Sunday morning! Enjoy the fresh catch of the day along with a glass of wine and a look at all the crafts of local artisans! And look...up in the sky...

## Bodega Bay, California

Third Sunday in April
9:00 AM - 6:00 PM

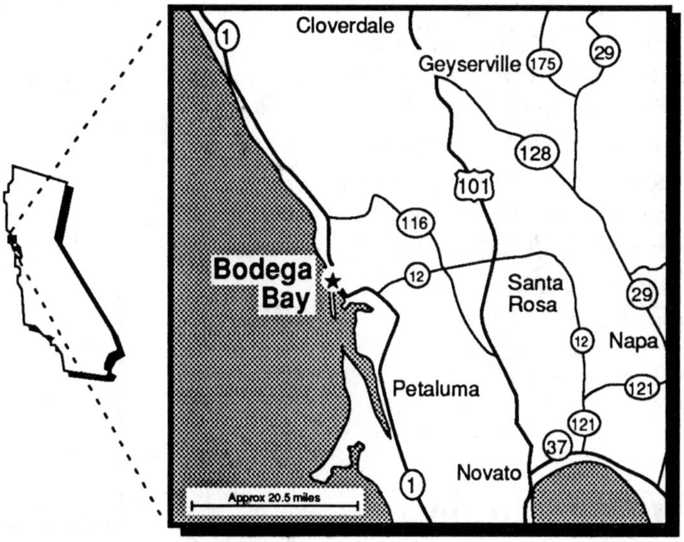


## What's goin' on...

Town population: **600**
Last year's attendance: **3,000**
Average outdoor temperature: **75°**
Festival location: **Westside Park**

*Up-to-date festival information is available from:*
*Bodega Bay Candies & Kites*
*(707) 875-3422*

- X Wine tasting/beer for sale
- X Food booths
- X Arts/crafts for sale
- X Live music
- Clowns
- X Face painters
- X Childrens games
- Animal exhibits/petting zoo
- Dogs allowed on leash
- Lost and found
- Bicycle racks
- First aid area available
- X Self-brought picnics allowed
- Self-brought alcohol allowed
- Stroller/wheelchair rentals available

- X Parade: boat parade
- Parking fee
- Entrance fee
- X Camping facilities: 1 mile
- X Boating facilities: Bodega Bay
- X RV facilities w/ hookups: 1 mile
- X Accomodations in town: Taylor's Estero Vista Inn
- X Restaurants in town

# *Lamb Derby*

"BAAA, BAAA, BLACK SHEEP have you any wool?" That little lambie-pie just may be at the Willows **Lamb Derby** festival being sheared—right now! This tradition of sheep-dog competitions, demos of sheepherding and sheep sheering began in 1932! But these are just the "watching" parts of the festival—the really good stuff is being marinated and barbecued!

## Willows, California

First Monday through Sunday in May
Daily noon - 9:00 PM

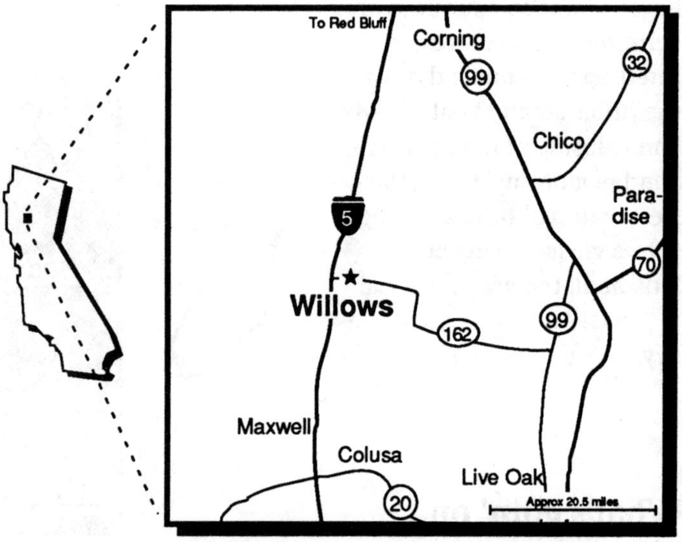


*Up-to-date festival information is available from:*
*Willows Chamber of Commerce*
*(916) 934-8150*

## What's goin' on...

Town population: **6,000**
Last year's attendance: **N/A**
Average outdoor temperature: **75°**
Festival location: **Downtown**

| | |
|---|---|
| X | Wine tasting/beer for sale |
| X | Food booths |
| X | Arts/crafts for sale |
| X | Live music |
| X | Clowns |
| X | Face painters |
| X | Childrens games |
| X | Animal exhibits/petting zoo |
| X | Dogs allowed on leash |
| | Lost and found |
| | Bicycle racks |
| | First aid area available |
| X | Self-brought picnics allowed |
| | Self-brought alcohol allowed |
| | Stroller/wheelchair rentals available |

| | |
|---|---|
| X | Parade: (time & date not avbl.) |
| | Parking fee |
| | Entrance fee |
| X | Camping facilities: [illegible] miles |
| X | Boating facilities: Stony Gorge Res. |
| X | RV facilities w/ hookups: 3 miles |
| X | Accomodations in town |
| X | Restaurants in town |

# *Olivehurst Spring Festival*

THE LITTLE LEAGUE PANcake breakfast launches the **Olivehurst Spring Festival**. Handicrafts, art and food booths line 9th Avenue in this beautiful mountain town. There are museums throughout Yuba County waiting to be explored, or check out the nearby waterways—teemed with fish and waterfowl to challenge fly fisherpeople and outdoorspeople!

## Olivehurst, California

Second weekend in May

Daily 7:00 AM till you're tired!

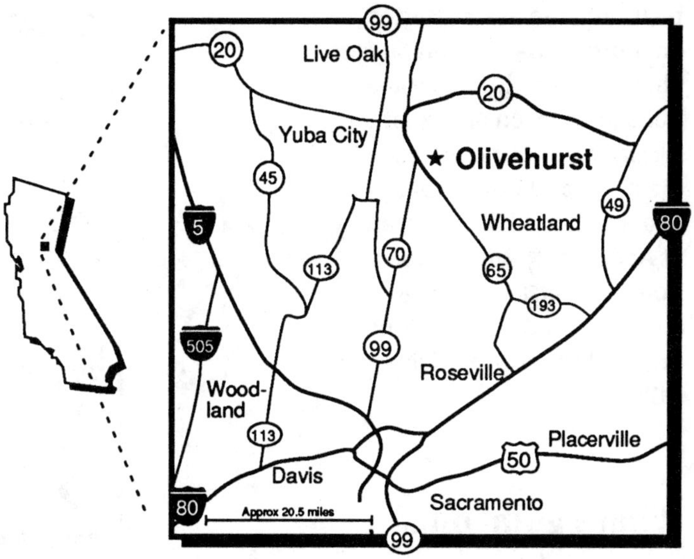


## What's goin' on...

Town population: **9,000**

Last year's attendance: **10,000**

Average outdoor temperature: **78°**

Festival location: **Park & Community Center**

☞ *Up-to-date festival information is available from:*
*Olivehurst Chamber of Commerce*
*(916) 743-6501*

| | |
|---|---|
| X | Wine tasting/beer for sale |
| X | Food booths |
| X | Arts/crafts for sale |
| X | Live music |
| X | Clowns |
| X | Face painters |
| X | Childrens games |
| | Animal exhibits/petting zoo |
| | Dogs allowed on leash |
| | Lost and found |
| X | Bicycle racks |
| | First aid area available |
| X | Self-brought picnics allowed |
| | Self-brought alcohol allowed |
| | Stroller/wheelchair rentals available |

| | |
|---|---|
| X | Parade: Sat. 11:00 AM on 9th St. |
| | Parking fee |
| | Entrance fee |
| X | Camping facilities: 1 mile |
| X | Boating facilities: Collins Lake |
| X | RV facilities w/ hookups: 1 mile |
| X | Accomodations in town<br>Bonanza Inn, Marysville Motor Lodge, The Oxbow |
| X | Restaurants in town<br>Daikoku, Cannery, The Eagle's Nest, China Moon |

# *Sutter Buttes Day*

**SUTTER BUTTES DAY** IS A terrific way to honor "the world's smallest mountain range!" Both unique and beautiful, the Sutter Buttes lie on a broad plain about 50 feet above sea level. The mountains are a circular roseate formation about nine miles in diameter and cover some 75 square miles. The celebration, at Acacia and Butte House Roads in Sutter, offers good food and cold beer. Unique arts and crafts are offered for sale.

## Sutter, California

Second Saturday in May
10:00 AM - 4:00 PM

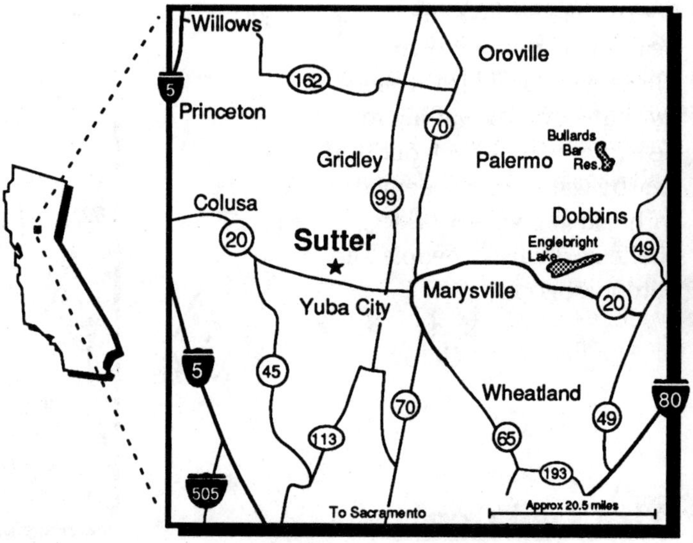


*Up-to-date festival information is available from:*
*Sutter Chamber of Commerce*
*(916) 743-6501*

## What's goin' on...

Town population: **2,225**
Last year's attendance: **2,000**
Average outdoor temperature: **70°**
Festival location: **Downtown**

- X Wine tasting/beer for sale
- X Food booths
- X Arts/crafts for sale
- X Live music
- X Clowns
- X Face painters
- X Childrens games
- Animal exhibits/petting zoo
- Dogs allowed on leash
- Lost and found
- Bicycle racks
- First aid area available
- X Self-brought picnics allowed
- Self-brought alcohol allowed
- Stroller/wheelchair rentals available

- X Parade: Sat. 10:00 AM downtown
- Parking fee
- Entrance fee
- X Camping facilities: 2 miles
- X Boating facilities: Sacramento River
- X RV facilities w/ hookups: In town
- X Accomodations in town
- X Restaurants in town

# *Windsor Day Festival*

IT'S A FINE LITTLE TOWN, that Windsor is! Well then, come on down and check out the **Windsor Day Festival**—where you can try your french fries with some home-made catsup from the Catsup Cook-Off Contest! There's live entertainment and food, crafts, and even game booths for the kids. While visiting, take a drive up to beautiful Lake Sonoma for an afternoon picnic, or check out the new Doom Flume Waterslides!

## Windsor, California

Second Saturday in May
10:00 AM - 5:00 PM

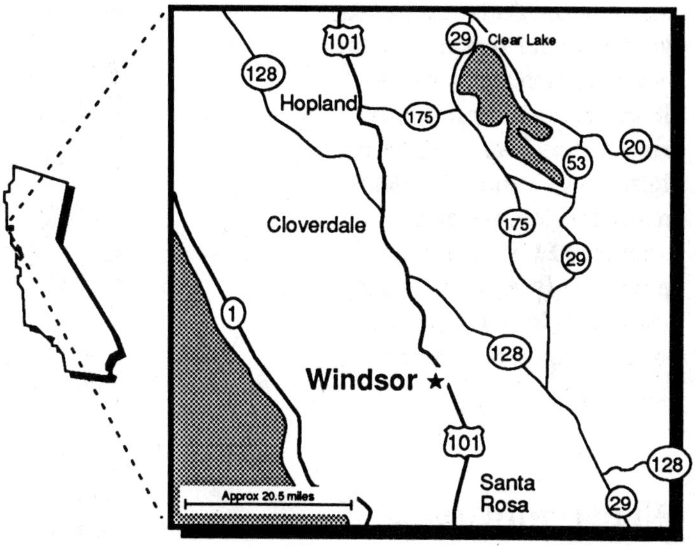


## What's goin' on...

Town population: **8,500**
Last year's attendance: **2,000**
Average outdoor temperature: **78°**
Festival location: **Keiser Park**

*Up-to-date festival information is available from:*
*Windsor Chamber of Commerce*
*(707) 838-7285*

| | |
|---|---|
| ✗ | Wine tasting/beer for sale |
| ✗ | Food booths |
| ✗ | Arts/crafts for sale |
| ✗ | Live music |
| ✗ | Clowns |
| ✗ | Face painters |
| ✗ | Childrens games |
| ✗ | Animal exhibits/petting zoo |
| ✗ | Dogs allowed on leash |
| ✗ | Lost and found |
| ✗ | Bicycle racks |
| ✗ | First aid area available |
| ✗ | Self-brought picnics allowed |
| | Self-brought alcohol allowed |
| | Stroller/wheelchair rentals available |

| | |
|---|---|
| ✗ | Parade: 10:00 AM downtown |
| | Parking fee |
| | Entrance fee |
| ✗ | Camping facilities: 10 miles |
| ✗ | Boating facilities: Lake Sonoma |
| ✗ | RV facilities w/ hookups: 1 mile |
| ✗ | Accomodations in town<br>Country Meadow Inn |
| ✗ | Restaurants in town<br>John Ash & Company |

# *Be-Bop & Brew*

AT THE **BE-BOP AND BREW**, you'll taste beers brought in by nearly 20 microbrewers from California, Oregon, and Washington. Four jazz bands will keep your mood light as you chat with the brewers themselves and sample the fruits of their labor! Many of these beers cannot be found in stores—like the great Steelhead Extra Pale Ale from Mad River Brewing Company! This is a splendid tribute to superb brewers! ***Cheers!***

## Arcata, California

Mother's Day
Noon - 6:00 PM

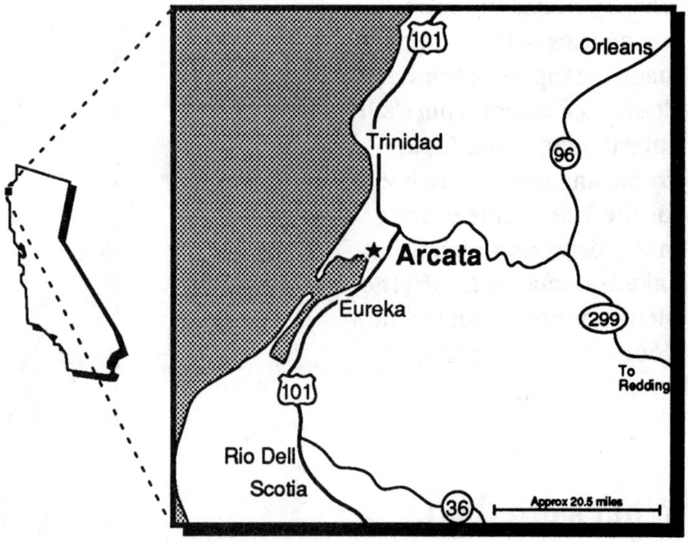


*Up-to-date festival information is available from:*
*Arcata Chamber of Commerce*
*(707) 822-3619*

## What's goin' on...

Town population: **15,000**
Last year's attendance: **3,000**
Average outdoor temperature: **60°**
Festival location: **Redwood Community Park**

- ✗ Wine tasting/beer for sale
- ✗ Food booths
- Arts/crafts for sale
- ✗ Live music
- Clowns
- Face painters
- Childrens games
- Animal exhibits/petting zoo
- ✗ Dogs allowed on leash
- ✗ Lost and found
- ✗ Bicycle racks
- First aid area available
- ✗ Self-brought picnics allowed
- ✗ Self-brought alcohol allowed
- Stroller/wheelchair rentals available

- Parade
- Parking fee
- ✗ Entrance fee: Adults $10; Kids $5
- ✗ Camping facilities. 17 miles
- ✗ Boating facilities: Humboldt Bay
- ✗ RV facilities w/ hookups: 3 miles
- ✗ Accomodations in town
  Red Lion, The Plough & Stars Country Inn B&B, The Lady Anne B&B, Super 8
- ✗ Restaurants in town
  Humboldt Brewery, Ottavio's, Abruzzi, Golden Harvest Cafe, Wildflower Cafe, In the Best of Taste

# *Red Suspenders Days*

**RED SUSPENDERS DAYS IN** Gridley offers small-town old-time fun such as bed races, a mule show, and a firemen's muster. Runs of 5K and 10K provide a more contemporary touch. This all-day Saturday event starts with a pancake breakfast and extends well into the balmy night with a moonlit dance until midnight. Among the craft-booth temptations are stitchery, stained glass, and pressed flowers.

## Gridley, California

Third Saturday in May
7:00 AM - 1:00 AM

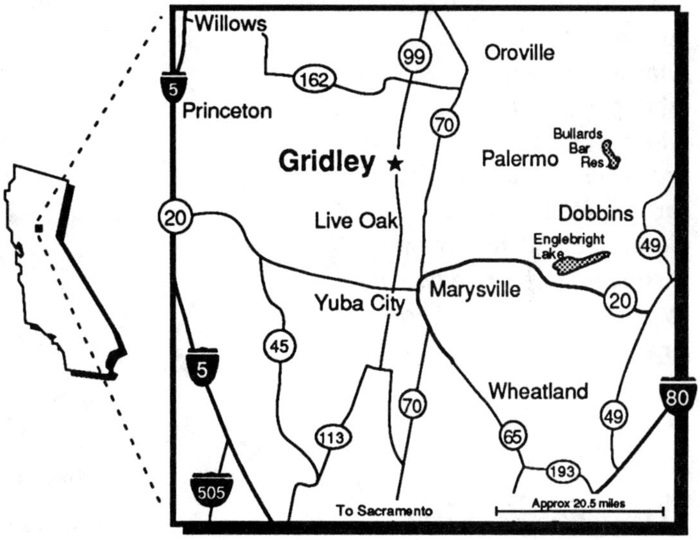


*Up-to-date festival information is available from:*
*Gridley Chamber of Commerce*
*(916) 846-3142*

## What's goin' on...

Town population: **4,400**
Last year's attendance: **10,000**
Average outdoor temperature: **85°**
Festival location: **Downtown park**

| | |
|---|---|
| | Wine tasting/beer for sale |
| ✗ | Food booths |
| ✗ | Arts/crafts for sale |
| ✗ | Live music |
| | Clowns |
| ✗ | Face painters |
| ✗ | Childrens games |
| | Animal exhibits/petting zoo |
| | Dogs allowed on leash |
| | Lost and found |
| | Bicycle racks |
| ✗ | First aid area available |
| ✗ | Self-brought picnics allowed |
| ✗ | Self-brought alcohol allowed |
| | Stroller/wheelchair rentals available |

| | |
|---|---|
| ✗ | Parade: 10:00 AM on Hazel & Virginia |
| | Parking fee |
| | Entrance fee |
| | Camping facilities |
| | Boating facilities |
| | RV facilities w/ hookups |
| ✗ | Accomodations in town<br>McCracken's Inn, Pacific Motel, Thresher Mansion |
| ✗ | Restaurants in town<br>Casa Lupe, Rib City, Furrows, Jerry's |

# *Community Festival & Collectors Car Show*

WILLITS' **COMMUNITY Festival & Collectors' Car Show** takes place in a little community where Highway 101 narrows down to a two-lane road to go through this charming town. Parducci winery will be on hand to whet your appetite, while you snack on the various goodies for sale. Willits is home to the Skunk Train, which snakes through immense redwoods to the coastal town of Fort Bragg.

## Willits, California

Third Saturday in May
10:00 AM - 6:00 PM

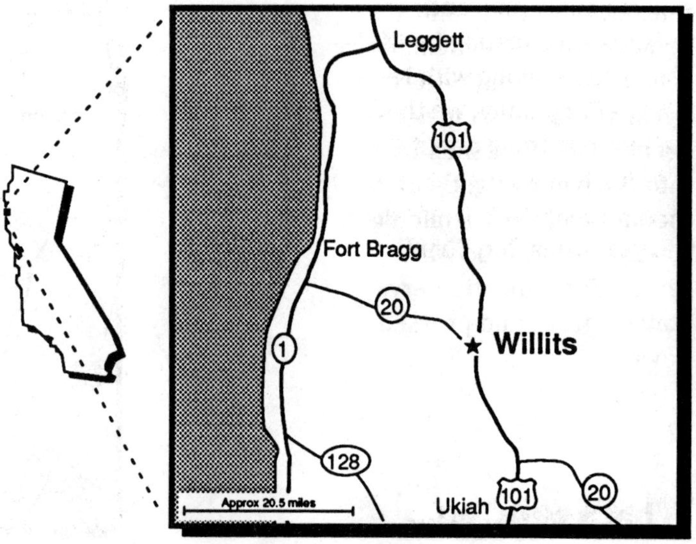


*Up-to-date festival information is available from:*
*Willits Chamber of Commerce*
*(707) 459-7910*

## What's goin' on...

Town population: **5,100**
Last year's attendance: **2,000**
Average outdoor temperature: **80°**
Festival location: **Downtown**

| | |
|---|---|
| ✗ | Wine tasting/beer for sale |
| ✗ | Food booths |
| ✗ | Arts/crafts for sale |
| ✗ | Live music |
| | Clowns |
| | Face painters |
| | Childrens games |
| | Animal exhibits/petting zoo |
| | Dogs allowed on leash |
| ✗ | Lost and found |
| | Bicycle racks |
| | First aid area available |
| ✗ | Self-brought picnics allowed |
| | Self-brought alcohol allowed |
| | Stroller/wheelchair rentals available |

| | |
|---|---|
| | Parade |
| | Parking fee |
| | Entrance fee |
| ✗ | Camping facilities. 2 miles |
| ✗ | Boating facilities: Lake Mendocino |
| ✗ | RV facilities w/ hookups: 2 miles |
| ✗ | Accomodations in town<br>Old West Inn, Brooktrail Lodge |
| ✗ | Restaurants in town<br>Old West Inn, Brooktrail Lodge |

# *Windsor Laff-Off*

LANDMARK VINEYARDS marks the spot for the **Windsor Laff-Off!** This hysterical evening of comedy begins at 6:00 p.m. and features wine tasting by the host winery, along with local talent. (Personally, we think the funniest thing about this little festival was that the person to contact for more information is Ben Funn!)

## Windsor, California

Third Saturday in May
6:00 PM - 9:00 PM

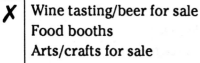

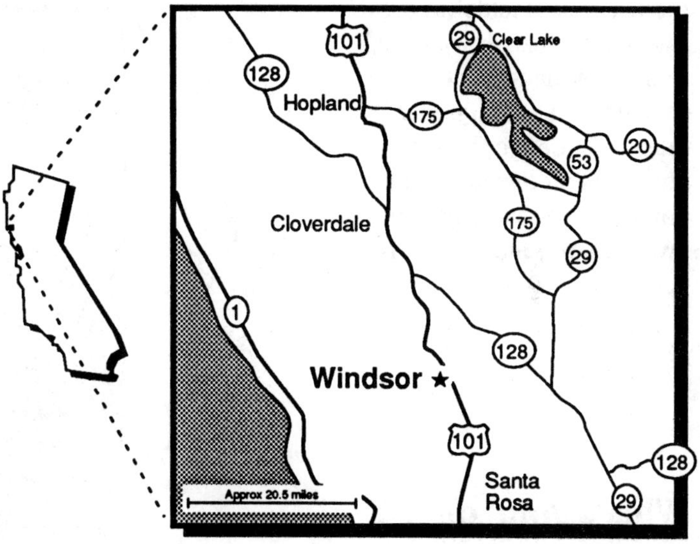


*Up-to-date festival information is available from:*
*Windsor Chamber of Commerce*
*(707) 838-7285*

## What's goin' on...

Town population: **8,500**
Last year's attendance: **300**
Average outdoor temperature: **75°**
Festival location: **Landmark Vineyards**

| | |
|---|---|
| X | Wine tasting/beer for sale |
| | Food booths |
| | Arts/crafts for sale |
| X | Live music |
| X | Clowns |
| | Face painters |
| | Childrens games |
| | Animal exhibits/petting zoo |
| | Dogs allowed on leash |
| | Lost and found |
| X | Bicycle racks |
| X | First aid area available |
| X | Self-brought picnics allowed |
| | Self-brought alcohol allowed |
| | Stroller/wheelchair rentals available |

| | |
|---|---|
| | Parade |
| | Parking fee |
| X | Entrance fee: Adults $5; Kids free |
| X | Camping facilities: 1 mile |
| X | Boating facilities: Lake Sonoma |
| X | RV facilities w/ hookups: 1 mile |
| X | Accomodations in town |
| X | Restaurants in town<br>Kevin's, Casey's Place |

# *Russian River Wine Festival*

HOW ABOUT WE MEET YOU at the **Russian River Wine Festival** in Healdsburg this year? Taking place at the picturesque Healdsburg Historical Plaza downtown, this is the place to do some serious wine tasting! Jazz music will dance through your ears all day long while you enjoy the winemakers favorites and munch on the goodies.

## Healdsburg, California

Sunday following Mother's Day
Noon - 5:00 PM

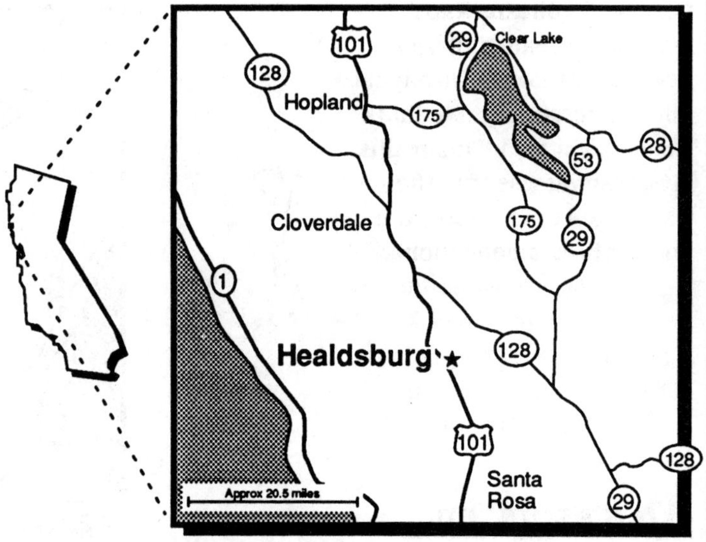


*Up-to-date festival information is available from:*
*Healdsburg Chamber of Commerce*
*(707) 433-6935*

## What's goin' on...

Town population: **9,800**
Last year's attendance: **4,000**
Average outdoor temperature: **83°**
Festival location: **Historic Plaza Park**

| | |
|---|---|
| X | Wine tasting/beer for sale |
| X | Food booths |
| X | Arts/crafts for sale |
| X | Live music |
| | Clowns |
| | Face painters |
| | Childrens games |
| | Animal exhibits/petting zoo |
| | Dogs allowed on leash |
| X | Lost and found |
| X | Bicycle racks |
| | First aid area available |
| X | Self-brought picnics allowed |
| | Self-brought alcohol allowed |
| | Stroller/wheelchair rentals available |

| | |
|---|---|
| | Parade |
| | Parking fee |
| | Entrance fee |
| X | Camping facilities: 5 10 miles |
| X | Boating facilities: Lake Sonoma |
| X | RV facilities w/ hookups: 10 miles |
| X | Accomodations in town<br>Dry Creek Inn, Healdsburg Inn, Haydon House, Grape Leaf Inn, Madrona Manor |
| X | Restaurants in town<br>Plaza Grill, Tre Scalini, Jacob Horner |

# *The* *Great Arcata-to-Ferndale Cross-Country Kinetic Sculpture Race*

HERE IT IS: THE ZANIEST FUN to hit Humboldt County each year! **"The Great Arcata-to-Ferndale Cross-Country Kinetic Sculpture Race"** begins at Arcata's Plaza at the noon whistle on Saturday (but there's an awfully fun dance on Friday night)! This people-powered race (allowing absolutely no batteries or motors)—in a collection of vehicles that must endure mud flats, sand dunes, Humboldt Bay, and the Eel River over a three-day period! And what works of *art* they are...

## Arcata, California

Memorial Day weekend (beginning Friday)
Hours vary

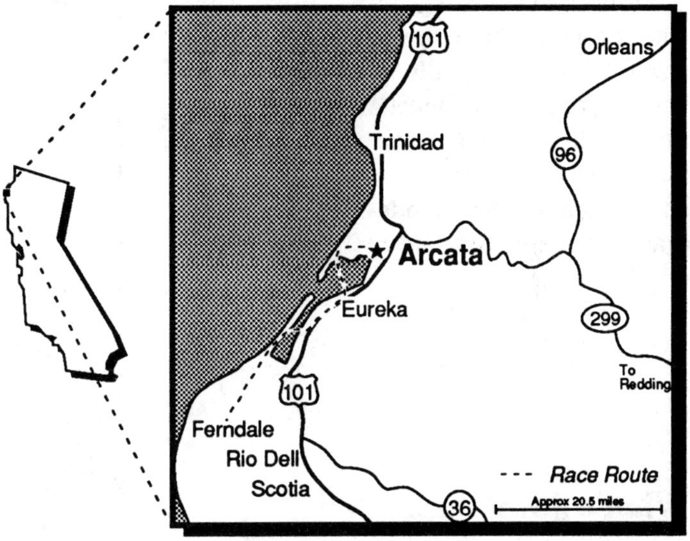


## What's goin' on...

Town population: **15,000**
Last year's attendance: **6,000**
Average outdoor temperature: **65°**
Festival location: **Citywide**

*Up-to-date festival information is available from:*
*Arcata Chamber of Commerce*
*(707) 822-3619*

| | |
|---|---|
| | Wine tasting/beer for sale |
| | Food booths |
| | Arts/crafts for sale |
| | Live music |
| | Clowns |
| | Face painters |
| | Childrens games |
| | Animal exhibits/petting zoo |
| | Dogs allowed on leash |
| | Lost and found |
| | Bicycle racks |
| | First aid area available |
| X | Self-brought picnics allowed |
| | Self-brought alcohol allowed |
| | Stroller/wheelchair rentals available |

| | |
|---|---|
| | Parade |
| | Parking fee |
| | Entrance fee |
| X | Camping facilities: 17 miles |
| X | Boating facilities: Humboldt Bay |
| X | RV facilities w/ hookups: 3 miles |
| X | Accomodations in town<br>Red Lion, The Plough & Stars Country Inn B&B, The Lady Anne B&B, Super 8 |
| X | Restaurants in town<br>Humboldt Brewery, Ottavio's, Abruzzi, Golden Harvest Cafe, Crosswinds, V&N Burger Bar |

# *Clear Lake Revival 1950's Car Show & Dance*

SITUATED ON CALIFORNIA'S largest natural lake, Lakeport hosts the **Clear Lake Revival 1950's Car Show & Dance!** Your day gets a kick start with a pancake breakfast and wraps up with ponytails bobbing at the 50s dance! All the time in between can be filled with wine tasting, shopping at the handmade-craft and art booths, and drooling over the mint-condition cars on display.

## Lakeport, California

First weekend in June
Hours vary

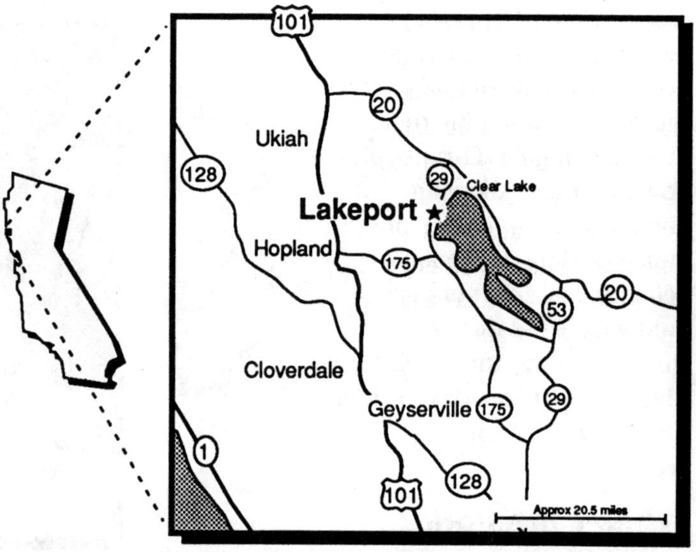


## What's goin' on...

Town population: **5,000**
Last year's attendance: **2,000**
Average outdoor temperature: **80°**
Festival location: **Fairgrounds**

*Up-to-date festival information is available from:*
*Lakeport Chamber of Commerce*
*(707) 263-6131*

| | |
|---|---|
| X | Wine tasting/beer for sale |
| X | Food booths |
| X | Arts/crafts for sale |
| X | Live music |
| | Clowns |
| | Face painters |
| | Childrens games |
| | Animal exhibits/petting zoo |
| | Dogs allowed on leash |
| | Lost and found |
| X | Bicycle racks |
| | First aid area available |
| X | Self-brought picnics allowed |
| X | Self-brought alcohol allowed |
| | Stroller/wheelchair rentals available |

| | |
|---|---|
| X | Parade: Sat. 7:00 PM on Main St. |
| | Parking fee |
| X | Entrance fee: Adults $3; Under 10 free |
| X | Camping facilities: In town |
| X | Boating facilities: Lake Mendocino |
| X | RV facilities w/ hookups: In town |
| | Accomodations in town |
| X | Restaurants in town<br>Park Place, Robin Hill, Anthony's Rainbow, Narrows |

# *Pony Express Days*

**PONY EXPRESS DAYS IN** McKinleyville is a whole lot more than just acknowledging this Pony Express stop of the mid-1800s! There's lots of good food, and booths filled with one-of-a-kind items such as jewelry, wearable art, leather goods, floral displays, and paintings. This niche of California is saturated with talented artists who enjoy the tranquility of the area the roar of the ocean!

## McKinleyville, California

First weekend in June
Daily 10:00 AM - 5:00 PM

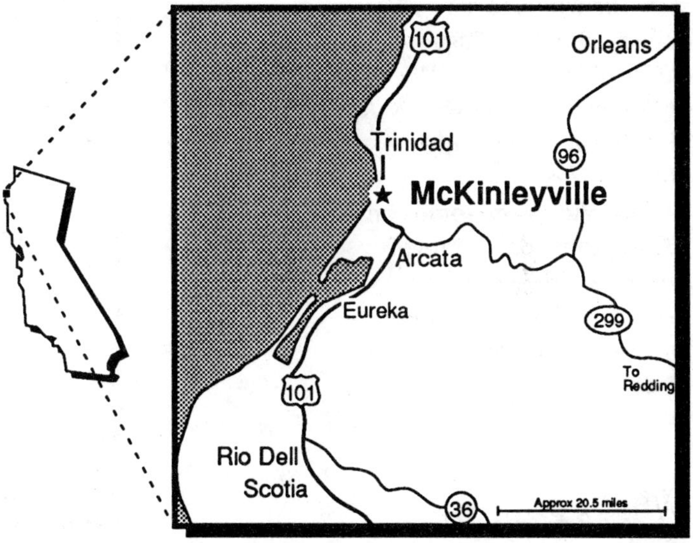


*Up-to-date festival information is available from:*
*McKinleyville Chamber of Commerce*
*(707) 839-1592*

## What's goin' on...

Town population: **14,000**
Last year's attendance: **1,500**
Average outdoor temperature: **68°**
Festival location: **Shopping Center**

| | |
|---|---|
| ✗ | Wine tasting/beer for sale |
| ✗ | Food booths |
| ✗ | Arts/crafts for sale |
| ✗ | Live music |
| | Clowns |
| | Face painters |
| ✗ | Childrens games |
| | Animal exhibits/petting zoo |
| ✗ | Dogs allowed on leash |
| ✗ | Lost and found |
| ✗ | Bicycle racks |
| ✗ | First aid area available |
| ✗ | Self-brought picnics allowed |
| | Self-brought alcohol allowed |
| | Stroller/wheelchair rentals available |

| | |
|---|---|
| ✗ | Parade: (time & date not avbl.) |
| | Parking fee |
| | Entrance fee |
| ✗ | Camping facilities |
| ✗ | Boating facilities: Humboldt Bay |
| ✗ | RV facilities w/ hookups |
| ✗ | Accomodations in town<br>Bella Vista Motel |
| ✗ | Restaurants in town |

# *Festival '91*

**FESTIVAL '91** IN RED BLUFF takes place at the fairgrounds where music is provided by local artists. Take a stroll to view the wood carvings, jewelry, and paintings for sale. Red Bluff's "hysterical" heritage can ve relived by visiting the Kelly Griggs Museum, or taking in the various Victorian homes on a driving tour. The home of William B. Ide, California pioneer, lies two miles northeast of Red Bluff as part of a state Historic Park.

## Red Bluff, California

First Saturday in June
10:00 AM - 5:00 PM

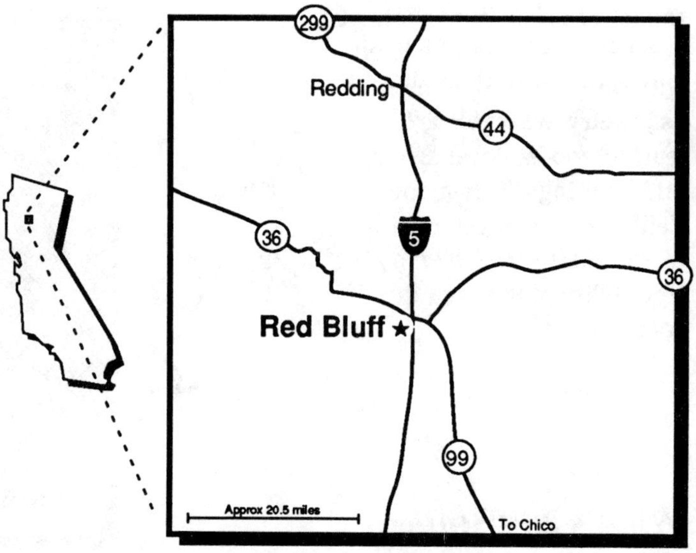


*Up-to-date festival information is available from:*
*Red Bluff Chamber of Commerce*
*(916) 527-6220*

## What's goin' on...

Town population: **12,000**
Last year's attendance: **4,000**
Average outdoor temperature: **90°**
Festival location:**Fairgrounds**

- X Wine tasting/beer for sale
- X Food booths
- X Arts/crafts for sale
- X Live music
- X Clowns
- Face painters
- Childrens games
- Animal exhibits/petting zoo
- Dogs allowed on leash
- X Lost and found
- X Bicycle racks
- X First aid area available
- X Self-brought picnics allowed
- X Self-brought alcohol allowed
- Stroller/wheelchair rentals available

- Parade
- Parking fee
- Entrance fee
- X Camping facilities: 1 mile
- X Boating facilities: Sacramento River
- X RV facilities w/ hookups: 1 mile
- X Accomodations in town
  Faulkner House B&B
- X Restaurants in town
  Blondie's, Francisco's, Hong Kong, Riverside Inn

# Teddy Bear Picnic

"IF YOU GO DOWN TO THE woods today, you'd better not go alone..." because the **Teddy Bear Picnic** is being held at Beachfront Park in Crescent City. This is a great place to go with the kids. With the smell of salt in the air, you can see all the teddy bears you could possibly imagine! Vendors have teddies for sale, and there are free games for the kids as well.

## Crescent City, California

Second Friday and Saturday in June
Daily 10:00 AM - 6:00 PM

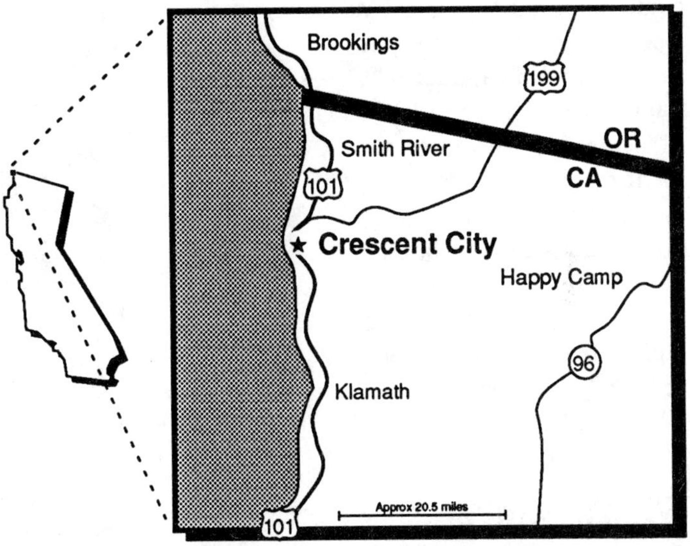


## What's goin' on...

Town population: **4,100**
Last year's attendance: **3,000**
Average outdoor temperature: **63°**
Festival location: **Beachfront Park**

*Up-to-date festival information is available from:*
*Crescent City Chamber of Commerce*
*(707) 464-3174*

| | |
|---|---|
| | Wine tasting/beer for sale |
| X | Food booths |
| | Arts/crafts for sale |
| | Live music |
| X | Clowns |
| X | Face painters |
| X | Childrens games |
| | Animal exhibits/petting zoo |
| | Dogs allowed on leash |
| | Lost and found |
| | Bicycle racks |
| | First aid area available |
| X | Self-brought picnics allowed |
| | Self-brought alcohol allowed |
| | Stroller/wheelchair rentals available |

| | |
|---|---|
| X | Parade: Sat. 10:00 AM downtown |
| | Parking fee |
| | Entrance fee |
| X | Camping facilities: 1 mile |
| X | Boating facilities: harbor |
| X | RV facilities w/ hookups: 1 mile |
| X | Accomodations in town<br>Breakers Motel, Camp Marigold, Harbor Motel, El Patio, Curly Redwood Lodge, B&Bs |
| X | Restaurants in town<br>Alias Jones, Harbor View Grotto, China Hut, Rowland's, Ship Ashore, Wakefields |

# *Humboldt Folklife Festival*

DUBBED AS A "CELEBRATION of folk music, dance, and song" the **Humboldt Folklife Festival**! Free childcare is available 10:00 AM - 5:00 PM; free bus service to-and-from Arcata City Hall and Lazy "L" Ranch every half-hour 9:30 AM - 1:00 AM. The entertainment ranges from country swing, old time fiddle, bluegrass, and Scottish Country Dance, to ragtime guitar, Israeli dance, and folk dancing. (Entrance fees: General: $8; HFS Members: $6; Under 12, over 60: free.)

## Arcata, California

Second Saturday in June
10:00 AM - 1:00 AM

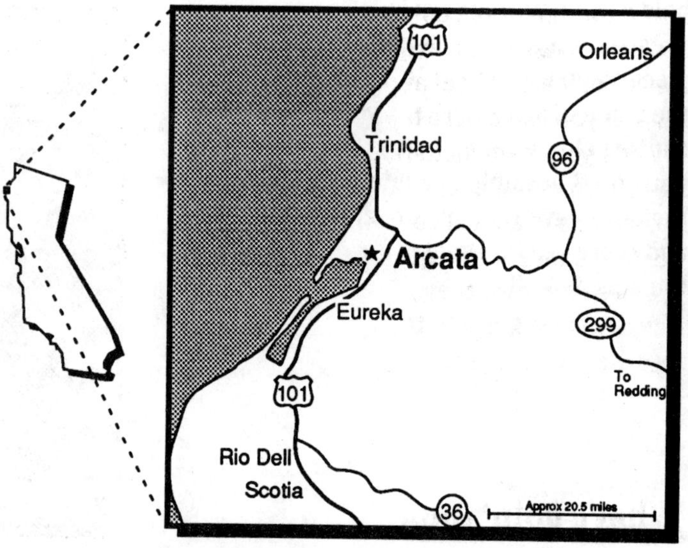


*Up-to-date festival information is available from:*
*Arcata Chamber of Commerce*
*(707) 822-3619*

## What's goin' on...

Town population: **15,000**
Last year's attendance: **500**
Average outdoor temperature: **70°**
Festival location: **Lazy "L" Ranch**

- ✗ Wine tasting/beer for sale
- ✗ Food booths
- Arts/crafts for sale
- ✗ Live music
- Clowns
- Face painters
- ✗ Childrens games
- ✗ Animal exhibits/petting zoo
- Dogs allowed on leash
- ✗ Lost and found
- ✗ Bicycle racks
- ✗ First aid area available
- ✗ Self-brought picnics allowed
- ✗ Self-brought alcohol allowed
- Stroller/wheelchair rentals available

- Parade
- Parking fee
- ✗ Entrance fee: see paragraph
- ✗ Camping facilities: 17 miles
- ✗ Boating facilities: Humboldt Bay
- ✗ RV facilities w/ hookups: 3 miles
- ✗ Accomodations in town
  Red Lion, The Plough & Stars Country Inn B&B, The Lady Anne B&B, Super 8
- ✗ Restaurants in town
  Humboldt Brewery, Ottavio's, Abruzzi, Golden Harvest Cafe, Crosswinds, V&N Burger Bar

# Luau

SMACK-DAB ON THE SACRAmento River is the town of Los Molinas—and an annual **Luau**. The trusty Volunteer Fire Department of Los Molinos cooks up an exquisite Hawaiian feast of beef and pork. If you leave here hungry, it's your own fault! But there's time to dance it off to the sounds of a local country western band. In this quaint and friendly town they welcome new faces to their Saturday-night event.

## Los Molinos, California

Second Saturday in June
6:00 PM - 11:00 PM

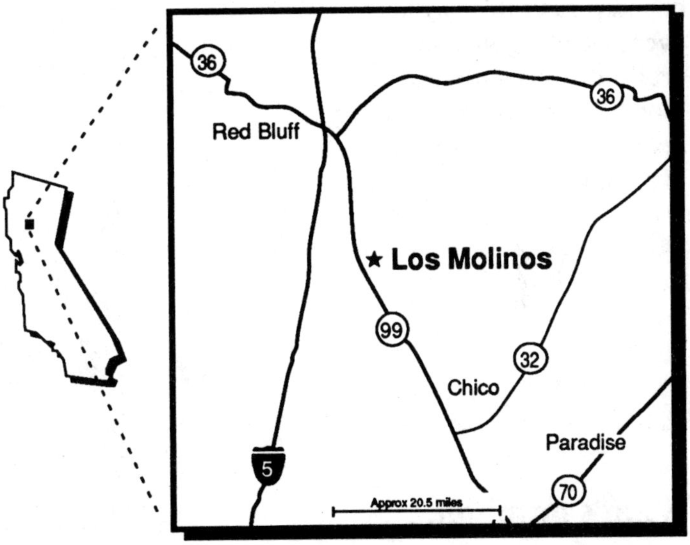


*Up-to-date festival information is available from:*
*Los Molinos Chamber of Commerce*
*(916) 384-2251*

## What's goin' on...

Town population: **1,400**
Last year's attendance: **450**
Average outdoor temperature: **90°**
Festival location: **Mill Creek Park**

| | |
|---|---|
| X | Wine tasting/beer for sale |
| X | Food booths |
| | Arts/crafts for sale |
| X | Live music |
| | Clowns |
| | Face painters |
| | Childrens games |
| X | Animal exhibits/petting zoo |
| | Dogs allowed on leash |
| | Lost and found |
| | Bicycle racks |
| | First aid area available |
| X | Self-brought picnics allowed |
| X | Self-brought alcohol allowed |
| | Stroller/wheelchair rentals available |

| | |
|---|---|
| X | Parade: 6:00 at the Park |
| | Parking fee |
| | Entrance fee |
| X | Camping facilities: On-site |
| X | Boating facilities: Sacramento River |
| X | RV facilities w/ hookups: On-site |
| X | Accomodations in town<br>Garden Valley Motel |
| X | Restaurants in town<br>Berry's Restaurant, The DePo, Burger Shack, N/B Cafe |

# *Great Grape Stampede*

YOU'LL SEE AND TASTE LOTS of grapes at the **Great Grape Stampede**! This charming area of California's wine country hosts this day-long event featuring wine tasting, arts and crafts, and lots of food to enjoy. While in the area be sure you take a tour of a few of the wineries!

## Windsor, California

Second Saturday in June
All day

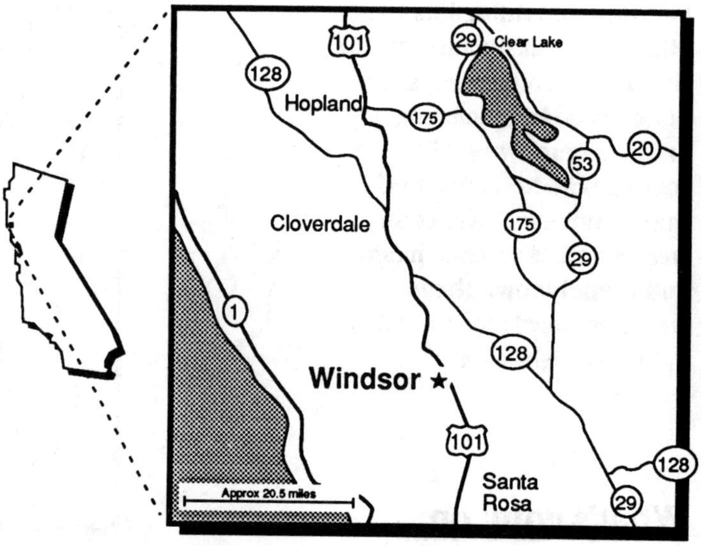


*Up-to-date festival information is available from:*
*Windsor Chamber of Commerce*
*(707) 838-7285*

## What's goin' on...

Town population: **8,500**
Last year's attendance: **400**
Average outdoor temperature: **78°**
Festival location: **Downtown**

| | |
|---|---|
| ✗ | Wine tasting/beer for sale |
| ✗ | Food booths |
| ✗ | Arts/crafts for sale |
| ✗ | Live music |
| | Clowns |
| | Face painters |
| | Childrens games |
| | Animal exhibits/petting zoo |
| | Dogs allowed on leash |
| ✗ | Lost and found |
| | Bicycle racks |
| ✗ | First aid area available |
| ✗ | Self-brought picnics allowed |
| | Self-brought alcohol allowed |
| | Stroller/wheelchair rentals available |

| | |
|---|---|
| | Parade |
| | Parking fee |
| ✗ | Entrance fee: (prices not avbl.) |
| ✗ | Camping facilities: 2 miles |
| ✗ | Boating facilities: Lake Sonoma |
| ✗ | RV facilities w/ hookups: 4 miles |
| ✗ | Accomodations in town |
| ✗ | Restaurants in town |

# *Railroad Days*

AH, DUNSMUIR! THERE'S *NO* place like Dunsmuir! Come see for yourself at **Railroad Days!** This town goes into overtime providing lots to do: Miss Dunsmuir Beauty pagent, carnival rides, antique plane fly-over, steam engine exhibits, river race, horse and carriage rides, ethnic food booths, sidewalk sale, fishing derby, and, if you still have any energy left, a 2K and 5K run! *Great fun!*

## Dunsmuir, California

Third weekend in June (beginning Thursday)
Hours vary (Sat. till 1:00 AM)

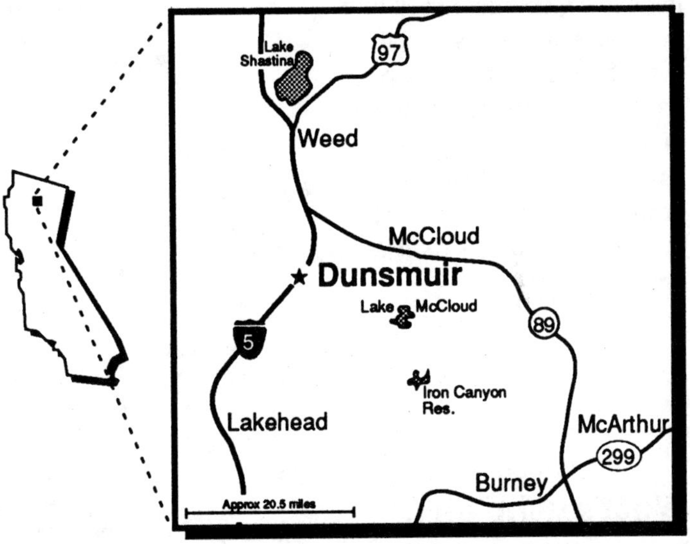


## What's goin' on...

Town population: **2,800**
Last year's attendance: **10,000**
Average outdoor temperature: **78°**
Festival location: **Downtown, park, river**

*Up-to-date festival information is available from:*
*Dunsmuir Chamber of Commerce*
*(916) 235-2177*

- X Wine tasting/beer for sale
- X Food booths
- X Arts/crafts for sale
- X Live music
- X Clowns
- X Face painters
- X Childrens games
- X Animal exhibits/petting zoo
- X Dogs allowed on leash
- X Lost and found
- X Bicycle racks
- X First aid area available
- X Self-brought picnics allowed
- Self-brought alcohol allowed
- Stroller/wheelchair rentals available

- X Parade: Sat. noon on Main St.
- Parking fee
- Entrance fee
- X Camping facilities: 2 miles
- X Boating facilities: Lake, river
- X RV facilities w/ hookups: In town
- X Accomodations in town
  Dunsmuir Inn, Clementine's, TraveLodge, Cave Springs
- X Restaurants in town
  Joaquin Miller, Gary's Pizza

# *Carnevale*

WHETHER IT'S A BOCCE ball tournament, an ax-throwing contest, a horseshoe tournament, or a log-cutting contest you'll find them all at **Carnevale** in mid-June. Music from the Navy band, fiddle tunes, and good ol' rock 'n' roll will fill the air as you fill your tummies with Polish sausage, ribs, barbecued chicken, and *exquisite* cheesecake!

## Weed, California

Third weekend in June
Hours vary

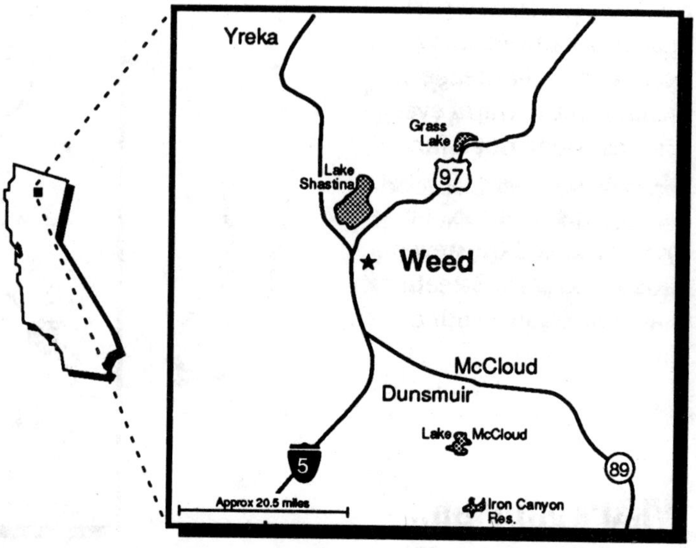


*Up-to-date festival information is available from:*
*Weed Chamber of Commerce*
*(916) 938-4624*

## What's goin' on...

Town population: **3,000**
Last year's attendance: **3,000**
Average outdoor temperature: **80°**
Festival location: **Bel Air Park**

| | |
|---|---|
| ✗ | Wine tasting/beer for sale |
| ✗ | Food booths |
| ✗ | Arts/crafts for sale |
| ✗ | Live music |
| ✗ | Clowns |
| ✗ | Face painters |
| ✗ | Childrens games |
| ✗ | Animal exhibits/petting zoo |
| ✗ | Dogs allowed on leash |
| ✗ | Lost and found |
| ✗ | Bicycle racks |
| ✗ | First aid area available |
| ✗ | Self-brought picnics allowed |
| ✗ | Self-brought alcohol allowed |
| ✗ | Stroller/wheelchair rentals available |

| | |
|---|---|
| ✗ | Parade: Sat. noon downtown |
| | Parking fee |
| | Entrance fee |
| ✗ | Camping facilities. 9 miles |
| ✗ | Boating facilities: Lake Shastina |
| ✗ | RV facilities w/ hookups: In town |
| ✗ | Accomodations in town |
| ✗ | Restaurants in town<br>Silva's, Hi Lo, "Y" Ranch Ocean Cowboy, California Pizza |

# *Warner Mountain Round-Up*

THE **WARNER MOUNTAIN Round-Up** in Cedarville is the biggest one-day rodeo in these United States! There's a wild-horse race and performances by the Redding Rodeo Drill Team. A barbecue and dancing in the warm evening breezes round out a fun-filled day. The old Cressler Bonner trading post is located in the town park, and the new one is situated on Main Street. This is a *friendly* town with an old-fashioned flair!

## Cedarville, California

Saturday prior to Father's Day
1:00 PM - 10:00 PM

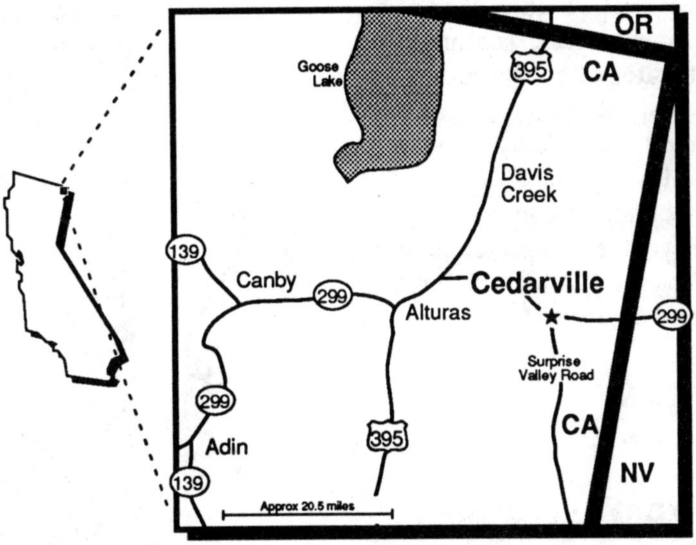


## What's goin' on...

Town population: **1,200**
Last year's attendance: **N/A**
Average outdoor temperature: **90°**
Festival location: **Fairgrounds**

*Up-to-date festival information is available from:*
*Cedarville Chamber of Commerce*
*(916) 233-2819*

| | |
|---|---|
| X | Wine tasting/beer for sale |
| X | Food booths |
| | Arts/crafts for sale |
| | Live music |
| | Clowns |
| | Face painters |
| | Childrens games |
| X | Animal exhibits/petting zoo |
| | Dogs allowed on leash |
| | Lost and found |
| | Bicycle racks |
| X | First aid area available |
| X | Self-brought picnics allowed |
| | Self-brought alcohol allowed |
| | Stroller/wheelchair rentals available |

| | |
|---|---|
| | Parade |
| | Parking fee |
| X | Entrance fee: $7 |
| X | Camping facilities: 20 miles |
| X | Boating facilities: Big Sage Res. |
| X | RV facilities w/ hookups: In town |
| X | Accomodations in town<br>Sunrise Motel |
| X | Restaurants in town<br>Golden's Restaurant, Don's Valley Burger |

# *Scandinavian Mid-Summer Festival*

IN THE OLD SCANDINAVIAN tradition, the summer solstice is celebrated at the **Mid-Summer Scandinavian Festival.** Parades, food, dances, music, costumes, and theater with a Scandinavian twist will delight you all day long along Main Street on Saturday and at the Fairgrounds on Sunday. The Ferndale Historic Committee boasts of 24 historic buildings and churches.

## Ferndale, California

Third weekend in June

Daily 10:00 AM - 4:00 PM

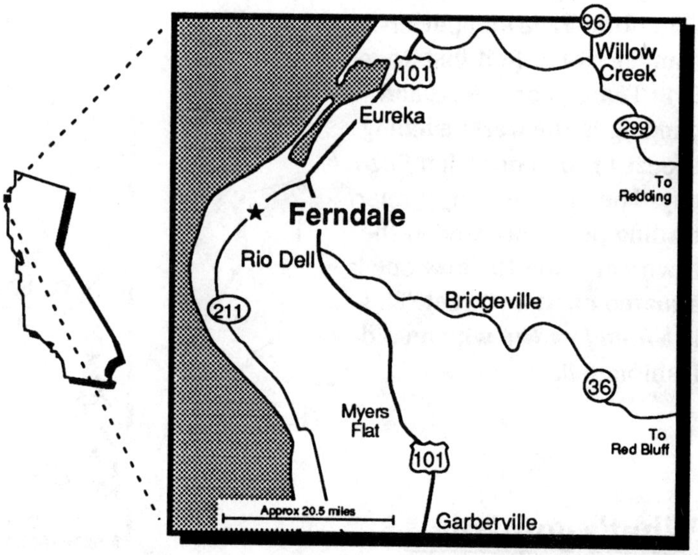


## What's goin' on...

Town population: **1,400**

Last year's attendance: **1,000**

Average outdoor temperature: **65°**

Festival location: **Downtown**

*Up-to-date festival information is available from:*
*Ferndale Chamber of Commerce*
*(707) 786-4477*

| | |
|---|---|
| | Wine tasting/beer for sale |
| ✗ | Food booths |
| ✗ | Arts/crafts for sale |
| ✗ | Live music |
| | Clowns |
| | Face painters |
| | Childrens games |
| | Animal exhibits/petting zoo |
| ✗ | Dogs allowed on leash |
| | Lost and found |
| | Bicycle racks |
| | First aid area available |
| ✗ | Self-brought picnics allowed |
| | Self-brought alcohol allowed |
| | Stroller/wheelchair rentals available |

| | |
|---|---|
| | Parade |
| | Parking fee |
| | Entrance fee |
| ✗ | Camping facilities: 5 miles |
| | Boating facilities |
| ✗ | RV facilities w/ hookups: 1 mile |
| ✗ | Accomodations in town<br>Victoria Village Inn, Ferndale B&B, Francis Creek Inn, Gingerbread Mansion Inn |
| ✗ | Restaurants in town<br>Fern Cafe, Diane's Cafe, Roman's, Victorian Village Inn |

N O R T H E R N

# *Summer Arts Festival & Jazz on the Lake*

YEOWZA! THE ANNUAL **Benbow Summer Arts Festival** is a delightful place to spend a June weekend in Northern California! Benbow Recreation Area is just a smidgen south of Garberville. The Festival includes handicrafts from local artists, food creations ranging from American to Mexican to Japanese, and entertainment all day. Saturday night marks **Jazz on the Lake**, with an outrageous outdoor concert!

## Garberville, California

Fourth weekend in June
Daily 10:00 AM - 6:00 PM

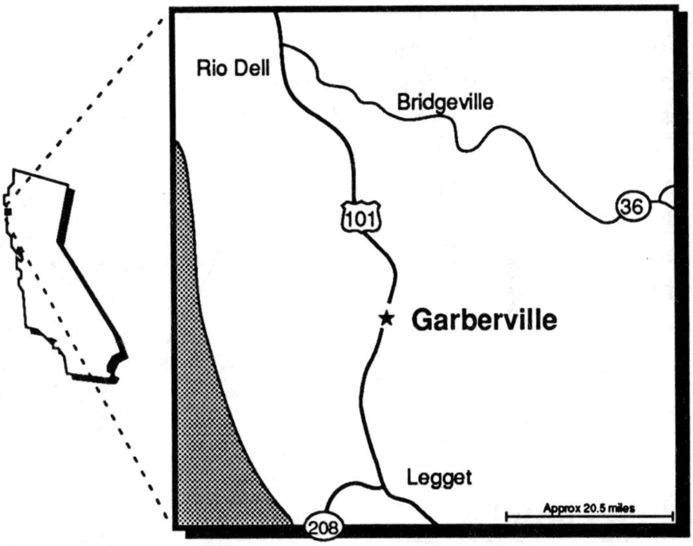


*Up-to-date festival information is available from:*
*Garberville Chamber of Commerce*
*(707) 923-2613*

## What's goin' on...

Town population: **1,000**
Last year's attendance: **N/A**
Average outdoor temperature: **85°**
Festival location: **Benbow Park**

| | |
|---|---|
| | Wine tasting/beer for sale |
| ✗ | Food booths |
| ✗ | Arts/crafts for sale |
| ✗ | Live music |
| ✗ | Clowns |
| ✗ | Face painters |
| ✗ | Childrens games |
| | Animal exhibits/petting zoo |
| ✗ | Dogs allowed on leash |
| ✗ | Lost and found |
| | Bicycle racks |
| ✗ | First aid area available |
| ✗ | Self-brought picnics allowed |
| ✗ | Self-brought alcohol allowed |
| | Stroller/wheelchair rentals available |

| | |
|---|---|
| | Parade |
| ✗ | Parking fee: $1 |
| ✗ | Entrance fee: $1 |
| ✗ | Camping facilities: On-site |
| ✗ | Boating facilities: Benbow Lake (canoes) |
| ✗ | RV facilities w/ hookups: On-site |
| ✗ | Accomodations in town<br>Benbow Inn, Hartsook Inn |
| ✗ | Restaurants in town<br>Benbow Inn, Brass Rail, Waterwheel, Woodrow's |

# *Jenner Festival of the Arts*

IT'S A SPECIAL WEEKEND IN California when a town more than quinduples it's population for a festival! Such a phenomenon happens for the **Jenner Festival of Arts**. Top quality abounds this festival of art, crafts, and ethnic food dishes. Over a dozen Sonoma county wineries will keep your souvenir wine glass filled while you tap your toes to the live jazz music.

## Jenner, California

Fourth weekend in June
Daily 10:00 AM - 6:00 PM

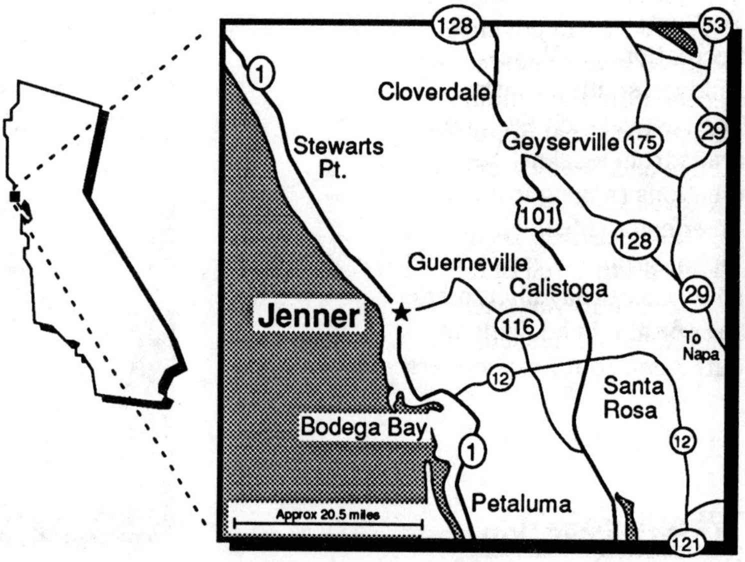


*Up-to-date festival information is available from:*
*Jenner Community Club*
*(707) 865-2689*

## What's goin' on...

Town population: **200**
Last year's attendance: **4,500**
Average outdoor temperature: **70°**
Festival location: **Downtown field**

| | |
|---|---|
| X | Wine tasting/beer for sale |
| X | Food booths |
| X | Arts/crafts for sale |
| X | Live music |
| X | Clowns |
| X | Face painters |
| | Childrens games |
| | Animal exhibits/petting zoo |
| X | Dogs allowed on leash |
| | Lost and found |
| | Bicycle racks |
| | First aid area available |
| X | Self-brought picnics allowed |
| X | Self-brought alcohol allowed |
| | Stroller/wheelchair rentals available |

| | |
|---|---|
| | Parade |
| | Parking fee |
| | Entrance fee |
| X | Camping facilities: 4 miles |
| X | Boating facilities: Russian River |
| X | RV facilities w/ hookups: 4 miles |
| X | Accomodations in town<br>Lazy River Motel, Murphy's Jenner B&B |
| X | Restaurants in town<br>Jenner by the Sea, River's End |

# *Rough & Ready Secession Day Celebration*

YOUR TEENAGERS AREN'T the *only* ones who've rebelled against the Establishment! In 1850, the town of Rough and Ready, weary of government-imposed taxes, decided to secede from the Union. Hence, the Great Republic of Rough and Ready was born—for three short months, that is! This **Secession Days Celebration** is full of fun and surprises for everyone—and should not be missed!

## Rough & Ready, California

Fourth Sunday in June
7:30 AM - 6:00 PM

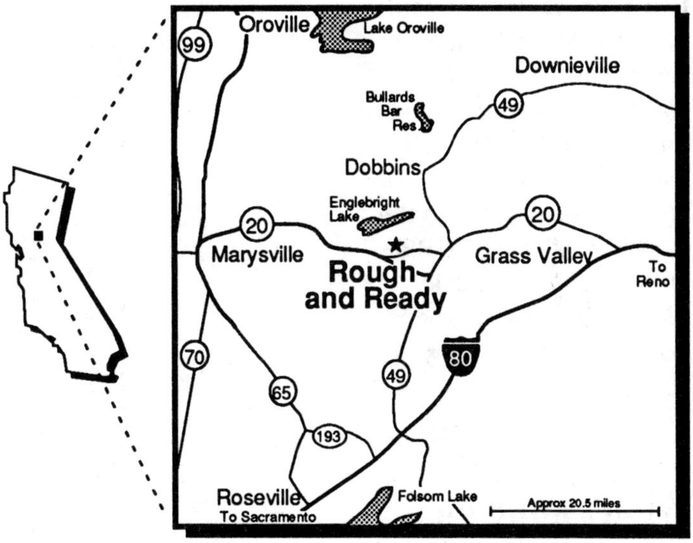


☞ *Up-to-date festival information is available from:*
*Rough & Ready Chamber of Commerce*
*(916) 273-9774*

## What's goin' on...

Town population: **1,508**
Last year's attendance: **4,000**
Average outdoor temperature: **85°**
Festival location: **Center of town**

| | |
|---|---|
| X | Wine tasting/beer for sale |
| X | Food booths |
| X | Arts/crafts for sale |
| X | Live music |
| X | Clowns |
| | Face painters |
| X | Childrens games |
| | Animal exhibits/petting zoo |
| X | Dogs allowed on leash |
| | Lost and found |
| | Bicycle racks |
| | First aid area available |
| X | Self-brought picnics allowed |
| | Self-brought alcohol allowed |
| | Stroller/wheelchair rentals available |

| | |
|---|---|
| X | Parade: (time & date not avbl.) |
| | Parking fee |
| | Entrance fee |
| X | Camping facilities: 4 miles |
| X | Boating facilities: Lake Wildwood |
| X | RV facilities w/ hookups: 4 miles |
| X | Accomodations in town |
| X | Restaurants in town<br>Midget Kitchen, Mexican Villa |

# *Paul Bunyan Mountain Festival*

LEAVE IT TO A WONDERFUL little California town to have the biggest festival of them all! The **Paul Bunyan Mountain Festival** is all its name implies! They do things around here in a *B-I-G* way...from the barbecued ribs on the grill to the hand-carved wood sculptures and country-style crafts, to the Junior Mountain Bike Ride and live country-music playing! Westwood was the hometown to Mr. Bunyan!

## Westwood, California

Last weekend in June (beginning Friday)
Hours vary

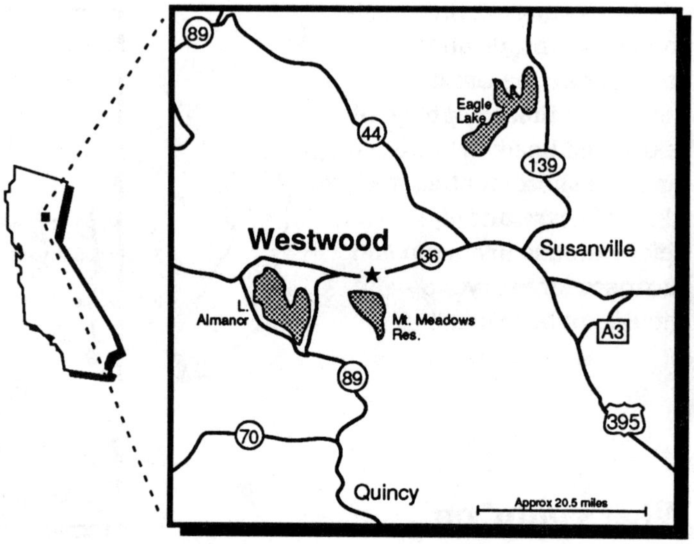


*Up-to-date festival information is available from:*
*Westwood Chamber of Commerce*
*(916) 256-2456*

## What's goin' on...

Town population: **2,000**
Last year's attendance: **10,000**
Average outdoor temperature: **87°**
Festival location: **Town Park**

| | |
|---|---|
| X | Wine tasting/beer for sale |
| X | Food booths |
| X | Arts/crafts for sale |
| X | Live music |
| | Clowns |
| X | Face painters |
| X | Childrens games |
| X | Animal exhibits/petting zoo |
| X | Dogs allowed on leash |
| X | Lost and found |
| | Bicycle racks |
| X | First aid area available |
| X | Self-brought picnics allowed |
| | Self-brought alcohol allowed |
| | Stroller/wheelchair rentals available |

| | |
|---|---|
| X | Parade: Sat. noon on 3rd Street |
| | Parking fee |
| X | Entrance fee: S & K $1; A $2 |
| X | Camping facilities: 5 miles |
| X | Boating facilities: Lake Almanor |
| X | RV facilities w/ hookups: 5 miles |
| X | Accomodations in town |
| X | Restaurants in town<br>Village Inn, Buffalo Chips, The Kopper Kettle |

# *Sonoma County Hot Air Balloon Classic*

WHAT DO PIPER SONOMA, Chalk Hill, and Chateau DeBaun all have in common? They are great wineries offering tastings at the **Sonoma County Hot Air Balloon Classic**! Looking up and seeing zillions of brightly colored balloons dot the blue sky is a sight to behold! And there's lots of shopping to do at the booths filled with art and crafts. The tunes playing are jazz, rock, and country. BIG FUN! And we're not just full of hot air...

## Windsor, California

Last weekend in June (beginning Friday)
Fri. 5:00 PM - late; Sat. & Sun. 6:00 AM - 6:00 PM

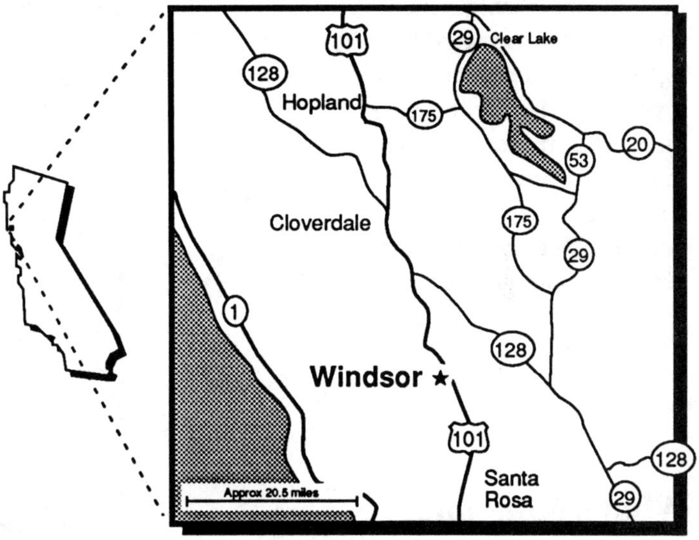


## What's goin' on...

Town population: **8,500**
Last year's attendance: **20,000**
Average outdoor temperature: **70°**
Festival location: **Windsor Golf Course**

*Up-to-date festival information is available from:*
*Windsor Chamber of Commerce*
*(707) 838-7285*

| | |
|---|---|
| X | Wine tasting/beer for sale |
| X | Food booths |
| X | Arts/crafts for sale |
| X | Live music |
| X | Clowns |
| X | Face painters |
| X | Childrens games |
| | Animal exhibits/petting zoo |
| | Dogs allowed on leash |
| X | Lost and found |
| | Bicycle racks |
| X | First aid area available |
| | Self-brought picnics allowed |
| | Self-brought alcohol allowed |
| | Stroller/wheelchair rentals available |

| | |
|---|---|
| | Parade |
| | Parking fee |
| X | Entrance fee: $3; Under 6 free |
| X | Camping facilities: 10 miles |
| X | Boating facilities: Lake Sonoma |
| X | RV facilities w/ hookups: 1 mile |
| X | Accomodations in town<br>Country Meadow Inn |
| X | Restaurants in town<br>John Ash & Company |

# *Burney Basin Days*

WHERE CAN YOU SEE AN actual Ugly Dog Contest? At **Burney Basin Days** in Burney, California! This friendly community in gorgeous Shasta County is anything but ugly—located next to the incredible McArthur Burney Falls. The streams and rivers in the area are ranked tenth in the world for trout fishing, and nearby Lake Britton is great for canoeing and waterskiing.

## Burney, California

Last weekend in June
Hours vary

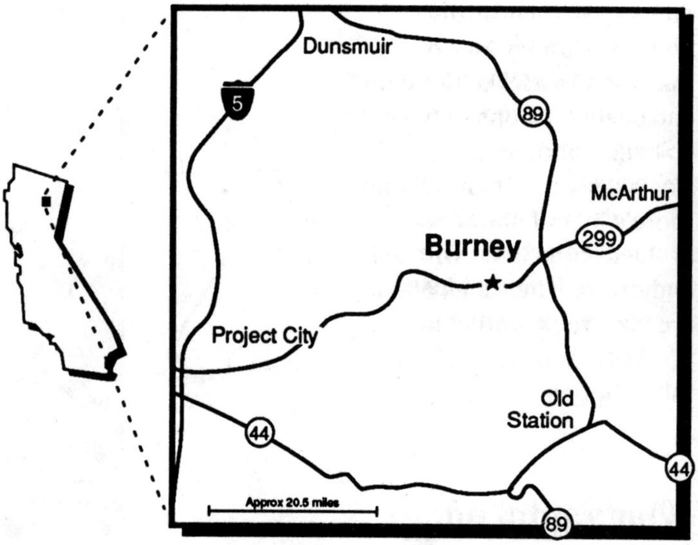


*Up-to-date festival information is available from:*
*Burney Chamber of Commerce*
*(916) 335-2111*

## What's goin' on...

Town population: **5,000**
Last year's attendance: **N/A**
Average outdoor temperature: **80°**
Festival location: **N/A**

| | |
|---|---|
| X | Wine tasting/beer for sale |
| X | Food booths |
| X | Arts/crafts for sale |
| X | Live music |
| X | Clowns |
| X | Face painters |
| X | Childrens games |
| X | Animal exhibits/petting zoo |
| | Dogs allowed on leash |
| X | Lost and found |
| | Bicycle racks |
| X | First aid area available |
| | Self-brought picnics allowed |
| | Self-brought alcohol allowed |
| | Stroller/wheelchair rentals available |

| | |
|---|---|
| X | Parade: (date & time not avbl.) |
| | Parking fee |
| | Entrance fee |
| X | Camping facilities: 5 miles |
| X | Boating facilities: Lake Britton |
| X | RV facilities w/ hookups: 12 miles |
| X | Accomodations in town |
| X | Restaurants in town<br>BJ's, Sam's Pizza, Outpost, Rex Club |

# *Frontier Days & Rodeo*

GET BACK TO THE BASICS OF small-town fun at **Frontier Days & Rodeo** in Willits! Located just a few miles from scenic Lake Mendocino, Frontier Days offers live music at this weekend event, along with a rodeo, and an evening street dance and barbecue. Craft booths are filled with handmade items from skilled artists. The Mendocino County Museum is one not to miss while visiting.

## Willits, California

Third & Fourth of July

7/3 7:00 PM - 10:00 PM; 7/4 9:00 AM - 6:00 PM

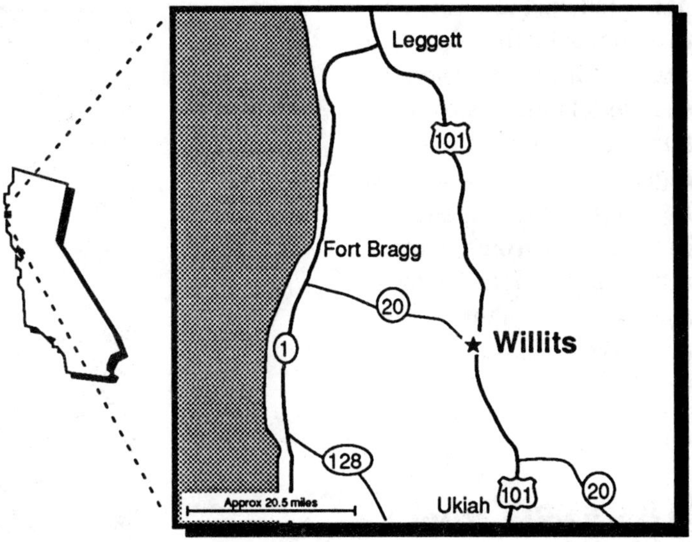


## What's goin' on...

Town population: **5,100**

Last year's attendance: **8,000**

Average outdoor temperature: **82°**

Festival location: **Rodeo grounds/downtown**

*Up-to-date festival information is available from:*
*Willits Chamber of Commerce*
*(707) 459-4113*

| | |
|---|---|
| X | Wine tasting/beer for sale |
| X | Food booths |
| X | Arts/crafts for sale |
| X | Live music |
| | Clowns |
| | Face painters |
| | Childrens games |
| | Animal exhibits/petting zoo |
| | Dogs allowed on leash |
| X | Lost and found |
| | Bicycle racks |
| X | First aid area available |
| X | Self-brought picnics allowed |
| | Self-brought alcohol allowed |
| | Stroller/wheelchair rentals available |

| | |
|---|---|
| X | Parade: On the 4th 11:00 AM on Main St. |
| | Parking fee |
| X | Entrance fee: Varies by event |
| X | Camping facilities: 1 mile |
| X | Boating facilities: Lake Mendocino |
| X | RV facilities w/ hookups: 1 mile |
| X | Accomodations in town<br>The Doll House B&B, San Sovci B&B |
| X | Restaurants in town<br>Brooktrails Lodge |

# *Fourth of July Plaza Fair & Waterfront Day*

THE **FOURTH OF JULY Plaza Fair & Waterfront Day** in downtown Arcata is a true-blue hometown event! Moms, dads, and kids all show up for this annual birthday party to snack on interesting goodies such as falafels and tofu burgers, along with the regulars such as all-American hot dogs and ice cream. Unique items from talented artists of Northern California are for sale. Don't miss the fireworks display.

## Arcata, California

Fourth of July
10:00 AM - 7:00 PM

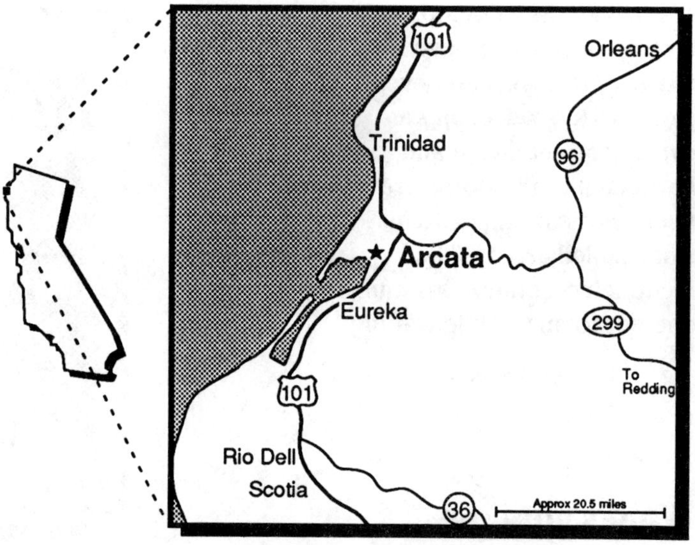


*Up-to-date festival information is available from:*
*Arcata Chamber of Commerce*
*(707) 822-3619*

## What's goin' on...

Town population: **15,000**
Last year's attendance: **3,000**
Average outdoor temperature: **65°**
Festival location: **Plaza**

- X Wine tasting/beer for sale
- X Food booths
- X Arts/crafts for sale
- X Live music
- X Clowns
- X Face painters
- X Childrens games
- X Animal exhibits/petting zoo
- Dogs allowed on leash
- X Lost and found
- X Bicycle racks
- X First aid area available
- X Self-brought picnics allowed
- Self-brought alcohol allowed
- Stroller/wheelchair rentals available

- Parade
- Parking fee
- Entrance fee
- X Camping facilities, 17 miles
- X Boating facilities: Humboldt Bay
- X RV facilities w/ hookups: 3 miles
- X Accomodations in town
  Red Lion, The Plough & Stars Country Inn B&B, The Lady Anne B&B, Super 8
- X Restaurants in town
  Humboldt Brewery, Ottavio's, Abruzzi, Golden Harvest Cafe, Crosswinds, V&N Burger Bar

# *Brownsville Mountain Fair*

LOOKIN' FOR SOME GOOD, old-fashioned country fun? Then come on out for the **Brownsville Mountain Fair!** There are events such as mud wrestling and a logging show...and for your tamer part, there's bingo, dancing, and a softball tournament. This all starts on the Fourth and lasts through the weekend. There's yummy food and more than 80 arts-and-crafts booths for you to enjoy. Yep! *We're havin' some fun now!*

## Brownsville, California

July 4th weekend
Daily 8:30 AM - 6:00 PM

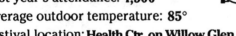

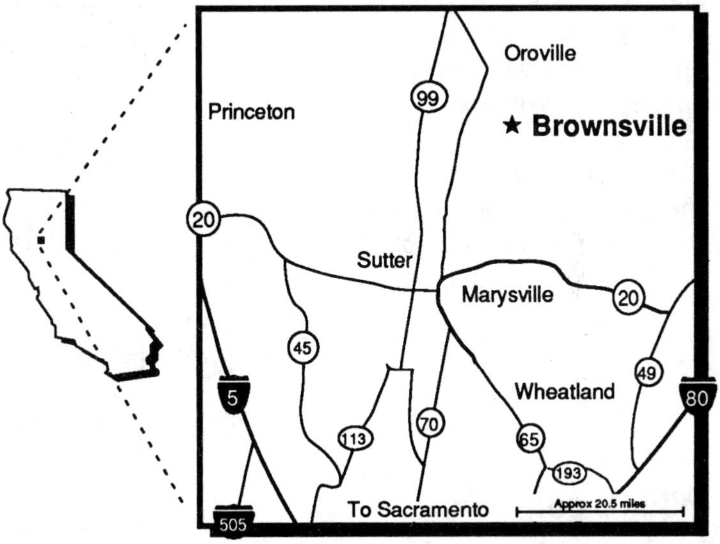


☞ *Up-to-date festival information is available from:*
*Brownsville Chamber of Commerce*
*(916) 743-6501*

## What's goin' on...

Town population: **1,000**
Last year's attendance: **4,500**
Average outdoor temperature: **85°**
Festival location: **Health Ctr. on Willow Glen**

- ✗ Wine tasting/beer for sale
- ✗ Food booths
- ✗ Arts/crafts for sale
- ✗ Live music
- ✗ Clowns
- ✗ Face painters
- ✗ Childrens games
- Animal exhibits/petting zoo
- Dogs allowed on leash
- Lost and found
- Bicycle racks
- ✗ First aid area available
- Self-brought picnics allowed
- Self-brought alcohol allowed
- ✗ Stroller/wheelchair rentals available

- Parade
- Parking fee
- ✗ Entrance fee: Adults $1; Kids 25¢
- ✗ Camping facilities: 15 miles
- ✗ Boating facilities: Collins Lake
- ✗ RV facilities w/ hookups: 15 miles
- ✗ Accomodations in town
  Mt. Seasons, Gold Cup Lodge
- ✗ Restaurants in town
  Rainbow Gold Cup Lodge, Pine Tree

# *Fourth of July Celebration*

**THE FOURTH OF JULY Celebration** is a bang-up time in Crescent City! With a huge art show and sale, logging show, contests, and taste-tempting food booths, to choose from—what more could you possibly want? Fireworks, you ask? Yes, Crescent City even lights up the skies in the evening with the biggest fireworks display on California's north coast!

## Crescent City, California

Fourth of July
10:00 AM - 10:30 PM

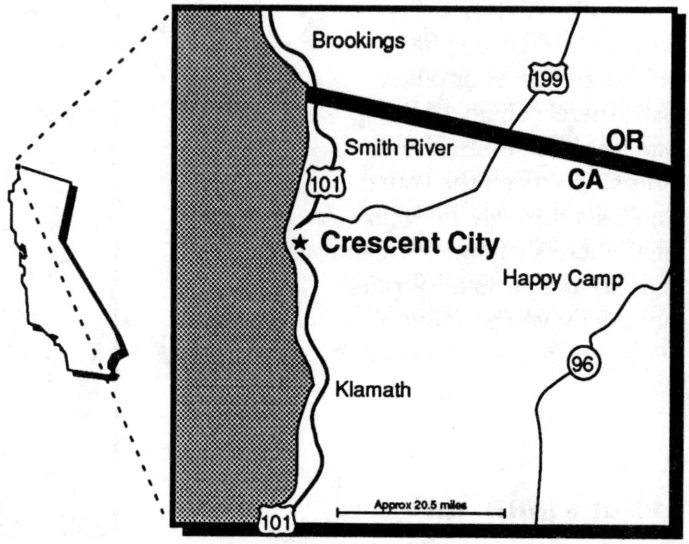


*Up-to-date festival information is available from:*
*Crescent City Chamber of Commerce*
*(707) 464-3174*

## What's goin' on...

Town population: **4,100**
Last year's attendance: **10,000**
Average outdoor temperature: **65°**
Festival location: **Beachfront Park**

- ✗ Wine tasting/beer for sale
- ✗ Food booths
- ✗ Arts/crafts for sale
- ✗ Live music
- ✗ Clowns
- ✗ Face painters
- ✗ Childrens games
- Animal exhibits/petting zoo
- ✗ Dogs allowed on leash
- ✗ Lost and found
- Bicycle racks
- ✗ First aid area available
- ✗ Self-brought picnics allowed
- Self-brought alcohol allowed
- Stroller/wheelchair rentals available

- ✗ Parade: 10:00 AM downtown
- Parking fee
- Entrance fee
- ✗ Camping facilities: 1 mile
- ✗ Boating facilities: harbor
- ✗ RV facilities w/ hookups: 1 mile
- ✗ Accomodations in town
  Breakers Motel, Camp Marigold, Harbor Motel, El Patio, Curly Redwood Lodge
- ✗ Restaurants in town
  Alias Jones, Harbor View Grotto, China Hut, Rowland's, Ship Ashore, Wakefields

# Fourth of July Celebration

DOWNIEVILLE HAS celebrations nearly year 'round, so why not a rip-roaring **Fourth of July Celebration**! Heck, this little community where the Yuba River runs right through town has been celebrating America's birthday this way since the late 1800s!! Fireworks and a dance when night falls. There's a flea market to browse through during the day and fireworks and a dance when night falls.

## Downieville, California

Fourth of July
10:00 AM - 5:00 PM

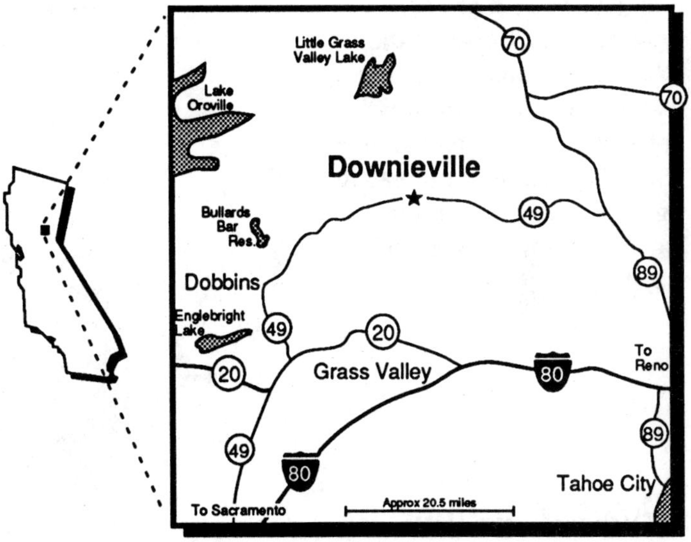


## What's goin' on...

Town population: **3,300**
Last year's attendance: **N/A**
Average outdoor temperature: **85°**
Festival location: **Downtown**

*Up-to-date festival information is available from:*
*Downieville Chamber of Commerce*
*(916) 289-3560*

| | |
|---|---|
| | Wine tasting/beer for sale |
| ✗ | Food booths |
| ✗ | Arts/crafts for sale |
| ✗ | Live music |
| | Clowns |
| | Face painters |
| ✗ | Childrens games |
| | Animal exhibits/petting zoo |
| ✗ | Dogs allowed on leash |
| | Lost and found |
| | Bicycle racks |
| ✗ | First aid area available |
| ✗ | Self-brought picnics allowed |
| | Self-brought alcohol allowed |
| | Stroller/wheelchair rentals available |

| | |
|---|---|
| ✗ | Parade: Noon downtown |
| | Parking fee |
| | Entrance fee |
| ✗ | Camping facilities: 3 miles |
| | Boating facilities |
| ✗ | RV facilities w/ hookups: 13 miles |
| ✗ | Accomodations in town<br>Dyers Resort, Riverside Motel, Robinsons, Downieville Motor Inn, The Lure |
| ✗ | Restaurants in town<br>Forks, Riverview Pizza, Coyoteville |

# *Kenwood Fourth of July Celebration*

IN THE HEART OF THE Golden State's breathtaking wine country lies the little town of Kenwood with a really fun **Fourth of July Celebration**! Check out the "Not Yet Famous" Chili Cook-off and then flex your muscles at the World Championship Pillow Fights (yes, you read it right)! A bike tour visiting local wineries is a wonderful way to end the day.

## Kenwood, California

Fourth of July
9:00 AM - 5:00 PM

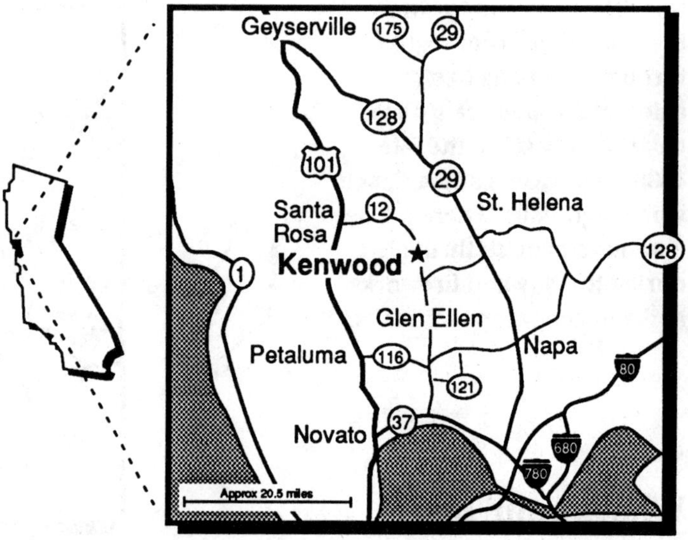


*Up-to-date festival information is available from:*
*Kenwood Chamber of Commerce*
*(707) 571-8071*

## What's goin' on...

Town population: **1,250**
Last year's attendance: **15,000**
Average outdoor temperature: **95°**
Festival location: **Plaza Park**

| | |
|---|---|
| ✗ | Wine tasting/beer for sale |
| ✗ | Food booths |
| ✗ | Arts/crafts for sale |
| ✗ | Live music |
| | Clowns |
| ✗ | Face painters |
| ✗ | Childrens games |
| | Animal exhibits/petting zoo |
| ✗ | Dogs allowed on leash |
| ✗ | Lost and found |
| | Bicycle racks |
| ✗ | First aid area available |
| ✗ | Self-brought picnics allowed |
| | Self-brought alcohol allowed |
| | Stroller/wheelchair rentals available |

| | |
|---|---|
| ✗ | Parade: 10:00 AM on Warm Springs Bl. |
| ✗ | Parking fee: $2 |
| ✗ | Entrance fee: $1 |
| | Camping facilities |
| | Boating facilities |
| | RV facilities w/ hookups |
| | Accomodations in town |
| ✗ | Restaurants in town<br>Vineyards Inn, Kenwood Restaurant, Orestes Garden Bear Lodge |

# *Fourth of July Parade*

THE **ANNUAL FOURTH OF July Parade** brings small town America back to life in Mendocino. Homemade floats, lots of marchers, a horse or two, baton twirlers and the Mendocino Fire Department's shiny fire engines proceed down Main Street past the historic Kelley House and Ford House. The view just beyond the parade is the spectacular Mendocino Bay.

## Mendocino, California

Fourth of July
Noon - 4:00 PM

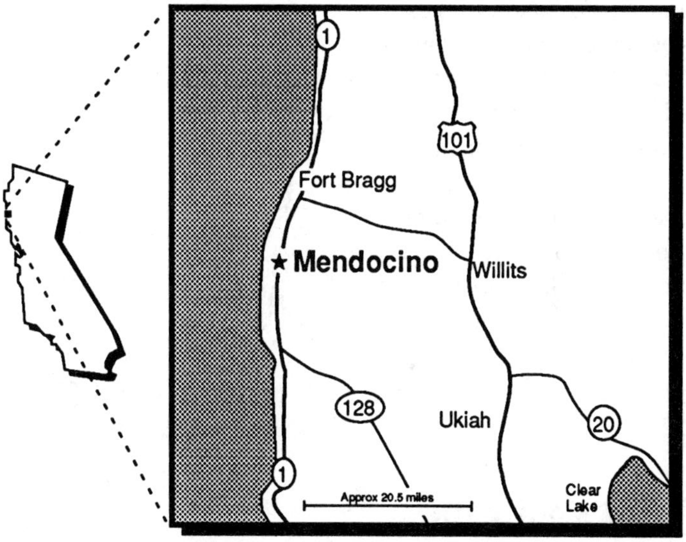


*Up-to-date festival information is available from:*
*Mendocino Chamber of Commerce*
*(707) 964-3153*

## What's goin' on...

Town population: **1,000**
Last year's attendance: **1,000**
Average outdoor temperature: **60°**
Festival location: **Downtown**

| | |
|---|---|
| ✗ | Wine tasting/beer for sale |
| ✗ | Food booths |
| ✗ | Arts/crafts for sale |
| ✗ | Live music |
| | Clowns |
| | Face painters |
| | Childrens games |
| | Animal exhibits/petting zoo |
| ✗ | Dogs allowed on leash |
| | Lost and found |
| ✗ | Bicycle racks |
| | First aid area available |
| ✗ | Self-brought picnics allowed |
| | Self-brought alcohol allowed |
| | Stroller/wheelchair rentals available |

| | |
|---|---|
| ✗ | Parade: Noon on Main St. |
| | Parking fee |
| | Entrance fee |
| ✗ | Camping facilities: 1 mile |
| ✗ | Boating facilities: Ocean/River |
| ✗ | RV facilities w/ hookups: 8 miles |
| ✗ | Accomodations in town<br>Blackberry Inn, Sea Gull Inn, 1021 Main Street, Mendocino Farmhouse B&B, Hill House |
| ✗ | Restaurants in town<br>Cafe Beaujolais, Hill House Inn, 955 Ukiah, MacCallum House, Chocolate Moosse |

# *Fourth of July Parade & Celebration*

"...FROM EVERY MOUNTAIN-side, let freedom ring!" It rings loud and clear at the **Fourth of July Parade & Celebration** in Nevada City! This rustic town really knows how to turn on the red, white, and blue for a great celebration! You'll see a colorful and patriotic parade, eat hot dogs, nachos, burritos, stuffed potatoes, nose around at the art and craft items for sale, and watch an explosion of fireworks in the evening!

## Nevada City, California

Fourth of July
10:00 AM - 7:00 PM

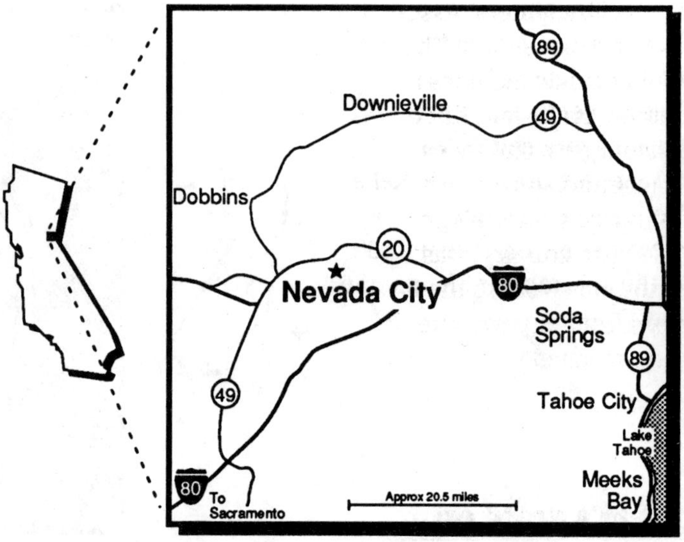


## What's goin' on...

Town population: **2,770**
Last year's attendance: **N/A**
Average outdoor temperature: **90°**
Festival location: **Downtown/Fairgrounds**

*Up-to-date festival information is available from:*
*Nevada City Chamber of Commerce*
*(916) 265-2692*

| | |
|---|---|
| X | Wine tasting/beer for sale |
| X | Food booths |
| X | Arts/crafts for sale |
| X | Live music |
| X | Clowns |
| X | Face painters |
| X | Childrens games |
| X | Animal exhibits/petting zoo |
| X | Dogs allowed on leash |
| X | Lost and found |
| X | Bicycle racks |
| X | First aid area available |
| X | Self-brought picnics allowed |
| | Self-brought alcohol allowed |
| X | Stroller/wheelchair rentals available |

| | |
|---|---|
| X | Parade |
| | Parking fee |
| X | Entrance fee |
| X | Camping facilities |
| X | Boating facilities |
| | RV facilities w/ hookups |
| X | Accomodations in town<br>The National Hotel, Le Petit Chateau, Grandmere's Inn, Red Castle |
| X | Restaurants in town<br>The Willo, York Street Blues, Friar Tuck's, Cowboy Pizza, The Apple Fare, Selaya's |

# *Fourth of July Firefighters Picnic*

WANT A REAL SMALL TOWN celebration? Come on down to the **Fourth of July Firefighters Picnic** sponsored by the Firefighters' Association and Lions Club. This all-day picnic includes a parade, crafts fair, hot dogs, hamburgers, and tacos. Wheatland, gateway to California's "Mother Lode" gold rush country, was host to the survivors to the ill-fated Donner party after they were rescued in 1846.

## Wheatland, California

Fourth of July
10:00 AM - 6:00 PM

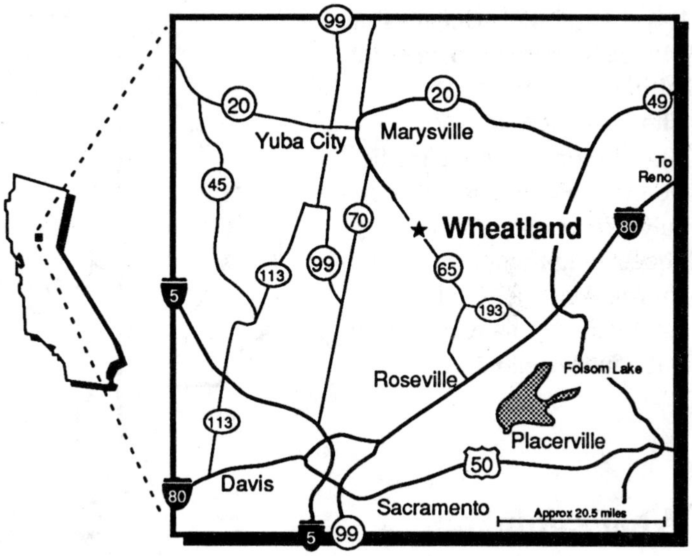


*Up-to-date festival information is available from:*
*Wheatland Chamber of Commerce*
*(we don't have a phone no.)*

## What's goin' on...

Town population: **1,474**
Last year's attendance: **350**
Average outdoor temperature: **96°**
Festival location: **Downtown**

| | |
|---|---|
| | Wine tasting/beer for sale |
| X | Food booths |
| X | Arts/crafts for sale |
| X | Live music |
| | Clowns |
| | Face painters |
| X | Childrens games |
| X | Animal exhibits/petting zoo |
| X | Dogs allowed on leash |
| X | Lost and found |
| X | Bicycle racks |
| X | First aid area available |
| X | Self-brought picnics allowed |
| | Self-brought alcohol allowed |
| | Stroller/wheelchair rentals available |

| | |
|---|---|
| | Parade |
| | Parking fee |
| | Entrance fee |
| X | Camping facilities: 7 miles |
| X | Boating facilities: Camp Far West Lake |
| X | RV facilities w/ hookups: 7 miles |
| | Accomodations in town |
| X | Restaurants in town<br>Morena's |

# *Fandango Days*

LONG AGO, WAGON TRAINS entered California at its northeastern corner. On sighting Goose Lake, thinking it was the Pacific Ocean, some pioneers stopped to celebrate with a Fandango dance. That's why the town of Alturas continues the tradition with **Fandango Days** in July! Water sports, horseshoes, Ping-Pong tournaments, a buffalo barbecue and dancing round out a full weekend.

## Alturas, California

First full weekend in July
Daily 10:00 AM - 7:30 PM

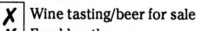

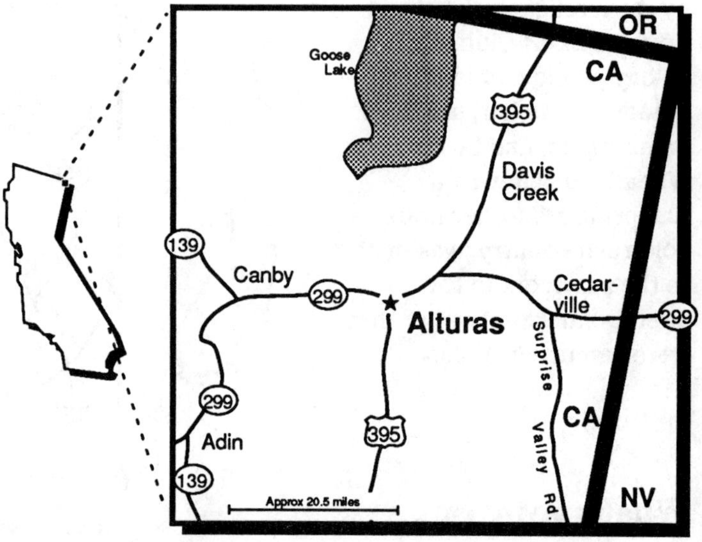


*Up-to-date festival information is available from:*
*Alturas Chamber of Commerce*
*(916) 233-2819*

## What's goin' on...

Town population: **3,025**
Last year's attendance: **N/A**
Average outdoor temperature: **85°**
Festival location: **California Pines Lodge**

- X Wine tasting/beer for sale
- X Food booths
- X Arts/crafts for sale
- X Live music
- X Clowns
- X Face painters
- X Childrens games
- X Animal exhibits/petting zoo
- X Dogs allowed on leash
- X Lost and found
- Bicycle racks
- X First aid area available
- X Self-brought picnics allowed
- Self-brought alcohol allowed
- Stroller/wheelchair rentals available

- X Parade: Sat. 11:00 AM on Main St.
- Parking fee
- Entrance fee
- X Camping facilities: 20 miles
- X Boating facilities: Big Sage Res.
- X RV facilities w/ hookups: In town
- X Accomodations in town
  Sunrise Motel
- X Restaurants in town
  Golden's Restaurant, Don's Valley Burger

# *World's Largest Salmon Barbecue*

FISH LOVERS UNITE! FORT Bragg holds the **World's Largest Salmon Barbecue** each year at Noyo Harbor, home of Fort Bragg's fishing fleet! Fort Bragg is home of the largest redwood mill in the world as well as of the famous Skunk Train, which chugs along 40 miles of track through majestic redwood forests to the town of Willits. Nearby is Georgia-Pacific Corporation's nursery, where more than three million redwood seedlings are grown for planting.

## Fort Bragg, California

First Saturday in July
10:00 AM - 11:00 PM

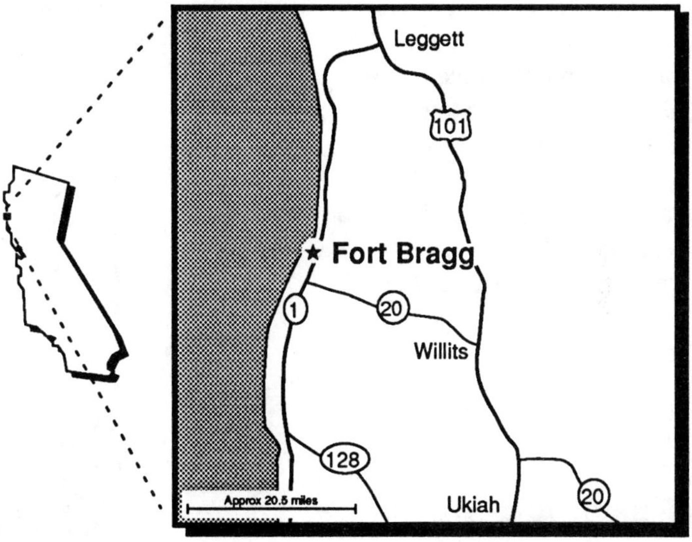


*Up-to-date festival information is available from:*
*Fort Bragg Chamber of Commerce*
*(800)-7-COAST-0*

## What's goin' on...

Town population: **5,019**
Last year's attendance: **5,000**
Average outdoor temperature: **85°**
Festival location: **Noyo Harbor**

| | |
|---|---|
| X | Wine tasting/beer for sale |
| X | Food booths |
| | Arts/crafts for sale |
| X | Live music |
| | Clowns |
| | Face painters |
| | Childrens games |
| | Animal exhibits/petting zoo |
| X | Dogs allowed on leash |
| | Lost and found |
| | Bicycle racks |
| | First aid area available |
| | Self-brought picnics allowed |
| | Self-brought alcohol allowed |
| | Stroller/wheelchair rentals available |

| | |
|---|---|
| | Parade |
| | Parking fee |
| X | Entrance fee: Adults $9; Kids $4 |
| X | Camping facilities: 1 mile |
| X | Boating facilities: Pacific Ocean |
| X | RV facilities w/ hookups: 1 mile |
| X | Accomodations in town<br>Fort Bragg Motel, Pudding Creek Inn B&B, Grey Whale Inn, Anchor Lodge |
| X | Restaurants in town<br>The Restaurant, D'Aurelio & Sons, Noyo River Restaurant, Wharf Restaurant, Cap'n Flints |

# *Lake County Rodeo*

THE **LAKE COUNTY RODEO** is great fun for the whole family! Located at the Fairgrounds, this two-day event is your typical country rodeo...complete with a Saturday-night dance beginning at 9:00. Indian jewelry, hats, T-shirts, and other western items are for sale...and, of course, there's a western-style barbecue! Don't forget that there are a bunch of wineries in the area to tour too!

## Lakeport, California

First Saturday in July
10:00 AM - 11:00 PM

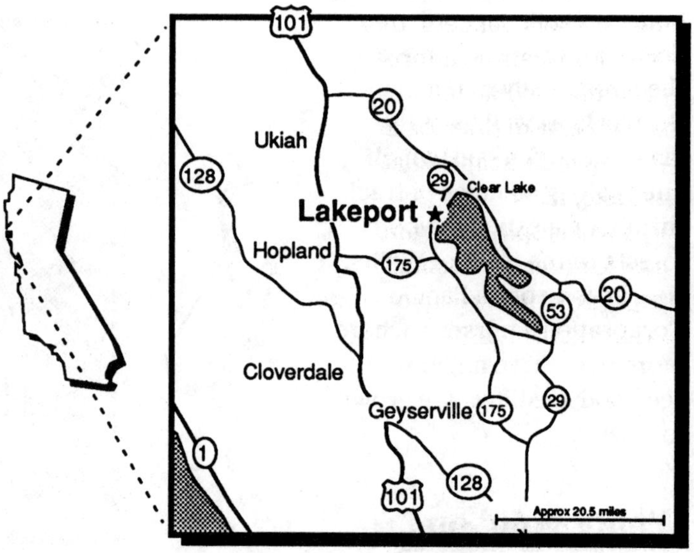


*Up-to-date festival information is available from:*
*Lakeport Chamber of Commerce*
*(707) 263-6131*

## What's goin' on...

Town population: **3,675**
Last year's attendance: **3,500**
Average outdoor temperature: **85°**
Festival location: **Fairgrounds**

| | |
|---|---|
| X | Wine tasting/beer for sale |
| X | Food booths |
| X | Arts/crafts for sale |
| | Live music |
| | Clowns |
| X | Face painters |
| X | Childrens games |
| X | Animal exhibits/petting zoo |
| | Dogs allowed on leash |
| X | Lost and found |
| X | Bicycle racks |
| X | First aid area available |
| X | Self-brought picnics allowed |
| | Self-brought alcohol allowed |
| X | Stroller/wheelchair rentals available |

| | |
|---|---|
| X | Parade: Sat. 1:00 PM on Main St. |
| X | Parking fee: $1 |
| X | Entrance fee: S $5; A $6; K $3 |
| X | Camping facilities: In town |
| X | Boating facilities: Clear Lake |
| X | RV facilities w/ hookups: In town |
| X | Accomodations in town |
| X | Restaurants in town<br>Park Place, Anthony's, Narrows Lodge, Robin Hill |

# *Obon Festival*

MARYSVILLE BUDDIST Church on B Street is where you'll find the **Obon Festival**! Complete with Japanese music and folk dancers, this celebration lasts all afternoon on Saturday. While in Marysville, take time for a walk or paddleboat ride at Ellis Lake, where friendly ducks will stop to chat and quack for bread and small bluegill practically leap onto your fishhooks!

## Marysville, California

First weekend in July
Daily 3:00 PM - 9:00 PM

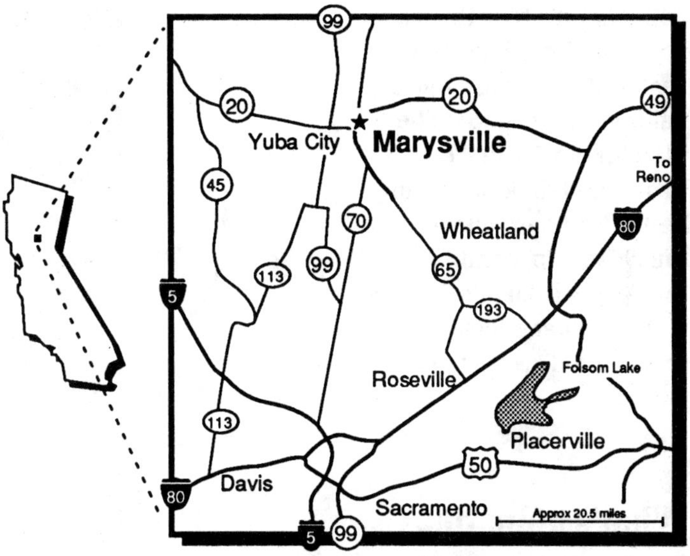


## What's goin' on...

Town population: **12,000**
Last year's attendance: **600**
Average outdoor temperature: **92°**
Festival location: **Marysville Buddist Festival**

*Up-to-date festival information is available from:*
*Marysville Chamber of Commerce*
*(916) 743-6501*

| | |
|---|---|
| ✗ | Wine tasting/beer for sale |
| | Food booths |
| | Arts/crafts for sale |
| ✗ | Live music |
| | Clowns |
| | Face painters |
| | Childrens games |
| | Animal exhibits/petting zoo |
| | Dogs allowed on leash |
| ✗ | Lost and found |
| | Bicycle racks |
| | First aid area available |
| | Self-brought picnics allowed |
| | Self-brought alcohol allowed |
| | Stroller/wheelchair rentals available |

| | |
|---|---|
| | Parade |
| | Parking fee |
| | Entrance fee |
| ✗ | Camping facilities: 1 mile |
| ✗ | Boating facilities: Collins Lake |
| ✗ | RV facilities w/ hookups: 1 mile |
| ✗ | Accomodations in town<br>Bonanza Inn, Marysville Motor Lodge, The Oxbow |
| ✗ | Restaurants in town<br>Daikoku, Cannery, The Eagle's Nest, China Moon |

# *Mendocino Music Festival*

THE HISTORIC VILLAGE OF Mendocino sits on a headland overlooking the magnificent north coastline. The 19th-century New England style buildings have been restored and house fine art galleries, and shops. The **Mendocino Music Festival** has gained national prominence for its excellent musicianship, combining musicians from San Francisco Symphony and local talent, under the direction of Allan Pollack.

## Mendocino, California

July 10th - 20th
Evenings at 8:00 PM

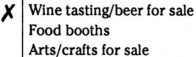

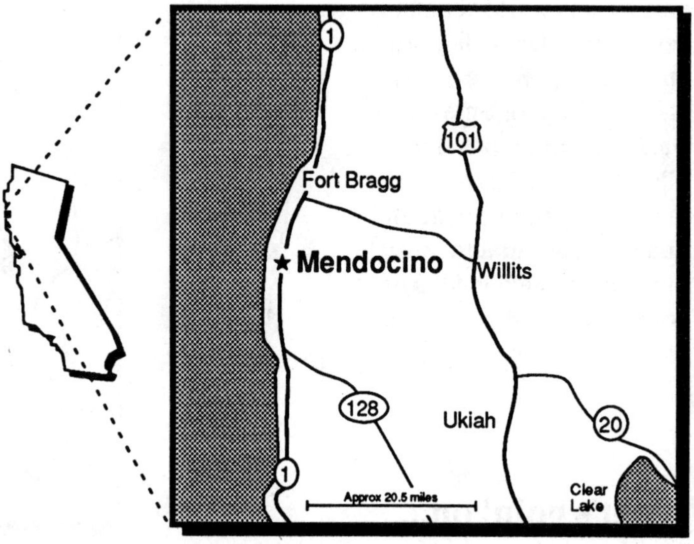


## What's goin' on...

Town population: **1,000**
Last year's attendance: **5,000**
Average outdoor temperature: **60°**
Festival location: **State headlands in town**

*Up-to-date festival information is available from:*
*Mendocino Chamber of Commerce*
*(707) 964-3153*

- X Wine tasting/beer for sale
- Food booths
- Arts/crafts for sale
- X Live music
- Clowns
- Face painters
- Childrens games
- Animal exhibits/petting zoo
- Dogs allowed on leash
- Lost and found
- Bicycle racks
- First aid area available
- Self-brought picnics allowed
- Self-brought alcohol allowed
- X Stroller/wheelchair rentals available

- Parade
- Parking fee
- X Entrance fee: (prices not avbl.)
- X Camping facilities: 1 mile
- X Boating facilities: Ocean/River
- X RV facilities w/ hookups: 8 miles
- X Accomodations in town
  Agate Cove Inn B&B, Sears House, Reed Manor, Mendocino Farmhouse B&B, Hill House
- X Restaurants in town
  Cafe Beaujolais, Hill House Inn, 955 Ukiah, MacCallum House, Chocolate Moosse

# *Wine Country Film Festival*

THIS ANNUAL **WINE COUNTRY Film Festival** is remarkable—it's jammed packed with exciting films from around the world! The first three days (Fri. - Sun.) are in Healdsburg, then, the festival hops to Calistoga (Tues. - Thurs.), and ends in Petaluma (Fri. - Sun.). (These town maps are elsewhere in the book). Please call the number provided to receive ticket information. Then come up and vote for your favorites!

## Glen Ellen, California

Second weekend to the third weekend in July
Hours vary

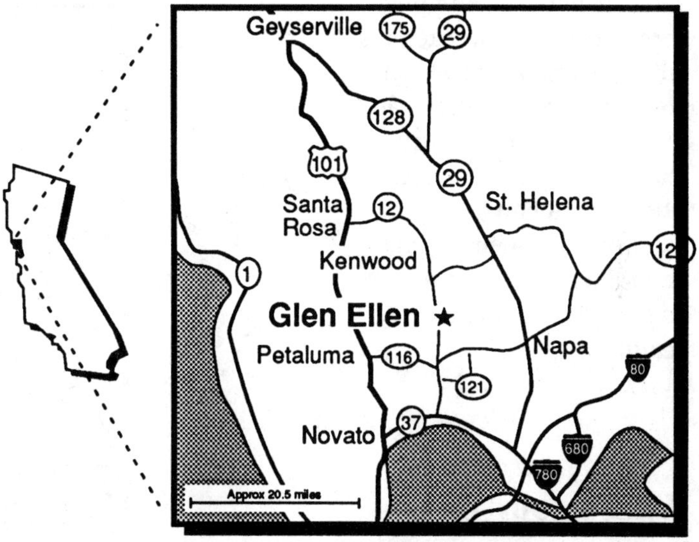


*Up-to-date festival information is available from:*
*Glen Ellen Wine Co. Film Festival*
*(707) 935-FILM*

## What's goin' on...

Town population: **N/A**
Last year's attendance: **15,000**
Average outdoor temperature: **79°**
Festival location: **Napa & Sonoma Counties**

| | |
|---|---|
| X | Wine tasting/beer for sale |
| X | Food booths |
| X | Arts/crafts for sale |
| X | Live music |
| | Clowns |
| | Face painters |
| | Childrens games |
| | Animal exhibits/petting zoo |
| | Dogs allowed on leash |
| | Lost and found |
| | Bicycle racks |
| | First aid area available |
| | Self-brought picnics allowed |
| | Self-brought alcohol allowed |
| | Stroller/wheelchair rentals available |

| | |
|---|---|
| | Parade |
| | Parking fee |
| X | Entrance fee: Varies $5 - 100 |
| X | Camping facilities: 5-10 miles |
| X | Boating facilities: Lake Sonoma |
| X | RV facilities w/ hookups: 20 miles |
| X | Accomodations in town |
| X | Restaurants in town |

# *Masten Ramsey Stockhorse Jubilee*

THE **MASTEN RAMSEY Stockhorse Jubilee** spotlights working stock, cutting and snaffle-bit horses, cattle penning, and trail and pleasure horses. The weekend is full of events open to both junior and senior riders, and also features a three-man-team event. It's all in a county where you'll find fresh, cool mountain air; scenic beauty; and wilderness areas where *no* motorized vehicles *dare* venture!

## Alturas, California

Second weekend in July
Hours vary

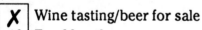

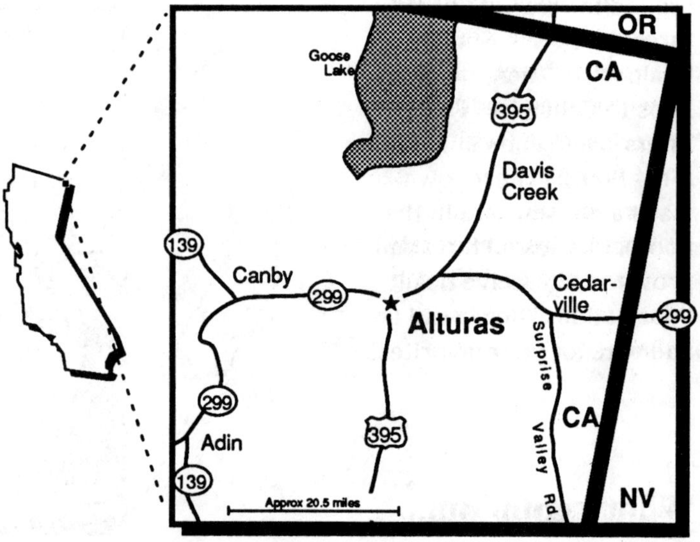


*Up-to-date festival information is available from:*
*Alturas Chamber of Commerce*
*(916) 233-2819*

## What's goin' on...

Town population: **3,025**
Last year's attendance: **N/A**
Average outdoor temperature: **85°**
Festival location: **Jr. Livestock Grounds**

- X Wine tasting/beer for sale
- X Food booths
- Arts/crafts for sale
- X Live music
- X Clowns
- Face painters
- Childrens games
- X Animal exhibits/petting zoo
- X Dogs allowed on leash
- X Lost and found
- Bicycle racks
- X First aid area available
- X Self-brought picnics allowed
- Self-brought alcohol allowed
- Stroller/wheelchair rentals available

- Parade
- Parking fee
- X Entrance fee: $6
- X Camping facilities: In town
- X Boating facilities: Dorris Res.
- X RV facilities w/ hookups: In town
- X Accomodations in town
  Court Motel, Hacienda Motel, Dunes Motel
- X Restaurants in town
  The Alamo, Betty's Country Kitchen, The Brass Nail

# *Lake County Wine & Food Renaissance*

THE LAKE COUNTY FAIRgrounds are the place to be for the annual **Lake County Wine & Food Renaissance.** This gala event features the products of the Kendall Jackson, Konocti, Guenoc, and Channing Rudd Cellars wineries, along with gourmet food booths of French, Italian, American, and German cultures. Clear Lake State Park and the Lake County Museum are other sites to take in.

## Lakeport, California

Second Saturday in July
1:00 PM - 5:00 PM

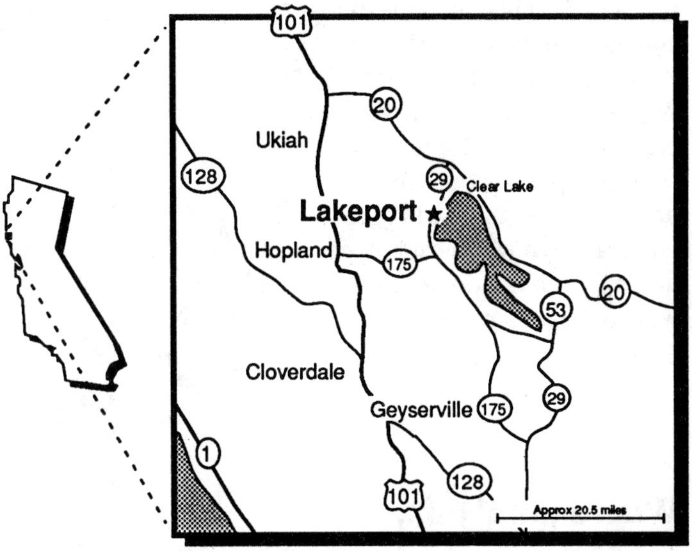


*Up-to-date festival information is available from:*
*Lakeport Chamber of Commerce*
*(707) 263-6131*

## What's goin' on...

Town population: **3,675**
Last year's attendance: **2,000**
Average outdoor temperature: **85°**
Festival location: **Fairgrounds**

| | |
|---|---|
| ✗ | Wine tasting/beer for sale |
| ✗ | Food booths |
| ✗ | Arts/crafts for sale |
| | Live music |
| ✗ | Clowns |
| ✗ | Face painters |
| ✗ | Childrens games |
| | Animal exhibits/petting zoo |
| ✗ | Dogs allowed on leash |
| ✗ | Lost and found |
| ✗ | Bicycle racks |
| ✗ | First aid area available |
| | Self-brought picnics allowed |
| | Self-brought alcohol allowed |
| ✗ | Stroller/wheelchair rentals available |

| | |
|---|---|
| | Parade |
| ✗ | Parking fee: $1 |
| ✗ | Entrance fee: $15 |
| ✗ | Camping facilities: In town |
| ✗ | Boating facilities: Clear Lake |
| ✗ | RV facilities w/ hookups: In town |
| ✗ | Accomodations in town |
| ✗ | Restaurants in town<br>Robin Hill, Park Place, Anthony's |

# *Shakespearean Festival at Benbow*

"TO BE OR NOT TO BE..." AT the **Shakespearean Festival at Benbow** Lake "...that is the question." The answer is YES! Dress in Elizabethan style and come north to celebrate the English poet and dramatist William Shakespeare. This celebration, amid huge redwood trees with their heavenly fragrance, will take you back to a wonderful place in time. This is a delightful way to spend a pleasant evening!

## Garberville, California

Last weekend in July (beginning Thursday)
Evenings

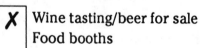

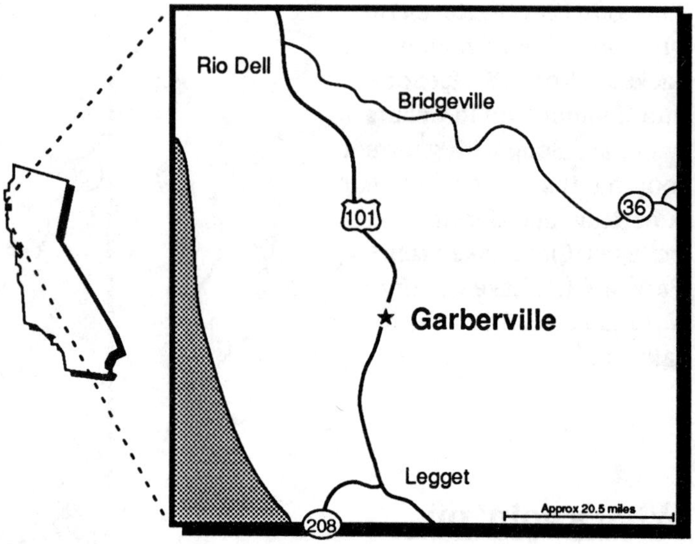


*Up-to-date festival information is available from:*
*Garberville Chamber of Commerce*
*(707) 923-2613*

## What's goin' on...

Town population: **1,000**
Last year's attendance: **N/A**
Average outdoor temperature: **70° eves**
Festival location: **Lakeside**

| | |
|---|---|
| ✗ | Wine tasting/beer for sale |
| | Food booths |
| | Arts/crafts for sale |
| ✗ | Live music |
| | Clowns |
| | Face painters |
| | Childrens games |
| | Animal exhibits/petting zoo |
| | Dogs allowed on leash |
| | Lost and found |
| | Bicycle racks |
| ✗ | First aid area available |
| ✗ | Self-brought picnics allowed |
| ✗ | Self-brought alcohol allowed |
| | Stroller/wheelchair rentals available |

| | |
|---|---|
| | Parade |
| | Parking fee |
| ✗ | Entrance fee: (prices not avbl.) |
| ✗ | Camping facilities: On-site |
| ✗ | Boating facilities: Benbow Lake (canoes) |
| ✗ | RV facilities w/ hookups: On-site |
| ✗ | Accomodations in town<br>Benbow Inn, Hartsook Inn |
| ✗ | Restaurants in town<br>Benbow Inn, Hartsook Inn, Woodrow's Waterwheel, Sicilitos |

# *Great Historic Hotel Bicycle Race & Criterium*

TUCKED AWAY IN THE tippy-top right-hand corner of California is the rustic town of Alturas with its **Great Historical Hotel Bicycle Race & Criterium.** It sure sounds like a full weekend of fun for the entire family! Not far from Alturas lies the 6,000-acre National Wildlife Refuge for migrating fowl and other wildlife (hunting is permitted on 1,440 acres of the refuge).

## Alturas, California

Fourth weekend in July
Daily 8:00 AM - 7:30 PM

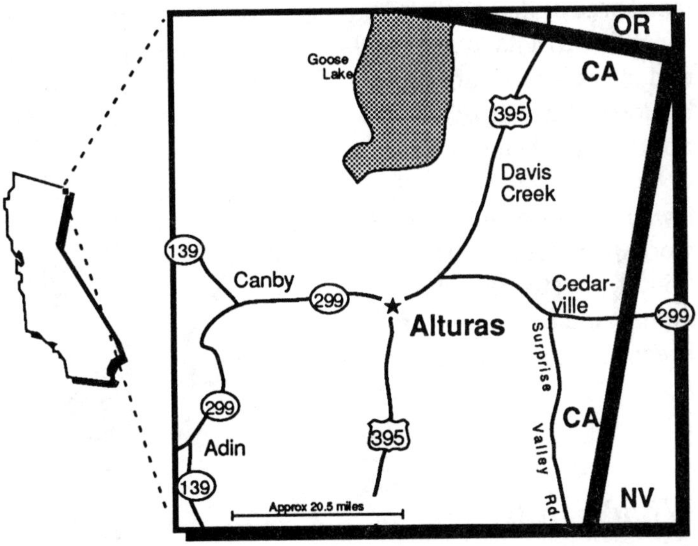


## What's goin' on...

Town population: **3,025**
Last year's attendance: **N/A**
Average outdoor temperature: **85°**
Festival location: **N/A**

*Up-to-date festival information is available from:*
*Alturas Chamber of Commerce*
*(916) 233-2819*

| | |
|---|---|
| | Wine tasting/beer for sale |
| | Food booths |
| | Arts/crafts for sale |
| | Live music |
| | Clowns |
| | Face painters |
| | Childrens games |
| | Animal exhibits/petting zoo |
| X | Dogs allowed on leash |
| | Lost and found |
| | Bicycle racks |
| X | First aid area available |
| | Self-brought picnics allowed |
| | Self-brought alcohol allowed |
| | Stroller/wheelchair rentals available |

| | |
|---|---|
| | Parade |
| | Parking fee |
| X | Entrance fee: $6 & up |
| X | Camping facilities: In town |
| X | Boating facilities: Dorris Res. |
| X | RV facilities w/ hookups: In town |
| X | Accomodations in town<br>Court Hotel, Hacienda Motel, Dunes Motel |
| X | Restaurants in town<br>The Alamo, Betty's Country Kitchen, The Brass Nail |

# *Wildwood Days*

**WILDWOOD DAYS** IN THE Rio Dell-Scotia area is a premier event for locals and vacationers alike! This relaxed area of California hosts tours through its lumber mills and offers fossil bluffs to explore. The festival's crafts booths include teddy bears, dolls, stone art, handmade jewelry, pottery, and woodwork items for sale. The food booths are stocked with homemade pies, Indian fry bread, chili, and lots more!

## Rio Dell-Scotia, California

First weekend in August (beginning Friday)
Daily 10:00 AM - 6:00 PM

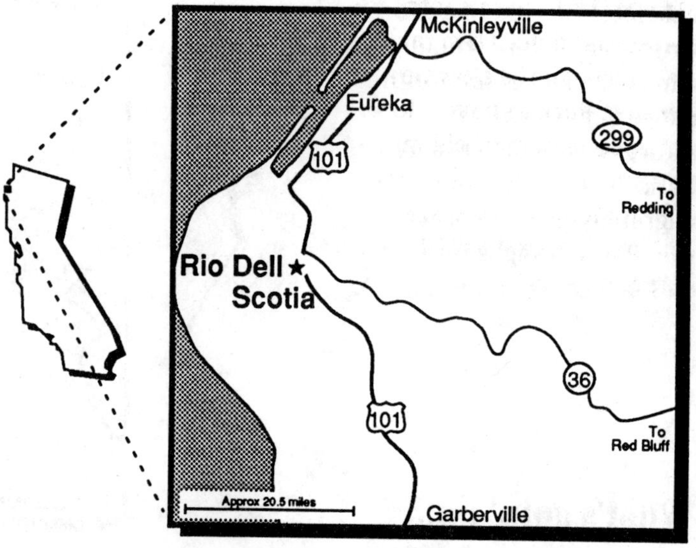


## What's goin' on...

Town population: **3,500**
Last year's attendance: **3,000**
Average outdoor temperature: **68°**
Festival location: **Downtown Rio Dell**

*Up-to-date festival information is available from:*
*Rio Dell-Scotia Chamber of Commerce*
*(707) 764-3436*

- ✗ Wine tasting/beer for sale
- ✗ Food booths
- ✗ Arts/crafts for sale
- ✗ Live music
- ✗ Clowns
- ✗ Face painters
- ✗ Childrens games
- Animal exhibits/petting zoo
- Dogs allowed on leash
- ✗ Lost and found
- ✗ Bicycle racks
- ✗ First aid area available
- Self-brought picnics allowed
- Self-brought alcohol allowed
- Stroller/wheelchair rentals available

- ✗ Parade: Sat. 11:00 AM downtown Rio Dell
- Parking fee
- Entrance fee
- ✗ Camping facilities: In town
- ✗ Boating facilities: Van Duzen River
- ✗ RV facilities w/ hookups: In town
- ✗ Accomodations in town
  Scotia Inn
- ✗ Restaurants in town
  Scotia Inn

# Miners Day

TO COMMEMORATE THE rich heritage of California's mining history, quaint Downieville annually salutes **Miners Day**! There's lots to eat, see, and do! Then take a walk through the Downieville Heritage Park to have a look at the collection of old mining equipment, including a steam boiler, monitor hose, stamp mill, and ore cart full of quartz chunks.

## Downieville, California

First Saturday in August
10:00 AM - 11:00 PM

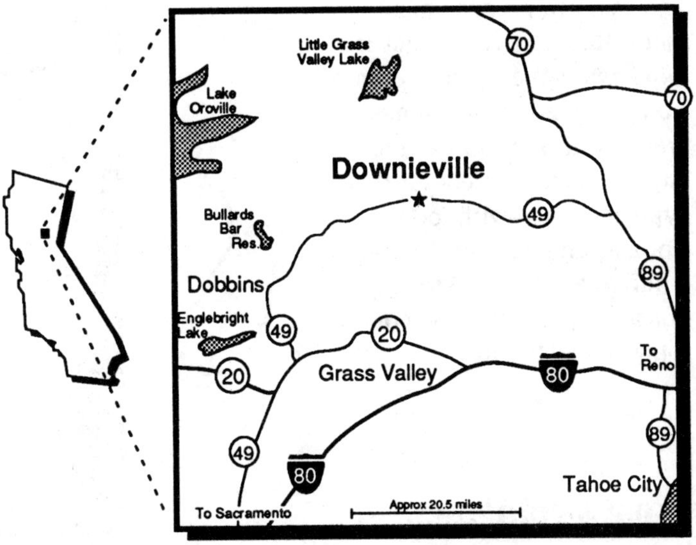


☞ *Up-to-date festival information is available from: Downieville Chamber of Commerce (916) 289-3560*

## What's goin' on...

Town population: **3,300**
Last year's attendance: **N/A**
Average outdoor temperature: **80°**
Festival location: **Downtown**

- [ ] Wine tasting/beer for sale
- [x] Food booths
- [x] Arts/crafts for sale
- [x] Live music
- [ ] Clowns
- [ ] Face painters
- [x] Childrens games
- [x] Animal exhibits/petting zoo
- [x] Dogs allowed on leash
- [ ] Lost and found
- [ ] Bicycle racks
- [ ] First aid area available
- [x] Self-brought picnics allowed
- [ ] Self-brought alcohol allowed
- [ ] Stroller/wheelchair rentals available

- [x] Parade: Noon on Main St.
- [ ] Parking fee
- [ ] Entrance fee
- [x] Camping facilities: 3 miles
- [ ] Boating facilities
- [x] RV facilities w/ hookups: 13 miles
- [x] Accomodations in town
  Dyers Resort, Riverside Motel, Robinsons, Downieville Motor Inn, The Lure
- [x] Restaurants in town
  Forks, Riverview Pizza, Coyoteville

# *Reggae on the River*

**REGGAE ON THE RIVER** IS the largest outdoor reggae event on the Pacific Coast! Featuring top-name American and Jamaican reggae musicians, this musical adventure will have you on your feet in no time. The warm summer weather at Benbow Lake in August is just perfect for this type of event—with food booths ranging from tofuburgers to sushi to egg rolls! And, give the golf course a try during the day.

## Garberville, California

First Saturday in August
Noon - 10:00 PM

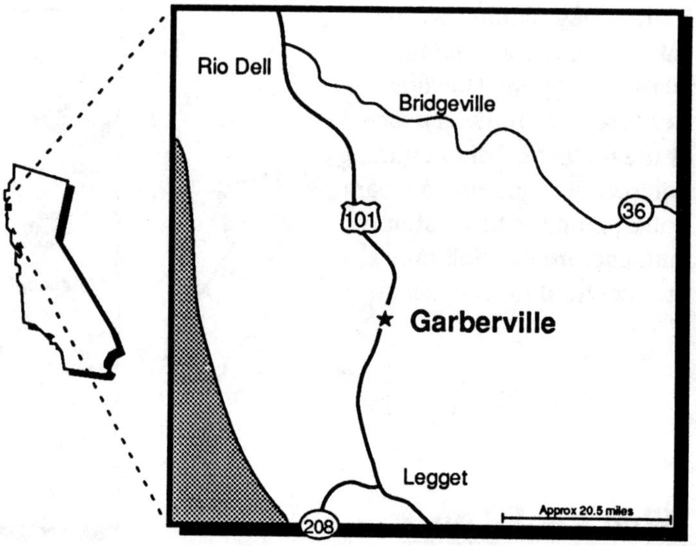


*Up-to-date festival information is available from:*
*Garberville Chamber of Commerce*
*(707) 923-2613*

## What's goin' on...

Town population: **10,000**
Last year's attendance: **N/A**
Average outdoor temperature: **85°**
Festival location: **Benbow Lake**

| | |
|---|---|
| X | Wine tasting/beer for sale |
| | Food booths |
| X | Arts/crafts for sale |
| X | Live music |
| | Clowns |
| X | Face painters |
| X | Childrens games |
| | Animal exhibits/petting zoo |
| X | Dogs allowed on leash |
| X | Lost and found |
| | Bicycle racks |
| X | First aid area available |
| X | Self-brought picnics allowed |
| X | Self-brought alcohol allowed |
| | Stroller/wheelchair rentals available |

| | |
|---|---|
| | Parade |
| | Parking fee |
| X | Entrance fee: $20; $18 in adv. |
| X | Camping facilities: On-site |
| X | Boating facilities: Benbow Lake (canoes) |
| X | RV facilities w/ hookups: On-site |
| X | Accomodations in town<br>Benbow Inn, Hartsook Inn |
| X | Restaurants in town<br>Waterwheel, Woodrow's, Sicilitos, Brass Rail |

# *Salmon Festival*

THE KLAMATH **SALMON Festival** is a celebration of the valuable salmon resource, featuring Hydro-Fobia Boat Races and an Indian barbecue salmon feast, live entertainment, a huge logging show, and arts and crafts. In addition to abundant salmon in the Northern California waters, you'll find trout, sturgeon, perch, smelt, ling cod, crab, and razor clams.

## Klamath, California

First weekend in August
Daily 10:00 AM - 6:00 PM

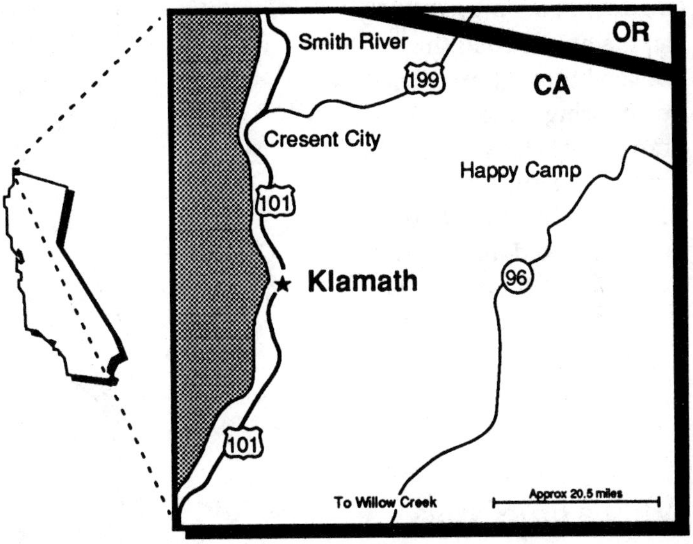


## What's goin' on...

Town population: **700**
Last year's attendance: **2,000**
Average outdoor temperature: **60°**
Festival location: **N/A**

*Up-to-date festival information is available from:*
*Klamath Chamber of Commerce*
*(707) 465-2224*

| | |
|---|---|
| X | Wine tasting/beer for sale |
| X | Food booths |
| X | Arts/crafts for sale |
| X | Live music |
| | Clowns |
| X | Face painters |
| X | Childrens games |
| | Animal exhibits/petting zoo |
| X | Dogs allowed on leash |
| X | Lost and found |
| X | Bicycle racks |
| X | First aid area available |
| X | Self-brought picnics allowed |
| | Self-brought alcohol allowed |
| | Stroller/wheelchair rentals available |

| | |
|---|---|
| X | Parade: Sun. 10:00 AM downtown |
| | Parking fee |
| | Entrance fee |
| X | Camping facilities: On-site |
| X | Boating facilities: Klamath River |
| X | RV facilities w/ hookups: 1 mile |
| X | Accomodations in town<br>Camp Marigold, Motel Trees |
| X | Restaurants in town |

# *Annie & Mary Day*

BLUE LAKE, A SMALL TOWN on California's beautiful North Coast, celebrates **Annie and Mary Day**—commemorating the bright gals who virtually ran the old railroad that chugged through Blue Lake to neighboring lumber mills. Start off the day with a lumberjack breakfast at 7:30 AM, then it's a day filled with barbecues, old-time fiddles, and lots of railroading history.

## Blue Lake, California

First Sunday in August
8:30 AM - 6:00 PM

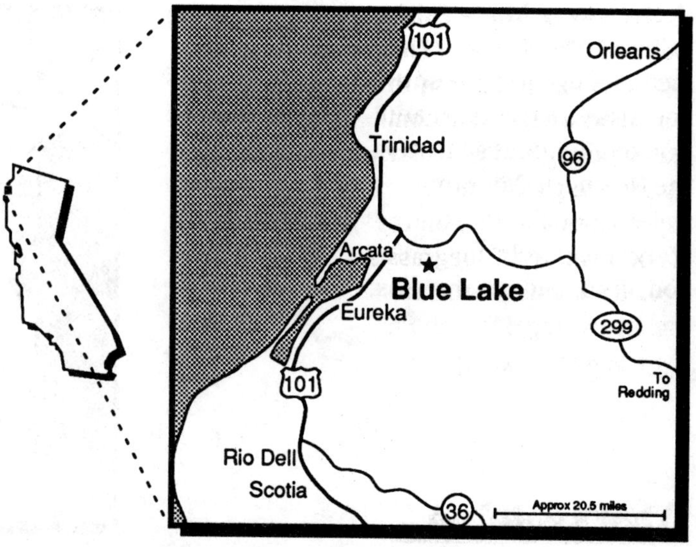


## What's goin' on...

Town population: **1,308**
Last year's attendance: **2,000**
Average outdoor temperature: **75°**
Festival location: **Downtown**

*Up-to-date festival information is available from:*
*Blue Lake Chamber of Commerce*
*(707) 668-5567*

| | |
|---|---|
| X | Wine tasting/beer for sale |
| X | Food booths |
| X | Arts/crafts for sale |
| X | Live music |
| X | Clowns |
| X | Face painters |
| X | Childrens games |
| X | Animal exhibits/petting zoo |
| | Dogs allowed on leash |
| X | Lost and found |
| X | Bicycle racks |
| X | First aid area available |
| X | Self-brought picnics allowed |
| | Self-brought alcohol allowed |
| | Stroller/wheelchair rentals available |

| | |
|---|---|
| X | Parade: Sun.—10:00 downtown |
| | Parking fee |
| | Entrance fee |
| X | Camping facilities: 15 miles |
| X | Boating facilities: Mad River |
| X | RV facilities w/ hookups: 15 miles |
| | Accomodations in town |
| X | Restaurants in town<br>Pizza Mill, Blue Lake Restaurant |

# *Gravenstein Apple Fair*

JUST SOUTH OF NORTHERN California's wine country lies Sebastopol...where the entire area turns out for the **Gravenstein Apple Fair!** Dubbed *The Sweetest Little Fair in Sonoma County,* this fun-filled weekend accommodates young and old alike. There are gigantic apple sculptures and "life on the farm" displays. Bluegrass and country music fill the air at the lively Ragle Ranch Park for the weekend too!

## Sebastopol, California

Second weekend in August
Daily 10:00 AM - 6:00 PM

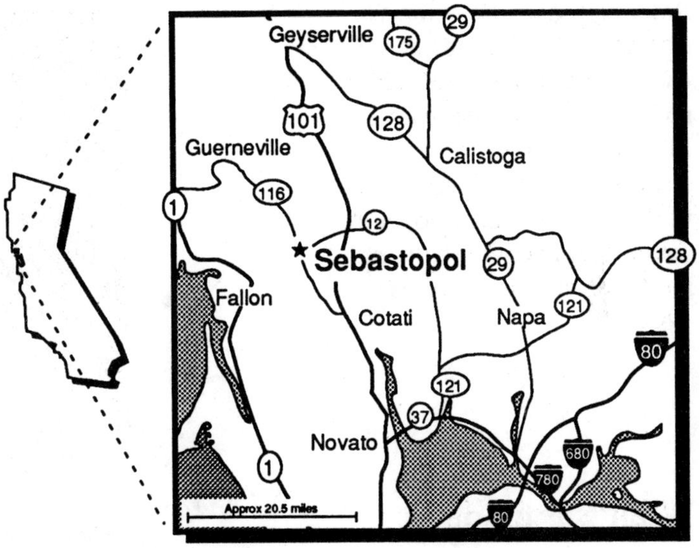


## What's goin' on...

Town population: **3,595**
Last year's attendance: **20,000**
Average outdoor temperature: **80°**
Festival location: **Eagle Ranch Park**

*Up-to-date festival information is available from:*
*Sebastopol Chamber of Commerce*
*(707) 823-3032*

- [x] Wine tasting/beer for sale
- [x] Food booths
- [x] Arts/crafts for sale
- [x] Live music
- [x] Clowns
- [x] Face painters
- [x] Childrens games
- [x] Animal exhibits/petting zoo
- [x] Dogs allowed on leash
- [x] Lost and found
- [x] Bicycle racks
- [x] First aid area available
- [x] Self-brought picnics allowed
- [ ] Self-brought alcohol allowed
- [ ] Stroller/wheelchair rentals available

- [ ] Parade
- [ ] Parking fee
- [x] Entrance fee: Adults $2.50; Kids free
- [x] Camping facilities: 10 miles
- [x] Boating facilities: Clear Lake
- [x] RV facilities w/ hookups: 10 miles
- [x] Accomodations in town
  The Strout House B&B
- [x] Restaurants in town
  Truffles, Chez Peyo, Maestro's

# *SEER— Solar Energy Expo & Rally*

SO, WHAT HAVE YOU DONE lately to help save our Mother Earthship? Coming to the **SEER—Solar Energy Expo & Rally** may give you some ***hot*** ideas! Included in the two-day extravaganza is a solar car road rally featuring some of the nation's most innovated solar/electric powered vehicles. This is an enjoyable way to spend a weekend and learn something useful, as well!

## Willits, California

Second weekend in August
Daily 8:00 AM - 6:00 PM

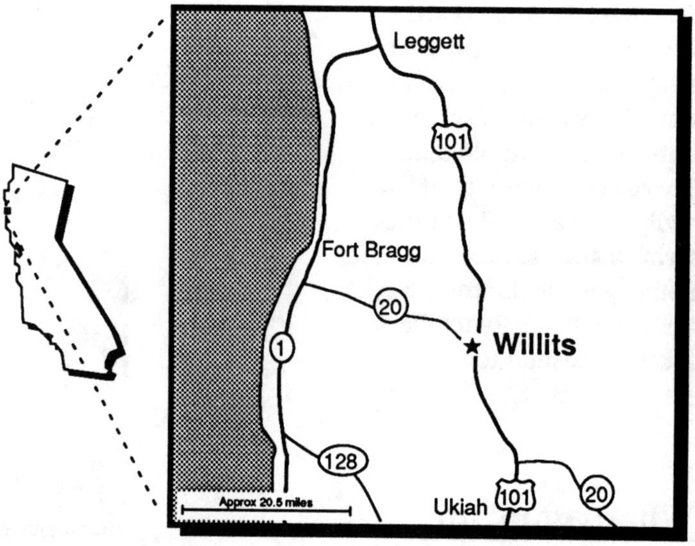


*Up-to-date festival information is available from:*
*Willits Chamber of Commerce*
*(707) 459-7910*

## What's goin' on...

Town population: **5,100**
Last year's attendance: **4,000**
Average outdoor temperature: **85°**
Festival location: **Expo grounds**

| | |
|---|---|
| | Wine tasting/beer for sale |
| X | Food booths |
| X | Arts/crafts for sale |
| X | Live music |
| | Clowns |
| | Face painters |
| X | Childrens games |
| | Animal exhibits/petting zoo |
| | Dogs allowed on leash |
| X | Lost and found |
| | Bicycle racks |
| X | First aid area available |
| X | Self-brought picnics allowed |
| | Self-brought alcohol allowed |
| | Stroller/wheelchair rentals available |

| | |
|---|---|
| | Parade |
| X | Parking fee: $1 |
| X | Entrance fee: Adults $5; Kids $2.50 |
| X | Camping facilities: 1 mile |
| X | Boating facilities: Lake Mendocino |
| X | RV facilities w/ hookups: 1 mile |
| X | Accomodations in town<br>The Doll House B&B, San Sovci B&B |
| X | Restaurants in town<br>Brooktrails Lodge |

# Modoc County Fair

WAY UP IN THE EXTREME northeastern corner of this great state lies the unparalleled scenic beauty of Cedarville, which boasts the **Modoc County Fair**! This land of Indian lore offers 255 miles of trout streams and more than 4,000 acres of lakes and reservoirs abundantly filled with trophy-sized rainbow and brown trout. Obviously, there is a great deal more than just the County Fair to lure you there!

## Cedarville, California

Fourth weekend in August (beginning Thursday)
Hours vary

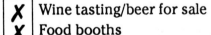

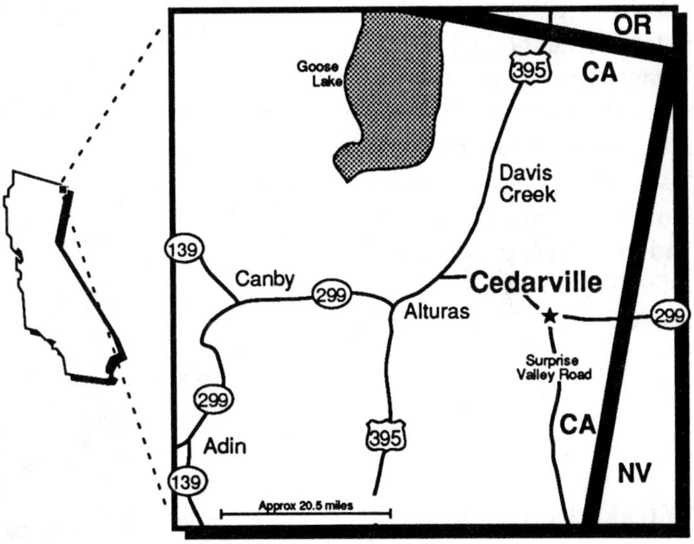


*Up-to-date festival information is available from:*
*Cedarville Chamber of Commerce*
*(916) 233-2819*

## What's goin' on...

Town population: **1,200**
Last year's attendance: **N/A**
Average outdoor temperature: **90°**
Festival location: **Fairgrounds**

| | |
|---|---|
| X | Wine tasting/beer for sale |
| X | Food booths |
| X | Arts/crafts for sale |
| X | Live music |
| X | Clowns |
| X | Face painters |
| X | Childrens games |
| X | Animal exhibits/petting zoo |
| X | Dogs allowed on leash |
| X | Lost and found |
| | Bicycle racks |
| X | First aid area available |
| | Self-brought picnics allowed |
| | Self-brought alcohol allowed |
| | Stroller/wheelchair rentals available |

| | |
|---|---|
| X | Parade: Sun. 10:00 AM on Main St. |
| | Parking fee |
| | Entrance fee |
| X | Camping facilities: 20 miles |
| X | Boating facilities: Big Sage Res. |
| X | RV facilities w/ hookups: 20 miles |
| X | Accomodations in town<br>Sunrise Motel |
| X | Restaurants in town<br>Don's Valley Burger, Golden's Restaurant |

# *Cypress Lane Jazz Festival*

LANDMARK VINEYARDS once again presents the **Cypress Lane Jazz Festival!** Bring your own blankets, lawn chairs—even a picnic—and enjoy the full-bodied wines being served as you relax to the sounds of some top-notch jazz. For example, the 1989 festival featured The Bill Saks Band of Romance, Bob Lucas, and Armand & Louise with Friends. For ticket information call the American Cancer Society.

## Windsor, California

Third Saturday in August
Noon - 6:00 PM

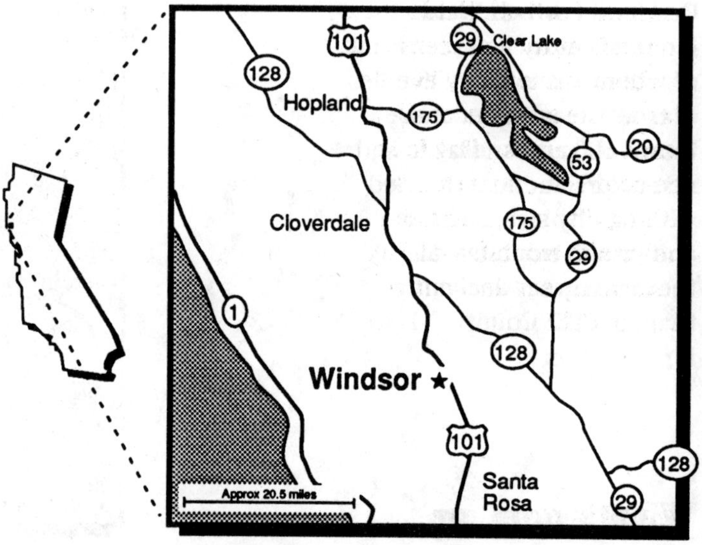


*Up-to-date festival information is available from:*
*Windsor Area Cancer Society*
*(707) 545-6720*

## What's goin' on...

Town population: **8,500**
Last year's attendance: **N/A**
Average outdoor temperature: **88°**
Festival location: **Landmark Vineyards**

| | |
|---|---|
| ✗ | Wine tasting/beer for sale |
| ✗ | Food booths |
| | Arts/crafts for sale |
| ✗ | Live music |
| | Clowns |
| | Face painters |
| | Childrens games |
| | Animal exhibits/petting zoo |
| | Dogs allowed on leash |
| | Lost and found |
| | Bicycle racks |
| | First aid area available |
| ✗ | Self-brought picnics allowed |
| ✗ | Self-brought alcohol allowed |
| | Stroller/wheelchair rentals available |

| | |
|---|---|
| | Parade |
| | Parking fee |
| ✗ | Entrance fee: A $10; Under 12 free |
| ✗ | Camping facilities: 8 miles |
| ✗ | Boating facilities: Lake Sonoma |
| ✗ | RV facilities w/ hookups: 8 miles |
| ✗ | Accomodations in town |
| ✗ | Restaurants in town |

# *Seafood Festival*

WITH THE KLAMATH AND Smith Rivers only a few miles away, it's only fitting that Crescent City hosts the **Seafood Festival**. Held annually at the Crescent City Harbor, this two-day event has all the makings of a fine Festival...outstanding food, ice-cold beer, interesting fishing displays, and fine arts-and-crafts exhibits—all taking place in a very *enchanting* area of California!

## Crescent City, California

Labor Day weekend

Daily noon - 5:00 PM

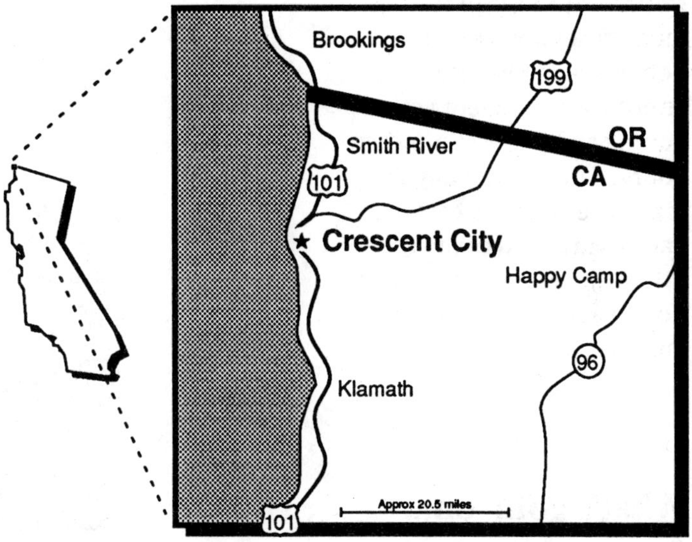


*Up-to-date festival information is available from:*
*Crescent City Chamber of Commerce*
*(707) 464-3174*

## What's goin' on...

Town population: **4,100**
Last year's attendance: **3,000**
Average outdoor temperature: **63°**
Festival location: **Harbor**

| | |
|---|---|
| X | Wine tasting/beer for sale |
| X | Food booths |
| | Arts/crafts for sale |
| X | Live music |
| X | Clowns |
| X | Face painters |
| X | Childrens games |
| X | Animal exhibits/petting zoo |
| X | Dogs allowed on leash |
| | Lost and found |
| | Bicycle racks |
| | First aid area available |
| | Self-brought picnics allowed |
| | Self-brought alcohol allowed |
| | Stroller/wheelchair rentals available |

| | |
|---|---|
| | Parade |
| | Parking fee |
| | Entrance fee |
| X | Camping facilities: 1 mile |
| X | Boating facilities: harbor |
| X | RV facilities w/ hookups: 1 mile |
| X | Accomodations in town<br>Breakers Motel, Camp Marigold, Harbor Motel, El Patio, Curly Redwood Lodge |
| X | Restaurants in town<br>Alias Jones, Harbor View Grotto, China Hut, Rowland's, Ship Ashore, Wakefields |

# *Septemberfest*

AUTUMN ISN'T AUTUMN without **Septemberfest** in Downieville. The day-long revelry starts out with donkey rides for the kids in the morning and ends with donkey racing in the afternoon...complete with betting and prizes! Enjoy yourself during the day on Main Street, inspecting the various arts and crafts on display and munching on hot dogs, nachos, hamburgers, and the like.

## Downieville, California

Saturday and Sunday of Labor Day weekend
Daily 9:00 AM - 6:00 PM

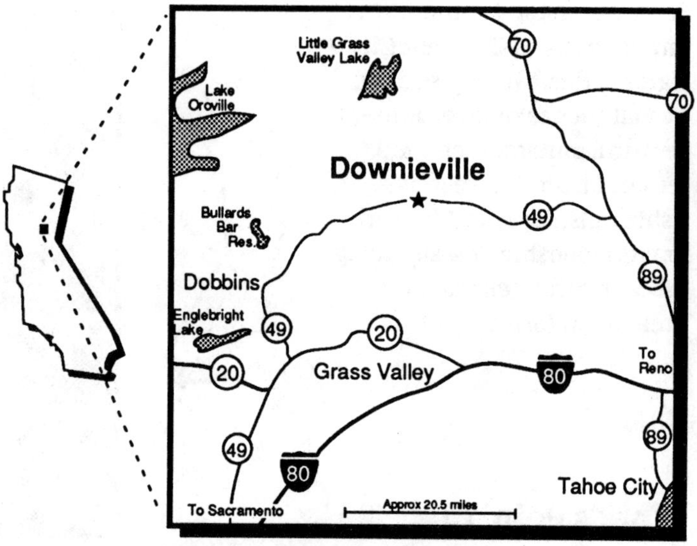


*Up-to-date festival information is available from:*
*Downieville Chamber of Commerce*
*(916) 289-3560*

## What's goin' on...

Town population: **3,300**
Last year's attendance: **N/A**
Average outdoor temperature: **80°**
Festival location: **Downtown**

- ✗ Wine tasting/beer for sale
- ✗ Food booths
- ✗ Arts/crafts for sale
- ✗ Live music
- ✗ Clowns
- Face painters
- Childrens games
- Animal exhibits/petting zoo
- ✗ Dogs allowed on leash
- Lost and found
- Bicycle racks
- ✗ First aid area available
- Self-brought picnics allowed
- Self-brought alcohol allowed
- Stroller/wheelchair rentals available

- Parade
- Parking fee
- Entrance fee
- ✗ Camping facilities: 3 miles
- ✗ Boating facilities
- ✗ RV facilities w/ hookups: 13 miles
- ✗ Accomodations in town
  Dyers Resort, Riverside Motel, Robinsons, Downieville Motor Inn, The Lure
- ✗ Restaurants in town
  Forks, Riverview Pizza, Coyoteville

# *Paul Bunyan Days*

THE BOOTS WORN AT **PAUL Bunyan Days** in Fort Bragg are definitely not made for walkin'! Nope...these here boots are made for the logging show you'll see on Sunday! There's also square dancing, a demolition derby, a gem-and-mineral show, kiddie games, and an outrageous water fight between the Fort Bragg Volunteer Fire Department and the Willits Volunteer Fire Dept.—that's on Saturday and not one to miss!

## Fort Bragg, California

Labor Day weekend
Daily 10:00 AM - 6:00 PM

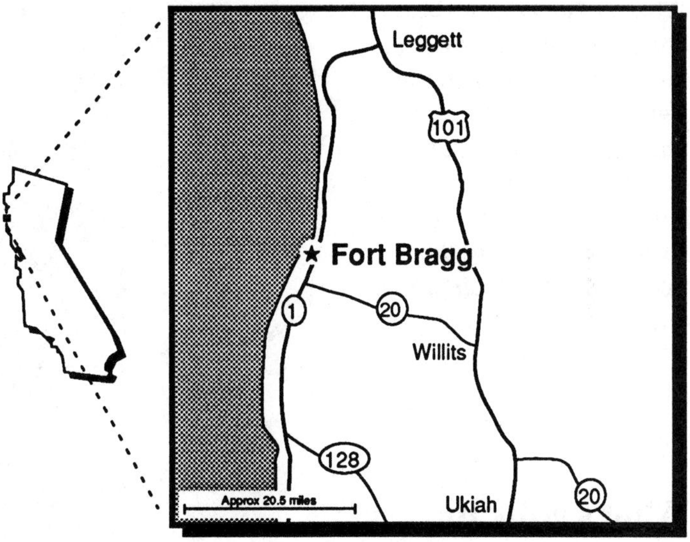


*Up-to-date festival information is available from:*
*Fort Bragg Chamber of Commerce*
*(800)-7-COAST-0*

## What's goin' on...

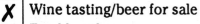

Town population: **5,019**
Last year's attendance: **N/A**
Average outdoor temperature: **65°**
Festival location: **Downtown**

| | |
|---|---|
| X | Wine tasting/beer for sale |
| X | Food booths |
| X | Arts/crafts for sale |
| X | Live music |
| | Clowns |
| X | Face painters |
| X | Childrens games |
| | Animal exhibits/petting zoo |
| X | Dogs allowed on leash |
| | Lost and found |
| X | Bicycle racks |
| X | First aid area available |
| X | Self-brought picnics allowed |
| | Self-brought alcohol allowed |
| | Stroller/wheelchair rentals available |

| | |
|---|---|
| X | Parade: Mon. noon on Main St. |
| | Parking fee |
| X | Entrance fee: To some, not all, events |
| X | Camping facilities: 1 mile |
| X | Boating facilities: Noyo River |
| X | RV facilities w/ hookups: 1 mile |
| X | Accomodations in town<br>Vista Manor Lodge, Old Coast Hotel, Surf Motel, Avalon House B&B, Barbary Coast Inn B&B |
| X | Restaurants in town<br>The Restaurant, D'Aurelio & Sons, Noyo River Restaurant, Wharf Restaurant, Cap'n Flints |

# *Jenner Whale of a Gala*

"BEAUTIFUL JENNER-BY-THE-Sea" is what this town should have been named. Judge for yourself at the **Jenner Whale of a Gala** celebration! Situated on the coast at the mouth of the Russian River, Jenner is a tranquil place chock-full of talented craftspersons. Pottery, silk, jewelry, handmade clothing, wood- and leatherwork booths line the club grounds while jazz music wafts through the salty air.

## Jenner, California

Saturday and Sunday prior to Labor Day
Daily 10:00 AM - 6:00 PM

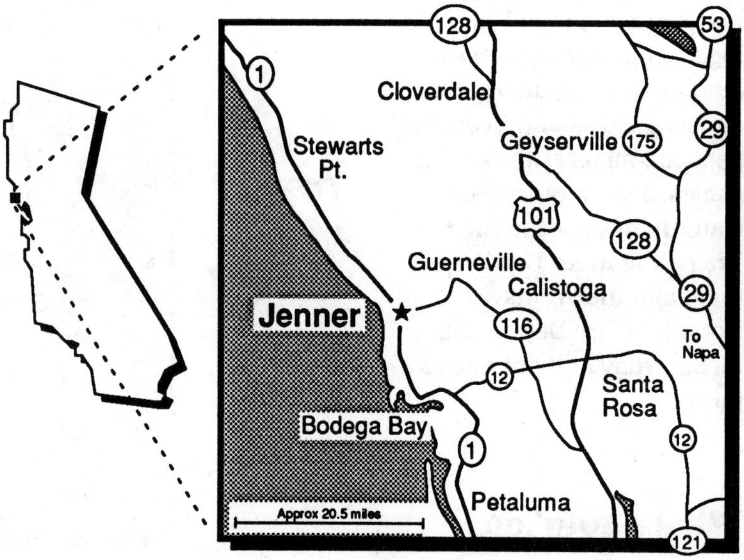


## What's goin' on...

Town population: **200**
Last year's attendance: **2,000**
Average outdoor temperature: **70°**
Festival location: **Club grounds downtown**

*Up-to-date festival information is available from:*
*Jenner Community Club*
*(707) 865-2689*

| | |
|---|---|
| X | Wine tasting/beer for sale |
| X | Food booths |
| X | Arts/crafts for sale |
| X | Live music |
| X | Clowns |
| X | Face painters |
| X | Childrens games |
| | Animal exhibits/petting zoo |
| X | Dogs allowed on leash |
| | Lost and found |
| | Bicycle racks |
| | First aid area available |
| X | Self-brought picnics allowed |
| X | Self-brought alcohol allowed |
| X | Stroller/wheelchair rentals available |

| | |
|---|---|
| | Parade |
| | Parking fee |
| | Entrance fee |
| X | Camping facilities: 4 miles |
| X | Boating facilities: Russian River |
| X | RV facilities w/ hookups: 4 miles |
| X | Accomodations in town<br>Lazy River Motel, Murphy's Jenner Inn |
| X | Restaurants in town<br>Jenner by the Sea, River's End, Bridgehaven |

# *Arts, Crafts, & Collectibles*

STAINED GLASS AND CERAMics are just an example of the craft booths available at the **Arts, Crafts, & Collectibles** festival. Montague is an original Southern Pacific railroad town where the depot has been restored into a museum. Most of the buildings are over 100 years old, with an original soda fountain dating back to 1947—specializing in 1¢ candy.

## Montague, California

Sunday prior to Labor Day
9:00 AM - 3:00 PM

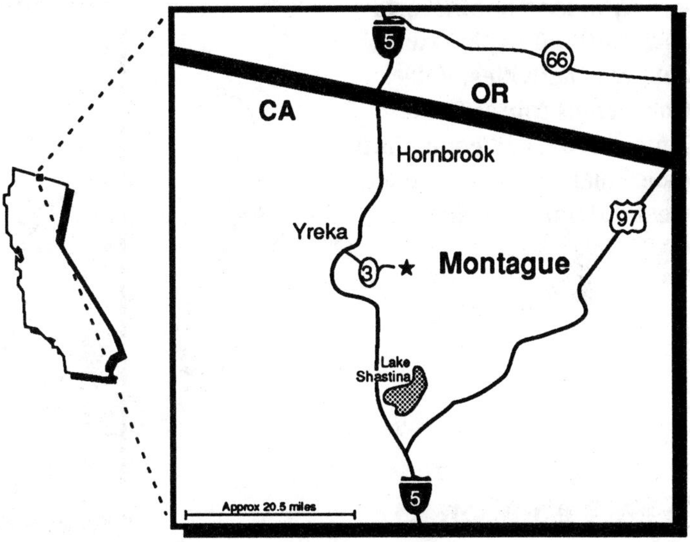


*Up-to-date festival information is available from:*
*Montague Chamber of Commerce*
*(916) 275-8862*

## What's goin' on...

Town population: **1,300**
Last year's attendance: **400**
Average outdoor temperature: **80°**
Festival location: **N/A**

| | |
|---|---|
| X | Wine tasting/beer for sale |
| X | Food booths |
| X | Arts/crafts for sale |
| X | Live music |
| X | Clowns |
| X | Face painters |
| X | Childrens games |
| | Animal exhibits/petting zoo |
| X | Dogs allowed on leash |
| X | Lost and found |
| X | Bicycle racks |
| X | First aid area available |
| X | Self-brought picnics allowed |
| | Self-brought alcohol allowed |
| | Stroller/wheelchair rentals available |

| | |
|---|---|
| | Parade |
| | Parking fee |
| | Entrance fee |
| X | Camping facilities: 5 miles |
| X | Boating facilities: Lake Shastina |
| X | RV facilities w/ hookups: 5 miles |
| | Accomodations in town |
| X | Restaurants in town<br>Ed's Cafe, The Boston Shaft, Wah Lee's |

# *Arts in the Park*

THE SACRAMENTO RIVER provides a picture-perfect backdrop for **Arts in the Park**. Entertainment all day, a variety of food booths, arts and crafts galore, fun run, childrens activities, Valley Oaks tennis tournament, junior rodeo, and community dance makes this a fun-filled weekend not to be missed!

## Red Bluff, California

First full weekend in September

Sat. 10:00 AM - 8:00 PM; Sun. 10:00 AM - 6:00 PM

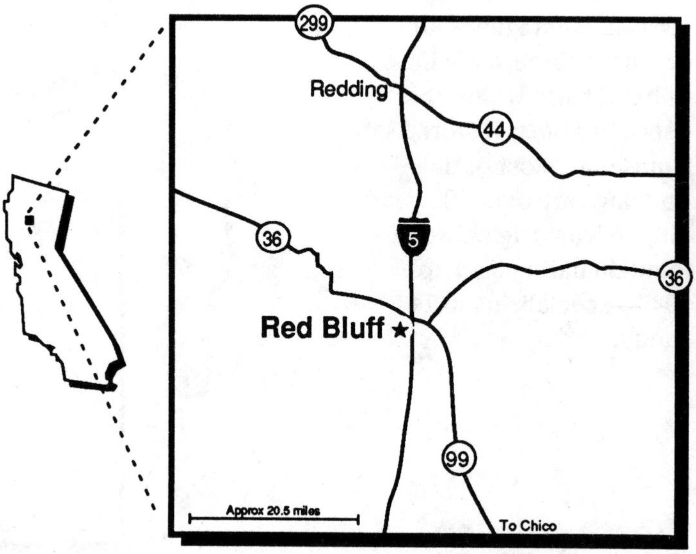


*Up-to-date festival information is available from:*
*Red Bluff Chamber of Commerce*
*(916) 527-6220*

## What's goin' on...

Town population: **12,100**
Last year's attendance: **2,000**
Average outdoor temperature: **90°**
Festival location: **City Park**

| | |
|---|---|
| | Wine tasting/beer for sale |
| X | Food booths |
| X | Arts/crafts for sale |
| X | Live music |
| X | Clowns |
| X | Face painters |
| X | Childrens games |
| | Animal exhibits/petting zoo |
| | Dogs allowed on leash |
| X | Lost and found |
| | Bicycle racks |
| | First aid area available |
| X | Self-brought picnics allowed |
| | Self-brought alcohol allowed |
| | Stroller/wheelchair rentals available |

| | |
|---|---|
| | Parade |
| | Parking fee |
| | Entrance fee |
| X | Camping facilities: 2 miles |
| X | Boating facilities: Sacramento River |
| X | RV facilities w/ hookups: 2 miles |
| X | Accomodations in town<br>Faulkner House B&B |
| X | Restaurants in town<br>Blondie's, Francisco's, Riverside Inn |

# *Tehama County Museum Jubilee*

JUST WHEN THE KIDS GET settled back into school, whisk them away for a weekend of fun at the **Tehama County Museum Jubilee**! The petting zoo is a popular attraction for all ages, and for you crafty types, there are booths overflowing with wood sculptures, paintings, woven fabrics, jewelry, silk and dried flower arrangements, and lots, lots more!

## Tehama, California

Weekend following Labor Day
Sat. 10:00 AM - 4:00 PM; Sun. noon - 4:00 PM

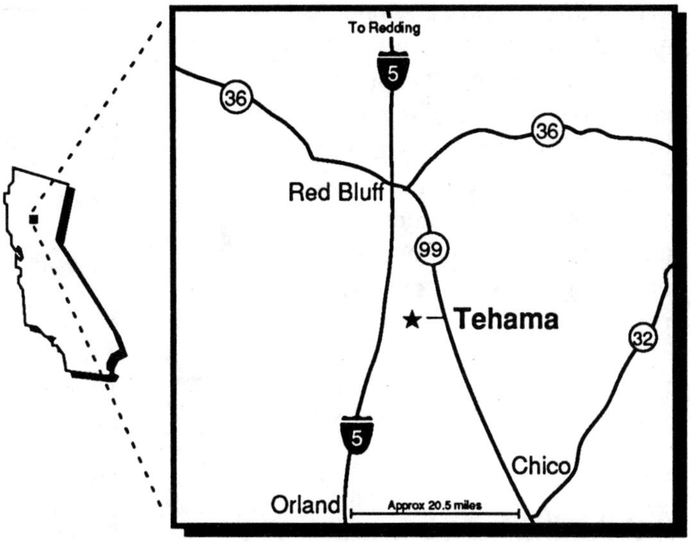


*Up-to-date festival information is available from:*
*Tehama Chamber of Commerce*
*(916) 384-2251*

## What's goin' on...

Town population: **350**
Last year's attendance: **800**
Average outdoor temperature: **90°**
Festival location: **Tehama Co. Museum**

| | |
|---|---|
| ✗ | Wine tasting/beer for sale |
| ✗ | Food booths |
| ✗ | Arts/crafts for sale |
| ✗ | Live music |
| ✗ | Clowns |
| ✗ | Face painters |
| ✗ | Childrens games |
| ✗ | Animal exhibits/petting zoo |
| | Dogs allowed on leash |
| ✗ | Lost and found |
| | Bicycle racks |
| ✗ | First aid area available |
| | Self-brought picnics allowed |
| | Self-brought alcohol allowed |
| | Stroller/wheelchair rentals available |

| | |
|---|---|
| ✗ | Parade: Sat. 10:00 AM near Habert Park |
| | Parking fee |
| | Entrance fee |
| ✗ | Camping facilities: 1 mile |
| ✗ | Boating facilities: Sacramento River |
| ✗ | RV facilities w/ hookups: 1 mile |
| ✗ | Accomodations in town<br>Garden Valley Motel, Los Molinos |
| ✗ | Restaurants in town<br>Berry's, N & B |

# *Willits Logging Show*

SO YOU LIKE BIG DUDES, EH? Well, this is you're kinda show! The **Willits Logging Show** features some of the world's finest loggers competing in the following events: The axe throw; obstacle pole; choker set; hot saw competition; double hand buck; Jack & Jill (huh?); and chopping! *Whew!* And for the grand finale...local teams compete for the perpetual Tug-of-War trophy.

## Willits, California

First Saturday in September
2:00 PM - 5:00 PM

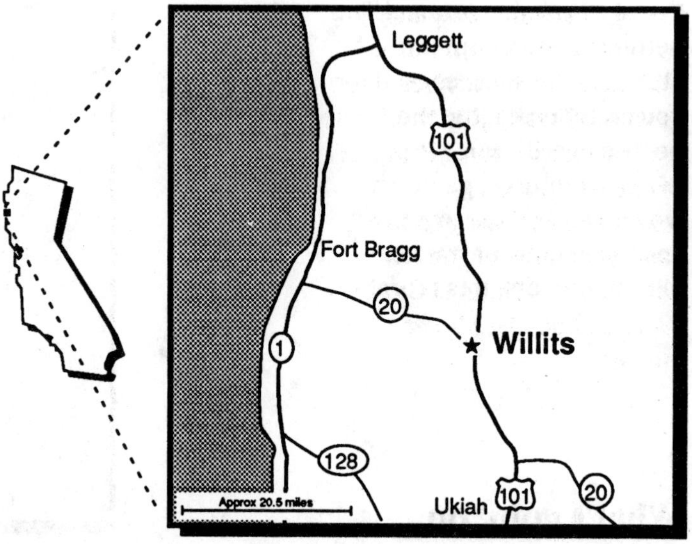


## What's goin' on...

Town population: **5,100**
Last year's attendance: **400**
Average outdoor temperature: **75°**
Festival location: **Rodeo grounds**

*Up-to-date festival information is available from:*
*Willits Chamber of Commerce*
*(707) 459-7910*

- X Wine tasting/beer for sale
- X Food booths
- X Arts/crafts for sale
- Live music
- Clowns
- Face painters
- Childrens games
- Animal exhibits/petting zoo
- Dogs allowed on leash
- X Lost and found
- Bicycle racks
- X First aid area available
- Self-brought picnics allowed
- Self-brought alcohol allowed
- Stroller/wheelchair rentals available

- Parade
- Parking fee
- X Entrance fee: $2
- X Camping facilities: 1 mile
- X Boating facilities: Lake Mendocino
- X RV facilities w/ hookups: 1 mile
- X Accomodations in town
  The Doll House B&B, San Sovci B&B
- X Restaurants in town
  Brooktrails Lodge

# *Prune Festival*

PRUNE PASTA? PRUNE yogurt? And Rory's Rip-Roading Prune Chili? You betcha...you'll find it all at the **Prune Festival.** Yuba and Sutter Counties turn purple with pride in September when prunes officially join the food-festival circuit. Meet Prunella Prune or sip a prune milkshake and sway to the red-hot sounds of the Professor Plum and Natural Gas Jazz Dixieland bands. *It's very moving!*

## Yuba City, California

Second weekend in September
Daily 10:00 AM - 7:00 PM

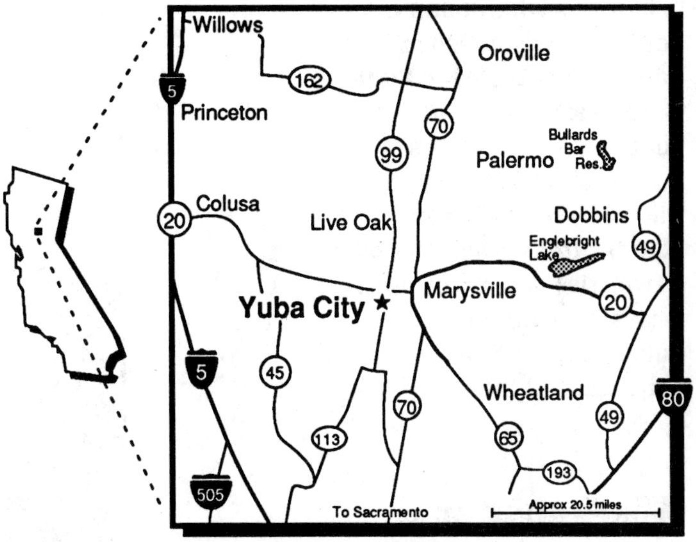


## What's goin' on...

Town population: **29,000**
Last year's attendance: **25,000**
Average outdoor temperature: **90°**
Festival location: **Yuba-Sutter Fairgrounds**

*Up-to-date festival information is available from:*
*Yuba City Chamber of Commerce*
*(916) 743-6501*

- ✗ Wine tasting/beer for sale
- ✗ Food booths
- ✗ Arts/crafts for sale
- ✗ Live music
- ✗ Clowns
- ✗ Face painters
- ✗ Childrens games
- ✗ Animal exhibits/petting zoo
- Dogs allowed on leash
- ✗ Lost and found
- ✗ Bicycle racks
- ✗ First aid area available
- Self-brought picnics allowed
- Self-brought alcohol allowed
- ✗ Stroller/wheelchair rentals available

- Parade
- Parking fee
- ✗ Entrance fee: S & K $3; A $5
- ✗ Camping facilities: 2 miles
- ✗ Boating facilities: Collins Lake
- ✗ RV facilities w/ hookups: 2 miles
- ✗ Accomodations in town
  Bonanza, Yuba City Motor Inn, Wicks B&B, Harkey House
- ✗ Restaurants in town
  Full House, Al's, Lucio's, The Refuge, Ruthy's

# *Wine Festival & Crafts Fair*

## Napa, California
Sunday following Labor Day
10:00 AM - 5:30 PM

AH! THE SIGHTS, SOUNDS, and smells of Napa Valley are exquisite! There's no place in the world quite like California's wine country. Come see for yourself at Napa's very own **Wine Festival & Crafts Fair.** Two hundred arts and crafts booths, and 24 food booths will nicely round out an 8-hour Saturday. There are over 40 wineries in the area open for tasting and/or tours! Ummmm...love that bouquet...and those *legs*!!

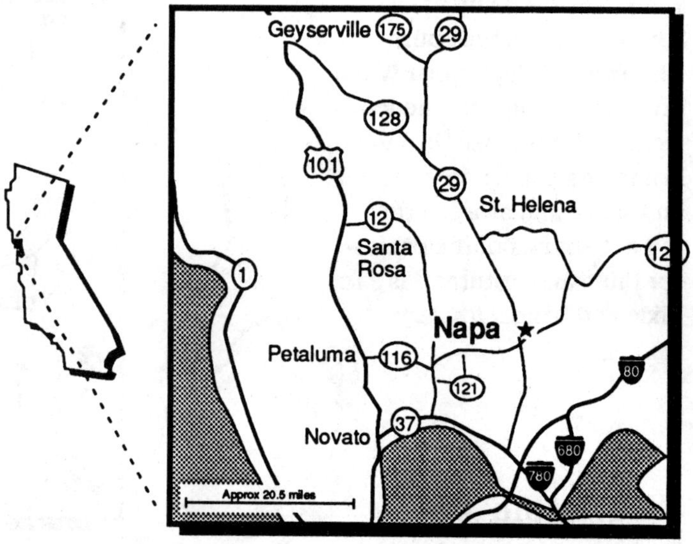


*Up-to-date festival information is available from:*
*Napa Chamber of Commerce*
*(707) 226-7455*

## What's goin' on...
Town population: **58,500**
Last year's attendance: **N/A**
Average outdoor temperature: **70°**
Festival location: **Napa City Center**

- ✗ Wine tasting/beer for sale
- ✗ Food booths
- ✗ Arts/crafts for sale
- ✗ Live music
- ✗ Clowns
- ✗ Face painters
- Childrens games
- Animal exhibits/petting zoo
- Dogs allowed on leash
- ✗ Lost and found
- Bicycle racks
- First aid area available
- Self-brought picnics allowed
- Self-brought alcohol allowed
- Stroller/wheelchair rentals available

- Parade
- Parking fee
- Entrance fee
- ✗ Camping facilities: 20 miles
- ✗ Boating facilities: Lake Berryessa
- ✗ RV facilities w/ hookups: 5 miles
- ✗ Accomodations in town
  Elm House Inn B&B, Chablis Lodge B&B, John Muir Inn, Embassy Suites
- ✗ Restaurants in town
  Long John Silvers, Jonesy's Steak House, La Crepe Cafe, Napa Valley Inn, Red Hen Cantina

# *Constitution Day Parade & Celebration*

GREAT MEN, EXTRAordinary women and revolutionary ideas made this great nation what it is today—come re-live a moment in history at Nevada City's **Constitution Day Parade and Celebration**! This is the largest parade of its kind in Northern California, taking place in one of California's most treasured towns. The National Hotel, in operation since 1856, is California's oldest hotel.

## Nevada City, California

Sunday following Labor Day
All day

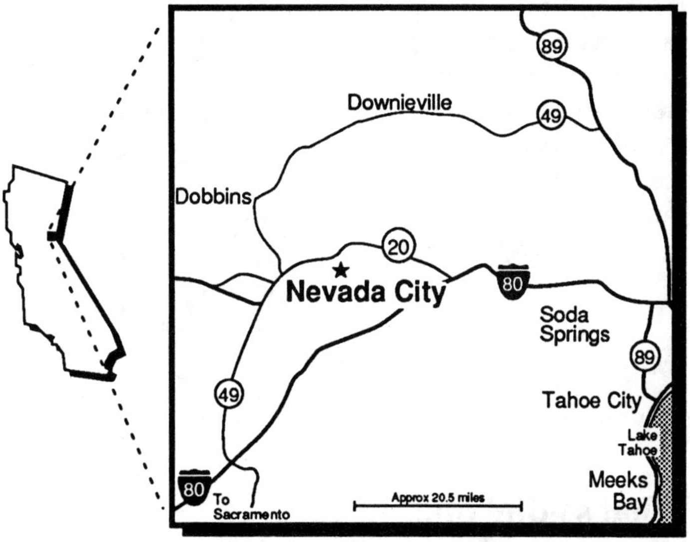


## What's goin' on...

Town population: **2,770**
Last year's attendance: **8,000**
Average outdoor temperature: **92°**
Festival location: **Downtown**

*Up-to-date festival information is available from:*
*Nevada City Chamber of Commerce*
*(916) 265-2692*

- ✗ Wine tasting/beer for sale
- ✗ Food booths
- ✗ Arts/crafts for sale
- ✗ Live music
- ✗ Clowns
- ✗ Face painters
- Childrens games
- Animal exhibits/petting zoo
- ✗ Dogs allowed on leash
- ✗ Lost and found
- Bicycle racks
- ✗ First aid area available
- ✗ Self-brought picnics allowed
- ✗ Self-brought alcohol allowed
- Stroller/wheelchair rentals available

- ✗ Parade: 1:00 downtown
- Parking fee
- Entrance fee
- ✗ Camping facilities: 5 miles
- ✗ Boating facilities: Englebright Lake
- ✗ RV facilities w/ hookups: 5 miles
- ✗ Accomodations in town
  Grandmere's Inn B&B, Flume's End B&B, Downey House B&B, The Parsonage B&B
- ✗ Restaurants in town
  The Willo, York Street Blues, National Hotel, Friar Tuck's, Cirino's Restaurant

# *Pasta Cook-Off & Sausage Challenge*

YUMMMMM! IT'S A TASTY, and delightful afternoon when Weed rolls out the **Pasta Cook-Off & Sausage Challenge**! Test the pasta and sausage for yourself, sip cappuccino or espresso, and view the paintings and crafts for sale. Be sure to allow some time to visit the Black Butte Saloon.

## Weed, California

Second Saturday in September
1:30 PM - 7:30 PM

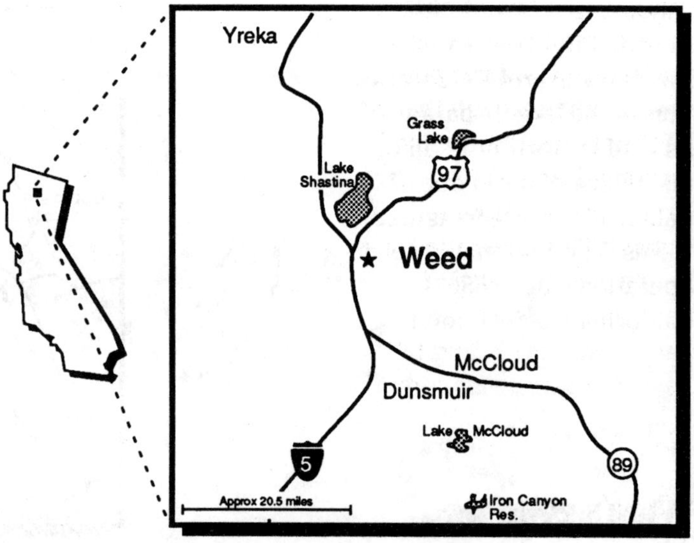


*Up-to-date festival information is available from:*
*Weed Chamber of Commerce*
*(916) 938-4624*

## What's goin' on...

Town population: **3,000**
Last year's attendance: **150**
Average outdoor temperature: **80°**
Festival location: **Heart Federal Parking Lot**

- X Wine tasting/beer for sale
- X Food booths
- X Arts/crafts for sale
- X Live music
- Clowns
- Face painters
- Childrens games
- Animal exhibits/petting zoo
- Dogs allowed on leash
- Lost and found
- X Bicycle racks
- First aid area available
- Self-brought picnics allowed
- Self-brought alcohol allowed
- Stroller/wheelchair rentals available

- Parade
- Parking fee
- Entrance fee
- X Camping facilities: 9 miles
- X Boating facilities: Lake Shastina
- X RV facilities w/ hookups: In town
- Accomodations in town
- X Restaurants in town
  Silva's, Hi Lo, "Y" Ranch Ocean Cowboy, California Pizza

# *Wine Tasting & Arts Festival*

EVERY TOWN STARTS A tradition sometime...and 1991 marks McCloud's 3rd annual **Wine Tasting and Arts Festival!** (It's been a roaring success each year.) Classical musicians play during the day as you stroll through the McCloud Guest House inspecting the works of artists Virgil Harton and Anne Kincaid. This energetic little town sits at the base of majestic Mt. Shasta, so you can imagine the hiking trails just waiting to be explored!

## McCloud, California

Second Saturday in September
Noon - 4:00 PM

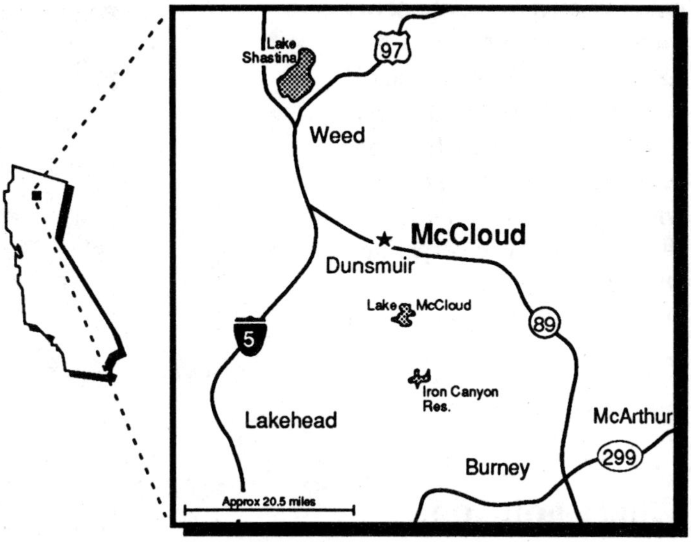


*Up-to-date festival information is available from:*
*McCloud Chamber of Commerce*
*(916) 964-2471*

## What's goin' on...

Town population: **1,700**
Last year's attendance: **N/A**
Average outdoor temperature: **85°**
Festival location: **McCloud Guest House**

| | |
|---|---|
| X | Wine tasting/beer for sale |
| X | Food booths |
| X | Arts/crafts for sale |
| X | Live music |
| | Clowns |
| | Face painters |
| | Childrens games |
| | Animal exhibits/petting zoo |
| | Dogs allowed on leash |
| | Lost and found |
| | Bicycle racks |
| | First aid area available |
| | Self-brought picnics allowed |
| | Self-brought alcohol allowed |
| | Stroller/wheelchair rentals available |

| | |
|---|---|
| | Parade |
| | Parking fee |
| X | Entrance fee: Adults $7 - 10 |
| X | Camping facilities: 3 miles |
| X | Boating facilities: Lake Shastina |
| X | RV facilities w/ hookups: 3 miles |
| X | Accomodations in town<br>Francois Grey Squirrel Inn B&B, Star Meadow Lodge, McCloud Guest House, McCloud Hotel |
| X | Restaurants in town<br>McCloud Guest House, McCloud Soda Shoppe, Francois Grey Squirrel Inn |

# *North Country Fair*

THE **NORTH COUNTRY FAIR** at Arcata Plaza offers assorted activities on the Sunday nearest to the autumn equinox. Dell Arte School of Mime performers are on hand, along with a couple of country-and-western bands. Tofu burgers, sushi, hot dogs, pizza, and tacos are served with the locally made beer of the Humboldt Brewery! The Oliveira and Fieldbrook wineries will also be on hand.

## Arcata, California

Sunday nearest to the Autumn Equinox
10:00 AM - 6:00 PM

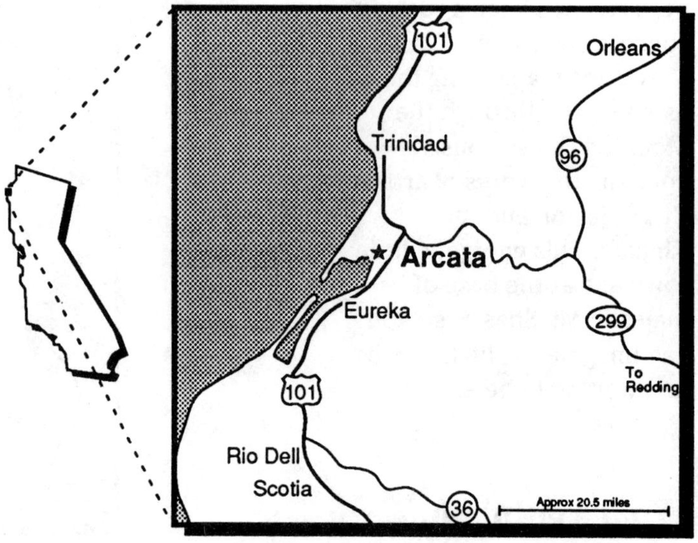


*Up-to-date festival information is available from:*
*Arcata Chamber of Commerce*
*(707) 822-3619*

## What's goin' on...

Town population: **15,000**
Last year's attendance: **7,500**
Average outdoor temperature: **70°**
Festival location: **Plaza**

- X Wine tasting/beer for sale
- X Food booths
- X Arts/crafts for sale
- X Live music
- X Clowns
- X Face painters
- X Childrens games
- X Animal exhibits/petting zoo
- Dogs allowed on leash
- X Lost and found
- X Bicycle racks
- X First aid area available
- X Self-brought picnics allowed
- Self-brought alcohol allowed
- Stroller/wheelchair rentals available

- X Parade: Sat. & Sun. 3:00 PM at the Plaza
- Parking fee
- Entrance fee
- X Camping facilities. 17 miles
- X Boating facilities: Humboldt Bay
- X RV facilities w/ hookups: 7 miles
- X Accomodations in town
  Red Lion, The Plough & Stars Country Inn B&B, The Lady Anne B&B, Super 8
- X Restaurants in town
  Humboldt Brewery, Ottavio's, Abruzzi, Golden Harvest Cafe, Crosswinds, V&N Burger Bar

# Beer & Sausage Festival

SURROUNDED BY VINEYARDS at the northern end of the world-famous Napa Valley is the picturesque town of Calistoga—home to the **Beer and Sausage Festival**! This town puts on a German facade complete with hot mustard and pretzels, German beers, and a variety of sausage sandwiches. Other stuff to do in town? There's lots! Mud baths, biking, great shopping, and ballooning!

## Calistoga, California

First Saturday in October
1:00 PM - 5:00 PM

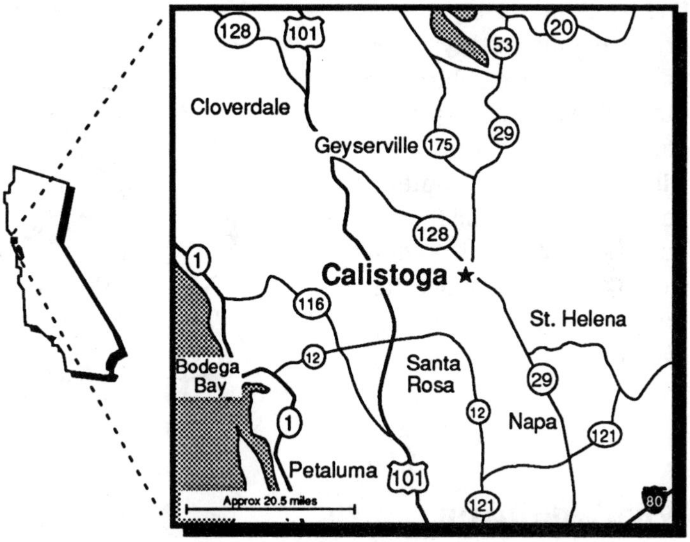


## What's goin' on...

Town population: **4,300**
Last year's attendance: **950**
Average outdoor temperature: **80°**
Festival location: **Napa County Fairgrounds**

*Up-to-date festival information is available from:*
*Calistoga Chamber of Commerce*
*(707) 942-6333*

| | |
|---|---|
| ✗ | Wine tasting/beer for sale |
| ✗ | Food booths |
| | Arts/crafts for sale |
| ✗ | Live music |
| | Clowns |
| | Face painters |
| | Childrens games |
| | Animal exhibits/petting zoo |
| | Dogs allowed on leash |
| | Lost and found |
| ✗ | Bicycle racks |
| | First aid area available |
| | Self-brought picnics allowed |
| | Self-brought alcohol allowed |
| | Stroller/wheelchair rentals available |

| | |
|---|---|
| | Parade |
| | Parking fee |
| ✗ | Entrance fee: (prices not avbl.) |
| ✗ | Camping facilities: 4 miles |
| ✗ | Boating facilities: Clear Lake |
| ✗ | RV facilities w/ hookups: 4 miles |
| ✗ | Accomodations in town<br>Indian Springs, Pine Street Inn & Spa, Wishingwell Inn, Hideaway Cottages |
| ✗ | Restaurants in town<br>Depot Restaurant & Wine Garden, Soo Yuan Restaurant |

# *Fall Colors Quilt Show*

THE STARS OF THE MOUNtain Star Quilters put on the **Fall Colors Quilt Show** in Downieville each year. You'll find a unique variety of creative quilts, teddy bears, handcrafted sweatshirts, and other fabric items to purchase—and, of course, there will be some mouth-watering goodies to snack on! If quilting's not your bag, don't worry—this charming little town has something for everyone!

## Downieville, California

First weekend in October
Daily 10:00 AM - 5:00 PM

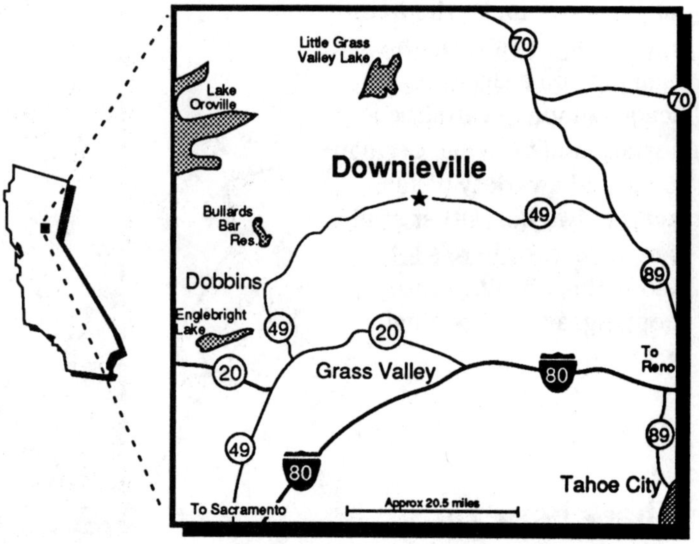


## What's goin' on...

Town population: **3,300**
Last year's attendance: **N/A**
Average outdoor temperature: **70°**
Festival location: **Community Hall**

*Up-to-date festival information is available from:*
*Downieville Chamber of Commerce*
*(916) 289-3560*

| | |
|---|---|
| | Wine tasting/beer for sale |
| X | Food booths |
| X | Arts/crafts for sale |
| | Live music |
| | Clowns |
| | Face painters |
| | Childrens games |
| | Animal exhibits/petting zoo |
| | Dogs allowed on leash |
| | Lost and found |
| | Bicycle racks |
| | First aid area available |
| | Self-brought picnics allowed |
| | Self-brought alcohol allowed |
| | Stroller/wheelchair rentals available |

| | |
|---|---|
| | Parade |
| | Parking fee |
| | Entrance fee |
| X | Camping facilities [illegible] miles |
| X | Boating facilities |
| X | RV facilities w/ hookups: 13 miles |
| X | Accomodations in town<br>Dyers Resort, Riverside Motel, Robinsons, Downieville Motor Inn, The Lure |
| X | Restaurants in town<br>Forks, Riverview Pizza, Coyoteville |

# *Beckwourth Western Days Festival*

A TEN-GALLON HAT, SPURS, and a shiny pair of boots will render you inconspicuous at the **Beckwourth Western Days Festival!** Western and native Indian vittles, art, and crafts will be available as you kick up your spurs to a little bluegrass music. After a stroll downtown, take a gander at the museums, historical sites, and beautiful Sutter Buttes (the smallest mountain range in the world)!

## Marysville, California

First weekend in October
Daily 10:00 AM - 7:00 PM

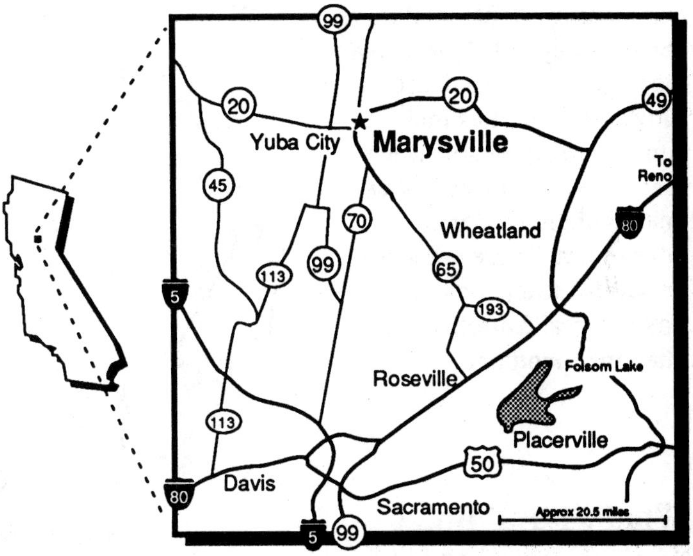


## What's goin' on...

Town population: **12,000**
Last year's attendance: **N/A**
Average outdoor temperature: **78°**
Festival location: **Riverfront Park/downtown**

*Up-to-date festival information is available from:*
*Marysville Chamber of Commerce*
*(916) 743-6501*

| | |
|---|---|
| X | Wine tasting/beer for sale |
| X | Food booths |
| X | Arts/crafts for sale |
| X | Live music |
| | Clowns |
| | Face painters |
| X | Childrens games |
| X | Animal exhibits/petting zoo |
| | Dogs allowed on leash |
| X | Lost and found |
| X | Bicycle racks |
| X | First aid area available |
| | Self-brought picnics allowed |
| | Self-brought alcohol allowed |
| | Stroller/wheelchair rentals available |

| | |
|---|---|
| X | Parade: Sat. 9:00 AM downtown |
| | Parking fee |
| X | Entrance fee: $3 |
| X | Camping facilities: 1 mile |
| X | Boating facilities: Collins Lake |
| X | RV facilities w/ hookups: 1 mile |
| X | Accomodations in town<br>Bonanza Inn, Marysville Motor Lodge, The Oxbow |
| X | Restaurants in town<br>Daikoku, Cannery, The Eagle's Nest, China Moon |

# *Johnny Appleseed Days*

PARADISE IS ALL ITS NAME implies! This picturesque town, nestled in the Sierra Nevada, kicks off October with **Johnny Appleseed Days.** Start the day out right with a big ol' pancake breakfast. Afternoon activities include contests, an apple-pie & ice cream social, a three-to-five-mile Apple Ridge Run, and door prizes. There are game booths for the younguns and arts-and-crafts booths that offer only handmade items.

## Paradise, California

First Saturday in October
9:00 AM - 5:00 PM

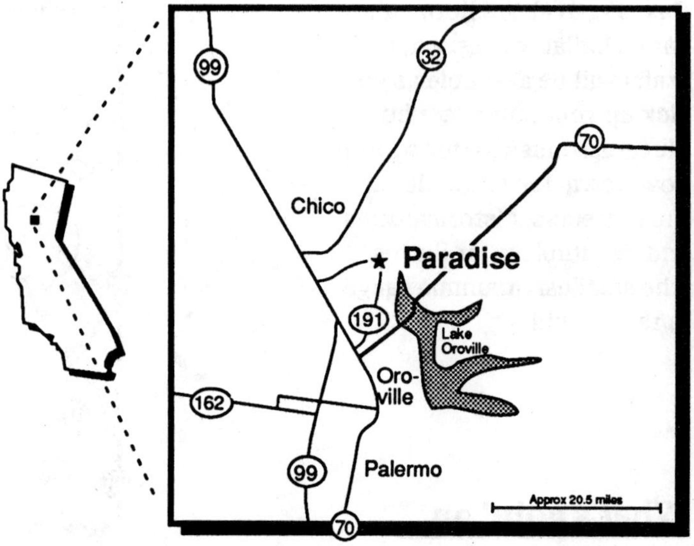


*Up-to-date festival information is available from:*
*Paradise Chamber of Commerce*
*(916) 877-9356*

## What's goin' on...

Town population: **39,000**
Last year's attendance: **20,000**
Average outdoor temperature: **90°**
Festival location: **Park**

| | |
|---|---|
| | Wine tasting/beer for sale |
| ✗ | Food booths |
| ✗ | Arts/crafts for sale |
| ✗ | Live music |
| | Clowns |
| ✗ | Face painters |
| ✗ | Childrens games |
| | Animal exhibits/petting zoo |
| | Dogs allowed on leash |
| ✗ | Lost and found |
| | Bicycle racks |
| ✗ | First aid area available |
| | Self-brought picnics allowed |
| | Self-brought alcohol allowed |
| | Stroller/wheelchair rentals available |

| | |
|---|---|
| | Parade |
| | Parking fee |
| | Entrance fee |
| ✗ | Camping facilities: 10 miles |
| ✗ | Boating facilities: Lake Oroville |
| ✗ | RV facilities w/ hookups: 10 miles |
| ✗ | Accomodations in town<br>Palos Verdes, Ponderosa Gardens |
| ✗ | Restaurants in town<br>Villa Roma, Pinocchio's, Cornicopia |

# *Oktoberfest*

## Lakeport, California

First weekend in October
Hours vary

MAIN STREET GETS DECKED out to the hilt for **Oktoberfest!** Lakeport folks enjoy this young festival (it only began in 1989) that alerts all to the beginning of fall. The vineyards' leaves begin to turn color as the wineries serve up their favorite wines at the two-day event. And, of course, there's German beer, knockwurst, pretzels, strudels...and lots more—even German tunes!

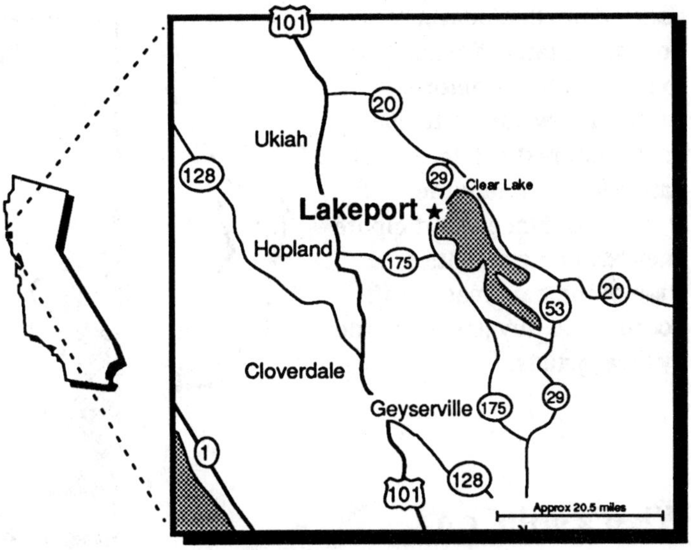


*Up-to-date festival information is available from:*
*Lakeport Chamber of Commerce*
*(707) 263-6131*

## What's goin' on...

Town population: **5,000**
Last year's attendance: **3,000**
Average outdoor temperature: **78°**
Festival location: **Main Street**

- ✗ Wine tasting/beer for sale
- ✗ Food booths
- ✗ Arts/crafts for sale
- ✗ Live music
- ✗ Clowns
- ✗ Face painters
- Childrens games
- Animal exhibits/petting zoo
- ✗ Dogs allowed on leash
- Lost and found
- Bicycle racks
- ✗ First aid area available
- ✗ Self-brought picnics allowed
- Self-brought alcohol allowed
- Stroller/wheelchair rentals available

- Parade
- Parking fee
- Entrance fee
- ✗ Camping facilities: In town
- ✗ Boating facilities: Clear Lake
- ✗ RV facilities w/ hookups: In town
- ✗ Accomodations in town
- ✗ Restaurants in town
  Anthony's, Park Place, Rainbow Restaurant, Narrows Restaurant

# *Indian Summer Festival*

WHAT BETTER PLACE THAN Cotati—named for a native American tribe—for the **Indian Summer Festival.** Located north of Marin County, Cotati is the gateway to the northern California wine country. Listen to live music, enjoy the delectable native foods, watch the traditional dances, participate in entertaining activities, shop at the handmade-craft booths, and buy jewelry made by local artists.

## Cotati, California

Second weekend in October
Daily 10:00 AM - 5:00 PM

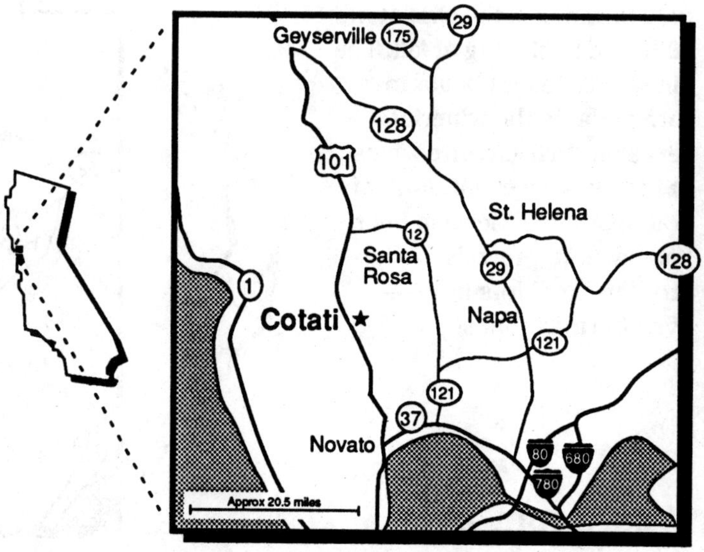


*Up-to-date festival information is available from:*
*Cotati Chamber of Commerce*
*(707) 795-5508*

## What's goin' on...

Town population: **5,500**
Last year's attendance: **1,000**
Average outdoor temperature: **65°**
Festival location: **Park**

| | |
|---|---|
| | Wine tasting/beer for sale |
| ✗ | Food booths |
| ✗ | Arts/crafts for sale |
| ✗ | Live music |
| | Clowns |
| | Face painters |
| | Childrens games |
| | Animal exhibits/petting zoo |
| ✗ | Dogs allowed on leash |
| ✗ | Lost and found |
| ✗ | Bicycle racks |
| ✗ | First aid area available |
| | Self-brought picnics allowed |
| | Self-brought alcohol allowed |
| | Stroller/wheelchair rentals available |

| | |
|---|---|
| | Parade |
| | Parking fee |
| | Entrance fee |
| ✗ | Camping facilities: 30 miles |
| | Boating facilities |
| ✗ | RV facilities w/ hookups: 7 miles |
| | Accomodations in town |
| ✗ | Restaurants in town<br>Tengu's, Markey's Restaurant, Rafa's Mexican Food |

# Beer & Sausage Fest

CALIFORNIA IS BIG ON gourmet...and this **Beer & Sausage Fest** is no exception! The gourmet mustards are *fabulous*, as are the cheeses, breads, sausages, and beers set out for taste tests. The Russian River is nearby for canoeing and full boating facilities are available at Lake Sonoma.

## Healdsburg, California

Third Saturday in October
4:00 PM - 7:00 PM

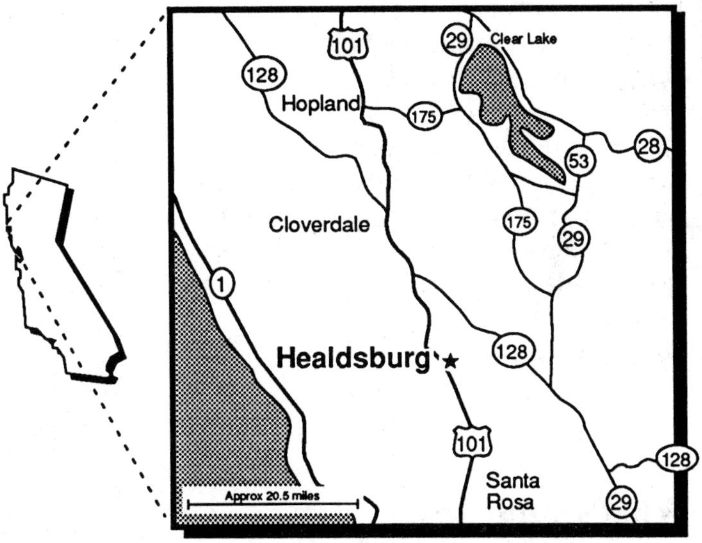


*Up-to-date festival information is available from:*
*Healdsburg Soroptimists of Healdsburg*
*(707) 433-6935*

## What's goin' on...

Town population: **10,000**
Last year's attendance: **600**
Average outdoor temperature: **75°**
Festival location: **Villa Chanticleer**

| | |
|---|---|
| X | Wine tasting/beer for sale |
| X | Food booths |
| X | Arts/crafts for sale |
| X | Live music |
| | Clowns |
| | Face painters |
| | Childrens games |
| | Animal exhibits/petting zoo |
| | Dogs allowed on leash |
| X | Lost and found |
| X | Bicycle racks |
| X | First aid area available |
| | Self-brought picnics allowed |
| | Self-brought alcohol allowed |
| | Stroller/wheelchair rentals available |

| | |
|---|---|
| | Parade |
| | Parking fee |
| | Entrance fee |
| X | Camping facilities: 5 - 10 miles |
| X | Boating facilities: Lake Sonoma |
| X | RV facilities w/ hookups: 10 miles |
| X | Accomodations in town<br>Dry Creek Inn, Healdsburg Inn, Haydon House, Grape Leaf Inn, Madrona Manor |
| X | Restaurants in town<br>Plaza Grill, Tre Scalini, Jacob Horner |

# *Fall Color Tour*

SOON AFTER THE GRAPES have been harvested in Northern California, Geyserville hosts its annual **Fall Color Tour**, showing off the spectacular amber golds and reds of the leaves left on the vines. This small community starts the day with the Volunteer Fire Department's serving a pancake breakfast. Later, one-of-a-kind handicrafts can be found for sale at the exhibits that line Geyserville Avenue.

## Geyserville, California

Fourth Saturday in October
9:00 AM - 6:00 PM

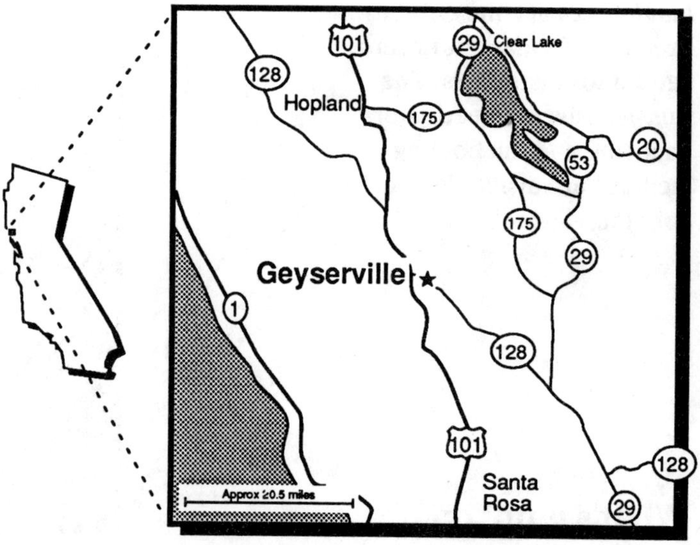


*Up-to-date festival information is available from:*
*Geyserville Chamber of Commerce*
*(707) 857-3745*

## What's goin' on...

Town population: **1,000**
Last year's attendance: **N/A**
Average outdoor temperature: **80°**
Festival location: **Geyserville Ave.**

- X Wine tasting/beer for sale
- X Food booths
- X Arts/crafts for sale
- X Live music
- X Clowns
- X Face painters
- X Childrens games
- Animal exhibits/petting zoo
- X Dogs allowed on leash
- Lost and found
- Bicycle racks
- X First aid area available
- Self-brought picnics allowed
- Self-brought alcohol allowed
- Stroller/wheelchair rentals available

- Parade
- Parking fee
- Entrance fee
- X Camping facilities: 10 miles
- X Boating facilities: Clear Lake
- X RV facilities w/ hookups: 10 miles
- X Accomodations in town
  Campbell Ranch Inn B&B, Hope-Bosworth B&B, Hope-Merril House B&B
- X Restaurants in town
  The Rex

# *Christmas Crafts Faire*

OPEN YOUR CHRISTMAS season at the tenth annual **Christmas Crafts Faire** in Guerneville. Three large rooms will be filled with over 125 booths of hand-painted silk scarves, jewelry, pottery, Christmas decorations, dolls, and much more. Proceeds will benefit the River Citizens Sewer Committee, a non-profit environmental organization working to keep the Russian River clean.

## Guerneville, California

Thanksgiving weekend
Daily 10:00 AM - 5:00 PM

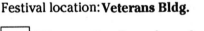

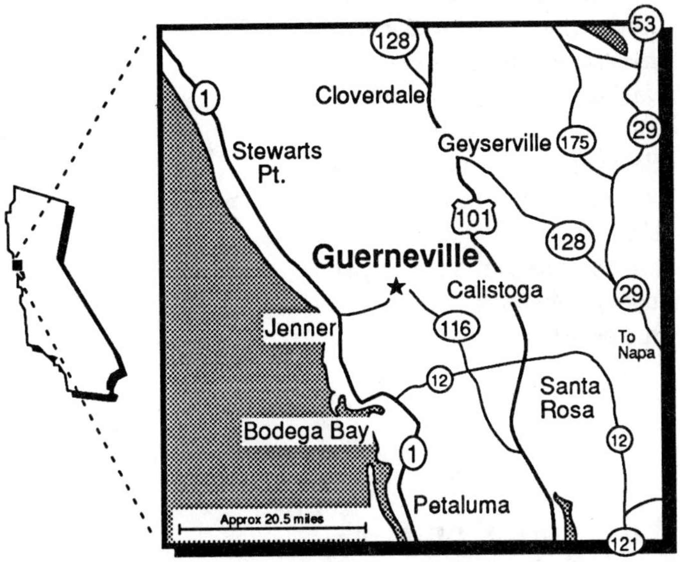


## What's goin' on...

Town population: **3,000**
Last year's attendance: **N/A**
Average outdoor temperature: **N/A indoor**
Festival location: **Veterans Bldg.**

*Up-to-date festival information is available from:*
*Guerneville Sonoma Co. Visitor Center*
*(707) 575-1191*

| | |
|---|---|
| | Wine tasting/beer for sale |
| X | Food booths |
| X | Arts/crafts for sale |
| X | Live music |
| | Clowns |
| | Face painters |
| | Childrens games |
| | Animal exhibits/petting zoo |
| | Dogs allowed on leash |
| | Lost and found |
| X | Bicycle racks |
| | First aid area available |
| X | Self-brought picnics allowed |
| | Self-brought alcohol allowed |
| | Stroller/wheelchair rentals available |

| | |
|---|---|
| | Parade |
| | Parking fee |
| | Entrance fee |
| X | Camping facilities: 10 miles |
| X | Boating facilities: Russian River |
| X | RV facilities w/ hookups: 10 miles |
| X | Accomodations in town<br>Healdsburg Inn on the Plaza, Lytton Springs Inn, Belle de Jour Inn, Frampton House B&B |
| X | Restaurants in town |

# *Artists' Christmas Fair*

WHILE THE FAMILY'S STILL gathered, and energized from the Thanksgiving dinner, why not take a drive into Nevada City for the annual **Artist's Christmas Fair**? This erstwhile town in the heart of California's Gold Country, offers one of the most unique Victorian Christmas fairs of all! Bedecked in lights, glitter and yuletide trimmings, all of Nevada City *loves* Christmastime!

## Nevada City, California

Weekend following Thanksgiving (beginning Fri.)
Daily 10:00 AM - 5:00 PM

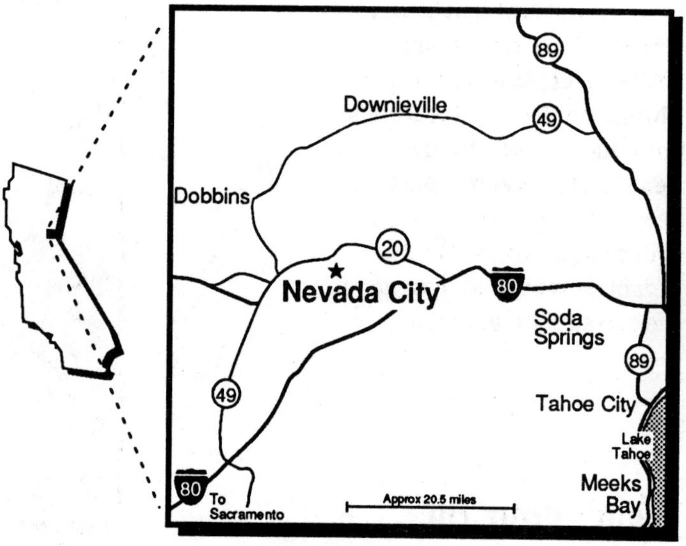


*Up-to-date festival information is available from:*
*Nevada City Chamber of Commerce*
*(316) 265-2692*

## What's goin' on...

Town population: **2,770**
Last year's attendance: **N/A**
Average outdoor temperature: **42°**
Festival location: **Downtown**

| | |
|---|---|
| X | Wine tasting/beer for sale |
| X | Food booths |
| X | Arts/crafts for sale |
| X | Live music |
| | Clowns |
| | Face painters |
| | Childrens games |
| | Animal exhibits/petting zoo |
| X | Dogs allowed on leash |
| | Lost and found |
| X | Bicycle racks |
| | First aid area available |
| | Self-brought picnics allowed |
| | Self-brought alcohol allowed |
| | Stroller/wheelchair rentals available |

| | |
|---|---|
| | Parade |
| | Parking fee |
| | Entrance fee |
| X | Camping facilities: 10 miles |
| X | Boating facilities: Scotts Flat Res. |
| X | RV facilities w/ hookups: 10 miles |
| X | Accomodations in town<br>Downey House B&B, Piety Hill Inn B&B, Red Castle Inn B&B, Grandmere's Inn |
| X | Restaurants in town<br>Moore's Diner, The Country Rose, The Coach House, The Apple Fare, Cowboy Pizza |

# *Victorian Christmas*

LOCATED IN ONE OF THE most charming cities in the Gold Country, Nevada City rolls back the calendar for their **Victorian Christmas** celebration. Dressed in Victorian costumes, the town's merchants decorate their shops and window fronts to reflect the spirit that lives here year round—community involvement! What a splendid way to spend a Wednesday evening!

## Nevada City, California

Wednesday evenings in December *and* the Sunday prior to Christmas

Weds. 6:00 PM - 9:00 PM; Sun. 1:00 PM - 5:00 PM

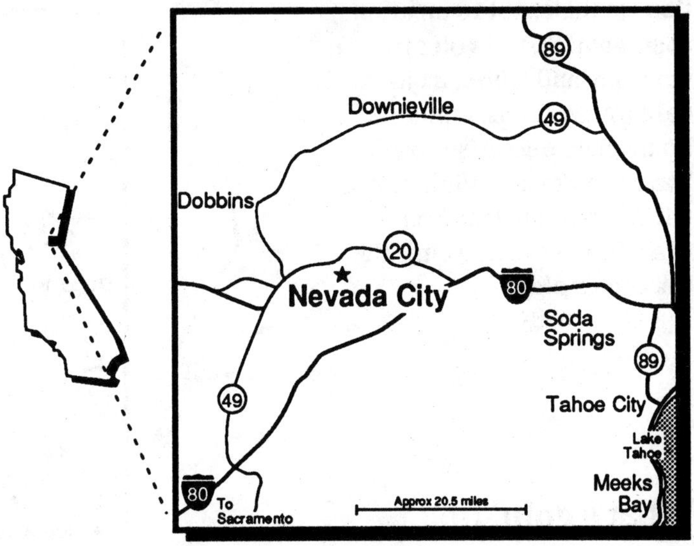


## What's goin' on...

Town population: **2,770**

Last year's attendance: **N/A**

Average outdoor temperature: **42°**

Festival location: **Downtown**

*Up-to-date festival information is available from:*
*Nevada City Chamber of Commerce*
*(316) 265-2692*

| | |
|---|---|
| X | Wine tasting/beer for sale |
| X | Food booths |
| X | Arts/crafts for sale |
| X | Live music |
| X | Clowns |
| X | Face painters |
| | Childrens games |
| | Animal exhibits/petting zoo |
| X | Dogs allowed on leash |
| | Lost and found |
| | Bicycle racks |
| | First aid area available |
| | Self-brought picnics allowed |
| | Self-brought alcohol allowed |
| | Stroller/wheelchair rentals available |

| | |
|---|---|
| | Parade |
| | Parking fee |
| | Entrance fee |
| X | Camping facilities: 10 miles |
| X | Boating facilities: Scotts Flat Res. |
| X | RV facilities w/ hookups: 10 miles |
| X | Accomodations in town<br>Campbell Ranch Inn B&B, Hope-Bosworth B&B, Hope-Merril House B&B, Flume's End B&B |
| X | Restaurants in town<br>The Willo, The Apple Fare, National Hotel, P.J.'s of Nevada City |

# *Holiday-On-Main-Street*

**HOLIDAY-ON-MAIN-STREET** in Downieville is a festive holiday celebration! There are all kinds of Christmas decorations for sale, not to mention angels and Santa. You can buy jams and jellies, fruitcakes, sweet rolls, and other homemade desserts too! Santa arrives on a vintage fire truck in the afternoon and again in the evening after the Christmas play.

## Downieville, California

Second Saturday in December
10:00 AM - 9:00 PM

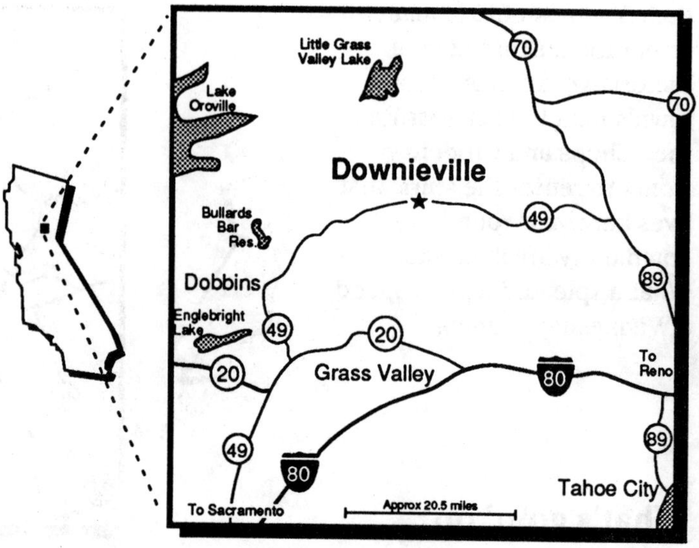


## What's goin' on...

Town population: **3,300**
Last year's attendance: **N/A**
Average outdoor temperature: **45°**
Festival location: **Downtown**

*Up-to-date festival information is available from:*
*Downieville Chamber of Commerce*
*(916) 289-3560*

| | |
|---|---|
| | Wine tasting/beer for sale |
| X | Food booths |
| X | Arts/crafts for sale |
| X | Live music |
| X | Clowns |
| | Face painters |
| | Childrens games |
| | Animal exhibits/petting zoo |
| | Dogs allowed on leash |
| | Lost and found |
| | Bicycle racks |
| | First aid area available |
| | Self-brought picnics allowed |
| | Self-brought alcohol allowed |
| | Stroller/wheelchair rentals available |

| | |
|---|---|
| | Parade |
| | Parking fee |
| | Entrance fee |
| X | Camping facilities: 3 miles |
| X | Boating facilities |
| X | RV facilities w/ hookups: 13 miles |
| X | Accomodations in town: Dyers Resort, Riverside Motel, Robinsons, Downieville Motor Inn, The Lure |
| X | Restaurants in town: Forks, Riverview Pizza, Coyoteville |

# *Winter Arts Faire*

SOME EXCEPTIONAL SHOPping can be done while the savory scent of hot mulled wine wafts through the air, and the nippy chill of winter is on the other side of the Community Center's door! This annual **Winter Arts Faire** summons Santa Claus from the North Pole to entertain the kiddies...while *you* hunt down the perfect handmade gift for Aunt Gertie!

## Redway, California

Second weekend in December
Hours vary

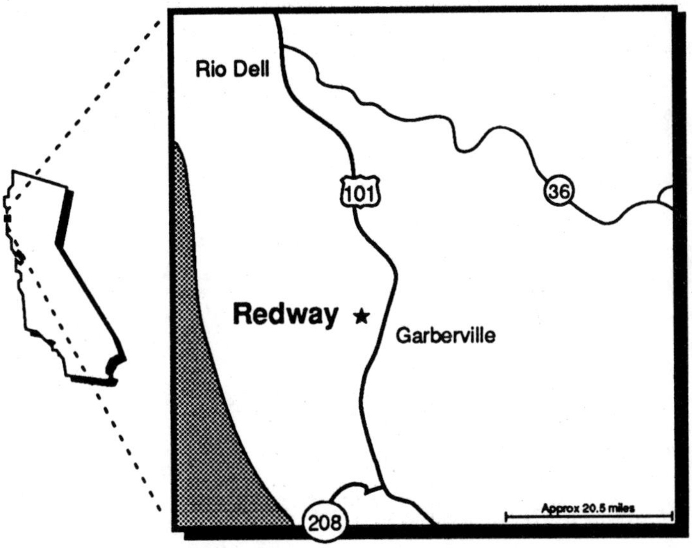


## What's goin' on...

Town population: **1,094**
Last year's attendance: **N/A**
Average outdoor temperature: **50°**
Festival location: **Community Center**

*Up-to-date festival information is available from:*
*Redway Chamber of Commerce*
*(707) 923-2533*

| | |
|---|---|
| X | Wine tasting/beer for sale |
| X | Food booths |
| X | Arts/crafts for sale |
| X | Live music |
| X | Clowns |
| X | Face painters |
| X | Childrens games |
| | Animal exhibits/petting zoo |
| X | Dogs allowed on leash |
| X | Lost and found |
| X | Bicycle racks |
| X | First aid area available |
| | Self-brought picnics allowed |
| | Self-brought alcohol allowed |
| | Stroller/wheelchair rentals available |

| | |
|---|---|
| | Parade |
| | Parking fee |
| X | Entrance fee: $1 |
| X | Camping facilities: 2 miles |
| X | Boating facilities: Benbow Lake |
| X | RV facilities w/ hookups: 2 miles |
| X | Accomodations in town |
| X | Restaurants in town |

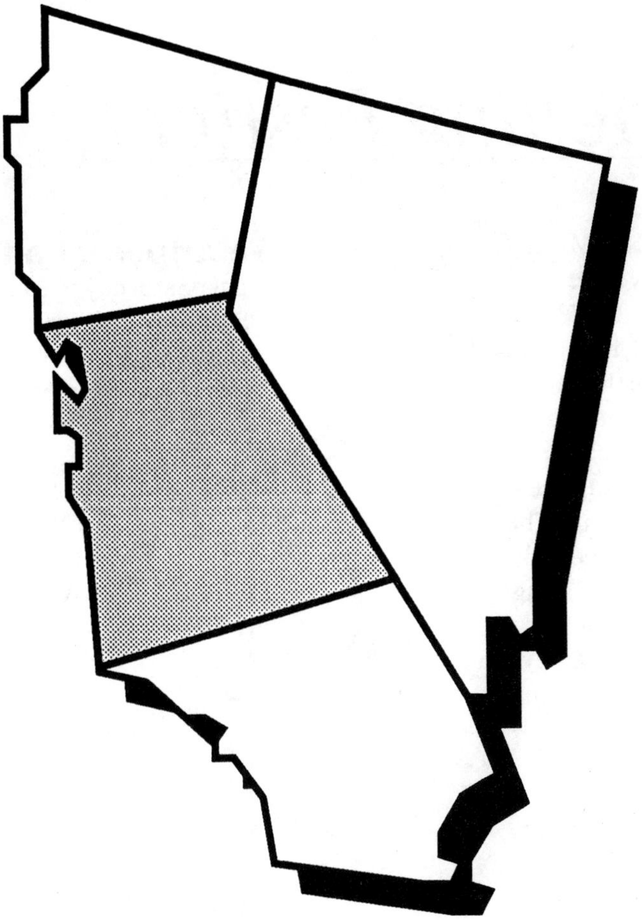

# Central California

# *Storytelling Festival*

LEAVE IT TO CHARMING Mariposa to have the **Storytelling Festival!** Hear tales told by premier national storytellers, participate in the open Story Swap, or watch enchanted children listen intently during the Children's Story Hour. The evening performance is one not to miss in this alluring little town nestled in the foothills of the Sierra Nevada Mountains. Quilts and puppets are on display, too.

## Mariposa, California

Last Saturday in January through the first Saturday in February
Hours vary

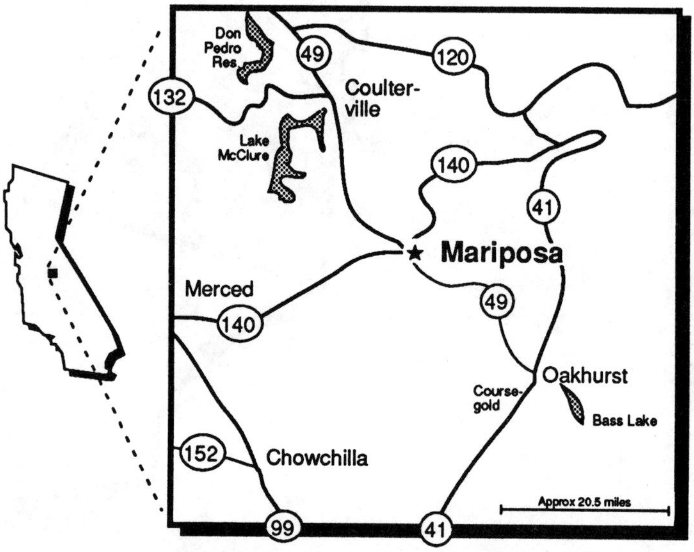


## What's goin' on...

Town population: **2,500**
Last year's attendance: **1,050**
Average outdoor temperature: **65°**
Festival location: **Fairgrounds**

*Up-to-date festival information is available from:*
*Mariposa Chamber of Commerce*
*(209) 966-2456*

| | |
|---|---|
| ✗ | Wine tasting/beer for sale |
| ✗ | Food booths |
| ✗ | Arts/crafts for sale |
| | Live music |
| | Clowns |
| | Face painters |
| | Childrens games |
| | Animal exhibits/petting zoo |
| | Dogs allowed on leash |
| ✗ | Lost and found |
| | Bicycle racks |
| | First aid area available |
| ✗ | Self-brought picnics allowed |
| | Self-brought alcohol allowed |
| | Stroller/wheelchair rentals available |

| | |
|---|---|
| | Parade |
| | Parking fee |
| ✗ | Entrance fee: (prices not avbl.) |
| ✗ | Camping facilities: On site |
| ✗ | Boating facilities: Merced River |
| ✗ | RV facilities w/ hookups: On-site |
| ✗ | Accomodations in town<br>Boulder Creek B&B, Granny's Garden B&B, Pilgrims Inn B&B, Meadow Creek Ranch B&B |
| ✗ | Restaurants in town |

# *Newark Art & Wine Festival*

IT'S NOT EXACTLY COLD outside...*c'mon this is California!* But, since Californians **do** like to festival hop year 'round, Newark offers their **Newark Art & Wine Festival** indoors! Five Livermore wineries are on hand so that you can taste their very best Chards, Zins, Cabs, and Blancs! And dine on some homemade treats while you enjoy the jazz music wafting through the recycled air!

## Newark, California

First weekend in February
Fri. & Sat. 10:00 AM - 9:00 PM; Sun. 11:00 AM - 5:00 PM

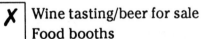

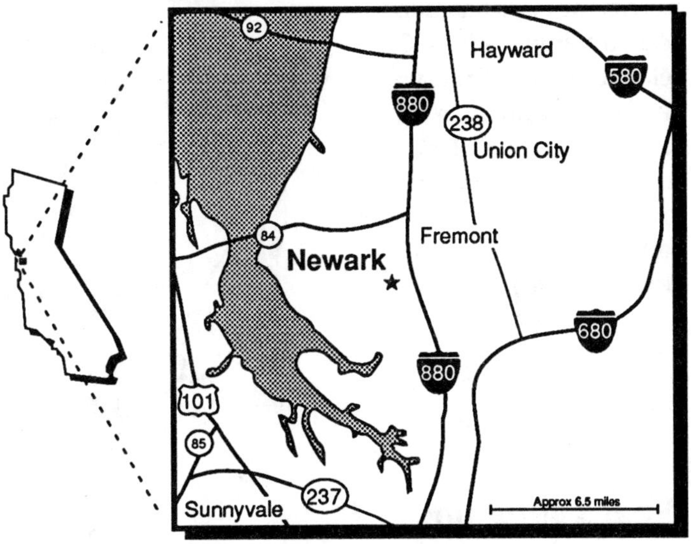


*Up-to-date festival information is available from:*
*Newark Chamber of Commerce*
*(415) 657-9555*

## What's goin' on...

Town population: **39.250**
Last year's attendance: **N/A**
Average outdoor temperature: **65°**
Festival location: **Newark Mall**

| | |
|---|---|
| X | Wine tasting/beer for sale |
| | Food booths |
| X | Arts/crafts for sale |
| X | Live music |
| | Clowns |
| | Face painters |
| | Childrens games |
| | Animal exhibits/petting zoo |
| | Dogs allowed on leash |
| X | Lost and found |
| X | Bicycle racks |
| X | First aid area available |
| | Self-brought picnics allowed |
| | Self-brought alcohol allowed |
| | Stroller/wheelchair rentals available |

| | |
|---|---|
| | Parade |
| | Parking fee |
| | Entrance fee |
| | Camping facilities |
| | Boating facilities |
| | RV facilities w/ hookups |
| X | Accomodations in town<br>Days Inn, Thunderbird Inn, Hilton, EZ8 |
| X | Restaurants in town<br>Nijo Castle, Chevy's, Wang's, El Burro |

# *Mardi Gras*

NEW ORLEANS ISN'T THE only town in these United States to celebrate **Mardi Gras**! Masks, music, and merriment mark San Luis Obispo's annual Mardi Gras celebration in February. The decade-old festivities usher in Lent with a cheerful join-the-crowd parade, followed by the richly costumed Maskers' Ball, with its spicy Cajun dinner and jazzy sounds.

## San Luis Obispo, California

Beginning of Lent
7:15 PM - midnight

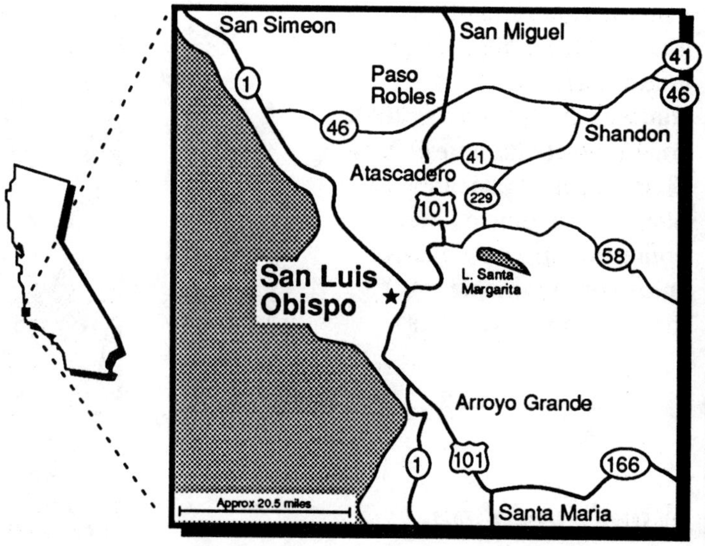


## What's goin' on...

Town population: **41,000**
Last year's attendance: **12,500**
Average outdoor temperature: **60°**
Festival location: **Downtown**

☞ *Up-to-date festival information is available from: San Luis Obispo Chamber of Commerce (805) 543-1323*

| | |
|---|---|
| X | Wine tasting/beer for sale |
| | Food booths |
| X | Arts/crafts for sale |
| X | Live music |
| X | Clowns |
| | Face painters |
| | Childrens games |
| | Animal exhibits/petting zoo |
| X | Dogs allowed on leash |
| | Lost and found |
| X | Bicycle racks |
| | First aid area available |
| X | Self-brought picnics allowed |
| | Self-brought alcohol allowed |
| | Stroller/wheelchair rentals available |

| | |
|---|---|
| X | Parade: (time & date not avbl.) |
| | Parking fee |
| X | Entrance fee: Masker's Ball $20 |
| X | Camping facilities: 15 miles |
| X | Boating facilities: Lakes and ocean |
| X | RV facilities w/ hookups: 15 miles |
| X | Accomodations in town<br>Madonna Inn, Peach Tree Inn, Garden St. B&B |
| X | Restaurants in town<br>Apple Farm, Hudson's Grill, Chef Em's, Cafe Roma, Brubeck's |

# *Migration Festival*

NATURAL BRIDGES STATE Beach hosts the annual **Migration Festival**! There are wonderful photographic and entomological displays explaining the life cycle and migration habits of the monarch butterfly and the whale, skits, and music! This is a celebration of all creatures—great and small—who pass through Santa Cruz on their migration journeys!

## Santa Cruz, California

Second Saturday in February
10:00 AM - 4:00 PM

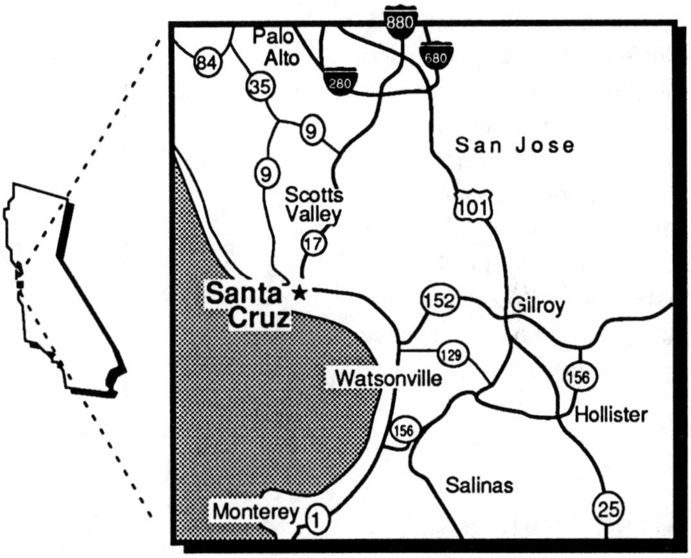


## What's goin' on...

Town population: **50,000**
Last year's attendance: **3,500**
Average outdoor temperature: **65°**
Festival location: **Natural Bridges State Park**

*Up-to-date festival information is available from:*
*Santa Cruz Visitors Bureau*
*(408) 425-1234*

- [ ] Wine tasting/beer for sale
- [x] Food booths
- [ ] Arts/crafts for sale
- [ ] Live music
- [ ] Clowns
- [ ] Face painters
- [x] Childrens games
- [ ] Animal exhibits/petting zoo
- [ ] Dogs allowed on leash
- [x] Lost and found
- [x] Bicycle racks
- [x] First aid area available
- [x] Self-brought picnics allowed
- [ ] Self-brought alcohol allowed
- [ ] Stroller/wheelchair rentals available

- [ ] Parade
- [x] Parking fee: $6 per car
- [ ] Entrance fee
- [x] Camping facilities: 2 miles
- [x] Boating facilities: Santa Cruz Harbor
- [x] RV facilities w/ hookups: 3 miles
- [x] Accomodations in town
- [x] Restaurants in town
  Aldo's, Crow's Nest

C E N T R A L

# *Mustard Festival*

BACK BY POPULAR DEMAND is the well liked **Mustard Festival!** Perched high atop the Santa Cruz Mountains, Congress Springs vineyards offers an spectacular view of the blooming mustard fields! Bring a picnic, but leave the mustard off the sammies, cuz after your do a little mustard and wine sampling...you're sure to find just the right tastes to complement your lunch! The free shuttle leaves from Saratoga High.

## Saratoga, California

President's Day weekend (three days)
Daily 11:00 AM - 4:00 PM

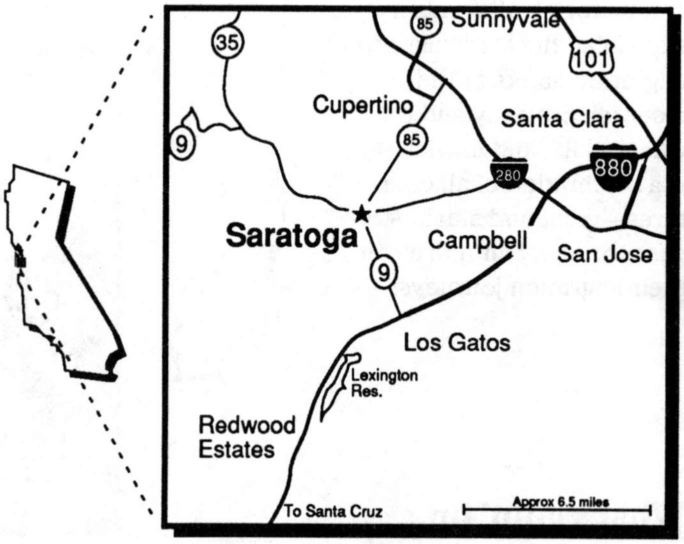


## What's goin' on...

Town population: **30,000**
Last year's attendance: **1,200**
Average outdoor temperature: **75°**
Festival location: **Congress Springs Winery**

*Up-to-date festival information is available from:*
*Saratoga Congress Springs Winery*
*(408) 867-1409*

| | |
|---|---|
| X | Wine tasting/beer for sale |
| X | Food booths |
| X | Arts/crafts for sale |
| X | Live music |
| | Clowns |
| | Face painters |
| | Childrens games |
| | Animal exhibits/petting zoo |
| | Dogs allowed on leash |
| | Lost and found |
| | Bicycle racks |
| | First aid area available |
| X | Self-brought picnics allowed |
| | Self-brought alcohol allowed |
| | Stroller/wheelchair rentals available |

| | |
|---|---|
| | Parade |
| X | Parking fee: $4 |
| | Entrance fee |
| X | Camping facilities: 20 miles |
| | Boating facilities |
| X | RV facilities w/ hookups: 7 miles |
| X | Accomodations in town<br>Saratoga Motel, The Inn at Saratoga |
| X | Restaurants in town<br>Bella Mia, La Mere Michelle, The Plumed Horse, Le Mouton Noir, The Adriatic, The Village Rendevous |

# *Almond Blossom Festival*

OOOH. THOSE TASTY LITTLE nuggets...how we love them so! The annual **Almond Blossom Festival** is, without a doubt, one of California's most beautiful festivals! The trees in full bloom are the honored attraction—but the real stuff—like the chicken bar-b-que, wine tasting, craft and art displays, giant street parade, Diaper Derby, and ham & pancake breakfast—is what the townfolks come out for! How 'bout you, too!

## Ripon, California

Fourth weekend in February (beginning Friday)
Hours vary

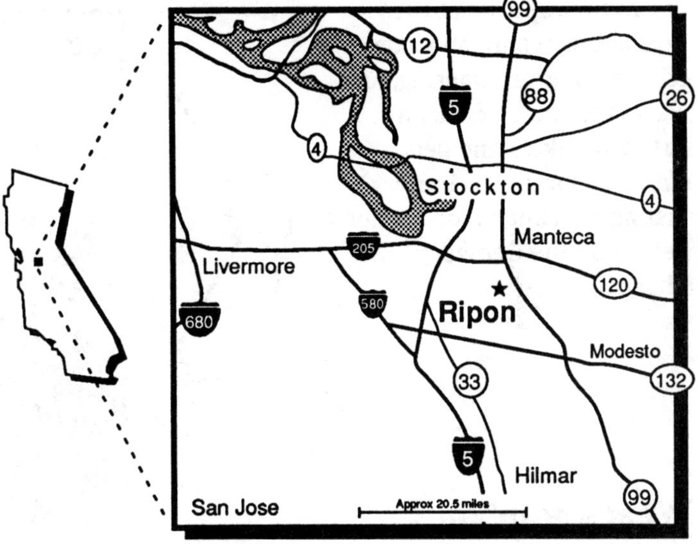


*Up-to-date festival information is available from:*
*Ripon Chamber of Commerce*
*(209) 599-7519*



## What's goin' on...

Town population: **7,500**
Last year's attendance: **35,000**
Average outdoor temperature: **70°**
Festival location: **Citywide**

| | |
|---|---|
| X | Wine tasting/beer for sale |
| X | Food booths |
| X | Arts/crafts for sale |
| X | Live music |
| | Clowns |
| | Face painters |
| X | Childrens games |
| | Animal exhibits/petting zoo |
| | Dogs allowed on leash |
| | Lost and found |
| | Bicycle racks |
| | First aid area available |
| | Self-brought picnics allowed |
| | Self-brought alcohol allowed |
| | Stroller/wheelchair rentals available |

| | |
|---|---|
| X | Parade: (date & time not avbl.) |
| | Parking fee |
| | Entrance fee |
| X | Camping facilities: 3 miles |
| X | Boating facilities: Oakwood Lake |
| X | RV facilities w/ hookups: 3 miles |
| X | Accomodations in town |
| X | Restaurants in town |

# *Clam Chowder Cook-Off & Chowder Chase*

DUST OFF YOUR RUNNING shoes and take off for the **Chowder Chase & Clam Chowder Cook-Off!** This all-day event happens at the Boardwalk, where all kinds of chowders are simmering, just waiting for tasters. Buy a batch of tickets and get started on some serious tasting! Call ahead for further details on the Chowder Chase.

## Santa Cruz, California

Fourth Saturday in February
11:00 AM - 5:00 Pm

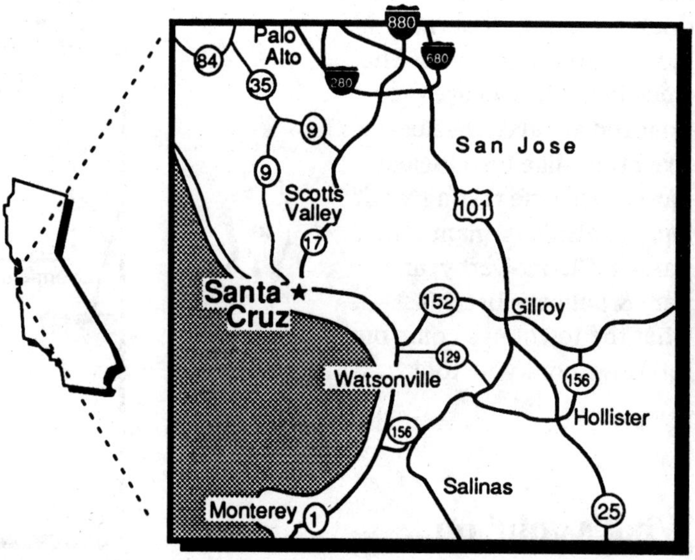


## What's goin' on...

Town population: **48,000**
Last year's attendance: **10,000**
Average outdoor temperature: **70°**
Festival location: **Santa Cruz Boardwalk**

*Up-to-date festival information is available from:*
*Santa Cruz Visitors Bureau*
*(408) 425-1234*

- ✗ Wine tasting/beer for sale
- ✗ Food booths
- Arts/crafts for sale
- Live music
- Clowns
- Face painters
- ✗ Childrens games
- Animal exhibits/petting zoo
- ✗ Dogs allowed on leash
- ✗ Lost and found
- ✗ Bicycle racks
- ✗ First aid area available
- Self-brought picnics allowed
- Self-brought alcohol allowed
- ✗ Stroller/wheelchair rentals available

- Parade
- ✗ Parking fee: $5
- ✗ Entrance fee: tasting kit
- ✗ Camping facilities: 2 miles
- ✗ Boating facilities: Santa Cruz Harbor
- ✗ RV facilities w/ hookups: In town
- ✗ Accomodations in town
  Dream Inn, Chaminade, Babbling Brook B&B, Pleasure Point Inn B&B
- ✗ Restaurants in town
  Sea Cloud, Casa Blanca, Chez Renee, Crow's Nest

# *SNOWFEST*

HERE? IN CALIFORNIA? YEP—the largest winter carnival in the west is called **SNOWFEST** and it's right nearby! This celebration of fun, snow, and sun features a fish fry, and wild game barbecue, Craft Faire, music from the 50's and 60's (at the dances), a dress-up-your-dog contest, two large parades, snow golf and snow soft- ball (you have to see it to believe it!), and lots, lots more! *This'll wear you out!*

## Tahoe City, California

First Friday through the second Sunday in March

Hours vary

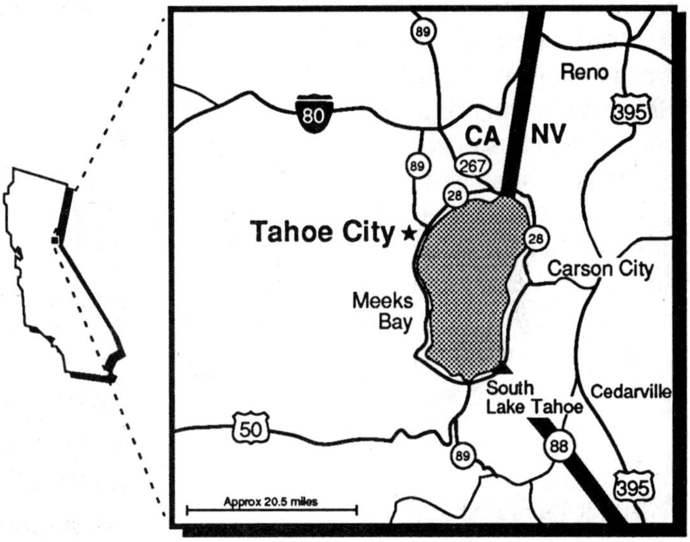


## What's goin' on...

Town population: **11,000**
Last year's attendance: **90,000**
Average outdoor temperature: **44°**
Festival location: **Citywide**

*Up-to-date festival information is available from:*
*Tahoe City Chamber of Commerce*
*(916) 583-2371*

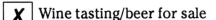

| | |
|---|---|
| X | Wine tasting/beer for sale |
| X | Food booths |
| X | Arts/crafts for sale |
| X | Live music |
| X | Clowns |
| X | Face painters |
| X | Childrens games |
| | Animal exhibits/petting zoo |
| X | Dogs allowed on leash |
| X | Lost and found |
| | Bicycle racks |
| | First aid area available |
| X | Self-brought picnics allowed |
| | Self-brought alcohol allowed |
| | Stroller/wheelchair rentals available |

| | |
|---|---|
| X | Parade: (time & date not avbl.) |
| | Parking fee |
| X | Entrance fee: Some, not all, events |
| X | Camping facilities: In town |
| X | Boating facilities: Lake Tahoe |
| X | RV facilities w/ hookups: In town |
| X | Accomodations in town<br>Cottage Inn at Lake Tahoe B&B, Mayfield House B&B, Sunnyside Inn |
| X | Restaurants in town<br>Rosie's Cafe, The Chart House, Jake's on the Lake, Sunnyside |

# *Sonoma County Folk Festival*

BURSTING WITH STUFF TO do, the **Sonoma County Folk Festival** promises more to do than listen to music! This festival falls in the heart of California's wine country...so of course the festival offers wine tasting, entertainment, dancers, and lots of good food to eat! Outside the Luther Burbank Center there's even more to explore—Jack London's home and grounds (a nearby state park), parks, museums, and wineries.

## Santa Rosa, California

Second and third weekends in March
Fri. 8:00 PM - midnight; Sat. 11:00 AM - midnight; Sun. noon - 10:00 PM

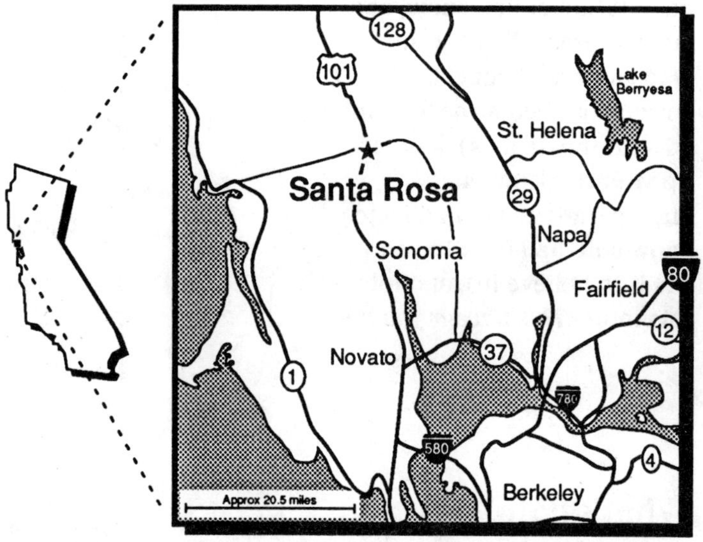

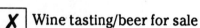

*Up-to-date festival information is available from:*
*Santa Rosa Visitors Bureau*
*(707) 575-1191*

## What's goin' on...

Town population: **100,000**
Last year's attendance: **5,000**
Average outdoor temperature: **65°**
Festival location: **Luther Burbank Center**

| | |
|---|---|
| ✗ | Wine tasting/beer for sale |
| ✗ | Food booths |
| | Arts/crafts for sale |
| ✗ | Live music |
| | Clowns |
| | Face painters |
| ✗ | Childrens games |
| | Animal exhibits/petting zoo |
| | Dogs allowed on leash |
| ✗ | Lost and found |
| ✗ | Bicycle racks |
| | First aid area available |
| ✗ | Self-brought picnics allowed |
| | Self-brought alcohol allowed |
| | Stroller/wheelchair rentals available |

| | |
|---|---|
| | Parade |
| | Parking fee |
| ✗ | Entrance fee: (prices not avbl.) |
| ✗ | Camping facilities: 10 miles |
| ✗ | Boating facilities: Russian River |
| ✗ | RV facilities w/ hookups: 10 miles |
| ✗ | Accomodations in town<br>Red Lion, Doubletree, El Rancho |
| ✗ | Restaurants in town<br>John Ash |

# *Blake Jones Trout Derby*

THIS IS A BLIND BOGEY—THE best kind in our book! Any size fish could win you the grand prize! An actual fish is caught the day before the **Blake Jones Trout Derby**, weighed and measured by a Notary Republic. So no one know what size fish will win! If your fish weighs in and measures in closest to the prior days catch...you could win "An Angler's Dream Come True"—worth $500! Kids, adults, women, Seniors...git on down here!

## Bishop, California

Second Sunday in March
Daily dawn - dusk

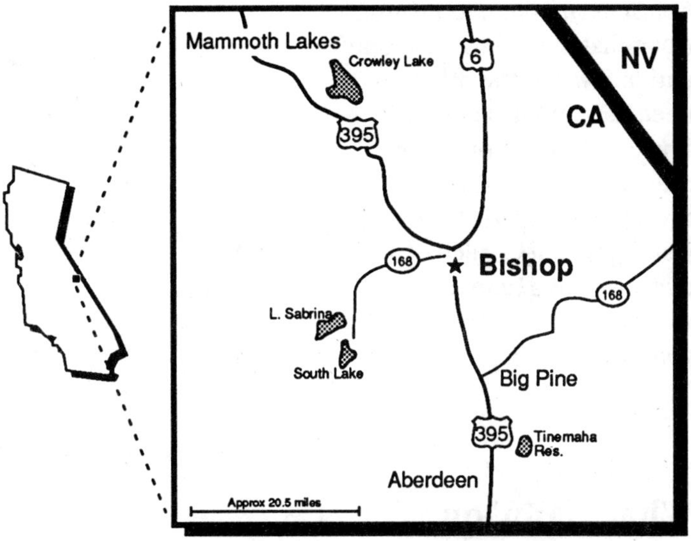


## What's goin' on...

Town population: **8,000**
Last year's attendance: **650**
Average outdoor temperature: **72°**
Festival location: **Pleasant Valley Reservoir**

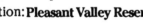

*Up-to-date festival information is available from:*
*Bishop Chamber of Commerce*
*(619) 873-8405*

| | |
|---|---|
| | Wine tasting/beer for sale |
| X | Food booths |
| | Arts/crafts for sale |
| | Live music |
| | Clowns |
| | Face painters |
| | Childrens games |
| | Animal exhibits/petting zoo |
| X | Dogs allowed on leash |
| | Lost and found |
| | Bicycle racks |
| | First aid area available |
| X | Self-brought picnics allowed |
| | Self-brought alcohol allowed |
| | Stroller/wheelchair rentals available |

| | |
|---|---|
| X | Parade |
| | Parking fee |
| X | Entrance fee: donations, please! |
| X | Camping facilities: On-site |
| X | Boating facilities: Lake Sabrina |
| X | RV facilities w/ hookups: On-site |
| X | Accomodations in town<br>Matlick House, Chalfant House |
| X | Restaurants in town<br>Whiskey Creek, Firehouse Grill, BBQ Bills, Jack's Waffle Shop, Bishop Grill |

C
E
N
T
R
A
L

# *Dandelion Days*

AH, THE PERFECT LITTLE gold country town of Jackson, has a perfectly fine festival—**Dandelion Days**! This celebration of fun, food, and frolic that stretches from one end of town to the other has been happening since 1975. The teriaki steak-on-a-sticks are fab and the antique browsing is *superb*! While visiting this little slice of paradise, take time to stop at the museum for a look old gold mining relics.

## Jackson, California

Third weekend in March
Daily 9:00 AM - 5:00 PM

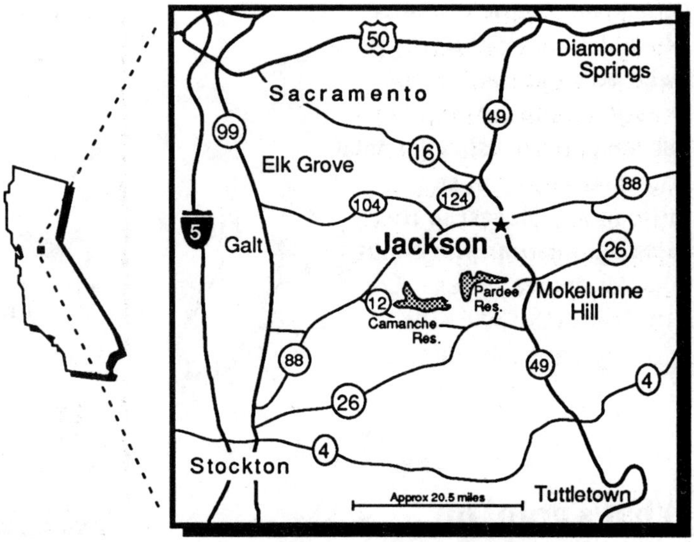


*Up-to-date festival information is available from:*
*Jackson Chamber of Commerce*
*(209) 223-0350*

## What's goin' on...

Town population: **3,500**
Last year's attendance: **15,000**
Average outdoor temperature: **75°**
Festival location: **Main Street**

- X Wine tasting/beer for sale
- X Food booths
- X Arts/crafts for sale
- X Live music
- X Clowns
- X Face painters
- Childrens games
- X Animal exhibits/petting zoo
- X Dogs allowed on leash
- X Lost and found
- X Bicycle racks
- X First aid area available
- X Self-brought picnics allowed
- Self-brought alcohol allowed
- Stroller/wheelchair rentals available

- Parade
- Parking fee
- Entrance fee
- X Camping facilities: 10 miles
- X Boating facilities: Lake Amador
- X RV facilities w/ hookups: 10 miles
- X Accomodations in town
  Ann Mari's Country Inn B&B, Broadway Hotel, The Wedgewood Inn B&B, Windrose Inn B&B
- X Restaurants in town

# Lemoore Crazy Days

IT'S A PLANE! IT'S A BIRD! No...it's just the crazy folks in Lemoore at **Crazy Days!** Spring has sprung and it's time to celebrate! These wacky lunatics have a heckuva good time at the annual parade—and then let the fun and frivolity spill over into their craft and food booths! You'll find the downtown completely upside down over this crazy festival!

## Lemoore, California

Third weekend in March (beginning Friday)
Hours vary

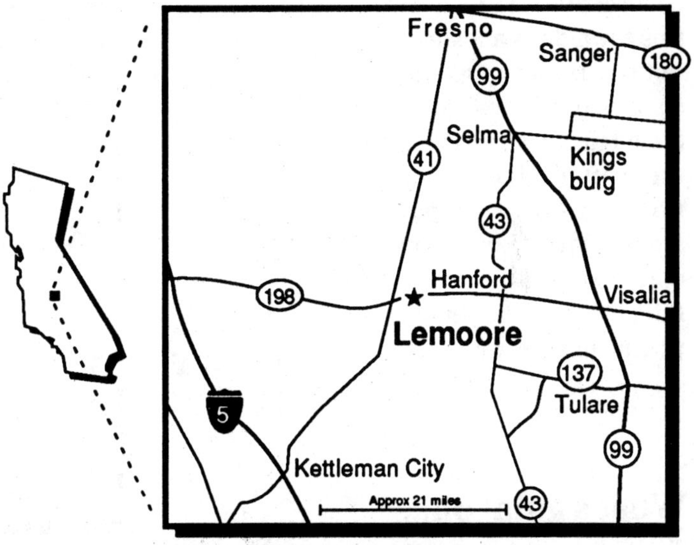


*Up-to-date festival information is available from:*
*Lemoore Chamber of Commerce*
*(209) 924-6401*

## What's goin' on...

Town population: **14,100**
Last year's attendance: **N/A**
Average outdoor temperature: **67°**
Festival location: **Downtown**

| | |
|---|---|
| | Wine tasting/beer for sale |
| ✗ | Food booths |
| ✗ | Arts/crafts for sale |
| ✗ | Live music |
| ✗ | Clowns |
| ✗ | Face painters |
| | Childrens games |
| ✗ | Animal exhibits/petting zoo |
| ✗ | Dogs allowed on leash |
| | Lost and found |
| | Bicycle racks |
| | First aid area available |
| | Self-brought picnics allowed |
| | Self-brought alcohol allowed |
| | Stroller/wheelchair rentals available |

| | |
|---|---|
| | Parade |
| | Parking fee |
| | Entrance fee |
| | Camping facilities |
| | Boating facilities |
| | RV facilities w/ hookups |
| ✗ | Accomodations in town<br>Vineyard Inn Motel |
| ✗ | Restaurants in town<br>The Cotton Mill, The Granary, Vineyard Inn, Casa Ortega, Vejar's |

C E N T R A L

# *Big Hat Day Festival*

DUST OFF THAT OLD HAT UP in the attic—you knew you were saving it for something! Well, how 'bout the **Big Hat Day Festival** in Clovis? Yep, this town does a festival right—serving up goodies such as homemade ice cream, Indian tacos, shaved ice, and the "battle of the barbecued ribs" cook-off (even the losers are fabulous)! You'll find country crafts for sale and a little bit of country music ringing in your ears too!

## Clovis, California

First Saturday in April
9:00 AM - 5:00 PM

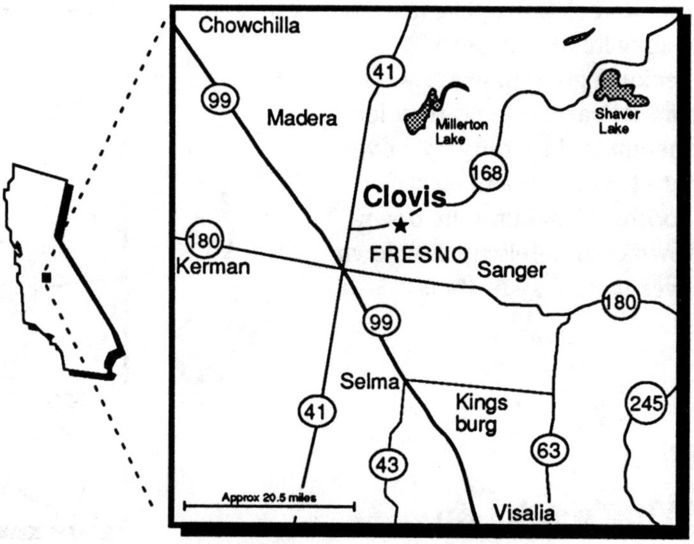


## What's goin' on...

Town population: **48,000**
Last year's attendance: **35,000**
Average outdoor temperature: **75°**
Festival location: **Clovis Old Town**

☞ *Up-to-date festival information is available from:*
*Clovis Chamber of Commerce*
*(209) 299-7273*

| | |
|---|---|
| ✗ | Wine tasting/beer for sale |
| ✗ | Food booths |
| ✗ | Arts/crafts for sale |
| ✗ | Live music |
| ✗ | Clowns |
| ✗ | Face painters |
| ✗ | Childrens games |
| ✗ | Animal exhibits/petting zoo |
| ✗ | Dogs allowed on leash |
| ✗ | Lost and found |
| ✗ | Bicycle racks |
| ✗ | First aid area available |
| ✗ | Self-brought picnics allowed |
| | Self-brought alcohol allowed |
| | Stroller/wheelchair rentals available |

| | |
|---|---|
| | Parade |
| | Parking fee |
| | Entrance fee |
| ✗ | Camping facilities: 25 miles |
| ✗ | Boating facilities: Millerton Lake |
| ✗ | RV facilities w/ hookups: 25 miles |
| ✗ | Accomodations in town<br>Rodeo Lodge |
| ✗ | Restaurants in town |

# *Opening Day on the Straits*

THE WATERFRONT TOWN OF Benicia may have lost its bid to be the major port on San Francisco Bay in the early 1850s...but it hosts the **Opening Day on the Straits**! This tradition began in 1979 and is especially fun for sailors and nautical buffs! Bring your picnic and beach chairs down to the marina for the entertaining and sometimes wacky boat parade and show! There's a steak and chicken barbecue in the evening.

## Benicia, California

Second Saturday in April
10:00 AM - 10:00 PM

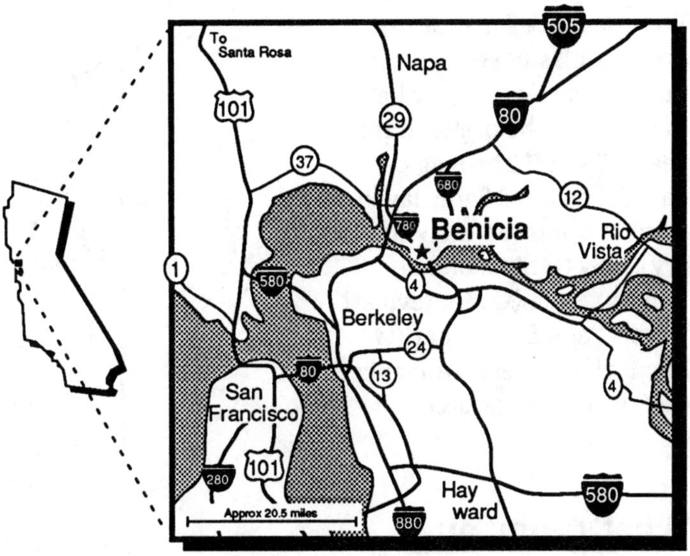


*Up-to-date festival information is available from:*
*Benicia Chamber of Commerce*
*(707) 745-2120*

## What's goin' on...

Town population: **24,000**
Last year's attendance: **10,000**
Average outdoor temperature: **75°**
Festival location: **Marina/Yacht Club**

| | |
|---|---|
| ✗ | Wine tasting/beer for sale |
| ✗ | Food booths |
| ✗ | Arts/crafts for sale |
| ✗ | Live music |
| | Clowns |
| | Face painters |
| | Childrens games |
| | Animal exhibits/petting zoo |
| ✗ | Dogs allowed on leash |
| | Lost and found |
| | Bicycle racks |
| | First aid area available |
| ✗ | Self-brought picnics allowed |
| | Self-brought alcohol allowed |
| | Stroller/wheelchair rentals available |

| | |
|---|---|
| ✗ | Parade: Boat parade on the Straits |
| | Parking fee |
| | Entrance fee |
| | Camping facilities |
| ✗ | Boating facilities: Straits |
| | RV facilities w/ hookups |
| ✗ | Accomodations in town<br>The Union Hotel B&B, Captain Dillinham's Inn B&B, Benicia Inn |
| ✗ | Restaurants in town |

# *Music at the Wineries*

ARE YOU UP FOR A LITTLE jazz, with a splash of Chardonnay? That's what's in store for you at **Music at the Wineries**. The Amador Arts Council folks have been really busy to make each year better than the one before! And this year's GREAT! The magic dates? The third Saturday in April (@ Sobon Estate Winery), May (@ Shenandoah Winery), June (@ Montevina Winery) and September (@ Montevina Winery). Advanced reservations suggested!

## Plymouth, California

See the paragraph
11:00 AM - 3:00 PM

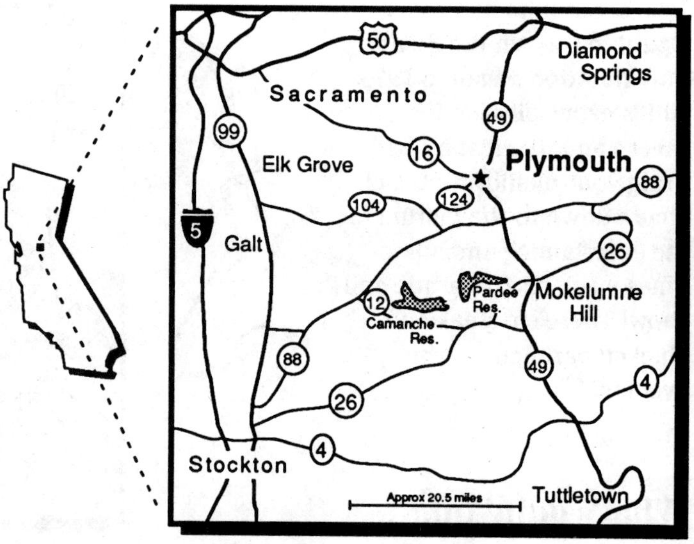


*Up-to-date festival information is available from:*
*Plymouth Arts Council*
*(209) 267-0211*

## What's goin' on...

Town population: **1,000**
Last year's attendance: **800**
Average outdoor temperature: **85°**
Festival location: **Local Wineries**

- X Wine tasting/beer for sale
- X Food booths
- X Arts/crafts for sale
- X Live music
- Clowns
- Face painters
- Childrens games
- Animal exhibits/petting zoo
- Dogs allowed on leash
- Lost and found
- Bicycle racks
- First aid area available
- Self-brought picnics allowed
- Self-brought alcohol allowed
- Stroller/wheelchair rentals available

- Parade
- Parking fee
- X Entrance fee $12
- X Camping facilities: In town
- X Boating facilities: Lake Amador
- X RV facilities w/ hookups: In town
- X Accomodations in town
  Shenandoah Village Motel
- X Restaurants in town

# *Springville Western Week and Sierra Rodeo*

"YIPPIE-I-EEE!" FEARLESS frontiersmen and drugstore dudes and dames...round up your ponies, cinch up the saddle and head the **Springville Western Week and Sierra Rodeo**! The first Saturday will find teamsters and trail tramps reenacting the Jackass Mail Run from Porterville to Springville. Then the following weekend "Big Hat" days kicks-off with a parade, followed by zillions of fun events!

## Springville, California

Third Saturday (Jackass Mail Run) and fourth weekend (Big Hat days & rodeo) in April
Hours vary

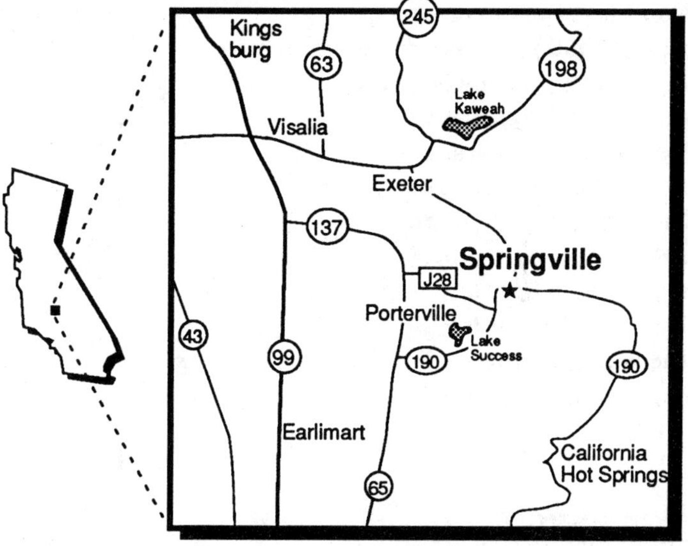


## What's goin' on...

Town population: **1,800**
Last year's attendance: **20,000**
Average outdoor temperature: **70°**
Festival location: **Citywide**

*Up-to-date festival information is available from:*
*Springville Chamber of Commerce*
*(209) 539-2312*

| | |
|---|---|
| ✗ | Wine tasting/beer for sale |
| ✗ | Food booths |
| ✗ | Arts/crafts for sale |
| ✗ | Live music |
| | Clowns |
| ✗ | Face painters |
| | Childrens games |
| | Animal exhibits/petting zoo |
| | Dogs allowed on leash |
| ✗ | Lost and found |
| | Bicycle racks |
| | First aid area available |
| | Self-brought picnics allowed |
| | Self-brought alcohol allowed |
| | Stroller/wheelchair rentals available |

| | |
|---|---|
| ✗ | Parade: 2nd Sat. 10:00 AM on Main St. |
| | Parking fee |
| ✗ | Entrance fee: Rodeo: A $7; K $3 |
| ✗ | Camping facilities: 3 miles |
| ✗ | Boating facilities: Lake Success |
| ✗ | RV facilities w/ hookups: 3 miles |
| ✗ | Accomodations in town |
| ✗ | Restaurants in town |

# *Clovis Championship Rodeo*

REAL COWBOYS AND REAL cowgirls! Yep, there's nothing phony about the annual **Clovis Championship Rodeo**. Come join the riders for a 6:00 AM (a what?) Pancake Breakfast, where real cowboys eat flapjacks, bacon, and eggs. Next stop? The parade on Clovis and Pollasky Streets. Then...the real thing! You'll see calf roping and bronc riding and smell the tri-tip barbecue! This is big fun for the whole family.

## Clovis, California

Fourth weekend in April
Hours vary

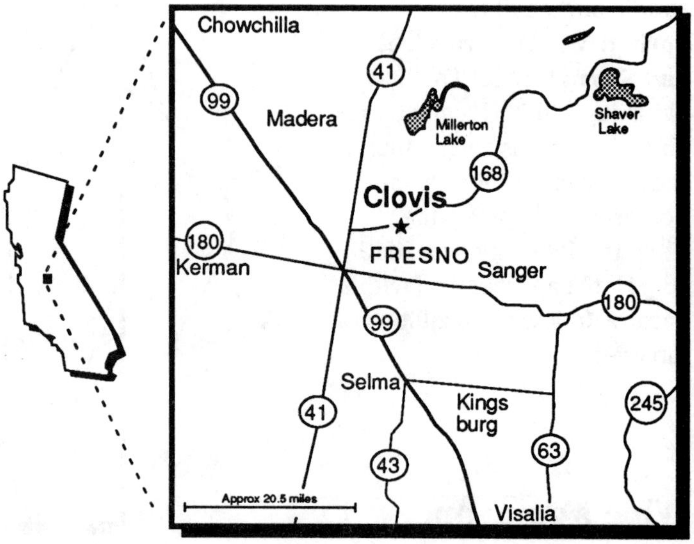


## What's goin' on...

Town population: **48,000**
Last year's attendance: **15,000**
Average outdoor temperature: **75°**
Festival location: **Rodeo Grounds**

*Up-to-date festival information is available from:*
*Clovis Chamber of Commerce*
*(209) 299-7273*

- ✗ Wine tasting/beer for sale
- ✗ Food booths
- Arts/crafts for sale
- ✗ Live music
- ✗ Clowns
- Face painters
- Childrens games
- ✗ Animal exhibits/petting zoo
- Dogs allowed on leash
- Lost and found
- Bicycle racks
- First aid area available
- Self-brought picnics allowed
- Self-brought alcohol allowed
- Stroller/wheelchair rentals available

- ✗ Parade: Sat. 10:00 AM downtown
- Parking fee
- ✗ Entrance fee: (prices not avbl.)
- ✗ Camping facilities: 25 miles
- ✗ Boating facilities: Millerton Lake
- ✗ RV facilities w/ hookups: 25 miles
- ✗ Accomodations in town
  Rodeo Lodge
- ✗ Restaurants in town

# *Butter & Egg Days Parade*

JULIE'S GRAMMA ALWAYS said, "If it starts with a pound of butter and a dozen eggs, it's gotta be good!" So what's that make the **Butter and Eggs Days Parade**? Really great! Besides the yummy food (homemade pies and pastries, and barbecued meats and sausages), there are butter-churning demonstrations; a petting zoo; egg tosses; and, of course, a parade!

## Petaluma, California

Last Saturday in April
11:00 AM - 5:00 PM

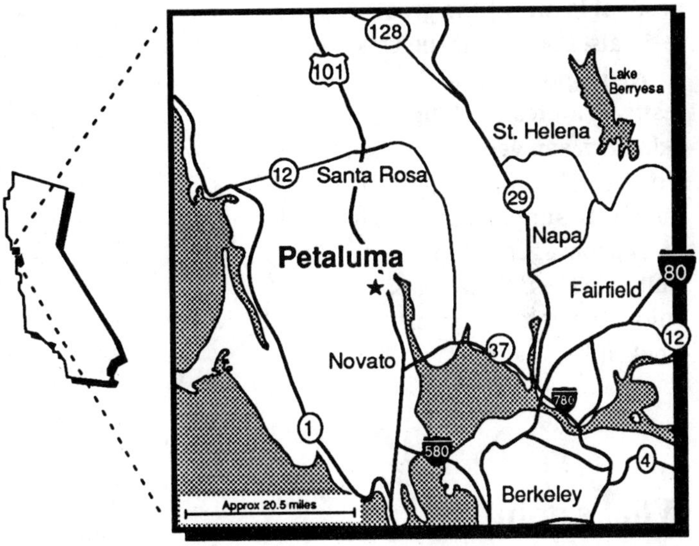




## What's goin' on...

Town population: **42,000**
Last year's attendance: **5,000**
Average outdoor temperature: **75°**
Festival location: **Downtown**

*Up-to-date festival information is available from:*
*Petaluma Chamber of Commerce*
*(707) 762-2785*

| | |
|---|---|
| X | Wine tasting/beer for sale |
| X | Food booths |
| | Arts/crafts for sale |
| X | Live music |
| X | Clowns |
| X | Face painters |
| X | Childrens games |
| X | Animal exhibits/petting zoo |
| X | Dogs allowed on leash |
| X | Lost and found |
| X | Bicycle racks |
| X | First aid area available |
| X | Self-brought picnics allowed |
| | Self-brought alcohol allowed |
| | Stroller/wheelchair rentals available |

| | |
|---|---|
| X | Parade: Noon on Petaluma Ave. |
| | Parking fee |
| | Entrance fee |
| X | Camping facilities: 5 miles |
| X | Boating facilities: River, lake, and bay |
| X | RV facilities w/ hookups: 5 miles |
| X | Accomodations in town<br>Best Western, Quality Inn, Motel 6, Cavanagh Cottage B&B, 7th St. Inn B&B |
| X | Restaurants in town<br>Petrucci's, Tempura House, Steamer Gold, Cattlemen's, Fino's,Original Marvin's |

# *Asparagus Festival*

ASPARAGUS PASTA? ASPARAGUS lasagne? Asparagus soups, salads, and everything asparagussed! The **Asparagus Festival** is one of the great festivals! Located at the Oak Grove Regional Park, this festival salutes the long, skinny, green veggie your kids won't eat! Did you know that California supplies over 70% of all asparagus sold in these United States? Come out and enjoy this comical green weekend!

## Stockton, California

Fourth weekend in April
Daily 10:00 AM - 6:00 PM

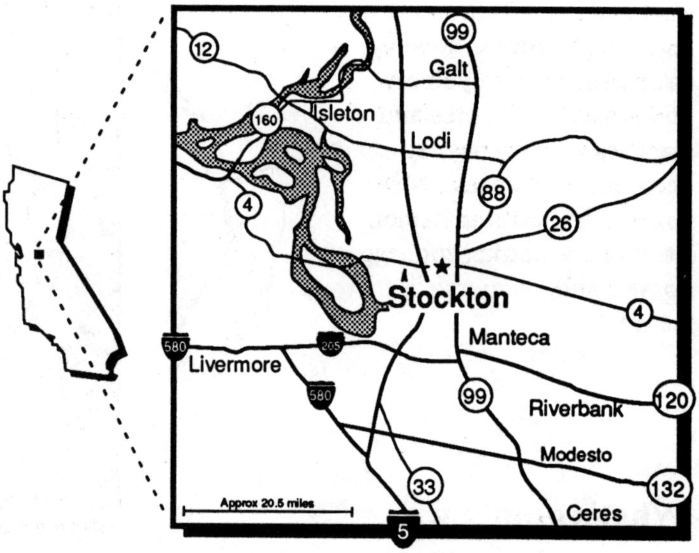


*Up-to-date festival information is available from:*
*Stockton Chamber of Commerce*
*(209) 466-7066*

## What's goin' on...

Town population: **150,000**
Last year's attendance: **70,000**
Average outdoor temperature: **80°**
Festival location: **Oak Grove Park**

- X Wine tasting/beer for sale
- X Food booths
- X Arts/crafts for sale
- X Live music
- X Clowns
- X Face painters
- X Childrens games
- X Animal exhibits/petting zoo
- Dogs allowed on leash
- X Lost and found
- X Bicycle racks
- X First aid area available
- X Self-brought picnics allowed
- Self-brought alcohol allowed
- Stroller/wheelchair rentals available

- Parade
- Parking fee
- Entrance fee
- X Camping facilities: 15 miles
- X Boating facilities: The Delta
- X RV facilities w/ hookups: 15 miles
- X Accomodations in town
  The Old Victorian Inn B&B, Holiday Inn, Allstar Inn
- X Restaurants in town

# *Spring Festival & Loyalty Day Parade*

COMING TO THE WINTON **Spring Festival** is a terrific way to welcome the blooming of beautiful flowers! Winton, a very small town with only *one* traffic light, claims to be the "friendliest town in all of California!" Arts-and-crafts exhibits have items for sale. Mexican, Portuguese, and American snacks are available, as are beer, wine, and soft drinks.

## Winton, California

Fourth weekend in April
Sat. 10:00 AM - 10:00 PM; Sun. 10:00 AM - 5:00 PM

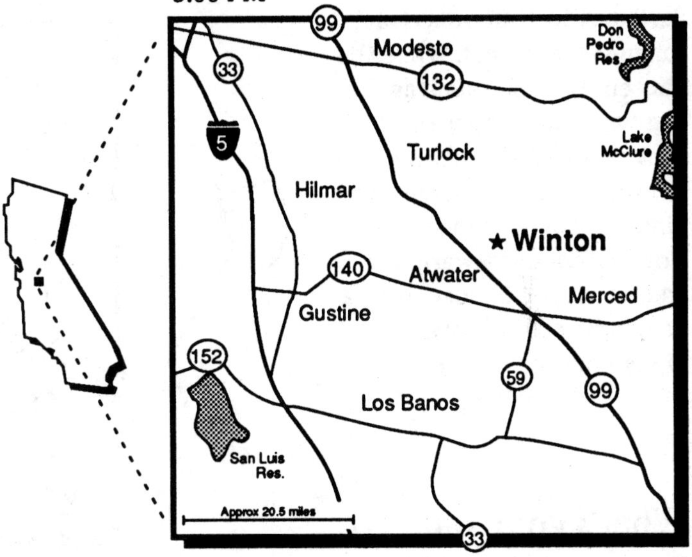


## What's goin' on...

Town population: **4,995**
Last year's attendance: **8,000**
Average outdoor temperature: **90°**
Festival location: **Park**

*Up-to-date festival information is available from:*
*Winton Chamber of Commerce*
*(209) 358-5615*

| | |
|---|---|
| ✗ | Wine tasting/beer for sale |
| ✗ | Food booths |
| ✗ | Arts/crafts for sale |
| ✗ | Live music |
| ✗ | Clowns |
| ✗ | Face painters |
| ✗ | Childrens games |
| | Animal exhibits/petting zoo |
| | Dogs allowed on leash |
| ✗ | Lost and found |
| | Bicycle racks |
| ✗ | First aid area available |
| ✗ | Self-brought picnics allowed |
| | Self-brought alcohol allowed |
| | Stroller/wheelchair rentals available |

| | |
|---|---|
| ✗ | Parade: (time & date not avbl.) |
| | Parking fee |
| | Entrance fee |
| ✗ | Camping facilities: 7 miles |
| ✗ | Boating facilities: Merced River |
| ✗ | RV facilities w/ hookups: 7 miles |
| ✗ | Accomodations in town |
| ✗ | Restaurants in town<br>Cook Stove, Tammy's |

C E N T R A L

# *Fair Oaks Fiesta*

VISIT OUR STATE'S CAPITAL after you drop by the **Fair Oaks Fiesta.** Enjoy foods of all nationalities, including Serbian, Mexican, American, Japanese, and Thai. While the kids enjoy games such as the egg toss and compete in the sack races, everyone can enjoy live entertainment of all kinds throughout the day. You can count on warm weather if you choose to do a little river rafting down the chilly American River.

## Fair Oaks, California

First weekend in May
Hours vary

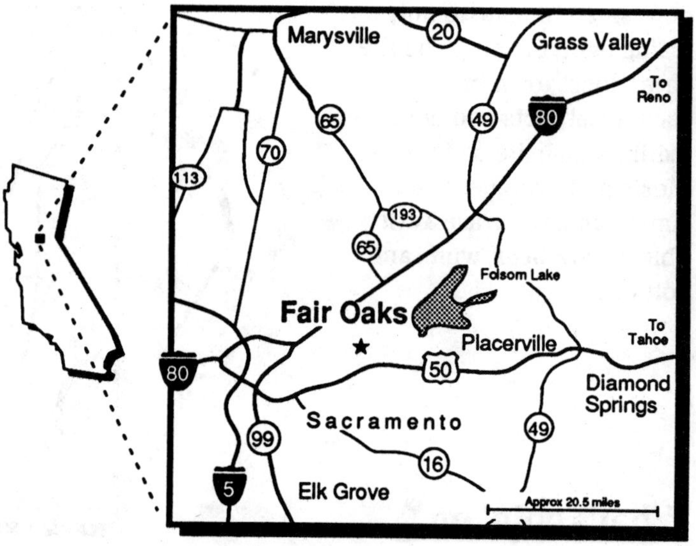


## What's goin' on...

Town population: **40,000**
Last year's attendance: **7,000**
Average outdoor temperature: **90°**
Festival location: **Fair Oaks Park**

*Up-to-date festival information is available from:*
*Fair Oaks Chamber of Commerce*
*(916) 967-2903*

| | |
|---|---|
| X | Wine tasting/beer for sale |
| X | Food booths |
| X | Arts/crafts for sale |
| X | Live music |
| X | Clowns |
| X | Face painters |
| X | Childrens games |
| | Animal exhibits/petting zoo |
| X | Dogs allowed on leash |
| | Lost and found |
| X | Bicycle racks |
| | First aid area available |
| | Self-brought picnics allowed |
| | Self-brought alcohol allowed |
| | Stroller/wheelchair rentals available |

| | |
|---|---|
| X | Parade: Sat. 10:00 AM Fair Oaks Park |
| | Parking fee |
| | Entrance fee |
| X | Camping facilities: [illegible] |
| X | Boating facilities: Folsom Lake |
| | RV facilities w/ hookups |
| X | Accomodations in town<br>Best Western Heritage Inn, Sheraton Sunrise Hotel |
| X | Restaurants in town<br>La Posta, Eat Your Vegetables, Michelmore's, Fair Oaks Cafe, Sports Bar & Grill |

# *Oldtimers Days*

**OLDTIMERS DAYS** IN Avenal begins with a colorful downtown parade and ends up at Floyd Rice Park! This community celebration comes complete with tri-tip barbecues, hot dogs, seafood cocktails, tacos, and the like; live music all day long; and artists and craftspersons displaying their handmade commodities. Located just 20 minutes from the famous Harris Ranch, Avenal is a friendly place!

## Avenal, California

First weekend in May (beginning Friday)
Hours vary

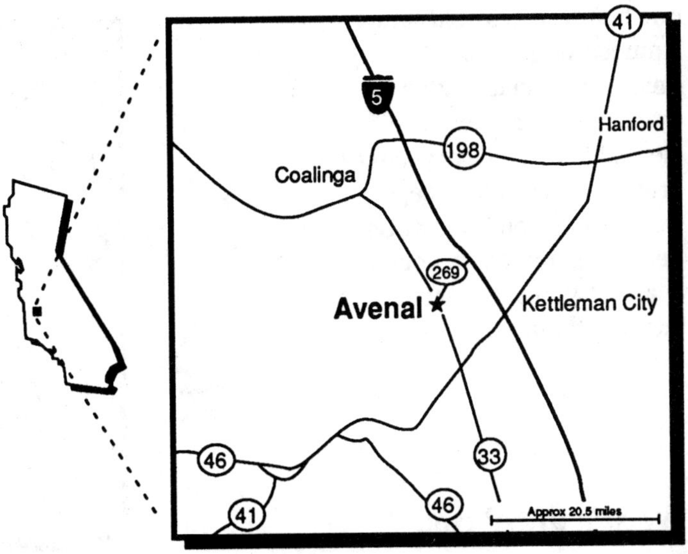


## What's goin' on...

Town population: **8,500**
Last year's attendance: **2,300**
Average outdoor temperature: **80°**
Festival location: **Floyd Rice Park**

*Up-to-date festival information is available from:*
*Avenal Chamber of Commerce*
*(209) 386-0690*

| | |
|---|---|
| X | Wine tasting/beer for sale |
| X | Food booths |
| X | Arts/crafts for sale |
| X | Live music |
| X | Clowns |
| X | Face painters |
| X | Childrens games |
| X | Animal exhibits/petting zoo |
| X | Dogs allowed on leash |
| X | Lost and found |
| | Bicycle racks |
| X | First aid area available |
| X | Self-brought picnics allowed |
| | Self-brought alcohol allowed |
| | Stroller/wheelchair rentals available |

| | |
|---|---|
| X | Parade: Sat. 10:00 AM on Kings St. |
| | Parking fee |
| | Entrance fee |
| | Camping facilities |
| | Boating facilities |
| X | RV facilities w/ hookups: In town |
| X | Accomodations in town<br>The Lodging House |
| X | Restaurants in town<br>Roger's Cafe, Ardo's, Creekside Inn, Pizza Factory |

CENTRAL

# *Ione Homecoming Picnic & Parade*

HERE IT IS! IONE'S BIG FESTIVAL of the year—and what a doozey it is! Nope—you sure won't get bored at this over one hundred year old **Ione Homecoming Picnic & Parade**! The celebration is overseen by the newly elected Miss Ione (pageant on Friday night)—who keeps a watchful eye on the carnival, bed races, art show, equestrian activities, barbecue, and dance! Git on out and enjoy it!

## Ione, California

First weekend in May (beginning Friday)
Hours vary

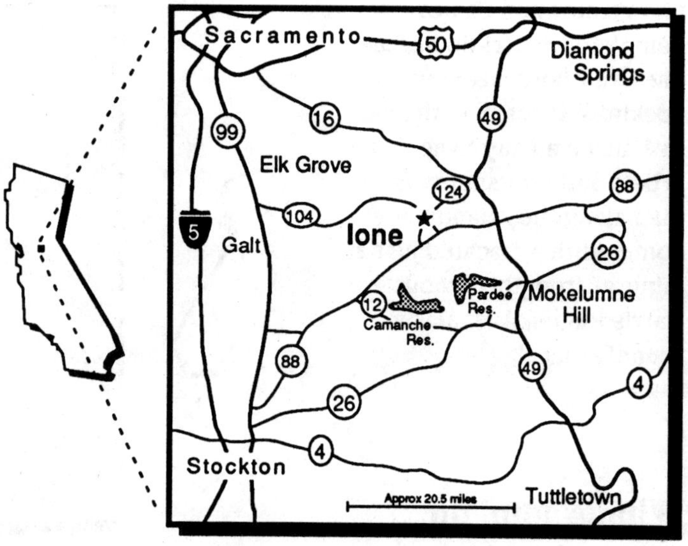


## What's goin' on...

Town population: **2,500**
Last year's attendance: **N/A**
Average outdoor temperature: **80°**
Festival location: **Howard Park**

*Up-to-date festival information is available from:*
*Ione Chamber of Commerce*
*(209) 223-0350*

- ✗ Wine tasting/beer for sale
- ✗ Food booths
- ✗ Arts/crafts for sale
- ✗ Live music
- ✗ Clowns
- Face painters
- ✗ Childrens games
- ✗ Animal exhibits/petting zoo
- Dogs allowed on leash
- ✗ Lost and found
- ✗ Bicycle racks
- ✗ First aid area available
- ✗ Self-brought picnics allowed
- Self-brought alcohol allowed
- Stroller/wheelchair rentals available

- ✗ Parade: Sat. (time not avbl.)
- Parking fee
- Entrance fee
- ✗ Camping facilities: 5 miles
- ✗ Boating facilities: Lake Amador
- ✗ RV facilities w/ hookups: 5 miles
- ✗ Accomodations in town
  The Heirloom B&B
- ✗ Restaurants in town

# *Ceres Street Faire*

IT'S A FUNNY-LOOKING name...and it's pronounced like the word serious—but, seriously folks, the town is everything *but*! The **Ceres Street Faire** is a heck of a good time—complete with entertainment all day long, ethnic-food booths cookin' up everything you can imagine, and craft booths filled with handmade items such as jewelry, hand-painted fabrics, silk arrangements, baskets, and leather and wood carvings.

## Ceres, California

First weekend in May
Sat. 8:00 AM - 5:00 PM; Sun. 8:00 AM - 4:00 PM

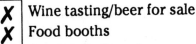

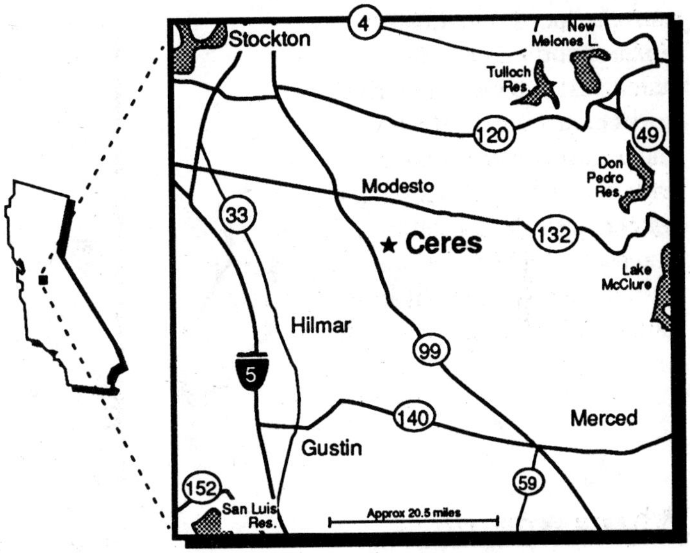


*Up-to-date festival information is available from:*
*Ceres Chamber of Commerce*
*(209) 537-2601*

## What's goin' on...

Town population: **26,000**
Last year's attendance: **N/A**
Average outdoor temperature: **80°**
Festival location: **Downtown**

| | |
|---|---|
| X | Wine tasting/beer for sale |
| X | Food booths |
| X | Arts/crafts for sale |
| X | Live music |
| X | Clowns |
| X | Face painters |
| | Childrens games |
| X | Animal exhibits/petting zoo |
| X | Dogs allowed on leash |
| X | Lost and found |
| X | Bicycle racks |
| X | First aid area available |
| X | Self-brought picnics allowed |
| X | Self-brought alcohol allowed |
| | Stroller/wheelchair rentals available |

| | |
|---|---|
| | Parade |
| | Parking fee |
| | Entrance fee |
| X | Camping facilities: 15 miles |
| X | Boating facilities: Turlock Lake |
| X | RV facilities w/ hookups: 15 miles |
| X | Accomodations in town<br>Blue Mill Motel, All Seasons Inn |
| X | Restaurants in town<br>Alfonso's, Peach Tree |

CENTRAL

# *Cinco de Mayo*

THE COMMEMORATE THE rich heritage of Delano, **Cinco de Mayo** has become an annual celebration. Besides relishing tacos, burritos, tamales, and other ethnic delicacies, you can enjoy the works of art and crafts for sale. Brightly colored dresses wave in the sunlight as female dancers interpret traditional dances. You'll hear several mariachi bands and a little rock 'n' roll!

## Delano, California

First weekend in May
Daily 10:00 AM - 11:00 PM

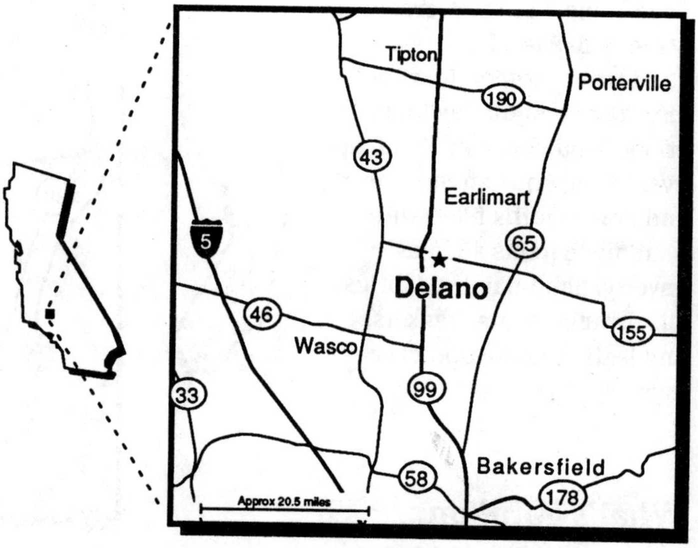


## What's goin' on...

Town population: **21,000**
Last year's attendance: **N/A**
Average outdoor temperature: **75°**
Festival location: **Memorial Park**

*Up-to-date festival information is available from:*
*Delano Chamber of Commerce*
*(805) 725-2518*

| | |
|---|---|
| ✗ | Wine tasting/beer for sale |
| ✗ | Food booths |
| ✗ | Arts/crafts for sale |
| ✗ | Live music |
| | Clowns |
| | Face painters |
| ✗ | Childrens games |
| | Animal exhibits/petting zoo |
| ✗ | Dogs allowed on leash |
| | Lost and found |
| ✗ | Bicycle racks |
| | First aid area available |
| ✗ | Self-brought picnics allowed |
| | Self-brought alcohol allowed |
| | Stroller/wheelchair rentals available |

| | |
|---|---|
| ✗ | Parade: (date & time not avbl.) |
| | Parking fee |
| ✗ | Entrance fee: $1 |
| ✗ | Camping facilities: 2 miles |
| ✗ | Boating facilities: Lake Success |
| ✗ | RV facilities w/ hookups: 2 miles |
| ✗ | Accomodations in town |
| ✗ | Restaurants in town |

# *Western Festival*

THE FIRST WEEKEND IN May is the time to be at Elk Grove Park—site of the Elk Grove **Western Festival**. This festival started out in the late 1950s as a fund-raiser for the elementary school and now has one of the best parades in the state, with more than 200 entrants and lasting about three hours! The local Gibson winery has a tasting room not too far from the park.

## Elk Grove, California

First weekend in May
Daily 11:00 AM - 6:00 PM

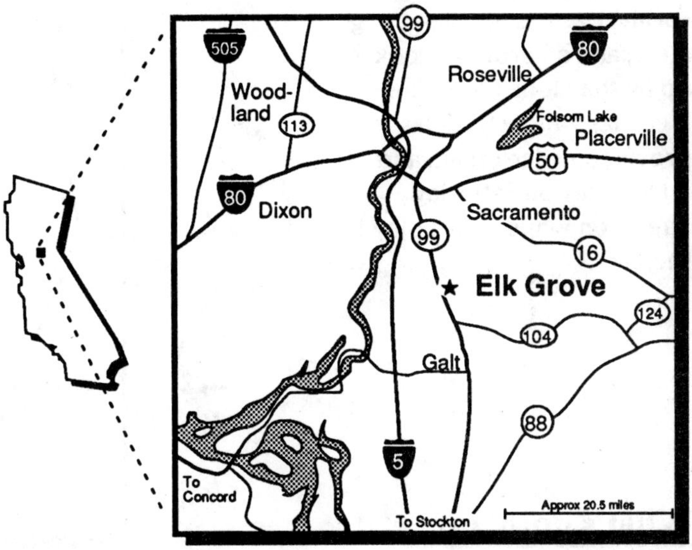


*Up-to-date festival information is available from:*
*Elk Grove Chamber of Commerce*
*(916) 685-3911*

## What's goin' on...

Town population: **32,000**
Last year's attendance: **17,000**
Average outdoor temperature: **93°**
Festival location: **Elk Grove Park**

| | |
|---|---|
| X | Wine tasting/beer for sale |
| X | Food booths |
| X | Arts/crafts for sale |
| X | Live music |
| | Clowns |
| X | Face painters |
| X | Childrens games |
| | Animal exhibits/petting zoo |
| X | Dogs allowed on leash |
| X | Lost and found |
| X | Bicycle racks |
| | First aid area available |
| X | Self-brought picnics allowed |
| | Self-brought alcohol allowed |
| | Stroller/wheelchair rentals available |

| | |
|---|---|
| X | Parade: Sat. 11:00 on Elk Street |
| | Parking fee |
| X | Entrance fee: $3 |
| X | Camping facilities: 30 miles |
| X | Boating facilities: The Delta |
| X | RV facilities w/ hookups: 30 miles |
| | Accomodations in town |
| X | Restaurants in town<br>Village Choice, The General Store, Stoney's, Vince's Ristorante |

CENTRAL

# *Spring Festival*

RIVERDALE FOLKS KICK-OFF their summer by heading on over to the **Spring Festival**. This two-day escapade has carnival games for the youngsters, and a barbecue cooked up by the Lions Club. The local dairy-industry folks provide free ice cream and milkshakes on Saturday afternoon while bands play in the park.

## Riverdale, California

First weekend in May
Hours vary

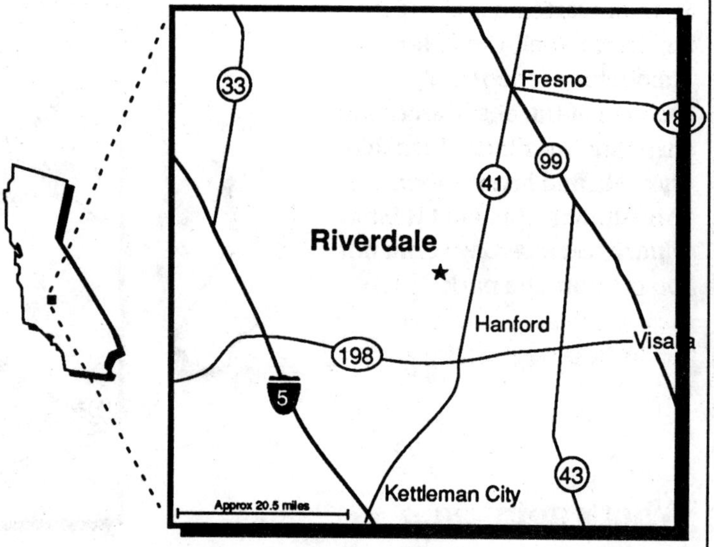


*Up-to-date festival information is available from:*
*Riverdale Chamber of Commerce*
*(we don't have a phone no.)*

## What's goin' on...

Town population: **1,866**
Last year's attendance: **2,000**
Average outdoor temperature: **85°**
Festival location: **Park**

| | |
|---|---|
| X | Wine tasting/beer for sale |
| X | Food booths |
| X | Arts/crafts for sale |
| X | Live music |
| X | Clowns |
| X | Face painters |
| X | Childrens games |
| | Animal exhibits/petting zoo |
| X | Dogs allowed on leash |
| | Lost and found |
| | Bicycle racks |
| X | First aid area available |
| X | Self-brought picnics allowed |
| | Self-brought alcohol allowed |
| | Stroller/wheelchair rentals available |

| | |
|---|---|
| X | Parade: Sat. 10:30 AM downtown |
| | Parking fee |
| | Entrance fee |
| X | Camping facilities [illegible] |
| X | Boating facilities: Pine Flat Res. |
| X | RV facilities w/ hookups: 25 miles |
| | Accomodations in town |
| X | Restaurants in town |

# *Selma Raisin Festival*

WHAT U.S. CROP IS GROWN exclusively in California's largest agricultural county?...and begins with an R? Come see for yourself at the Selma **Raisin Festival!** This friendly community began celebrating this wrinkly little fruit back in 1980, and it looks like it'll go on for years! This is loads of fun, with lots of raisin-oriented contests and competitions: count the raisins, raisin cook-off, and Raisin Queen crowning are just a few!

## Selma, California

First Saturday in May
9:00 AM - 10:00 PM

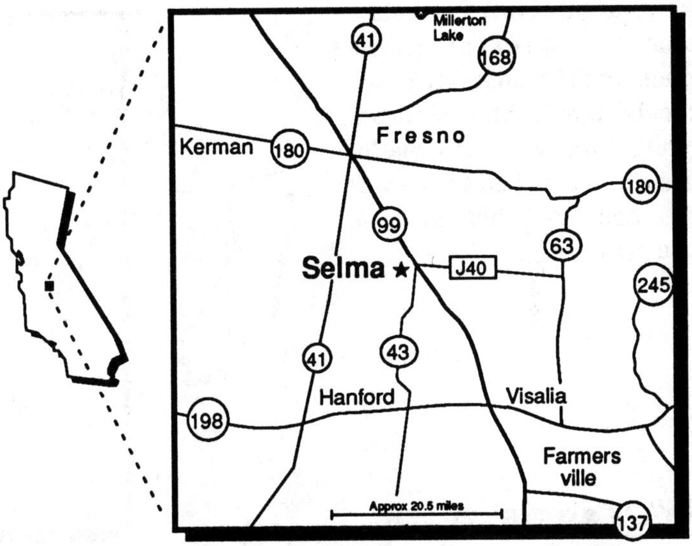


*Up-to-date festival information is available from:*
*Selma Chamber of Commerce*
*(209) 896-3315*

## What's goin' on...

Town population: **14,700**
Last year's attendance: **8,000**
Average outdoor temperature: **85°**
Festival location: **Pioneer Village**

| | |
|---|---|
| X | Wine tasting/beer for sale |
| X | Food booths |
| X | Arts/crafts for sale |
| X | Live music |
| X | Clowns |
| X | Face painters |
| X | Childrens games |
| X | Animal exhibits/petting zoo |
| | Dogs allowed on leash |
| X | Lost and found |
| X | Bicycle racks |
| X | First aid area available |
| | Self-brought picnics allowed |
| | Self-brought alcohol allowed |
| | Stroller/wheelchair rentals available |

| | |
|---|---|
| X | Parade: Sat. 10:00 AM downtown |
| X | Parking fee: $1 |
| | Entrance fee |
| X | Camping facilities: 10 miles |
| X | Boating facilities: Kings River |
| X | RV facilities w/ hookups: 10 miles |
| X | Accomodations in town<br>Super 8, Villager Inn |
| X | Restaurants in town<br>Sal's Mexican Restaurant, Arthur's |

CENTRAL

# *Western Week*

**WESTERN WEEK** IN Woodlake guarantees fun for the whole family! Located just west of Lake Kaweah in the warm central valley of California, Woodlake offers a tricycle race for the kiddies and craft booths filled with ceramics and wooden and homemade items. In addition, artists will be showing off their oils and watercolors.

## Woodlake, California

Second week of May
Hours vary

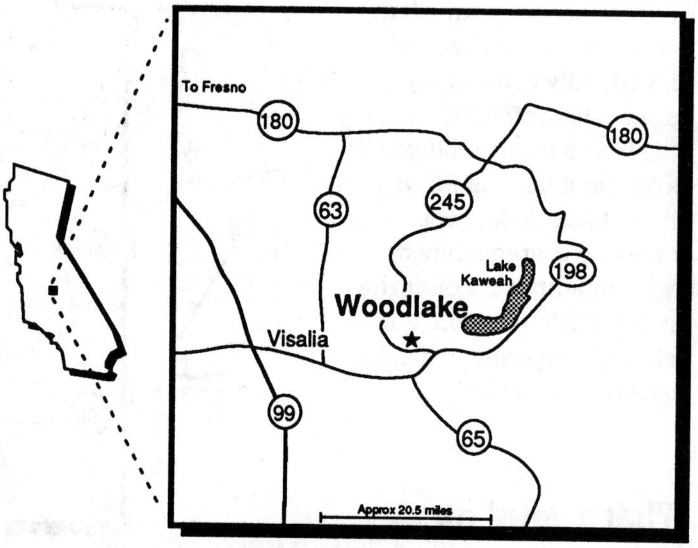


*Up-to-date festival information is available from:*
*Woodlake Chamber of Commerce*
*(209) 564-8055*

## What's goin' on...

Town population: **4,343**
Last year's attendance: **2,000**
Average outdoor temperature: **80°**
Festival location: **Townwide**

- ✗ Wine tasting/beer for sale
- ✗ Food booths
- ✗ Arts/crafts for sale
- ✗ Live music
- ✗ Clowns
- ✗ Face painters
- ✗ Childrens games
- Animal exhibits/petting zoo
- ✗ Dogs allowed on leash
- ✗ Lost and found
- ✗ Bicycle racks
- ✗ First aid area available
- Self-brought picnics allowed
- Self-brought alcohol allowed
- Stroller/wheelchair rentals available

- ✗ Parade: (date & time not avbl.)
- Parking fee
- Entrance fee
- ✗ Camping facilities: 20 miles
- ✗ Boating facilities: Kaweah Lake
- ✗ RV facilities w/ hookups: 20 miles
- Accomodations in town
- ✗ Restaurants in town
  La Villa, Great Star, New China, Dora's

# *Coyote Howl*

FOLKS FROM MARIPOSA County have been howling ever since the first annual **Coyote Howl** in 1985! They have wonderful art & craft booths, antiques & collectibles, food, music, carnival games, raffles, music, and lots of other entertainment. Prizes will be awarded to the most authentic coyote howlers—kids and adults. So sharpen your vocal cords and practice recreating the calls of our furry friends!

## Coulterville, California

Second weekend in May
Daily 10:00 AM - 6:00 PM

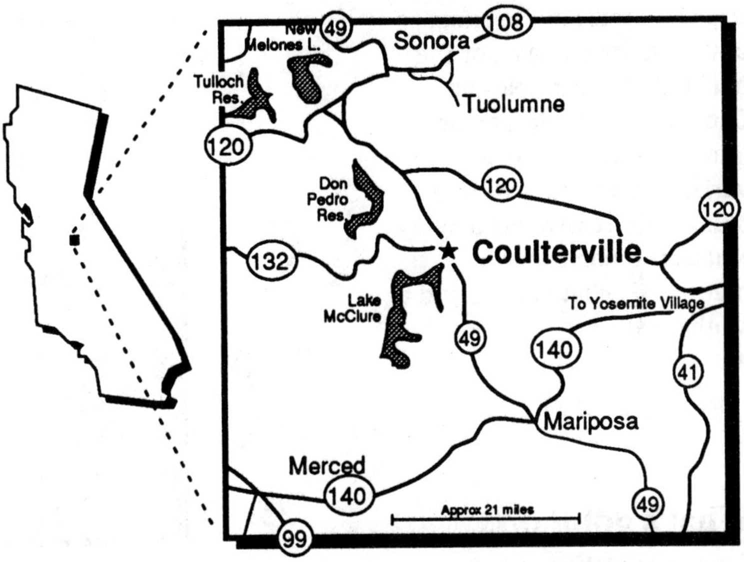


*Up-to-date festival information is available from:*
*Coulterville Visitor Center*
*(209) 878-3074*

## What's goin' on...

Town population: **3,000**
Last year's attendance: **2,500**
Average outdoor temperature: **80°**
Festival location: **Downtown**

| | |
|---|---|
| X | Wine tasting/beer for sale |
| X | Food booths |
| X | Arts/crafts for sale |
| X | Live music |
| | Clowns |
| | Face painters |
| X | Childrens games |
| X | Animal exhibits/petting zoo |
| | Dogs allowed on leash |
| | Lost and found |
| X | Bicycle racks |
| | First aid area available |
| X | Self-brought picnics allowed |
| | Self-brought alcohol allowed |
| | Stroller/wheelchair rentals available |

| | |
|---|---|
| X | Parade |
| | Parking fee |
| | Entrance fee |
| X | Camping facilities: 8 miles |
| | Boating facilities |
| X | RV facilities w/ hookups: 8 miles |
| X | Accomodations in town |
| X | Restaurants in town |

C
E
N
T
R
A
L

# *Hallcrest Bluegrass Art and Wine Festival*

THE **HALLCREST Bluegrass, Art and Wine Festival** at Hallcrest Vineyards is a terrific way to spend Mother's Day weekend! Sip the crisp, buttery Chardonnays, or the full-bodied Zinfandels and Cabernets, or their famous nonalcoholic premium varietal grape juice. All this, plus an impressive art display and a little homegrown bluegrass...what more could a Mother ask for?

## Felton, California

Second weekend in May
Daily 11:00 AM - 5:30 PM

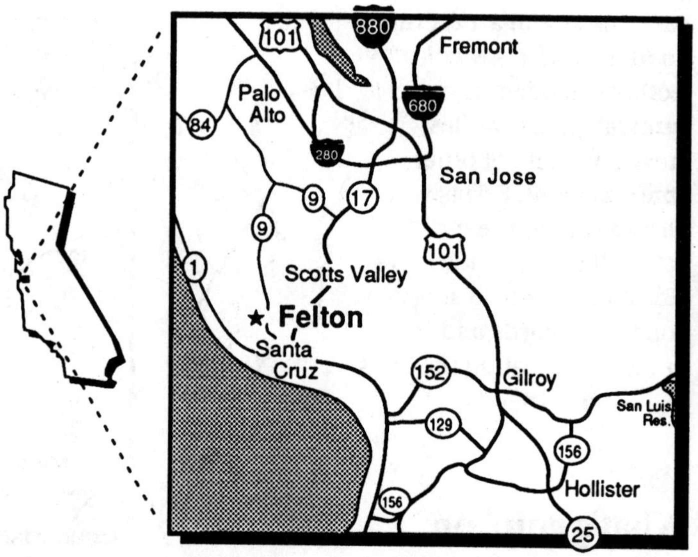


## What's goin' on...

Town population: **4,000**
Last year's attendance: **1,000**
Average outdoor temperature: **70°**
Festival location: **Hallcrest Vineyards**

*Up-to-date festival information is available from:*
*Felton Hallcrest Vineyards*
*(408) 335-4441*

- X Wine tasting/beer for sale
- X Food booths
- X Arts/crafts for sale
- X Live music
- Clowns
- Face painters
- Childrens games
- Animal exhibits/petting zoo
- Dogs allowed on leash
- Lost and found
- Bicycle racks
- First aid area available
- Self-brought picnics allowed
- Self-brought alcohol allowed
- Stroller/wheelchair rentals available

- Parade
- Parking fee
- X Entrance fee: $6; Under 21 free
- X Camping facilities: 5 miles
- X Boating facilities: Santa Cruz Harbor
- X RV facilities w/ hookups: 5 miles
- X Accomodations in town
  Fair View Manor B&B
- X Restaurants in town
  Mama Mia, Tampico, Whistle Inn

# *Classical-to-Jazz Under the Stars Concert*

SO YA WANNA TREAT MOM right on Mother's Day? How about the day before? Why not Lemoore's **Classical-to-Jazz Under the Stars Concert** on Saturday? There's nothing like a balmy evening and the perfect blend of music to soothe you. Bring your lawn chair, a picnic, and a bottle of wine if you'd like...

## Lemoore, California

Saturday prior to Mother's Day
4:00 PM - 11:00 PM

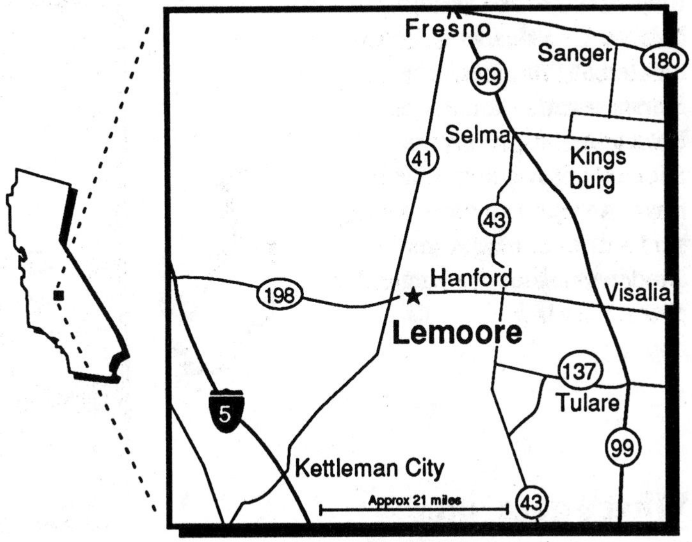


*Up-to-date festival information is available from:*
*Lemoore Chamber of Commerce*
*(209) 924-6401*

## What's goin' on...

Town population: **14,100**
Last year's attendance: **N/A**
Average outdoor temperature: **78°**
Festival location: **Downtown**

| | |
|---|---|
| | Wine tasting/beer for sale |
| X | Food booths |
| | Arts/crafts for sale |
| X | Live music |
| X | Clowns |
| | Face painters |
| | Childrens games |
| | Animal exhibits/petting zoo |
| X | Dogs allowed on leash |
| | Lost and found |
| | Bicycle racks |
| | First aid area available |
| X | Self-brought picnics allowed |
| X | Self-brought alcohol allowed |
| | Stroller/wheelchair rentals available |

| | |
|---|---|
| | Parade |
| | Parking fee |
| | Entrance fee |
| X | Camping facilities |
| X | Boating facilities |
| X | RV facilities w/ hookups |
| X | Accomodations in town<br>Vineyard Inn Motel |
| X | Restaurants in town<br>The Cotton Mill, The Granary, Vineyard Inn, Casa Ortega, Vejar's |

CENTRAL

# *Mother Lode Round-Up & Parade*

SONORA SWELLS WITH pride when the **Mother Lode Round-Up Rodeo & Parade** comes around! This intriguing town wants kids—young and old—to visit this wonderland located at the foot of the Sierra Nevada Mountains. Before the 2:00 PM rodeo on Sunday, enjoy a stroll through town, browse the antique shops or take a walk in the shadows of the towering pines. This is *truly* God's country!

## Sonora, California

Second weekend in May

Sat. 10:00 AM - 6:00 PM; Sun. 2:00 PM - 6:00 PM

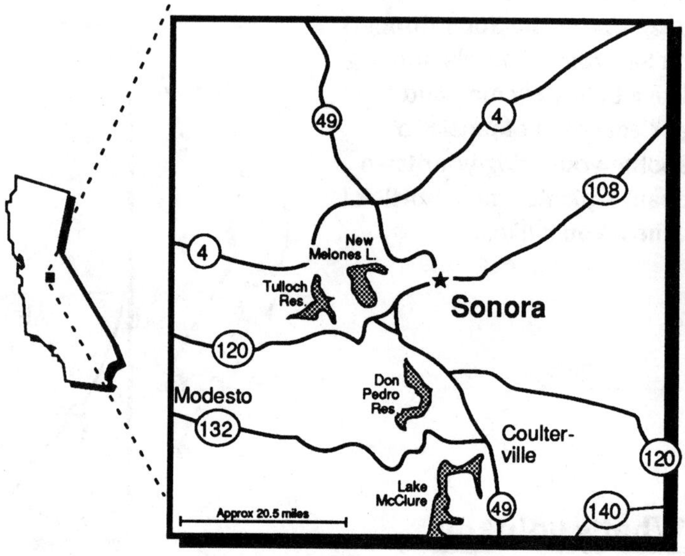


*Up-to-date festival information is available from:*
*Sonora Chamber of Commerce*
*(209) 532-4212*

## What's goin' on...

Town population: **3,247**
Last year's attendance: **10,000**
Average outdoor temperature: **68°**
Festival location: **Downtown**

- [ ] Wine tasting/beer for sale
- [ ] Food booths
- [ ] Arts/crafts for sale
- [ ] Live music
- [ ] Clowns
- [ ] Face painters
- [ ] Childrens games
- [ ] Animal exhibits/petting zoo
- [ ] Dogs allowed on leash
- [x] Lost and found
- [ ] Bicycle racks
- [x] First aid area available
- [x] Self-brought picnics allowed
- [ ] Self-brought alcohol allowed
- [ ] Stroller/wheelchair rentals available

- [x] Parade: Sat. 10:30 AM downtown
- [x] Parking fee: $5
- [x] Entrance fee: Adults $6; Kids $3
- [x] Camping facilities: 5 miles
- [x] Boating facilities: New Melones Res.
- [x] RV facilities w/ hookups: 3 miles
- [x] Accomodations in town
  Sonora Gold Lodge, The Palm Hotel, Oak Hill Ranch
- [x] Restaurants in town
  The Cove, Country Kitchen, Iron Door Saloon

# *Holy Ghost Festival*

YES, THERE REALLY IS A **Holy Ghost Festival** in Half Moon Bay! More popularly known as Charmarita (actually the name of a Portuguese folk dance), this event has been annually sponsored by the I.D.E.S. (The Society of the Divine Holy Spirit) since 1871. The all-day celebration greets thousands of visitors with free bread, meat, and wine on the spacious grounds of the I.D.E.S. Hall on Main Street in Half Moon Bay.

## Half Moon Bay, California

Second Sunday in May
10:00 AM - 5:00 PM

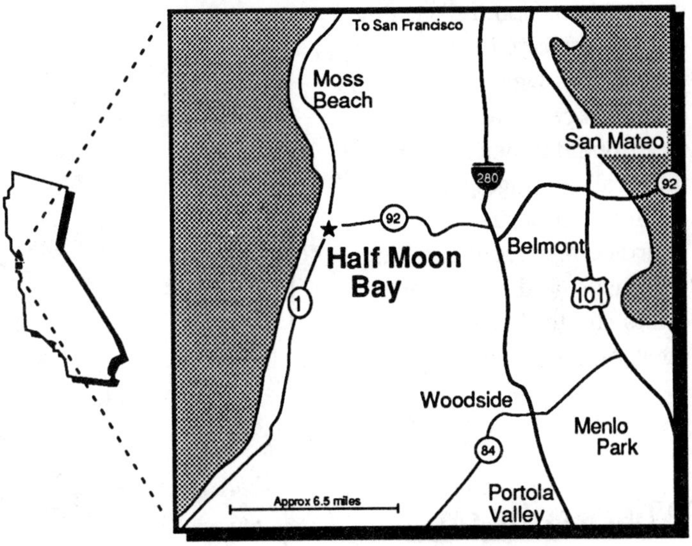


*Up-to-date festival information is available from:*
*Half Moon Bay Chamber of Commerce*
*(415) 726-5202*

## What's goin' on...

Town population: **7,282**
Last year's attendance: **N/A**
Average outdoor temperature: **70°**
Festival location: **I.D.E.S. Hall**

- X Wine tasting/beer for sale
- X Food booths
- Arts/crafts for sale
- X Live music
- Clowns
- Face painters
- Childrens games
- X Animal exhibits/petting zoo
- Dogs allowed on leash
- X Lost and found
- Bicycle racks
- X First aid area available
- X Self-brought picnics allowed
- Self-brought alcohol allowed
- Stroller/wheelchair rentals available

- X Parade: Sun. 10:00 AM on Main Street
- Parking fee
- Entrance fee
- X Camping facilities: 1 mile
- X Boating facilities: Half Moon Bay
- X RV facilities w/ hookups: 1 mile
- X Accomodations in town
  Half Moon Bay Lodge, Harbor View Inn, San Benito House
- X Restaurants in town
  The Miramar, Dan's Place, Moss Beach Distillery

# *La Fiesta*

**LA FIESTA** IN SAN LUIS Obispo is a 200-year-old traditional rite-of-spring celebration. The festivities begin with a bonfire burning of Zozobra, or Old Man Gloom, followed by five days of events celebrating the city's Spanish heritage. You'll find it all—a huge pancake breakfast, a barbecue, and beard contest. Add strolling mariachis, and an arts and crafts fair, and La Fiesta overflows with mucho gusto!

## San Luis Obispo, California

Third week in May (beginning Tuesday)
Hours vary

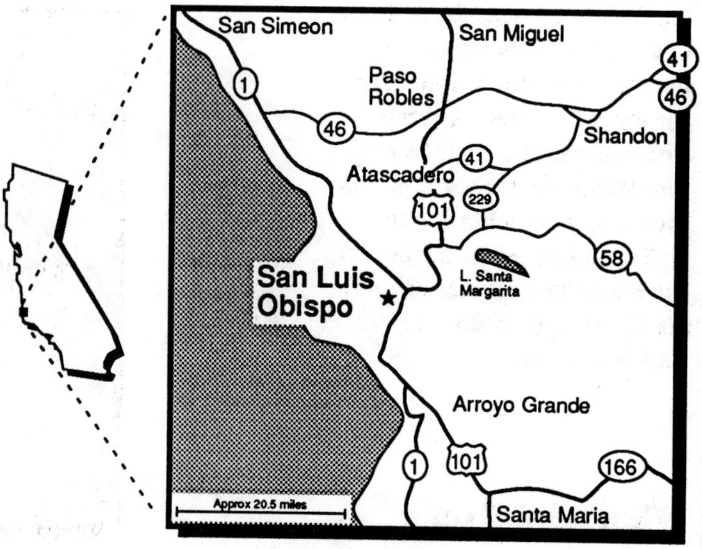


*Up-to-date festival information is available from:*
*San Luis Obispo Chamber of Commerce*
*(805) 543-1323*

## What's goin' on...

Town population: **41,000**
Last year's attendance: **40,000**
Average outdoor temperature: **75°**
Festival location: **Citywide**

- X Wine tasting/beer for sale
- X Food booths
- X Arts/crafts for sale
- X Live music
- X Clowns
- X Face painters
- X Childrens games
- X Animal exhibits/petting zoo
- X Dogs allowed on leash
- X Lost and found
- X Bicycle racks
- X First aid area available
- X Self-brought picnics allowed
- Self-brought alcohol allowed
- Stroller/wheelchair rentals available

- Parade
- Parking fee
- X Entrance fee: Varies $20 - 50
- X Camping facilities: 15 miles
- X Boating facilities: Lakes and ocean
- X RV facilities w/ hookups: 15 miles
- X Accomodations in town
  Madonna Inn, Peach Tree Inn, Garden St. B&B
- X Restaurants in town
  Apple Farm, Hudson's Grill, Chef Em's

# Salinas Valley Fair

BEFORE THE MERCURY reaches into the nineties, King City celebrates the **Salinas Valley Fair**! This is pretty much your standard fair, in standard fairgrounds, with standard fair rides, standard fair food, and standard fair entertainment! Got it? The area is famous for its produce...and you'll find really terrific prices at the local fruit and vegetable stands alongside the roads.

## King City, California

Third week in May
Daily 10:00 AM - 10:00 PM

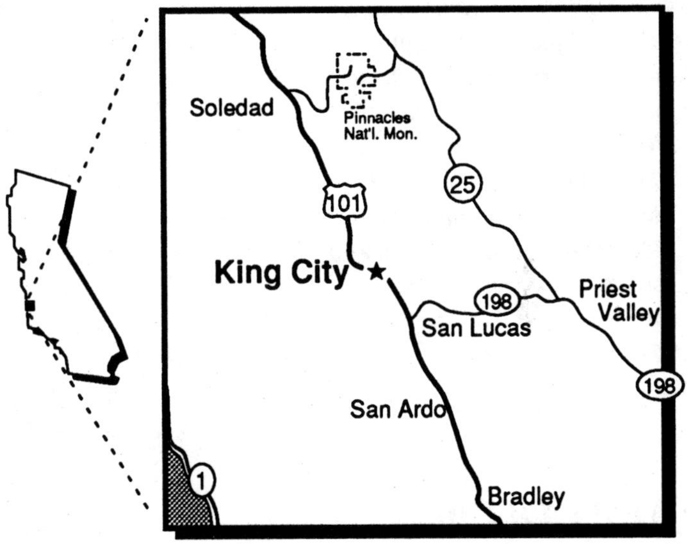


*Up-to-date festival information is available from:*
*King City Chamber of Commerce*
*(408) 385-3814*

## What's goin' on...

Town population: **7,800**
Last year's attendance: **50,000**
Average outdoor temperature: **80°**
Festival location: **Fairgrounds**

| | |
|---|---|
| X | Wine tasting/beer for sale |
| X | Food booths |
| X | Arts/crafts for sale |
| X | Live music |
| X | Clowns |
| X | Face painters |
| X | Childrens games |
| X | Animal exhibits/petting zoo |
| | Dogs allowed on leash |
| X | Lost and found |
| X | Bicycle racks |
| X | First aid area available |
| X | Self-brought picnics allowed |
| | Self-brought alcohol allowed |
| X | Stroller/wheelchair rentals available |

| | |
|---|---|
| | Parade |
| X | Parking fee: $2 |
| X | Entrance fee: Varies by day |
| X | Camping facilities: In town |
| X | Boating facilities: Lake and river |
| X | RV facilities w/ hookups: In town |
| X | Accomodations in town<br>Best Western, Keefer's, Silver Saddle, Sage Motel, Palm Motel, Crown DD Lodge |
| X | Restaurants in town<br>Guadalajara, El Zarape, Keefer's, City Cafe, China King, El Lugarcito |

CENTRAL

# Swedish Festival

KINGSBURG INVITES YOU TO their annual **Swedish Festival**. Swedish consular dignitaries, and guests from Kingsburg's sister city in Sweden are the honored guests. The quiet and clean town of Kingsburg features arts/crafts/souvenir shops, architecture in a Swedish (Tudor) motif, hanging flowerpots, flags, and dala horses on lampposts and boasts a city water tower in the form of a 60,000-gallon Swedish coffeepot!

## Kingsburg, California

Third weekend in May (beginning Thursday)
Hours vary

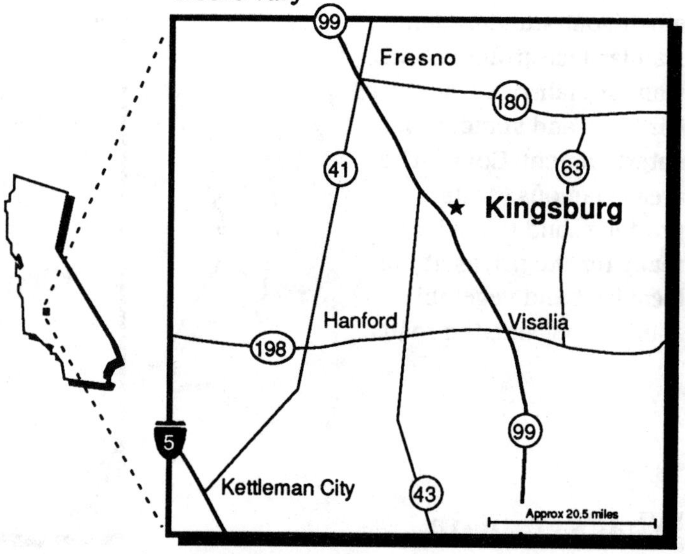


## What's goin' on...

Town population: **6,424**
Last year's attendance: **15,000**
Average outdoor temperature: **90°**
Festival location: **Memorial Park**

*Up-to-date festival information is available from:*
*Kingsburg Chamber of Commerce*
*(209) 897-2925*

| | |
|---|---|
| | Wine tasting/beer for sale |
| X | Food booths |
| X | Arts/crafts for sale |
| X | Live music |
| X | Clowns |
| X | Face painters |
| X | Childrens games |
| | Animal exhibits/petting zoo |
| X | Dogs allowed on leash |
| X | Lost and found |
| | Bicycle racks |
| X | First aid area available |
| X | Self-brought picnics allowed |
| | Self-brought alcohol allowed |
| | Stroller/wheelchair rentals available |

| | |
|---|---|
| X | Parade: Sat. 10:00 AM on Draper St. |
| | Parking fee |
| | Entrance fee |
| X | Camping facilities: In town |
| X | Boating facilities: Kings River |
| X | RV facilities w/ hookups: In town |
| | Accomodations in town |
| X | Restaurants in town<br>Riverland, Swedish Inn, The Valley Inn, Kady's Country Kitchen, The Dala House |

# *PowWow Days Country Faire*

LOTS OF CHIEFS, SQUAWS and little Indians will be out for the **PowWow Days Country Faire**! Strawberry shortcake, sausage sandwiches, hot dogs, tacos, ice cream, pasta, and nachos are just just a hint at what will be served up for lunch and dinner. The Saturday night dance features a little bit of country...and a little bit of rock 'n roll!

## Orangevale, California

Third weekend in May
Hours vary

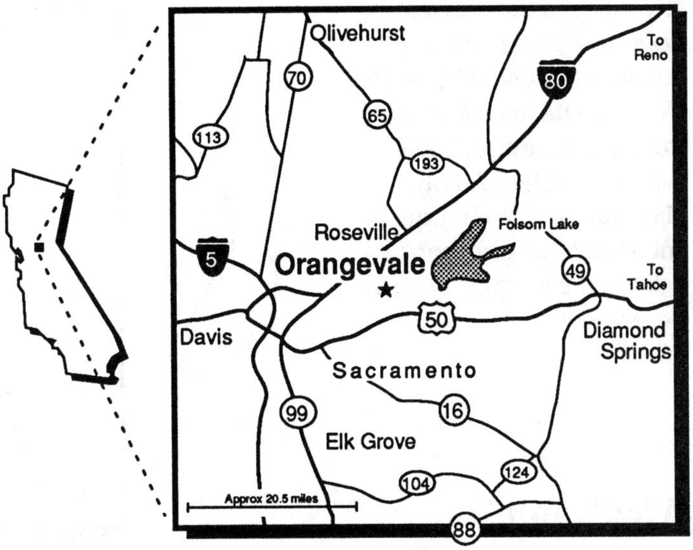


## What's goin' on...

Town population: **30,000**
Last year's attendance: **10,000**
Average outdoor temperature: **85°**
Festival location: **Community Park**

*Up-to-date festival information is available from:*
*Orangevale Chamber of Commerce*
*(916) 988-0175*

- X Wine tasting/beer for sale
- X Food booths
- X Arts/crafts for sale
- X Live music
- X Clowns
- X Face painters
- X Childrens games
- X Animal exhibits/petting zoo
- X Dogs allowed on leash
- X Lost and found
- Bicycle racks
- X First aid area available
- X Self-brought picnics allowed
- Self-brought alcohol allowed
- Stroller/wheelchair rentals available

- X Parade: Sat. 9:00 AM on Greenback Ln.
- X Parking fee: $1
- Entrance fee
- X Camping facilities: 1 mile
- X Boating facilities: Lake Folsom
- X RV facilities w/ hookups: 1 mile
- X Accomodations in town
  Economy Inn
- X Restaurants in town
  Campfire Cafe, Three Amigos, Orangetree Cafe

# *Prune Festival*

THE **PRUNE FESTIVAL** comes complete with live jazz bands all day long. With food booths featuring such items as prune mustard, prune cake, and prune jam, the quaint little town of Campbell closes off its main street for this two-day event. Local wineries such as J. Lohr, Mirrasou, Weibel, Troquato, and Glen Ellen are spotlighted. It's a fun and *moving* experience!

## Campbell, California

Third weekend in May
Daily 10:00 AM - 6:00 PM

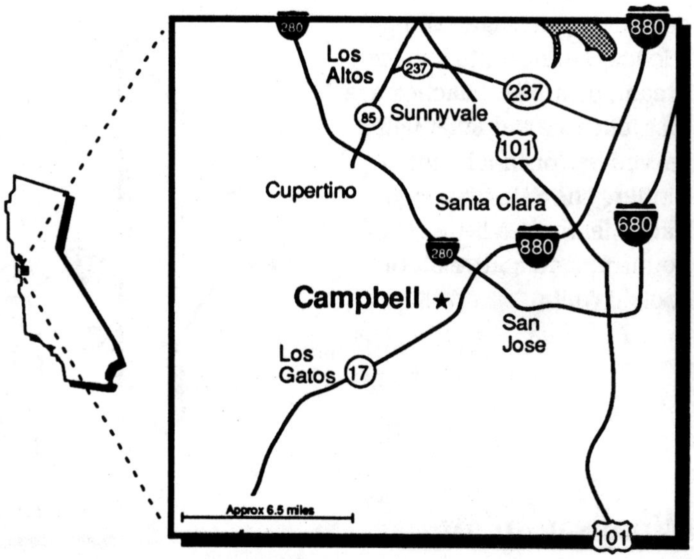


*Up-to-date festival information is available from:*
*Campbell Chamber of Commerce*
*(408) 378-6252*

## What's goin' on...

Town population: **27067**
Last year's attendance: **38,000**
Average outdoor temperature: **78°**
Festival location: **Downtown**

- X Wine tasting/beer for sale
- X Food booths
- X Arts/crafts for sale
- X Live music
- X Clowns
- X Face painters
- X Childrens games
- X Animal exhibits/petting zoo
- X Dogs allowed on leash
- X Lost and found
- Bicycle racks
- X First aid area available
- Self-brought picnics allowed
- Self-brought alcohol allowed
- Stroller/wheelchair rentals available

- Parade
- Parking fee
- Entrance fee
- X Camping facilities: 20 miles
- Boating facilities
- X RV facilities w/ hookups: 20 miles
- X Accomodations in town
  Campbell Inn
- X Restaurants in town
  Jersey's, Martha's Vineyards, Spoons, Campbell House

# *Americafest*

**AMERICAFEST** IS IN ITS FIRST year! Along with barbecues, a new- and classic-car show, dancing, country music, childrens games, and craft booths, there are also a few things downtown to explore. Such as the 80 antique dealers in a six-block radius, the Clovis-Big Dry Creek Historical Museum, and the cobblestone streets. Wild Water Adventure water slides are seven miles east of Clovis, too.

## Clovis, California

Third Saturday in May
9:00 AM - 5:00 PM

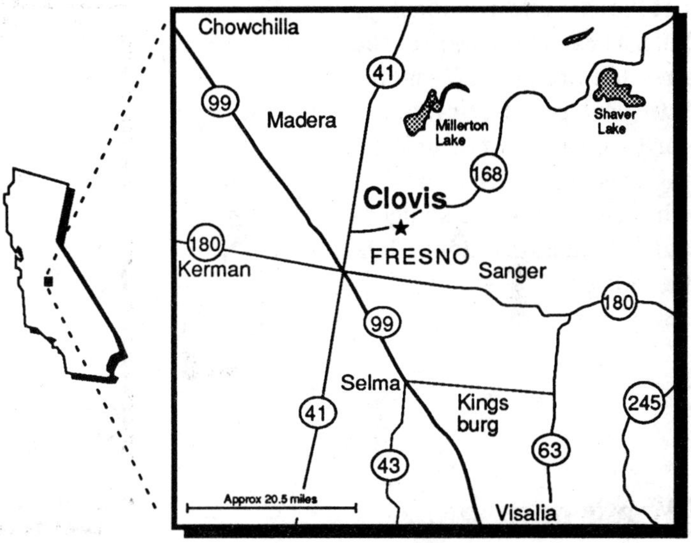


*Up-to-date festival information is available from:*
*Clovis Chamber of Commerce*
*(209) 299-7273*

## What's goin' on...

Town population: **33,000**
Last year's attendance: **20,000**
Average outdoor temperature: **85°**
Festival location: **Old Town Clovis**

| | |
|---|---|
| X | Wine tasting/beer for sale |
| X | Food booths |
| X | Arts/crafts for sale |
| X | Live music |
| X | Clowns |
| X | Face painters |
| X | Childrens games |
| | Animal exhibits/petting zoo |
| X | Dogs allowed on leash |
| X | Lost and found |
| | Bicycle racks |
| X | First aid area available |
| X | Self-brought picnics allowed |
| | Self-brought alcohol allowed |
| | Stroller/wheelchair rentals available |

| | |
|---|---|
| | Parade |
| | Parking fee |
| | Entrance fee |
| X | Camping facilities |
| X | Boating facilities: Millerton Lake |
| X | RV facilities w/ hookups |
| X | Accomodations in town<br>Rodeo Lodge |
| X | Restaurants in town<br>Cottage Cafe, La Posada, 500 Club, Wine & Rack Shack, Wong's Jade Garden, Sal's |

CENTRAL

# *Mayfest*

THERE'S SOMETHING FOR everyone at the Los Altos **Mayfest**! You can take a seat and watch the 43rd annual Pet Parade, or stroll through Lincoln Park for a look at the Arts and Crafts Show and do a little wine tasting, or rise early on Sunday morning for the pancake breakfast and see what old knickknacks might amuse you at the Lions Club Flea Market.

## Los Altos, California

Third weekend in May
Daily 10:00 AM - 5:00 PM

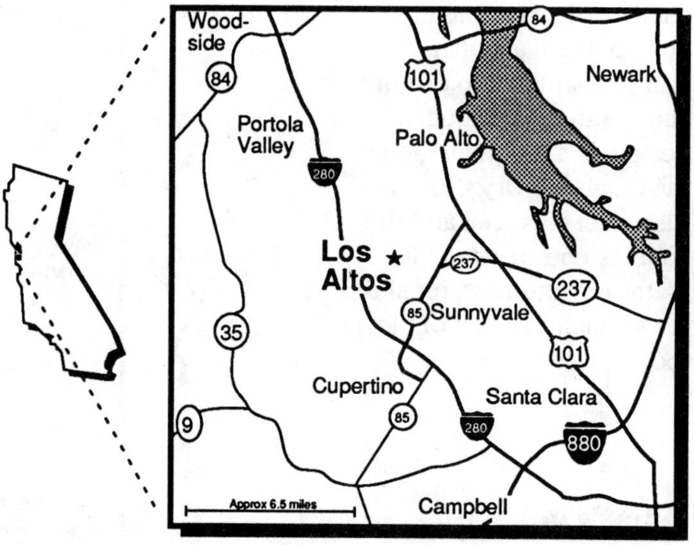


*Up-to-date festival information is available from:*
*Los Altos Chamber of Commerce*
*(415) 948-1455*

## What's goin' on...

Town population: **27,583**
Last year's attendance: **10,000**
Average outdoor temperature: **70°**
Festival location: **Lincoln Park**

| | |
|---|---|
| X | Wine tasting/beer for sale |
| X | Food booths |
| X | Arts/crafts for sale |
| X | Live music |
| | Clowns |
| | Face painters |
| | Childrens games |
| | Animal exhibits/petting zoo |
| X | Dogs allowed on leash |
| | Lost and found |
| | Bicycle racks |
| | First aid area available |
| | Self-brought picnics allowed |
| | Self-brought alcohol allowed |
| | Stroller/wheelchair rentals available |

| | |
|---|---|
| X | Parade: Sat. 10:00 AM downtown |
| | Parking fee |
| | Entrance fee |
| | Camping facilities |
| | Boating facilities |
| | RV facilities w/ hookups |
| | Accomodations in town |
| X | Restaurants in town<br>Armadillo Willy's, Los Altos Bar & Grill, Arno's |

# *Paso Robles Wine Festival*

BLUEGRASS, COUNTRY, JAZZ, and popular music waft through the air as you mosey from winery (booth) to winery (booth), sampling the 22 local wineries' finest at the **Paso Robles Wine Festival!** All this happens at City Park downtown, where the local restaurants and service groups will be on hand offering delicious food to complement the fermented grape juice!

## Paso Robles, California

Third weekend in May
Daily noon - 5:00 PM

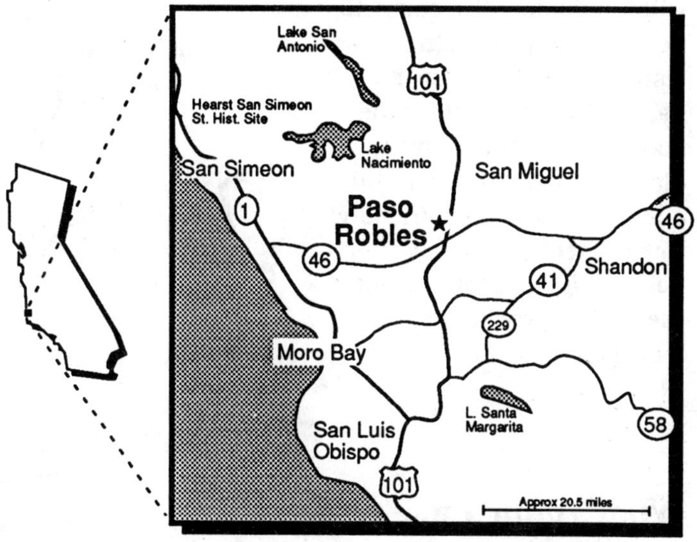


## What's goin' on...

Town population: **17,000**
Last year's attendance: **13,000**
Average outdoor temperature: **80°**
Festival location: **City Park**

*Up-to-date festival information is available from:*
*Paso Robles Chamber of Commerce*
*(805) 238-0506*

| | |
|---|---|
| X | Wine tasting/beer for sale |
| X | Food booths |
| | Arts/crafts for sale |
| X | Live music |
| | Clowns |
| X | Face painters |
| | Childrens games |
| | Animal exhibits/petting zoo |
| | Dogs allowed on leash |
| X | Lost and found |
| X | Bicycle racks |
| X | First aid area available |
| | Self-brought picnics allowed |
| | Self-brought alcohol allowed |
| | Stroller/wheelchair rentals available |

| | |
|---|---|
| | Parade |
| | Parking fee |
| X | Entrance fee: $10 |
| X | Camping facilities: 20 miles |
| X | Boating facilities: Lake San Antonio |
| X | RV facilities w/ hookups: In town |
| X | Accomodations in town: Almond View Inn, The Ranch, Darken Downs Equestre-Inn, Marianna Motel, TraveLodge |
| X | Restaurants in town: Maya Mexican Foods, O'Shea's Diner, Busi's Chianti Room, Annie's Dinner House & Saloon |

CENTRAL

# *Potato & Cotton Festival*

THE SHAFTER **POTATO & Cotton Festival** is a big event in this "agricultural paradise!" Lasting three days, beginning with the Junior Miss competition on Friday night, the festival offers a fun run, a Tasty Tators contest for the good cooks in town, and an old-fashioned box social and auction. This is a *real* friendly town, where people enjoy being with one another, and the festival promises to be lotsa fun!

## Shafter, California

Third weekend in May
Daily 10:00 AM - 7:00 PM

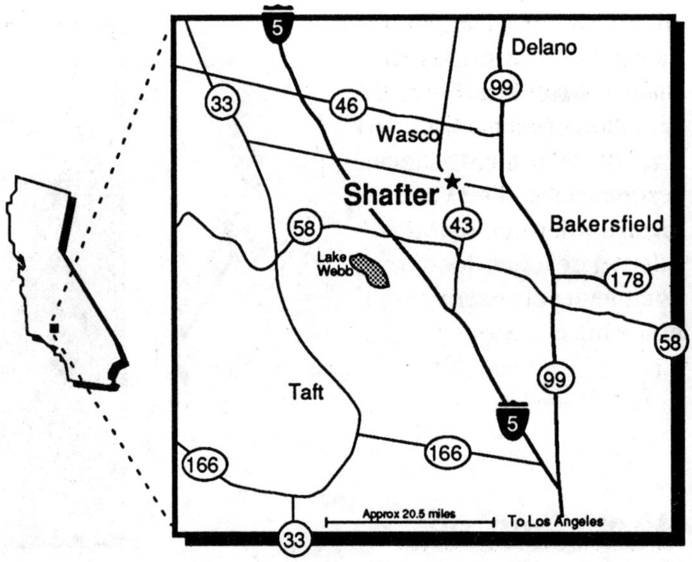


*Up-to-date festival information is available from:*
*Shafter Chamber of Commerce*
*(805) 746-2600*

## What's goin' on...

Town population: **8,000**
Last year's attendance: **3,500**
Average outdoor temperature: **75°**
Festival location: **Park**

| | |
|---|---|
| ✗ | Wine tasting/beer for sale |
| ✗ | Food booths |
| ✗ | Arts/crafts for sale |
| ✗ | Live music |
| | Clowns |
| | Face painters |
| | Childrens games |
| | Animal exhibits/petting zoo |
| | Dogs allowed on leash |
| | Lost and found |
| | Bicycle racks |
| | First aid area available |
| | Self-brought picnics allowed |
| | Self-brought alcohol allowed |
| | Stroller/wheelchair rentals available |

| | |
|---|---|
| ✗ | Parade: (date & time not avbl.) |
| | Parking fee |
| | Entrance fee |
| ✗ | Camping facilities: 10 miles |
| ✗ | Boating facilities: Lake Buena Vista |
| ✗ | RV facilities w/ hookups: 5 miles |
| ✗ | Accomodations in town |
| ✗ | Restaurants in town<br>Yee's Steak House |

# *Mill Valley Mountain Plays*

MT. TAM IS A GREAT PLACE to spend a Sunday afternoon, and an even greater place to spend the day if you're attending one of the Mountain Play Associations **Mill Valley Mountain Plays**. This tradition of reenacting Broadway musicals has been a ritual since 1913! Pack a picnic or try one of the sandwiches, hot dogs or pizzas for sale under these towering redwoods by the Pacific!

## Mill Valley, California

Last two Sundays in May; all Sundays in June
Beginning at 1:00 PM

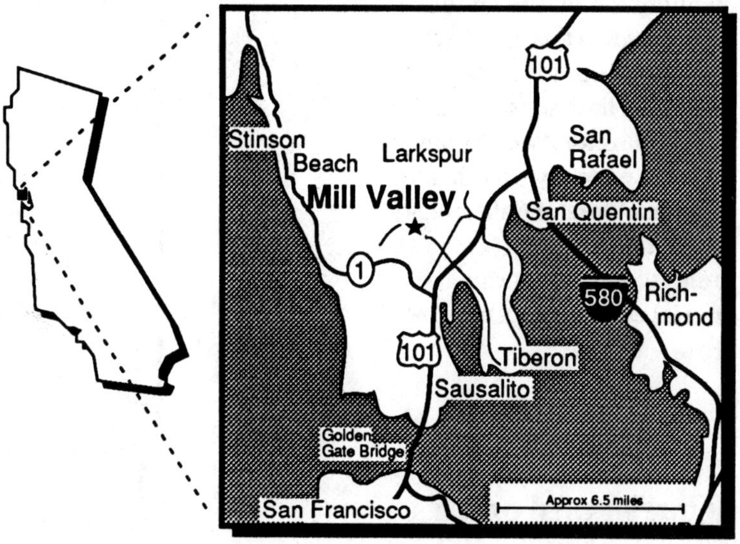


*Up-to-date festival information is available from:*
*Mill Valley Chamber of Commerce*
*(415) 472-7470*

## What's goin' on...

Town population: **47,000**
Last year's attendance: **22,000**
Average outdoor temperature: **75°**
Festival location: **Mt. Tamalpais State Park**

| | |
|---|---|
| | Wine tasting/beer for sale |
| X | Food booths |
| | Arts/crafts for sale |
| X | Live music |
| | Clowns |
| | Face painters |
| | Childrens games |
| | Animal exhibits/petting zoo |
| | Dogs allowed on leash |
| X | Lost and found |
| | Bicycle racks |
| X | First aid area available |
| X | Self-brought picnics allowed |
| X | Self-brought alcohol allowed |
| | Stroller/wheelchair rentals available |

| | |
|---|---|
| | Parade |
| | Parking fee |
| X | Entrance fee: Srs/Kids$10; Adults $15 |
| X | Camping facilities: 1 mile |
| | Boating facilities |
| | RV facilities w/ hookups |
| X | Accomodations in town<br>Mt. Home Inn, many B&Bs |
| X | Restaurants in town |

CENTRAL

# *Outdoor Antiques Faire*

IF YOU'RE PLAYING THE alphabet game...this is *ONE* word you're always looking for—antiQue! And if you're an antique buff, the **Outdoor Antiques Faire** is another thing you should be looking for! You'll find antiques and collectibles for every room in the house...and yard! This historical area of California—just north of San Francisco—embraces a special era of California

## San Anselmo, California

Third Sunday in May
9:00 AM - 4:00 PM

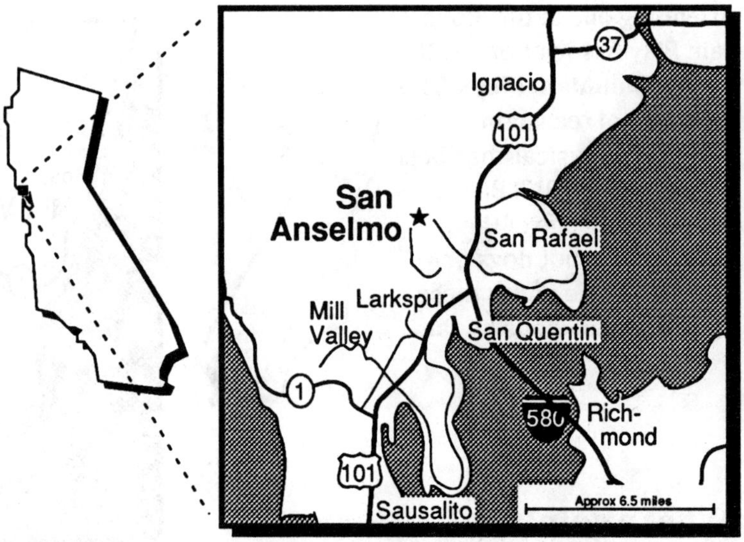


## What's goin' on...

Town population: **12,500**
Last year's attendance: **5,000**
Average outdoor temperature: **80°**
Festival location: **Creek Park**

*Up-to-date festival information is available from:*
*San Anselmo Chamber of Commerce*
*(415) 454-2510*

| | |
|---|---|
| | Wine tasting/beer for sale |
| ✗ | Food booths |
| | Arts/crafts for sale |
| | Live music |
| | Clowns |
| | Face painters |
| | Childrens games |
| | Animal exhibits/petting zoo |
| ✗ | Dogs allowed on leash |
| | Lost and found |
| ✗ | Bicycle racks |
| | First aid area available |
| ✗ | Self-brought picnics allowed |
| ✗ | Self-brought alcohol allowed |
| | Stroller/wheelchair rentals available |

| | |
|---|---|
| | Parade |
| | Parking fee |
| | Entrance fee |
| | Camping facilities |
| | Boating facilities |
| | RV facilities w/ hookups |
| ✗ | Accomodations in town |
| ✗ | Restaurants in town<br>Comforts, Rossetti's, Ted's, Hilda's, Ristorante al Fresco, The Bistro |

# *Festival of Wine*

CALIFORNIA'S IDEAL CLIMATE makes for perfect grapes! Perfect grapes make perfect wine! Perfect wine makes a for a perfect **Festival of Wine**! The enchanting town of Tiburon, created way back in 1884, has been hosting this revelry of wine enjoyment since 1984. Over forty wineries send their very best for your tasting pleasure, and local restaurants turn out, too, to offer goodies to munch on!

## Tiburon, California

Third Sunday in May
1:00 PM - 5:00 PM

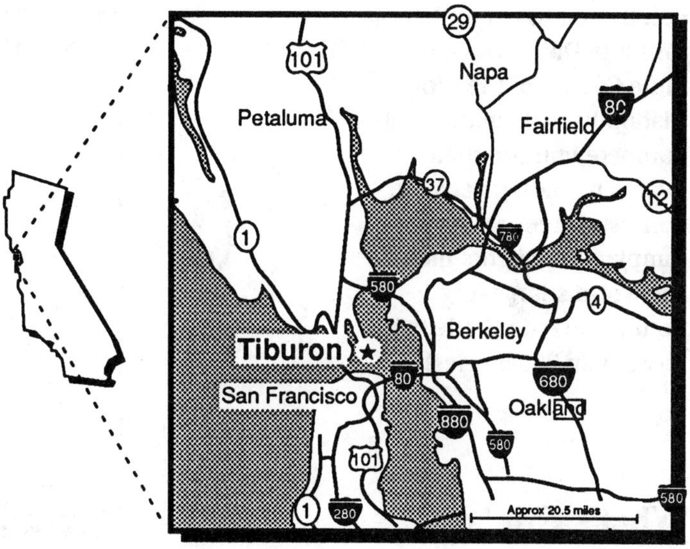


*Up-to-date festival information is available from:*
*Tiburon Chamber of Commerce*
*(415) 435-5633*

## What's goin' on...

Town population: **10,000**
Last year's attendance: **900**
Average outdoor temperature: **65°**
Festival location: **Pt. Tiburon Plaza**

- X Wine tasting/beer for sale
- X Food booths
- X Arts/crafts for sale
- X Live music
- Clowns
- Face painters
- Childrens games
- Animal exhibits/petting zoo
- X Dogs allowed on leash
- X Lost and found
- X Bicycle racks
- X First aid area available
- Self-brought picnics allowed
- Self-brought alcohol allowed
- Stroller/wheelchair rentals available

- Parade
- X Parking fee: $3
- X Entrance fee: Adults $13
- X Camping facilities: 20 miles
- X Boating facilities: San Francisco Bay
- X RV facilities w/ hookups: 20 miles
- X Accomodations in town
  Tiburon Lodge
- X Restaurants in town
  Servino Ristorante, Rooney's Cafe & Grill, Hearts & Flowers Cafe, New Morning Cafe

CENTRAL

# *Mule Days*

THE QUESTION IS: ARE *YOU* ready for the most raucous and outrageously fun mule party in the world? Well, if so, you'll need to get to Bishop for **Mule Days**! Known as the Mule Capital of the World, Bishop has 600 mules that compete in more than 94 events including packing contests, steer roping, and jumping. Highlights include the world's largest nonmotorized parade, with more than 250 entries!

## Bishop, California

Memorial Day weekend
Daily 8:00 AM - 9:00 PM

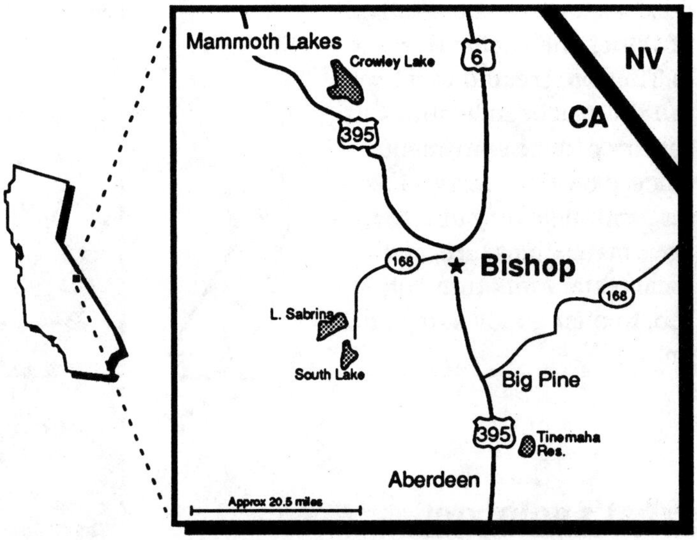


*Up-to-date festival information is available from:*
*Bishop Chamber of Commerce*
*(619) 873-8405*

## What's goin' on...

Town population: **3,800**
Last year's attendance: **40,000**
Average outdoor temperature: **75°**
Festival location: **Fairgrounds**

- ✗ Wine tasting/beer for sale
- ✗ Food booths
- ✗ Arts/crafts for sale
- ✗ Live music
- ✗ Clowns
- ✗ Face painters
- ✗ Childrens games
- ✗ Animal exhibits/petting zoo
- ✗ Dogs allowed on leash
- ✗ Lost and found
- ✗ Bicycle racks
- ✗ First aid area available
- ✗ Self-brought picnics allowed
- Self-brought alcohol allowed
- Stroller/wheelchair rentals available

- ✗ Parade: Sat. 10:00 AM downtown
- Parking fee
- ✗ Entrance fee: (prices not avbl.)
- ✗ Camping facilities: Fairgrounds
- ✗ Boating facilities
- ✗ RV facilities w/ hookups: 2 miles
- ✗ Accomodations in town
  Matlick House, Chalfant House
- ✗ Restaurants in town
  Whiskey Creek, Firehouse Grill, BBQ Bills, Jack's Waffle Shop, Bishop Grill

# *Horned Toad Derby*

DRIVE SOUTH IN 198 TO Coalinga for its annual **Horned Toad Race**—a tradition in town since 1936! When you reach town for the festival, you'll find horned-toad derby races that even *you* can participate in! In addition, there are adult tricycle races, a carnival, a golf tournament, water fights, and entertaining stage shows! The whole town turns out for this one!

## Coalinga, California

Memorial Day weekend (beginning Thursday)
Hours vary

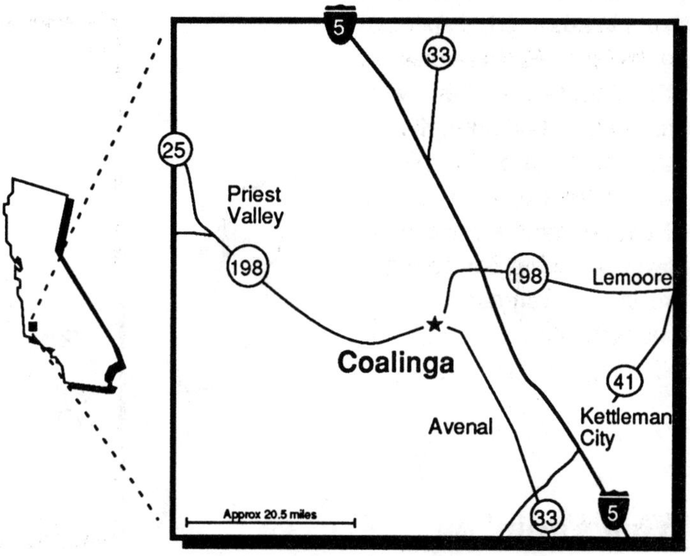


*Up-to-date festival information is available from:*
*Coalinga Chamber of Commerce*
*(209) 935-2948*

## What's goin' on...

Town population: **8,450**
Last year's attendance: **9,000**
Average outdoor temperature: **90°**
Festival location: **Downtown**

- X Wine tasting/beer for sale
- X Food booths
- X Arts/crafts for sale
- X Live music
- X Clowns
- X Face painters
- X Childrens games
- X Animal exhibits/petting zoo
- X Dogs allowed on leash
- X Lost and found
- Bicycle racks
- X First aid area available
- Self-brought picnics allowed
- Self-brought alcohol allowed
- Stroller/wheelchair rentals available

- X Parade: Sat 10:30 AM downtown
- Parking fee
- Entrance fee
- X Camping facilities: 15 miles
- Boating facilities
- X RV facilities w/ hookups: In town
- X Accomodations in town
  Harris Ranch Inn, Big Country Inn, Cambridge Inn
- X Restaurants in town
  Harris Ranch, Cambridge Inn, Red Robin

# *Boulder Creek Art & Wine Festival*

AFTER YOU'VE HAD YOUR fill of rides at the Santa Cruz Boardwalk, venture inland for the **Boulder Creek Art & Wine Festival**! This special event features three days filled with Golden State wine, splendid food, and joyful merriment in one of California's prettiest towns! This clean community boasts towering redwoods as big around as your car! Definitely a delight!

## Boulder Creek, California

Memorial Day weekend
Daily 11:00 AM - 4:00 PM

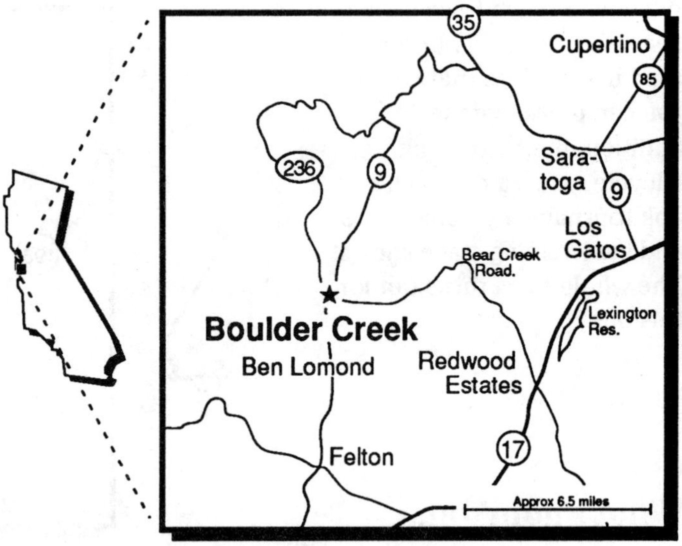


*Up-to-date festival information is available from:*
*Boulder Creek Chamber of Commerce*
*(408) 425-1234*

## What's goin' on...

Town population: **6,000**
Last year's attendance: **2,500**
Average outdoor temperature: **55°**
Festival location: **Downtown**

| | |
|---|---|
| ✗ | Wine tasting/beer for sale |
| ✗ | Food booths |
| ✗ | Arts/crafts for sale |
| ✗ | Live music |
| | Clowns |
| ✗ | Face painters |
| ✗ | Childrens games |
| ✗ | Animal exhibits/petting zoo |
| ✗ | Dogs allowed on leash |
| ✗ | Lost and found |
| ✗ | Bicycle racks |
| ✗ | First aid area available |
| | Self-brought picnics allowed |
| | Self-brought alcohol allowed |
| | Stroller/wheelchair rentals available |

| | |
|---|---|
| | Parade |
| | Parking fee |
| | Entrance fee |
| ✗ | Camping facilities: 4 miles |
| ✗ | Boating facilities: Santa Cruz Harbor |
| ✗ | RV facilities w/ hookups: 4 miles |
| ✗ | Accomodations in town<br>Boulder Creek Lodge |
| ✗ | Restaurants in town<br>Boulder Creek Lodge, Scopazzi Inn, |

# *Mountain Peddler's Antique & Collector's Fair*

NESTLED AT THE BOTTOM tip of the Yosemite National Forest lies the lively little town of Oakhurst—host to the **Mountain Peddler's Antique & Collector's Fair**! Heck, the town folks like this little get together so much, that it's held twice yearly! You'll find knick-knacks you've never seen or heard of before...but there's definitely something for everyone! And as they say, "one man's junk, is another man's treasure!"

## Oakhurst, California

Memorial Day weekend
Daily 8:00 AM - 5:00 PM

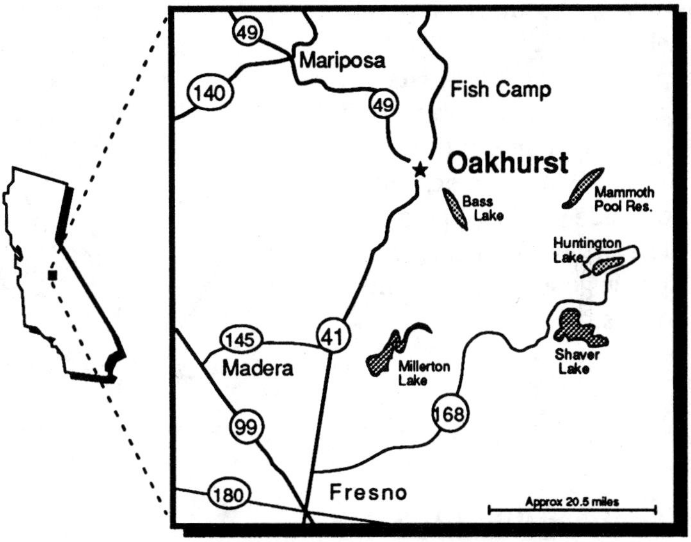


## What's goin' on...

Town population: **12,000**
Last year's attendance: **20,000**
Average outdoor temperature: **80°**
Festival location: **Downtown**

*Up-to-date festival information is available from:*
*Oakhurst Chamber of Commerce*
*(209) 683-7766*

- X Wine tasting/beer for sale
- X Food booths
- X Arts/crafts for sale
- X Live music
- Clowns
- Face painters
- Childrens games
- Animal exhibits/petting zoo
- Dogs allowed on leash
- Lost and found
- Bicycle racks
- First aid area available
- Self-brought picnics allowed
- Self-brought alcohol allowed
- Stroller/wheelchair rentals available

- Parade
- X Parking fee: $2 or free
- Entrance fee
- X Camping facilities: 5 miles
- X Boating facilities: Bass Lake
- X RV facilities w/ hookups: In town
- X Accomodations in town
  Shilo Inn, Best Western
- X Restaurants in town
  The Old Barn, Erna's Elderberry House, Golden Bit

CENTRAL

# *Heritage Day Festival*

YOUNG AND OLD ALIKE WILL enjoy themselves at Half Moon Bay's **Heritage Day Festival.** Many different ethnic groups have prepared delicious goodies to fill you up while coastside artists exhibit their handicrafts. Half Moon Bay, home of the Obester Winery, is rich with coastside produce stands of local farmers who cultivate fresh vegetables, fruits, and flowers.

## Half Moon Bay, California

Fourth Saturday in May
Noon - 6:00 PM

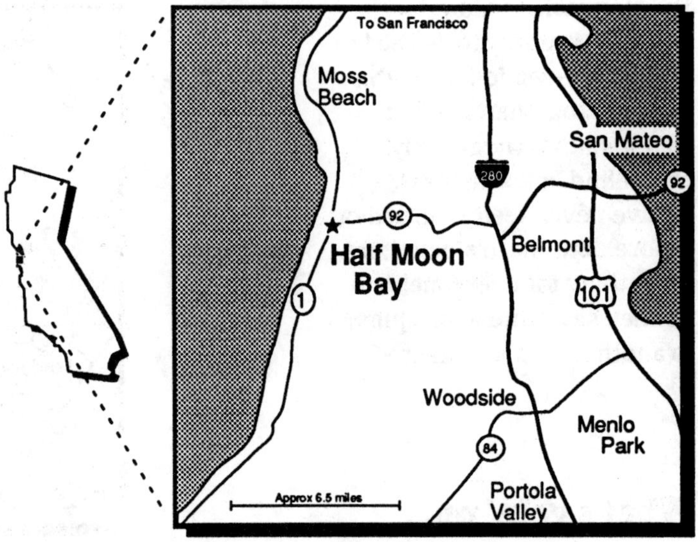


*Up-to-date festival information is available from:*
*Half Moon Bay Chamber of Commerce*
*(415) 726-5202*

## What's goin' on...

Town population: **7,282**
Last year's attendance: **N/A**
Average outdoor temperature: **70°**
Festival location: **Downtown**

| | |
|---|---|
| X | Wine tasting/beer for sale |
| X | Food booths |
| X | Arts/crafts for sale |
| X | Live music |
| | Clowns |
| X | Face painters |
| X | Childrens games |
| | Animal exhibits/petting zoo |
| | Dogs allowed on leash |
| X | Lost and found |
| X | Bicycle racks |
| X | First aid area available |
| | Self-brought picnics allowed |
| | Self-brought alcohol allowed |
| | Stroller/wheelchair rentals available |

| | |
|---|---|
| | Parade |
| | Parking fee |
| | Entrance fee |
| X | Camping facilities: 1 mile |
| X | Boating facilities: Half Moon Bay |
| X | RV facilities w/ hookups: 1 mile |
| X | Accomodations in town: Half Moon Bay Lodge, Harbor View Inn, San Benito House |
| X | Restaurants in town: Dan's Place, Abalone Shop, The Miramar, Moss Beach Distillery |

# *Mushroom Mardi Gras*

FUNGI? SCHROOMS? NO matter what you call 'em...you'll find zillions at the Morgan Hill **Mushroom Mardi Gras**! Needless to say, the dishes served are simply incredible—more than 40 kinds of mushroom delicacies, as well as fresh calamari and scampi. Wine tasting will be compliments of Guglielmo, San Martin, Pedrizetti, and Kirigin wineries. The music will run the gamut—from jazz to R&B.

## Morgan Hill, California

Sunday & Monday of Memorial Day weekend
10:00 AM - 5:00 PM

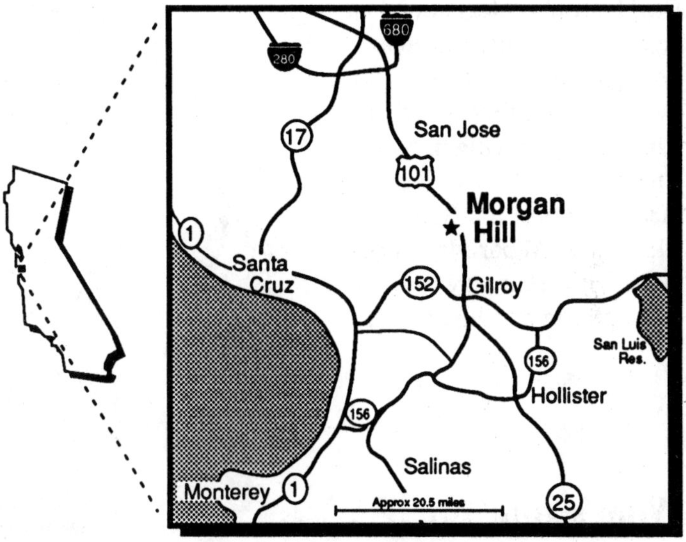


*Up-to-date festival information is available from:*
*Morgan Hill Chamber of Commerce*
*(408) 779-9444*

## What's goin' on...

Town population: **22,500**
Last year's attendance: **35,000**
Average outdoor temperature: **73°**
Festival location: **Park**

- X Wine tasting/beer for sale
- X Food booths
- X Arts/crafts for sale
- X Live music
- X Clowns
- X Face painters
- X Childrens games
- X Animal exhibits/petting zoo
- X Dogs allowed on leash
- X Lost and found
- Bicycle racks
- X First aid area available
- X Self-brought picnics allowed
- Self-brought alcohol allowed
- Stroller/wheelchair rentals available

- Parade
- Parking fee
- Entrance fee
- X Camping facilities: 5 miles
- X Boating facilities: Coyote Reservoir
- X RV facilities w/ hookups: 5 miles
- X Accomodations in town
  Best Western Country Inn, Country Rose B&B
- X Restaurants in town
  Flying Lady, Golden Oak, Ida's

# *Felton Remembers*

IF YOU LOOKED CLOSELY AT the date, you'd realize just exactly what **Felton Remembers** on this special Memorial Day! Felton's celebration is a wonderful tribute to those young men and women who have devoted their lives to America by serving in one of the armed services—particularly in light of the Gulf War! The 10:00 AM parade shoots right down Highway 9—through the middle of town.

## Felton, California

Memorial Day
9:30 - 4:30

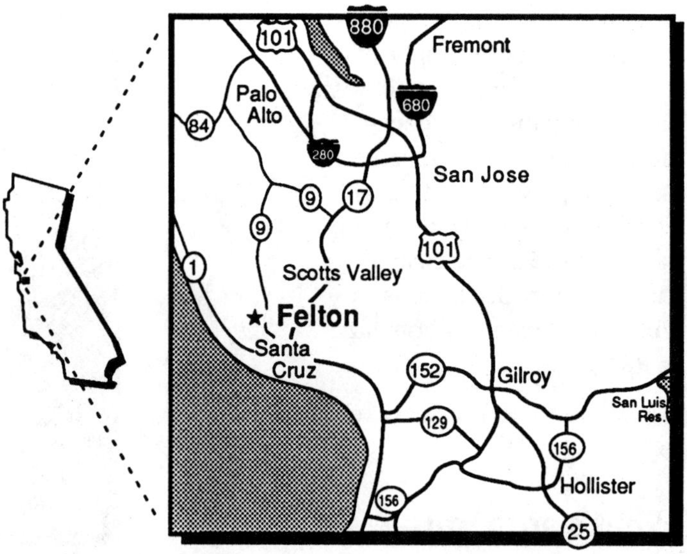


*Up-to-date festival information is available from:*
*Felton Chamber of Commerce*
*(408) 335-2764*

## What's goin' on...

Town population: **3,500**
Last year's attendance: **2,000**
Average outdoor temperature: **75°**
Festival location: **Downtown**

| | |
|---|---|
| X | Wine tasting/beer for sale |
| X | Food booths |
| X | Arts/crafts for sale |
| X | Live music |
| X | Clowns |
| X | Face painters |
| X | Childrens games |
| | Animal exhibits/petting zoo |
| X | Dogs allowed on leash |
| | Lost and found |
| | Bicycle racks |
| | First aid area available |
| X | Self-brought picnics allowed |
| | Self-brought alcohol allowed |
| | Stroller/wheelchair rentals available |

| | |
|---|---|
| X | Parade: Mon. 10:00 AM downtown |
| | Parking fee |
| | Entrance fee |
| X | Camping facilities. 1 mile |
| X | Boating facilities: Santa Cruz Harbor |
| X | RV facilities w/ hookups: 1 mile |
| X | Accomodations in town |
| X | Restaurants in town |

# Art in the Vineyard

WE HAPPEN TO LOVE BOTH wines and art...hence, the **Art in the Vineyard** festival at the Wente Brothers Winery will top our festival hopping itinerary! Over 35 local artists have put the finishing touches on their favorite pieces, especially chosen for this special event! Local restaurants have been invited as well to offer you a sampling of their finest cuisine, too! Commemorative wine glasses are for sale.

## Livermore, California

Memorial Day
11:00 AM - 5:00 PM

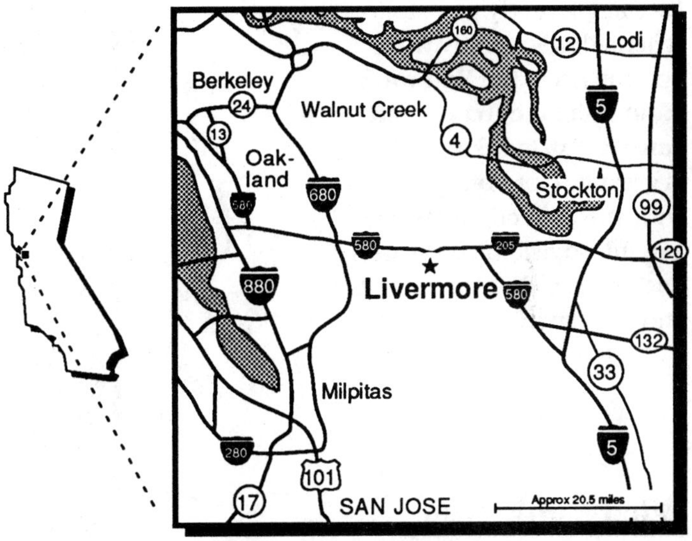


## What's goin' on...

Town population: **56,445**
Last year's attendance: **5,000**
Average outdoor temperature: **90°**
Festival location: **Wente Brothers Winery**

☞ *Up-to-date festival information is available from:*
*Livermore Chamber of Commerce*
*(415) 447-1606*

| | |
|---|---|
| X | Wine tasting/beer for sale |
| X | Food booths |
| X | Arts/crafts for sale |
| X | Live music |
| | Clowns |
| | Face painters |
| | Childrens games |
| | Animal exhibits/petting zoo |
| | Dogs allowed on leash |
| | Lost and found |
| X | Bicycle racks |
| | First aid area available |
| | Self-brought picnics allowed |
| | Self-brought alcohol allowed |
| | Stroller/wheelchair rentals available |

| | |
|---|---|
| | Parade |
| | Parking fee |
| | Entrance fee |
| X | Camping facilities: 11 miles |
| X | Boating facilities: Del Valle Res. |
| X | RV facilities w/ hookups: 11 miles |
| X | Accomodations in town<br>Townhouse Motel, Residence Inn, Holiday Inn |
| X | Restaurants in town<br>El Lorito, Le Coquelicot, Cruiser's, Beeb's Bar & Grill, Wente Sparkling Cellars Restaurant |

# *Redwood Mountain Fine Art & Craft Fair Music Festival*

IMAGINE REDWOODS AS BIG around as your house. Now picture yourself sitting in a fragrant grove of them listening intently to a story-teller—that's exactly what you can do at the **Redwood Mountain Fine Art & Craft Faire & Music Festival**. This is great fun for young and old, with music to captivate any ear, improvisational theater, fine art for sale, storytelling, and lots more!

## Ben Lomond, California

First weekend in June
Daily 10:00 AM - 6:00 PM

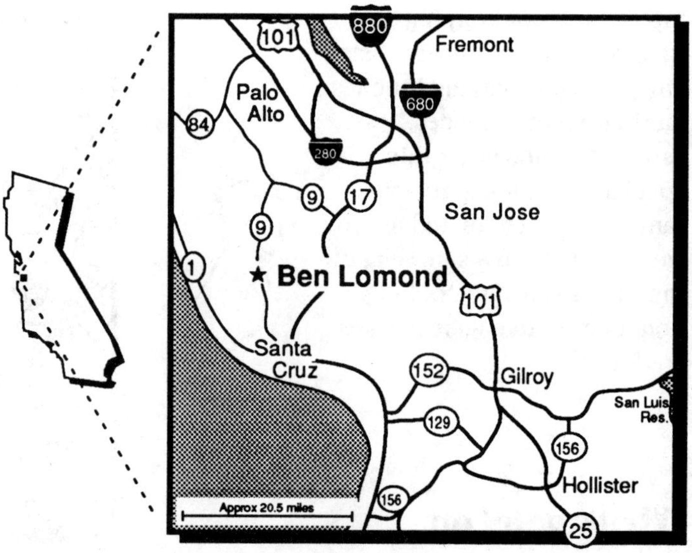


*Up-to-date festival information is available from:*
*Ben Lomond Chamber of Commerce*
*(408) 336-3600*

## What's goin' on...

Town population: **5,000**
Last year's attendance: **10,000**
Average outdoor temperature: **75°**
Festival location: **Park**

- ✗ Wine tasting/beer for sale
- ✗ Food booths
- ✗ Arts/crafts for sale
- ✗ Live music
- ✗ Clowns
- ✗ Face painters
- ✗ Childrens games
- Animal exhibits/petting zoo
- Dogs allowed on leash
- Lost and found
- Bicycle racks
- ✗ First aid area available
- ✗ Self-brought picnics allowed
- ✗ Self-brought alcohol allowed
- Stroller/wheelchair rentals available

- ✗ Parade
- Parking fee
- ✗ Entrance fee: $5; Under 12 free
- ✗ Camping facilities: 3 miles
- ✗ Boating facilities: Santa Cruz Harbor
- ✗ RV facilities w/ hookups: In town
- ✗ Accomodations in town
  Brookdale Lodge, Chateau des Fleurs B&B, Fairview Manor B&B
- ✗ Restaurants in town
  Señor Gomez, Tampico Grande, Trout Inn Scopozzie's, Mama Mia

# *Davis Street Faire*

HOME TO 45,000 BICYCLES—no it's not a small city in China—it's home to the University California at Davis...and home to the **Davis Street Faire**! A time for browsing and eating and laughing and dancing in the streets! Hamburgers, hot dogs, pizza, Thai dishes, and chili for the bellies, and lots of unique arts and crafts booths line the street. This is a nice way to kick off summer!

## Davis, California

First weekend in June
Daily 10:00 AM - 5:00 PM

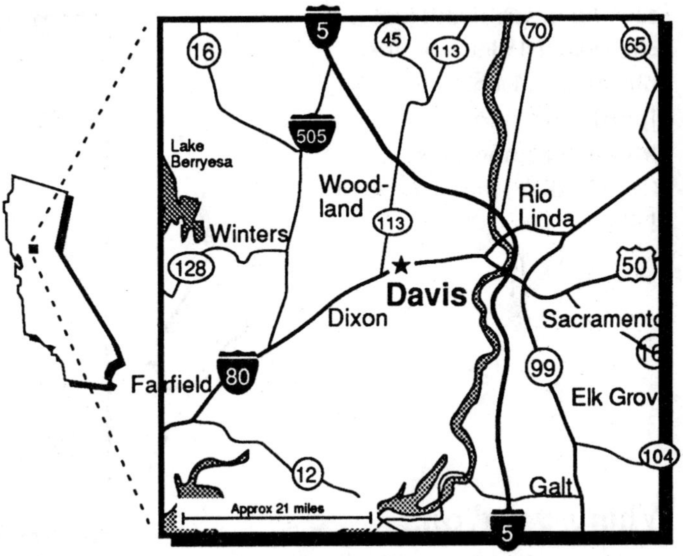


*Up-to-date festival information is available from:*
*Davis Chamber of Commerce*
*(916) 756-5160*



## What's goin' on...

Town population: **45,000**
Last year's attendance: **10,000**
Average outdoor temperature: **95°**
Festival location: **Downtown**

- X Wine tasting/beer for sale
- X Food booths
- X Arts/crafts for sale
- X Live music
- X Clowns
- X Face painters
- Childrens games
- Animal exhibits/petting zoo
- X Dogs allowed on leash
- Lost and found
- X Bicycle racks
- First aid area available
- X Self-brought picnics allowed
- Self-brought alcohol allowed
- Stroller/wheelchair rentals available

- Parade
- Parking fee
- Entrance fee
- X Camping facilities: 30 miles
- X Boating facilities: Lake Berryessa
- X RV facilities w/ hookups: 30 miles
- X Accomodations in town
  Ramada Inn, Aggie Inn, Campus Inn, Davis B&B, The Partridge Inn, University Lodge
- X Restaurants in town
  Ding How, The Graduate, Sudwerk's, Osaka Sushi, The Back Alley Brewery & Bistro

# *Strawberry Festival*

THE LUSCIOUS LITTLE FRUIT with the big, big taste is the center of attention at the **Strawberry Festival!** This is a really fun festival and just a little calorie-laden—white, milk, and dark chocolate-dipped strawberries, strawberry smoothies, tarts, SHORTCAKES, pie...you name it!

## Los Gatos, California

First weekend in June
Daily 11:00 AM - 5:00 PM

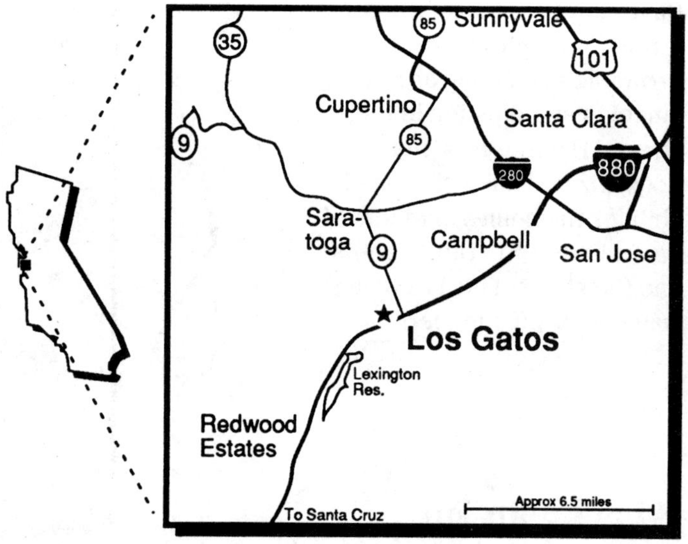


## What's goin' on...

Town population: **28,500**
Last year's attendance: **50,000**
Average outdoor temperature: **50°**
Festival location: **Downtown & Civic Center**

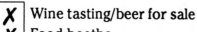

*Up-to-date festival information is available from:*
*Los Gatos Chamber of Commerce*
*(408) 354-9300*

| | |
|---|---|
| ✗ | Wine tasting/beer for sale |
| ✗ | Food booths |
| ✗ | Arts/crafts for sale |
| ✗ | Live music |
| | Clowns |
| ✗ | Face painters |
| | Childrens games |
| | Animal exhibits/petting zoo |
| ✗ | Dogs allowed on leash |
| ✗ | Lost and found |
| | Bicycle racks |
| ✗ | First aid area available |
| ✗ | Self-brought picnics allowed |
| | Self-brought alcohol allowed |
| | Stroller/wheelchair rentals available |

| | |
|---|---|
| | Parade |
| | Parking fee |
| | Entrance fee |
| ✗ | Camping facilities: 20 miles |
| ✗ | Boating facilities |
| ✗ | RV facilities w/ hookups: 3 miles |
| ✗ | Accomodations in town<br>Toll House, Los Gatos Lodge, La Hacienda Inn, Lodge at Villa Felice, Los Gatos Garden Inn |
| ✗ | Restaurants in town<br>The Chart House, C.B. Hannegan's, Fiorillo's, Mabel's Lantern House, Pedro's, The Diner |

# *Summerfest*

SUMMERTIME, SUMMERTIME, Sum-, Sum-, Summertime is a beautiful time in California! So, how 'bout heading to the charming little town of Los Gatos for **Summerfest**! Besides having all these food and craft booths at your fingertips—there's also great shopping in this charming little town! When you're ready to get away from the crowds, head over to Vasona Park to feed the ducks or rent a boat (small row- and sailboats) for a cruise around the lake.

## Los Gatos, California

June (call Chamber)
Daily 11:00 AM - 6:00 PM

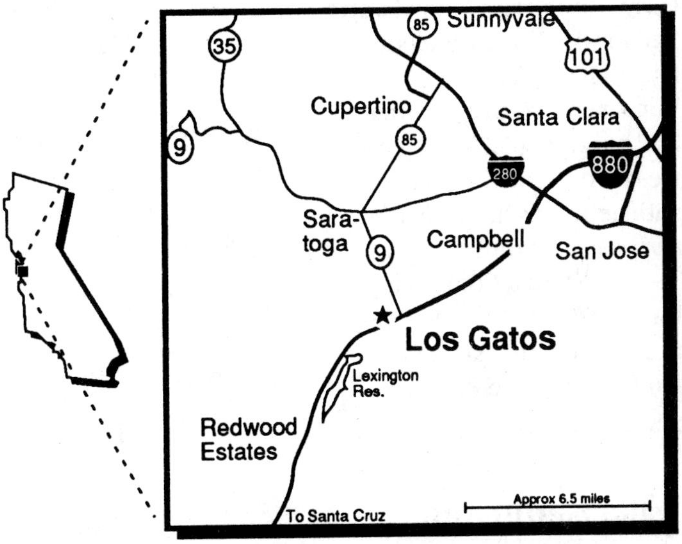


## What's goin' on...

Town population: **28,500**
Last year's attendance: **20,000**
Average outdoor temperature: **80°**
Festival location: **Old Town**

*Up-to-date festival information is available from:*
*Los Gatos Chamber of Commerce*
*(408) 354-9300*

| | |
|---|---|
| X | Wine tasting/beer for sale |
| X | Food booths |
| X | Arts/crafts for sale |
| X | Live music |
| X | Clowns |
| X | Face painters |
| | Childrens games |
| | Animal exhibits/petting zoo |
| | Dogs allowed on leash |
| X | Lost and found |
| | Bicycle racks |
| X | First aid area available |
| | Self-brought picnics allowed |
| | Self-brought alcohol allowed |
| | Stroller/wheelchair rentals available |

| | |
|---|---|
| | Parade |
| | Parking fee |
| | Entrance fee |
| X | Camping facilities: 20 miles |
| | Boating facilities |
| X | RV facilities w/ hookups: 3 miles |
| X | Accomodations in town<br>Toll House, Los Gatos Lodge, La Hacienda Inn, Lodge at Villa Felice, Los Gatos Garden Inn |
| X | Restaurants in town<br>The Chart House, C.B. Hannegan's, Fiorillo's, Mabel's Lantern House, Pedro's, The Diner |

# *Apricot Fiesta*

THE **APRICOT FIESTA** IN Patterson promises to be a weekend packed with all kinds of things to do! It's early—but drag yourself outta bed for the hot-air balloons launch from the Bonaaventure and Masonic Hall parking lots! The weekend's festivities continue with activities like a *Run for Apricots*, an Arm Wrestling Tourney, and a Community Dance. Patterson concludes the Fiesta with a skydiver *landing* on Circle Plaza...a spectacular event!

## Patterson, California

First weekend in June

Sat. 10:00 AM - 8:00 PM; Sun. 7:00 AM - 5:00 PM

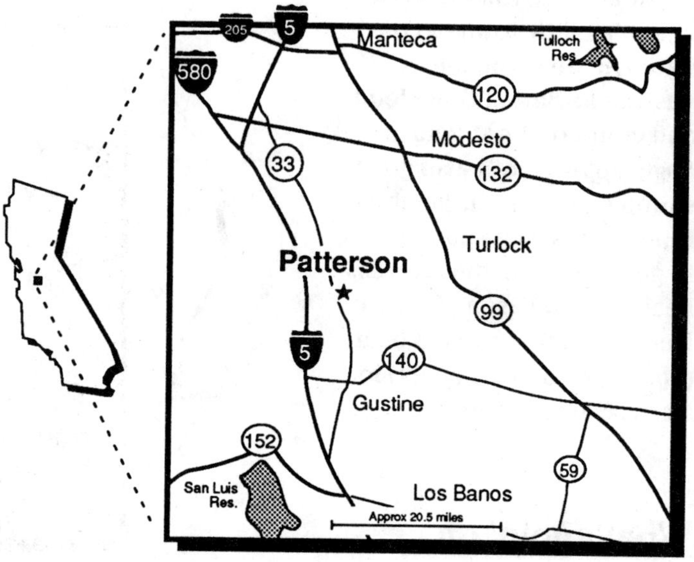


*Up-to-date festival information is available from:*
*Patterson Chamber of Commerce*
*(209) 892-2821*

## What's goin' on...

Town population: **8,700**
Last year's attendance: **25,000**
Average outdoor temperature: **90°**
Festival location: **Downtown park area**

| | |
|---|---|
| X | Wine tasting/beer for sale |
| X | Food booths |
| X | Arts/crafts for sale |
| X | Live music |
| X | Clowns |
| X | Face painters |
| X | Childrens games |
| X | Animal exhibits/petting zoo |
| X | Dogs allowed on leash |
| | Lost and found |
| | Bicycle racks |
| X | First aid area available |
| | Self-brought picnics allowed |
| | Self-brought alcohol allowed |
| | Stroller/wheelchair rentals available |

| | |
|---|---|
| X | Parade: Sat. 11:00 in the center of town |
| | Parking fee |
| | Entrance fee |
| X | Camping facilities: 8 miles |
| X | Boating facilities: San Luis Res. |
| X | RV facilities w/ hookups: 8 miles |
| X | Accomodations in town<br>Westley Hotel |
| X | Restaurants in town |

# *Western Weekend & 4-H Livestock Show*

LESS THAN AN HOURS DRIVE northwest of the Golden Gate Bridge lies the lazy and charming little town of Point Reyes Station—home to the **Western Weekend & 4-H Livestock Show**. There's lots to see, eat, and do! Saturday night, enjoy country tunes as you kick up your heels till the clock strikes midnight!

## Point Reyes Station, California

First weekend in June
Hours vary

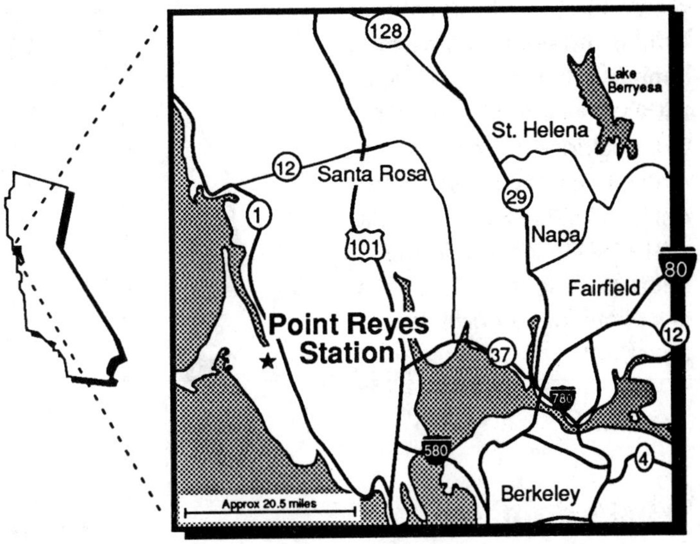


*Up-to-date festival information is available from: Point Reyes Station Chamber of Commerce (415) 663-9232*

## What's goin' on...

Town population: **1,100**
Last year's attendance: **2,500**
Average outdoor temperature: **65°**
Festival location: **Downtown**

| | |
|---|---|
| | Wine tasting/beer for sale |
| ✗ | Food booths |
| | Arts/crafts for sale |
| ✗ | Live music |
| ✗ | Clowns |
| | Face painters |
| | Childrens games |
| | Animal exhibits/petting zoo |
| ✗ | Dogs allowed on leash |
| ✗ | Lost and found |
| | Bicycle racks |
| ✗ | First aid area available |
| ✗ | Self-brought picnics allowed |
| ✗ | Self-brought alcohol allowed |
| | Stroller/wheelchair rentals available |

| | |
|---|---|
| ✗ | Parade: Sun. noon at Pt. Reyes Station |
| | Parking fee |
| | Entrance fee |
| ✗ | Camping facilities: 2 miles |
| ✗ | Boating facilities: Ocean |
| ✗ | RV facilities w/ hookups: 2 miles |
| ✗ | Accomodations in town |
| ✗ | Restaurants in town<br>Station House Cafe, Chez Madeline, Jerry's Farm House |

# *Sunnyvale Art & Wine Festival*

THE ANNUAL **SUNNYVALE Art & Wine Festival** is critical to a serious Festival Hopper! This festival has been expanded to include 475 of the United States select artists! Sample 24 wines (commemorative wine glass included) from California's leading wine makers and savor epicurian delights (...like Pennsylvania Ox Roast?). Located in the heart of "Silicon Valley," this is *still* one of California's finest!

## Sunnyvale, California

First full weekend in June
Daily 10:00 AM - 6:00 PM

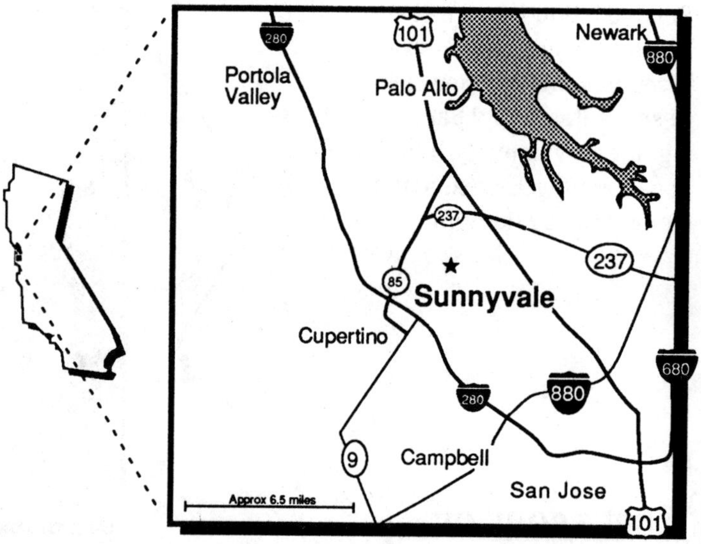


## What's goin' on...

Town population: **116,968**
Last year's attendance: **150,000**
Average outdoor temperature: **74°**
Festival location: **Downtown**

☞ *Up-to-date festival information is available from:*
*Sunnyvale Chamber of Commerce*
*(408) 736-4971*

| | |
|---|---|
| ✗ | Wine tasting/beer for sale |
| ✗ | Food booths |
| ✗ | Arts/crafts for sale |
| | Live music |
| | Clowns |
| ✗ | Face painters |
| ✗ | Childrens games |
| | Animal exhibits/petting zoo |
| | Dogs allowed on leash |
| ✗ | Lost and found |
| ✗ | Bicycle racks |
| ✗ | First aid area available |
| | Self-brought picnics allowed |
| | Self-brought alcohol allowed |
| | Stroller/wheelchair rentals available |

| | |
|---|---|
| | Parade |
| | Parking fee |
| | Entrance fee |
| ✗ | Camping facilities: 15 miles |
| | Boating facilities |
| ✗ | RV facilities w/ hookups: 2 miles |
| ✗ | Accomodations in town<br>Residence Inn, Sheraton, Maple Tree Inn, Sundowner Inn |
| ✗ | Restaurants in town<br>Tao Tao, Chevy's, California Cafe, American Joe's, Pacific Fresh, Coastline Cafe, El Faro |

# *Italian Picnic & Parade*

MAMA MIA! YOU DON'T HAVE to be Italian to come to the **Italian Picnic & Parade,** sponsored by the Italian Benevolent Society! But, you do have to like pasta—and what red-blooded American doesn't! You'll find pasta of all shapes and sizes in all colors of sauces—red, green, and white (**wow**...that might make a great flag, no?)! There are lots of fun games for the kids, too!

## Sutter Creek, California

First weekend in June
Hours vary

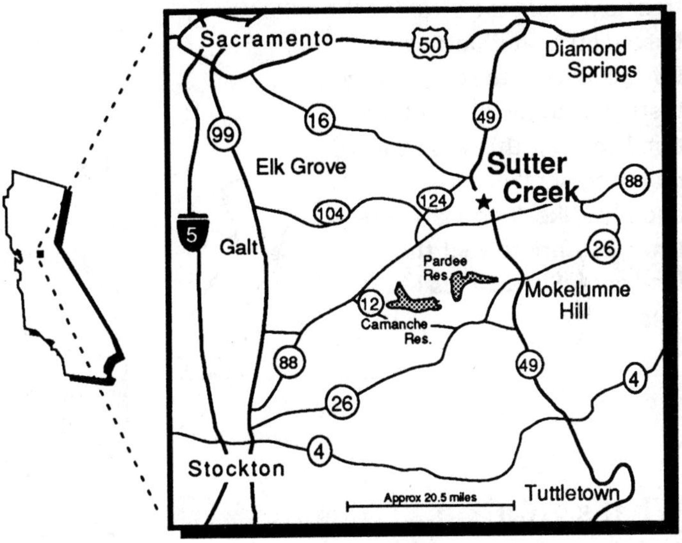


*Up-to-date festival information is available from:*
*Sutter Creek Chamber of Commerce*
*(209) 223-0353*

## What's goin' on...

Town population: **2,000**
Last year's attendance: **10,000**
Average outdoor temperature: **85°**
Festival location: **Park**

- X Wine tasting/beer for sale
- X Food booths
- Arts/crafts for sale
- Live music
- Clowns
- Face painters
- X Childrens games
- Animal exhibits/petting zoo
- X Dogs allowed on leash
- X Lost and found
- Bicycle racks
- X First aid area available
- X Self-brought picnics allowed
- X Self-brought alcohol allowed
- Stroller/wheelchair rentals available

- X Parade: Sun. 10:00 AM on Main St.
- Parking fee
- Entrance fee
- X Camping facilities: 9 miles
- X Boating facilities: Pardee Res.
- X RV facilities w/ hookups: 10 miles
- X Accomodations in town
  The Foxes in Sutter Creek B&B, Sutter Creek Inn B&B, The Hanford House B&B
- X Restaurants in town

# *Walnut Creek Art & Wine Festival*

THE TENTH ANNUAL **ART & Wine Festival** in Walnut Creek will be a weekend of festivities for the whole family to enjoy! From the strolling entertainers and petting zoo for the kiddies to robust-brew tasting from the Devil Mountain Brewery, this will be a day to remember for young and old alike. If you stop off in town, be sure to visit the Lindsey & Shadelands Museum.

## Walnut Creek, California

First weekend in June
Daily 11:00 AM - 6:00 PM

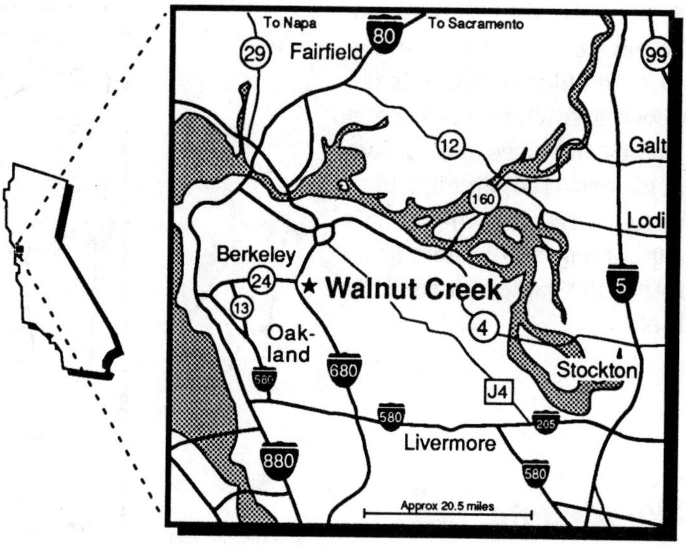


## What's goin' on...

Town population: **62,900**
Last year's attendance: **30,000**
Average outdoor temperature: **80°**
Festival location: **Heather Farms Park**

☞ *Up-to-date festival information is available from:*
*Walnut Creek Chamber of Commerce*
*(415) 934-2007*

| | |
|---|---|
| ✗ | Wine tasting/beer for sale |
| ✗ | Food booths |
| ✗ | Arts/crafts for sale |
| ✗ | Live music |
| | Clowns |
| | Face painters |
| | Childrens games |
| ✗ | Animal exhibits/petting zoo |
| | Dogs allowed on leash |
| ✗ | Lost and found |
| | Bicycle racks |
| | First aid area available |
| ✗ | Self-brought picnics allowed |
| | Self-brought alcohol allowed |
| | Stroller/wheelchair rentals available |

| | |
|---|---|
| | Parade |
| ✗ | Parking fee: $2 per car |
| | Entrance fee |
| ✗ | Camping facilities: 3 miles |
| ✗ | Boating facilities: Carquinez Straits |
| ✗ | RV facilities w/ hookups: 10 miles |
| ✗ | Accomodations in town<br>Doubletree, North Main Holiday Inn |
| ✗ | Restaurants in town<br>Scott's Seafood, Spiendini, Maximillian's, Max's Opera Cafe |

# *Flag Festival & Water Festival*

THE BANKS OF THE KINGS River are all decked out for the **Flag & Water Festival** in June. This impeccable little community is beautifully Swedish, and the folks who live here open their arms to tourists and visitors. The festival is highlighted by the boat parade down the river, and on the river banks you'll find food booths—and picnickers just soaking in the sights.

## Kingsburg, California

Second Saturday in June
9:00 AM - 5:00 PM

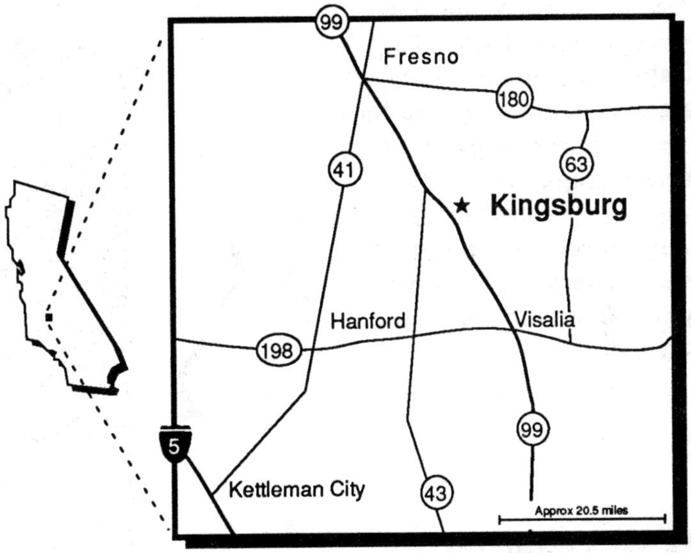


## What's goin' on...

Town population: **6,424**
Last year's attendance: **3,000**
Average outdoor temperature: **90°**
Festival location: **Kings River**

*Up-to-date festival information is available from:*
*Kingsburg Chamber of Commerce*
*(209) 897-2925*

| | |
|---|---|
| X | Wine tasting/beer for sale |
| X | Food booths |
| X | Arts/crafts for sale |
| X | Live music |
| | Clowns |
| X | Face painters |
| X | Childrens games |
| X | Animal exhibits/petting zoo |
| X | Dogs allowed on leash |
| X | Lost and found |
| X | Bicycle racks |
| X | First aid area available |
| X | Self-brought picnics allowed |
| X | Self-brought alcohol allowed |
| X | Stroller/wheelchair rentals available |

| | |
|---|---|
| | Parade |
| | Parking fee |
| X | Entrance fee: $3 |
| X | Camping facilities: In town |
| X | Boating facilities: Kings River |
| X | RV facilities w/ hookups: In town |
| X | Accomodations in town |
| X | Restaurants in town<br>Swedish Inn, Riverland, The Valley Inn, Kady's Country Kitchen |

# *World's Fastest Rodeo*

WAY BACK IN 1918 A TRADItion began in Livermore... the **World's Fastest Rodeo!** Besides rodeo events, this wild, Western celebration features country music on stage, and lots of fine Western art for your buying pleasure—bead work, clothing, paintings, photography, leatherwork, pottery, and handmade baskets. For you yokels out there, this sounds like lots of fun!

## Livermore, California

First weekend in June
Hours vary

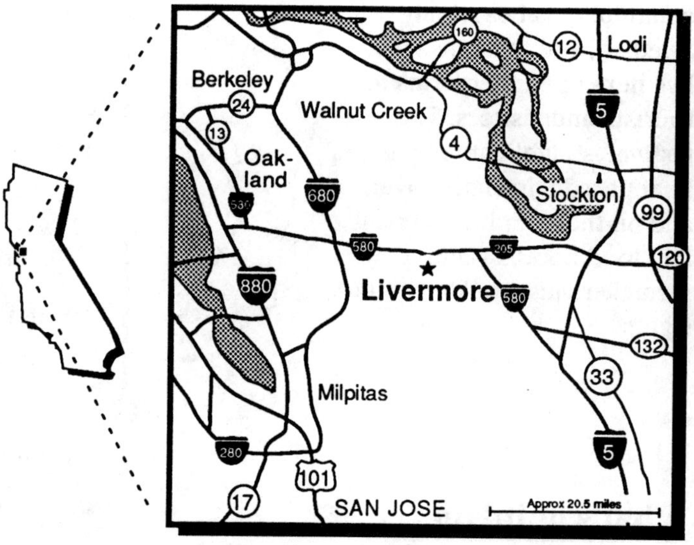


## What's goin' on...

Town population: **56,445**
Last year's attendance: **18,000**
Average outdoor temperature: **80°**
Festival location: **Robertson Park**

*Up-to-date festival information is available from:*
*Livermore Chamber of Commerce*
*(415) 447-1606*

| | |
|---|---|
| X | Wine tasting/beer for sale |
| X | Food booths |
| | Arts/crafts for sale |
| X | Live music |
| | Clowns |
| | Face painters |
| | Childrens games |
| | Animal exhibits/petting zoo |
| | Dogs allowed on leash |
| X | Lost and found |
| | Bicycle racks |
| X | First aid area available |
| | Self-brought picnics allowed |
| | Self-brought alcohol allowed |
| | Stroller/wheelchair rentals available |

| | |
|---|---|
| X | Parade: Sat. 10:00 AM on Second St. |
| | Parking fee |
| X | Entrance fee: $2 |
| X | Camping facilities: 11 miles |
| X | Boating facilities: Del Valle Res. |
| X | RV facilities w/ hookups: 11 miles |
| X | Accomodations in town<br>Townhouse Motel, Residence Inn, Holiday Inn |
| X | Restaurants in town<br>El Lorito, Le Coquelicot, Cruiser's, Beeb's Bar & Grill, Wente Sparkling Cellars Restaurant |

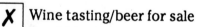

# *Pacific Fine Arts*

SAN CARLOS PICKED A FINE time for the **Pacific Fine Arts Fair!** This is a high-quality fine-arts festival, one not to miss if you enjoy wandering among booths of ceramics, fabric and paper art, stained glass, watercolor and oil paintings, and fine sculpture. The food booths focus on barbecued chicken and beef, Chinese, Thai, Greek, and Mexican delicacies!

## San Carlos, California

Second weekend in June
Daily 9:00 AM - 5:00 PM

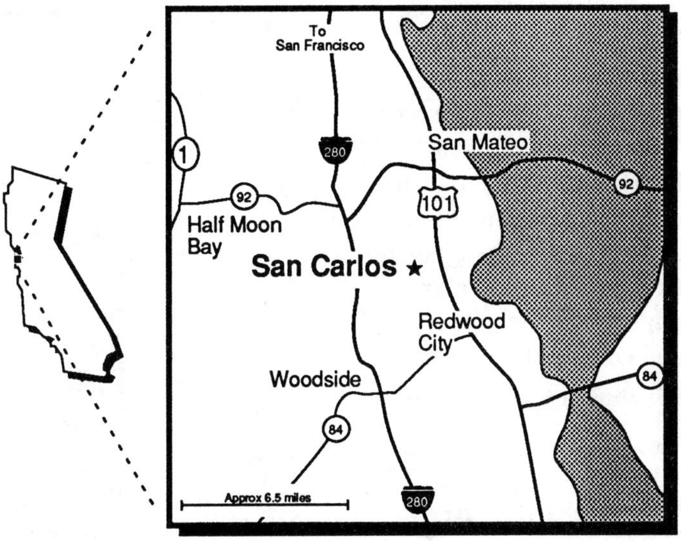


## What's goin' on...

Town population: **26,000**
Last year's attendance: **10,000**
Average outdoor temperature: **80°**
Festival location: **Laurel St.**

*Up-to-date festival information is available from:*
*San Carlos Chamber of Commerce*
*(415) 593-1068*

| | |
|---|---|
| | Wine tasting/beer for sale |
| X | Food booths |
| X | Arts/crafts for sale |
| | Live music |
| | Clowns |
| | Face painters |
| | Childrens games |
| | Animal exhibits/petting zoo |
| X | Dogs allowed on leash |
| | Lost and found |
| X | Bicycle racks |
| | First aid area available |
| | Self-brought picnics allowed |
| | Self-brought alcohol allowed |
| | Stroller/wheelchair rentals available |

| | |
|---|---|
| | Parade |
| | Parking fee |
| | Entrance fee |
| X | Camping facilities: 30 miles |
| X | Boating facilities: San Francisco Bay |
| X | RV facilities w/ hookups: 30 miles |
| X | Accomodations in town<br>Dunfey, Holiday Inn, San Carlos Inn |
| X | Restaurants in town<br>Salvatore's, Pete's Harbor, Capers, Messina's, San Carlos Joe's |

# *Health & Harmony Music & Arts Festival*

WANDERING MISTRALS, stilt walkers, psychic readers, wholistic health practioners, Motown music and California-natural food will lift your spirits at the **Health & Harmony Music & Arts Festival** in unique Sonoma County. Born of the 60's, this festival has now grown to encompass the needs and actions of the 90's by demon-strating a sincere interest in impro- ving the quality of life and concern for Mother Earth.

## Santa Rosa, California

Second weekend in June
Daily: 10:00 AM - 7:00 PM

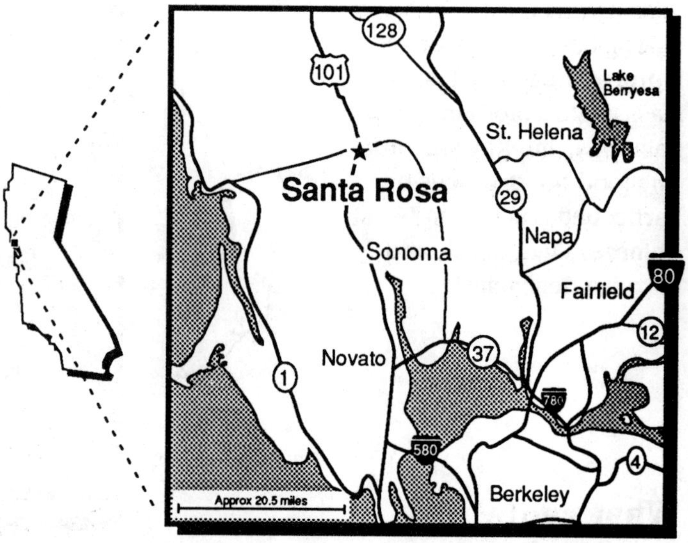


*Up-to-date festival information is available from:*
*Santa Rosa Wishing Well Productions*
*(707) 575-9355*

## What's goin' on...

Town population: **100,000**
Last year's attendance: **15,000**
Average outdoor temperature: **78°**
Festival location: **Fairgrounds**

| | |
|---|---|
| X | Wine tasting/beer for sale |
| X | Food booths |
| X | Arts/crafts for sale |
| X | Live music |
| X | Clowns |
| X | Face painters |
| X | Childrens games |
| X | Animal exhibits/petting zoo |
| | Dogs allowed on leash |
| X | Lost and found |
| X | Bicycle racks |
| X | First aid area available |
| X | Self-brought picnics allowed |
| | Self-brought alcohol allowed |
| | Stroller/wheelchair rentals available |

| | |
|---|---|
| | Parade |
| X | Parking fee: $1.00 |
| X | Entrance fee: S $4; A $6; K $2 |
| X | Camping facilities: On site |
| X | Boating facilities: Lake Sonoma |
| X | RV facilities w/ hookups: On-site |
| X | Accomodations in town<br>Red Lion, Doubletree, El Rancho |
| X | Restaurants in town<br>John Ash |

# *Junefest*

LOS OSOS FOLKS TELL US that their **Junefest** is "as old as the hills, and twice as dusty!" Heck, sign us up...that sounds like big fun! Located just ten short miles from beautiful Morro Bay, this crazy little town puts on quite a celebration: barbecued chicken and ribs, Mexican and Oriental food, rock 'n' roll and country music, and good times for all!

## Los Osos, California

Second Sunday in June
9:00 AM - 5:00 PM

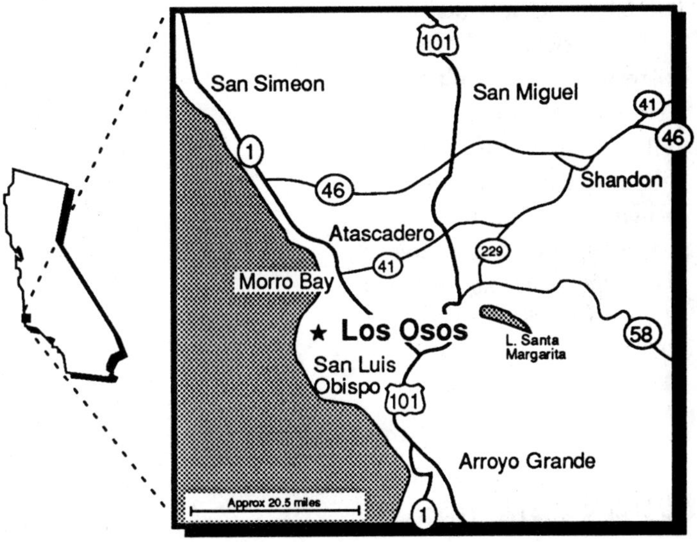




## What's goin' on...

Town population: **16,000**
Last year's attendance: **7,000**
Average outdoor temperature: **70°**
Festival location: **Downtown Baywood**

*Up-to-date festival information is available from:*
*Los Osos Chamber of Commerce*
*(805) 528-4884*

| | |
|---|---|
| ✗ | Wine tasting/beer for sale |
| ✗ | Food booths |
| ✗ | Arts/crafts for sale |
| ✗ | Live music |
| | Clowns |
| ✗ | Face painters |
| | Childrens games |
| | Animal exhibits/petting zoo |
| ✗ | Dogs allowed on leash |
| | Lost and found |
| | Bicycle racks |
| ✗ | First aid area available |
| ✗ | Self-brought picnics allowed |
| | Self-brought alcohol allowed |
| | Stroller/wheelchair rentals available |

| | |
|---|---|
| | Parade |
| | Parking fee |
| | Entrance fee |
| ✗ | Camping facilities: 5 miles |
| ✗ | Boating facilities: 3 miles |
| ✗ | RV facilities w/ hookups: 5 miles |
| ✗ | Accomodations in town<br>Baywood Lodge B&B, Julia's B&B, Blue Heron Motel |
| ✗ | Restaurants in town<br>Don Edwardo's, Sculptured Egg, Rodney's, Salty Pelican, Rodney's |

# *Crawdad Festival*

YOU CAN EAT 'EM PICKLED, fried, cajun'ed, boiled, or sauteed—just don't eat these tasty little crustaceans raw! The **Isleton Crawdad Festival** is where you can try the little critters if you haven't before—and boy, are they delicious! The festival highlights are the crowning of the Crawdad Queen, river raft racers, the crawdad cook-off and eating contest, and arts crafts booths!

## Isleton, California

Third weekend in June (beginning Friday)
Fri. 6:00 PM - midnight; Sat. 9:00 AM - 1:00 AM; Sun. 9:00 AM - 6:00 PM

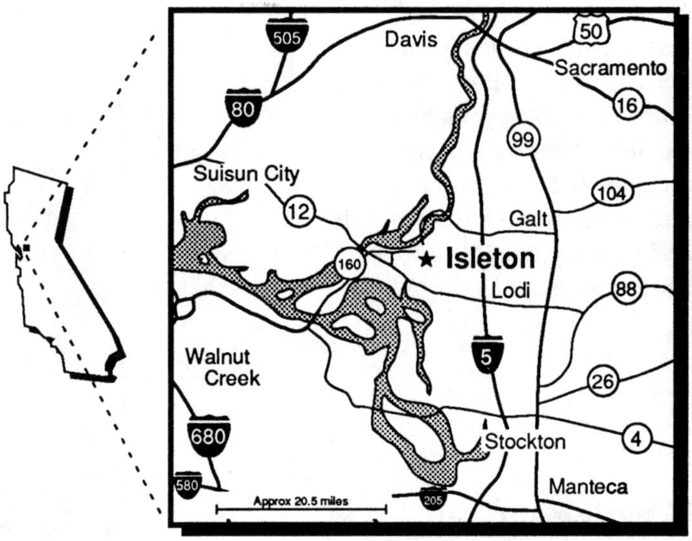


## What's goin' on...

Town population: **902**
Last year's attendance: **75,000**
Average outdoor temperature: **80°**
Festival location: **Main Street**

☞ *Up-to-date festival information is available from:*
*Isleton Chamber of Commerce*
*(916) 777-6503*

| | |
|---|---|
| ✗ | Wine tasting/beer for sale |
| ✗ | Food booths |
| ✗ | Arts/crafts for sale |
| ✗ | Live music |
| | Clowns |
| ✗ | Face painters |
| ✗ | Childrens games |
| | Animal exhibits/petting zoo |
| | Dogs allowed on leash |
| ✗ | Lost and found |
| | Bicycle racks |
| ✗ | First aid area available |
| | Self-brought picnics allowed |
| | Self-brought alcohol allowed |
| | Stroller/wheelchair rentals available |

| | |
|---|---|
| ✗ | Parade: (date & time not avbl.) |
| ✗ | Parking fee: $3 |
| | Entrance fee |
| ✗ | Camping facilities: 10 miles |
| ✗ | Boating facilities: The Delta |
| ✗ | RV facilities w/ hookups: 10 miles |
| ✗ | Accomodations in town |
| ✗ | Restaurants in town |

# *Hilmar Dairy Festival*

IN THE HEART OF CALIFORNIA's dairy land is where you'll appropriately find the **Hilmar Dairy Festival.** You can find loads of events all day to participate in—cow milking, cow mooing, De-Calf-Alon relays, a pet parade, and the Little Milk Maid and Little Milk Man contests. Baked goods, hot dogs, linguica samos, ice cream, and free milk are among the tasties for your tummies.

## Hilmar, California

Third Saturday in June
10:00 AM - 5:00 PM

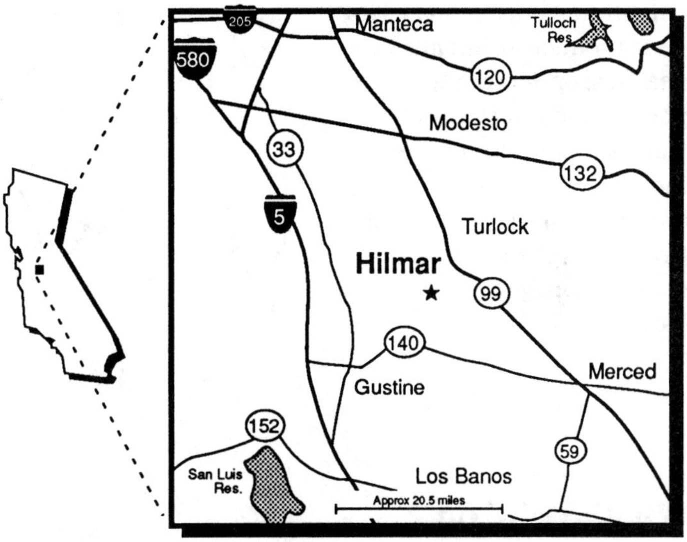


*Up-to-date festival information is available from:*
*Hilmar Chamber of Commerce*
*(209) 668-0719*

## What's goin' on...

Town population: **2,500**
Last year's attendance: **5,000**
Average outdoor temperature: **85°**
Festival location: **Hilmar High**

| | |
|---|---|
| X | Wine tasting/beer for sale |
| X | Food booths |
| X | Arts/crafts for sale |
| X | Live music |
| | Clowns |
| X | Face painters |
| X | Childrens games |
| X | Animal exhibits/petting zoo |
| X | Dogs allowed on leash |
| X | Lost and found |
| | Bicycle racks |
| | First aid area available |
| | Self-brought picnics allowed |
| | Self-brought alcohol allowed |
| | Stroller/wheelchair rentals available |

| | |
|---|---|
| | Parade |
| | Parking fee |
| | Entrance fee |
| X | Camping facilities: 6 miles |
| X | Boating facilities: 30 - 50 miles |
| X | RV facilities w/ hookups: 6 miles |
| | Accomodations in town |
| X | Restaurants in town<br>Ranch House, Deana & Sousa's |

# *Modesto á la Carte*

MODESTO, KNOWN AS HOME of the world's largest winery—E. & J. Gallo is also home to **Modesto á la Carte** in June. Celebrating the abundance of local produce—almonds, peaches, apricots, grains, grapes, and tomatoes, this feast is fit for a king (queen, too!). Director/producer George Lucas wrote American Graffiti based on his experiences cruising the streets of Modesto.

## Modesto, California

Third weekend in June
Daily 10:00 AM - 7:00 PM

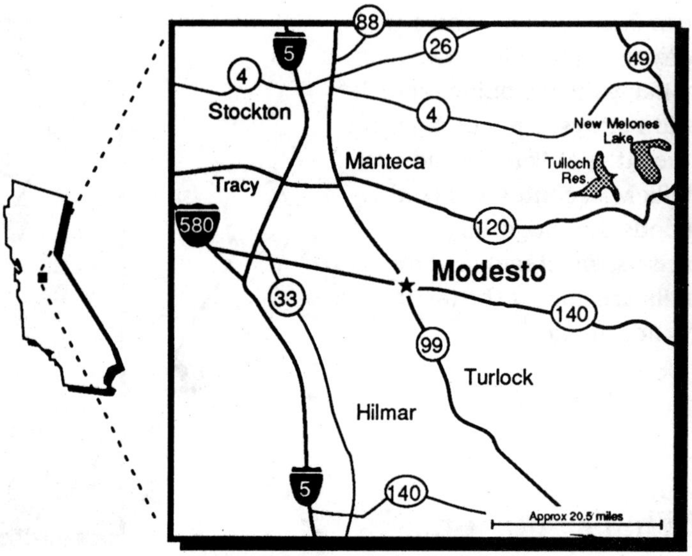


*Up-to-date festival information is available from:*
*Modesto Chamber of Commerce*
*(209) 577-5757*

## What's goin' on...

Town population: **152,100**
Last year's attendance: **18,000**
Average outdoor temperature: **90°**
Festival location: **Along "I" Street**

| | |
|---|---|
| ✗ | Wine tasting/beer for sale |
| ✗ | Food booths |
| ✗ | Arts/crafts for sale |
| ✗ | Live music |
| ✗ | Clowns |
| ✗ | Face painters |
| ✗ | Childrens games |
| ✗ | Animal exhibits/petting zoo |
| | Dogs allowed on leash |
| ✗ | Lost and found |
| | Bicycle racks |
| ✗ | First aid area available |
| | Self-brought picnics allowed |
| | Self-brought alcohol allowed |
| | Stroller/wheelchair rentals available |

| | |
|---|---|
| | Parade |
| | Parking fee |
| ✗ | Entrance fee: Srs/Kids $2; Adults $4 |
| ✗ | Camping facilities: 15 miles |
| ✗ | Boating facilities: Turlock Lake |
| ✗ | RV facilities w/ hookups: 17 miles |
| ✗ | Accomodations in town<br>Red Lion, Holiday Inn, Best Western, Capri Inn, Lexington Inn, Capri Inn, Super 8, Mallards Inn |
| ✗ | Restaurants in town |

# *Dairy Festival*

NOT TO BE OUTDONE BY the folks in Hilmar and Irwindale, Tulare has a **Dairy Festival** of its own—complete with milk-drinking and cow-milking contests! Enjoy a visit to the animal exhibit exhibit and petting zoo, with furry friends such a goats, sheep, calves, and bulls. There are lots of cow-theme crafts, along with all sorts of dairy products for lunch.

## Tulare, California

Second weekend in June
Daily 9:00 AM - 8:00 PM

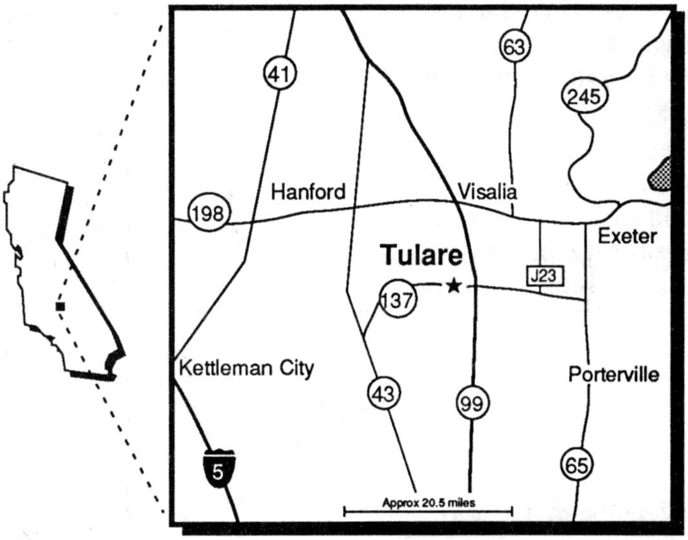


## What's goin' on...

Town population: **29,655**
Last year's attendance: **5,000**
Average outdoor temperature: **80°**
Festival location: **Zumwalt Park**

*Up-to-date festival information is available from:*
*Tulare Chamber of Commerce*
*(209) 686-1547*

| | |
|---|---|
| X | Wine tasting/beer for sale |
| X | Food booths |
| X | Arts/crafts for sale |
| X | Live music |
| X | Clowns |
| X | Face painters |
| X | Childrens games |
| X | Animal exhibits/petting zoo |
| | Dogs allowed on leash |
| X | Lost and found |
| X | Bicycle racks |
| | First aid area available |
| X | Self-brought picnics allowed |
| | Self-brought alcohol allowed |
| | Stroller/wheelchair rentals available |

| | |
|---|---|
| X | Parade Sat. 11:00 AM near the Park |
| | Parking fee |
| | Entrance fee |
| X | Camping facilities: 3 miles |
| X | Boating facilities: Lake Success |
| X | RV facilities w/ hookups: 5 miles |
| X | Accomodations in town |
| X | Restaurants in town |

# *Burrito Bash, Arts & Crafts Festival*

IT'S NEARLY TEN YEARS OLD and it just keeps getting better each year! The **Burrito Bash, Arts & Crafts Festival** in Watsonville is a bash all right! All the local artists will be here showing off their unique artistry—glass, wood, clay, paint, and leather. Bend your elbow with a cold beer, and suck down a couple of really tasty burritos on—ready for this —homemade tortillas! (Yum! Our favorite!)

## Watsonville, California

Third weekend in June
Dailly 10:00 AM - 7:00 PM

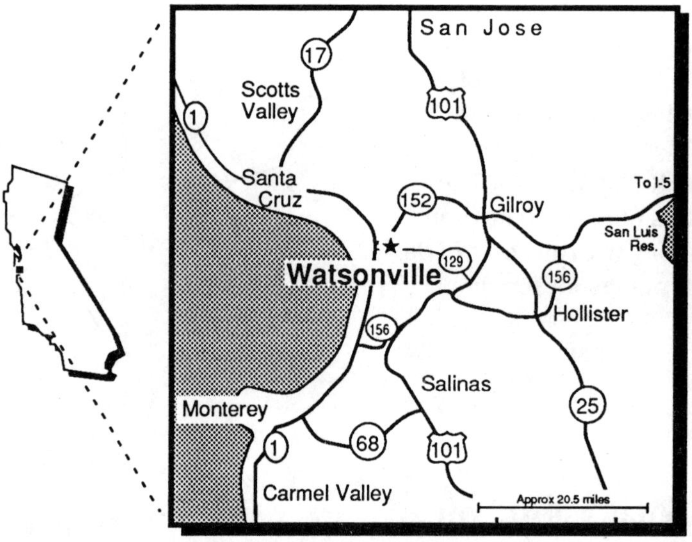


*Up-to-date festival information is available from:*
*Watsonville Chamber of Commerce*
*(408) 425-1234*

## What's goin' on...

Town population: **30,250**
Last year's attendance: **20,000**
Average outdoor temperature: **65°**
Festival location: **Fairgrounds**

| | |
|---|---|
| X | Wine tasting/beer for sale |
| X | Food booths |
| X | Arts/crafts for sale |
| X | Live music |
| X | Clowns |
| X | Face painters |
| X | Childrens games |
| | Animal exhibits/petting zoo |
| | Dogs allowed on leash |
| X | Lost and found |
| | Bicycle racks |
| X | First aid area available |
| | Self-brought picnics allowed |
| | Self-brought alcohol allowed |
| | Stroller/wheelchair rentals available |

| | |
|---|---|
| | Parade |
| | Parking fee |
| X | Entrance fee: S & K $3; A $4 |
| X | Camping facilities: 5 miles |
| X | Boating facilities: Pinto Lake |
| X | RV facilities w/ hookups: 5 miles |
| X | Accomodations in town<br>National 9 Motel, Mid-Town Motel |
| X | Restaurants in town<br>Miramar Grill, Del Monte Cafe, Beach Street, Golden Ricksha, EDO |

# *Art Under the Oaks*

AFTER YOU SERVE DAD breakfast in bed, pull the weeds, and mow the lawn...how about an afternoon of **Art Under the Oaks** in Livermore? Father's Day is special and what a great way to get outside (...and out of any other chores) and enjoy the day! Free hors d'oeuvres, harp music and fabulous art...how can you go wrong? (Although my dad would prefer his smelly ol' cowboy hat, horseshoes and a barbecue!)

## Livermore, California

Father's Day
11:00 AM - 4:00 PM

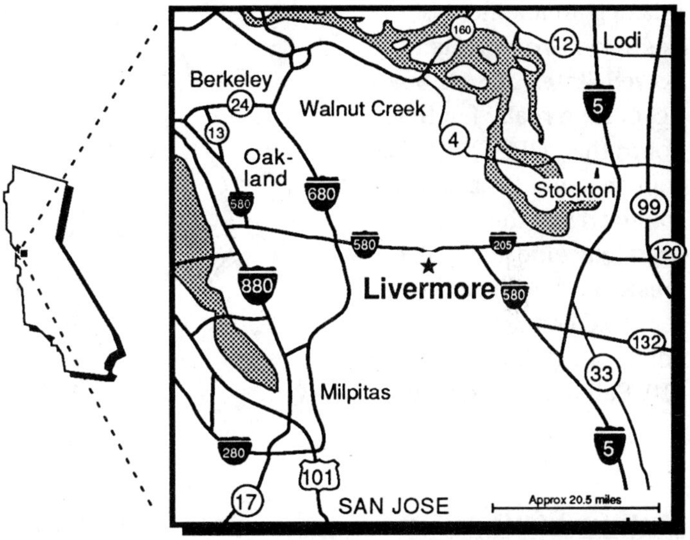


*Up-to-date festival information is available from:*
*Livermore Chamber of Commerce*
*(415) 447-1606*

## What's goin' on...

Town population: **56,445**
Last year's attendance: **18,000**
Average outdoor temperature: **80°**
Festival location: **Downtown Park**

- X Wine tasting/beer for sale
- X Food booths
- X Arts/crafts for sale
- X Live music
- Clowns
- Face painters
- Childrens games
- Animal exhibits/petting zoo
- Dogs allowed on leash
- Lost and found
- X Bicycle racks
- First aid area available
- Self-brought picnics allowed
- Self-brought alcohol allowed
- Stroller/wheelchair rentals available

- Parade
- Parking fee
- Entrance fee
- X Camping facilities: 11 miles
- X Boating facilities: Del Valle Res.
- X RV facilities w/ hookups: 11 miles
- X Accomodations in town
  Townhouse Motel, Residence Inn, Holiday Inn
- X Restaurants in town
  El Lorito, Le Coquelicot, Cruiser's, Beeb's Bar & Grill, Wente Sparkling Cellars Restaurant

# *Pops for Pops*

TREAT DAD TO THE **POPS for Pops** concert—a free concert sponsored by the Santa Cruz Symphony in the relaxing atmosphere of Redwood Grove at Henry Cowell State Park. Or buy a ticket for a really fun time—board the POPS EXPRESS train in Santa Cruz and ride round-trip to the park, taste premium wine, enjoy live music on the trip, and get reserved concert seating: adults, $25; children (3-15), $10. Call to order tickets.

## Santa Cruz, California

Father's Day
2:00 PM - 6:00 PM

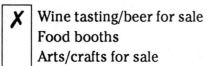

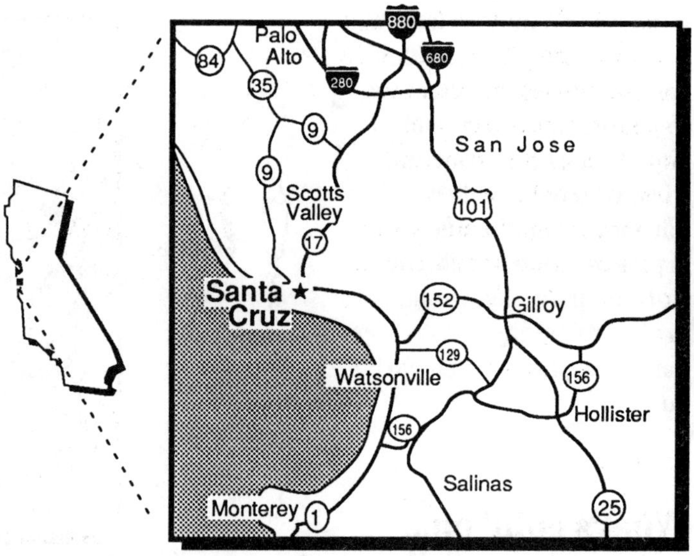


## What's goin' on...

Town population: **48,000**
Last year's attendance: **2,000**
Average outdoor temperature: **75°**
Festival location: **Henry Cowell State Park**

*Up-to-date festival information is available from:*
*Santa Cruz Symphony Office*
*(408) 462-0553*

X Wine tasting/beer for sale
Food booths
Arts/crafts for sale
X Live music
Clowns
Face painters
Childrens games
Animal exhibits/petting zoo
Dogs allowed on leash
Lost and found
X Bicycle racks
First aid area available
X Self-brought picnics allowed
X Self-brought alcohol allowed
Stroller/wheelchair rentals available

Parade
X Parking fee: $3 per car in Park
X Entrance fee: (train ride)
X Camping facilities: On-site
X Boating facilities: Santa Cruz Harbor
X RV facilities w/ hookups: On-site
X Accomodations in town
Dream Inn, Babbling Brook B&B, Pleasure Point B&B, The Darling House B&B

X Restaurants in town
Crow's Nest, Aldo's

# *Sonoma Marin Fair*

GENERALLY A FAIR IS A FAIR, is a fair, is a fair! But these smaller towns north of San Francisco offer a hometown twists that's quite refreshing! The **Sonoma Marin Fair** is no exception—as you can see from the official Festival Hopper's checklist below! They nearly have it all...including the notorious Ugly Dog Contest and Llama-Rama!

## Petaluma, California

Third week in June
Daily 10:00 AM - midnight

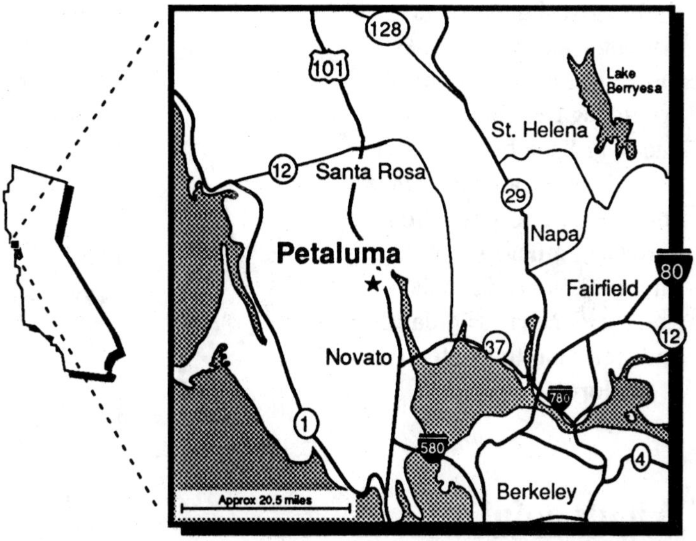


*Up-to-date festival information is available from:*
*Petaluma Chamber of Commerce*
*(707) 762-2785*

## What's goin' on...

Town population: **42,000**
Last year's attendance: **67,824**
Average outdoor temperature: **80°**
Festival location: **Fairgrounds**

| | |
|---|---|
| | Wine tasting/beer for sale |
| ✗ | Food booths |
| ✗ | Arts/crafts for sale |
| ✗ | Live music |
| ✗ | Clowns |
| ✗ | Face painters |
| ✗ | Childrens games |
| ✗ | Animal exhibits/petting zoo |
| | Dogs allowed on leash |
| ✗ | Lost and found |
| ✗ | Bicycle racks |
| ✗ | First aid area available |
| ✗ | Self-brought picnics allowed |
| | Self-brought alcohol allowed |
| ✗ | Stroller/wheelchair rentals available |

| | |
|---|---|
| | Parade |
| ✗ | Parking fee: $2 |
| ✗ | Entrance fee: Adults $5; Kids $2.50 |
| ✗ | Camping facilities: 5 miles |
| ✗ | Boating facilities: River, lake, and bay |
| ✗ | RV facilities w/ hookups: 5 miles |
| ✗ | Accomodations in town<br>Best Western, Quality Inn, Motel 6, Cavanagh Cottage B&B, 7th St. Inn B&B |
| ✗ | Restaurants in town<br>De Schmire, Steamer Gold Landing, Aram's, Cattlemen's, Fino's, Graziano's, Sonoma Joe's |

# *Ruby Jubilee*

CALLING ALL FESTIVAL hoppers! Calling all festival hoppers! Alert! Alert! The **Ruby Jubilee** is the first year that North Highlands is hosting a festival! So, be there! The different booths are taking the shape of barbecue grills, a beer garden, pizzeria, and booths of arts and crafts. There will be a variety of music and dancing till midnight on Saturday! Good luck North Highlands, and welcome to the festivals of California!

## North Highlands, California

Fourth weekend in June
Daily 10:00 AM - 8:00 PM

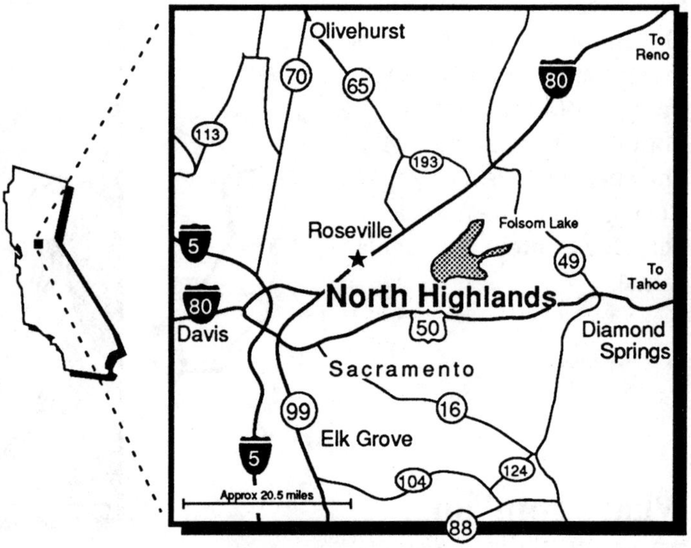


## What's goin' on...

Town population: **60,000**
Last year's attendance: **N/A**
Average outdoor temperature: **85°**
Festival location: **(call Chamber)**

*Up-to-date festival information is available from:*
*North Highlands Chamber of Commerce*
*(916) 334-2214*

- X Wine tasting/beer for sale
- X Food booths
- X Arts/crafts for sale
- X Live music
- X Clowns
- X Face painters
- X Childrens games
- X Animal exhibits/petting zoo
- Dogs allowed on leash
- X Lost and found
- X Bicycle racks
- X First aid area available
- X Self-brought picnics allowed
- X Self-brought alcohol allowed
- Stroller/wheelchair rentals available

- Parade
- Parking fee
- X Entrance fee: $3 per car
- X Camping facilities: 15 miles
- X Boating facilities: Lake/River
- X RV facilities w/ hookups: 15 miles
- X Accomodations in town
- X Restaurants in town
  Blue Oak, Marash's, Pizza Arena, Po Folks

# *Wine Festival*

CALIFORNIA'S GOLD COUNTRY, like her Napa Valley wine country, is blessed with a perfect grape-growing climate. So, it's only fitting that Plymouth show off it's varietal grapes at the **Wine Festival.** Besides wine tasting, there are the Mercer Caverns to visit—just south of town, and if you are an antique hunter, this entire area has nifty little shops to check out.

## Plymouth, California

Fourth weekend in June
11:00 AM - 7:00 PM

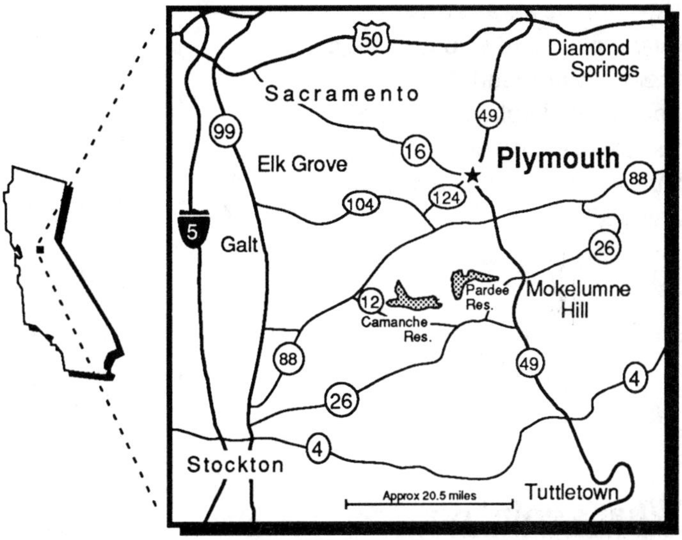


## What's goin' on...

Town population: **1,000**
Last year's attendance: **N/A**
Average outdoor temperature: **90°**
Festival location: **Fairgrounds**

*Up-to-date festival information is available from: Plymouth Chamber of Commerce (209) 223-0350*

| | |
|---|---|
| X | Wine tasting/beer for sale |
| X | Food booths |
| | Arts/crafts for sale |
| X | Live music |
| | Clowns |
| | Face painters |
| | Childrens games |
| | Animal exhibits/petting zoo |
| | Dogs allowed on leash |
| | Lost and found |
| | Bicycle racks |
| | First aid area available |
| | Self-brought picnics allowed |
| | Self-brought alcohol allowed |
| | Stroller/wheelchair rentals available |

| | |
|---|---|
| | Parade |
| | Parking fee |
| X | Entrance fee: (prices not avbl.) |
| X | Camping facilities: In town |
| X | Boating facilities: Lake Amador |
| X | RV facilities w/ hookups: In town |
| X | Accomodations in town<br>Shenandoah Village Hotel |
| X | Restaurants in town |

# *Bay Hill Champagne Festival*

JAZZ UP YOUR WEEKEND with a trip over to San Bruno for the **Bay Hill Champagne Festival**! Jazzy sounds waft through the air as you sip champagne and stroll through the many arts and crafts booths on display. Do bring the children, dahlink—there's a carnival that will keep them amused!

## San Bruno, California

Fourth weekend in June
Daily 10:00 AM - 5:00 PM

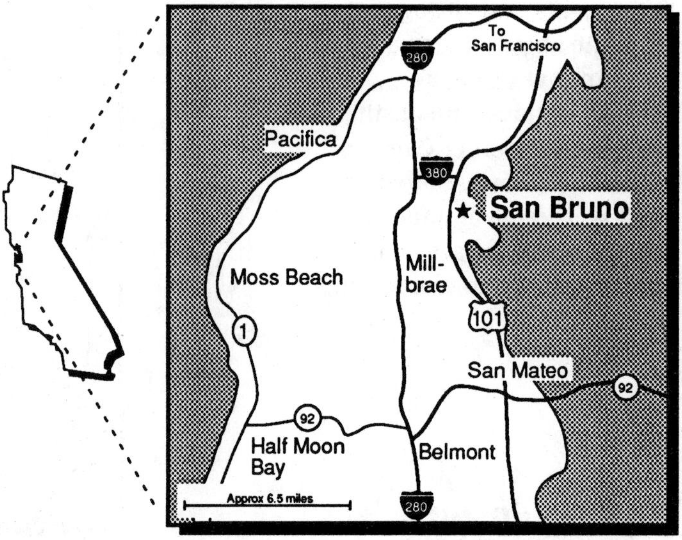


## What's goin' on...

Town population: **35,600**
Last year's attendance: **25,000**
Average outdoor temperature: **70°**
Festival location: **Office Park**

*Up-to-date festival information is available from:*
*San Bruno Chamber of Commerce*
*(415) 588-0180*

| | | | |
|---|---|---|---|
| X | Wine tasting/beer for sale | | Parade |
| X | Food booths | | Parking fee |
| X | Arts/crafts for sale | | Entrance fee |
| X | Live music | | Camping facilities |
| X | Clowns | X | Boating facilities: San Francisco Bay |
| X | Face painters | | RV facilities w/ hookups |
| X | Childrens games | X | Accomodations in town<br>Marriott |
| X | Animal exhibits/petting zoo | | |
| | Dogs allowed on leash | | |
| X | Lost and found | | |
| X | Bicycle racks | X | Restaurants in town |
| X | First aid area available | | |
| X | Self-brought picnics allowed | | |
| | Self-brought alcohol allowed | | |
| | Stroller/wheelchair rentals available | | |

# *Joyce Becker's Soap Opera Festival*

NOW, THIS IS NO ORDINARY festival! No arts-and-crafts booths. No food booths (well, we weren't counting the Boardwalk's!). No face painters. No bean-bag toss. But at **Joyce Becker's Soap Opera Festival**, you'll get the dirt on all the soap stars and what's happening on the sets. This is a must for soapie fans! (Thank goodness it's a *weekend* festival!)

## Santa Cruz, California

Fourth weekend in June
Daily 1:00 - 5:00 PM

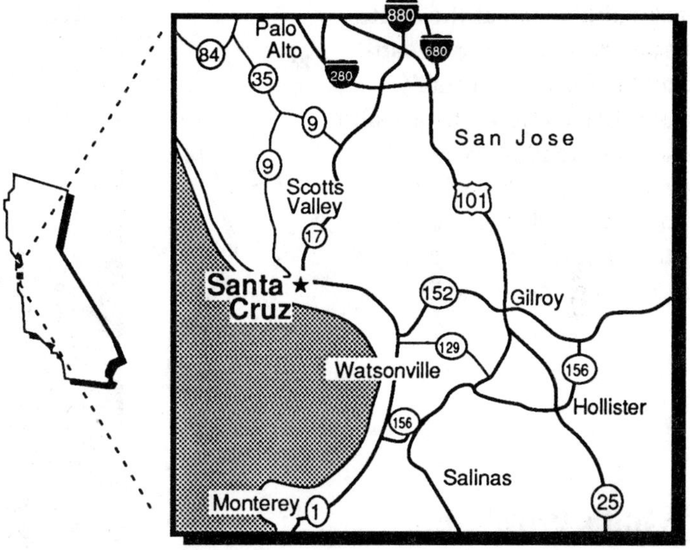


*Up-to-date festival information is available from:*
*Santa Cruz Visitors Bureau*
*(408) 425-1234*

## What's goin' on...

Town population: **48,000**
Last year's attendance: **15,000**
Average outdoor temperature: **75°**
Festival location: **Santa Cruz Boardwalk**

| | |
|---|---|
| X | Wine tasting/beer for sale |
| X | Food booths |
| | Arts/crafts for sale |
| | Live music |
| | Clowns |
| | Face painters |
| | Childrens games |
| | Animal exhibits/petting zoo |
| | Dogs allowed on leash |
| | Lost and found |
| X | Bicycle racks |
| | First aid area available |
| X | Self-brought picnics allowed |
| | Self-brought alcohol allowed |
| | Stroller/wheelchair rentals available |

| | |
|---|---|
| | Parade |
| X | Parking fee: meters |
| | Entrance fee |
| X | Camping facilities: 2 miles |
| X | Boating facilities: Santa Cruz Harbor |
| X | RV facilities w/ hookups: In town |
| X | Accomodations in town<br>Dream Inn, Chaminade, Babbling Brook B&B, Cliff Crest B&B, Pleasure Point Inn B&B |
| X | Restaurants in town<br>Sea Cloud, Casa Blanca, Chez Renee, Crow's Nest, Aldo's |

# *Santa Cruz County Vinter's Festival*

BRING YOUR OWN PICNIC and grab a glass of wine for a relaxing afternoon among thousand-year-old redwoods or on the beach at the **Santa Cruz County Vinter's Festival!** This festival actually takes place county-wide—and at a few locations—so call beforehand to see what's happening where. Santa Cruz offers fun during the day and in the evening at the Boardwalk.

## Santa Cruz, California

Fourth weekend in June
Daily 11:00 AM - 5:00 PM

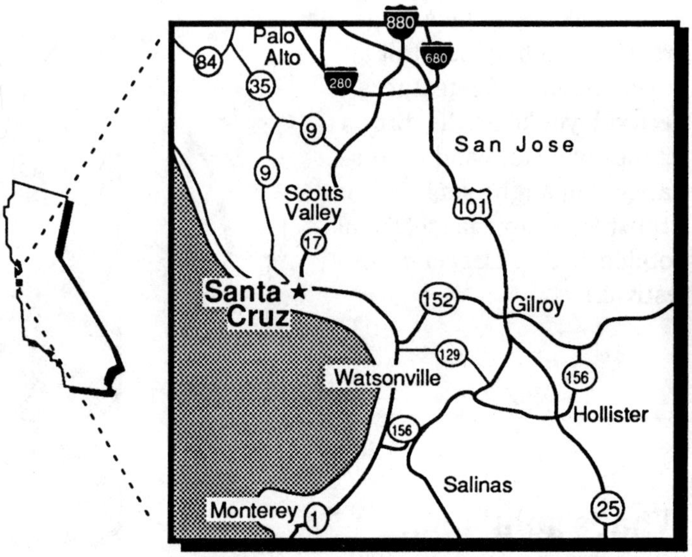


*Up-to-date festival information is available from:*
*Santa Cruz Visitors Bureau*
*(408) 425-1234*

## What's goin' on...

Town population: **235,300**
Last year's attendance: **2,800**
Average outdoor temperature: **65°**
Festival location: **Various locations in co.**

| | |
|---|---|
| X | Wine tasting/beer for sale |
| X | Food booths |
| | Arts/crafts for sale |
| X | Live music |
| | Clowns |
| | Face painters |
| | Childrens games |
| | Animal exhibits/petting zoo |
| | Dogs allowed on leash |
| X | Lost and found |
| X | Bicycle racks |
| X | First aid area available |
| X | Self-brought picnics allowed |
| | Self-brought alcohol allowed |
| | Stroller/wheelchair rentals available |

| | |
|---|---|
| X | Parade |
| X | Parking fee: meters |
| X | Entrance fee: $10 includes glass |
| X | Camping facilities: 2 miles |
| X | Boating facilities: Santa Cruz Harbor |
| X | RV facilities w/ hookups: 4 miles |
| X | Accomodations in town<br>Many B&Bs, TraveLodge Riviera, Sunset Inn, Chaminade, Best Western Torch-Lite Inn |
| X | Restaurants in town<br>Seabright Brewery, Pontiac Grill, Adolph's, Crow's Nest, Aldo's, Hindquarter, Miramar |

# *Novato Art, Wine & Music Festival*

"FOR THE TIME OF YOUR life" get your fanny on down to the **Novato Art, Wine & Music Festival!** Well, that's what they tell *us* anyway...and over 200 artists and craftspeople are counting on you too! Nestled in a valley surrounded by forested hills, this town is just south of the famous Napa valley—who sends 30 of her top wineries to complement the tasty food served. This makes for a fun weekend!

## Novato, California

Fourth weekend in June
Daily 10:00 AM - 6:00 PM

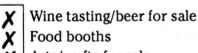

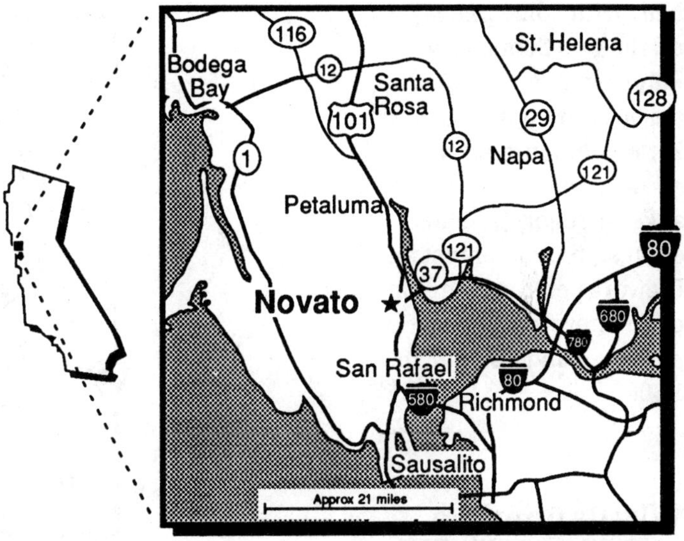


*Up-to-date festival information is available from:*
*Novato Chamber of Commerce*
*(415) 897-1164*



## What's goin' on...

Town population: **50,000**
Last year's attendance: **20,000**
Average outdoor temperature: **78°**
Festival location: **Downtown on Grant Ave.**

| | |
|---|---|
| X | Wine tasting/beer for sale |
| X | Food booths |
| X | Arts/crafts for sale |
| X | Live music |
| X | Clowns |
| X | Face painters |
| | Childrens games |
| | Animal exhibits/petting zoo |
| | Dogs allowed on leash |
| X | Lost and found |
| | Bicycle racks |
| X | First aid area available |
| | Self-brought picnics allowed |
| | Self-brought alcohol allowed |
| X | Stroller/wheelchair rentals available |

| | |
|---|---|
| | Parade |
| | Parking fee |
| | Entrance fee |
| X | Camping facilities: 9 miles |
| X | Boating facilities: 2 miles |
| | RV facilities w/ hookups |
| X | Accomodations in town<br>Quality Inn, TraveLodge, Skylark Motel, Novato Motel |
| X | Restaurants in town<br>Hilltop Cafe, Santa Fe Mary's |

# *Rocklin Jubilee*

ROCK ON IN ROCKLIN AT the **Rocklin Jubilee**! Wake your feet up on the 5K or 10K run at 7:00 AM, then fill you belly with some pancakes hot off the Cub Scout's grill! Entertainment includes a magic show, aerobics and karate demonstrations, pet show (there's even a look-alikes category), frisbee contest, beard contest and fireworks extravaganza at dark! There's also a tri-tip barbecue and dancing till 1:30!

## Rocklin, California

Last Saturday in June
7:00 AM - 1:30 AM

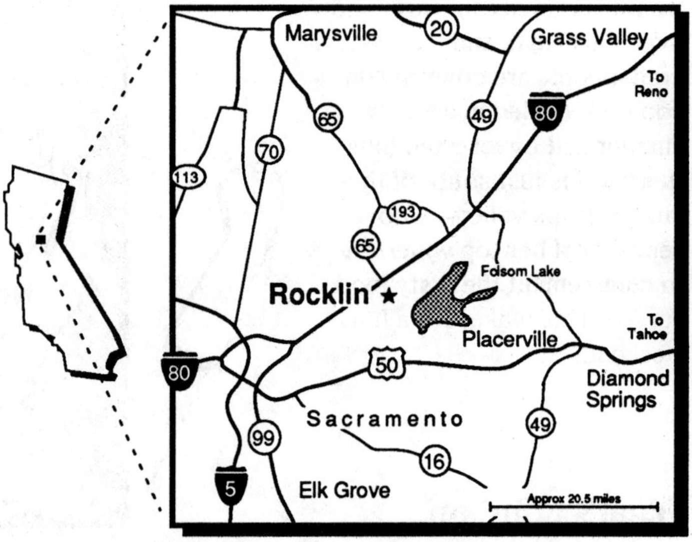


## What's goin' on...

Town population: **16,000**
Last year's attendance: **5,500**
Average outdoor temperature: **100°**
Festival location: **Johnson Springview Park**

*Up-to-date festival information is available from:*
*Rocklin Chamber of Commerce*
*(916) 624-2548*

| | |
|---|---|
| ✗ | Wine tasting/beer for sale |
| ✗ | Food booths |
| ✗ | Arts/crafts for sale |
| ✗ | Live music |
| ✗ | Clowns |
| ✗ | Face painters |
| ✗ | Childrens games |
| | Animal exhibits/petting zoo |
| ✗ | Dogs allowed on leash |
| ✗ | Lost and found |
| | Bicycle racks |
| | First aid area available |
| ✗ | Self-brought picnics allowed |
| | Self-brought alcohol allowed |
| | Stroller/wheelchair rentals available |

| | |
|---|---|
| ✗ | Parade: Sat. 10:00 AM on Pacific St. |
| | Parking fee |
| | Entrance fee |
| ✗ | Camping facilities 7 miles |
| ✗ | Boating facilities: Folsom Lake |
| ✗ | RV facilities w/ hookups: 7 miles |
| ✗ | Accomodations in town<br>First Choice Inn |
| ✗ | Restaurants in town<br>Michael's, Cattleman's, Headquarter House |

# *Saratoga Blossom Festival*

THE QUAINT AND FRIENDLY village of Saratoga pulls out all the stops for their annual **Blossom Festival**—featuring the California poppy on the commemorative wine glasses. The festival is a revival of the 1900-1940 Blossom Festival, when people came to Saratoga by train and horse and buggy. Eighteen restaurants fill the little village—five of them boast a 4-star rating!

## Saratoga, California

Last Saturday in June
11:00 AM - 5:00 PM

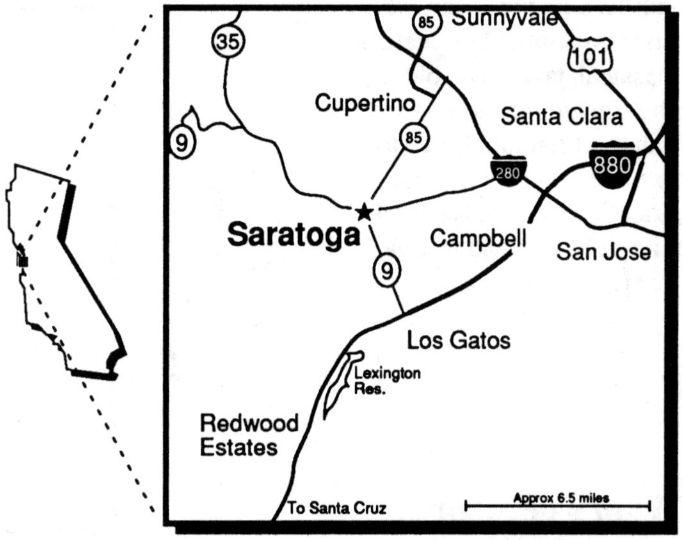


## What's goin' on...

Town population: **30,000**
Last year's attendance: **10,000**
Average outdoor temperature: **78°**
Festival location: **Big Basin Way**

*Up-to-date festival information is available from:*
*Saratoga Saratoga Village Assn.*
*(408) 867-9417*

- X Wine tasting/beer for sale
- X Food booths
- X Arts/crafts for sale
- X Live music
- Clowns
- X Face painters
- Childrens games
- X Animal exhibits/petting zoo
- Dogs allowed on leash
- X Lost and found
- X Bicycle racks
- X First aid area available
- Self-brought picnics allowed
- Self-brought alcohol allowed
- Stroller/wheelchair rentals available

- Parade
- Parking fee
- Entrance fee
- X Camping facilities: 20 miles
- Boating facilities
- X RV facilities w/ hookups: 7 miles
- X Accomodations in town
  Saratoga Motel, The Inn at Saratoga
- X Restaurants in town
  Bella Mia, La Mere Michelle, The Plumed Horse, Le Mouton Noir, The Adriatic, The Village Rendevous

# *Lake Tahoe Summer Music Festival*

THERE'S ALMOST TOO MUCH to do during the day—but save your nights for the **Lake Tahoe Summer Music Festival!** This festival runs July through September, featuring classical, jazz, rock, oldies, rhythm and blues, and jazz. Call the Chamber office for exact times, performers, prices and dates. We hope this eight-year-old festival lasts forever!

## Tahoe City, California

July through Labor Day
Evenings

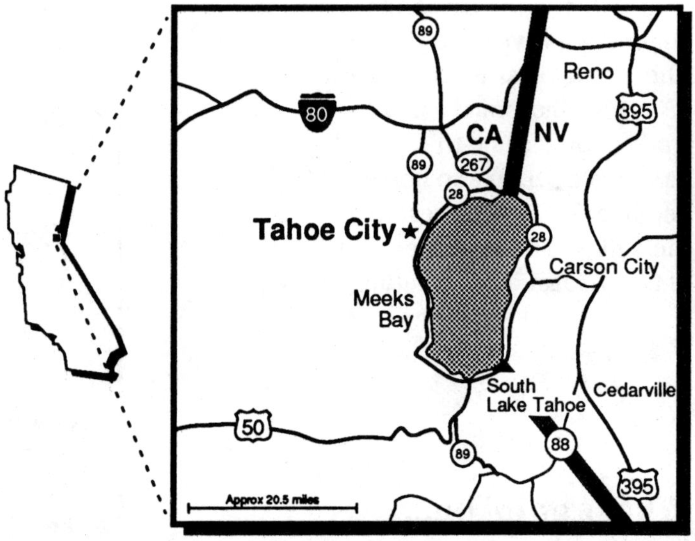


*Up-to-date festival information is available from:*
*Tahoe City Chamber of Commerce*
*(916) 583-2371*

## What's goin' on...

Town population: **11,000**
Last year's attendance: **3,000**
Average outdoor temperature: **45°**
Festival location: **Lakeside**

| | |
|---|---|
| X | Wine tasting/beer for sale |
| | Food booths |
| | Arts/crafts for sale |
| | Live music |
| | Clowns |
| | Face painters |
| | Childrens games |
| | Animal exhibits/petting zoo |
| | Dogs allowed on leash |
| X | Lost and found |
| | Bicycle racks |
| | First aid area available |
| X | Self-brought picnics allowed |
| X | Self-brought alcohol allowed |
| | Stroller/wheelchair rentals available |

| | |
|---|---|
| | Parade |
| | Parking fee |
| X | Entrance fee: prices vary |
| X | Camping facilities: 8 miles |
| X | Boating facilities: Lake Tahoe |
| X | RV facilities w/ hookups: 8 miles |
| X | Accomodations in town<br>Sunnyside Inn, Cottage Inn B&B, Mayfield House B&B |
| X | Restaurants in town<br>Sunnyside, Jake's on the Lake, Rosie's Cafe |

# *Folsom PRCA Championship Rodeo & Fourth of July Festival*

THIS POPULAR FIVE-DAY event is much more than a festival. The **Folsom PRCA Championship Rodeo & Fourth of July Festival** offers a carnival for the kids and plenty of entertainment at the rodeo! Country music will float through the air as ribs, chicken and real beef are cooked to perfection on the barbies! Take a walk on historic Sutter Street for a variety of antique stores and boutiques. (Fee for rodeo: Adults $9.50; Kids $4.50)

## Folsom, California

First Wednesday through Sunday in July

Daily: Festival & carnival all day; Rodeo 8:00 PM - 11:00 PM

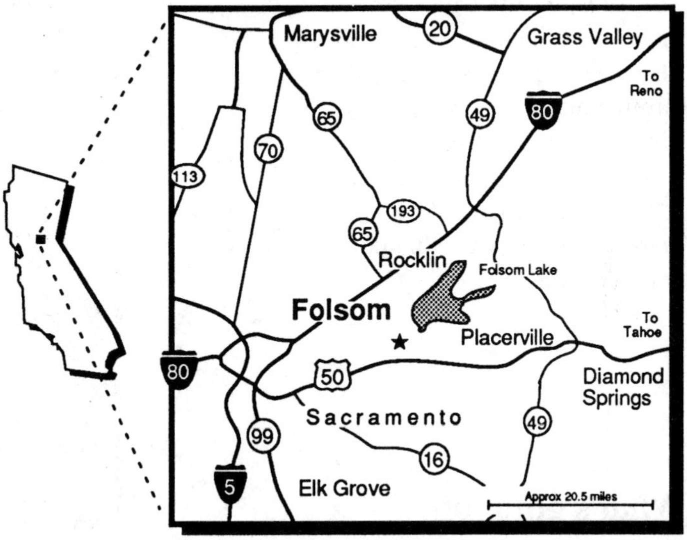


## What's goin' on...

Town population: **25,647**

Last year's attendance: **40,000**

Average outdoor temperature: **90°**

Festival location: **Folsom City Park**

*Up-to-date festival information is available from:*
*Folsom Chamber of Commerce*
*(916) 985-2698*

- X Wine tasting/beer for sale
- X Food booths
- Arts/crafts for sale
- X Live music
- X Clowns
- Face painters
- X Childrens games
- Animal exhibits/petting zoo
- Dogs allowed on leash
- X Lost and found
- X Bicycle racks
- X First aid area available
- Self-brought picnics allowed
- Self-brought alcohol allowed
- Stroller/wheelchair rentals available

- Parade
- X Parking fee: $2
- X Entrance fee: Rodeo only
- X Camping facilities: 4 miles
- X Boating facilities: Folsom Lake
- RV facilities w/ hookups
- X Accomodations in town
  Economy Inn, Sheraton, Plum Tree Inn B&B
- X Restaurants in town
  The Cliffhouse, Hacienda, Christofs, Pater Yagers, Marmalades, On The Wind Rose

# *Antioch Stars & Stripes Day*

TWENTY THOUSAND PEOPLE can't be wrong! That was the attendance record for the 1990 **Antioch Stars and Stripes Day**...and this year promises to be bigger and better than ever! Everything's happening downtown: plenty of food, arts-and-crafts booths, contests, live music, games for the kids, and a fireworks display that'll knock yer socks off!

## Antioch, California

Fourth of July
11:00 AM - 11:00 PM

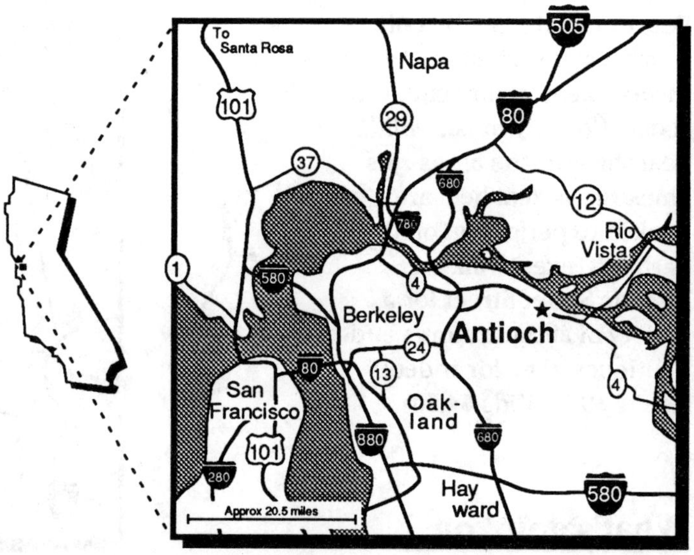


## What's goin' on...

Town population: **55,000**
Last year's attendance: **20,000**
Average outdoor temperature: **92°**
Festival location: **Downtown**

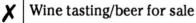

*Up-to-date festival information is available from:*
*Antioch Chamber of Commerce*
*(415) 757-1800*

| | |
|---|---|
| X | Wine tasting/beer for sale |
| X | Food booths |
| X | Arts/crafts for sale |
| X | Live music |
| X | Clowns |
| X | Face painters |
| X | Childrens games |
| | Animal exhibits/petting zoo |
| X | Dogs allowed on leash |
| X | Lost and found |
| | Bicycle racks |
| X | First aid area available |
| X | Self-brought picnics allowed |
| | Self-brought alcohol allowed |
| | Stroller/wheelchair rentals available |

| | |
|---|---|
| | Parade |
| | Parking fee |
| | Entrance fee |
| X | Camping facilities: 5 miles |
| X | Boating facilities: The Delta |
| X | RV facilities w/ hookups: 5 miles |
| X | Accomodations in town<br>All Seasons Inn, Hillcrest Motel, Best Western Heritage Inn |
| X | Restaurants in town<br>Rudy's Restaurant, Scula Pasta, The New Mecca |

# *Fourth of July Festival*

SNUGGLED UP TO THE north side of Mt. Diablo is the cozy town of Clayton, with a bang-up annual **Fourth of July Festival**. Clayton celebrates our nation's birthday in regal style, starting with a flapjack breakfast served at 8:00 a.m. Then take your place on Main Street's sidewalk for the parade. After that the craft and art booths will be beckoning you! These folks really roll out the red carpet!

## Clayton, California

Fourth of July
8:00 AM - 9:00 PM

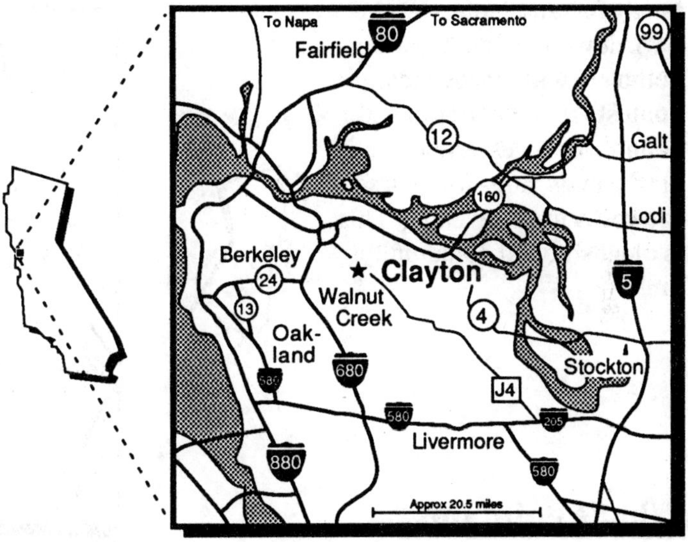


*Up-to-date festival information is available from:*
*Clayton Chamber of Commerce*
*(415) 672-3622*

## What's goin' on...

Town population: **7,200**
Last year's attendance: **4,000**
Average outdoor temperature: **90°**
Festival location: **Downtown**

| | |
|---|---|
| X | Wine tasting/beer for sale |
| X | Food booths |
| X | Arts/crafts for sale |
| X | Live music |
| X | Clowns |
| X | Face painters |
| X | Childrens games |
| | Animal exhibits/petting zoo |
| X | Dogs allowed on leash |
| X | Lost and found |
| | Bicycle racks |
| X | First aid area available |
| X | Self-brought picnics allowed |
| X | Self-brought alcohol allowed |
| | Stroller/wheelchair rentals available |

| | |
|---|---|
| X | Parade 10:00 AM on Main St. |
| | Parking fee |
| | Entrance fee |
| X | Camping facilities: 8 miles |
| X | Boating facilities: The Delta |
| | RV facilities w/ hookups |
| | Accomodations in town |
| X | Restaurants in town<br>Black Diamond, La Cocotte |

# *Fourth of July— Family Fun in the Park*

WE PROMISE YOU A "BANG-up" time at the **Family Fun in the Park** celebration on the Fourth of July! Join in the family fun and fanfare at the park downtown all day long—complete with barbecues, contests and competitions, country-and-western music, kids' games, and—of course—fireworks in the evening! This is old-fashioned community fun!

## Exeter, California

Fourth of July
10:00 AM - 4:00 PM

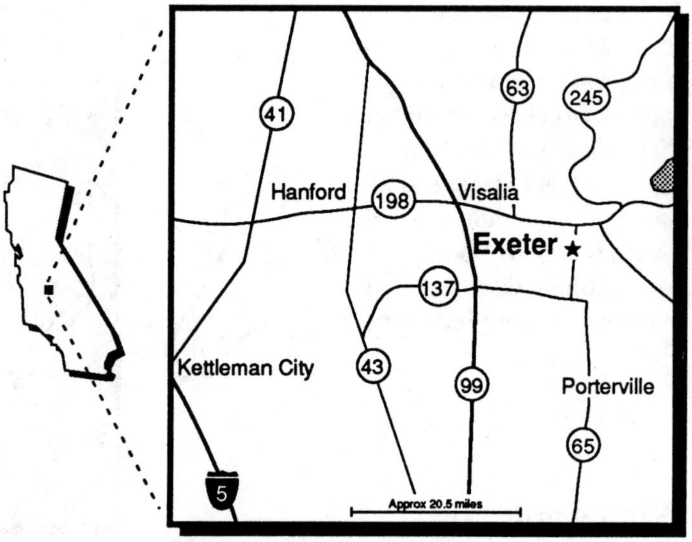


## What's goin' on...

Town population: **7,491**
Last year's attendance: **N/A**
Average outdoor temperature: **100°**
Festival location: **Park**

*Up-to-date festival information is available from:*
*Exeter Chamber of Commerce*
*(209) 592-2919*

| | |
|---|---|
| X | Wine tasting/beer for sale |
| X | Food booths |
| X | Arts/crafts for sale |
| X | Live music |
| | Clowns |
| X | Face painters |
| X | Childrens games |
| | Animal exhibits/petting zoo |
| | Dogs allowed on leash |
| | Lost and found |
| | Bicycle racks |
| X | First aid area available |
| | Self-brought picnics allowed |
| | Self-brought alcohol allowed |
| | Stroller/wheelchair rentals available |

| | |
|---|---|
| | Parade |
| | Parking fee |
| | Entrance fee |
| X | Camping facilities: 10 miles |
| X | Boating facilities: Lake Kaweah |
| X | RV facilities w/ hookups: 6 miles |
| X | Accomodations in town<br>Kaweah Motel |
| X | Restaurants in town |

# *Ol' Fashioned Fourth of July*

YOU'RE INVITED TO SPEND an **Ol' Fashioned Fourth of July** in Half Moon Bay. A parade, fireworks at El Granada Beach at dark, entertainment at the Community/Senior Center, and food and crafts booths are all part of the day's celebration. This area offers numerous activities for the whole family—such as camping at the beautiful Half Moon Bay State Beach and stables for horseback riding (yes...on the beach...and it's a gas!).

## Half Moon Bay, California

Fourth of July
Noon - 6:00 PM

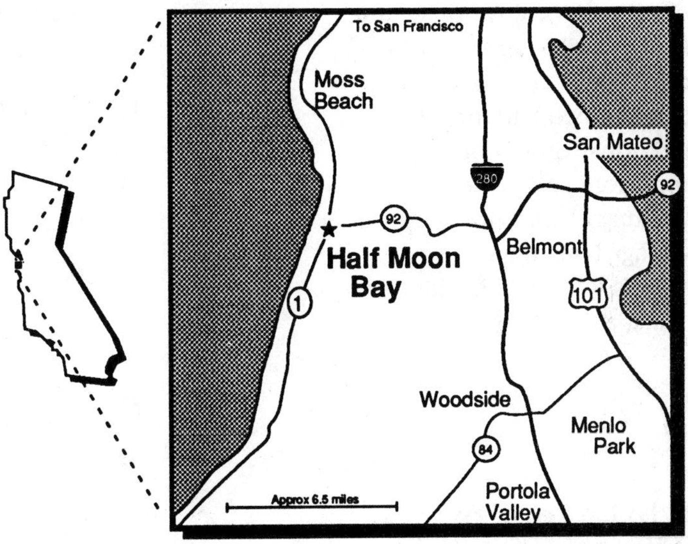


*Up-to-date festival information is available from:*
*Half Moon Bay Chamber of Commerce*
*(415) 726-5202*

## What's goin' on...

Town population: **7,282**
Last year's attendance: **N/A**
Average outdoor temperature: **70°**
Festival location: **El Granada Beach**

| | |
|---|---|
| | Wine tasting/beer for sale |
| | Food booths |
| X | Arts/crafts for sale |
| X | Live music |
| | Clowns |
| | Face painters |
| | Childrens games |
| | Animal exhibits/petting zoo |
| | Dogs allowed on leash |
| X | Lost and found |
| | Bicycle racks |
| X | First aid area available |
| X | Self-brought picnics allowed |
| | Self-brought alcohol allowed |
| | Stroller/wheelchair rentals available |

| | |
|---|---|
| X | Parade: Wed. noon on Main St. |
| | Parking fee |
| | Entrance fee |
| X | Camping facilities: 1 mile |
| X | Boating facilities: Half Moon Bay |
| X | RV facilities w/ hookups: 1 mile |
| X | Accomodations in town<br>Harbor View Inn, The Mill Rose Inn, Julie's B&B |
| X | Restaurants in town<br>Main Street Grill, Pasta Moon, Old Princeton Landing |

# *Valley Heritage Day*

HAVE YOU EVER BEEN TO A "pink bean" cook-off? Well, then **Valley Heritage Day** is a must! In addition to the cook-off, you can enjoy homemade sausage, ribs, and lots of other barbecued taste treats! San Lorenzo Park boasts a historical agriculture museum, old school house, working blacksmith shop, and vintage train depot—so there's lots to do besides eat, drink, and be merry!

## King City, California

Fourth of July
8:00 AM - 6:00 PM

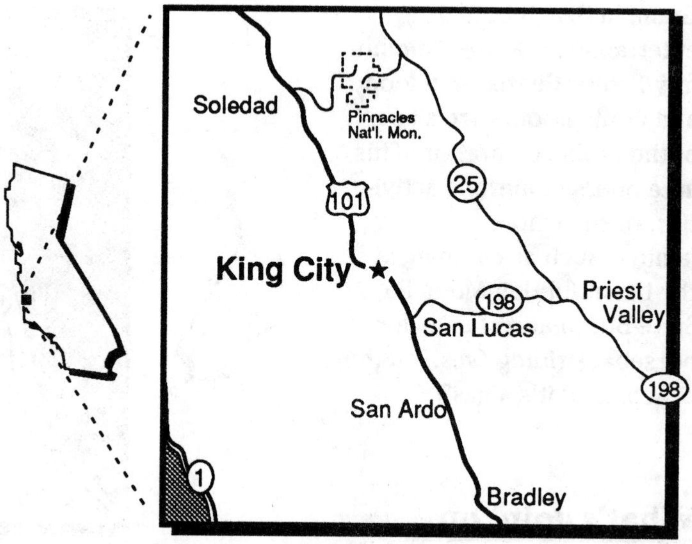


## What's goin' on...

Town population: **7,800**
Last year's attendance: **5,000**
Average outdoor temperature: **85°**
Festival location: **San Lorenzo Park**

*Up-to-date festival information is available from:*
*King City Chamber of Commerce*
*(408) 385-3814*

| | |
|---|---|
| ✗ | Wine tasting/beer for sale |
| ✗ | Food booths |
| ✗ | Arts/crafts for sale |
| ✗ | Live music |
| | Clowns |
| ✗ | Face painters |
| ✗ | Childrens games |
| | Animal exhibits/petting zoo |
| | Dogs allowed on leash |
| ✗ | Lost and found |
| | Bicycle racks |
| ✗ | First aid area available |
| ✗ | Self-brought picnics allowed |
| | Self-brought alcohol allowed |
| | Stroller/wheelchair rentals available |

| | |
|---|---|
| ✗ | Parade: On the 4th 10:00 AM downtown |
| ✗ | Parking fee: $3 |
| | Entrance fee |
| ✗ | Camping facilities: On site |
| ✗ | Boating facilities: Lake and river |
| ✗ | RV facilities w/ hookups: On-site |
| ✗ | Accomodations in town<br>Best Western, Keefer's, Silver Saddle, Sage Motel, Palm Motel, Crown DD Lodge |
| ✗ | Restaurants in town<br>Guadalajara, El Zarape, Keefer's, City Cafe, China King, El Lugarcito |

# *Old Fashioned Fourth of July*

LOTS OF OLD FASHIONED fun can be found just south of downtown Livermore at the annual **Old Fashioned Fourth of July** get together. The music begins at noon—'bout the same time the barbecues are j-u-u-u-st right for a burger or a dog. Or if it's homemade strawberry shortcake you crave, well this is the place to be!

## Livermore, California

Fourth of July
Noon - 10:00 PM

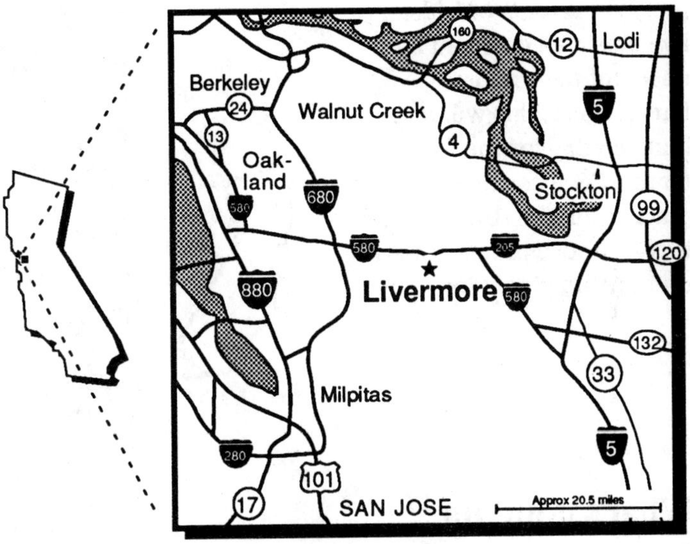


## What's goin' on...

Town population: **56,445**
Last year's attendance: **8,000**
Average outdoor temperature: **80°**
Festival location: **Gardella Gardens**

*Up-to-date festival information is available from:*
*Livermore Chamber of Commerce*
*(415) 447-1606*

| | |
|---|---|
| X | Wine tasting/beer for sale |
| X | Food booths |
| | Arts/crafts for sale |
| X | Live music |
| X | Clowns |
| | Face painters |
| X | Childrens games |
| | Animal exhibits/petting zoo |
| X | Dogs allowed on leash |
| X | Lost and found |
| X | Bicycle racks |
| X | First aid area available |
| X | Self-brought picnics allowed |
| | Self-brought alcohol allowed |
| | Stroller/wheelchair rentals available |

| | |
|---|---|
| | Parade |
| | Parking fee |
| X | Entrance fee: S & K 50¢; A $2 |
| X | Camping facilities: 11 miles |
| X | Boating facilities: Del Valle Res. |
| X | RV facilities w/ hookups: 11 miles |
| X | Accomodations in town<br>Townhouse Motel, Residence Inn, Holiday Inn |
| X | Restaurants in town<br>El Lorito, Le Coquelicot, Cruiser's, Beeb's Bar & Grill, Wente Sparkling Cellars Restaurant |

CENTRAL

# *Fourth of July Fiesta*

YOU'LL FIND ACTION IN Frontierland Park at the **Fourth of July Fiesta** in this coastal town. Complete with pony rides for the kiddies, live music all day, and barbecued hot dogs and hamburgers, this will be a bang-up day for the whole family. Pacifica can be a foggy place in July, so bring a jacket if you choose to take a walk on the Municipal Pier.

## Pacifica, California

Fourth of July
11:00 AM - 5:00 PM

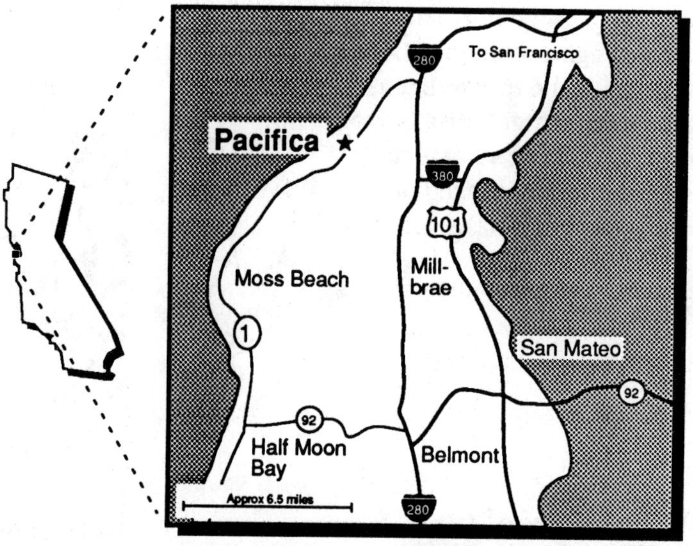


*Up-to-date festival information is available from:*
*Pacifica Chamber of Commerce*
*(415) 355-4122*

## What's goin' on...

Town population: **40,000**
Last year's attendance: **N/a**
Average outdoor temperature: **65°**
Festival location: **Frontierland Park**

- ✗ Wine tasting/beer for sale
- ✗ Food booths
- ✗ Arts/crafts for sale
- Live music
- ✗ Clowns
- ✗ Face painters
- ✗ Childrens games
- Animal exhibits/petting zoo
- ✗ Dogs allowed on leash
- ✗ Lost and found
- ✗ Bicycle racks
- ✗ First aid area available
- ✗ Self-brought picnics allowed
- Self-brought alcohol allowed
- Stroller/wheelchair rentals available

- Parade
- Parking fee
- Entrance fee
- ✗ Camping facilities: 15 miles
- ✗ Boating facilities: Half Moon Bay
- ✗ RV facilities w/ hookups: 1 mile
- ✗ Accomodations in town
  Nick's Sea Breeze Motel, Lighthouse Hotel, Pacifica Motor Inn, Sea View Motor Lodge
- ✗ Restaurants in town
  Moonraker, Nick's, Sharp Park Restaurant, Balistreri's

# *Tapestry in Talent*

"DO YOU KNOW THE WAY to San Jose.?.." We sure hope so, because that's where you'll find the **Tapestry in Talent** festival of the arts. Historically the oldest city in California, this town of many cultures offers a festival with a huge spectrum of arts and crafts...and incredible food booths as well! Besides the festival, take a tour through the Rosicrucian Museum and notorious Winchester Mystery House.

## San Jose, California

Weekend closest to the Fourth of July
Daily 10:00 AM - 6:00 PM

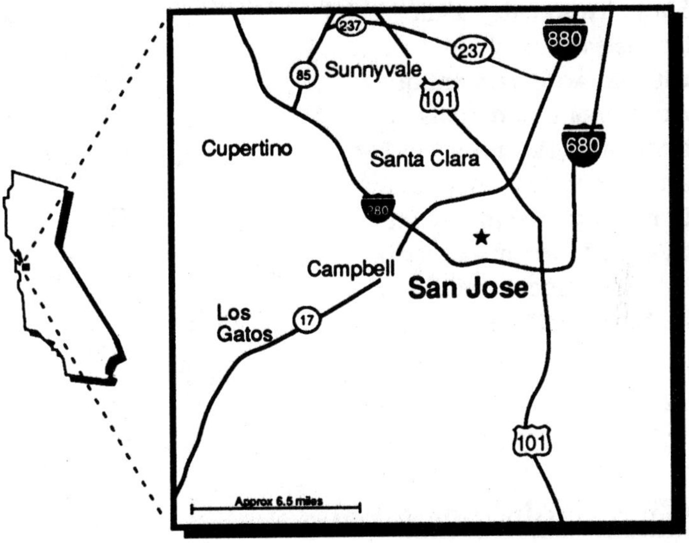


*Up-to-date festival information is available from:*
*San Jose Tapestry in Talent*
*(408) 293-9727*

## What's goin' on...

Town population: **650,000**
Last year's attendance: **100,000**
Average outdoor temperature: **90°**
Festival location: **Downtown**

| | |
|---|---|
| X | Wine tasting/beer for sale |
| X | Food booths |
| X | Arts/crafts for sale |
| X | Live music |
| X | Clowns |
| X | Face painters |
| X | Childrens games |
| X | Animal exhibits/petting zoo |
| | Dogs allowed on leash |
| X | Lost and found |
| X | Bicycle racks |
| X | First aid area available |
| | Self-brought picnics allowed |
| | Self-brought alcohol allowed |
| | Stroller/wheelchair rentals available |

| | |
|---|---|
| | Parade |
| | Parking fee |
| | Entrance fee |
| X | Camping facilities: 35 miles |
| | Boating facilities |
| X | RV facilities w/ hookups: 2 miles |
| X | Accomodations in town<br>Red Lion, The Briar Rose B&B |
| X | Restaurants in town<br>D.B. Cooper's, Paolo's, Original Joe's, Gordon Biersch Gardens |

C
E
N
T
R
A
L

# *Oakdale Antique & Craft Show*

JUST INSIDE THE STANISLAUS County line is the charming town of Oakdale—host to the **Oakdale Antique & Craft Show**. This all-day affair begins early at Wood Park with extraordinary antiques and one-of-a-kind crafts in addition to the more familiar arts and crafts available. Don't forget to stop by the Oakdale Museum and the Hershey Chocolate Factory for their terrific tours!

## Oakdale, California

Weekend following the Fourth of July
6:00 AM - 5:00 PM

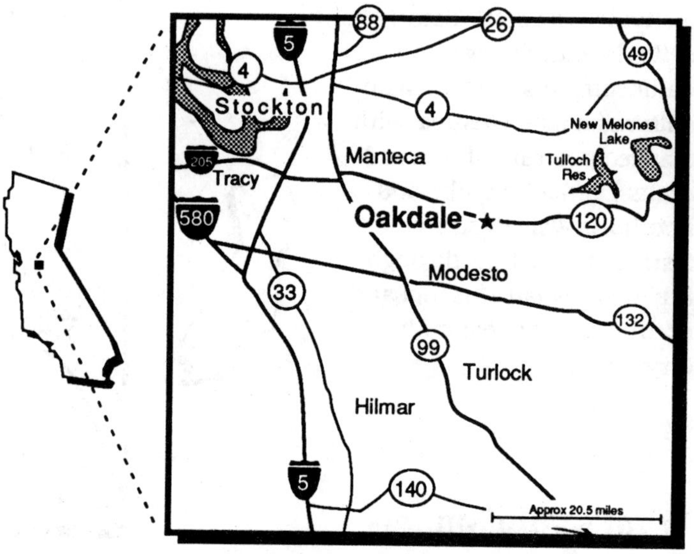


## What's goin' on...

Town population: **11,600**
Last year's attendance: **6,000**
Average outdoor temperature: **90°**
Festival location: **Wood Park**

*Up-to-date festival information is available from:*
*Oakdale Chamber of Commerce*
*(209) 847-2244*

| | |
|---|---|
| ✗ | Wine tasting/beer for sale |
| ✗ | Food booths |
| ✗ | Arts/crafts for sale |
| ✗ | Live music |
| | Clowns |
| | Face painters |
| | Childrens games |
| ✗ | Animal exhibits/petting zoo |
| | Dogs allowed on leash |
| ✗ | Lost and found |
| | Bicycle racks |
| | First aid area available |
| | Self-brought picnics allowed |
| | Self-brought alcohol allowed |
| | Stroller/wheelchair rentals available |

| | |
|---|---|
| | Parade |
| | Parking fee |
| | Entrance fee |
| ✗ | Camping facilities, 6 miles |
| ✗ | Boating facilities: Oakdale Lake |
| ✗ | RV facilities w/ hookups: 6 miles |
| ✗ | Accomodations in town<br>Ramada Inn, Holiday Motel, Oakdale Motel |
| ✗ | Restaurants in town<br>Nutcracker, Betty-Dee's, Sonia's Mexican |

# *Fairfield Kite Festival*

LOOK UP IN THE SKY...IT looks like there are huge dots of confetti suspended in mid-air! This **Fairfield Kite Festival** is a blast! Kids love it. Dads love it. Everybody loves kite-flying. Bring your own kite for some expert advice on the techniques of the sport, or just come down for the afternoon—there's *plenty* to watch!

## Fairfield, California

Second weekend in July
All day

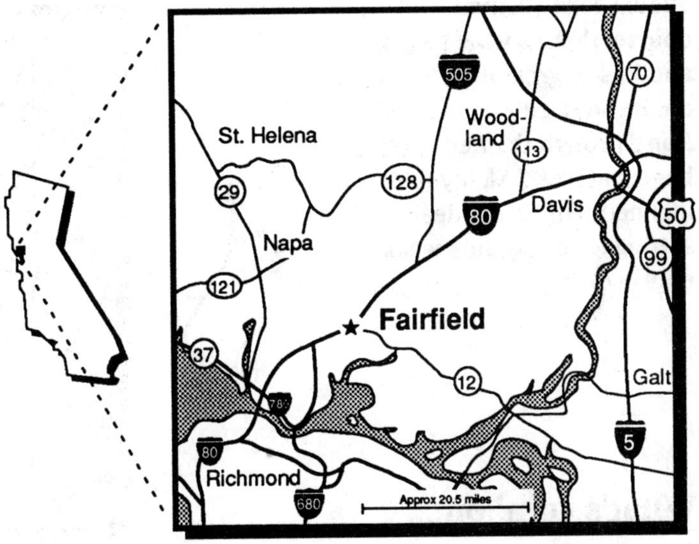


## What's goin' on...

Town population: **59,000**
Last year's attendance: **N/A**
Average outdoor temperature: **80°**
Festival location: **Solano College**

*Up-to-date festival information is available from:*
*Fairfield Chamber of Commerce*
*(707) 425-4625*

| | |
|---|---|
| X | Wine tasting/beer for sale |
| X | Food booths |
| X | Arts/crafts for sale |
| X | Live music |
| | Clowns |
| | Face painters |
| X | Childrens games |
| | Animal exhibits/petting zoo |
| | Dogs allowed on leash |
| | Lost and found |
| | Bicycle racks |
| | First aid area available |
| X | Self-brought picnics allowed |
| | Self-brought alcohol allowed |
| | Stroller/wheelchair rentals available |

| | |
|---|---|
| | Parade |
| | Parking fee |
| | Entrance fee |
| X | Camping facilities: 10 miles |
| X | Boating facilities: Lake Berryessa |
| X | RV facilities w/ hookups: 10 miles |
| X | Accomodations in town |
| X | Restaurants in town<br>Wild Willey's I-Scream & Samwiches, Gordito's, The Nut Tree, Chauncey's |

CENTRAL

# *Jazz Festival*

JUST 15 MINUTES FROM Santa Cruz, nestled upon a sunlit knoll, the historic Hallcrest Vineyards holds its annual **Jazz Festival.** Of course, there's wine tasting and lots of great food to snack on! Be advised that the 10K Run Through the Redwoods begins at 9:00 AM, if you're so inclined! This is an ideal setting for a lazy July weekend!

## Felton, California

Second weekend in July
Daily 11:00 AM - 5:30 PM

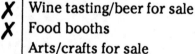

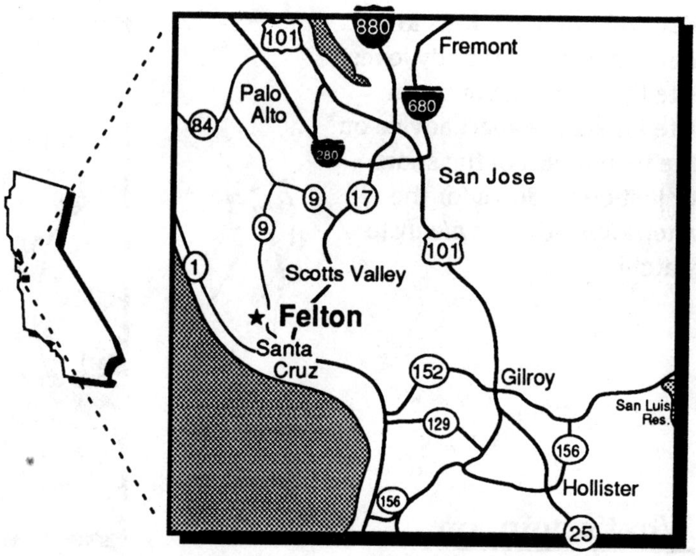


## What's goin' on...

Town population: **4,000**
Last year's attendance: **1,000**
Average outdoor temperature: **75°**
Festival location: **Hallcrest Winery**

*Up-to-date festival information is available from:*
*Felton Chamber of Commerce*
*(408) 335-4441*

| | |
|---|---|
| X | Wine tasting/beer for sale |
| X | Food booths |
| | Arts/crafts for sale |
| X | Live music |
| | Clowns |
| | Face painters |
| | Childrens games |
| | Animal exhibits/petting zoo |
| | Dogs allowed on leash |
| X | Lost and found |
| | Bicycle racks |
| | First aid area available |
| X | Self-brought picnics allowed |
| | Self-brought alcohol allowed |
| | Stroller/wheelchair rentals available |

| | |
|---|---|
| | Parade |
| | Parking fee |
| | Entrance fee: $6; Under 21 free |
| X | Camping facilities: 5 miles |
| X | Boating facilities: Santa Cruz Harbor |
| X | RV facilities w/ hookups: 5 miles |
| X | Accomodations in town<br>Fairview Manor B&B |
| X | Restaurants in town<br>Mama Mia, Tampico, Whistle Inn |

# *Arts & Wine Festival*

THE STATELY COMMUNITY of Los Altos annually holds an **Arts & Wine Festival** that's a cut above the rest! The tree-lined Main and State Streets are turned into one gigantic art gallery, featuring outstanding, well-known artists and photographers. The local restaurants are cooking up some hearty dishes and a few California wineries are on hand to indulge you while jazz drifts through the warm summer air.

## Los Altos, California

Second weekend in July
Daily 10:00 AM - 5:00 PM

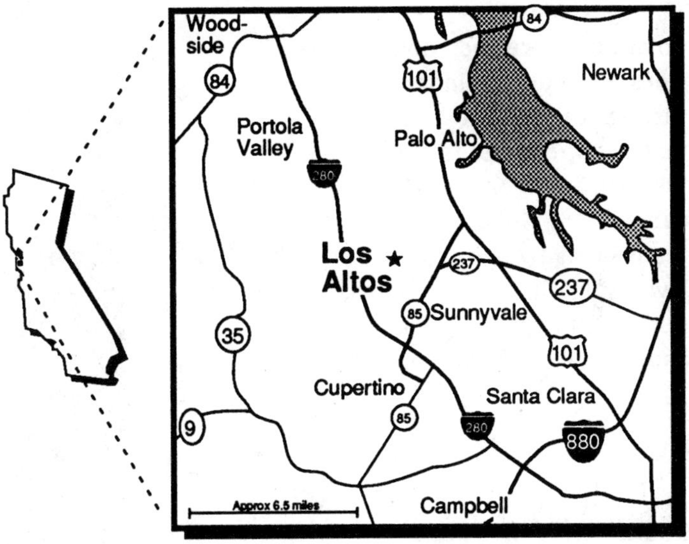


*Up-to-date festival information is available from:*
*Los Altos Chamber of Commerce*
*(415) 948-1455*

## What's goin' on...

Town population: **27,583**
Last year's attendance: **N/A**
Average outdoor temperature: **85°**
Festival location: **Main & State Streets**

| | |
|---|---|
| X | Wine tasting/beer for sale |
| X | Food booths |
| X | Arts/crafts for sale |
| X | Live music |
| | Clowns |
| X | Face painters |
| | Childrens games |
| | Animal exhibits/petting zoo |
| X | Dogs allowed on leash |
| X | Lost and found |
| X | Bicycle racks |
| X | First aid area available |
| X | Self-brought picnics allowed |
| | Self-brought alcohol allowed |
| | Stroller/wheelchair rentals available |

| | |
|---|---|
| | Parade |
| | Parking fee |
| | Entrance fee |
| X | Camping facilities: 20 miles |
| | Boating facilities |
| X | RV facilities w/ hookups: 10 miles |
| | Accomodations in town |
| X | Restaurants in town<br>Mac's Tea Room, Arno's, Black Forest Inn |

C
E
N
T
R
A
L

# *Sonoma Summer Arts & Crafts Faire*

THIS TWO-DAY CELEBRATION is a cut above the rest! Well, actually...*Somona County* is a cut above the rest! There's so much to see and do around here...bal loon rides, museums, wander through the redwoods, wine taste, shop, or attend the **Sonoma Summer Arts & Crafts Faire**! Great food and really great art abounds—jewelry, leatherwork, clothes, pottery, and glass works. Simply put...*delightful!*

## Santa Rosa, California

Second weekend in July
Daily 10:00 AM - 5:00 PM

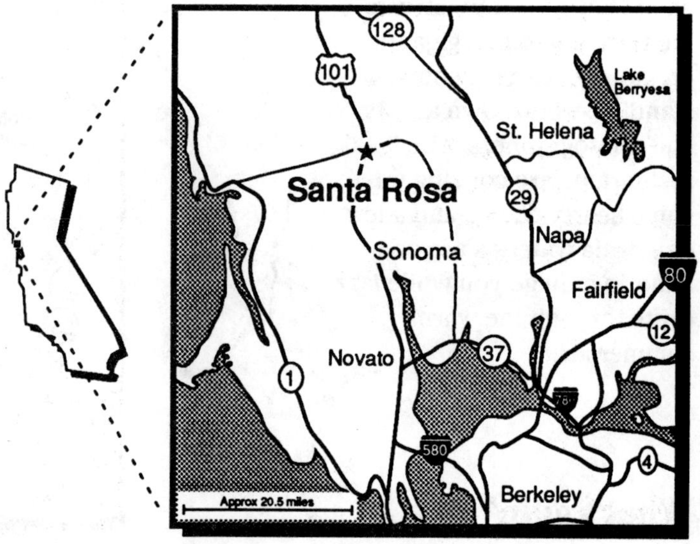


## What's goin' on...

Town population: **100,000**
Last year's attendance: **4,000**
Average outdoor temperature: **85°**
Festival location: **Field off Hwy. 101**

*Up-to-date festival information is available from:*
*Santa Rosa Visitors Bureau*
*(707) 575-1191*

- Wine tasting/beer for sale
- X Food booths
- X Arts/crafts for sale
- X Live music
- X Clowns
- X Face painters
- X Childrens games
- Animal exhibits/petting zoo
- X Dogs allowed on leash
- X Lost and found
- X Bicycle racks
- First aid area available
- X Self-brought picnics allowed
- Self-brought alcohol allowed
- Stroller/wheelchair rentals available

- Parade
- Parking fee
- Entrance fee
- X Camping facilities, 10 miles
- X Boating facilities: Russian River
- X RV facilities w/ hookups: 10 miles
- X Accomodations in town: Red Lion, Doubletree, El Rancho
- X Restaurants in town: John Ash

# *Christmas in July Benefit Jazz Festival*

YOU CAN COUNT ON BIG fun in the little towns of Amador County—and Sutter Creek is no exception when it introduces it's **Christmas in July Benefit Jazz Festival**. In its eleventh year, this all-day festival has the reputation for bringing in top jazz bands from all over California. Enjoy the wine tasting and lunch available, or bring you own!

## Sutter Creek, California

Second Saturday in July
10:00 AM - 6:00 PM

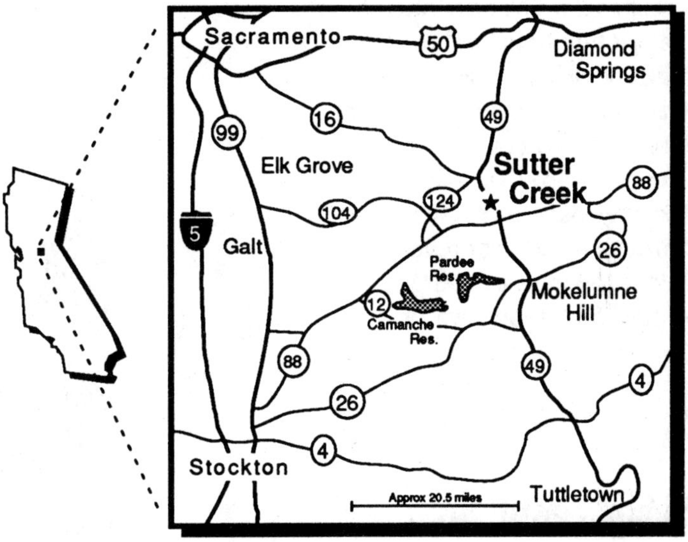


*Up-to-date festival information is available from:*
*Sutter Creek Chamber of Commerce*
*(209) 223-0350*

## What's goin' on...

Town population: **2,000**
Last year's attendance: **N/A**
Average outdoor temperature: **85°**
Festival location: **Park**

- X Wine tasting/beer for sale
- X Food booths
- Arts/crafts for sale
- Live music
- Clowns
- Face painters
- Childrens games
- Animal exhibits/petting zoo
- Dogs allowed on leash
- Lost and found
- Bicycle racks
- X First aid area available
- X Self-brought picnics allowed
- X Self-brought alcohol allowed
- Stroller/wheelchair rentals available

- Parade
- Parking fee
- X Entrance fee: $7.50
- X Camping facilities: 10 miles
- X Boating facilities: Pardee Res.
- X RV facilities w/ hookups: 10 miles
- X Accomodations in town
  Sutter Creek Inn B&B, The Hanford House B&B, The Foxes in Sutter Creek B&B
- X Restaurants in town

C E N T R A L

# *Sonoma Valley Wine Festival & Liberty 100K Bicycle Race*

START OFF A WARM JULY day with a brish 100K bike race, and then enjoy wine tasting in the afternoon while you mingle. The **Sonoma Valley Wine Festival & Liberty 100K Bicycle Race** features good eats, fine wines, wonderful jazz music, and bicycle shorts! Weeeee! Eldridge lies just north of Sonoma—offering great hiking, biking, shopping, dining, and people-watching!

**Sonoma, California**
Second Sunday in July
7:00 AM - 6:00 PM

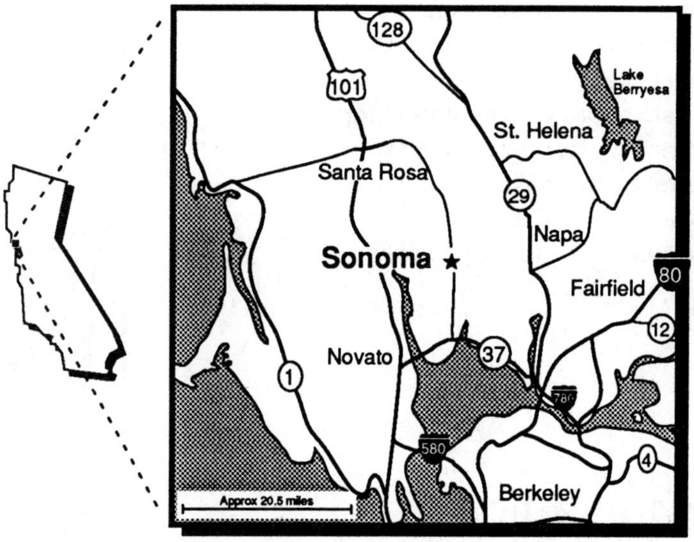


## What's goin' on...

Town population: **10,000**
Last year's attendance: **2,800**
Average outdoor temperature: **85°**
Festival location: **Sonoma Development Ctr.**

*Up-to-date festival information is available from:*
*Sonoma Chamber of Commerce*
*(707) 996-1033*

| | |
|---|---|
| X | Wine tasting/beer for sale |
| X | Food booths |
| X | Arts/crafts for sale |
| X | Live music |
| X | Clowns |
| X | Face painters |
| | Childrens games |
| | Animal exhibits/petting zoo |
| X | Dogs allowed on leash |
| X | Lost and found |
| | Bicycle racks |
| X | First aid area available |
| X | Self-brought picnics allowed |
| | Self-brought alcohol allowed |
| | Stroller/wheelchair rentals available |

| | |
|---|---|
| | Parade |
| | Parking fee |
| X | Entrance fee: S $5; A $10; K free |
| X | Camping facilities: 5 miles |
| X | Boating facilities: Lake Sonoma |
| X | RV facilities w/ hookups: In town |
| X | Accomodations in town: London Lodge, Sonoma Valley Inn, Sonoma Mission Inn |
| X | Restaurants in town |

# *Cabrillo Music Festival*

THE **CABRILLO MUSIC Festival** is a favorite among Santa Cruz County locals—and has been for 28 years now! Featuring top-name classical and modern artists, this festival's hours and locations vary from day to day (call Chamber for dates, times, and prices). While in town, enjoy the Santa Cruz Boardwalk—survivor of the 1989 earthquake.

## Aptos, California

Third Thursday through the fourth Sunday in July
Hours vary depending on location

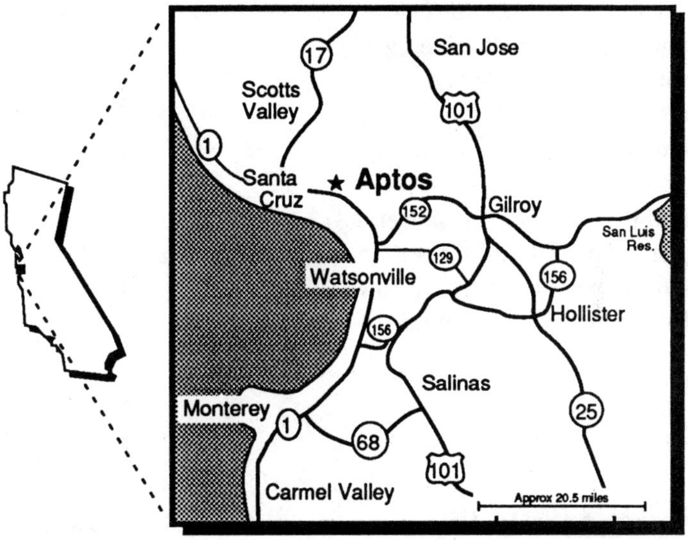


## What's goin' on...

Town population: **55,000**
Last year's attendance: **6,000**
Average outdoor temperature: **75°**
Festival location: **Various**

*Up-to-date festival information is available from:*
*Aptos Chamber of Commerce*
*(408) 688-1467*

| | |
|---|---|
| | Wine tasting/beer for sale |
| | Food booths |
| | Arts/crafts for sale |
| X | Live music |
| | Clowns |
| | Face painters |
| | Childrens games |
| | Animal exhibits/petting zoo |
| | Dogs allowed on leash |
| | Lost and found |
| X | Bicycle racks |
| | First aid area available |
| X | Self-brought picnics allowed |
| | Self-brought alcohol allowed |
| | Stroller/wheelchair rentals available |

| | |
|---|---|
| | Parade |
| | Parking fee |
| X | Entrance fee: $3-19 |
| X | Camping facilities: In town |
| X | Boating facilities: Santa Cruz Harbor |
| X | RV facilities w/ hookups: In town |
| X | Accomodations in town<br>Apple Lane Inn B&B, Mangels House B&B |
| X | Restaurants in town<br>Manuel's, Aptos Gayle's, Shadowbrook |

# *Eastern Sierra Tri-County Fair*

BOATING, FISHING, MOUNTAIN climbing, hiking, and the **Eastern Sierra Tri-County Fair**...what more could you ask for in outdoor fun? How about really great mixed grill? And country- and-western music so you can dance your fanny off? Or art exhibits by pros such as Richard Coons and Russ Marwin? Children's games? You'll find all of that and lots more! Come on down for some real country fun!

## Bishop, California

Third weekend in July (beginning Thursday)
Daily noon - midnight

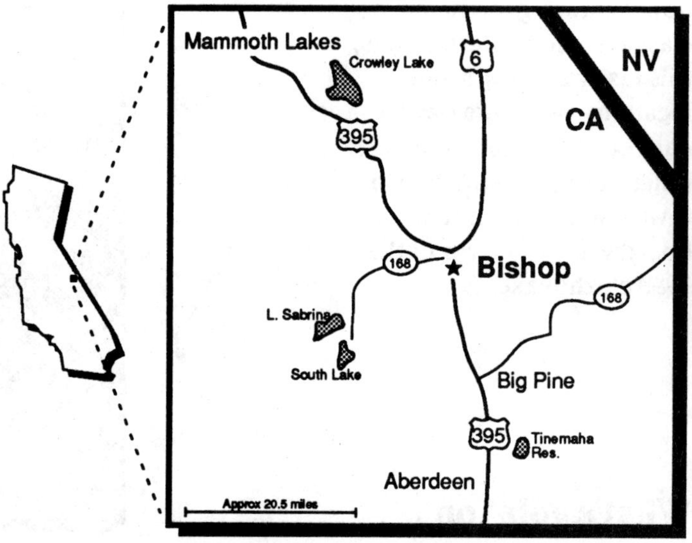


## What's goin' on...

Town population: **8,000**
Last year's attendance: **25,000**
Average outdoor temperature: **95°**
Festival location: **Fairgrounds**

*Up-to-date festival information is available from:*
*Bishop Chamber of Commerce*
*(619) 873-8405*

- X Wine tasting/beer for sale
- X Food booths
- X Arts/crafts for sale
- X Live music
- X Clowns
- X Face painters
- X Childrens games
- X Animal exhibits/petting zoo
- Dogs allowed on leash
- X Lost and found
- X Bicycle racks
- X First aid area available
- Self-brought picnics allowed
- Self-brought alcohol allowed
- Stroller/wheelchair rentals available

- X Parade: Sat. 10:00 AM on Home St.
- Parking fee
- Entrance fee
- X Camping facilities: On-site
- X Boating facilities: Lake Sabrina
- X RV facilities w/ hookups: On-site
- X Accomodations in town
  Matlick House, Chalfant House
- X Restaurants in town
  Whiskey Creek, Firehouse Grill, BBQ Bills, Jack's Waffle Shop, Bishop Grill

# *A Connoisseur's Market Place*

MENLO PARK CALLS IT A **Connoisseur's Market Place**...but we just call it outrageous! What a way to sample fine international cuisine from 25 of the Peninsula's restaurants—delicacies such as blue-corn quesadillas, stuffed mushrooms, Hawaiian shaved ice, strawberry tarts, and gobs more! Learn to cook with the Bay Area's great chefs and shop till you drop at more than 200 arts-and-crafts booths!

## Menlo Park, California

Third weekend in July
Daily 10:00 AM - 6:00 PM

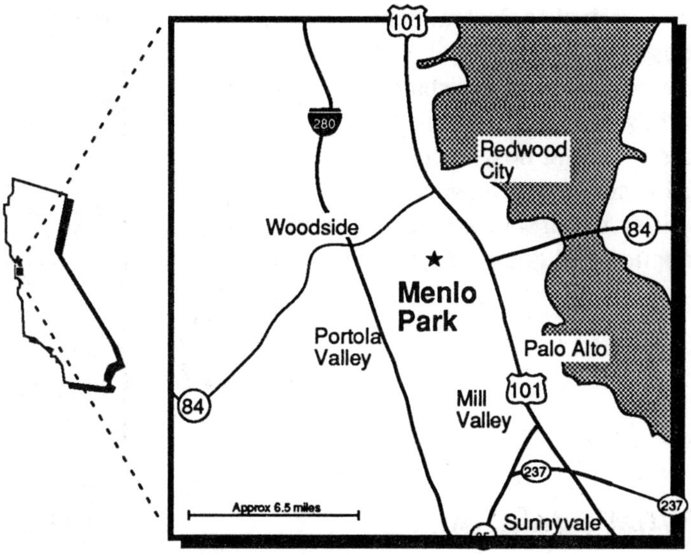


*Up-to-date festival information is available from:*
*Menlo Park Chamber of Commerce*
*(415) 325-2818*

## What's goin' on...

Town population: **26,580**
Last year's attendance: **21,000**
Average outdoor temperature: **78°**
Festival location: **Downtown**

| | |
|---|---|
| X | Wine tasting/beer for sale |
| X | Food booths |
| X | Arts/crafts for sale |
| X | Live music |
| X | Clowns |
| X | Face painters |
| X | Childrens games |
| | Animal exhibits/petting zoo |
| | Dogs allowed on leash |
| X | Lost and found |
| X | Bicycle racks |
| X | First aid area available |
| | Self-brought picnics allowed |
| | Self-brought alcohol allowed |
| | Stroller/wheelchair rentals available |

| | |
|---|---|
| | Parade |
| | Parking fee |
| | Entrance fee |
| X | Camping facilities: 20 miles |
| X | Boating facilities: Pete's Harbor |
| X | RV facilities w/ hookups: 20 miles |
| X | Accomodations in town |
| X | Restaurants in town |

C E N T R A L

# *Central Coast Wine Classic*

SAN LUIS OBISPO COMBINES relaxation with excitement at the annual **Central Coast Wine Classic**. This little town on California's Central Coast has been a stopping-off point for coastal travelers since the 1700s. This unique wine-tasting event hosts more than 75 wineries of the Central Valley, along with a wine auction and gourmet dinner.

## San Luis Obispo, California

Third weekend in June
Hours vary

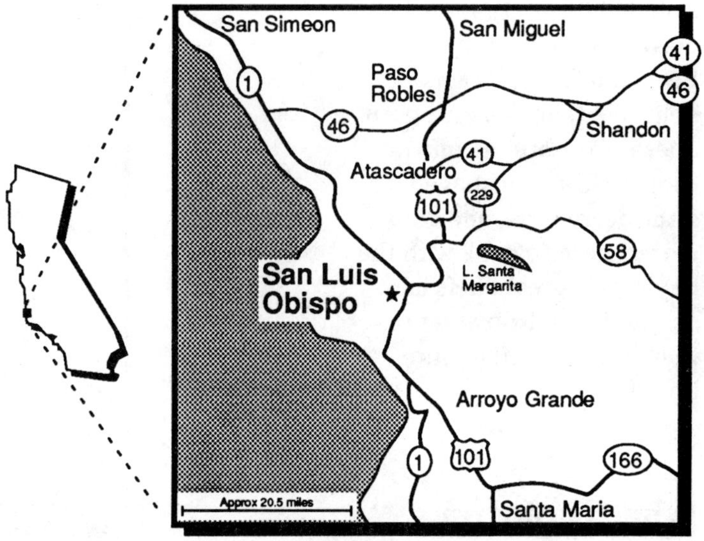


## What's goin' on...

Town population: **41,000**
Last year's attendance: **1,800**
Average outdoor temperature: **75°**
Festival location: **San Luis Bay Resort**

*Up-to-date festival information is available from:*
*San Luis Obispo Chamber of Commerce*
*(805) 543-1323*

| | |
|---|---|
| ✗ | Wine tasting/beer for sale |
| ✗ | Food booths |
| | Arts/crafts for sale |
| ✗ | Live music |
| | Clowns |
| | Face painters |
| | Childrens games |
| | Animal exhibits/petting zoo |
| | Dogs allowed on leash |
| ✗ | Lost and found |
| ✗ | Bicycle racks |
| | First aid area available |
| ✗ | Self-brought picnics allowed |
| | Self-brought alcohol allowed |
| | Stroller/wheelchair rentals available |

| | |
|---|---|
| | Parade |
| | Parking fee |
| ✗ | Entrance fee: $20-50 |
| ✗ | Camping facilities: 15 miles |
| ✗ | Boating facilities: Lakes and ocean |
| ✗ | RV facilities w/ hookups: 15 miles |
| ✗ | Accomodations in town<br>Madonna Inn, Peach Tree Inn, Garden St. B&B |
| ✗ | Restaurants in town<br>Apple Farm, Hudson's Grill, Chef Em's |

# *Salute To The Arts*

FERTILE SOIL AND A MILD, sunny climate makes for a perfect environment for Sonoma's **Salute To The Arts**! This showcase of the winemaking, culinary, literary, visual, and performing arts will feature food and wine, music, outdoor theater, art shows, exhibits, and a gathering of authors in the Plaza. This makes for a delightful weekend in California's wine country.

## Sonoma, California

Third weekend in July (beginning Friday)
Daily Noon - 5:00 PM

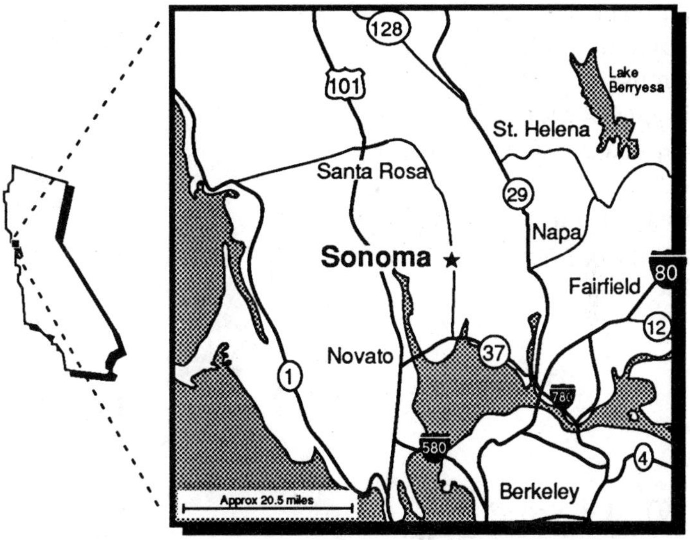


*Up-to-date festival information is available from:*
*Sonoma Chamber of Commerce*
*(707) 996-1033*

## What's goin' on...

Town population: **7,500**
Last year's attendance: **10,000**
Average outdoor temperature: **85°**
Festival location: **Sonoma Plaza**

| | |
|---|---|
| X | Wine tasting/beer for sale |
| X | Food booths |
| X | Arts/crafts for sale |
| X | Live music |
| | Clowns |
| | Face painters |
| | Childrens games |
| | Animal exhibits/petting zoo |
| | Dogs allowed on leash |
| X | Lost and found |
| X | Bicycle racks |
| X | First aid area available |
| X | Self-brought picnics allowed |
| | Self-brought alcohol allowed |
| | Stroller/wheelchair rentals available |

| | |
|---|---|
| | Parade |
| | Parking fee |
| | Entrance fee |
| X | Camping facilities: 10 miles |
| X | Boating facilities: Lake, river & bay |
| X | RV facilities w/ hookups: 30 miles |
| X | Accomodations in town: Sonoma Mission Inn, Westerbeke Ranch, Tanglewood House, Country Cottage |
| X | Restaurants in town: Barducci's Resorante, Gino's, T. J.'s Sonoma Grill and Bakery, Sonoma Sausage Company |

# *Strauss Festival*

IT WAS THE DREAM OF IRIS Zimbelman's—the **Strauss Festival**...on Strauss Island, no less! The costuming, music, and dancing are unlike anything you've seen before—a must for music lovers! There is special seating for handicapped and senior citizens; otherwise bring your blanket to sit on and picnics for enjoying three evenings under the stars! *Heavenly!*

## Elk Grove, California

Fourth weekend in July
Nightly 8:00 PM - 11:00 PM

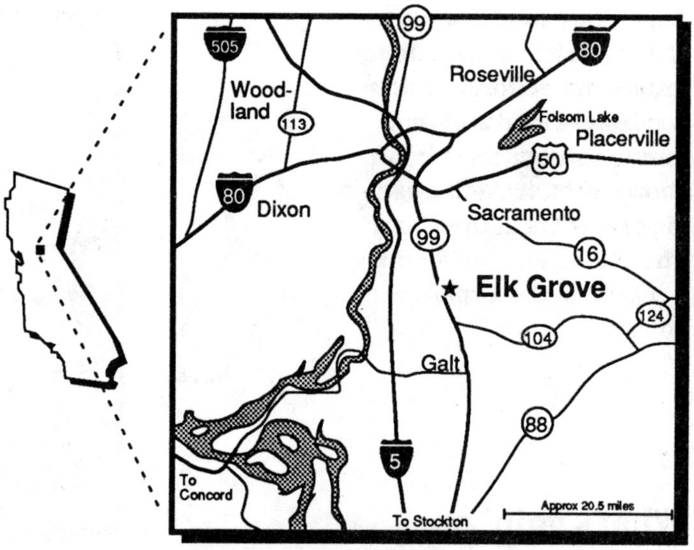


*Up-to-date festival information is available from:*
*Elk Grove Chamber of Commerce*
*(916) 685-3911*

## What's goin' on...

Town population: **32,000**
Last year's attendance: **3,000**
Average outdoor temperature: **97°**
Festival location: **Strauss Island**

| | |
|---|---|
| | Wine tasting/beer for sale |
| | Food booths |
| | Arts/crafts for sale |
| ✗ | Live music |
| | Clowns |
| | Face painters |
| | Childrens games |
| | Animal exhibits/petting zoo |
| ✗ | Dogs allowed on leash |
| ✗ | Lost and found |
| ✗ | Bicycle racks |
| | First aid area available |
| ✗ | Self-brought picnics allowed |
| | Self-brought alcohol allowed |
| | Stroller/wheelchair rentals available |

| | |
|---|---|
| | Parade |
| | Parking fee |
| ✗ | Entrance fee: $3 per car |
| | Camping facilities |
| | Boating facilities |
| | RV facilities w/ hookups |
| ✗ | Accomodations in town |
| ✗ | Restaurants in town<br>Village Choice, The General Store, Stoney's, Vince's Ristorante |

# *Amador County Fair*

ANOTHER ONE OF California's treasures is hidden in the once-gold-filled nooks and crannies of Amador County. The **Amador County Fair** is a real country experience up and out of the hustle-bustle of our 8-to-5 lives! Attracting over 30,000 people each year, this festival is pushing it's half-century mark.

## Plymouth, California

Last weekend in July (beginning Thursday)
Daily 9:00 AM - midnight

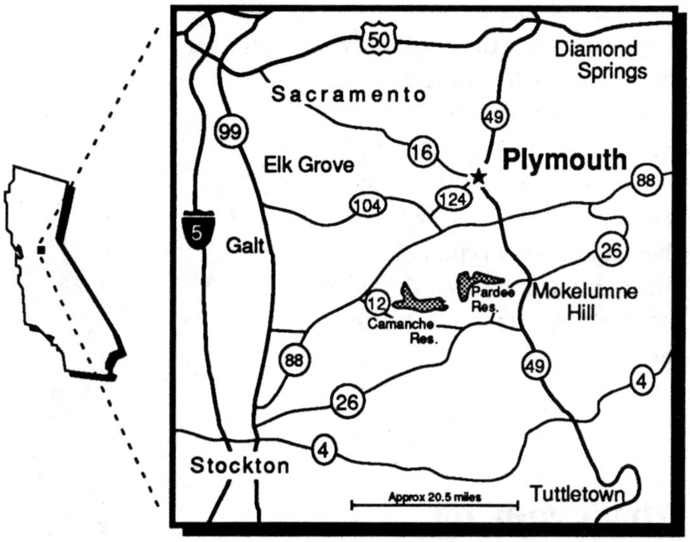


*Up-to-date festival information is available from:*
*Plymouth Chamber of Commerce*
*(209) 223-0350*

## What's goin' on...

Town population: **1,000**
Last year's attendance: **30,000**
Average outdoor temperature: **95°**
Festival location: **Fairgrounds**

| | |
|---|---|
| ✗ | Wine tasting/beer for sale |
| ✗ | Food booths |
| ✗ | Arts/crafts for sale |
| ✗ | Live music |
| ✗ | Clowns |
| ✗ | Face painters |
| ✗ | Childrens games |
| | Animal exhibits/petting zoo |
| ✗ | Dogs allowed on leash |
| ✗ | Lost and found |
| ✗ | Bicycle racks |
| ✗ | First aid area available |
| ✗ | Self-brought picnics allowed |
| | Self-brought alcohol allowed |
| | Stroller/wheelchair rentals available |

| | |
|---|---|
| | Parade |
| ✗ | Parking fee: $1 |
| ✗ | Entrance fee: Adults $4; Kids $2 |
| ✗ | Camping facilities: In town |
| ✗ | Boating facilities: Lake Amador |
| ✗ | RV facilities w/ hookups: In town |
| ✗ | Accomodations in town |
| ✗ | Restaurants in town |

# *Garlic Festival*

IT'S THE GRANDDADDY OF them all—the Gilroy **Garlic Festival**! The 85 booths containing one-of-a-kind arts-and-crafts items are impressive, but they still play second fiddle to Gourmet Alley, where the "scented pearl" is in the wine, the ice cream, the fried calamari, and the other 100+ food booths! Live music of all types play during the three days. Brave the crowds; this is a must for garlic lovers!

## Gilroy, California

Last full weekend in July (beginning Friday)
Daily 10:00 AM - 6:00 PM

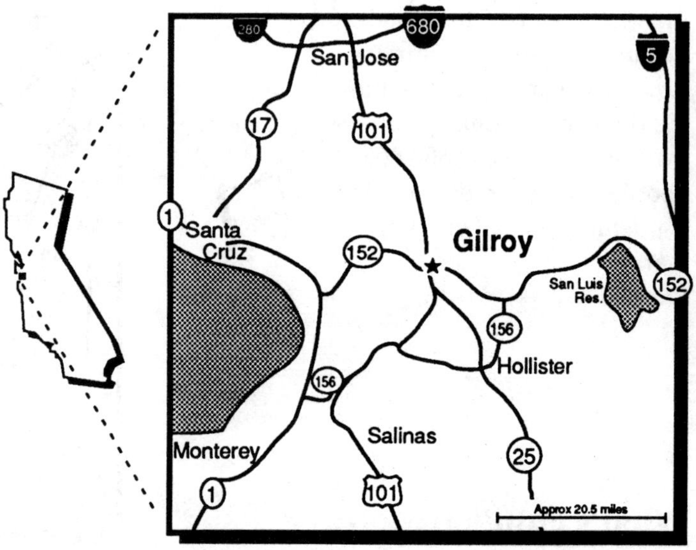


*Up-to-date festival information is available from:*
*Gilroy Visitors Bureau*
*(408) 842-6437*

## What's goin' on...

Town population: **30,000**
Last year's attendance: **142,000**
Average outdoor temperature: **90°**
Festival location: **Christmas Hill Park**

| | |
|---|---|
| X | Wine tasting/beer for sale |
| X | Food booths |
| X | Arts/crafts for sale |
| X | Live music |
| X | Clowns |
| X | Face painters |
| X | Childrens games |
| | Animal exhibits/petting zoo |
| | Dogs allowed on leash |
| X | Lost and found |
| | Bicycle racks |
| X | First aid area available |
| | Self-brought picnics allowed |
| | Self-brought alcohol allowed |
| | Stroller/wheelchair rentals available |

| | |
|---|---|
| | Parade |
| | Parking fee |
| X | Entrance fee: Srs/Kids $2; Adults $7 |
| X | Camping facilities: 15 miles |
| X | Boating facilities: Lake Coyote |
| X | RV facilities w/ hookups: 15 miles |
| X | Accomodations in town<br>Country Rose Inn B&B, Best Western, Casa de Fruta, Super 8, Motel 6 |
| X | Restaurants in town<br>Harvest Time, Diggers, Sandrinos |

# *Mozart Festival*

THE WORLD-RENOWNED **Mozart Festival** in San Luis Obispo, is a two-decades-old tribute to Wolfgang Amadeus Mozart, with more than 20 concerts and a study program. The week-long Festival is rich with the sounds of the classics, from chamber music to symphonies, at several locations in town. This is a lovely tribute to one of the world's greatest composers!

## San Luis Obispo, California

Last weekend in July through the first weekend in August
Hours vary

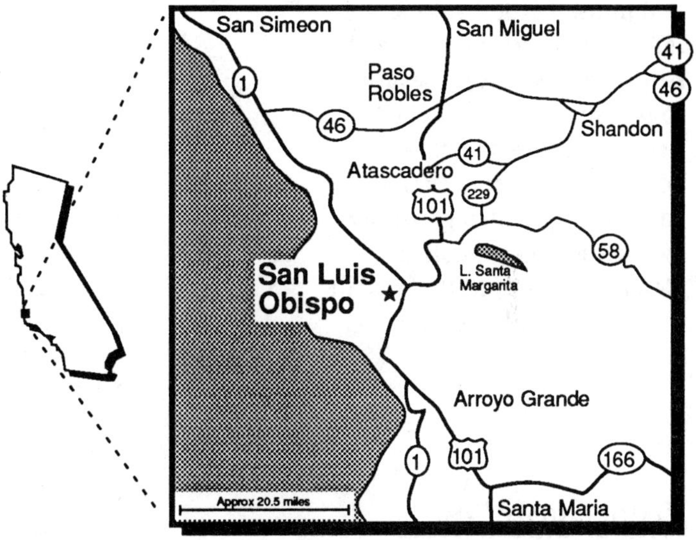


## What's goin' on...

Town population: **41,000**
Last year's attendance: **10,000**
Average outdoor temperature: **75°**
Festival location: **Countywide**

*Up-to-date festival information is available from:*
*San Luis Obispo Chamber of Commerce*
*(805) 543-1323*

| | |
|---|---|
| | Wine tasting/beer for sale |
| | Food booths |
| | Arts/crafts for sale |
| ✗ | Live music |
| | Clowns |
| | Face painters |
| | Childrens games |
| | Animal exhibits/petting zoo |
| ✗ | Dogs allowed on leash |
| | Lost and found |
| | Bicycle racks |
| | First aid area available |
| ✗ | Self-brought picnics allowed |
| | Self-brought alcohol allowed |
| | Stroller/wheelchair rentals available |

| | |
|---|---|
| | Parade |
| | Parking fee |
| ✗ | Entrance fee: Varies |
| ✗ | Camping facilities: 15 miles |
| ✗ | Boating facilities: Lakes and ocean |
| ✗ | RV facilities w/ hookups: 15 miles |
| ✗ | Accomodations in town<br>Madonna Inn, Peach Tree Inn, Garden St. B&B |
| ✗ | Restaurants in town<br>Apple Farm, Hudson's Grill, Chef Em's, Cafe Roma, Brubeck's |

# *Music from Bear Valley*

SET IN A SPECTACULAR mountain setting, **Music from Bear Valley** combines the best of the classics, opera, and pops. Nestled among the tall trees of the high-Sierra ski resort Bear Valley, it is sure to please music enthusiasts and pleasure seekers! In addition to the concerts, you can also enjoy hiking, fishing, swimming, tennis, golf, and clean mountain air! Please call for the different packages available.

## Bear Valley, California

Last weekend in July through the second weekend in August
Hours vary

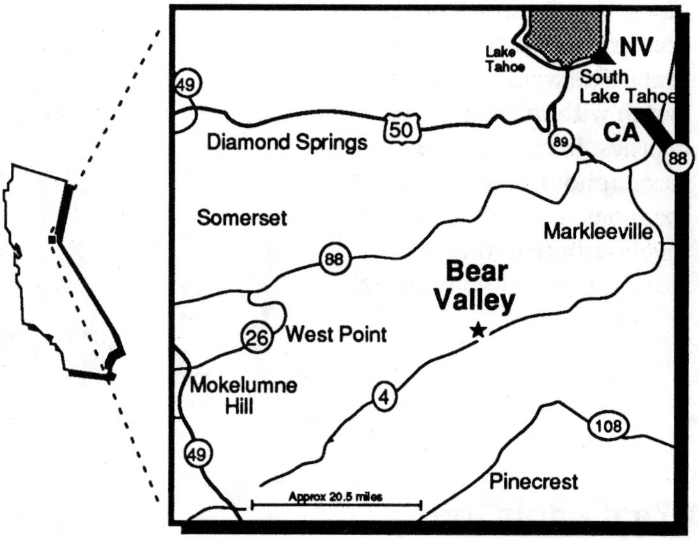


*Up-to-date festival information is available from:*
*Bear Valley Lodge*
*(209) 753-2325*

## What's goin' on...

Town population: **50,000**
Last year's attendance: **35,000**
Average outdoor temperature: **70°**
Festival location: **Bear Valley resort**

- X Wine tasting/beer for sale
- X Food booths
- X Arts/crafts for sale
- X Live music
- Clowns
- Face painters
- Childrens games
- Animal exhibits/petting zoo
- X Dogs allowed on leash
- Lost and found
- Bicycle racks
- First aid area available
- X Self-brought picnics allowed
- X Self-brought alcohol allowed
- Stroller/wheelchair rentals available

- Parade
- Parking fee
- X Entrance fee: $7 - $8
- X Camping facilities: 2 miles
- X Boating facilities: Salt Springs Res.
- X RV facilities w/ hookups: 15 miles
- X Accomodations in town
  Bear Valley Lodge
- X Restaurants in town
  Bear Valley Lodge

# *Art & Wine Festival*

CHARLIE CHAPLIN LIKED THE area so much that he filmed The Little Tramp here—maybe it's time you too came to see what Fremont has to offer, at the **Art & Wine Festival**. Located at the southern end of BART (Bay Area Rapid Transit), the festival offers music, ethnic cuisine, wine tasting, and many arts-and-crafts booths.

## Fremont, California

Last weekend in July
Daily 10:00 AM - 5:00 PM

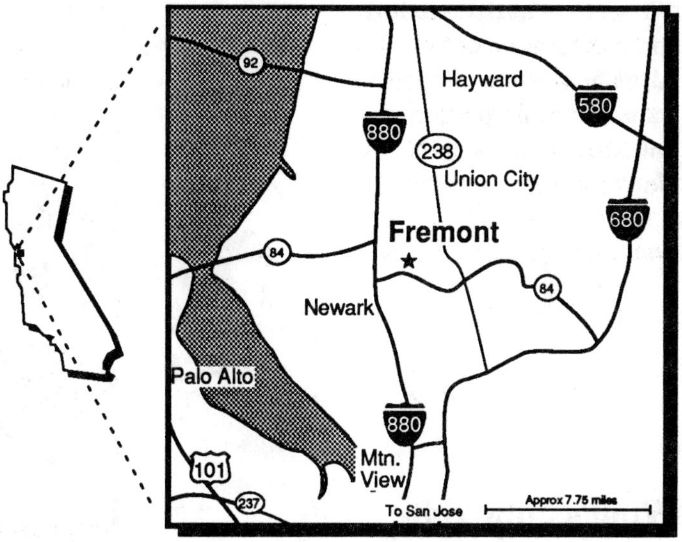




## What's goin' on...

Town population: **172,400**
Last year's attendance: **150,000**
Average outdoor temperature: **75°**
Festival location: **Paseo Padre & Mowry**

*Up-to-date festival information is available from:*
*Fremont Chamber of Commerce*
*(415) 657-1355*

| | |
|---|---|
| ✗ | Wine tasting/beer for sale |
| ✗ | Food booths |
| ✗ | Arts/crafts for sale |
| ✗ | Live music |
| ✗ | Clowns |
| ✗ | Face painters |
| | Childrens games |
| | Animal exhibits/petting zoo |
| ✗ | Dogs allowed on leash |
| | Lost and found |
| ✗ | Bicycle racks |
| ✗ | First aid area available |
| ✗ | Self-brought picnics allowed |
| | Self-brought alcohol allowed |
| | Stroller/wheelchair rentals available |

| | |
|---|---|
| | Parade |
| | Parking fee |
| | Entrance fee |
| | Camping facilities |
| ✗ | Boating facilities: Del Valle Res. |
| | RV facilities w/ hookups |
| ✗ | Accomodations in town<br>Lord Bradley's Inn B&B, Quality Inn, Courtyard by Marriott |
| ✗ | Restaurants in town |

# *Wings of Charity Airshow*

ARE YOU READY FOR SOME bird watching? I mean real big, beautiful, chrome birds? Then make your way to the **Wings for Charity Airshow** for an afternoon of fun. Airplane posters, models, pins, and other paraphernalia will be on display and for sale. Don't forget your camera!

## Livermore, California

Last weekend in July
Daily 8:00 AM - 4:00 PM

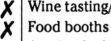

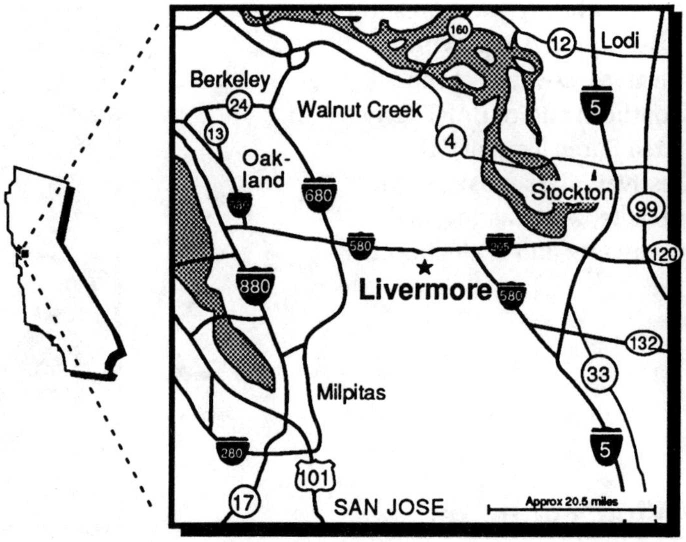


## What's goin' on...

Town population: **56,445**
Last year's attendance: **8,000**
Average outdoor temperature: **90°**
Festival location: **Livermore Muni. Airport**

*Up-to-date festival information is available from:*
*Livermore Chamber of Commerce*
*(415) 447-1606*

| | |
|---|---|
| X | Wine tasting/beer for sale |
| X | Food booths |
| | Arts/crafts for sale |
| | Live music |
| | Clowns |
| | Face painters |
| | Childrens games |
| | Animal exhibits/petting zoo |
| | Dogs allowed on leash |
| X | Lost and found |
| | Bicycle racks |
| X | First aid area available |
| X | Self-brought picnics allowed |
| | Self-brought alcohol allowed |
| X | Stroller/wheelchair rentals available |

| | |
|---|---|
| | Parade |
| | Parking fee |
| X | Entrance fee: S & K $2; $4 |
| X | Camping facilities: 11 miles |
| X | Boating facilities: Del Valle Res. |
| X | RV facilities w/ hookups: 11 miles |
| X | Accomodations in town<br>Townhouse Motel, Residence Inn, Holiday Inn |
| X | Restaurants in town<br>El Lorito, Le Coquelicot, Garcia's of Scottsdale, Livermore Seafood Restaurant |

# *California Mid-State Fair*

THIRTEEN SPECTACULAR days make up the **California Mid-State Fair**! No other fair in California has quite the musical line-up this one offers—Kenny Rogers, Sting, Rod Stewart, Bob Hope, Clint Black, and Kenny G.! WOW! While enjoying California's central coast, drive along the country roads, savor the rural atmosphere, and stop to sample the ambience of over 25 wineries.

## Paso Robles, California

Thirteen days in August (exact date not set)
Hours vary

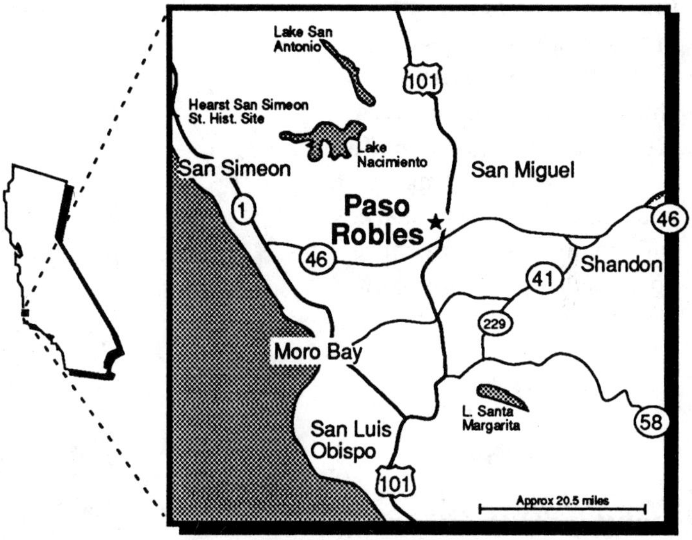


*Up-to-date festival information is available from:*
*Paso Robles Chamber of Commerce*
*(805) 238-0506*



## What's goin' on...

Town population: **18,000**
Last year's attendance: **435,000**
Average outdoor temperature: **95°**
Festival location: **Fairgrounds**

| | |
|---|---|
| ✗ | Wine tasting/beer for sale |
| ✗ | Food booths |
| ✗ | Arts/crafts for sale |
| ✗ | Live music |
| ✗ | Clowns |
| ✗ | Face painters |
| ✗ | Childrens games |
| ✗ | Animal exhibits/petting zoo |
| | Dogs allowed on leash |
| ✗ | Lost and found |
| | Bicycle racks |
| ✗ | First aid area available |
| ✗ | Self-brought picnics allowed |
| | Self-brought alcohol allowed |
| ✗ | Stroller/wheelchair rentals available |

| | |
|---|---|
| | Parade |
| ✗ | Parking fee: $3 |
| ✗ | Entrance fee: $5 |
| ✗ | Camping facilities: 20 miles |
| ✗ | Boating facilities: Lake San Antonio |
| ✗ | RV facilities w/ hookups: In town |
| ✗ | Accomodations in town<br>Roseleith, Country House Inn, Adelaide Motor Inn, Avalon Motel, Padre Oaks |
| ✗ | Restaurants in town<br>Templeton Corner, Wilson's, Wellsona House, Pepe's Mexican Restaurant |

# *Shakespeare Under the Stars*

JUST 12 MILES NORTH OF San Francisco lies the "burb" known as San Rafael...home to the Marin Shakespeare Company who annually produce the **Shakespeare Under the Stars** series. T-shirts, buttons, and posters are for sale, along with coffee, desserts, and soft drinks. So if you like your Shake- speare with something a little more noteworthy, pack your own picnic and bring a bottle of wine!

## San Rafael, California

Month of August (call for eaxct dates and times)
Evenings

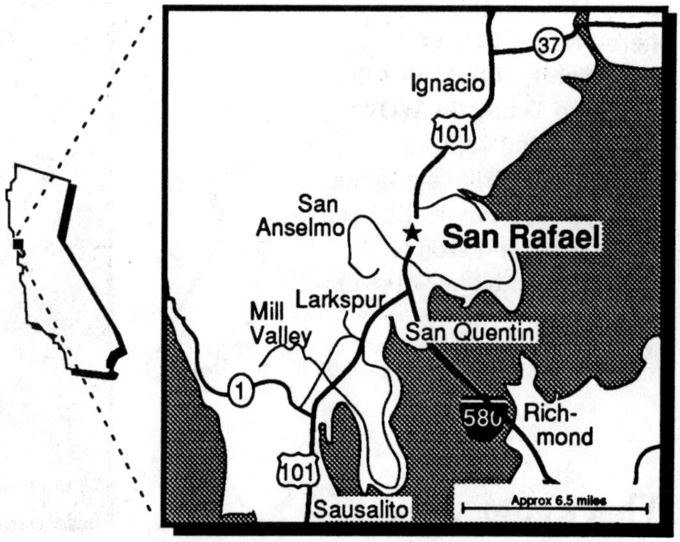


*Up-to-date festival information is available from:*
*San Rafael Marin Shakespeare Company*
*(415) 472-7470*

## What's goin' on...

Town population: **40,000**
Last year's attendance: **3,700**
Average outdoor temperature: **65°**
Festival location: **Forest Meadows Ampith.**

| | |
|---|---|
| | Wine tasting/beer for sale |
| ✗ | Food booths |
| | Arts/crafts for sale |
| ✗ | Live music |
| | Clowns |
| | Face painters |
| | Childrens games |
| | Animal exhibits/petting zoo |
| ✗ | Dogs allowed on leash |
| | Lost and found |
| | Bicycle racks |
| | First aid area available |
| ✗ | Self-brought picnics allowed |
| ✗ | Self-brought alcohol allowed |
| | Stroller/wheelchair rentals available |

| | |
|---|---|
| | Parade |
| | Parking fee |
| ✗ | Entrance fee: S & K $10; A $12 |
| ✗ | Camping facilities: 10 miles |
| ✗ | Boating facilities: San Francisco Bay |
| ✗ | RV facilities w/ hookups: 10 miles |
| ✗ | Accomodations in town<br>Panama Hotel, Embassy Suites |
| ✗ | Restaurants in town<br>La Toscana, Carlo Restaurant |

# *Calamari Festival*

SOME FOLKS ARE INTO cows, some folks are into pigs, and believe it or not...some folks are into squid! This slimey little creatures can be cooked up into some appetizing dishes—come see for yourself at the the 12th International **Calamari Festival**! Featuring squid art and Wednesday night cabarets, this month-long festival offers a variety of events. Call the Visitor's Bureau for the exact scoop.

## Santa Cruz, California

Month of August
Hours vary

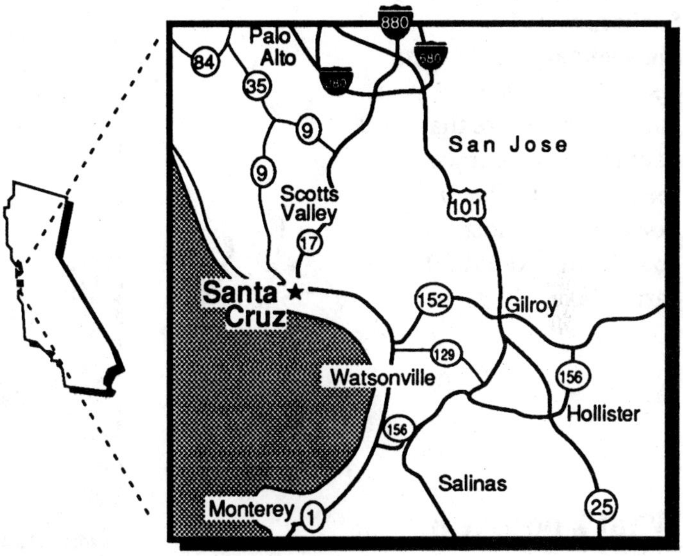


*Up-to-date festival information is available from:*
*Santa Cruz Visitors Bureau*
*(408) 425-1234*

## What's goin' on...

Town population: **51,000**
Last year's attendance: **25,000**
Average outdoor temperature: **70°**
Festival location: **India Joze Restaurant**

- ✗ Wine tasting/beer for sale
- ✗ Food booths
- ✗ Arts/crafts for sale
- ✗ Live music
- Clowns
- Face painters
- Childrens games
- Animal exhibits/petting zoo
- Dogs allowed on leash
- Lost and found
- ✗ Bicycle racks
- ✗ First aid area available
- Self-brought picnics allowed
- Self-brought alcohol allowed
- Stroller/wheelchair rentals available

- Parade
- Parking fee
- Entrance fee
- ✗ Camping facilities: 2 miles
- ✗ Boating facilities: Santa Cruz Harbor
- ✗ RV facilities w/ hookups: 4 miles
- ✗ Accomodations in town
  Hitching Post Motel, Holiday Inn, Lanai Motor Lodge, Dream Inn, many B&Bs
- ✗ Restaurants in town
  Crow's Nest, Aldo's, Hindquarter, Miramar, Sea Cloud, El Paisano Tamales, Anna Maria's

# *Shakespeare Santa Cruz*

ALL SHAKESPEARE BUFFS report to the U.C.S.C. Performing Arts complex for 35 days of (nearly) non-stop Shakespeare! The **Shakespeare Santa Cruz** festival is in it's ninth year, and attracts more than 22,000 people. While in town, visit the Santa Cruz Pier and Beach Boardwalk—whose roller coaster survived the 1989 earthquake.

## Santa Cruz, California

Month of August
Hours vary

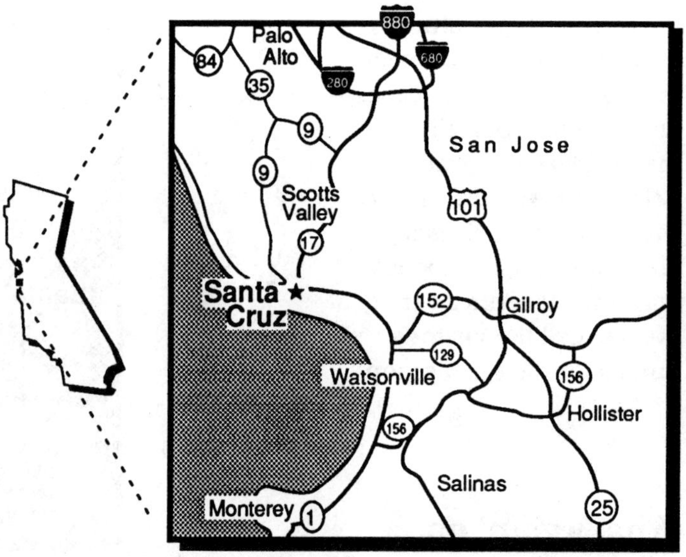


*Up-to-date festival information is available from:*
*Santa Cruz Visitors Bureau*
*(408) 425-1234*

## What's goin' on...

Town population: **51,000**
Last year's attendance: **25,000**
Average outdoor temperature: **70°**
Festival location: **U.C.S.C.**

| | |
|---|---|
| X | Wine tasting/beer for sale |
| X | Food booths |
| X | Arts/crafts for sale |
| | Live music |
| | Clowns |
| | Face painters |
| | Childrens games |
| | Animal exhibits/petting zoo |
| | Dogs allowed on leash |
| X | Lost and found |
| X | Bicycle racks |
| X | First aid area available |
| X | Self-brought picnics allowed |
| X | Self-brought alcohol allowed |
| | Stroller/wheelchair rentals available |

| | |
|---|---|
| | Parade |
| | Parking fee |
| X | Entrance fee: (prices not avbl.) |
| X | Camping facilities: 2 miles |
| X | Boating facilities: Santa Cruz Harbor |
| X | RV facilities w/ hookups: 4 miles |
| X | Accomodations in town<br>Hitching Post Motel, Holiday Inn, Lanai Motor Lodge, Dream Inn, many B&Bs |
| X | Restaurants in town<br>Crow's Nest, Aldo's, Hindquarter, Miramar, Sea Cloud, El Paisano Tamales, Anna Maria's |

# *Petaluma Summermusic Festival*

AH, SUMMER! THE GOLDEN hills, the peaceful river meandering through the Victorian town, cool lawns stretching before splendid old mansions, the bucolic sounds of chickens and cows and...Opera, African Drums, Mandolins, Brass Choir, and Celtic Harp! Ah, the **Petaluma Summermusic Festival** takes place in Victorian homes, Cinnabar Theater, gardens, an old schoolhouse, and the Community Center.

## Petaluma, California

Three weeks in August
Hours vary

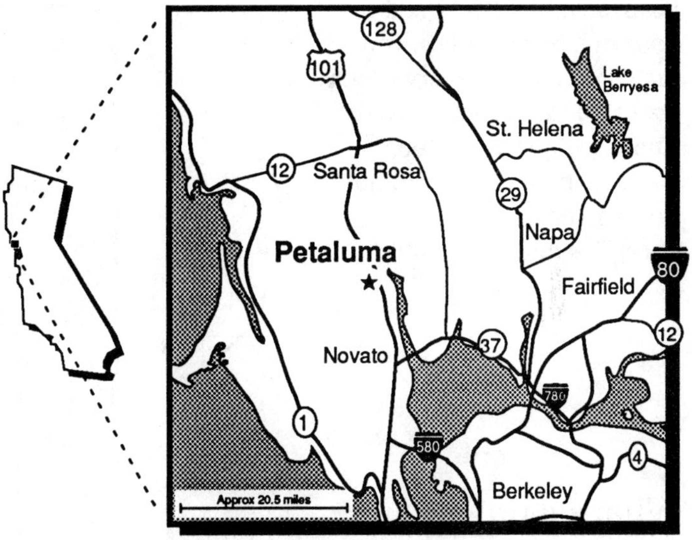


☞ *Up-to-date festival information is available from:*
*Petaluma Chamber of Commerce*
*(707) 762-2785*

## What's goin' on...

Town population: **42,000**
Last year's attendance: **3,000**
Average outdoor temperature: **78°**
Festival location: **Citywide**

| | |
|---|---|
| X | Wine tasting/beer for sale |
| | Food booths |
| | Arts/crafts for sale |
| X | Live music |
| | Clowns |
| | Face painters |
| | Childrens games |
| | Animal exhibits/petting zoo |
| | Dogs allowed on leash |
| | Lost and found |
| | Bicycle racks |
| | First aid area available |
| X | Self-brought picnics allowed |
| | Self-brought alcohol allowed |
| | Stroller/wheelchair rentals available |

| | |
|---|---|
| | Parade |
| | Parking fee |
| X | Entrance fee: Varies $8 - 20 |
| X | Camping facilities: 5 miles |
| X | Boating facilities: River, lake, and bay |
| X | RV facilities w/ hookups: 5 miles |
| X | Accomodations in town: Best Western, Quality Inn, Motel 6, Cavanagh Cottage B&B, 7th St. Inn B&B |
| X | Restaurants in town: Petrucci's, Tempura House, Steamer Gold, Cattlemen's, Fino's, Original Marvin's |

# *Lambtown U.S.A. Festival*

BETCHA DIDN'T KNOW THAT **Lambtown U.S.A.** was right here in California. Yep, home of the Dixon Lambtown U.S.A. Festival! And talk about a cook-off...holy smokes, you'll find lamb cooked every which way, and talk about fantastic! There's wine tasting too, along with handmade crafts and artistic items to pore over. The music? Country!

## Dixon, California

First weekend in August
10:00 AM - 7:00 PM

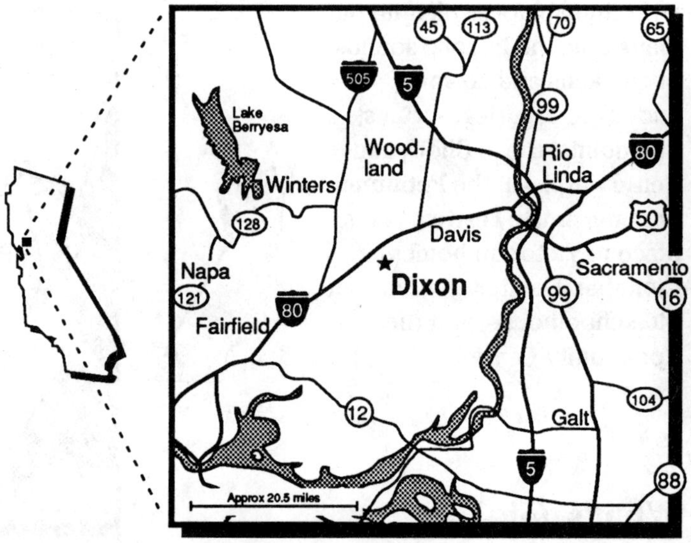


*Up-to-date festival information is available from:*
*Dixon Chamber of Commerce*
*(916) 678-2650*

## What's goin' on...

Town population: **11,000**
Last year's attendance: **8,000**
Average outdoor temperature: **90°**
Festival location: **Fairgrounds**

| | |
|---|---|
| ✗ | Wine tasting/beer for sale |
| ✗ | Food booths |
| ✗ | Arts/crafts for sale |
| ✗ | Live music |
| ✗ | Clowns |
| ✗ | Face painters |
| ✗ | Childrens games |
| ✗ | Animal exhibits/petting zoo |
| | Dogs allowed on leash |
| ✗ | Lost and found |
| | Bicycle racks |
| ✗ | First aid area available |
| | Self-brought picnics allowed |
| | Self-brought alcohol allowed |
| | Stroller/wheelchair rentals available |

| | |
|---|---|
| | Parade |
| | Parking fee |
| ✗ | Entrance fee: Srs. $2; Adults $4 |
| | Camping facilities |
| | Boating facilities |
| ✗ | RV facilities w/ hookups: On site |
| | Accomodations in town |
| ✗ | Restaurants in town<br>Chevy's, Kim and Ned's, Country Oak, Cattlemen's |

# *California Dry Bean Festival*

THE **CALIFORNIA DRY Bean Festival** has turned into one of California's outstanding festivals! Festival hoppers come from all over to test the zillions of bean recipes conjured up especially for this weekend! Other nourishment comes in the form of beer; calamari; ribs; kabobs; and yummy ethnic foods. There's lots of live music and very talented puppeteers to keep you entertained.

## Tracy, California

First weekend in August
Daily 10:00 AM - 7:00 PM

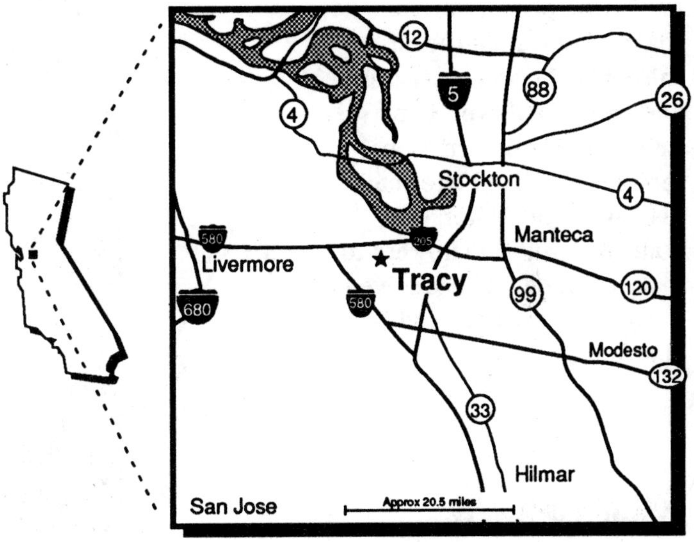


## What's goin' on...

Town population: **37,000**
Last year's attendance: **42,000**
Average outdoor temperature: **94°**
Festival location: **Downtown**

*Up-to-date festival information is available from:*
*Tracy Chamber of Commerce*
*(209) 835-2131*

| | |
|---|---|
| X | Wine tasting/beer for sale |
| X | Food booths |
| X | Arts/crafts for sale |
| X | Live music |
| X | Clowns |
| X | Face painters |
| X | Childrens games |
| X | Animal exhibits/petting zoo |
| | Dogs allowed on leash |
| X | Lost and found |
| | Bicycle racks |
| X | First aid area available |
| | Self-brought picnics allowed |
| | Self-brought alcohol allowed |
| | Stroller/wheelchair rentals available |

| | |
|---|---|
| | Parade |
| | Parking fee |
| X | Entrance fee: S & K $2; A $4 |
| X | Camping facilities: 20 miles |
| X | Boating facilities: San Joaquin River |
| X | RV facilities w/ hookups: 20 miles |
| X | Accomodations in town<br>Tracy Inn, Motel 6, Motel Orleans, Motel Hacienda, Royal Motel |
| X | Restaurants in town<br>Tracy Inn, Opera House, Horseshoe, Brooks Ranch |

# *Gladiola Festival*

THE **GLADIOLA FESTIVAL** wakes you up with the scrumptious smells of a pancake breakfast. But this is hardly the primary aroma that curls through the air, as this festival features fragrant and beautiful flower displays! Crafts booths, international-food booths, and historical displays of old Union City combined with the flowers to make a full day. There's even a tennis tournament and 5–10K run!

## Union City, California

First weekend in August
Daily 10:00 AM - 6:00 PM

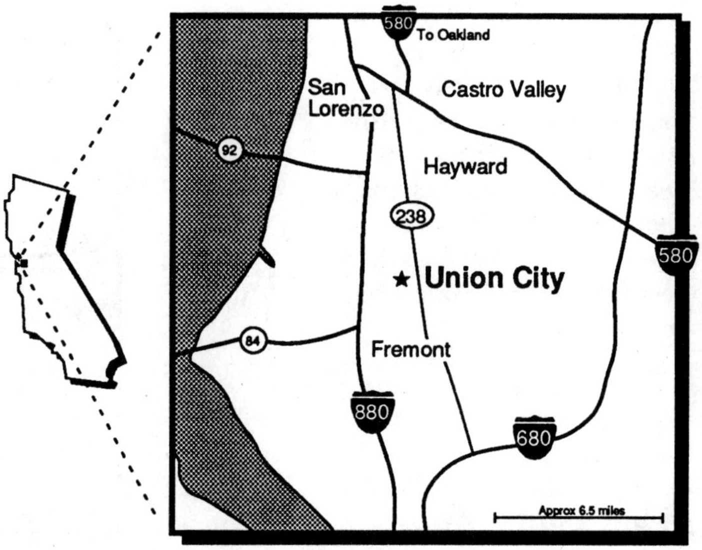


*Up-to-date festival information is available from:*
*Union City Chamber of Commerce*
*(415) 471-3115*

## What's goin' on...

Town population: **39,406**
Last year's attendance: **N/A**
Average outdoor temperature: **73°**
Festival location: **Downtown**

| | |
|---|---|
| ✗ | Wine tasting/beer for sale |
| ✗ | Food booths |
| ✗ | Arts/crafts for sale |
| ✗ | Live music |
| ✗ | Clowns |
| ✗ | Face painters |
| ✗ | Childrens games |
| | Animal exhibits/petting zoo |
| | Dogs allowed on leash |
| | Lost and found |
| ✗ | Bicycle racks |
| | First aid area available |
| ✗ | Self-brought picnics allowed |
| | Self-brought alcohol allowed |
| | Stroller/wheelchair rentals available |

| | |
|---|---|
| | Parade |
| | Parking fee |
| | Entrance fee |
| ✗ | Camping facilities: 15 miles |
| ✗ | Boating facilities: San Francisco Bay |
| | RV facilities w/ hookups |
| ✗ | Accomodations in town |
| ✗ | Restaurants in town |

# *Arts & Crafts Festival*

BASS LAKE'S ANNUAL **Arts & Crafts Festival** is a revelry of amusement! Located amid the huge granite boulders of southern Yosemite National Park, Bass Lake is an ideal waterskiing lake. The Festival features the artwork of Ron Smith, Lucy Poff, Rita Watkins, and Jewel Shoulders and food booths of all ethnic varieties. Whatta great way to spend a Saturday outdoors!

## Bass Lake, California

Second weekend in August
Sat. 10:00 AM - 8:00 PM; Sun. 10:00 AM - 4:00 PM

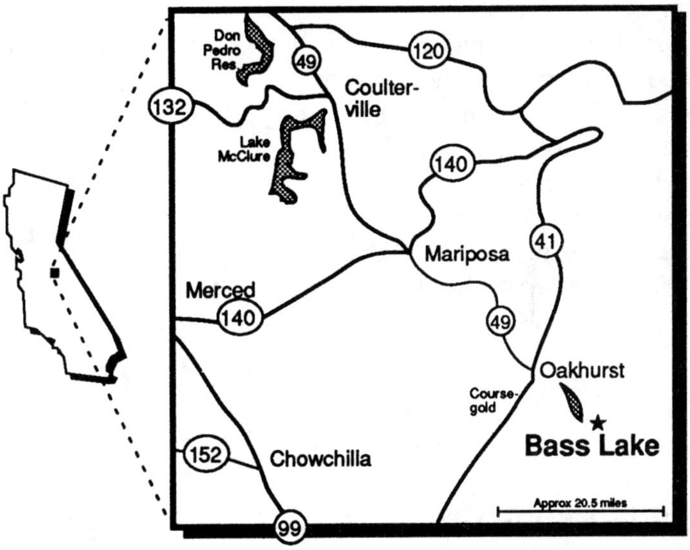


*Up-to-date festival information is available from:*
*Bass Lake Chamber of Commerce*
*(209) 642-3676*

## What's goin' on...

Town population: **500**
Last year's attendance: **2,500**
Average outdoor temperature: **85°**
Festival location: **Pines Village**

| | |
|---|---|
| | Wine tasting/beer for sale |
| X | Food booths |
| X | Arts/crafts for sale |
| X | Live music |
| | Clowns |
| X | Face painters |
| | Childrens games |
| | Animal exhibits/petting zoo |
| X | Dogs allowed on leash |
| | Lost and found |
| | Bicycle racks |
| X | First aid area available |
| X | Self-brought picnics allowed |
| | Self-brought alcohol allowed |
| | Stroller/wheelchair rentals available |

| | |
|---|---|
| | Parade |
| | Parking fee |
| | Entrance fee |
| X | Camping facilities: 3 miles |
| X | Boating facilities: Bass Lake |
| X | RV facilities w/ hookups: 6 miles |
| X | Accomodations in town<br>Pines Chalet |
| X | Restaurants in town<br>Pines Restaurant |

# Cupertino Country Festival

THE **CUPERTINO COUNTRY Festival** happens right in our backyard! The local wineries sell wine by the glass (souvenir wine glasses are available), while the food booths serve delicacies ranging from frozen yogurt to Philly cheesesteaks to fajitas to fried calamari! Yum! Artists coming from far and wide for this entertaining event fill the 300 arts-and-crafts booths.

## Cupertino, California

Second weekend in August
Daily 10:00 AM - 5:00 PM

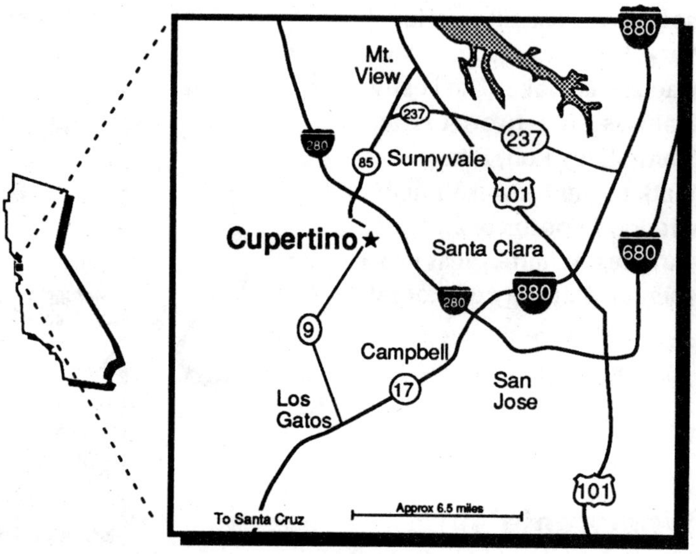


## What's goin' on...

Town population: **39,650**
Last year's attendance: **25,000**
Average outdoor temperature: **85°**
Festival location: **City Hall**

*Up-to-date festival information is available from:*
*Cupertino Chamber of Commerce*
*(408) 252-7054*

- ✗ Wine tasting/beer for sale
- ✗ Food booths
- ✗ Arts/crafts for sale
- ✗ Live music
- ✗ Clowns
- ✗ Face painters
- ✗ Childrens games
- Animal exhibits/petting zoo
- ✗ Dogs allowed on leash
- ✗ Lost and found
- ✗ Bicycle racks
- ✗ First aid area available
- Self-brought picnics allowed
- Self-brought alcohol allowed
- Stroller/wheelchair rentals available

- Parade
- Parking fee
- Entrance fee
- ✗ Camping facilities: 5 miles
- Boating facilities
- ✗ RV facilities w/ hookups: 10 miles
- ✗ Accomodations in town
  Cupertino Inn, Woodmark Hotel
- ✗ Restaurants in town
  Sports City Cafe, Pizzeria Uno's, T.G.I.F.'s, P.J. Mulligan's, Florentine's, Fontana's

# *Old Adobe Fiesta*

AFTER ATTENDING THE **Old Adobe Fiesta**, you will have a vivid understanding of how Petaluma life was in the early California rancho era. Continue to the historic downtown area to see the Iron Front buildings built in the late 1800's. The free, self-guided walking tour brochure "Streets of Petaluma" will guide you to some 38 points of interest in the downtown area. Visit the Petaluma Museum to see history.

## Petaluma, California

Second Sunday in August
11:00 AM - 4:00 PM

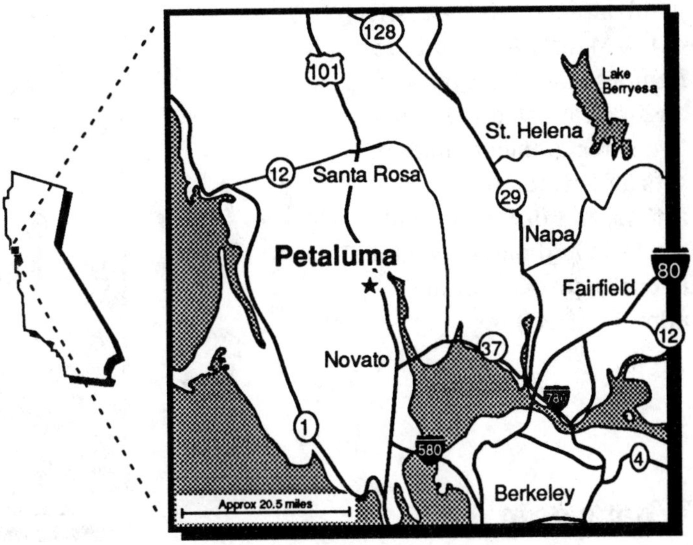


## What's goin' on...

Town population: **42,000**
Last year's attendance: **4,000**
Average outdoor temperature: **73°**
Festival location: **Adobe State Park**

*Up-to-date festival information is available from:*
*Petaluma Chamber of Commerce*
*(707) 762-2785*

| | |
|---|---|
| | Wine tasting/beer for sale |
| X | Food booths |
| X | Arts/crafts for sale |
| | Live music |
| | Clowns |
| | Face painters |
| X | Childrens games |
| X | Animal exhibits/petting zoo |
| | Dogs allowed on leash |
| | Lost and found |
| | Bicycle racks |
| | First aid area available |
| X | Self-brought picnics allowed |
| | Self-brought alcohol allowed |
| | Stroller/wheelchair rentals available |

| | |
|---|---|
| | Parade |
| | Parking fee |
| X | Entrance fee: Adults $2 |
| X | Camping facilities: 5 miles |
| X | Boating facilities: River, lake, and bay |
| X | RV facilities w/ hookups: 5 miles |
| X | Accomodations in town<br>Best Western, Quality Inn, Motel 6, Cavanaugh Cottage B&B, 7th St. Inn B&B |
| X | Restaurants in town<br>Petrucci's, Tempura House, Aram's, Cattlemen's, Fino's, Graziano's, Sonoma Joe's |

C
E
N
T
R
A
L

# *Saint Lawrence Festival*

GENTLEMEN, HOIST YOUR lady over your shoulder and retreat to the **Saint Lawrence Festival!** This re-creation of a guild faire and village festival of the Middle Ages and the Rennaissance features games and pageantry, continuous live entertainment, unique arts and crafts by local artists, and fine wines and ales! Oh, and please *do* come in costume! (Kids under 5 admitted free!)

## Ben Lomond, California

Third weekend in August
Daily 10:00 AM - 6:00 PM

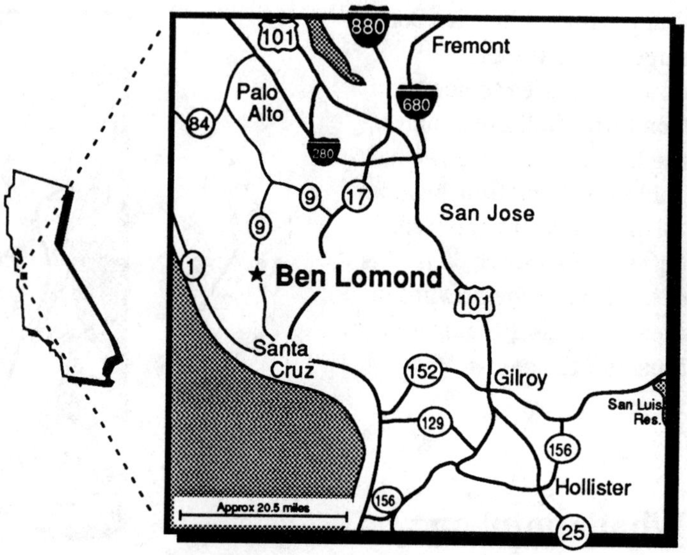


*Up-to-date festival information is available from:*
*Ben Lomond Chamber of Commerce*
*(408) 336-3600*

## What's goin' on...

Town population: **1,200**
Last year's attendance: **N/A**
Average outdoor temperature: **78°**
Festival location: **St. Lawrence Glen**

| | |
|---|---|
| ✗ | Wine tasting/beer for sale |
| ✗ | Food booths |
| ✗ | Arts/crafts for sale |
| ✗ | Live music |
| | Clowns |
| ✗ | Face painters |
| ✗ | Childrens games |
| | Animal exhibits/petting zoo |
| | Dogs allowed on leash |
| | Lost and found |
| ✗ | Bicycle racks |
| | First aid area available |
| ✗ | Self-brought picnics allowed |
| | Self-brought alcohol allowed |
| | Stroller/wheelchair rentals available |

| | |
|---|---|
| ✗ | Parade: Processions twice daily |
| | Parking fee |
| ✗ | Entrance fee: S $4; A $5; 5-12 $2 |
| ✗ | Camping facilities: 1 mile |
| ✗ | Boating facilities: Santa Cruz Harbor |
| ✗ | RV facilities w/ hookups: 2 miles |
| ✗ | Accomodations in town<br>Fern River Resort, Chateau des Fleurs B&B |
| ✗ | Restaurants in town<br>J.J.'s, Mama Mia's, Tyrolian Inn, Shang-Hai Restaurant |

# *Beach Party*

DUBBED THE "MOST magnificent beach in the world," Grover City offers lots to do besides the annual **Beach Party**! You can horseback ride, surf, fly kites, or visit beautiful Pismo Beach. And at the Beach Party, you can enjoy food stands featuring tri-tip sandwiches, clam chowder, hamburgers, and ice cream. Handcrafted clothes, jewelry, paintings, and special photography will also be for sale.

## Grover City, California

Third Saturday in August
11:00 AM - 4:30 PM

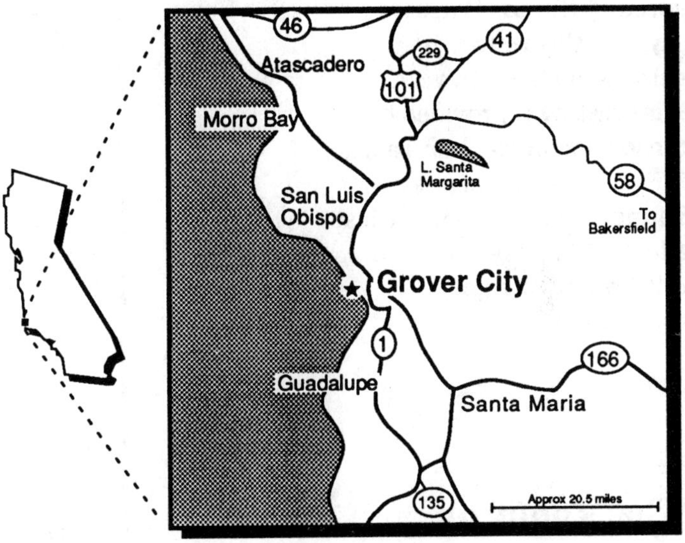


### What's goin' on...

Town population: **11,000**
Last year's attendance: **5,000**
Average outdoor temperature: **73°**
Festival location: **Picnic area at beach**

*Up-to-date festival information is available from:*
*Grover City Chamber of Commerce*
*(805) 489-9091*

- [x] Wine tasting/beer for sale
- [x] Food booths
- [x] Arts/crafts for sale
- [x] Live music
- [x] Clowns
- [x] Face painters
- [x] Childrens games
- [x] Animal exhibits/petting zoo
- [x] Dogs allowed on leash
- [x] Lost and found
- [x] Bicycle racks
- [x] First aid area available
- [x] Self-brought picnics allowed
- [ ] Self-brought alcohol allowed
- [ ] Stroller/wheelchair rentals available

- [ ] Parade
- [ ] Parking fee
- [ ] Entrance fee
- [x] Camping facilities: 1 mile
- [x] Boating facilities: Avila Bay
- [x] RV facilities w/ hookups: 1 mile
- [x] Accomodations in town
  Oak Park Resort, Knights Inn, Motel 6, Quality Suites
- [x] Restaurants in town
  The Quarterback, Spanish Seas, Pismo Joe's, Shore Cliff, Genovese's, Sea Venture

# *Fiesta de Artes*

THE SPANISH THEME OF **Fiesta de Artes** is appropriate for the picturesque town of Los Gatos—The Cats! Sponsored by the Los Gatos Jaycees, this festival is celebrating it's 25th year! Wine tasting is provided by ten local vinters—Ivan Tamas, Kirigin Cellars, Congress Springs, and Mirassou are just a few. This artsy town does this festival up right!

## Los Gatos, California

Third weekend in August
Daily 11:00 AM - 6:00 PM

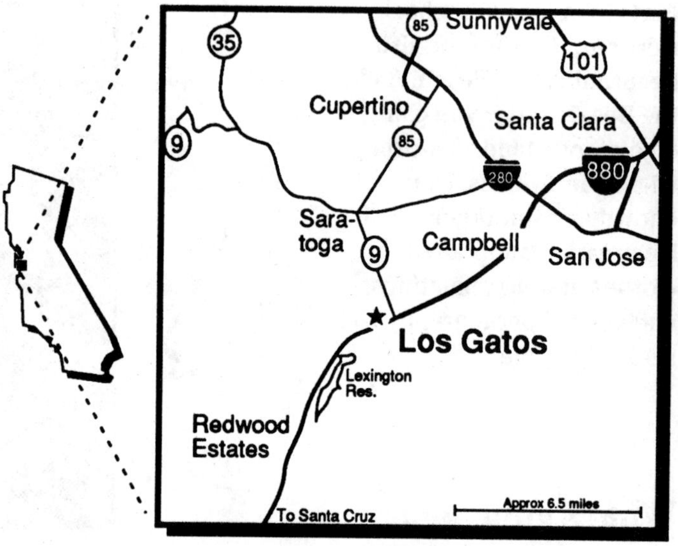


*Up-to-date festival information is available from:*
*Los Gatos Chamber of Commerce*
*(408) 354-9300*

## What's goin' on...

Town population: **28,500**
Last year's attendance: **20,000**
Average outdoor temperature: **85°**
Festival location: **Old Town**

- ✗ Wine tasting/beer for sale
- ✗ Food booths
- ✗ Arts/crafts for sale
- ✗ Live music
- ✗ Clowns
- ✗ Face painters
- Childrens games
- Animal exhibits/petting zoo
- Dogs allowed on leash
- ✗ Lost and found
- Bicycle racks
- ✗ First aid area available
- Self-brought picnics allowed
- Self-brought alcohol allowed
- Stroller/wheelchair rentals available

- Parade
- Parking fee
- Entrance fee
- ✗ Camping facilities: 20 miles
- ✗ Boating facilities
- ✗ RV facilities w/ hookups: 3 miles
- ✗ Accomodations in town
  Toll House, Los Gatos Lodge, La Hacienda Inn, Lodge at Villa Felice, Los Gatos Garden Inn
- ✗ Restaurants in town
  The Chart House, C.B. Hannegan's, Fiorillo's, Mabel's Lantern House, Pedro's, The Diner

# *Milpitas Art & Wine Fetival*

CALIFORNIA MAKES THE finest wines around...and if you don't believe us Californians, see for yourself at the **Milpitas Art & Wine Festival!** Yesiree, lift your glasses to the sky as you salute the vineyards of J. Lohr, Wente, Elliston, Troquato, Stony Ridge and Mirrasou! Ant there are food booths galore, too—Thai, calamari, Polish, Japanese, hamburgers and hotdogs, and sweets! But, remember...you came here to see the art!

## Milpitas, California

Third weekend in August
Daily 10:00 AM - 5:00 PM

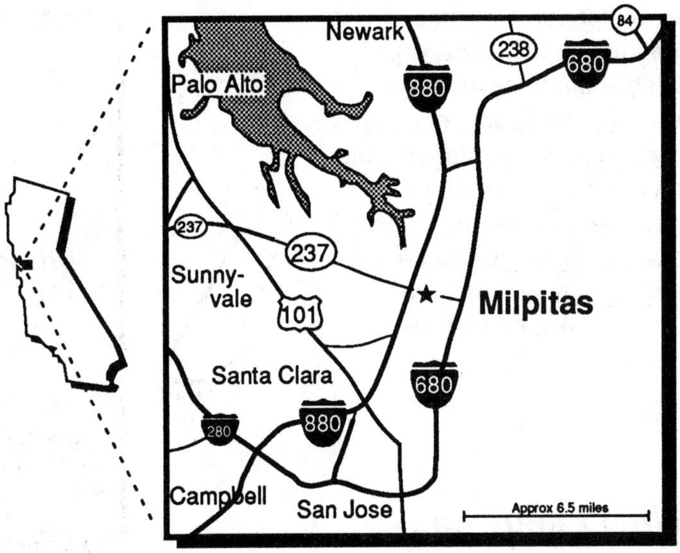


*Up-to-date festival information is available from:*
*Milpitas Chamber of Commerce*
*(408) 262-2613*

## What's goin' on...

Town population: **49,250**
Last year's attendance: **45,000**
Average outdoor temperature: **78°**
Festival location: **Downtown**

- ✗ Wine tasting/beer for sale
- ✗ Food booths
- ✗ Arts/crafts for sale
- ✗ Live music
- ✗ Clowns
- ✗ Face painters
- Childrens games
- Animal exhibits/petting zoo
- ✗ Dogs allowed on leash
- ✗ Lost and found
- Bicycle racks
- ✗ First aid area available
- ✗ Self-brought picnics allowed
- Self-brought alcohol allowed
- Stroller/wheelchair rentals available

- Parade
- Parking fee
- Entrance fee
- Camping facilities
- Boating facilities
- ✗ RV facilities w/ hookups: 8 miles
- ✗ Accomodations in town
  Beverly Heritage, Sheraton, Embassy Suites, Holiday Inn
- ✗ Restaurants in town
  Brandon's, Zahir's Cafe, Tivoli Restaurant, The Club at Summitpointe

# *Petaluma River Festival*

RISE AND SHINE FOR THE 7:00 AM pancake breakfast that launches the **Petaluma River Festival**. Wow... there's lots to do here all day long! After feasting on hotcakes, eggs, bacon, and juice, make your way over to booths of country crafts and art. For lunch, dine on Greek, Thai, or Mexican food—or good ol' fried chicken. Dance in the streets, beneath a starlit sky, from 8 till midnight. Perfect score below...*YEOWZA!*

## Petaluma, California

Third Saturday in August
7:00 AM - midnight

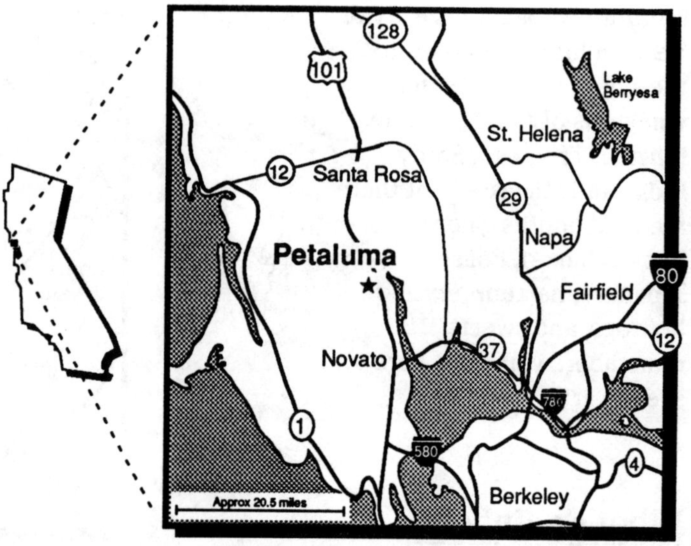


*Up-to-date festival information is available from:*
*Petaluma Chamber of Commerce*
*(707) 762-2785*

## What's goin' on...

Town population: **42,000**
Last year's attendance: **10,000**
Average outdoor temperature: **83°**
Festival location: **Downtown**

| | |
|---|---|
| ✗ | Wine tasting/beer for sale |
| ✗ | Food booths |
| ✗ | Arts/crafts for sale |
| ✗ | Live music |
| ✗ | Clowns |
| ✗ | Face painters |
| ✗ | Childrens games |
| ✗ | Animal exhibits/petting zoo |
| ✗ | Dogs allowed on leash |
| ✗ | Lost and found |
| ✗ | Bicycle racks |
| ✗ | First aid area available |
| ✗ | Self-brought picnics allowed |
| ✗ | Self-brought alcohol allowed |
| ✗ | Stroller/wheelchair rentals available |

| | |
|---|---|
| | Parade |
| | Parking fee |
| ✗ | Entrance fee: Adults $2; Kids free |
| ✗ | Camping facilities, 5 miles |
| ✗ | Boating facilities: River, lake, and bay |
| ✗ | RV facilities w/ hookups: 5 miles |
| ✗ | Accomodations in town<br>Best Western, Quality Inn, Motel 6, Cavanagh Cottage B&B, 7th St. Inn B&B |
| ✗ | Restaurants in town<br>Petrucci's, Tempura House, Steamer Gold, Cattlemen's, Fino's,Original Marvin's |

# *Day on the Monterey Bay Regatta*

MORE THAN 1,000 SPINNAkers billowing and 1,500 sailors will take to the big blue seas for the annual United Way **Day on the Monterey Bay Regattta.** Prices: $35 per individual sailings (inc: seabag, lunch, barbecue, steak dinner); $15 for barbecue steak dinner only! There's more than just sailing too—banjo band, raffles, and nautical flea market! Interested in sailing? Call for more information.

## Santa Cruz, California

Third Saturday in August
Early till late!

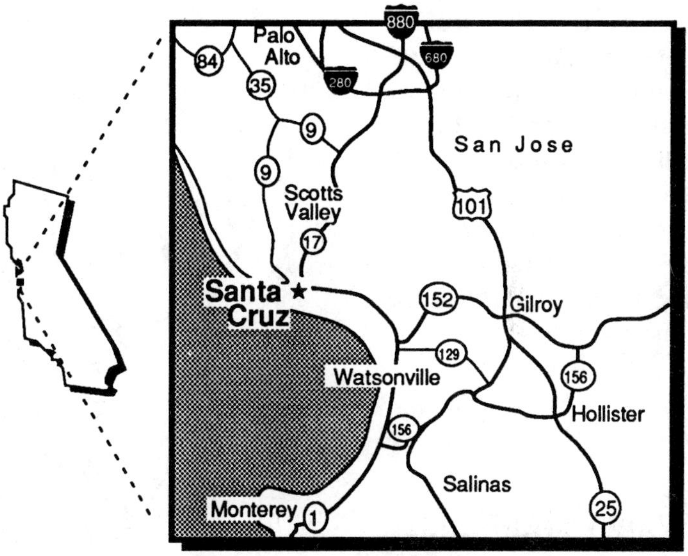

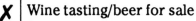

*Up-to-date festival information is available from:*
*Santa Cruz Yacht Harbor*
*(408) 688-2082*

## What's goin' on...

Town population: **45,000**
Last year's attendance: **1,500**
Average outdoor temperature: **75°**
Festival location: **Santa Cruz Yacht Harbor**

| | |
|---|---|
| X | Wine tasting/beer for sale |
| X | Food booths |
| | Arts/crafts for sale |
| X | Live music |
| | Clowns |
| | Face painters |
| | Childrens games |
| | Animal exhibits/petting zoo |
| X | Dogs allowed on leash |
| | Lost and found |
| X | Bicycle racks |
| | First aid area available |
| X | Self-brought picnics allowed |
| X | Self-brought alcohol allowed |
| | Stroller/wheelchair rentals available |

| | |
|---|---|
| | Parade |
| | Parking fee |
| X | Entrance fee: see paragraph |
| X | Camping facilities: 5 miles |
| X | Boating facilities: Monterey Bay |
| X | RV facilities w/ hookups: 5 miles |
| X | Accomodations in town<br>Babbling Brook B&B, Cliff Crest B&B, Chateau Victorian B&B, The Darling House B&B |
| X | Restaurants in town<br>Aldo's, Crow's Nest |

# *South San Francisco Art & Wine Festival*

NOT ONLY DOES THE **SOUTH San Francisco Art & Wine Festival** headline great wine and distinguished art, but it also has a chili cook-off on Saturday and a classic-car show on Sunday. This little-sister town of the "the City" will host food booths with Italian, Mexican, Chinese, Japanese, and Hawaiian favorites and has a petting zoo for the youngsters to enjoy.

## So. San Francisco, California

Third weekend in August
Daily 10:00 AM - 6:00 PM

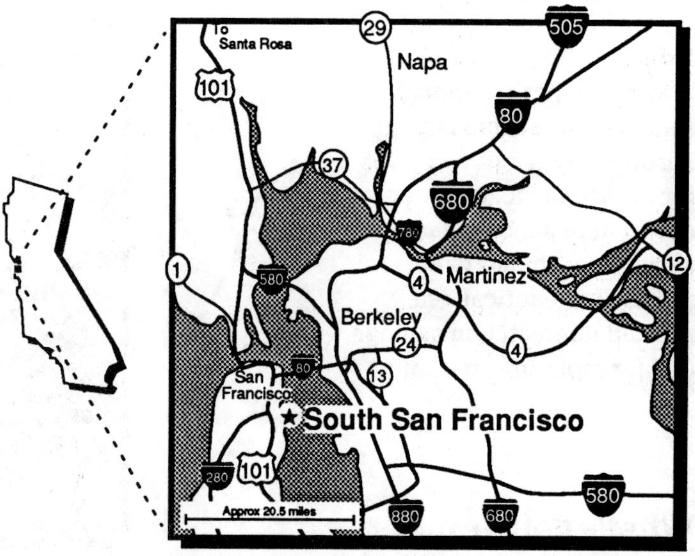


*Up-to-date festival information is available from:*
*So. San Francisco Chamber of Commerce*
*(415) 588-1911*

## What's goin' on...

Town population: **50,000**
Last year's attendance: **50,000**
Average outdoor temperature: **68°**
Festival location: **Downtown**

| | | | |
|---|---|---|---|
| X | Wine tasting/beer for sale | | Parade |
| X | Food booths | | Parking fee |
| X | Arts/crafts for sale | | Entrance fee |
| X | Live music | X | Camping facilities: [illegible] miles |
| X | Clowns | X | Boating facilities: San Francisco Bay |
| X | Face painters | X | RV facilities w/ hookups: 3 miles |
| X | Childrens games | X | Accomodations in town |
| X | Animal exhibits/petting zoo | | Grovesnor |
| | Dogs allowed on leash | | |
| X | Lost and found | | |
| X | Bicycle racks | | |
| X | First aid area available | X | Restaurants in town |
| | Self-brought picnics allowed | | |
| | Self-brought alcohol allowed | | |
| | Stroller/wheelchair rentals available | | |

# *Auburn Area Funk Soap Box Derby*

A WHAT? YES YOU READ IT right! Auburn is the proud host to the **Auburn Area Bunk Soap Box Derby**! This hilarious and exciting event is unique, fun, and very suspenseful! "It's time to match wits with the most creative minds and the most devious mechanical wizards of mischief," says Auburn's Mayor Bud Pisarek. The entrance rules are only a half-a-page long...so you know there will be loads of zany entries!

## Auburn, California

Third Sunday in August
8:30 AM - 6:30 PM

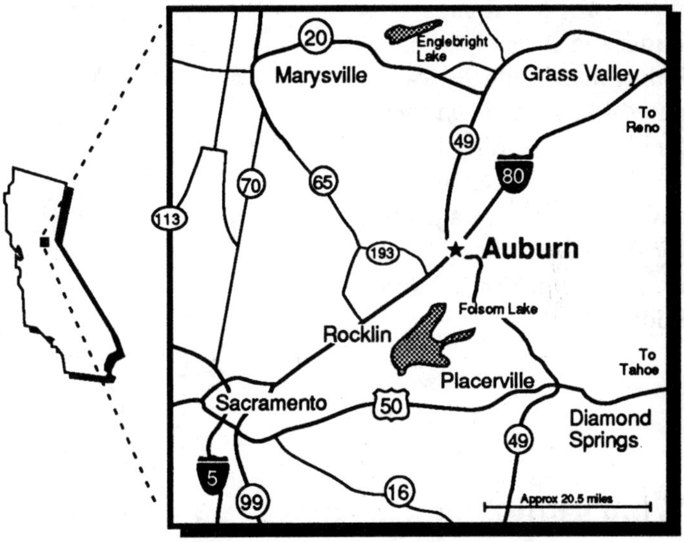


## What's goin' on...

Town population: **7,500**
Last year's attendance: **N/A**
Average outdoor temperature: **85°**
Festival location: **Lincoln Way**

☞ *Up-to-date festival information is available from:*
*Auburn Chamber of Commerce*
*(916) 885-5616*

| | |
|---|---|
| X | Wine tasting/beer for sale |
| X | Food booths |
| X | Arts/crafts for sale |
| X | Live music |
| X | Clowns |
| | Face painters |
| | Childrens games |
| | Animal exhibits/petting zoo |
| X | Dogs allowed on leash |
| | Lost and found |
| | Bicycle racks |
| X | First aid area available |
| X | Self-brought picnics allowed |
| | Self-brought alcohol allowed |
| | Stroller/wheelchair rentals available |

| | |
|---|---|
| | Parade |
| | Parking fee |
| | Entrance fee: No fee to watch |
| X | Camping facilities: In town |
| X | Boating facilities: Folsom Lake |
| X | RV facilities w/ hookups: In town |
| X | Accomodations in town: The Dry Creek Inn B&B, Lincoln House B&B, Old Auburn Inn B&B, Power's Mansion Inn B&B |
| X | Restaurants in town: Lou La Bonte's, Cafe Chaos, The Koffee Kup, Edelweiss Restaurant |

# Cantaloupe Roundup

FIREBAUGH IS THE HOME OF the California **Cantaloupe Roundup** in August. Let your hair down and dance the night away to live music under the stars of Firebaugh's balmy nights. Ideally located—50 miles from the Sierras and 30 miles from the Pacific Coast—this little town's festival has a carnival for the kids, crafts, and "the best Mexican food around" till midnight!

## Firebaugh, California

Fourth weekend in August (beginning Thursday)
Hours vary

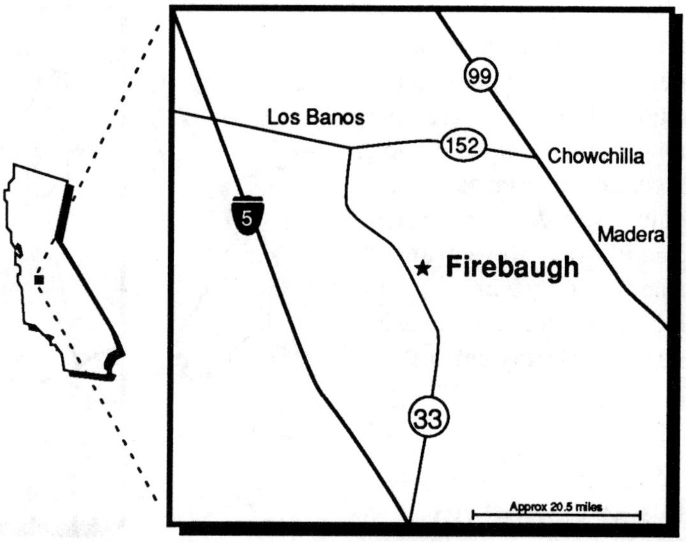


## What's goin' on...

Town population: **3,740**
Last year's attendance: **8,000**
Average outdoor temperature: **90°**
Festival location: **Downtown**

*Up-to-date festival information is available from:*
*Firebaugh Chamber of Commerce*
*(209) 659-3701*

- X Wine tasting/beer for sale
- X Food booths
- X Arts/crafts for sale
- X Live music
- X Clowns
- X Face painters
- X Childrens games
- Animal exhibits/petting zoo
- X Dogs allowed on leash
- X Lost and found
- Bicycle racks
- X First aid area available
- X Self-brought picnics allowed
- Self-brought alcohol allowed
- Stroller/wheelchair rentals available

- X Parade: Sat. noon downtown
- Parking fee
- Entrance fee
- X Camping facilities: 10 miles
- X Boating facilities: Madera Lake
- X RV facilities w/ hookups: 8 miles
- Accomodations in town
- X Restaurants in town
  El Capitan, Jack's Prime Time, Miguel's, Firebaugh Restaurant

# *Gilroy Hispanic Cultural Festival*

THREE STAGES OF FREE entertainment are scattered throughout the **Gilroy Hispanic Cultural Festival.** "Para Los Niños" includes carnival rides, petting zoo, piñata breaking, puppet shows and much more. For you mouth-watering adults, there are gourmet Hispanic food booths from Mexico, Spain, South and Central America.

## Gilroy, California

Last full weekend in August
Daily 10:00 AM - 7:00 PM

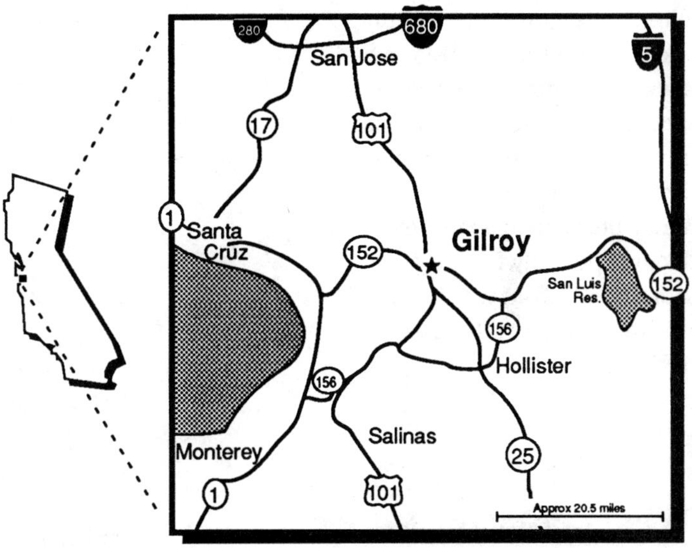


## What's goin' on...

Town population: **30,000**
Last year's attendance: **142,000**
Average outdoor temperature: **90°**
Festival location: **Christmas Hill Park**

*Up-to-date festival information is available from:*
*Gilroy Hispanic Chamber*
*(408) 848-5780*

| | |
|---|---|
| ✗ | Wine tasting/beer for sale |
| ✗ | Food booths |
| ✗ | Arts/crafts for sale |
| ✗ | Live music |
| ✗ | Clowns |
| ✗ | Face painters |
| ✗ | Childrens games |
| ✗ | Animal exhibits/petting zoo |
| | Dogs allowed on leash |
| ✗ | Lost and found |
| | Bicycle racks |
| ✗ | First aid area available |
| | Self-brought picnics allowed |
| | Self-brought alcohol allowed |
| | Stroller/wheelchair rentals available |

| | |
|---|---|
| ✗ | Parade |
| | Parking fee |
| ✗ | Entrance fee: S $4; A $5; K $1 |
| ✗ | Camping facilities: 15 miles |
| ✗ | Boating facilities: Lake Coyote |
| ✗ | RV facilities w/ hookups: 15 miles |
| ✗ | Accomodations in town<br>Country Rose Inn B&B, Best Western, Casa de Fruta, Super 8, Motel 6 |
| ✗ | Restaurants in town<br>Harvest Time, Diggers, Sandrinos |

CENTRAL

# *Scotts Valley Pioneer Days*

**PIONEER DAYS** BEGAN IN 1987, and it's been a roaring success, so they plan to make it even bigger and better! You'll encounter entertaining clowns and mimes, feast on fresh calamari and strawberry shortcake, enjoy the live jazz music, survey the handmade crafts for sale, and take in the early pioneering exhibits! This is an especially friendly community that welcomes all visitors! (Kids under 5 admitted free.)

## Scotts Valley, California

Fourth weekend in August
Daily 10:00 AM - 6:00 PM

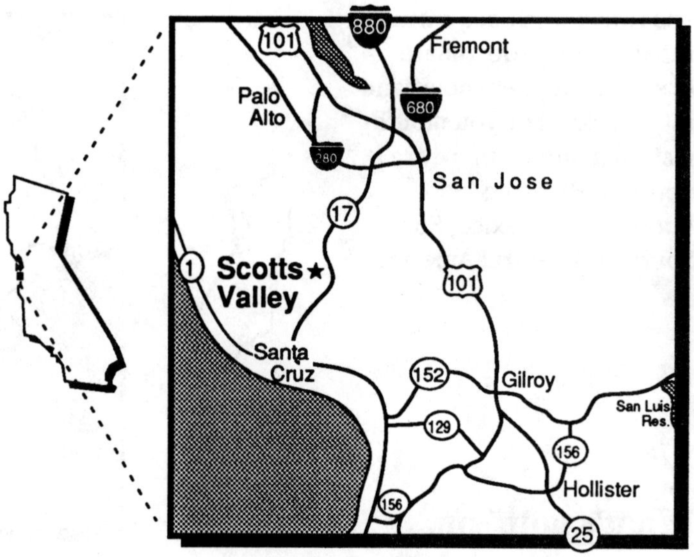


*Up-to-date festival information is available from:*
*Scotts Valley Chamber of Commerce*
*(408) 438-1010*

## What's goin' on...

Town population: **9,085**
Last year's attendance: **4,000**
Average outdoor temperature: **78°**
Festival location: **Siltanen Park**

- ✗ Wine tasting/beer for sale
- ✗ Food booths
- ✗ Arts/crafts for sale
- ✗ Live music
- ✗ Clowns
- ✗ Face painters
- ✗ Childrens games
- ✗ Animal exhibits/petting zoo
- ✗ Dogs allowed on leash
- ✗ Lost and found
- ✗ Bicycle racks
- ✗ First aid area available
- Self-brought picnics allowed
- Self-brought alcohol allowed
- Stroller/wheelchair rentals available

- ✗ Parade: (date & time not avbl.)
- Parking fee
- ✗ Entrance fee: S $3; A $5; 6-11 $2
- ✗ Camping facilities: 1 mile
- ✗ Boating facilities: Santa Cruz Harbor
- ✗ RV facilities w/ hookups: 1 mile
- ✗ Accomodations in town
  Best Western, Chateau des Fleurs
- ✗ Restaurants in town
  Zanotto's Pasta and More, Peachwood's Bar & Grill, Backstage Restaurant, ABC Chinese

# *Wild West Rodeo Weekend*

THE ANNUAL **WILD WEST Rodeo Weekend** takes place in Bishop on Labor Day weekend—just like it has been since 1930. Set in the beautiful Sierra Nevada Mountains, Bishop offers two PRCA rodeos, teen dance, carnival, barbecue, chili cook-off— followed by a chili dinner that'll knock you outta your saddle—bed races, and dances galore! Oh, and let's not forget the unforgettable Lion's Pancake Breakfast! This is serious all-American fun!

## Bishop, California

Labor Day weekend
Daily 9:30 AM - 9:00 PM

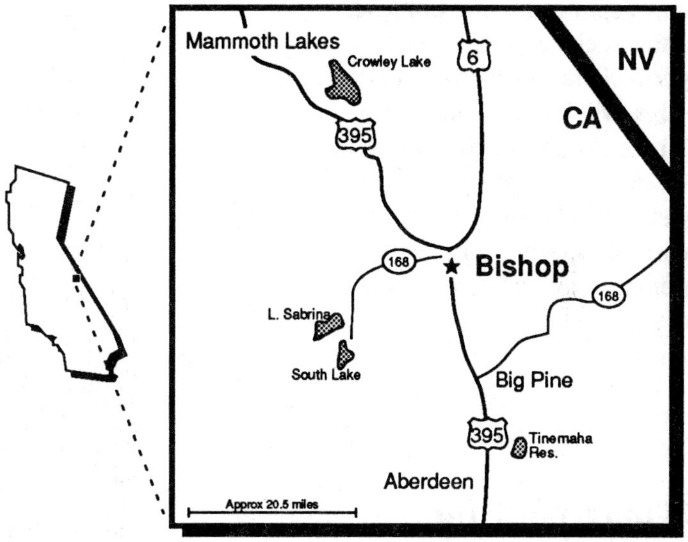


*Up-to-date festival information is available from:*
*Bishop Chamber of Commerce*
*(619) 873-8405*

## What's goin' on...

Town population: **3,800**
Last year's attendance: **25,000**
Average outdoor temperature: **95°**
Festival location: **Fairgrounds**

- X Wine tasting/beer for sale
- X Food booths
- X Arts/crafts for sale
- X Live music
- X Clowns
- Face painters
- X Childrens games
- Animal exhibits/petting zoo
- X Dogs allowed on leash
- X Lost and found
- X Bicycle racks
- X First aid area available
- X Self-brought picnics allowed
- Self-brought alcohol allowed
- Stroller/wheelchair rentals available

- X Parade: Sat. 10:00 AM on Main St.
- Parking fee
- X Entrance fee: (prices not avbl.)
- X Camping facilities: Fairgrounds
- Boating facilities
- X RV facilities w/ hookups: 2 miles
- X Accomodations in town
  Matlick House, Chalfant House
- X Restaurants in town
  Whiskey Creek, Firehouse Grill, BBQ Bills, Jack's Waffle Shop, Bishop Grill

# *Fall Fest*

TODOS SANTOS PARK IS THE site of Concord's **Fall Fest** over the Labor Day weekend. Food booths featuring Mexican, Japanese, Thai, Chinese, and Greek cuisine, as well as good ol' hamburgers and hot dogs, will be on hand. There's lots to do: listen to music, taste wines, sample cook-off–winning chili, or just hang out with the clowns, jugglers, puppeteers, and face painters!

## Concord, California

Labor Day weekend
Daily 10:00 AM - 10:00 PM

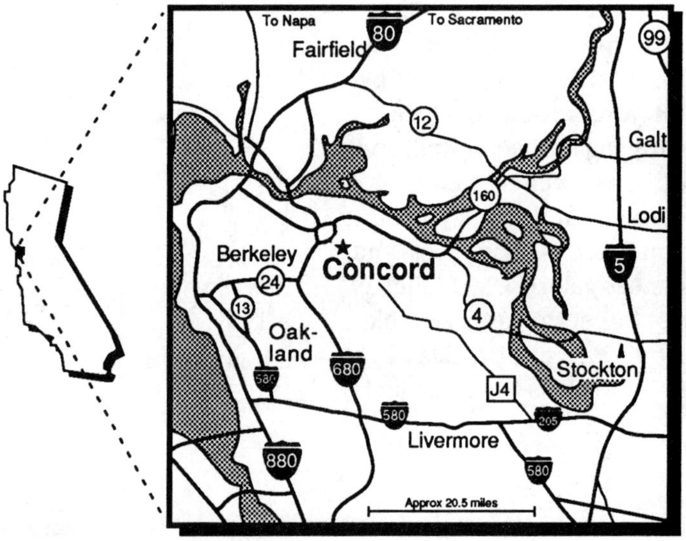


*Up-to-date festival information is available from:*
*Concord Chamber of Commerce*
*(415) 684-1496*

## What's goin' on...

Town population: **108,000**
Last year's attendance: **6,000**
Average outdoor temperature: **85°**
Festival location: **Todos Santos Park**

- ✗ Wine tasting/beer for sale
- ✗ Food booths
- ✗ Arts/crafts for sale
- ✗ Live music
- ✗ Clowns
- ✗ Face painters
- ✗ Childrens games
- Animal exhibits/petting zoo
- ✗ Dogs allowed on leash
- ✗ Lost and found
- Bicycle racks
- ✗ First aid area available
- ✗ Self-brought picnics allowed
- Self-brought alcohol allowed
- Stroller/wheelchair rentals available

- Parade
- ✗ Parking fee: $1
- Entrance fee
- Camping facilities
- ✗ Boating facilities: Straits
- ✗ RV facilities w/ hookups: In town
- ✗ Accomodations in town
  Concord Hilton, Concord Inn, Heritage Inn Concord, Easy 8 Motel, Trees Inn
- ✗ Restaurants in town
  Benihana's, El Morocco, Charley Brown's, Pacific Fresh

# *Harvest Festival*

LIVERMORE FEATURES nine local wineries in and around the towns of Pleasanton, Livermore, and Sunol at the annual **Harvest Festival**. Each winery has events and entertainment during the Labor Day weekend in celebration of the top-quality grapes harvested: Cabernet Sauvignon, Sauvignon Blanc, and Chardonnay. The $10. entry fee includes shuttle, souvenir glass, and program.

## Livermore, California

Labor Day weekend
Daily noon - 5:00 PM

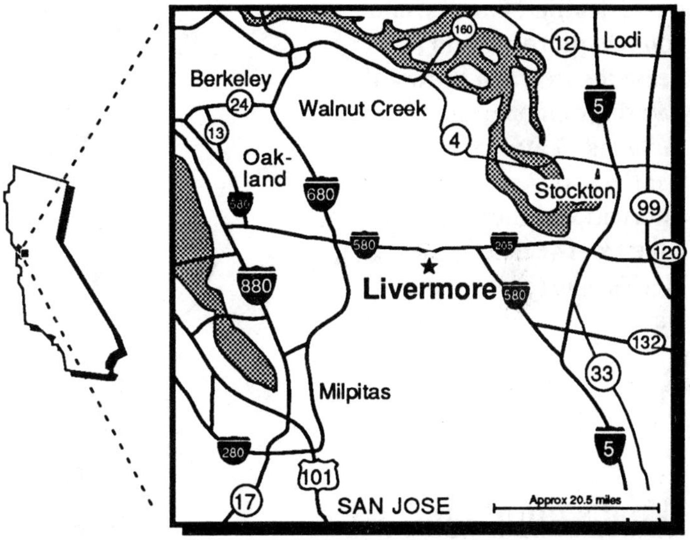


CENTRAL

## What's goin' on...

Town population: **56,445**
Last year's attendance: **10,000**
Average outdoor temperature: **82°**
Festival location: **Robertson Park/Wineries**

*Up-to-date festival information is available from:*
*Livermore Chamber of Commerce*
*(415) 447-1606*

| | |
|---|---|
| X | Wine tasting/beer for sale |
| X | Food booths |
| X | Arts/crafts for sale |
| X | Live music |
| X | Clowns |
| X | Face painters |
| | Childrens games |
| | Animal exhibits/petting zoo |
| | Dogs allowed on leash |
| | Lost and found |
| X | Bicycle racks |
| | First aid area available |
| | Self-brought picnics allowed |
| | Self-brought alcohol allowed |
| | Stroller/wheelchair rentals available |

| | |
|---|---|
| | Parade |
| | Parking fee |
| X | Entrance fee: See notes |
| X | Camping facilities: 11 miles |
| X | Boating facilities: Del Valle Res. |
| X | RV facilities w/ hookups: 11 miles |
| X | Accomodations in town<br>Townhouse Motel, Residence Inn, Holiday Inn |
| X | Restaurants in town<br>El Lorito, Le Coquelicot, Cruiser's, Beeb's Bar & Grill, Wente Sparkling Cellars Restaurant |

# *Millbrae Art & Wine Festival*

THE ANNUAL **MILLBRAE ART & Wine Festival** features exceptional crafts: jewelry, ceramics, stained glass, wood, leather, flowers, and soft sculpture. Artists also bring their oil and watercolor paintings, photographs, and etchings. Featuring food booths with American and international themes, and wine from selected vineyards, all this takes place on Broadway.

## Millbrae, California

Saturday and Sunday of Labor Day weekend
Daily 10:00 AM - 6:00 PM

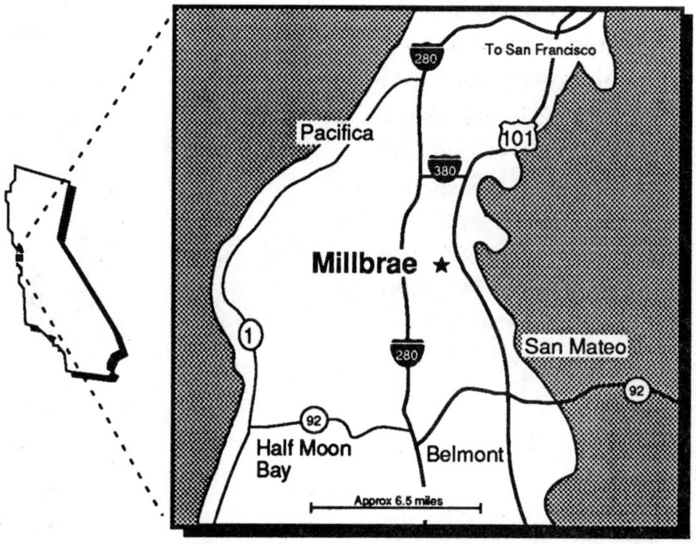


*Up-to-date festival information is available from:*
*Millbrae Chamber of Commerce*
*(415) 697-7324*

## What's goin' on...

Town population: **21,250**
Last year's attendance: **100,000**
Average outdoor temperature: **80°**
Festival location: **Downtown**

| | |
|---|---|
| ✗ | Wine tasting/beer for sale |
| ✗ | Food booths |
| ✗ | Arts/crafts for sale |
| ✗ | Live music |
| | Clowns |
| ✗ | Face painters |
| ✗ | Childrens games |
| | Animal exhibits/petting zoo |
| ✗ | Dogs allowed on leash |
| ✗ | Lost and found |
| | Bicycle racks |
| ✗ | First aid area available |
| ✗ | Self-brought picnics allowed |
| | Self-brought alcohol allowed |
| | Stroller/wheelchair rentals available |

| | |
|---|---|
| | Parade |
| | Parking fee |
| | Entrance fee |
| | Camping facilities |
| ✗ | Boating facilities: San Francisco Bay |
| | RV facilities w/ hookups |
| ✗ | Accomodations in town<br>El Rancho Inn, TraveLodge, Clarion Hotel, Westin Hotel |
| ✗ | Restaurants in town<br>Ray's Place, Hong Kong Flower Lounge, 16 Mile House, Terrace Cafe |

# *Mountain Peddler's Antique & Collector's Fair*

NESTLED AT THE BOTTOM tip of the Yosemite National Forest lies the lively little town of Oakhurst—host to the **Mountain Peddler's Antique & Collector's Fair**! Heck, the town folks like this little get together so much, that it's held twice yearly! You'll find knick-knacks you've never seen or heard of before...but there's definitely some- thing for everyone! And as they say, "one man's junk, is another man's treasure!"

## Oakhurst, California

Labor Day weekend
Daily 8:00 AM - 5:00 PM

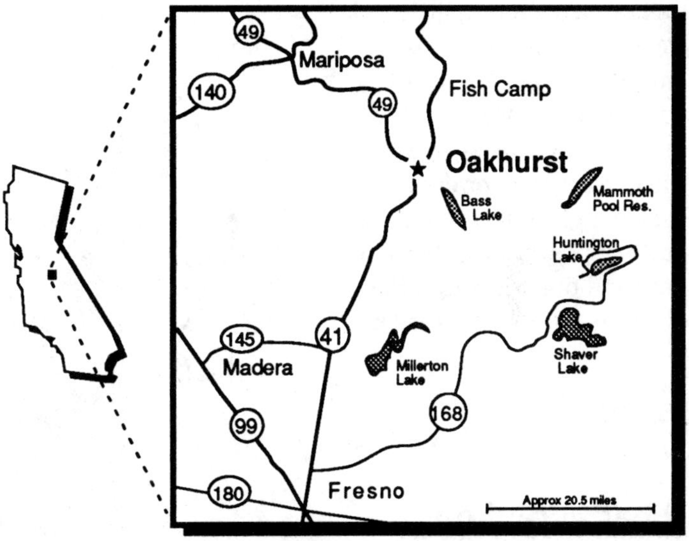


## What's goin' on...

Town population: **12,000**
Last year's attendance: **20,000**
Average outdoor temperature: **80°**
Festival location: **Downtown**

*Up-to-date festival information is available from: Oakhurst Chamber of Commerce (209) 683-7766*

- X Wine tasting/beer for sale
- X Food booths
- X Arts/crafts for sale
- X Live music
- Clowns
- Face painters
- Childrens games
- Animal exhibits/petting zoo
- Dogs allowed on leash
- Lost and found
- Bicycle racks
- First aid area available
- Self-brought picnics allowed
- Self-brought alcohol allowed
- Stroller/wheelchair rentals available

- Parade
- X Parking fee: $2 or free
- Entrance fee
- X Camping facilities: 5 miles
- X Boating facilities: Bass Lake
- X RV facilities w/ hookups: In town
- X Accomodations in town
  Shilo Inn, Best Western
- X Restaurants in town
  The Old Barn, Erna's Elderberry House, Golden Bit

# *Sausalito Art Festival*

THIS IS ALMOST AN ELEGANT affair! The **Sausalito Art Festival**, which began back in 1951, is held in one of California's alluring little waterfront towns. Full of antique and gift shops, the community is made up primarily of artists—making the fine arts and crafts for sale extra special. There is a Festival poster for sale each year and puppet shows that even the adults will treasure.

## Sausalito, California

Labor Day (three-day) weekend
Daily 10:00 AM - 6:00 PM

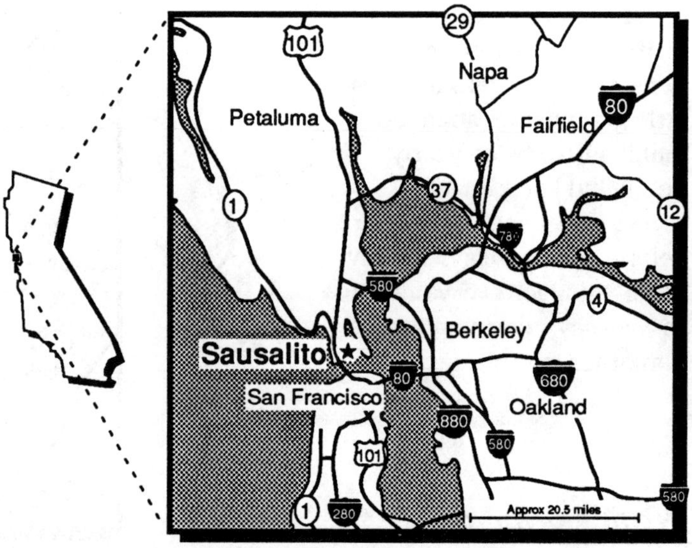


## What's goin' on...

Town population: **7,500**
Last year's attendance: **50,000**
Average outdoor temperature: **70°**
Festival location: **Marinship Park**

*Up-to-date festival information is available from:*
*Sausalito Chamber of Commerce*
*(415) 332-0505*

- X Wine tasting/beer for sale
- X Food booths
- X Arts/crafts for sale
- X Live music
- X Clowns
- X Face painters
- X Childrens games
- Animal exhibits/petting zoo
- Dogs allowed on leash
- X Lost and found
- X Bicycle racks
- X First aid area available
- Self-brought picnics allowed
- Self-brought alcohol allowed
- Stroller/wheelchair rentals available

- Parade
- X Parking fee: $3
- X Entrance fee: S & K $2; A $4
- X Camping facilities: 10 miles
- X Boating facilities: San Francisco Bay
- X RV facilities w/ hookups: 15 miles
- X Accomodations in town
  Casa Madrone, Alta Mira, Sausalito Hotel
- X Restaurants in town
  Houlihan's, Spinnaker

# *Apple Hill Festival*

WHAT AN INCREDIBLE SMELL permeates the air when you head up Hwy. 50 to the **Apple Hill Festival!** Sixteen bake shops and seven cider mills churn out mouth-watering goodies beginning in early September when the Golden Delicious apples are ready to harvest! Delectable specialties range from apple pie and apple almond bars to apple cheese cake and apple butter! Bring one back for your teacher!

## Camino, California

Labor Day to Christmas
Hours vary

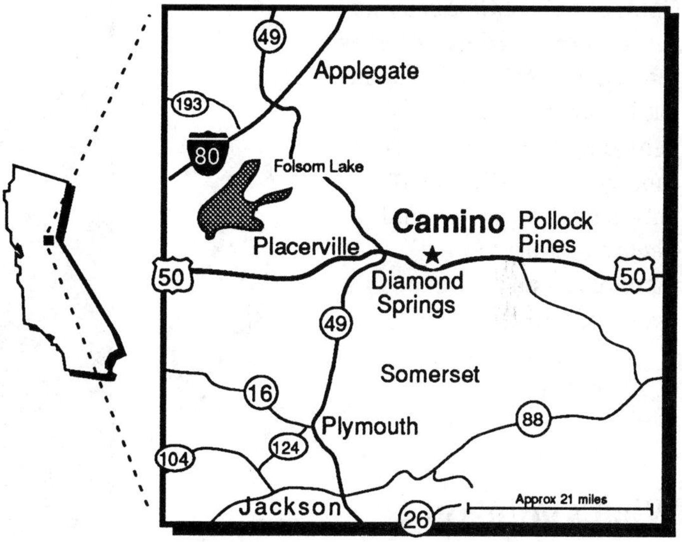


*Up-to-date festival information is available from:*
*Camino Apple Hill Growers Assn.*
*(916) 622-9595*

## What's goin' on...

Town population: **9,000**
Last year's attendance: **N/A**
Average outdoor temperature: **65°**
Festival location: **Apple Hill**

| | |
|---|---|
| | Wine tasting/beer for sale |
| X | Food booths |
| X | Arts/crafts for sale |
| | Live music |
| | Clowns |
| | Face painters |
| X | Childrens games |
| X | Animal exhibits/petting zoo |
| X | Dogs allowed on leash |
| | Lost and found |
| | Bicycle racks |
| | First aid area available |
| X | Self-brought picnics allowed |
| | Self-brought alcohol allowed |
| | Stroller/wheelchair rentals available |

| | |
|---|---|
| | Parade |
| | Parking fee |
| | Entrance fee |
| X | Camping facilities: 6 miles |
| | Boating facilities |
| X | RV facilities w/ hookups: 6 miles |
| | Accomodations in town |
| | Restaurants in town |

# *Wild Game Barbecue*

WOULD YOU TRY BARBECUED rattlesnake? If so, you'd better git on over to the **Wild Game Barbecue** in San Luis Obispo! This SLO Sportsmen's Assn.- sponsored event takes place at Cuesta Park. Besides wild boar, rattlesnake, elk, venison, buffalo, albacore tuna, and bear, there will be not-so-exotic chicken and beef to tempt your tastebuds—all barbecued on oakwood grills!

## San Luis Obispo, California

September (call Chamber for exact date)
Noon - 3:00 PM

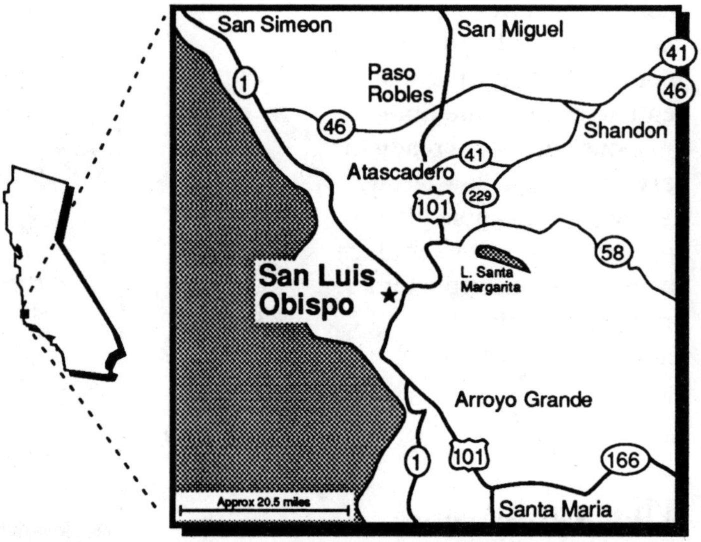


## What's goin' on...

Town population: **41,000**
Last year's attendance: **2,500**
Average outdoor temperature: **70°**
Festival location: **Cuesta Park**

*Up-to-date festival information is available from:*
*San Luis Obispo Chamber of Commerce*
*(805) 543-1323*

- ✗ Wine tasting/beer for sale
- ✗ Food booths
- Arts/crafts for sale
- Live music
- Clowns
- Face painters
- Childrens games
- Animal exhibits/petting zoo
- Dogs allowed on leash
- Lost and found
- ✗ Bicycle racks
- First aid area available
- Self-brought picnics allowed
- Self-brought alcohol allowed
- Stroller/wheelchair rentals available

- Parade
- Parking fee
- Entrance fee
- ✗ Camping facilities: 15 miles
- ✗ Boating facilities: Lakes and ocean
- ✗ RV facilities w/ hookups: 15 miles
- ✗ Accomodations in town
  Madonna Inn, Peach Tree Inn, Garden St. B&B
- ✗ Restaurants in town
  Apple Farm, Hudson's Grill, Chef Em's, Cafe Roma, Brubeck's

# *Labor Day Country Bazaar*

MAIN STREET IS LINED WITH booths selling everything from antiques and armadillos to zen and sulu charms at the **Labor Day Country Bazaar**. There are food and drink booths, a dunk tank, drawings for boats and other prizes. Diamond Springs says "come early & stay late...we promise an enjoyable time!"

## Diamond Springs, California

Labor Day
8:00 AM - 6:00 PM

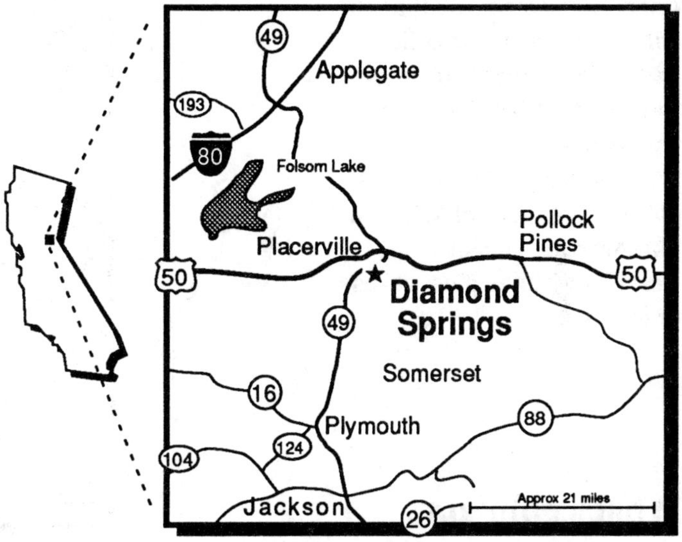


*Up-to-date festival information is available from:*
*Diamond Springs Community Assn.*
*(916) 621-1766*

## What's goin' on...

Town population: **2,000**
Last year's attendance: **2,500**
Average outdoor temperature: **95°**
Festival location: **Main St./Downtown**

| | |
|---|---|
| ✗ | Wine tasting/beer for sale |
| ✗ | Food booths |
| ✗ | Arts/crafts for sale |
| ✗ | Live music |
| | Clowns |
| ✗ | Face painters |
| | Childrens games |
| | Animal exhibits/petting zoo |
| ✗ | Dogs allowed on leash |
| ✗ | Lost and found |
| | Bicycle racks |
| ✗ | First aid area available |
| ✗ | Self-brought picnics allowed |
| | Self-brought alcohol allowed |
| | Stroller/wheelchair rentals available |

| | |
|---|---|
| ✗ | Parade: 1:00 PM on Main St. (Hwy. 49) |
| | Parking fee |
| | Entrance fee |
| ✗ | Camping facilities: 5 miles |
| ✗ | Boating facilities: Lake |
| ✗ | RV facilities w/ hookups: 10 miles |
| ✗ | Accomodations in town<br>Placerville Inn |
| ✗ | Restaurants in town<br>Diamond Motel, The Diggins, The Vineyard House |

# *Harvest Festival*

EVEN WE HAD TO LOOK THIS one up on the map! But...the Kerman **Harvest Festival** promises to be a memorable one! Not far from the Bianchi Vineyards, this town offers dances on Friday and Saturday night with a tri-tip barbecue. The carnival will thrill the kiddies while you savor the flavors of Mexican and American snacks and desserts such as pies, cakes, and ice cream.

## Kerman, California

Weekend following Labor Day (beginning Thurs.)
Thurs. & Fri. 5:00 PM - midnight; Sat. & Sun. noon - midnight

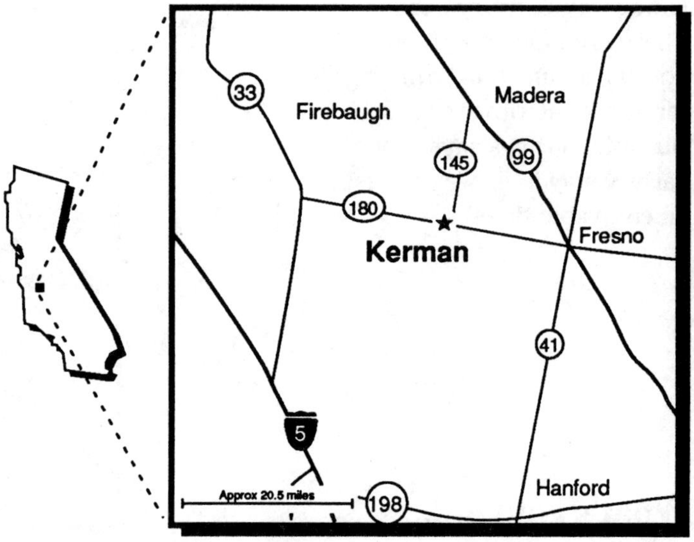


*Up-to-date festival information is available from:*
*Kerman Chamber of Commerce*
*(209) 846-6343*

## What's goin' on...

Town population: **4,800**
Last year's attendance: **10,000**
Average outdoor temperature: **100°**
Festival location: **Downtown park**

| | |
|---|---|
| X | Wine tasting/beer for sale |
| X | Food booths |
| X | Arts/crafts for sale |
| X | Live music |
| | Clowns |
| X | Face painters |
| X | Childrens games |
| | Animal exhibits/petting zoo |
| X | Dogs allowed on leash |
| X | Lost and found |
| | Bicycle racks |
| X | First aid area available |
| | Self-brought picnics allowed |
| | Self-brought alcohol allowed |
| | Stroller/wheelchair rentals available |

| | |
|---|---|
| X | Parade: Sat. 10:00 AM downtown |
| | Parking fee |
| X | Entrance fee: Adults \$2; Kids \$1 |
| | Camping facilities |
| | Boating facilities |
| | RV facilities w/ hookups |
| | Accomodations in town |
| | Restaurants in town |

# *Fall Festival*

THE ANNUAL **FALL FESTIVAL** in Castro Valley is a fabulous place to celebrate the coming of autumn. Offering a wide variety of live entertainment on three stages, it also has food booths representing all the ethnic groups you can think of, and arts and crafts galore. In addition, Lake Chabot—offering a wonderful place for picnicking, hiking, and boating—is only a few miles away.

## Castro Valley, California

Weekend following Labor Day
Daily 10:00 AM - 6:00 PM

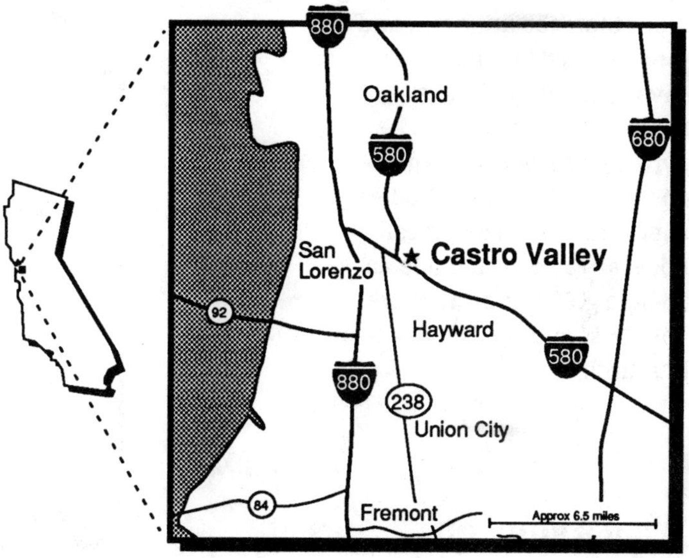


## What's goin' on...

Town population: **48,000**
Last year's attendance: **65,000**
Average outdoor temperature: **80°**
Festival location: **Outdoor shopping area**

*Up-to-date festival information is available from:*
*Castro Valley Chamber of Commerce*
*(415) 537-5300*

| | |
|---|---|
| ✗ | Wine tasting/beer for sale |
| ✗ | Food booths |
| ✗ | Arts/crafts for sale |
| ✗ | Live music |
| ✗ | Clowns |
| ✗ | Face painters |
| | Childrens games |
| | Animal exhibits/petting zoo |
| ✗ | Dogs allowed on leash |
| ✗ | Lost and found |
| | Bicycle racks |
| ✗ | First aid area available |
| ✗ | Self-brought picnics allowed |
| ✗ | Self-brought alcohol allowed |
| | Stroller/wheelchair rentals available |

| | |
|---|---|
| | Parade |
| | Parking fee |
| | Entrance fee |
| ✗ | Camping facilities: 3 miles |
| ✗ | Boating facilities: San Francisco Bay |
| ✗ | RV facilities w/ hookups: 3 miles |
| ✗ | Accomodations in town<br>TraveLodge, Rose Garden |
| ✗ | Restaurants in town |

# *Art & Wine Festival*

DOWNTOWN CASTRO Street is where you'll find the gigantic Mountain View **Art and Wine Festival**— featuring more than 450 art, craft, and food booths! Indulge in savory delights such as nachos, sausages, tacos, gyros, pizza, and homemade cookies and taste full-bodied wines from local wineries. Local attractions include an 18-hole golf course at Shoreline Park, and the NASA Ames Research Ctr.

## Mountain View, California

Weekend following Labor Day
Daily 10:00 AM - 5:00 PM

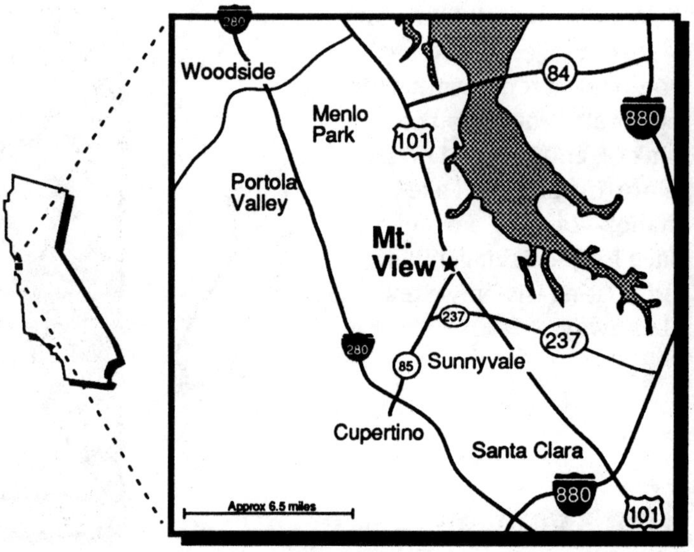


## What's goin' on...

Town population: **63,000**
Last year's attendance: **150,000**
Average outdoor temperature: **75°**
Festival location: **Downtown**

*Up-to-date festival information is available from:*
*Mountain View Chamber of Commerce*
*(415) 968-8378*

- ✗ Wine tasting/beer for sale
- ✗ Food booths
- ✗ Arts/crafts for sale
- Live music
- ✗ Clowns
- ✗ Face painters
- ✗ Childrens games
- ✗ Animal exhibits/petting zoo
- ✗ Dogs allowed on leash
- Lost and found
- Bicycle racks
- First aid area available
- ✗ Self-brought picnics allowed
- Self-brought alcohol allowed
- Stroller/wheelchair rentals available

- Parade
- Parking fee
- Entrance fee
- ✗ Camping facilities: 20 miles
- Boating facilities
- ✗ RV facilities w/ hookups: 10 miles
- ✗ Accomodations in town
- ✗ Restaurants in town
  Jacqueline's Cafe & Wine Bar, Chez TJ, Golden Wok

# *Tiburon Chili Festival*

AND IN 1884, THE WATERfront community of Tiburon was created! Ah, but this whimsical little town really heats up in September for the **Tiburon Chili Festival**! Take the 30-minute ferry ride from San Francisco. Better yet, make an entire day of it and take the ferry from Tiburon out to Angel Island for a bicycle ride. The Richardson Bay Wildlife Sanctuary, in Tiburon, is a wild place to visit too!

## Tiburon, California

First Saturday in September
11:00 AM - 4:00 PM

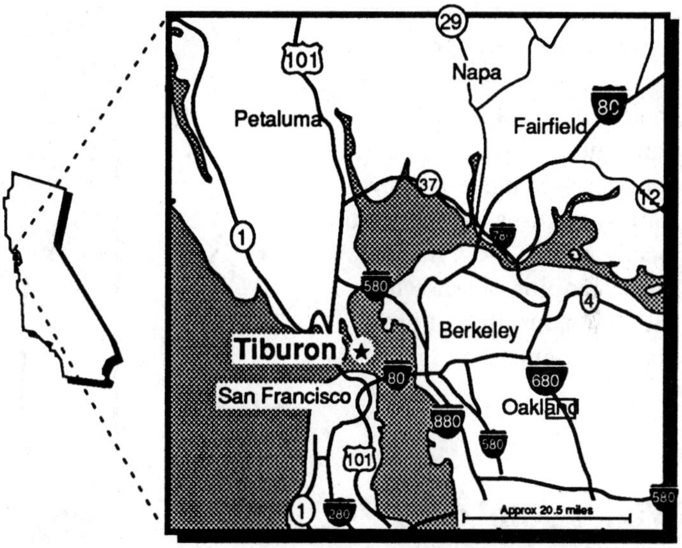


*Up-to-date festival information is available from:*
*Tiburon Chamber of Commerce*
*(415) 435-5633*

## What's goin' on...

Town population: **10,000**
Last year's attendance: **1,900**
Average outdoor temperature: **67°**
Festival location: **Outside Bank of America**

| | |
|---|---|
| X | Wine tasting/beer for sale |
| X | Food booths |
| | Arts/crafts for sale |
| X | Live music |
| X | Clowns |
| X | Face painters |
| X | Childrens games |
| X | Animal exhibits/petting zoo |
| X | Dogs allowed on leash |
| X | Lost and found |
| X | Bicycle racks |
| X | First aid area available |
| | Self-brought picnics allowed |
| | Self-brought alcohol allowed |
| | Stroller/wheelchair rentals available |

| | |
|---|---|
| | Parade |
| X | Parking fee: $3 |
| X | Entrance fee: Adults $4 |
| X | Camping facilities: 20 miles |
| X | Boating facilities: San Francisco Bay |
| X | RV facilities w/ hookups: 20 miles |
| X | Accomodations in town<br>Tiburon Lodge |
| X | Restaurants in town<br>Servino Ristorante, Rooney's Cafe & Grill, Hearts & Flowers Cafe, New Morning Cafe |

CENTRAL

# *Dairy & Poultry Festival*

WE DON'T THINK YOU'LL hear "a round of chicken 'n' dumplings for the brood, please" at Turlocks **Dairy & Poultry Festival**, but you're likely to hear lots of cock-a-doodle-doos! Nestled at the southern end of one of California's most pristine counties— Stanislaus—this festival features lots of great locally -grown food! And there's booths overflowing with dolls, furniture, floral displays, t-shirts, and more!

## Turlock, California

Weekend following Labor Day
Hours vary

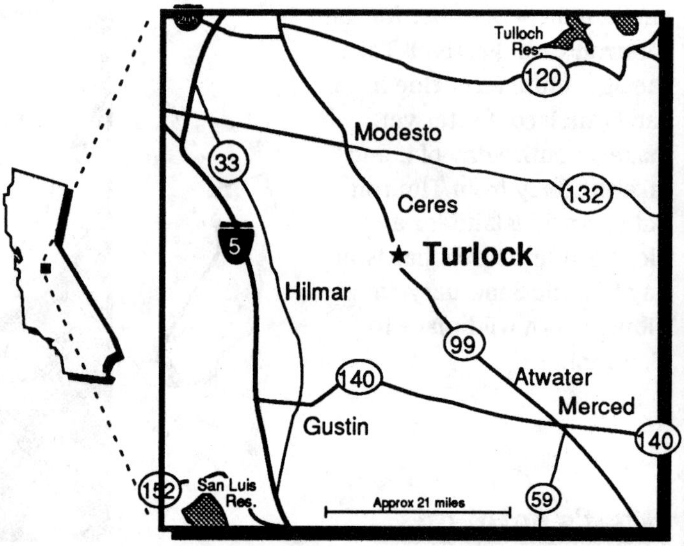


*Up-to-date festival information is available from:*
*Turlock Chamber of Commerce*
*(209) 632-2221*

## What's goin' on...

Town population: **41,000**
Last year's attendance: **4,000**
Average outdoor temperature: **73°**
Festival location: **Fairgrounds**

| | |
|---|---|
| X | Wine tasting/beer for sale |
| X | Food booths |
| X | Arts/crafts for sale |
| X | Live music |
| X | Clowns |
| X | Face painters |
| | Childrens games |
| | Animal exhibits/petting zoo |
| | Dogs allowed on leash |
| | Lost and found |
| | Bicycle racks |
| | First aid area available |
| | Self-brought picnics allowed |
| | Self-brought alcohol allowed |
| | Stroller/wheelchair rentals available |

| | |
|---|---|
| X | Parade: (time & date not avbl.) |
| X | Parking fee: $1 |
| X | Entrance fee: A $1; Under 12 free |
| | Camping facilities |
| | Boating facilities |
| | RV facilities w/ hookups |
| X | Accomodations in town |
| X | Restaurants in town |

# *Onion Festival*

THERE'S NOT A DRY EYE IN the house when the **Onion Festival** gets under way in Vacaville! This tasty festival features zany things like: Donovan Jon Fandre in the "dem-ONION- stration kitchen;" a model train for the kiddies to rides (sorry dad!); Onion Cook-off; raw onion eating contest; and games like "Wheel of Fortu-ONION!" There's even a dog-sitting service offered by the SPCA! Sounds like a great time! (Kids under 5 admitted free!)

## Vacaville, California

First full weekend in September

Sat. 10:00 AM - 7:00 PM; Sun. 10:00 AM - 5:00 PM

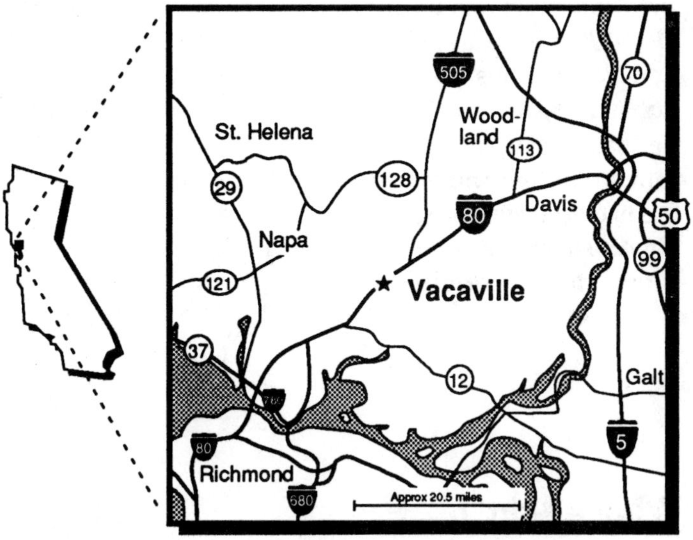


*Up-to-date festival information is available from:*
*Vacaville Chamber of Commerce*
*(707) 448-6424*

## What's goin' on...

Town population: **70,000**
Last year's attendance: **N/A**
Average outdoor temperature: **85°**
Festival location: **Pena Adobe Park**

| | |
|---|---|
| X | Wine tasting/beer for sale |
| X | Food booths |
| X | Arts/crafts for sale |
| X | Live music |
| X | Clowns |
| X | Face painters |
| X | Childrens games |
| X | Animal exhibits/petting zoo |
| X | Dogs allowed on leash |
| X | Lost and found |
| X | Bicycle racks |
| X | First aid area available |
| X | Self-brought picnics allowed |
| | Self-brought alcohol allowed |
| | Stroller/wheelchair rentals available |

| | |
|---|---|
| | Parade |
| | Parking fee |
| X | Entrance fee: S & K $2; A $5 |
| | Camping facilities |
| | Boating facilities |
| | RV facilities w/ hookups |
| X | Accomodations in town |
| X | Restaurants in town |

CENTRAL

# Oktoberfest

WELL, IT AIN'T QUITE YET, but the festivities are in full swing at the **Oktoberfest** celebration behind the Tyrolean Inn in Ben Lomond! In its 17th year, this celebration features music by The Hollanders and food by Germans—sausage, sauerkraut, bratwurst, and the like. And what would a big, fat sausage sandwich be without a cold German beer?

## Ben Lomond, California

Sunday following Labor Day
2:00 PM - 8:00 PM

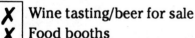

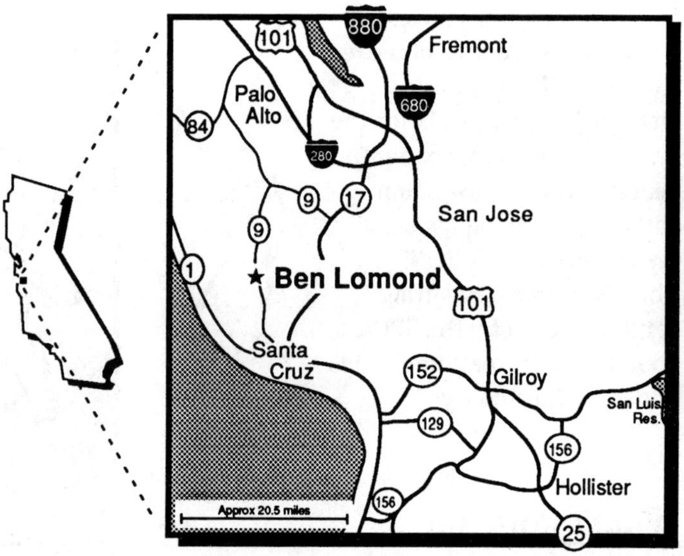


*Up-to-date festival information is available from:*
*Ben Lomond Tyrolean Inn*
*(408) 423-1111*

## What's goin' on...

Town population: **6,000**
Last year's attendance: **1,000**
Average outdoor temperature: **77°**
Festival location: **Outside Tyrolean Inn**

| | |
|---|---|
| ✗ | Wine tasting/beer for sale |
| ✗ | Food booths |
| | Arts/crafts for sale |
| ✗ | Live music |
| | Clowns |
| | Face painters |
| ✗ | Childrens games |
| | Animal exhibits/petting zoo |
| | Dogs allowed on leash |
| | Lost and found |
| | Bicycle racks |
| | First aid area available |
| | Self-brought picnics allowed |
| | Self-brought alcohol allowed |
| | Stroller/wheelchair rentals available |

| | |
|---|---|
| | Parade |
| | Parking fee |
| | Entrance fee |
| ✗ | Camping facilities: 2 miles |
| ✗ | Boating facilities: Loch Lomond |
| ✗ | RV facilities w/ hookups: 2 miles |
| ✗ | Accomodations in town<br>Tyrolean Inn, Fairview Manor |
| ✗ | Restaurants in town<br>Tyrolean Inn |

# *Begonia Festival & Parade*

THE PARADE ON SUNDAY IS definitely worth the trip to Capitola for the **Begonia Festival & Parade**! The photo of Garfield on the back of this book is just an example of the fantabulous floats that drift down the Soquel Creek behind the Shadowbrook restaurant. During the festival hours you'll see lots of colorful begonia displays and find all sorts of tantalizing taste treats!

## Capitola, California

Second Sunday in September
Hours vary

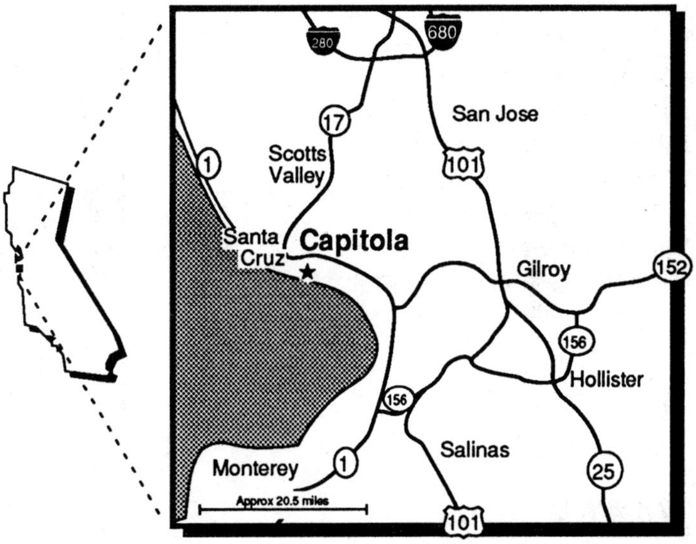


*Up-to-date festival information is available from:*
*Capitola Chamber of Commerce*
*(408) 475-6522*

## What's goin' on...

Town population: **10,450**
Last year's attendance: **12,000**
Average outdoor temperature: **70°**
Festival location: **Capitola Village**

| | |
|---|---|
| X | Wine tasting/beer for sale |
| X | Food booths |
| X | Arts/crafts for sale |
| X | Live music |
| | Clowns |
| | Face painters |
| | Childrens games |
| | Animal exhibits/petting zoo |
| X | Dogs allowed on leash |
| X | Lost and found |
| X | Bicycle racks |
| X | First aid area available |
| X | Self-brought picnics allowed |
| X | Self-brought alcohol allowed |
| | Stroller/wheelchair rentals available |

| | |
|---|---|
| X | Parade: 2nd Sun. 2:00 down Soquel Crk. |
| X | Parking fee: meters |
| | Entrance fee |
| X | Camping facilities: 5 miles |
| X | Boating facilities: Monterey Bay |
| X | RV facilities w/ hookups: 5 miles |
| X | Accomodations in town<br>Harbor Lights Motel, Capitola Inn, Inn at Depot Hill |
| X | Restaurants in town<br>Bandstand, Edgewater Club, Country Court Tea Room, Cedar House, Anna Maria's |

# *California Tomato Festival*

YOU SAY "TOE-MAY-TOE," I say "Toe-mah-toe"...and we all say **Tomato Festival!** Dixieland jazz music and heavenly jazz will play throughout the Festival while you try dried tomatoes, marinated tomatoes, tomato sauces over pasta, tomato juice and just plain naked! And let your feet do the Victorian home walking tour through town—'tis delightful!

## Woodland, California

Saturday following Labor Day
10:00 AM - 7:00 PM

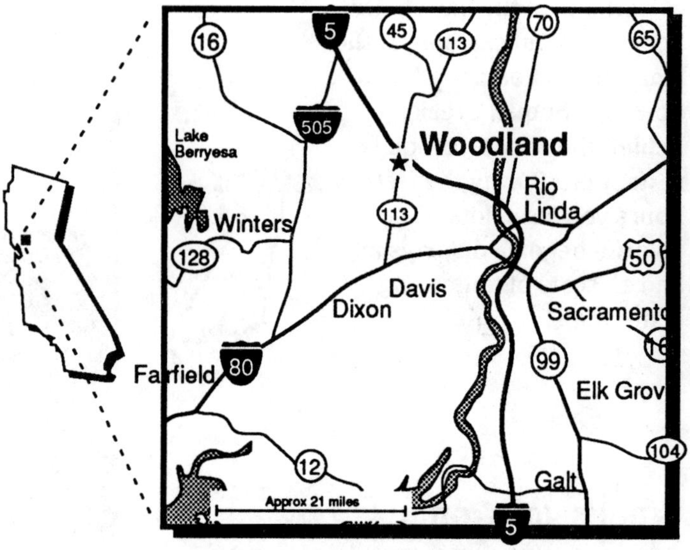


*Up-to-date festival information is available from:*
*Woodland Chamber of Commerce*
*(916) 662-7327*

## What's goin' on...

Town population: **38,980**
Last year's attendance: **5,000**
Average outdoor temperature: **85°**
Festival location: **Fairgrounds**

| | |
|---|---|
| X | Wine tasting/beer for sale |
| X | Food booths |
| X | Arts/crafts for sale |
| X | Live music |
| | Clowns |
| X | Face painters |
| | Childrens games |
| X | Animal exhibits/petting zoo |
| | Dogs allowed on leash |
| X | Lost and found |
| | Bicycle racks |
| X | First aid area available |
| | Self-brought picnics allowed |
| | Self-brought alcohol allowed |
| | Stroller/wheelchair rentals available |

| | |
|---|---|
| | Parade |
| | Parking fee |
| X | Entrance fee: $5 |
| X | Camping facilities: [illegible] miles |
| X | Boating facilities: Clear Lake |
| X | RV facilities w/ hookups: 15 miles |
| X | Accomodations in town<br>Cinderella Motel, Valley Oaks Motel |
| X | Restaurants in town<br>Morrison's, Pietro's, Lee's Chinese, Michelle's |

# Art in the Park

**ART IN THE PARK** AT Susana Park in Martinez is a blissful way to spend a Sunday afternoon. Local artists and craftpersons come out to show and sell their breathtaking wares. Martinez boasts more antique stores than any other town in beautiful Contra Costa County and is located near the Wildcat Canyon Recreation Park.

## Martinez, California

Third Sunday in September
10:00 AM - 5:00 PM

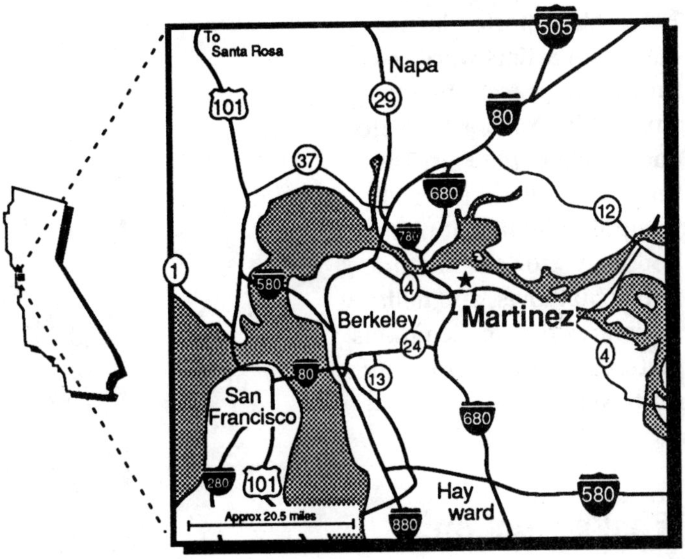


## What's goin' on...

Town population: **22,582**
Last year's attendance: **22,000**
Average outdoor temperature: **80°**
Festival location: **Susana Park**

*Up-to-date festival information is available from:*
*Martinez Chamber of Commerce*
*(415) 228-2345*

| | |
|---|---|
| X | Wine tasting/beer for sale |
| X | Food booths |
| X | Arts/crafts for sale |
| X | Live music |
| X | Clowns |
| X | Face painters |
| X | Childrens games |
| | Animal exhibits/petting zoo |
| | Dogs allowed on leash |
| | Lost and found |
| | Bicycle racks |
| X | First aid area available |
| X | Self-brought picnics allowed |
| | Self-brought alcohol allowed |
| X | Stroller/wheelchair rentals available |

| | |
|---|---|
| | Parade |
| X | Parking fee: meters or free |
| | Entrance fee |
| | Camping facilities |
| X | Boating facilities: Straits |
| | RV facilities w/ hookups |
| X | Accomodations in town |
| X | Restaurants in town<br>The Albatross, Cafe Romano, Amato's, Ferry Street Station, LeBeau's |

CENTRAL

# *Benicia Handicraft Fair*

## Benicia, California

Second Saturday following Labor Day
10:00 AM - 6:00 PM

FASCINATING BITS OF HISTORY are revealed by a tour through town and a Stopover at the **Benicia Handicraft Fair**! This historic place is *filled* with artists who look forward to presenting the fruits of their labor to visitors and guests at the Fair. Take time to check out the architecturally significant pioneer houses, Victorians, historic public buildings, and military structures that make up this picturesque Northern California town!

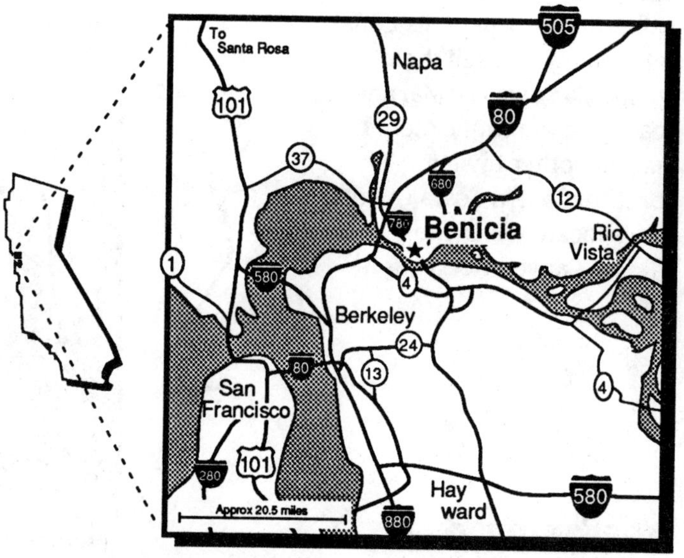


*Up-to-date festival information is available from:*
*Benicia Chamber of Commerce*
*(415) 745-2120*

## What's goin' on...

Town population: **23,000**
Last year's attendance: **15,000**
Average outdoor temperature: **75°**
Festival location: **First St.**

| | |
|---|---|
| ✗ | Wine tasting/beer for sale |
| ✗ | Food booths |
| ✗ | Arts/crafts for sale |
| | Live music |
| | Clowns |
| | Face painters |
| | Childrens games |
| | Animal exhibits/petting zoo |
| | Dogs allowed on leash |
| | Lost and found |
| | Bicycle racks |
| | First aid area available |
| | Self-brought picnics allowed |
| | Self-brought alcohol allowed |
| | Stroller/wheelchair rentals available |

| | |
|---|---|
| | Parade |
| | Parking fee |
| | Entrance fee |
| | Camping facilities |
| ✗ | Boating facilities: Straits |
| | RV facilities w/ hookups |
| ✗ | Accomodations in town |
| ✗ | Restaurants in town |

# *Art & Wine Festival*

AS CALIFORNIANS, WE *KNOW* that the best time at the beach is not the summertime but the (usually) sunny month of September! That's when Capitola hosts its annual **Art & Wine Festival.** Featuring unique craft items emphasizing the sand, sky, and sea, it also brings you live music and the opportunity to sample delicacies from ten local restaurants. This is really a *top-notch* festival!

## Capitola, California

Second weekend in September
Daily 10:00 AM - 6:00 PM

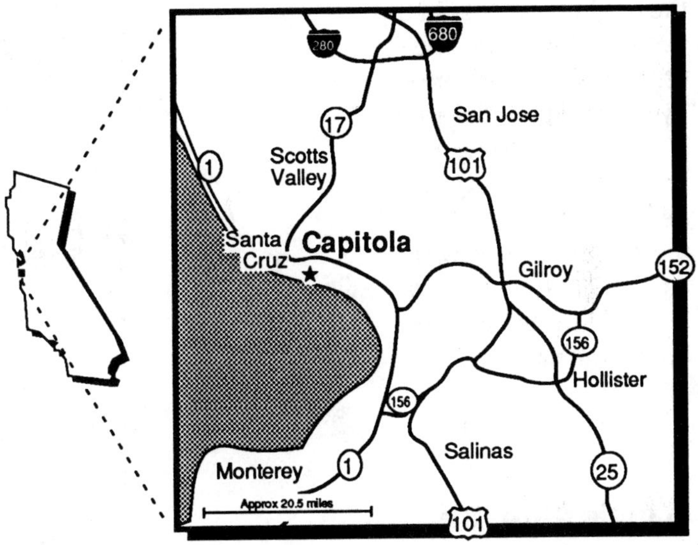


*Up-to-date festival information is available from:*
*Capitola Chamber of Commerce*
*(408) 475-6522*

## What's goin' on...

Town population: **10,000**
Last year's attendance: **20,000**
Average outdoor temperature: **68°**
Festival location: **Esplanade**

| | |
|---|---|
| X | Wine tasting/beer for sale |
| X | Food booths |
| X | Arts/crafts for sale |
| X | Live music |
| X | Clowns |
| | Face painters |
| | Childrens games |
| | Animal exhibits/petting zoo |
| X | Dogs allowed on leash |
| | Lost and found |
| X | Bicycle racks |
| | First aid area available |
| X | Self-brought picnics allowed |
| | Self-brought alcohol allowed |
| | Stroller/wheelchair rentals available |

| | |
|---|---|
| | Parade |
| X | Parking fee: meters |
| | Entrance fee |
| X | Camping facilities: 1 mile |
| X | Boating facilities: Monterey Bay |
| X | RV facilities w/ hookups: 1 mile |
| X | Accomodations in town |
| X | Restaurants in town<br>Shadowbrook, Adam's Rib, Margaritaville |

CENTRAL

# *Balloons Over the Valley*

**BALLOONS OVER THE VALley** is a spectacular event! Sixty hot-air balloons launch at dawn, splashing color over the bright blue skies of the valley and signaling the start of the day-long activities. Fly-bys of vintage and warbird aircraft, as well as antique and modern military aircraft demonstrations, will take place after the balloons launch. Pilots will be available to talk to the spectators during the day.

## Modesto, California

Second weekend in September
Daily 5:00 AM - noon

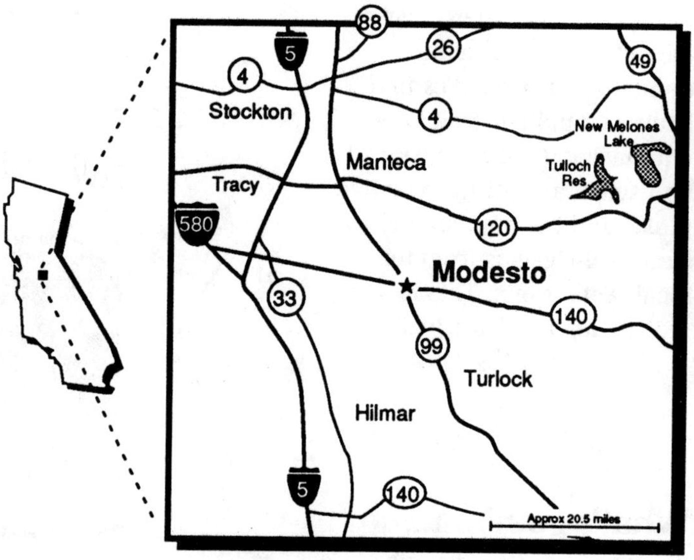


*Up-to-date festival information is available from:*
*Modesto Chamber of Commerce*
*(209) 577-5757*

## What's goin' on...

Town population: **106,602**
Last year's attendance: **25,000**
Average outdoor temperature: **85°**
Festival location: **Modesto Airport**

- ✗ Wine tasting/beer for sale
- ✗ Food booths
- ✗ Arts/crafts for sale
- Live music
- Clowns
- ✗ Face painters
- ✗ Childrens games
- Animal exhibits/petting zoo
- Dogs allowed on leash
- ✗ Lost and found
- Bicycle racks
- ✗ First aid area available
- Self-brought picnics allowed
- Self-brought alcohol allowed
- Stroller/wheelchair rentals available

- Parade
- Parking fee
- ✗ Entrance fee: Adults $5; Kids $2
- ✗ Camping facilities: 5 miles
- ✗ Boating facilities: New Melones
- ✗ RV facilities w/ hookups: 10 miles
- ✗ Accomodations in town
  Malaga House B&B
- ✗ Restaurants in town
  Mallard's, Cask & Cleaver's, Sundial, Acapulco

# *New York Landing Seafood Festival*

WE'VE ALL HEARD OUR share of fish stories, but this one's worth listening to! Manhattan and Boston clam chowder, barbecued oysters on the half shell marinated calamari, sushi, seafood gumbo...and more at the **New York Landing Seafood Festival**. Swarming with Bay area chefs, this is one of the *tastiest* festivals yet! Incidently, this auspicious little town of Pittsburg used to be known as New York Landing!

## Pittsburg, California

Second weekend in September
Daily 10:00 AM - 6:00 PM

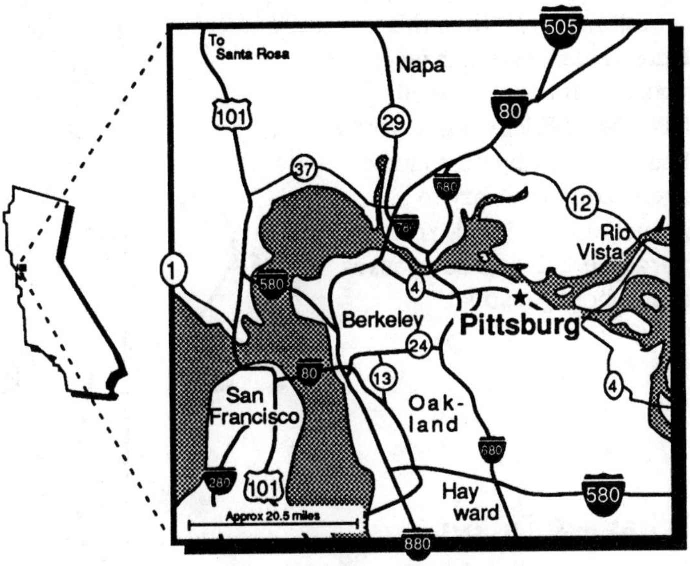


*Up-to-date festival information is available from:*
*Pittsburg Chamber of Commerce*
*(415) 432-7301*

## What's goin' on...

Town population: **50,000**
Last year's attendance: **80.000**
Average outdoor temperature: **80°**
Festival location: **Downtown**

- X Wine tasting/beer for sale
- X Food booths
- Arts/crafts for sale
- X Live music
- X Clowns
- X Face painters
- Childrens games
- Animal exhibits/petting zoo
- X Dogs allowed on leash
- X Lost and found
- Bicycle racks
- X First aid area available
- Self-brought picnics allowed
- Self-brought alcohol allowed
- Stroller/wheelchair rentals available

- Parade
- Parking fee
- X Entrance fee: $2
- Camping facilities
- X Boating facilities: San Francisco Bay
- X RV facilities w/ hookups: 1 mile
- X Accomodations in town
- X Restaurants in town
  New Mella Cafe, Snooker Pete's, Pactrino's

CENTRAL

# *Blue Grass Festival*

BRING YOUR OWN PICNIC or enjoy the food and drinks for sale at the Fairgrounds, but whatever you do...if you're a blue grass lover, then this **Blue Grass Festival** is where you'll want to be! Beginning at 6:00 PM on Friday night, you'll hear some of the best music ever—contemporary to gospel to traditional. You can purchase 1, 2, or 3-day passes to this young festival.

## Plymouth, California

**Third weekend in September (beginning Friday)**
**Hours vary**

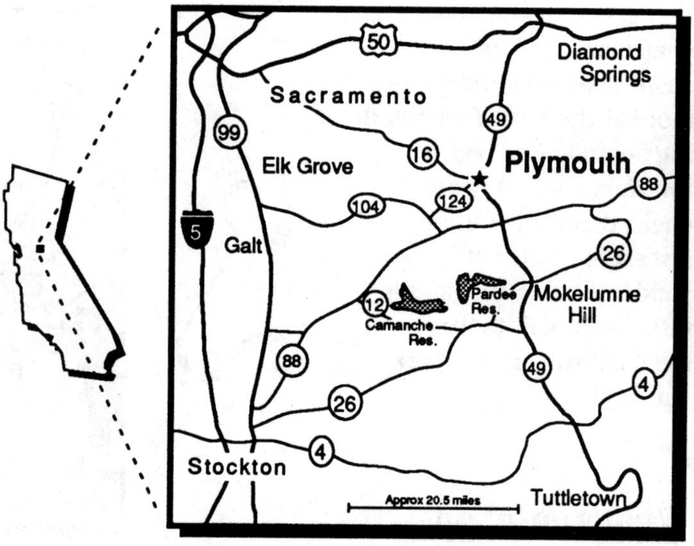


## What's goin' on...

Town population: **2,000**
Last year's attendance: **N/A**
Average outdoor temperature: **80°**
Festival location: **Fairgrounds**

*Up-to-date festival information is available from:*
*Plymouth Chamber of Commerce*
*(209) 223-0350*

| | |
|---|---|
| X | Wine tasting/beer for sale |
| X | Food booths |
| | Arts/crafts for sale |
| X | Live music |
| | Clowns |
| | Face painters |
| X | Childrens games |
| | Animal exhibits/petting zoo |
| | Dogs allowed on leash |
| X | Lost and found |
| | Bicycle racks |
| X | First aid area available |
| X | Self-brought picnics allowed |
| | Self-brought alcohol allowed |
| | Stroller/wheelchair rentals available |

| | |
|---|---|
| | Parade |
| X | Parking fee: (price not avbl.) |
| X | Entrance fee: (prices not avbl.) |
| X | Camping facilities: On-site |
| X | Boating facilities: Lake Amador |
| X | RV facilities w/ hookups: On-site |
| X | Accomodations in town |
| X | Restaurants in town |

# *Fall Festival*

JOURNEY TO THE ATWATER **Fall Festival** in sensational Merced County in September. Located near the famous Castle Air Museum, which houses the West Coast's largest display of aircraft, this festival hosts local bands, gospel singers, and square dancing, and . Local artists turn out to display their silk- and dried-flower arrangements, oil paintings, ceramics, and watercolors for your pleasure and/or purchase.

## Atwater, California

Third weekend in September
Daily 10:00 AM - 5:00 PM

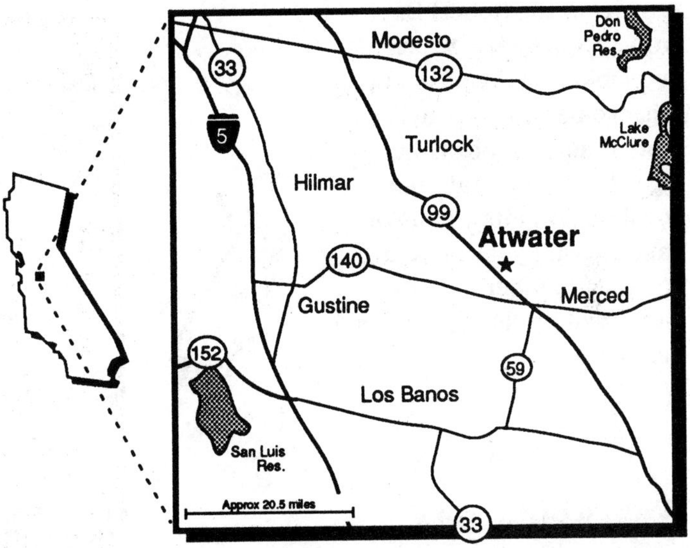


*Up-to-date festival information is available from:*
*Atwater Chamber of Commerce*
*(209) 358-4251*

## What's goin' on...

Town population: **20,541**
Last year's attendance: **20,000**
Average outdoor temperature: **85°**
Festival location: **Park**

- X Wine tasting/beer for sale
- X Food booths
- X Arts/crafts for sale
- X Live music
- X Clowns
- X Face painters
- X Childrens games
- X Animal exhibits/petting zoo
- X Dogs allowed on leash
- X Lost and found
- Bicycle racks
- X First aid area available
- Self-brought picnics allowed
- Self-brought alcohol allowed
- Stroller/wheelchair rentals available

- Parade
- Parking fee
- Entrance fee
- Camping facilities
- Boating facilities
- RV facilities w/ hookups
- Accomodations in town
- X Restaurants in town
  Granny's Pantry, Brooks Ranch

# *Burlingame Days by the Bay*

THE CITYSCAPE IS ONE OF California's most beautiful views—witness it for yourself at **Burlingame's Days by the Bay**! Set in the Robert B. Wooley State Park, which overlooks San Francisco Bay, this two-day event promises more than 300 booths bursting with art and craft items. Local restaurants will be on hand to whet your appetite, and the Chamber of Commerce will be selling famous California wines.

## Burlingame, California

Third weekend in September
Daily 10:00 AM - 5:00 PM

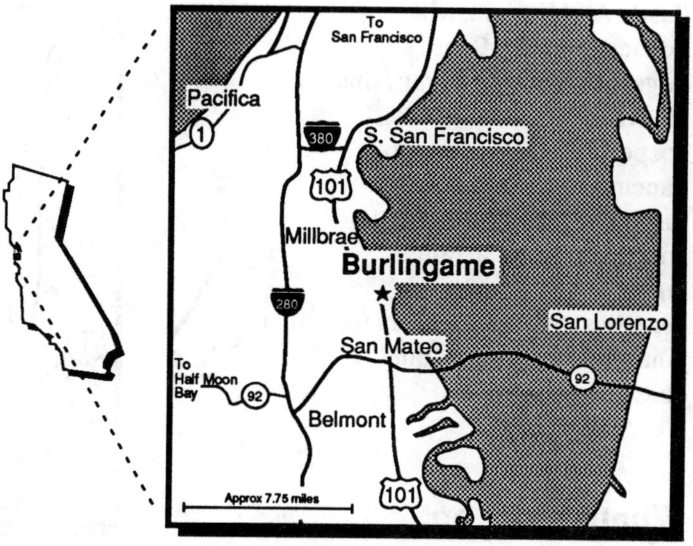


*Up-to-date festival information is available from:*
*Burlingame Chamber of Commerce*
*(415) 344-1735*

## What's goin' on...

Town population: **27,250**
Last year's attendance: **5,000**
Average outdoor temperature: **60°**
Festival location: **Wooley State Park**

| | |
|---|---|
| ✗ | Wine tasting/beer for sale |
| ✗ | Food booths |
| ✗ | Arts/crafts for sale |
| ✗ | Live music |
| ✗ | Clowns |
| ✗ | Face painters |
| ✗ | Childrens games |
| | Animal exhibits/petting zoo |
| ✗ | Dogs allowed on leash |
| ✗ | Lost and found |
| | Bicycle racks |
| ✗ | First aid area available |
| | Self-brought picnics allowed |
| | Self-brought alcohol allowed |
| | Stroller/wheelchair rentals available |

| | |
|---|---|
| | Parade |
| | Parking fee |
| | Entrance fee |
| | Camping facilities |
| ✗ | Boating facilities: Coyote Point Harbor |
| | RV facilities w/ hookups |
| ✗ | Accomodations in town<br>Sheraton, Days Inn, Embassy Suites |
| ✗ | Restaurants in town<br>Max's Opera Cafe, Partner's, Scalini, Bobby McGee's, The Fisherman |

# *Great Chili Cook-Off*

KEEP AN *EYE* ON THE COOKS at the **Great Chili Cook-Off!** Here the contestants *must* prepare their chili on-site while you enjoy the smells, music and roam through the arts-and-crafts booths. While the chili's simmering, you enjoy the squid, ice cream, and ethnic foods available till 4:00—that's when the judging starts!

## Carmel Valley, California

Third Saturday in September
10:00 AM - 6:00 PM

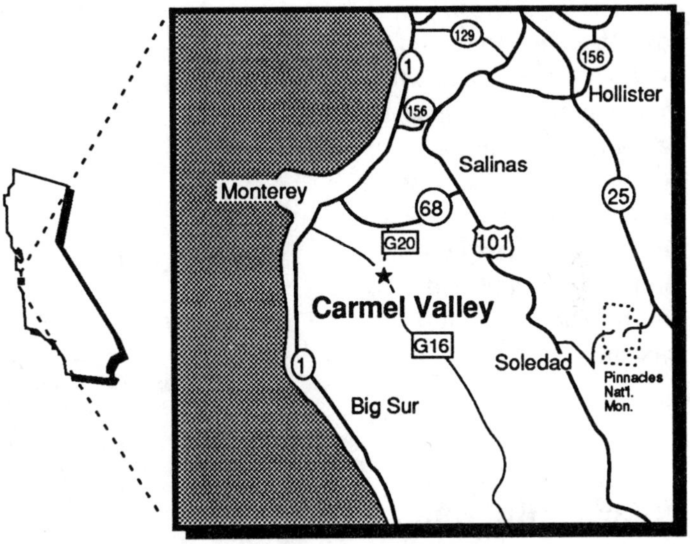


## What's goin' on...

Town population: **15,000**
Last year's attendance: **350**
Average outdoor temperature: **80°**
Festival location: **C.V. Comm. Youth Ctr.**

*Up-to-date festival information is available from:*
*Carmel Valley Chamber of Commerce*
*(408) 659-4000*

| | |
|---|---|
| X | Wine tasting/beer for sale |
| X | Food booths |
| X | Arts/crafts for sale |
| X | Live music |
| X | Clowns |
| X | Face painters |
| X | Childrens games |
| X | Animal exhibits/petting zoo |
| | Dogs allowed on leash |
| X | Lost and found |
| | Bicycle racks |
| X | First aid area available |
| X | Self-brought picnics allowed |
| | Self-brought alcohol allowed |
| | Stroller/wheelchair rentals available |

| | |
|---|---|
| | Parade |
| | Parking fee |
| | Entrance fee |
| X | Camping facilities: 10 miles |
| X | Boating facilities: Monterey Bay |
| X | RV facilities w/ hookups: 10 miles |
| X | Accomodations in town |
| X | Restaurants in town |

C E N T R A L

# *Founder's Day Celebration*

*LOTS FOR SALE IN Carmichael, California—10-acre tracts for $1,500 with 10% down on terms of $10 per month at 6% interest.* That advertisement appeared in the early 1900's—and with that in mind, Carmichael will celebrate its annual **Founder's Day Celebration.** This community (83 years old) birthday party boasts food booths, craft and art booths, and live country and rock music.

## Carmichael, California

Third Saturday in September
9:00 AM - 5:00 PM

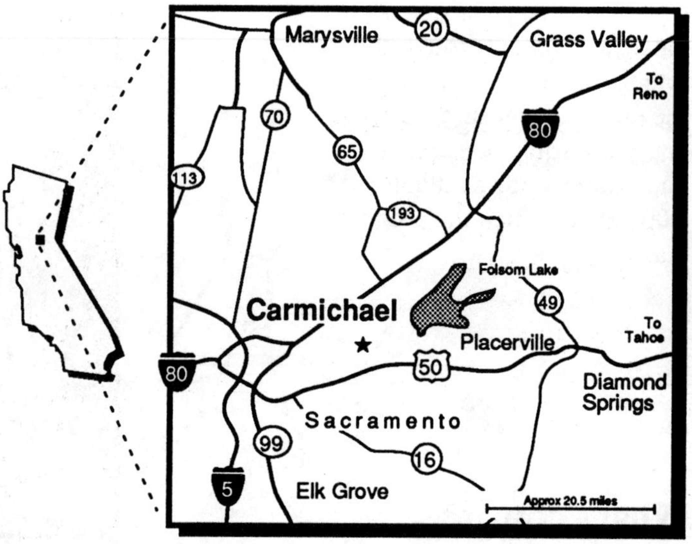


## What's goin' on...

Town population: **73,000**
Last year's attendance: **8,000**
Average outdoor temperature: **75°**
Festival location: **Carmichael Park**

*Up-to-date festival information is available from: Carmichael Chamber of Commerce (916) 481-1002*

| | |
|---|---|
| | Wine tasting/beer for sale |
| X | Food booths |
| X | Arts/crafts for sale |
| X | Live music |
| X | Clowns |
| X | Face painters |
| X | Childrens games |
| X | Animal exhibits/petting zoo |
| X | Dogs allowed on leash |
| X | Lost and found |
| | Bicycle racks |
| X | First aid area available |
| X | Self-brought picnics allowed |
| X | Self-brought alcohol allowed |
| | Stroller/wheelchair rentals available |

| | |
|---|---|
| | Parade |
| | Parking fee |
| | Entrance fee |
| X | Camping facilities: 10 miles |
| X | Boating facilities: Folsom Lake |
| X | RV facilities w/ hookups: 10 miles |
| X | Accomodations in town<br>Holiday Inn, La Quinta |
| X | Restaurants in town<br>Cafe Capri, Continental Cuisine, Chef Liu Hunan Cuisine |

# *Artichoke Festival*

AHA! THE **ARTICHOKE FESTIVAL** is a must for thistle lovers! You'll find artichokes fixed every which way, including stuffed, fried, marinated, and steamed ...*yum!* Local artists emerge to peddle their wares, along with makers of ceramics, dried flowers, and jewelry. The Monterey Bay is only five miles away, keeping Castroville at just the right temperature for Festival Hoppers.

## Castroville, California

Third weekend in September
Daily: 9:00 AM - 5:00 PM

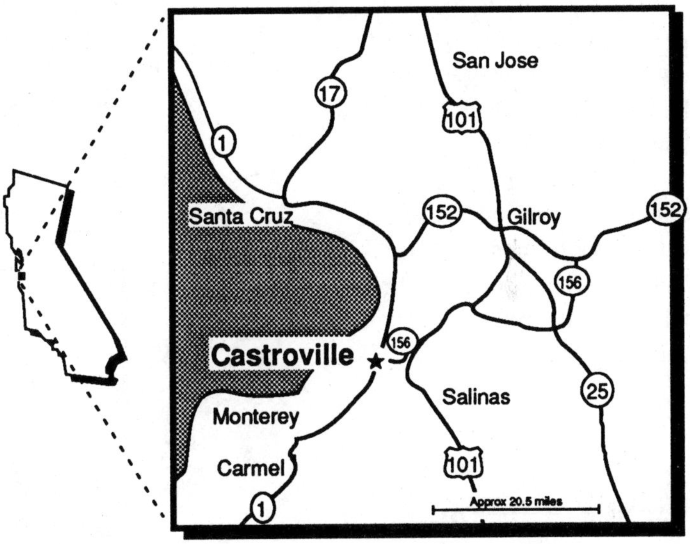


## What's goin' on...

Town population: **4,500**
Last year's attendance: **50,000**
Average outdoor temperature: **78°**
Festival location: **Community Center**

*Up-to-date festival information is available from:*
*Castroville Artichoke Festival*
*(408) 633-2465*

- ✗ Wine tasting/beer for sale
- ✗ Food booths
- ✗ Arts/crafts for sale
- ✗ Live music
- ✗ Clowns
- ✗ Face painters
- ✗ Childrens games
- Animal exhibits/petting zoo
- Dogs allowed on leash
- ✗ Lost and found
- Bicycle racks
- ✗ First aid area available
- ✗ Self-brought picnics allowed
- Self-brought alcohol allowed
- Stroller/wheelchair rentals available

- ✗ Parade: (time & date not avbl.)
- Parking fee
- ✗ Entrance fee: Adults $2; Kids free
- ✗ Camping facilities
- ✗ Boating facilities: Monterey Bay
- ✗ RV facilities w/ hookups: 15 miles
- ✗ Accomodations in town
- ✗ Restaurants in town
  Moss Landing Oyster Bar, Giant Artichoke, Central Texan, La Scuola

# *Gunfighter's Rendezvous*

DRESS IN 1800's STYLE AND bring the whole family down to the annual **Gunfighter's Rendezvous**! Here you'll see professional gunfighter groups, dressed in authentic western wear, performing shootouts and skits daily. Dance hall girls and slick-looking lawmen will also be casing the streets! There are raffles, food, music, art & crafts booths, and lots of real wild west flavor happening in these parts!

## Coulterville, California

Third weekend in September
Daily 10:00 AM - 6:00 PM

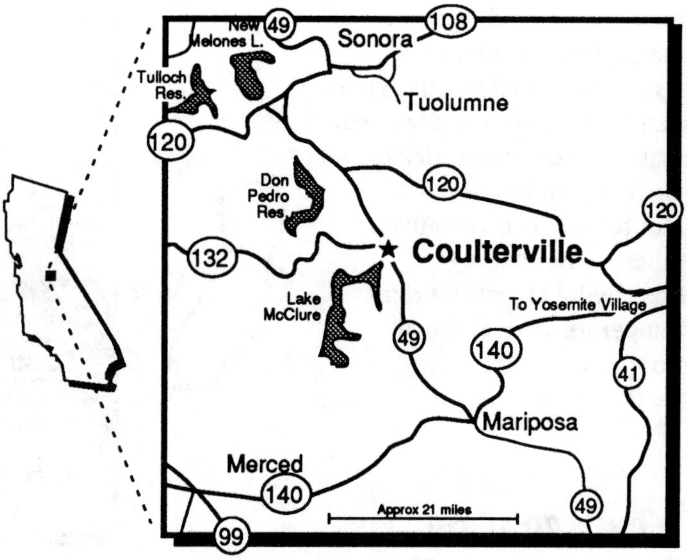


*Up-to-date festival information is available from:*
*Coulterville Visitor Center*
*(209) 878-3074*

## What's goin' on...

Town population: **3,000**
Last year's attendance: **2,500**
Average outdoor temperature: **80°**
Festival location: **Downtown**

| | |
|---|---|
| X | Wine tasting/beer for sale |
| X | Food booths |
| X | Arts/crafts for sale |
| X | Live music |
| | Clowns |
| | Face painters |
| | Childrens games |
| | Animal exhibits/petting zoo |
| X | Dogs allowed on leash |
| | Lost and found |
| X | Bicycle racks |
| | First aid area available |
| X | Self-brought picnics allowed |
| | Self-brought alcohol allowed |
| | Stroller/wheelchair rentals available |

| | |
|---|---|
| | Parade |
| | Parking fee |
| | Entrance fee |
| X | Camping facilities: 8 miles |
| X | Boating facilities |
| X | RV facilities w/ hookups: 8 miles |
| X | Accomodations in town |
| X | Restaurants in town |

# *1890's Days*

SOJOURN BACK IN TIME with the Oakdale colony for **1890's Days**! This old-fashioned, little town puts on quite a show for this one-day event! You'll find shopkeepers, restauranteers, and watering-hole tenders dressed to the nines in early-American apparel—even the kids get into the act. As you leave town, climb into the Sierra Nevada foothills for scenic beauty *beyond* compare.

## Oakdale, California

Third Saturday in September
10:00 AM - 3:00 PM

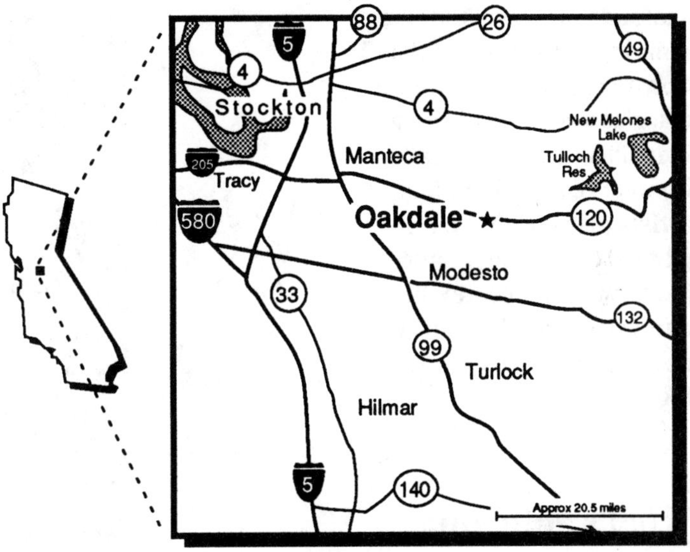


*Up-to-date festival information is available from:*
*Oakdale Chamber of Commerce*
*(209) 847-2244*

## What's goin' on...

Town population: **11,600**
Last year's attendance: **1,000**
Average outdoor temperature: **78°**
Festival location: **Downtown East F St.**

| | |
|---|---|
| | Wine tasting/beer for sale |
| X | Food booths |
| X | Arts/crafts for sale |
| X | Live music |
| | Clowns |
| | Face painters |
| X | Childrens games |
| | Animal exhibits/petting zoo |
| | Dogs allowed on leash |
| X | Lost and found |
| | Bicycle racks |
| | First aid area available |
| | Self-brought picnics allowed |
| | Self-brought alcohol allowed |
| | Stroller/wheelchair rentals available |

| | |
|---|---|
| | Parade |
| | Parking fee |
| | Entrance fee |
| X | Camping facilities: 6 miles |
| X | Boating facilities: Oakdale Lake |
| X | RV facilities w/ hookups: 6 miles |
| X | Accomodations in town<br>Ramada Inn, Holiday Motel, Oakdale Motel |
| X | Restaurants in town<br>Nutcracker, Betty-Dee's, Sonia's Mexican |

# *Pacific Coast Fog Fest*

DELICACIES SUCH AS BARBEcued oysters, salmon teriyaki, blackened shrimp, seafood gumbo, gyros, fog dogs, and seafood fajitas will tantalize your taste buds at the **Pacific Coast Fog Fest**. Burn off the calories with a walk along magnificent rows of crafts booths! Featured are fine artists displaying their glasswork, leather goods, jewelry, ceramics, textiles, and woodwork. This is one day the Pacificans *pray* for fog!

## Pacifica, California

Third weekend in September
Daily 10:00 AM - 6:00 PM

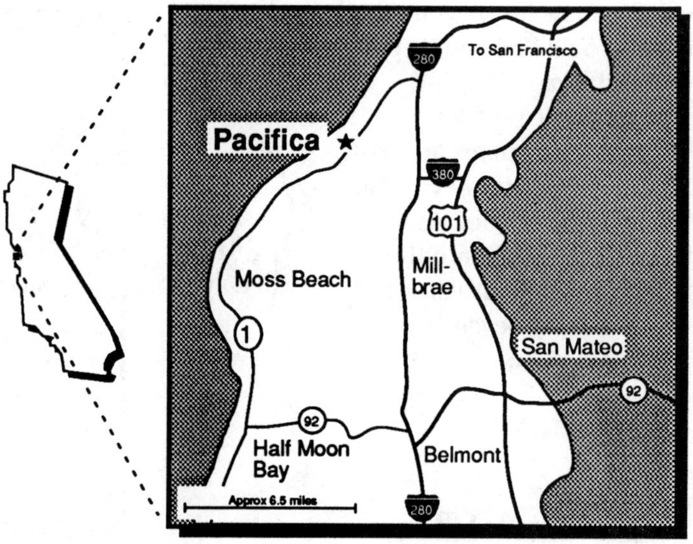


## What's goin' on...

Town population: **40,000**
Last year's attendance: **50,000**
Average outdoor temperature: **68°**
Festival location: **Palmetto Ave.**

*Up-to-date festival information is available from:*
*Pacifica Chamber of Commerce*
*(415) 355-4122*

- ✗ Wine tasting/beer for sale
- ✗ Food booths
- ✗ Arts/crafts for sale
- ✗ Live music
- ✗ Clowns
- ✗ Face painters
- ✗ Childrens games
- Animal exhibits/petting zoo
- Dogs allowed on leash
- ✗ Lost and found
- Bicycle racks
- ✗ First aid area available
- ✗ Self-brought picnics allowed
- Self-brought alcohol allowed
- Stroller/wheelchair rentals available

- ✗ Parade: Sat. on Palmetto Ave. (no time)
- Parking fee
- Entrance fee
- ✗ Camping facilities: 15 miles
- ✗ Boating facilities: Half Moon Bay
- ✗ RV facilities w/ hookups: 1 mile
- ✗ Accomodations in town
  Nick's Sea Breeze Motel, Lighthouse Hotel, Pacifica Motor Inn, Sea View Motor Lodge
- ✗ Restaurants in town
  Moonraker, Nick's, Sharp Park Restaurant, Balistreri's

# *Big Time Indian Days*

HAVE YOU EVER WITNESSED the Miwok ceremonial games and dances? You can at **Big Time Indian Days** in Pine Grove! Enjoy native American foods—fixed by native Americans! Explore the booths filled with craft items—many pertaining to a much simpler life. And let the kids roam around to play games and enjoy the music and dance.

## Pine Grove, California

Third weekend in September
Daily 10:00 AM - 6:00 PM

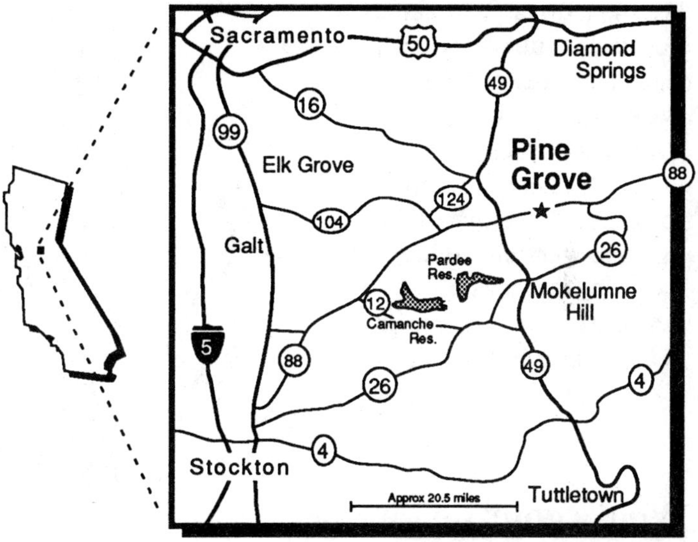


## What's goin' on...

Town population: **1,500**
Last year's attendance: **N/A**
Average outdoor temperature: **70°**
Festival location: **Park**

*Up-to-date festival information is available from:*
*Pine Grove Chamber of Commerce*
*(209) 223-0350*

| | |
|---|---|
| | Wine tasting/beer for sale |
| X | Food booths |
| X | Arts/crafts for sale |
| X | Live music |
| | Clowns |
| | Face painters |
| X | Childrens games |
| | Animal exhibits/petting zoo |
| | Dogs allowed on leash |
| X | Lost and found |
| | Bicycle racks |
| X | First aid area available |
| X | Self-brought picnics allowed |
| | Self-brought alcohol allowed |
| | Stroller/wheelchair rentals available |

| | |
|---|---|
| | Parade |
| X | Parking fee: $3 per car |
| | Entrance fee |
| X | Camping facilities: 3 miles |
| X | Boating facilities: Pardee Lake |
| X | RV facilities w/ hookups: 4 miles |
| X | Accomodations in town |
| X | Restaurants in town |

# *Heritage Days*

THE HISTORY OF PLEASANTON is proudly preserved, as shown by the turn-out of residents to Pleasanton's **Heritage Days**! Craft and food booths line downtown, while jazz musicians play nearby. Take a walk to see the classic Victorian houses which border the historical downtown area. Several motion pictures were filmed here including Rebecca of Sunnybrook Farms, starring Mary Pickford!

## Pleasanton, California

Third weekend in September
Daily 10:00 AM - 5:00 PM

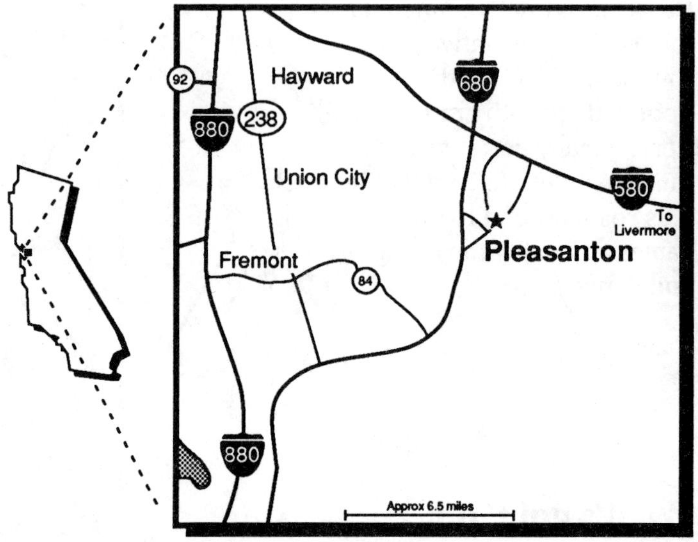


## What's goin' on...

Town population: **48,000**
Last year's attendance: **4,000**
Average outdoor temperature: **73°**
Festival location: **Downtown**

*Up-to-date festival information is available from:*
*Pleasanton Chamber of Commerce*
*(415) 846-5858*

| | |
|---|---|
| | Wine tasting/beer for sale |
| X | Food booths |
| X | Arts/crafts for sale |
| X | Live music |
| X | Clowns |
| X | Face painters |
| | Childrens games |
| X | Animal exhibits/petting zoo |
| X | Dogs allowed on leash |
| | Lost and found |
| | Bicycle racks |
| | First aid area available |
| | Self-brought picnics allowed |
| | Self-brought alcohol allowed |
| | Stroller/wheelchair rentals available |

| | |
|---|---|
| X | Parade: Sat. 12:00 PM on Main St. |
| | Parking fee |
| | Entrance fee |
| X | Camping facilities: 15 miles |
| X | Boating facilities: Del Valle Res. |
| X | RV facilities w/ hookups: 15 miles |
| X | Accomodations in town<br>The Plum Tree Inn B&B, Hilton, Holiday Inn, Super 8 |
| X | Restaurants in town<br>Pleasanton Hotel, Velvet Turtle, Casanova's, Maestro's |

# *Grape Bowl Festival*

CHRISTENED "THE NATIONAL Christmas Tree City," the friendly little town of Sanger—located a stone's throw from the Kings River and a few miles from Pine Flat Reservoir—annually hosts the **Grape Bowl Festival** to salute the grape! With craft booths featuring unique items such as redwood patio furniture and handmade dolls; it also offers all types of great food booths featuring grapes, grapes, grapes!

## Sanger, California

Third weekend in September

Sat. 10:00 AM - midnight; Sun. 10:00 AM - 6:00 PM

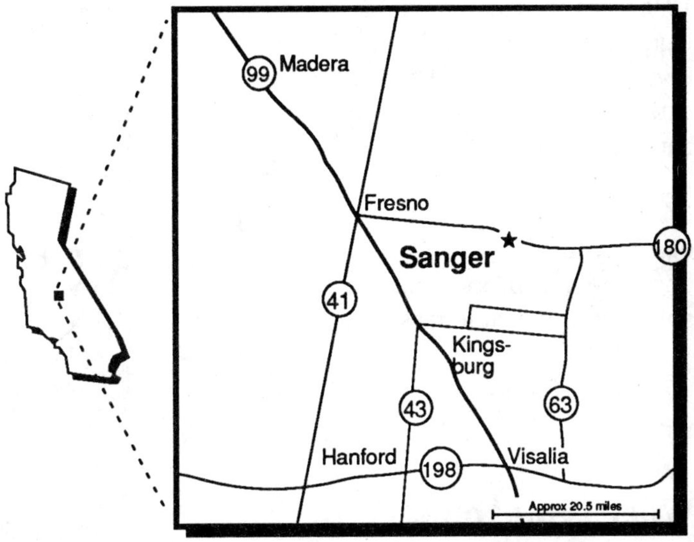




## What's goin' on...

Town population: **12,542**
Last year's attendance: **5,000**
Average outdoor temperature: **90°**
Festival location: **Citywide**

*Up-to-date festival information is available from:*
*Sanger Chamber of Commerce*
*(209) 875-4575*

| | |
|---|---|
| X | Wine tasting/beer for sale |
| X | Food booths |
| X | Arts/crafts for sale |
| X | Live music |
| | Clowns |
| X | Face painters |
| X | Childrens games |
| X | Animal exhibits/petting zoo |
| | Dogs allowed on leash |
| X | Lost and found |
| | Bicycle racks |
| X | First aid area available |
| | Self-brought picnics allowed |
| | Self-brought alcohol allowed |
| | Stroller/wheelchair rentals available |

| | |
|---|---|
| | Parade |
| X | Parking fee: $1 |
| X | Entrance fee: (prices not avbl.) |
| X | Camping facilities: 18 miles |
| X | Boating facilities: Kings River |
| X | RV facilities w/ hookups: 18 miles |
| X | Accomodations in town<br>Townhouse Motel |
| X | Restaurants in town<br>Wonder Valley Ranch Resort, Sherwood Inn, Your Place, Chapala |

# *Scotts Valley Living History Faire*

WOW! NOW THIS SOUNDS intriguing! Take a tour of the historic Scott house and the surrounding park—a 10,000 to 12,000 year old indian village—at the **Scotts Valley Living History Faire**. This active community just east of Santa Cruz began this festival in 1990. The booths house crafts for sale, as well as demonstrations of horseshoeing, broom making, spinning, and candle making.

## Scotts Valley, California

Third weekend in September
Daily: 10:00 AM - 5:00 PM

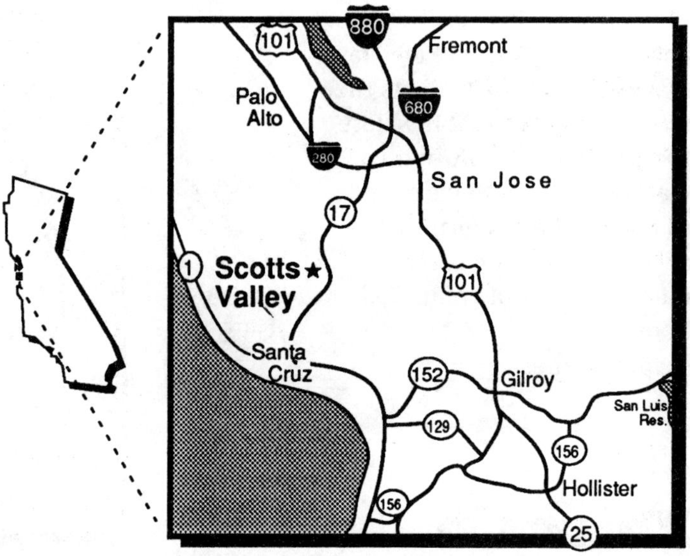


## What's goin' on...

Town population: **9,460**
Last year's attendance: **N/A**
Average outdoor temperature: **78°**
Festival location: **Scott House Park/City Hall**

☞ *Up-to-date festival information is available from:*
*Scotts Valley Chamber of Commerce*
*(408) 438-1010*

| | |
|---|---|
| | Wine tasting/beer for sale |
| X | Food booths |
| X | Arts/crafts for sale |
| X | Live music |
| X | Clowns |
| | Face painters |
| X | Childrens games |
| | Animal exhibits/petting zoo |
| | Dogs allowed on leash |
| X | Lost and found |
| | Bicycle racks |
| | First aid area available |
| | Self-brought picnics allowed |
| | Self-brought alcohol allowed |
| | Stroller/wheelchair rentals available |

| | |
|---|---|
| | Parade |
| | Parking fee |
| X | Entrance fee: $2 |
| X | Camping facilities: 3 miles |
| X | Boating facilities: Santa Cruz Harbor |
| X | RV facilities w/ hookups: 1 mile |
| X | Accomodations in town<br>Chateau des Fleures, Best Western Inn |
| X | Restaurants in town<br>Zanoto's Pasta & More, Peachwood's Bar & Grill, Backstage Restaurant, ABC Chinese |

# *A Taste of San Mateo*

THIS WILL BE THE BEST $30 bucks you've ever spent! At **A Taste of San Mateo**, the entire infield at Bay Meadows is transformed into a movable feast provided by the finest restaurants and the best wineries. This all-you-can-eat-and-drink affair highlights more than 60 Bay Area restaurants and 100 California wineries. All *this* and horse racing *too*!

## San Mateo, California

Fourth Sunday in September
Noon - 3:00 PM

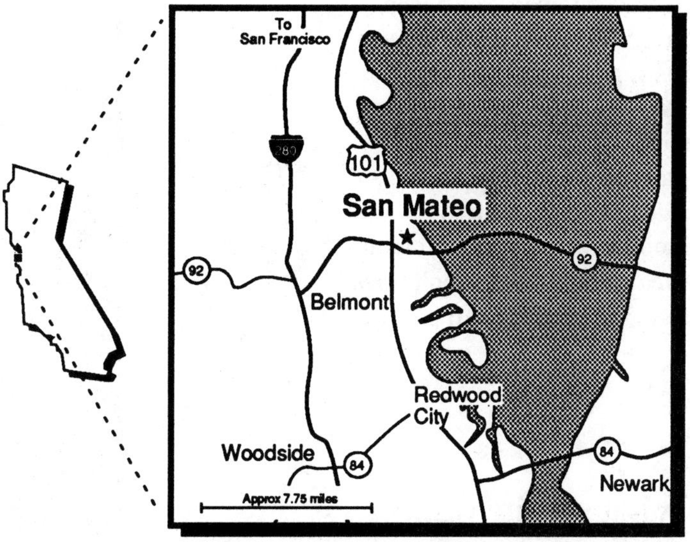


*Up-to-date festival information is available from:*
*San Mateo Chamber of Commerce*
*(415) 341-5679*

## What's goin' on...

Town population: **85,700**
Last year's attendance: **2,500**
Average outdoor temperature: **80°**
Festival location: **Bay Meadows Infield**

| | |
|---|---|
| X | Wine tasting/beer for sale |
| X | Food booths |
| | Arts/crafts for sale |
| X | Live music |
| | Clowns |
| | Face painters |
| | Childrens games |
| | Animal exhibits/petting zoo |
| | Dogs allowed on leash |
| X | Lost and found |
| | Bicycle racks |
| X | First aid area available |
| | Self-brought picnics allowed |
| | Self-brought alcohol allowed |
| | Stroller/wheelchair rentals available |

| | |
|---|---|
| | Parade |
| X | Parking fee: $2 |
| X | Entrance fee: $30 |
| | Camping facilities |
| X | Boating facilities: San Francisco Bay |
| X | RV facilities w/ hookups: 7 miles |
| X | Accomodations in town<br>Holiday Inn, Firestone Lodge, Ben Franklin Hotel, Residence Inn |
| X | Restaurants in town<br>321 Ellsworth, Bogie's, Mallard's Señor Pepe's, The Fish Market, Pot Sticker |

# *Valley of the Moon Vintage Festival*

HERALDED AS THE OLDEST wine harvest festival California, the **Valley of the Moon Vintage Festival** is—perhaps needless to say—*exquisite!* Treat yourself to fine wine tasting from dozens of outstanding local wineries and savor the tasty food! Hand-painted silk and hand-knit sweaters are just two examples of what you'll find at the crafts booths. Don't miss the grape stomp and parade!

## Sonoma, California

Last weekend in September (beginning Friday)
Hours vary

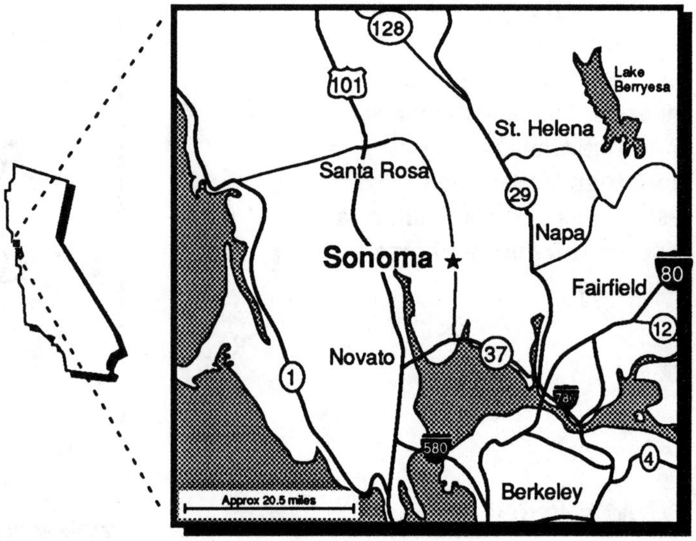


*Up-to-date festival information is available from:*
*Sonoma Chamber of Commerce*
*(707) 996-1033*

## What's goin' on...

Town population: **10,000**
Last year's attendance: **2,000**
Average outdoor temperature: **80°**
Festival location: **Sonoma Plaza**

- X Wine tasting/beer for sale
- X Food booths
- X Arts/crafts for sale
- X Live music
- Clowns
- Face painters
- Childrens games
- Animal exhibits/petting zoo
- Dogs allowed on leash
- X Lost and found
- X Bicycle racks
- First aid area available
- X Self-brought picnics allowed
- X Self-brought alcohol allowed
- Stroller/wheelchair rentals available

- X Parade: (date & time not avbl.)
- Parking fee
- Entrance fee
- X Camping facilities: 8 miles
- X Boating facilities
- X RV facilities w/ hookups: 1 mile
- X Accomodations in town
  Sonoma Hotel, Sonoma Mission Inn & Spa, El Pueblo Motel, Coopers Grove Ranch B&B
- X Restaurants in town
  Depot Hotel 1870, The Big Three, Grist Mill Inn, Magliulo's Restaurant, La Casa

# *Wild West Film Fest*

THE WEEKEND BEGINS AT the **Wild West Film Fest** with a Friday night gala honoring Western movie stars Roy Rogers and Dale Evans, followed by two days of Western film showing, movie memorabilia museum, live entertainment, film actor guests, and arts and crafts. A professional rodeo will entertain you on Sunday.

## Sonora, California

Last weekend in September
Hours vary

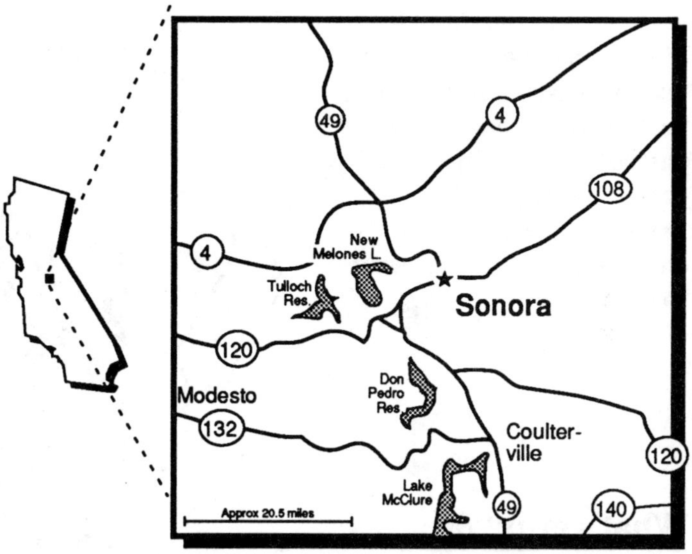


*Up-to-date festival information is available from:*
*Sonora Visitors Bureau*
*(209) 532-4212*

## What's goin' on...

Town population: **3,247**
Last year's attendance: **N/A**
Average outdoor temperature: **80°**
Festival location: **Tuolumne County**

| | |
|---|---|
| X | Wine tasting/beer for sale |
| X | Food booths |
| X | Arts/crafts for sale |
| X | Live music |
| | Clowns |
| | Face painters |
| | Childrens games |
| | Animal exhibits/petting zoo |
| | Dogs allowed on leash |
| | Lost and found |
| X | Bicycle racks |
| | First aid area available |
| X | Self-brought picnics allowed |
| | Self-brought alcohol allowed |
| | Stroller/wheelchair rentals available |

| | |
|---|---|
| | Parade |
| | Parking fee |
| | Entrance fee |
| X | Camping facilities: 10 miles |
| X | Boating facilities |
| X | RV facilities w/ hookups: 10 miles |
| X | Accomodations in town<br>Sonora Gold Lodge, The Palm Hotel, Oak Hill Ranch |
| X | Restaurants in town<br>The Cove, Country Kitchen, Iron Door Saloon |

# *River Town Jamboree*

IF IT'S THAT SMALL-TOWN feeling you crave, with big-time fun, then the **River Town Jamboree** is for you! Folks in the historical riverfront town of Antioch have been throwing this two-day party for five years now and have it down pat: contests, competitions, barbecues, music of all flavors, etc., etc., etc! This is an adventure you *won't* want to miss!

## Antioch, California

Last weekend in September
Daily 10:00 AM - 6:00 PM

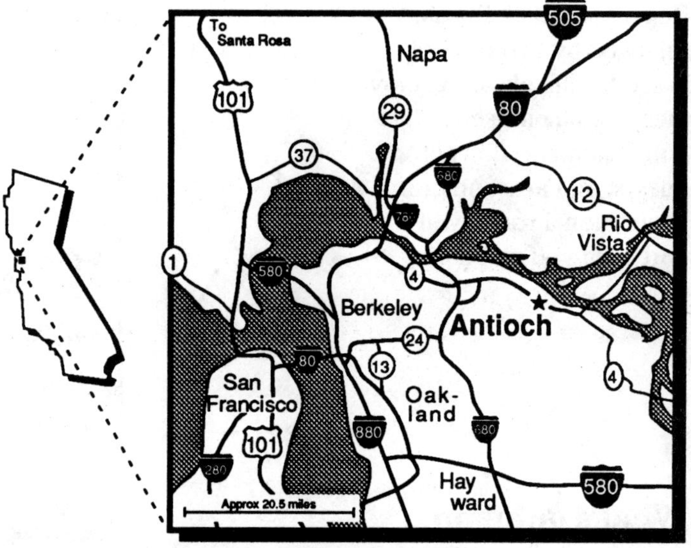


## What's goin' on...

Town population: **51,000**
Last year's attendance: **75,000**
Average outdoor temperature: **85°**
Festival location: **Downtown**

☞ *Up-to-date festival information is available from:*
*Antioch Chamber of Commerce*
*(415) 757-1800*

| | |
|---|---|
| ✗ | Wine tasting/beer for sale |
| ✗ | Food booths |
| ✗ | Arts/crafts for sale |
| ✗ | Live music |
| ✗ | Clowns |
| ✗ | Face painters |
| ✗ | Childrens games |
| ✗ | Animal exhibits/petting zoo |
| | Dogs allowed on leash |
| ✗ | Lost and found |
| | Bicycle racks |
| ✗ | First aid area available |
| ✗ | Self-brought picnics allowed |
| | Self-brought alcohol allowed |
| ✗ | Stroller/wheelchair rentals available |

| | |
|---|---|
| ✗ | Parade: (date & time not avbl.) |
| | Parking fee |
| | Entrance fee |
| | Camping facilities |
| ✗ | Boating facilities: Straits |
| | RV facilities w/ hookups |
| ✗ | Accomodations in town |
| ✗ | Restaurants in town<br>Potato Barge, Riverview Lodge, La Plaza, Ugly Duck |

# *Clovisfest*

ARE YOU FAMILIAR WITH the colorful autumn season in Clovis? Yes, California does have a noticable seasonal change! The falling leaves, bright orange pumpkins, gentle autumn breezes can all be found at **Clovisfest**! Believe us when we tell you that the tri-tip cook-off competi- tion is worth the drive! Jazz and country bands, old time fiddlers, a car show, helicop- ter rides...you name it, Clovisfest has it!

## Clovis, California

Last Saturday in September
9:00 AM - 5:00 PM

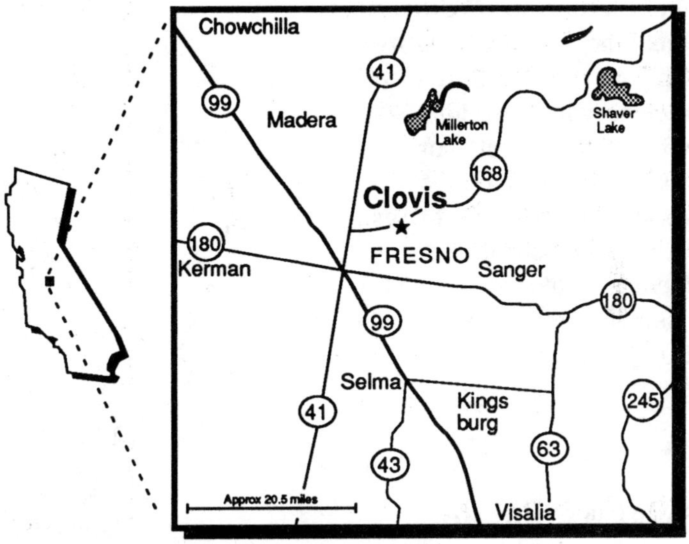


*Up-to-date festival information is available from:*
*Clovis Chamber of Commerce*
*(209) 299-7273*

## What's goin' on...

Town population: **33,000**
Last year's attendance: **20,000**
Average outdoor temperature: **85°**
Festival location: **Old Town Clovis**

| | |
|---|---|
| ✗ | Wine tasting/beer for sale |
| ✗ | Food booths |
| ✗ | Arts/crafts for sale |
| ✗ | Live music |
| ✗ | Clowns |
| ✗ | Face painters |
| ✗ | Childrens games |
| | Animal exhibits/petting zoo |
| ✗ | Dogs allowed on leash |
| ✗ | Lost and found |
| | Bicycle racks |
| ✗ | First aid area available |
| ✗ | Self-brought picnics allowed |
| | Self-brought alcohol allowed |
| | Stroller/wheelchair rentals available |

| | |
|---|---|
| | Parade |
| | Parking fee |
| ✗ | Entrance fee |
| | Camping facilities |
| ✗ | Boating facilities: Millerton Lake |
| | RV facilities w/ hookups |
| ✗ | Accomodations in town |
| ✗ | Restaurants in town<br>Chocolate Transfer Company, Wine & Rack Shack, Wong's Jade Garden, The Flume |

# *Raisin Festival*

IT'S ONLY APPROPRIATE that the ***real*** California Raisins get in on all of this merriment—and you'll find them at the **Raisin Festival!** Amid the food booths featuring gobs of raisin-based recipes, you'll also find teriyaki beef, Armenian dishes, Mexican food, and good ol' American hot dogs. Other nonraisin attractions include an old sawmill historical buildings and numerous fruit-packing houses.

## Dinuba, California

Last weekend in September
Fri. 3:00 PM - dark; Sat. & Sun. 8:00 AM - 11:00 PM

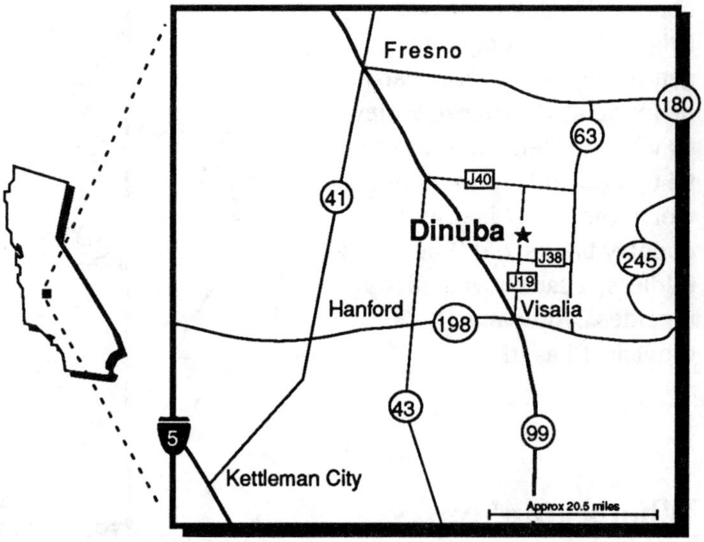


## What's goin' on...

Town population: **12,400**
Last year's attendance: **7,000**
Average outdoor temperature: **80°**
Festival location: **Park**

*Up-to-date festival information is available from:*
*Dinuba Chamber of Commerce*
*(209) 591-2707*

| | |
|---|---|
| ✗ | Wine tasting/beer for sale |
| ✗ | Food booths |
| ✗ | Arts/crafts for sale |
| ✗ | Live music |
| ✗ | Clowns |
| ✗ | Face painters |
| ✗ | Childrens games |
| | Animal exhibits/petting zoo |
| | Dogs allowed on leash |
| ✗ | Lost and found |
| | Bicycle racks |
| | First aid area available |
| ✗ | Self-brought picnics allowed |
| | Self-brought alcohol allowed |
| | Stroller/wheelchair rentals available |

| | |
|---|---|
| ✗ | Parade(time & date not avbl.) |
| | Parking fee |
| | Entrance fee |
| ✗ | Camping facilities: 6 miles |
| ✗ | Boating facilities: Kings River |
| ✗ | RV facilities w/ hookups: 10 miles |
| ✗ | Accomodations in town |
| ✗ | Restaurants in town<br>Lalo's, The Safari, New China Restaurant |

# *Petaluma Antique Street Faire*

PETALUMA'S TURN-OF-THE-century downtown is an enchanting site for the **Petaluma Antique Street Faire**! Iron Front buildings surround the 120 vendors displaying their wares. Specialty shopping and browsing for antiques go hand in hand in this quaint little community.

## Petaluma, California

Last Sunday in September
8:00 AM - 4:00 PM

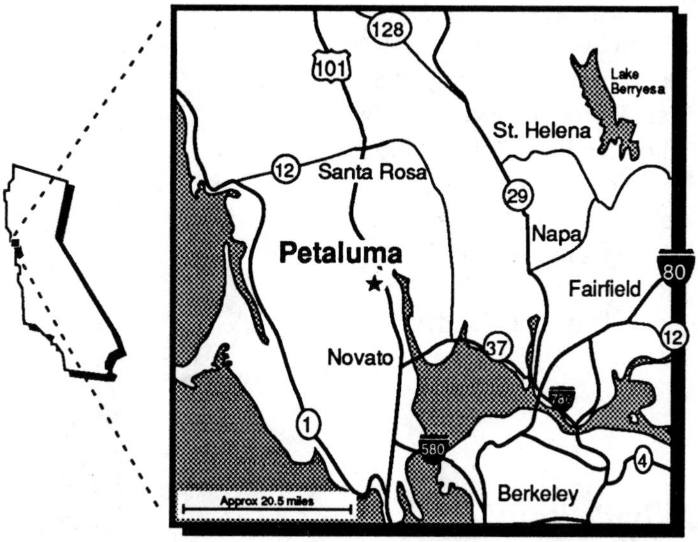


*Up-to-date festival information is available from:*
*Petaluma Chamber of Commerce*
*(707) 762-2785*

## What's goin' on...

Town population: **42,000**
Last year's attendance: **5,000**
Average outdoor temperature: **75°**
Festival location: **Downtown**

- X Wine tasting/beer for sale
- X Food booths
- X Arts/crafts for sale
- Live music
- Clowns
- Face painters
- Childrens games
- Animal exhibits/petting zoo
- X Dogs allowed on leash
- Lost and found
- X Bicycle racks
- First aid area available
- X Self-brought picnics allowed
- Self-brought alcohol allowed
- Stroller/wheelchair rentals available

- Parade
- Parking fee
- Entrance fee
- X Camping facilities: 5 miles
- X Boating facilities: River, lake, and bay
- X RV facilities w/ hookups: 5 miles
- X Accomodations in town
  Best Western, Quality Inn, Motel 6, Cavanagh Cottage B&B, 7th St. Inn B&B
- X Restaurants in town
  Petrucci's, Tempura House, Steamer Gold, Cattlemen's, Fino's, Original Marvin's

C E N T R A L

# *Italian Film Festival*

SHOWCASE THEATER IN THE Civic Center comes alive when the **Italian Film Festival** comes to life! This fabulous 2000-seat facility was designed by Frank Lloyd Wright, and is, in itself, worthy of a visit. Film buffs will not only enjoy the films, but the food and vino served is quite delicious too. There's good shopping in town, and a picturesque waterfront to picnic at during the day.

## San Rafael, California

Four Sunday nights in Oct. & Nov. (call Chamber for exact dates)
7:30 PM - 11:00 PM

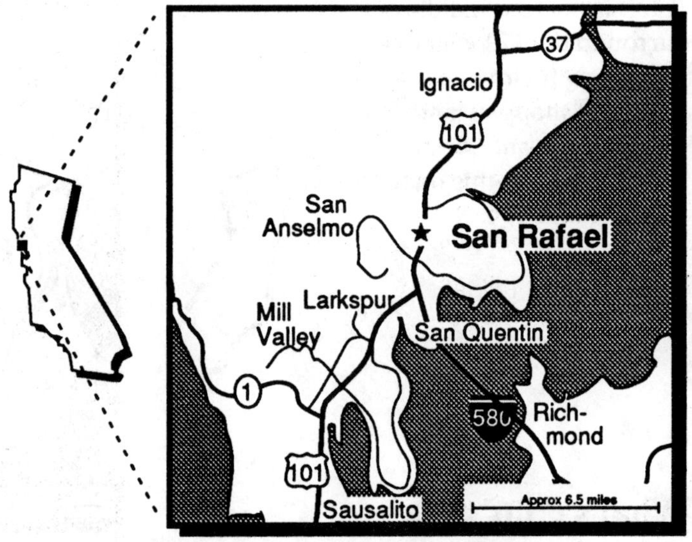


## What's goin' on...

Town population: **40,000**
Last year's attendance: **350**
Average outdoor temperature: **70°**
Festival location: **Marin Co. Civic Center**

*Up-to-date festival information is available from:*
*San Rafael Chamber of Commerce*
*(415) 454-4163*

- ✗ Wine tasting/beer for sale
- ✗ Food booths
- Arts/crafts for sale
- ✗ Live music
- Clowns
- Face painters
- Childrens games
- Animal exhibits/petting zoo
- Dogs allowed on leash
- Lost and found
- Bicycle racks
- ✗ First aid area available
- Self-brought picnics allowed
- Self-brought alcohol allowed
- Stroller/wheelchair rentals available

- Parade
- Parking fee
- ✗ Entrance fee: prices vary
- ✗ Camping facilities: 10 miles
- ✗ Boating facilities: San Francisco Bay
- ✗ RV facilities w/ hookups: 10 miles
- ✗ Accomodations in town
  Panama Hotel, Embassy Suites
- ✗ Restaurants in town
  La Toscana, Carlo Restaurant

# *Harvest Festival & Carnival*

VINEYARDS? IN FELTON? Well, folks, it is quite a bit south of the Napa Valley, but the fine wines produced at the Hallbrook Vineyards are worth the drive! Come down and see for yourself at the **Harvest Festival & Carnival** in October! Located just 15 minutes from Santa Cruz, this friendly little winery boasts *excellent* Chards, Zins, Cabs, and a luscious nonalcoholic premium varietal grape juice!

## Felton, California

First weekend in October
Daily 11:00 AM - 5:30 PM

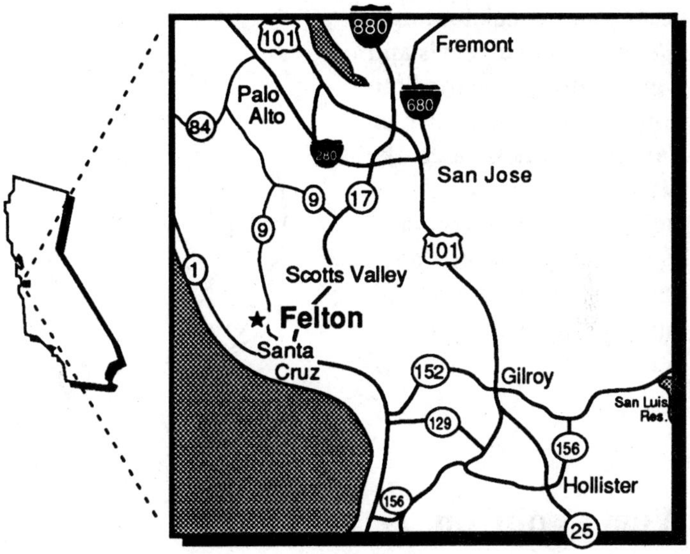


*Up-to-date festival information is available from:*
*Felton Chamber of Commerce*
*(408) 335-4441*

## What's goin' on...

Town population: **4,000**
Last year's attendance: **1,000**
Average outdoor temperature: **70°**
Festival location: **Hallcrest Vineyards**

- X Wine tasting/beer for sale
- X Food booths
- Arts/crafts for sale
- X Live music
- Clowns
- Face painters
- Childrens games
- Animal exhibits/petting zoo
- Dogs allowed on leash
- Lost and found
- Bicycle racks
- First aid area available
- X Self-brought picnics allowed
- Self-brought alcohol allowed
- Stroller/wheelchair rentals available

- Parade
- Parking fee
- X Entrance fee: $6; Under 12 free
- X Camping facilities: 5 miles
- X Boating facilities: Santa Cruz Harbor
- X RV facilities w/ hookups: 5 miles
- X Accomodations in town
  Fair View Manor B&B
- X Restaurants in town
  Mama Mia, Tampico, Whistle Inn

CENTRAL

# *Renaissance of Kings Faire*

THE SETTING: HANFORD-shire. The date: 1520. Young King Henry VIII, Queen Katherine of Aragon, and their court join the celebrating villagers in their revels and merriment. This is the fictitious setting of the town of Hanford's **Renaissance of Kings Faire**. Festivities include a knightly combat, traditional plays and dances, hearty victuals, and refreshing beverages! Truly a *royal* delight!

## Hanford, California

First weekend in October

Sat.10:00 AM - 6:00 PM; Sun. 10:00 AM - 5:00 PM

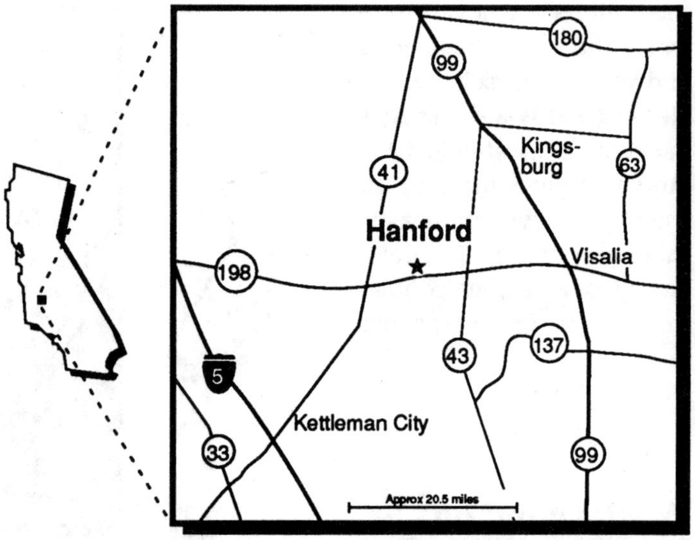


## What's goin' on...

Town population: **30,617**

Last year's attendance: **15,000**

Average outdoor temperature: **85°**

Festival location: **Civic Center Park**

*Up-to-date festival information is available from:*
*Hanford City Recreation Dept.*
*(209) 585-0483*

| | |
|---|---|
| X | Wine tasting/beer for sale |
| X | Food booths |
| X | Arts/crafts for sale |
| X | Live music |
| | Clowns |
| X | Face painters |
| X | Childrens games |
| | Animal exhibits/petting zoo |
| X | Dogs allowed on leash |
| X | Lost and found |
| X | Bicycle racks |
| X | First aid area available |
| X | Self-brought picnics allowed |
| | Self-brought alcohol allowed |
| | Stroller/wheelchair rentals available |

| | |
|---|---|
| X | Parade: Sat. & Sun. at noon |
| | Parking fee |
| | Entrance fee |
| X | Camping facilities: Fairgrounds |
| X | Boating facilities: 10 miles |
| X | RV facilities w/ hookups |
| X | Accomodations in town<br>Best Western, Irwin Street Inn |
| X | Restaurants in town<br>Imperial Dynasty, Justo's Basque, Irwin Street Inn, Hoosegow (old jail) |

# *Sunny Hills Grape Festival*

THE **SUNNY HILLS GRAPE Festival** is held right next to the Larkspur Landing Ferry—the ferry that runs between San Francisco and Larkspur. You'll find autumn and holiday decorations; needlepoint items; handmade quilts and clothing; silk and dried flower arrangements; and lots of great food booths. This is genuinely a nice way to spend a family weekend!

## Larkspur, California

First Saturday in October
10:00 AM - 5:00 PM

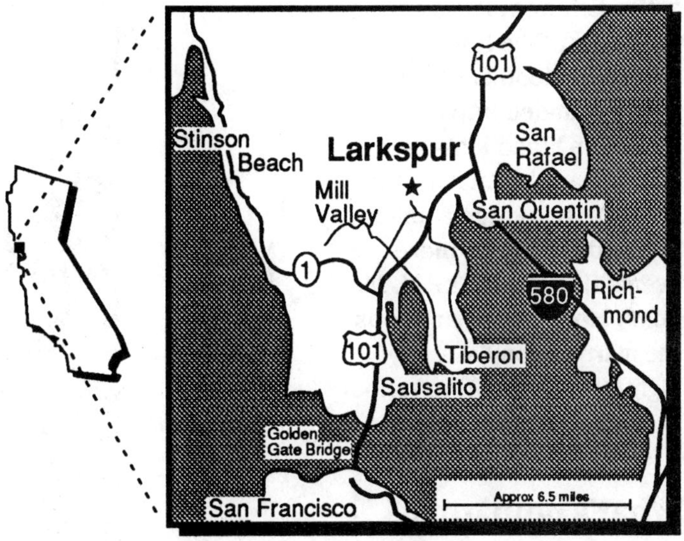


*Up-to-date festival information is available from:*
*Larkspur Visitors Bureau*
*(415) 472-7470*

## What's goin' on...

Town population: **10,000**
Last year's attendance: **3,000**
Average outdoor temperature: **78°**
Festival location: **Larkspur Landing area**

| | |
|---|---|
| X | Wine tasting/beer for sale |
| X | Food booths |
| X | Arts/crafts for sale |
| X | Live music |
| X | Clowns |
| X | Face painters |
| X | Childrens games |
| X | Animal exhibits/petting zoo |
| | Dogs allowed on leash |
| X | Lost and found |
| | Bicycle racks |
| X | First aid area available |
| X | Self-brought picnics allowed |
| X | Self-brought alcohol allowed |
| | Stroller/wheelchair rentals available |

| | |
|---|---|
| | Parade |
| | Parking fee |
| | Entrance fee |
| | Camping facilities |
| X | Boating facilities: San Francisco Bay |
| | RV facilities w/ hookups |
| X | Accomodations in town: Courtyard Marriott, Holiday Inn, Embassy Suites |
| X | Restaurants in town: Scoma's, Yet Wah, Lark Creek Inn, Remillards, Chevy's, Acapulco |

C
E
N
T
R
A
L

# *Harbor Festival*

THE **HARBOR FESTIVAL**, with its waterfront setting at Morro Bay, celebrates one of the few natural harbors and active fishing villages on the west coast. The festival's Wine & Seafood Faire has been expanded into a "main attraction" (and kick-off for October as National Seafood Month), with entertainment, arts and crafts and more events than ever. The M. M. Lucky Horseshoe Band tops the marquee on Saturday night. (Students bring school ID for $1 off entrance fee)

## Morro Bay, California

First weekend in October
Daily 10:00 AM - 6:00 PM

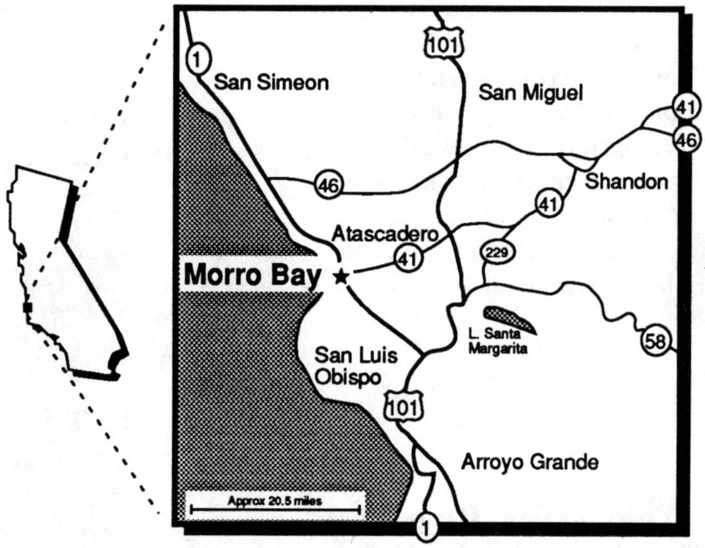


*Up-to-date festival information is available from:*
*Morro Bay Chamber of Commerce*
*(805) 772-4467*

## What's goin' on...

Town population: **9,064**
Last year's attendance: **16,000**
Average outdoor temperature: **70°**
Festival location: **Citywide**

| | |
|---|---|
| X | Wine tasting/beer for sale |
| X | Food booths |
| X | Arts/crafts for sale |
| X | Live music |
| X | Clowns |
| X | Face painters |
| X | Childrens games |
| X | Animal exhibits/petting zoo |
| X | Dogs allowed on leash |
| X | Lost and found |
| X | Bicycle racks |
| X | First aid area available |
| | Self-brought picnics allowed |
| | Self-brought alcohol allowed |
| | Stroller/wheelchair rentals available |

| | |
|---|---|
| | Parade |
| | Parking fee |
| X | Entrance fee: S $1; A $2; K free |
| X | Camping facilities: 3 miles |
| X | Boating facilities: Bay |
| X | RV facilities w/ hookups: 3 miles |
| X | Accomodations in town |
| X | Restaurants in town<br>Hungry Tiger, Bob's Fish 'n Chips, Dorn's |

# *Downtown Street Festival*

THIS IS ONE TO BRING THE kids to! The Children's Theater at the **Downtown Street Festival** in San Bruno is absolutely delightful! As is the food, wine, craft and art booths, and music! This festival's been attracting people since 1977 and over 75,000 people turn out each year to enjoy it!

## San Bruno, California

First weekend in October
Daily 10:00 AM - 5:00 PM

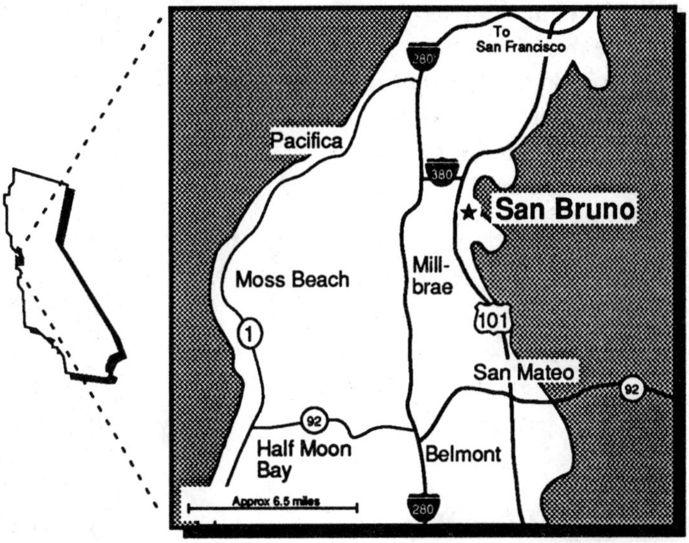


*Up-to-date festival information is available from:*
*San Bruno Chamber of Commerce*
*(415) 588-0180*

## What's goin' on...

Town population: **35,600**
Last year's attendance: **75,000**
Average outdoor temperature: **55°**
Festival location: **Citywide**

| | |
|---|---|
| X | Wine tasting/beer for sale |
| X | Food booths |
| X | Arts/crafts for sale |
| X | Live music |
| X | Clowns |
| X | Face painters |
| X | Childrens games |
| X | Animal exhibits/petting zoo |
| | Dogs allowed on leash |
| X | Lost and found |
| X | Bicycle racks |
| X | First aid area available |
| X | Self-brought picnics allowed |
| | Self-brought alcohol allowed |
| | Stroller/wheelchair rentals available |

| | |
|---|---|
| | Parade |
| | Parking fee |
| | Entrance fee |
| | Camping facilities |
| X | Boating facilities: San Francisco Bay |
| | RV facilities w/ hookups |
| X | Accomodations in town<br>Marriot |
| X | Restaurants in town<br>Artichoke Joes |

CENTRAL

# *Long Marine Lab Open House & Fall Fish Festival*

WHY NOT HEAD ON DOWN to the **Long Marine Lab Open House & Fall Fish Festival**—just for the halibut? Live music will entertain as you tour the premises—the bookstore and gift shops are open too. Barbecued fish, salads, beer, wine, and soft drinks will be available for lunch.

## Santa Cruz, California

First Saturday in October
10:00 AM - 4:00 AM

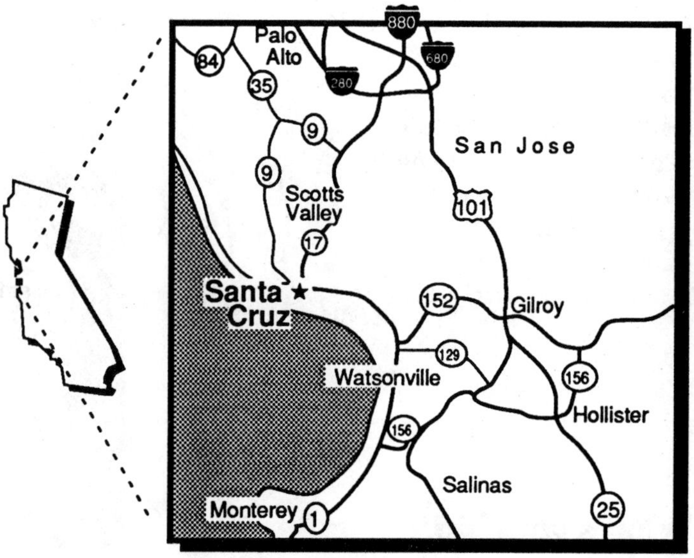


## What's goin' on...

Town population: **48,000**
Last year's attendance: **3,500**
Average outdoor temperature: **73°**
Festival location: **Long Marine Lab**

☞ *Up-to-date festival information is available from:*
*Santa Cruz Visitors Bureau*
*(408) 425-1234*

| | |
|---|---|
| X | Wine tasting/beer for sale |
| X | Food booths |
| | Arts/crafts for sale |
| X | Live music |
| | Clowns |
| | Face painters |
| | Childrens games |
| X | Animal exhibits/petting zoo |
| | Dogs allowed on leash |
| | Lost and found |
| | Bicycle racks |
| | First aid area available |
| | Self-brought picnics allowed |
| | Self-brought alcohol allowed |
| | Stroller/wheelchair rentals available |

| | |
|---|---|
| | Parade |
| | Parking fee |
| | Entrance fee |
| X | Camping facilities: [illegible] miles |
| X | Boating facilities: Santa Cruz Harbor |
| X | RV facilities w/ hookups: 5 miles |
| X | Accomodations in town |
| X | Restaurants in town<br>Riva's, Casablanca |

# *Wine & Cheese Expo*

THERE'S A WHOLE LOT more to Vallejo than the **Wine & Cheese Expo**! Home to Marine World/Africa U.S.A. and the Naval Historical Museum, this waterfront town puts on quite an Expo in the park. A dozen Napa Valley wineries will be on hand to share the fruits of their harvests, and in addition to cheese to taste, a variety of ethnic food is being prepared for your consumption. Yummy stuff!

## Vallejo, California

First weekend in October
Daily 10:00 AM - 5:00 PM

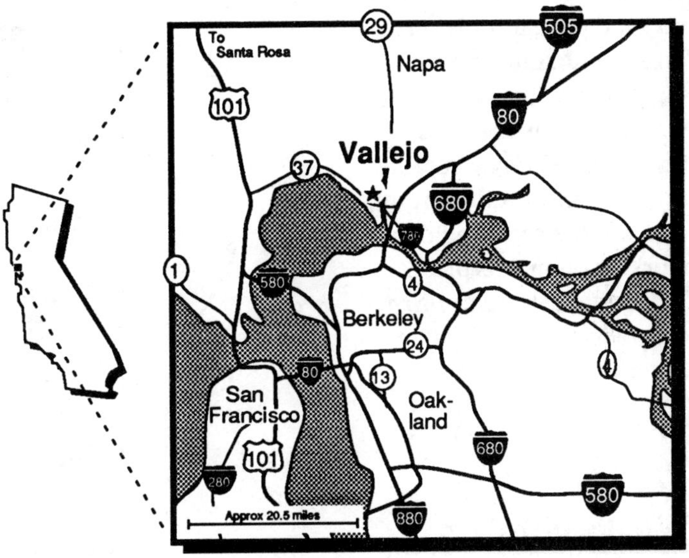


*Up-to-date festival information is available from:*
*Vallejo Chamber of Commerce*
*(707) 644-5551*

## What's goin' on...

Town population: **50,000**
Last year's attendance: **35,000**
Average outdoor temperature: **70°**
Festival location: **Park**

| | |
|---|---|
| X | Wine tasting/beer for sale |
| X | Food booths |
| X | Arts/crafts for sale |
| | Live music |
| X | Clowns |
| X | Face painters |
| | Childrens games |
| | Animal exhibits/petting zoo |
| X | Dogs allowed on leash |
| X | Lost and found |
| | Bicycle racks |
| X | First aid area available |
| X | Self-brought picnics allowed |
| | Self-brought alcohol allowed |
| | Stroller/wheelchair rentals available |

| | |
|---|---|
| | Parade |
| | Parking fee |
| | Entrance fee |
| X | Camping facilities: 5 miles |
| X | Boating facilities: San Francisco Bay |
| X | RV facilities w/ hookups: 5 miles |
| X | Accomodations in town<br>Comfort Inn, Holiday Inn |
| X | Restaurants in town<br>Wharf, Remark, Sardine Can, Alex's, Mario's |

CENTRAL

# *Festival '91*

ONE OF CALIFORNIA'S VERY best festivals is **Festival '91** in Livermore! Why: The craftspeople *must* demonstrate their particular craft on-site! Absolutely fascinating! You'll witness weavers working on their looms, jewelers creating wearable art, quilters stitching away, and woodcarvers tediously working on masterpieces! This is a weekend of ***pure*** creativity!

## Livermore, California

First weekend in October
Daily 11:00 AM - 5:00 PM

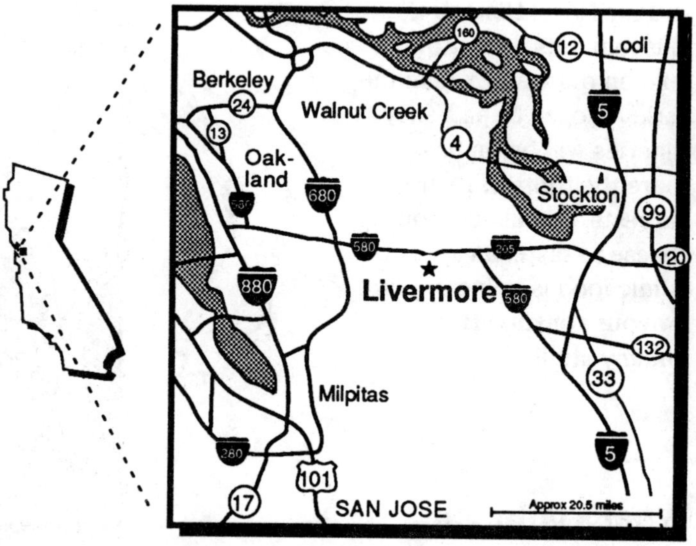


*Up-to-date festival information is available from:*
*Livermore Chamber of Commerce*
*(415) 447-1606*

## What's goin' on...

Town population: **56,445**
Last year's attendance: **6,000**
Average outdoor temperature: **80°**
Festival location: **"The Barn"**

- X Wine tasting/beer for sale
- X Food booths
- X Arts/crafts for sale
- X Live music
- X Clowns
- X Face painters
- X Childrens games
- Animal exhibits/petting zoo
- X Dogs allowed on leash
- X Lost and found
- X Bicycle racks
- First aid area available
- X Self-brought picnics allowed
- Self-brought alcohol allowed
- Stroller/wheelchair rentals available

- Parade
- Parking fee
- Entrance fee
- X Camping facilities, 11 miles
- X Boating facilities: Del Valle Res.
- X RV facilities w/ hookups: 11 miles
- X Accomodations in town
  Townhouse Motel, Residence Inn, Holiday Inn
- X Restaurants in town
  El Lorito, Le Coquelicot, Cruiser's, Beeb's Bar & Grill, Wente Sparkling Cellars Restaurant

# *Yountville Days Parade & Festival*

THE SLEEPY LITTLE VILLAGE of Yountville comes alive for **Yountville Days Parade & Festival!** This rather flat area of Napa Valley—perfect for bicycling—holds this annual event in the downtown park. Besides the local artists and craftspersons exhibiting for the day, there is terrific shopping in the quaint village. The wine is *exquisite*, of course, and the food booths offer delicious morsels!

## Yountville, California

First Sunday in October
11:00 AM - dusk

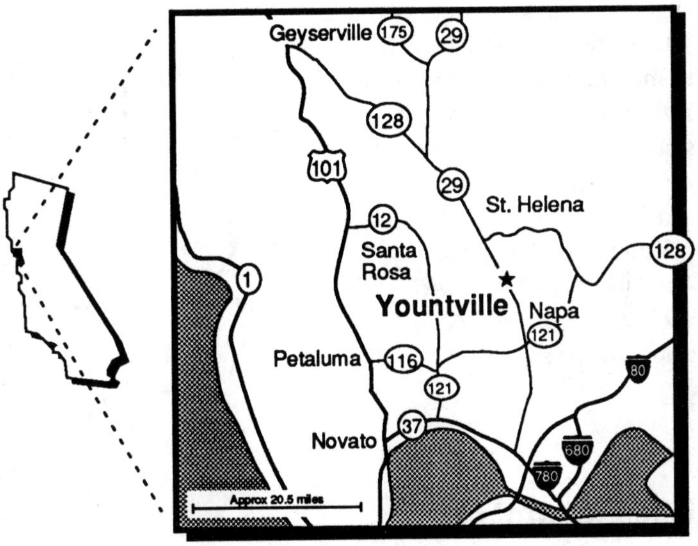


*Up-to-date festival information is available from:*
*Yountville Chamber of Commerce*
*(707) 944-0904*

## What's goin' on...

Town population: **3,000**
Last year's attendance: **4,200**
Average outdoor temperature: **80°**
Festival location: **Yountville Park**

| | |
|---|---|
| X | Wine tasting/beer for sale |
| X | Food booths |
| X | Arts/crafts for sale |
| X | Live music |
| X | Clowns |
| X | Face painters |
| X | Childrens games |
| X | Animal exhibits/petting zoo |
| | Dogs allowed on leash |
| | Lost and found |
| | Bicycle racks |
| | First aid area available |
| X | Self-brought picnics allowed |
| X | Self-brought alcohol allowed |
| | Stroller/wheelchair rentals available |

| | |
|---|---|
| X | Parade: 12:30 on Washington St. |
| | Parking fee |
| | Entrance fee |
| X | Camping facilities: 12 miles |
| X | Boating facilities: Lake Berryessa |
| X | RV facilities w/ hookups: 1 mile |
| X | Accomodations in town<br>Burgundy House Inn B&B, Rockhaven B&B |
| X | Restaurants in town |

# *Porterville Stagecoach Stampede*

Y'ALL COME OUT TO A REAL western bang-up celebration at the **Porterville Stagecoach Stampede**! Porterville was a *rowdy* stagecoach stop in the late 1800s and its time you come out and see what all the hullaboo is about! Lots of good home cooking, contests and raffles, and booths stuffed with lots of little pretties! And bring your dancin' shoes for a twirl around the dance floor—till midnight or so!

## Porterville, California

Second weekend in October
Daily 10:00 AM - midnight

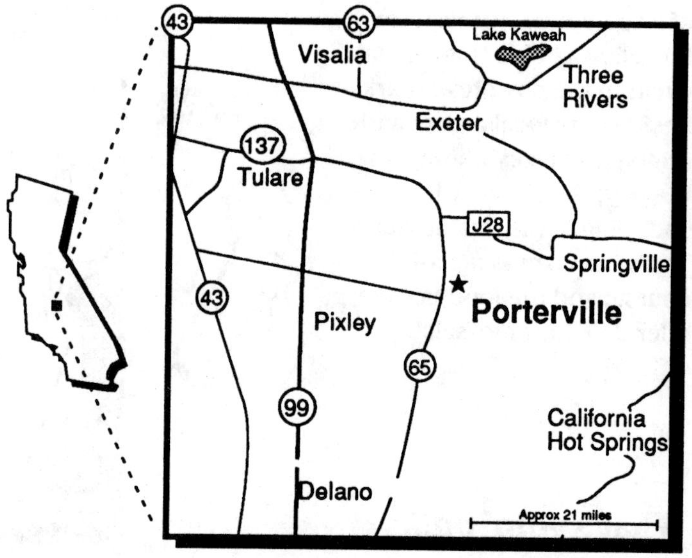


## What's goin' on...

Town population: **27,000**
Last year's attendance: **10,000**
Average outdoor temperature: **78°**
Festival location: **Fairgrounds**

*Up-to-date festival information is available from:*
*Porterville Chamber of Commerce*
*(209) 784-7502*

- ✗ Wine tasting/beer for sale
- ✗ Food booths
- ✗ Arts/crafts for sale
- ✗ Live music
- Clowns
- Face painters
- ✗ Childrens games
- ✗ Animal exhibits/petting zoo
- Dogs allowed on leash
- ✗ Lost and found
- Bicycle racks
- ✗ First aid area available
- Self-brought picnics allowed
- Self-brought alcohol allowed
- Stroller/wheelchair rentals available

- Parade
- Parking fee
- ✗ Entrance fee: S & K $3; A $5
- ✗ Camping facilities: 6 miles
- ✗ Boating facilities: Lake
- ✗ RV facilities w/ hookups: 6 miles
- ✗ Accomodations in town
  Sundance Inn, Paul Bunyan Lodge, Motel 6
- ✗ Restaurants in town
  Porterville Palace Hotel, The Oak Pit

# *Rio Vista Bass Derby*

THE WAYWARD HOME OF Humphrey the Humback whale is the site for the 44th **Rio Vista Bass Derby**! Exquisite art by Norma Bird, wood carvings by Pete Bennett and Steve Esperson, and ceramics by Sharon Gile are just a few of the well-known artists who display. This small town with a big heart has a great the little local museum, and be sure to stop in at Foster's Bighorn for some **BIG** surprises!

## Rio Vista, California

Second weekend in October
4:00 PM Friday - 8:00 PM Sunday

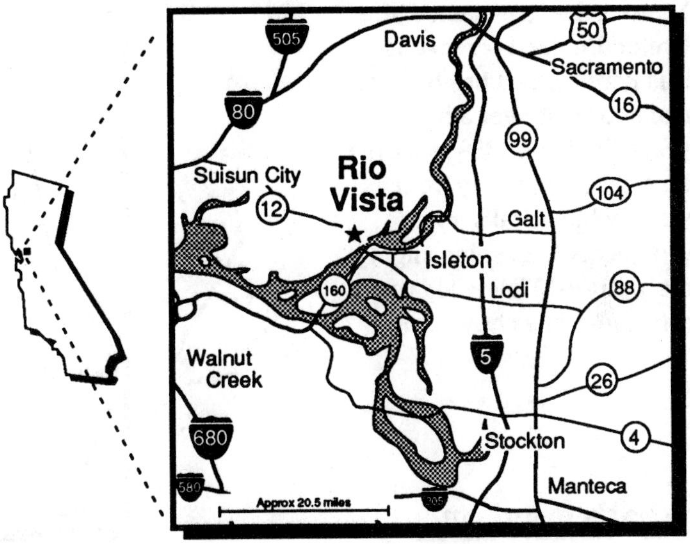


## What's goin' on...

Town population: **3,100**
Last year's attendance: **30,000**
Average outdoor temperature: **65°**
Festival location: **Downtown and the Delta**

*Up-to-date festival information is available from:*
*Rio Vista Chamber of Commerce*
*(707) 374-2700*

| | |
|---|---|
| X | Wine tasting/beer for sale |
| X | Food booths |
| X | Arts/crafts for sale |
| X | Live music |
| X | Clowns |
| | Face painters |
| X | Childrens games |
| X | Animal exhibits/petting zoo |
| X | Dogs allowed on leash |
| X | Lost and found |
| | Bicycle racks |
| X | First aid area available |
| X | Self-brought picnics allowed |
| | Self-brought alcohol allowed |
| | Stroller/wheelchair rentals available |

| | |
|---|---|
| X | Parade: Sun. 12:30 on Main St. |
| | Parking fee |
| X | Entrance fee: Derby & boat launch |
| X | Camping facilities: In town |
| X | Boating facilities: River |
| X | RV facilities w/ hookups: In town |
| X | Accomodations in town<br>Rio Sands, Vista Motel |
| X | Restaurants in town<br>Foster's Bighorn - The Point, Jessen's Cafe |

# *Exeter Fall Festival*

FOR ABOUT THE ZILLIONTH time—spark up the 'cue for the **Exeter Fall Festival**—the deep-pit barbecue, that is! Yesiree, Exeter—named after Exeter, England— reckons this here festival has been a ritual for just over a hundred years, since its 1888 founding Musical groups play from a stage, while local service groups cook up some mighty tasty vittles! Y'all enjoy the arts-and-crafts show, too!

## Exeter, California

Second Saturday in October
10:00 AM - 4:00 PM

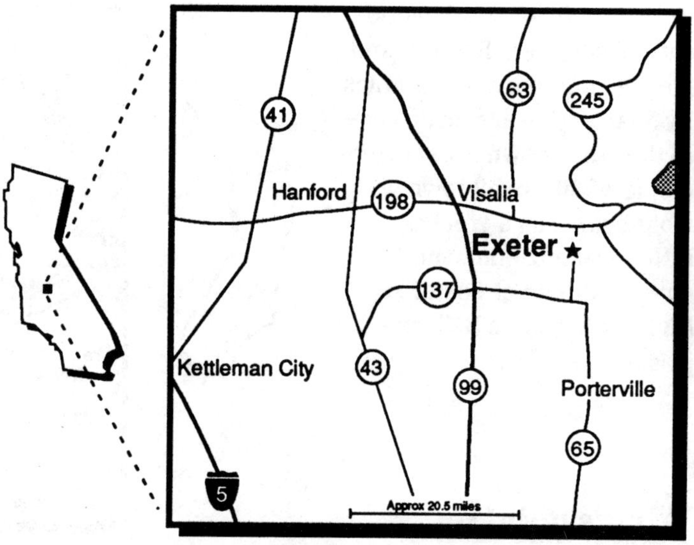


*Up-to-date festival information is available from:*
*Exeter Chamber of Commerce*
*(209) 592-2919*

## What's goin' on...

Town population: **7,491**
Last year's attendance: **N/A**
Average outdoor temperature: **90°**
Festival location: **Park**

- ✗ Wine tasting/beer for sale
- ✗ Food booths
- ✗ Arts/crafts for sale
- ✗ Live music
- Clowns
- ✗ Face painters
- Childrens games
- Animal exhibits/petting zoo
- ✗ Dogs allowed on leash
- Lost and found
- Bicycle racks
- ✗ First aid area available
- Self-brought picnics allowed
- Self-brought alcohol allowed
- Stroller/wheelchair rentals available

- ✗ Parade: (date & time not avbl.)
- Parking fee
- Entrance fee
- ✗ Camping facilities: 10 miles
- ✗ Boating facilities: Lake Kaweah
- ✗ RV facilities w/ hookups: 6 miles
- ✗ Accomodations in town
  Kaweah Motel
- Restaurants in town

# *Fowler Fall Festival*

TUCKED AWAY IN THE fruitful arm of California's Central Valley, Fowler offers the **Fowler Fall Festival** for visitors and townfolks alike. Sponsored by the Lions Club, this shindig boogies from the wee hours of the morning to the wee hours of the morning! For more recreation ideas, hit the Pine Flat Reservoir for fishing, swimming and boating.

## Fowler, California

Second Saturday in October
7:00 AM - 1:00 AM

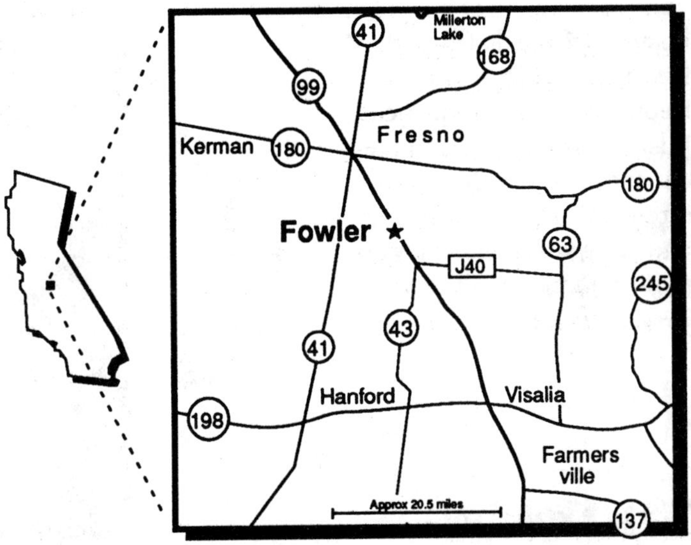


## What's goin' on...

Town population: **3,076**
Last year's attendance: **400**
Average outdoor temperature: **75°**
Festival location: **Merced St. & Third**

*Up-to-date festival information is available from:*
*Fowler Chamber of Commerce*
*(209) 233-4651*

| | |
|---|---|
| | Wine tasting/beer for sale |
| X | Food booths |
| X | Arts/crafts for sale |
| X | Live music |
| X | Clowns |
| X | Face painters |
| X | Childrens games |
| X | Animal exhibits/petting zoo |
| X | Dogs allowed on leash |
| | Lost and found |
| | Bicycle racks |
| X | First aid area available |
| | Self-brought picnics allowed |
| | Self-brought alcohol allowed |
| | Stroller/wheelchair rentals available |

| | |
|---|---|
| X | Parade: (date & time not avbl.) |
| | Parking fee |
| | Entrance fee |
| X | Camping facilities: 10 miles |
| X | Boating facilities: Pine Flat Res. |
| X | RV facilities w/ hookups: 10 miles |
| | Accomodations in town |
| | Restaurants in town |

# *Pioneer Day*

A GREAT TRADITION SINCE 1931, **Pioneer Day** pays tribute to local pioneers and their descendants. "Leave your pocketbook at home and come celebrate in friendship" is the motto of the Day. Dedicated citizens and local businesses fund the antique car show, whiskerino contest, street dance, roping contest, and store window displays of pioneer family traditions. *Yeowza...big fun!*

## Paso Robles, California

Saturday prior to Columbus Day (Oct.)
10:00 AM - 5:00 PM

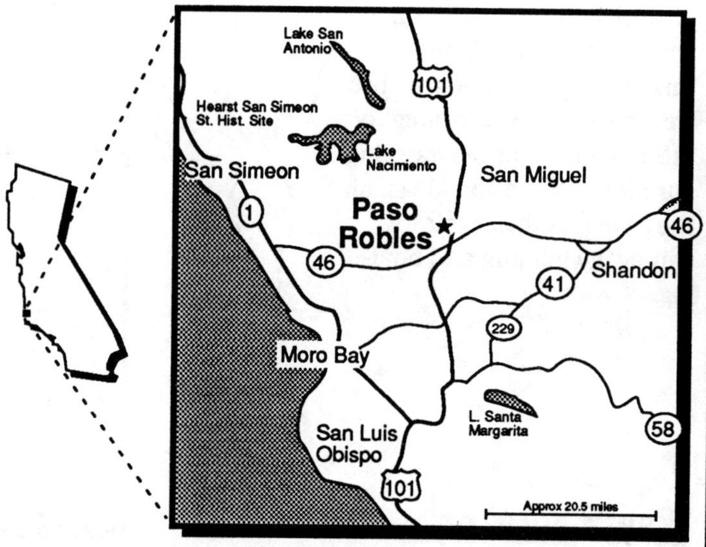


## What's goin' on...

Town population: **18,000**
Last year's attendance: **13,000**
Average outdoor temperature: **82°**
Festival location: **Downtown**

*Up-to-date festival information is available from:*
*Paso Robles Chamber of Commerce*
*(805) 238-0506*

| | |
|---|---|
| | Wine tasting/beer for sale |
| | Food booths |
| | Arts/crafts for sale |
| ✗ | Live music |
| ✗ | Clowns |
| | Face painters |
| | Childrens games |
| | Animal exhibits/petting zoo |
| | Dogs allowed on leash |
| ✗ | Lost and found |
| | Bicycle racks |
| | First aid area available |
| ✗ | Self-brought picnics allowed |
| | Self-brought alcohol allowed |
| | Stroller/wheelchair rentals available |

| | |
|---|---|
| ✗ | Parade: Sat. 10:00 AM downtown |
| | Parking fee |
| | Entrance fee |
| ✗ | Camping facilities: 20 miles |
| ✗ | Boating facilities: Lake San Antonio |
| ✗ | RV facilities w/ hookups: In town |
| ✗ | Accomodations in town<br>Roseleith, Country House Inn, Adelaide Motor Inn, Avalon Motel, Padre Oaks |
| ✗ | Restaurants in town<br>Templeton Corner, Wilson's, Wellsona House, Pepe's Mexican Restaurant |

# *Riverbank Cheese & Wine Expo*

IT'S STILL INDIAN SUMMER at **Riverbank's Cheese & Wine Expo**! More than 100,000 people can't be wrong in attending this weekend event featuring nearly 300 art, crafts, antique, and food vendors at the free street festival. Reserve tickets early for one of the seven tasting sessions "Taste the Cheese, Savor the Wine" ($15.00). Dixieland jazz and roving minstralls make the experience memorable!

## Riverbank, California

Second weekend in October
Daily 9:00 AM - 5:00 PM

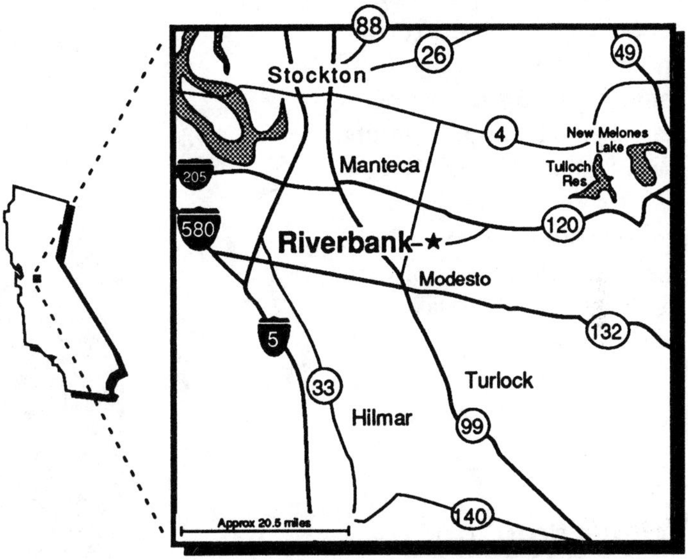


C
E
N
T
R
A
L

## What's goin' on...

Town population: **7,000**
Last year's attendance: **105,000**
Average outdoor temperature: **85°**
Festival location: **Downtown**

*Up-to-date festival information is available from:*
*Riverbank Chamber of Commerce*
*(209) 869-4541*

| | |
|---|---|
| X | Wine tasting/beer for sale |
| X | Food booths |
| X | Arts/crafts for sale |
| X | Live music |
| | Clowns |
| X | Face painters |
| | Childrens games |
| | Animal exhibits/petting zoo |
| X | Dogs allowed on leash |
| X | Lost and found |
| | Bicycle racks |
| X | First aid area available |
| | Self-brought picnics allowed |
| | Self-brought alcohol allowed |
| | Stroller/wheelchair rentals available |

| | |
|---|---|
| | Parade |
| X | Parking fee: $2.00 |
| | Entrance fee |
| X | Camping facilities: 15 miles |
| | Boating facilities |
| X | RV facilities w/ hookups: 15 miles |
| X | Accomodations in town<br>Ramada Inn, Holiday Motel (five miles away in Oakdale) |
| X | Restaurants in town<br>Ellis Restaurant, Pizza Plus, Elena's, El Ranchito |

# *Brussels Sprout Festival*

OH NO! THEY DIDN'T! Sprout-water taffy? Yep, they did it at the **Brussels Sprout Festival** in Santa Cruz. And it ain't too bad, neither! You'll find the bizarre and the usual—sprout pizza, sprout ice cream, marinated sprouts, sprout tacos, fried sprouts—every-which-way-but-loose sprouts! But you'll even find a few of those! These miniature cabbages are full of flavor!

## Santa Cruz, California

Second weekend in October
Daily 11:00 AM - 5:00 PM

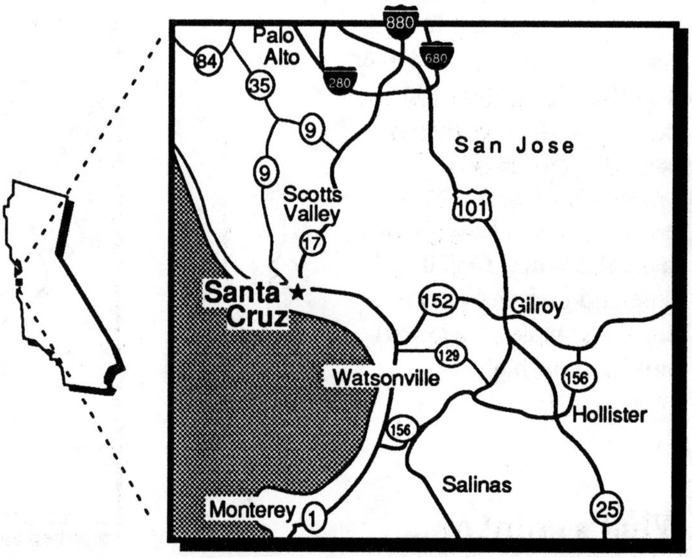


*Up-to-date festival information is available from:*
*Santa Cruz Visitors Bureau*
*(408) 425-1234*

## What's goin' on...

Town population: **51,000**
Last year's attendance: **30,000**
Average outdoor temperature: **65°**
Festival location: **Beach Boardwalk**

- X Wine tasting/beer for sale
- X Food booths
- X Arts/crafts for sale
- Live music
- X Clowns
- X Face painters
- X Childrens games
- Animal exhibits/petting zoo
- Dogs allowed on leash
- X Lost and found
- X Bicycle racks
- X First aid area available
- X Self-brought picnics allowed
- X Self-brought alcohol allowed
- X Stroller/wheelchair rentals available

- Parade
- X Parking fee: meters
- Entrance fee
- X Camping facilities: 10 miles
- X Boating facilities: Santa Cruz Harbor
- X RV facilities w/ hookups: 4 miles
- X Accomodations in town
  Many B&Bs, TraveLodge Riviera, Sunset Inn, Chaminade, Best Western Torch-Lite Inn
- X Restaurants in town
  Seabright Brewery, Pontiac Grill, Adolph's, Crow's Nest, Aldo's, Hindquarter, Miramar

# *Fiesta*

THE REEDLEY **FIESTA** IS terrific family event which must be attended! Nicknamed "The World's Fruit Basket," Reedley goes all out for this weekend of fun! Food booths along Gourmet Alley feature the best teriaki beef sticks around and outstanding tamales! Be sure to get to Pioneer Park in time for the 10:00 AM parade! Then hit Gourmet Garden Deli for an evening with the locals!

## Reedley, California

Second Saturday in October
10:00 AM - 6:00 PM

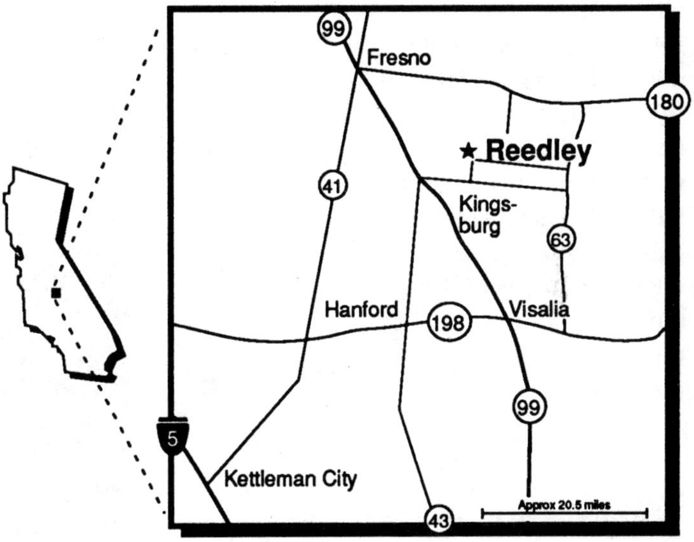


## What's goin' on...

Town population: **15,000**
Last year's attendance: **2,500**
Average outdoor temperature: **70°**
Festival location: **Citywide**

*Up-to-date festival information is available from:*
*Reedley Chamber of Commerce*
*(209) 638-3548*

| | |
|---|---|
| X | Wine tasting/beer for sale |
| X | Food booths |
| X | Arts/crafts for sale |
| X | Live music |
| X | Clowns |
| X | Face painters |
| X | Childrens games |
| X | Animal exhibits/petting zoo |
| X | Dogs allowed on leash |
| X | Lost and found |
| X | Bicycle racks |
| X | First aid area available |
| X | Self-brought picnics allowed |
| | Self-brought alcohol allowed |
| X | Stroller/wheelchair rentals available |

| | |
|---|---|
| X | Parade: Sat. 10:00 AM downtown |
| X | Parking fee |
| | Entrance fee |
| X | Camping facilities: Kings River |
| X | Boating facilities: Kings River |
| X | RV facilities w/ hookups: In town |
| X | Accomodations in town |
| X | Restaurants in town<br>Gourmet Garden Deli, Bear Club, Bub's Pub |

C
E
N
T
R
A
L

# *Welcome Back Monarch Day*

NATURAL BRIDGES STATE Beach hosts the annual **Welcome Back Monarch Day!** This awesome sight of a zillion winged creatures returning home is well worth a trip to Santa Cruz—both for the sights and for the education of it all! There are wonderful photo- graphic and entomological displays explaining the life cycle and migration habits of the monarch, hourly monarch tours, skits, and music! A *must* for the kids!

## Santa Cruz, California

Second Sunday in October
Noon - 4:00 PM

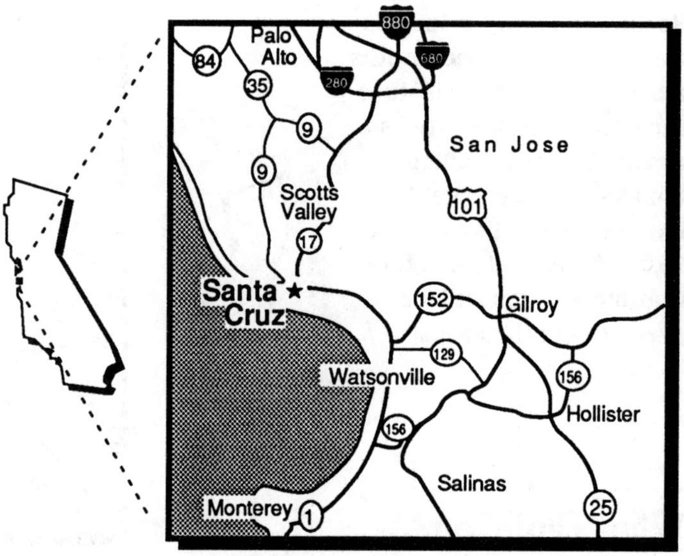


## What's goin' on...

Town population: **50,000**
Last year's attendance: **35,000**
Average outdoor temperature: **70°**
Festival location: **Natural Bridges State Park**

☞ *Up-to-date festival information is available from:*
*Santa Cruz Visitors Bureau*
*(408) 425-1234*

| | |
|---|---|
| | Wine tasting/beer for sale |
| ✗ | Food booths |
| | Arts/crafts for sale |
| ✗ | Live music |
| | Clowns |
| | Face painters |
| | Childrens games |
| | Animal exhibits/petting zoo |
| | Dogs allowed on leash |
| | Lost and found |
| ✗ | Bicycle racks |
| ✗ | First aid area available |
| ✗ | Self-brought picnics allowed |
| | Self-brought alcohol allowed |
| | Stroller/wheelchair rentals available |

| | |
|---|---|
| | Parade |
| ✗ | Parking fee: $6 per car |
| | Entrance fee |
| ✗ | Camping facilities: 2 miles |
| ✗ | Boating facilities: Santa Cruz Harbor |
| ✗ | RV facilities w/ hookups: 3 miles |
| ✗ | Accomodations in town |
| ✗ | Restaurants in town<br>Aldo's, Crow's Nest |

# *Slug Fest & Earthquake Anniversary*

SHAKE, RATTLE, 'N ROLL IS what the folks 'round these parts of California did in 1989! So they Santa Cruzians mixed two celebrations in one—**Slug Fest & Earthquake Anniversary**! The slug is the hailed mascot of UCSC, is a favorite among the locals, and is not the main ingredient in the dishes served! So leave your salt at home and come see how this community "bounced back" from the devastating quake of '89.

## Santa Cruz, California

Seventeenth of October
10:00 AM - 7:00 PM

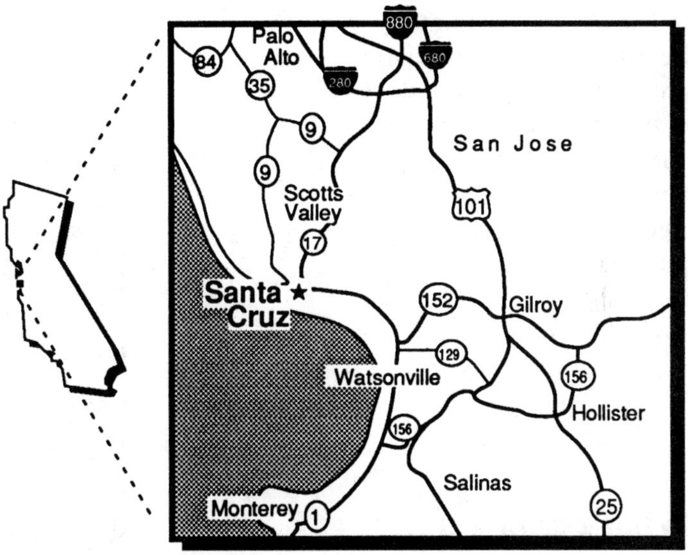


*Up-to-date festival information is available from:*
*Santa Cruz Visitors Bureau*
*(408) 425-1234*

## What's goin' on...

Town population: **50,000**
Last year's attendance: **N/A**
Average outdoor temperature: **70°**
Festival location: **Downtown**

- ✗ Wine tasting/beer for sale
- ✗ Food booths
- ✗ Arts/crafts for sale
- ✗ Live music
- Clowns
- Face painters
- ✗ Childrens games
- Animal exhibits/petting zoo
- ✗ Dogs allowed on leash
- Lost and found
- Bicycle racks
- First aid area available
- ✗ Self-brought picnics allowed
- Self-brought alcohol allowed
- Stroller/wheelchair rentals available

- Parade
- Parking fee
- Entrance fee
- ✗ Camping facilities: 2 miles
- ✗ Boating facilities: Santa Cruz Harbor
- ✗ RV facilities w/ hookups: 3 miles
- ✗ Accomodations in town
- ✗ Restaurants in town
  Aldo's, Crow's Nest

C E N T R A L

# *Atascadero Colony Days*

ATASCADERO LIES ADJACENT to the Los Padres National Forest and only 15 miles inland from the Pacific Ocean. **Atascadero Colony Days** is held to celebrate the unique founding and history of the Atascadero Colony in 1913. The day features a 2-hour parade, and follows with a concert, dancers, over 90 arts and crafts booths, firemens brigade and a whiskerino contest.

## Atascadero, California

Third Saturday in October
8:00 AM - 5:00 PM

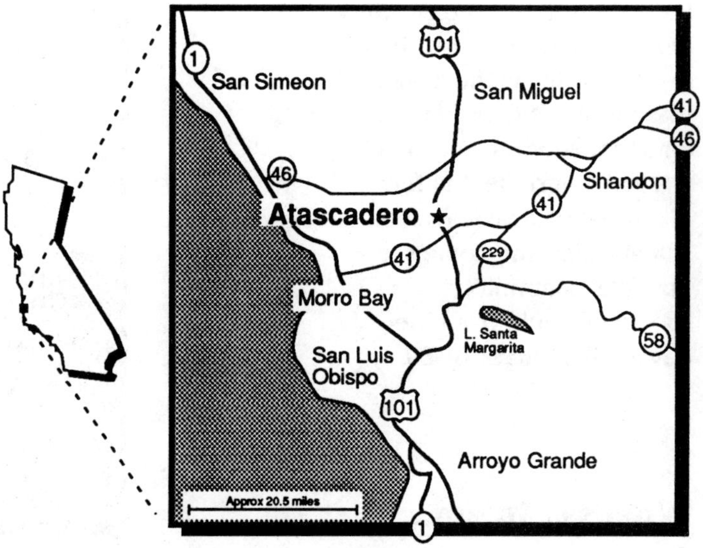


## What's goin' on...

Town population: **23,000**
Last year's attendance: **10,000**
Average outdoor temperature: **80°**
Festival location: **N/A**

*Up-to-date festival information is available from:*
*Atascadero Chamber of Commerce*
*(805) 466-2044*

| | |
|---|---|
| X | Wine tasting/beer for sale |
| X | Food booths |
| X | Arts/crafts for sale |
| X | Live music |
| X | Clowns |
| X | Face painters |
| X | Childrens games |
| | Animal exhibits/petting zoo |
| | Dogs allowed on leash |
| X | Lost and found |
| | Bicycle racks |
| X | First aid area available |
| X | Self-brought picnics allowed |
| | Self-brought alcohol allowed |
| | Stroller/wheelchair rentals available |

| | |
|---|---|
| X | Parade: 10:00 AM |
| | Parking fee |
| | Entrance fee |
| X | Camping facilities: 8 miles |
| X | Boating facilities: 8 miles |
| X | RV facilities w/ hookups: 10 miles |
| X | Accomodations in town<br>Best Western Colony Inn, Atascadero Inn, Rancho Tee |
| X | Restaurants in town<br>Martha's Steak House, China Star, Segreto's, LoLo's |

# *Pumpkin & Art Festival*

THE HALF MOON BAY **PUMPkin & Art Festival** is one of California's most popular events! The Festival grounds are sprinkled with more than 250 arts-and-crafts booths showcasing authentic handcrafted wares, 30 food-and-beverage booths, and an array of entertainment to delight you senses. Located on Main Street, the activities include live jazz and blue-grass music, puppet shows, mines, magicians, professional pumpkin carvers, and pumpkin-pie eating and pumpkin-carving contests.

## What's goin' on...

Town population: **7,282**
Last year's attendance: **350,000**
Average outdoor temperature: **70°**
Festival location: **Main Street**

## Half Moon Bay, California

Third weekend in October
Daily 10:00 AM - 5:00 PM

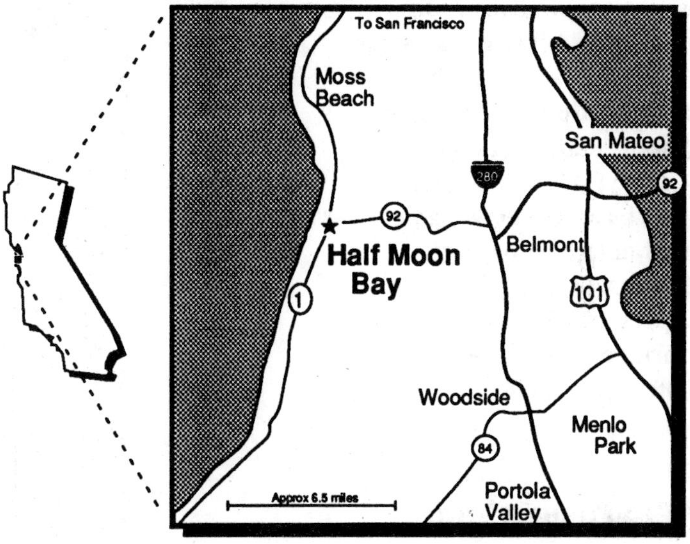


*Up-to-date festival information is available from:*
*Half Moon Bay Chamber of Commerce*
*(415) 726-5202*

| | |
|---|---|
| X | Wine tasting/beer for sale |
| X | Food booths |
| X | Arts/crafts for sale |
| X | Live music |
| X | Clowns |
| X | Face painters |
| X | Childrens games |
| X | Animal exhibits/petting zoo |
| X | Dogs allowed on leash |
| X | Lost and found |
| X | Bicycle racks |
| X | First aid area available |
| X | Self-brought picnics allowed |
| X | Self-brought alcohol allowed |
| X | Stroller/wheelchair rentals available |

| | |
|---|---|
| X | Parade: (date & time not avbl.) |
| | Parking fee |
| | Entrance fee |
| X | Camping facilities: 1 mile |
| X | Boating facilities: Half Moon Bay |
| X | RV facilities w/ hookups: 1 mile |
| X | Accomodations in town<br>Half Moon Bay Lode, Harbor View Inn, San Benito House |
| X | Restaurants in town<br>Dan's Place, The Abalone Shop, Moss Beach Distillery, The Miramar |

# *Springville Apple Festival*

EVERYTHING FROM APPLE butter to apple burritos... apple dolls...apple pies and cakes...candied apples... apple sauce...apple cider... Big Apple run...children's games! They're all found at the **Springville Apple Festival**—"Apple Capital of Tulare County!" More than 40 food booths and over 80 hand crafted arts and crafts booths. Cooking contests. Apple orchards with over 15 varieties to choose from. They have it all!

## Springville, California

Third weekend in October
Daily 10:00 AM - 4:00 PM

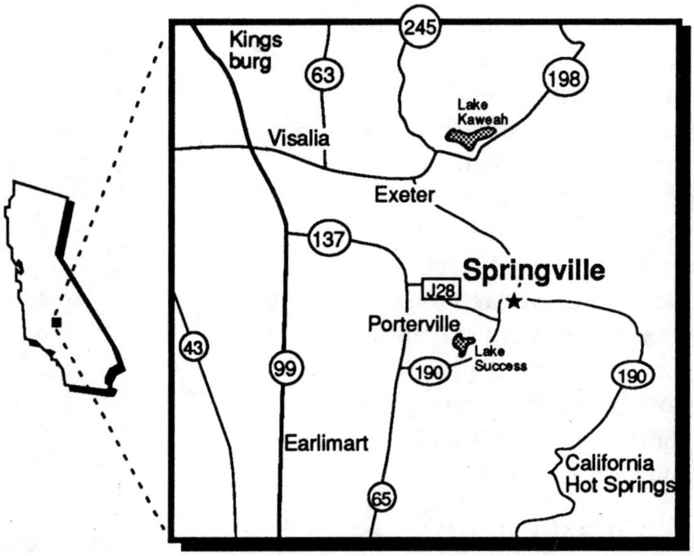


## What's goin' on...

Town population: **1,800**
Last year's attendance: **16,000**
Average outdoor temperature: **70°**
Festival location: **Main Street & Park**

*Up-to-date festival information is available from:*
*Springville Chamber of Commerce*
*(209) 539-2312*

| | |
|---|---|
| | Wine tasting/beer for sale |
| ✗ | Food booths |
| ✗ | Arts/crafts for sale |
| ✗ | Live music |
| ✗ | Clowns |
| ✗ | Face painters |
| ✗ | Childrens games |
| ✗ | Animal exhibits/petting zoo |
| ✗ | Dogs allowed on leash |
| | Lost and found |
| ✗ | Bicycle racks |
| | First aid area available |
| ✗ | Self-brought picnics allowed |
| | Self-brought alcohol allowed |
| | Stroller/wheelchair rentals available |

| | |
|---|---|
| | Parade |
| | Parking fee |
| | Entrance fee |
| ✗ | Camping facilities: 3 miles |
| ✗ | Boating facilities: Lake Success |
| ✗ | RV facilities w/ hookups: 3 miles |
| ✗ | Accomodations in town |
| ✗ | Restaurants in town |

# *Rocklin Harvest Craft Faire*

"OH BAKE ME A PUMPKIN Pie" is the theme of this years **Rocklin Harvest Craft Faire**. Scarecrows will be on hand to greet the entire family, the costume contest and carnival will delight the kids, and moms (and dads!) can enter the pumpkin pie and home-made bread baking contests. The Haunted Halloween House opens at 5:30 at the Finnish Temperance Hall.

## Rocklin, California

Saturday before Halloween
10:00 AM - 5:00 PM

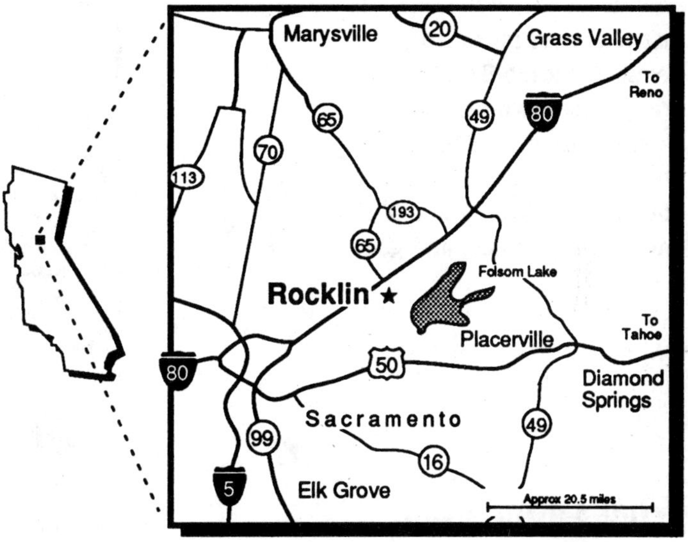


## What's goin' on...

Town population: **16,000**
Last year's attendance: **N/A**
Average outdoor temperature: **70°**
Festival location: **Community Center**

*Up-to-date festival information is available from:*
*Rocklin Chamber of Commerce*
*(916) 624-2548*

| | |
|---|---|
| | Wine tasting/beer for sale |
| X | Food booths |
| X | Arts/crafts for sale |
| X | Live music |
| | Clowns |
| X | Face painters |
| X | Childrens games |
| | Animal exhibits/petting zoo |
| | Dogs allowed on leash |
| | Lost and found |
| X | Bicycle racks |
| | First aid area available |
| X | Self-brought picnics allowed |
| | Self-brought alcohol allowed |
| | Stroller/wheelchair rentals available |

| | |
|---|---|
| | Parade |
| | Parking fee |
| | Entrance fee |
| X | Camping facilities: 7 miles |
| X | Boating facilities: Folsom Lake |
| X | RV facilities w/ hookups: 7 miles |
| X | Accomodations in town |
| X | Restaurants in town |

C
E
N
T
R
A
L

# *Octoberfest*

LOS OSOS FOLKS TELL US that their **Octoberfest** is "as old as the hills, and twice as dusty!" Heck, sign us up...that sounds like big fun! Located just ten short miles from beautiful Morro Bay, this crazy little town puts on quite a celebration: barbecued chicken and ribs, Mexican and Oriental food, rock 'n' roll and country music, and good times for all!

## Los Osos, California

Last Sunday in October
9:00 AM - 4:00 PM

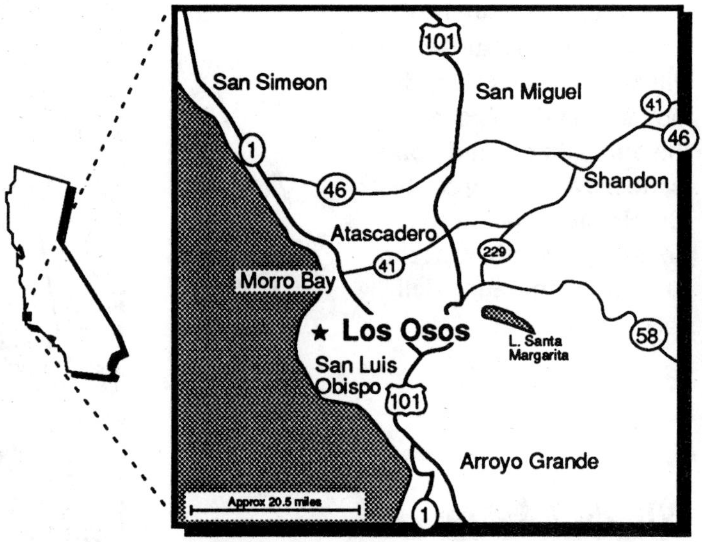


## What's goin' on...

Town population: **16,000**
Last year's attendance: **7,000**
Average outdoor temperature: **70°**
Festival location: **Baywood Park**

*Up-to-date festival information is available from:*
*Los Osos Chamber of Commerce*
*(805) 528-4884*

| | |
|---|---|
| ✗ | Wine tasting/beer for sale |
| ✗ | Food booths |
| ✗ | Arts/crafts for sale |
| ✗ | Live music |
| | Clowns |
| ✗ | Face painters |
| | Childrens games |
| ✗ | Animal exhibits/petting zoo |
| ✗ | Dogs allowed on leash |
| ✗ | Lost and found |
| | Bicycle racks |
| | First aid area available |
| ✗ | Self-brought picnics allowed |
| | Self-brought alcohol allowed |
| | Stroller/wheelchair rentals available |

| | |
|---|---|
| ✗ | Parade: (time & date not avbl.) |
| | Parking fee |
| | Entrance fee |
| ✗ | Camping facilities: 5 miles |
| ✗ | Boating facilities: 3 miles |
| ✗ | RV facilities w/ hookups: 5 miles |
| ✗ | Accomodations in town<br>Baywood B&B, Julia's B&B, Blue Heron Hotel |
| ✗ | Restaurants in town<br>Don Edwardo's, Sculptured Egg, Rodney's, Salty Pelican |

# Halloween Ghost Walk

FOR A REAL HOLLOWEEN adventure, gather up the kids, dress 'em up and go for a **Halloween Ghost Walk**! This is a scary night walk through downtown—complete with ghost stories, trick or treating, goblins, witches and ghosts!

## Clayton, California

Halloween eve
5:00 PM - 9:00 PM

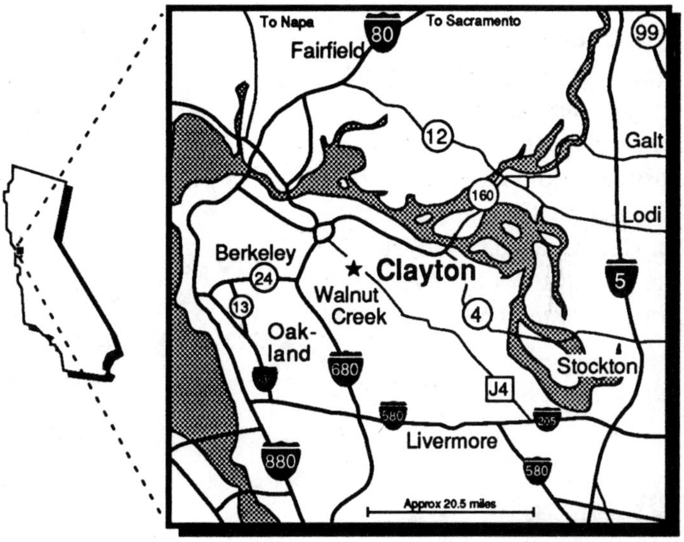


## What's goin' on...

Town population: **7,200**
Last year's attendance: **500**
Average outdoor temperature: **70°**
Festival location: **Downtown**

*Up-to-date festival information is available from:*
*Clayton Chamber of Commerce*
*(415) 672-3622*

| | |
|---|---|
| | Wine tasting/beer for sale |
| | Food booths |
| | Arts/crafts for sale |
| | Live music |
| | Clowns |
| | Face painters |
| | Childrens games |
| | Animal exhibits/petting zoo |
| ✗ | Dogs allowed on leash |
| | Lost and found |
| | Bicycle racks |
| | First aid area available |
| | Self-brought picnics allowed |
| | Self-brought alcohol allowed |
| | Stroller/wheelchair rentals available |

| | |
|---|---|
| | Parade |
| | Parking fee |
| | Entrance fee |
| ✗ | Camping facilities: 8 miles |
| ✗ | Boating facilities: The Delta |
| | RV facilities w/ hookups |
| | Accomodations in town |
| ✗ | Restaurants in town<br>Black Diamond, La Cocotte |

C
E
N
T
R
A
L

# *Galt Craft Faire*

THE WEATHER'S TURNED A little cooler and it's time to get busy whittling away on the ol' Christmas list! So why not head over to the **Galt Craft Faire** and have a peek at the handmade dolls, ceramics, art, hand-painted and tie-dyed clothing, wood carvings, quilts, and all kinds of other neat things just right for Christmas gifts! Oh, and the Galtians would never let you go home hungry... there's great eats, too!

## Galt, California

First Friday and Saturday in November
Fri. 6:00 PM - 9:00 PM; Sat. 10:00 AM - 6:00 PM

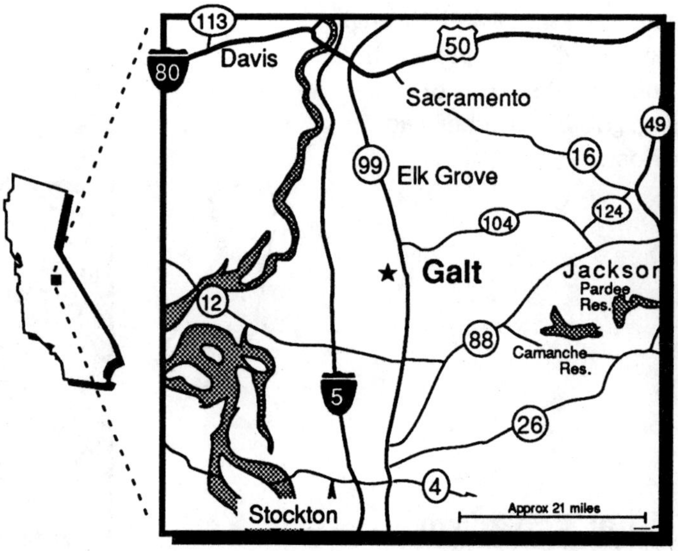


*Up-to-date festival information is available from:*
*Galt Chamber of Commerce*
*(209) 745-2529*

## What's goin' on...

Town population: **7,500**
Last year's attendance: **N/A**
Average outdoor temperature: **78°**
Festival location: **Civic Cener**

- [ ] Wine tasting/beer for sale
- [x] Food booths
- [x] Arts/crafts for sale
- [x] Live music
- [ ] Clowns
- [ ] Face painters
- [ ] Childrens games
- [ ] Animal exhibits/petting zoo
- [ ] Dogs allowed on leash
- [ ] Lost and found
- [ ] Bicycle racks
- [ ] First aid area available
- [ ] Self-brought picnics allowed
- [ ] Self-brought alcohol allowed
- [ ] Stroller/wheelchair rentals available

- [ ] Parade
- [ ] Parking fee
- [ ] Entrance fee
- [x] Camping facilities: 10 miles
- [x] Boating facilities: Delta
- [x] RV facilities w/ hookups: 10 miles
- [x] Accomodations in town
- [x] Restaurants in town
  Golden Acorn

# *Farmers Market Festival*

SAN RAFAEL HAS AN ABUNdance of marinas and recreational water-oriented sports, in addition to their annual **Farmers Market Festival** in November! This "burb" of "The City" offers more than just a "farmers market" atmosphere—there's lots of craft booths to shop and really great barbecued ribies, oysters, teriaki, and cheese-cake-on-a-stick dipped in chocolate (oh, *phule-e-e-e-ase!*). Yum! Yum!

## San Rafael, California

Every Thursday in November
6:00 PM - 9:00 PM

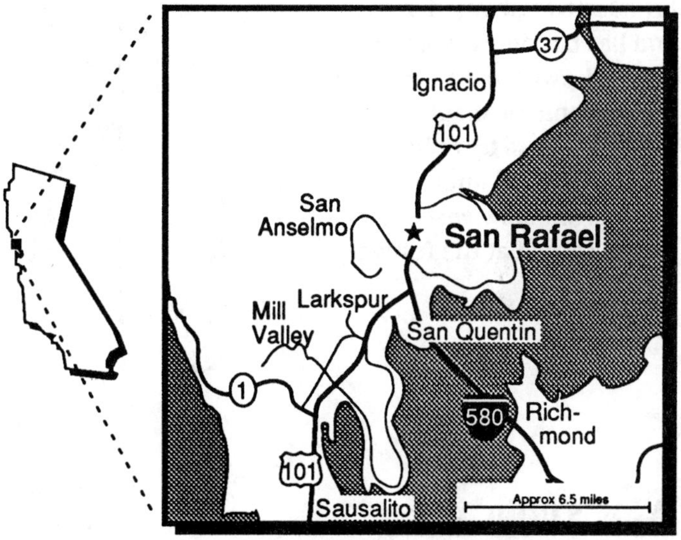


## What's goin' on...

Town population: **40,000**
Last year's attendance: **6,000**
Average outdoor temperature: **65°**
Festival location: **4th Street (downtown)**

*Up-to-date festival information is available from:*
*San Rafael Chamber of Commerce*
*(415) 454-4163*

| | |
|---|---|
| | Wine tasting/beer for sale |
| X | Food booths |
| X | Arts/crafts for sale |
| X | Live music |
| X | Clowns |
| X | Face painters |
| X | Childrens games |
| X | Animal exhibits/petting zoo |
| X | Dogs allowed on leash |
| X | Lost and found |
| X | Bicycle racks |
| X | First aid area available |
| X | Self-brought picnics allowed |
| | Self-brought alcohol allowed |
| | Stroller/wheelchair rentals available |

| | |
|---|---|
| | Parade |
| | Parking fee |
| | Entrance fee |
| X | Camping facilities: 10 miles |
| X | Boating facilities: San Francisco Bay |
| X | RV facilities w/ hookups: 10 miles |
| X | Accomodations in town<br>Panama Hotel, Embassy Suites |
| X | Restaurants in town<br>La Toscana, Carlo Restaurant |

C E N T R A L

# *20th Century Crafts Faire*

SOUTH OF MODESTO IS THE thriving metropolis of Hughson...home to the **20th Century Crafts Faire**! This little festival debuted in 1971, and has become a roaring success—with over 125 juried craftspeople on display! This California farm town harvests many fruits and nuts, so you can imaging how *terrific* the dishes served at the festival are!

## Hughson, California

Weekend before Thanksgiving
Daily 10:00 AM - 5:00 PM

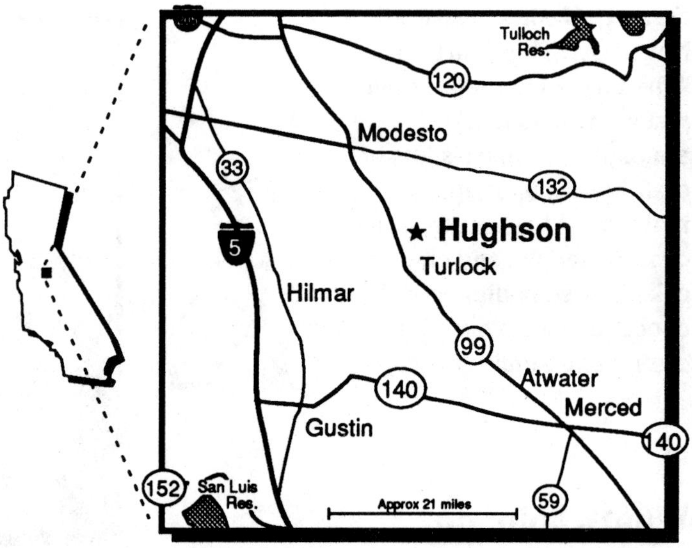


*Up-to-date festival information is available from:*
*Hughson 20th Century Club*
*(209) 883-0631*

## What's goin' on...

Town population: **3,500**
Last year's attendance: **13,500**
Average outdoor temperature: **65°**
Festival location: **High School**

| | |
|---|---|
| | Wine tasting/beer for sale |
| X | Food booths |
| X | Arts/crafts for sale |
| | Live music |
| | Clowns |
| X | Face painters |
| | Childrens games |
| | Animal exhibits/petting zoo |
| | Dogs allowed on leash |
| X | Lost and found |
| X | Bicycle racks |
| | First aid area available |
| X | Self-brought picnics allowed |
| | Self-brought alcohol allowed |
| | Stroller/wheelchair rentals available |

| | |
|---|---|
| | Parade |
| | Parking fee |
| | Entrance fee |
| X | Camping facilities: 15 miles |
| X | Boating facilities: 15 miles |
| X | RV facilities w/ hookups: 15 miles |
| | Accomodations in town |
| | Restaurants in town |

# *Beaujolais Nouveau Festival*

GET A SITTER AND COME down to one of the most beautiful resorts in Pebble Beach—the Inn at Spanish Bay! And if you can't spell "BEAUJOLAIS" you're probably to young to join us at the **Beaujolais Nouveau Festival!** This festival is in its infancy—it only began in 1989—but promises fabulous views, hors d'oeuvres, wine, classical music, and ambience! This is the one to take your guy or gal to...and leave the kiddies at home!

## Pebble Beach, California

Third Thursday in November
5:00 PM - 7:30 PM

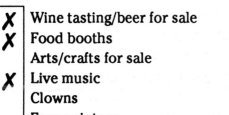

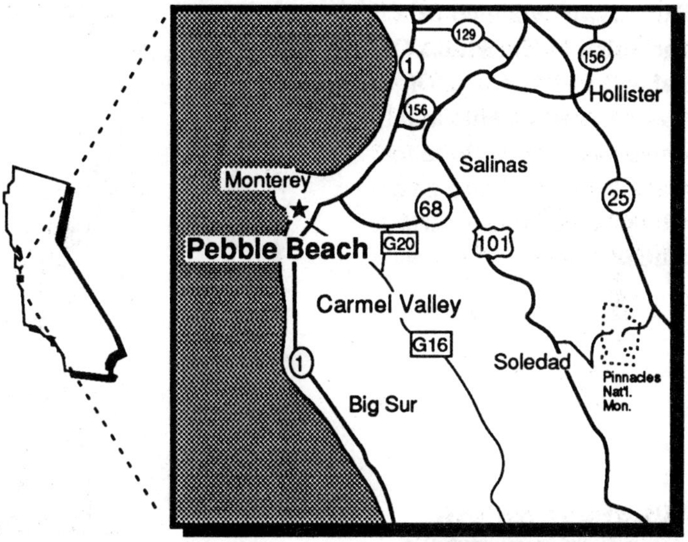


## What's goin' on...

Town population: **6,000**
Last year's attendance: **700**
Average outdoor temperature: **N/A-indoor**
Festival location: **The Inn at Spanish Bay**

*Up-to-date festival information is available from:*
*Pebble Beach Chamber of Commerce*
*(408) 649-2723*

| | |
|---|---|
| ✗ | Wine tasting/beer for sale |
| ✗ | Food booths |
| | Arts/crafts for sale |
| ✗ | Live music |
| | Clowns |
| | Face painters |
| | Childrens games |
| | Animal exhibits/petting zoo |
| | Dogs allowed on leash |
| ✗ | Lost and found |
| | Bicycle racks |
| | First aid area available |
| | Self-brought picnics allowed |
| | Self-brought alcohol allowed |
| | Stroller/wheelchair rentals available |

| | |
|---|---|
| | Parade |
| | Parking fee |
| ✗ | Entrance fee: $35 |
| ✗ | Camping facilities: 15 miles |
| ✗ | Boating facilities: Monterey Bay |
| ✗ | RV facilities w/ hookups: 15 miles |
| ✗ | Accomodations in town |
| ✗ | Restaurants in town |

CENTRAL

# *Spirit of Christmas Crafts Faire & Celebration*

BE ENTERTAINED BY THE likes of Maria Muldaur and David Auerbach, or the Hildigrini Puppets and Scorby The Clown, while you shop the **Spirit of Christmas Crafts Faire & Celebration.** Of course Frosty, Santa and the elves will also be there to greet you. The Faire has been a tradition in these parts since 1976!

## Santa Rosa, California

First two weekends in December

Friday noon - 9:00 PM; Sat. & Sun. 10:00 AM - 7:00 PM

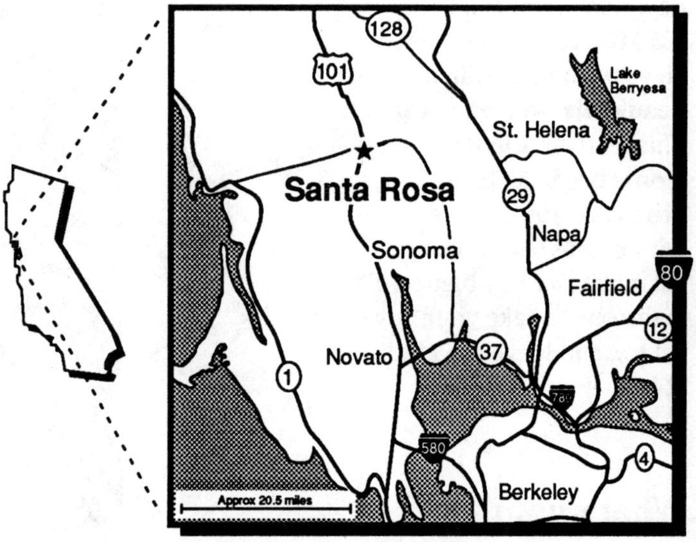


## What's goin' on...

Town population: **100,000**

Last year's attendance: **30,000**

Average outdoor temperature: **65°**

Festival location: **Fairgrounds**

*Up-to-date festival information is available from: Santa Rosa Wishing Well Productions (707) 575-9355*

| | |
|---|---|
| X | Wine tasting/beer for sale |
| X | Food booths |
| X | Arts/crafts for sale |
| X | Live music |
| X | Clowns |
| X | Face painters |
| X | Childrens games |
| | Animal exhibits/petting zoo |
| | Dogs allowed on leash |
| X | Lost and found |
| X | Bicycle racks |
| X | First aid area available |
| X | Self-brought picnics allowed |
| | Self-brought alcohol allowed |
| | Stroller/wheelchair rentals available |

| | |
|---|---|
| | Parade |
| X | Parking fee: $1 |
| X | Entrance fee: S $2; A $3; K $1 |
| X | Camping facilities: On-site |
| X | Boating facilities: Lake Sonoma |
| X | RV facilities w/ hookups: On-site |
| X | Accomodations in town<br>Red Lion, Doubletree, El Rancho |
| X | Restaurants in town<br>John Ash |

# *Christmas Open House*

TURN OUT WITH THE LOCAL yokels of Lemoore for the **Christmas Open House** celebration! Thanksgiving's over and it's time to delve into that Christmas list that's been taking a back seat to all of your other activities! There are booths filled with appetizing goodies to keep your motor going, and unique handmade items to spend your money on! Gee...what more could you ask for?

## Lemoore, California

Sunday following Thanksgiving Day
Noon - 4:00 PM

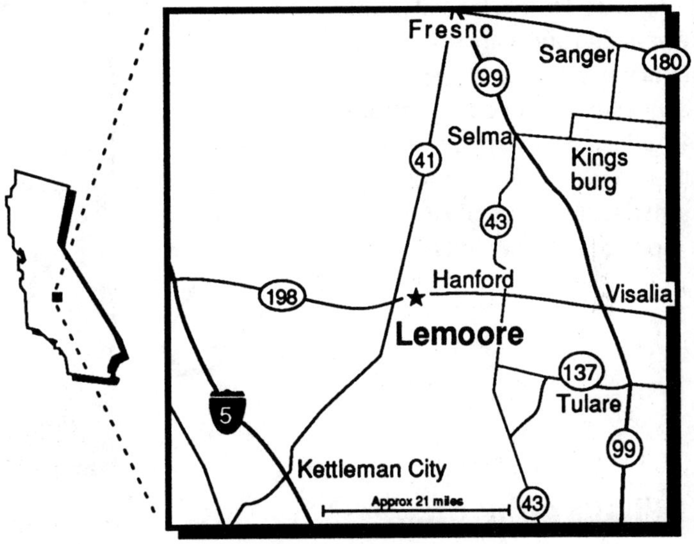


## What's goin' on...

Town population: **14,100**
Last year's attendance: **N/A**
Average outdoor temperature: **44°**
Festival location: **Downtown**

*Up-to-date festival information is available from:*
*Lemoore Chamber of Commerce*
*(209) 924-6401*

| | |
|---|---|
| X | Wine tasting/beer for sale |
| X | Food booths |
| X | Arts/crafts for sale |
| X | Live music |
| X | Clowns |
| X | Face painters |
| X | Childrens games |
| | Animal exhibits/petting zoo |
| X | Dogs allowed on leash |
| | Lost and found |
| | Bicycle racks |
| | First aid area available |
| | Self-brought picnics allowed |
| | Self-brought alcohol allowed |
| | Stroller/wheelchair rentals available |

| | |
|---|---|
| | Parade |
| | Parking fee |
| | Entrance fee |
| X | Camping facilities |
| X | Boating facilities |
| X | RV facilities w/ hookups |
| X | Accomodations in town<br>Vineyard Inn Motel |
| X | Restaurants in town<br>The Cotton Mill, The Granary, Vineyard Inn, Casa Ortega, Vejar's |

# *Heritage Homes Christmas Parlour Tour*

SIX TURN-OF-THE-CENTURY Victorian homes will be open for the seventh annual **Heritage Homes Christmas Parlour Tour.** The self-guided walking tour features six parlours, profusely arrayed with holiday decor. Costumed guides greet visitors with information on the architecture and history of each home. Dress warmly!

## Petaluma, California

First or second Sunday in December (call Chamber)
6:00 PM - 9:00 PM

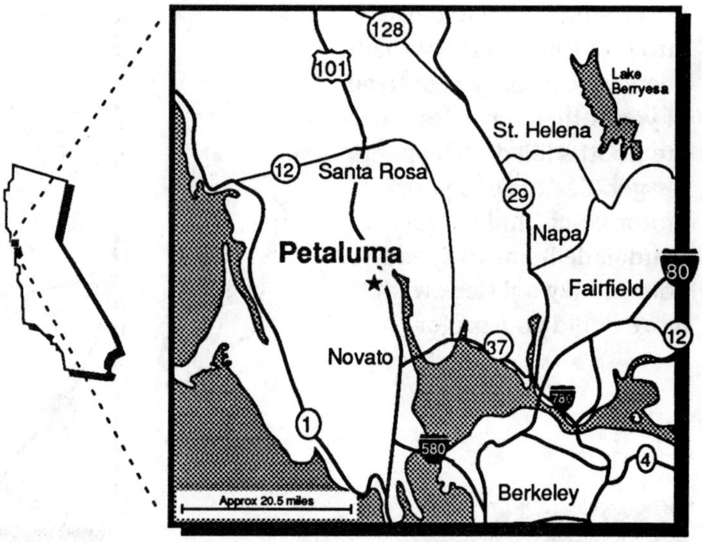


## What's goin' on...

Town population: **42,000**
Last year's attendance: **3,000**
Average outdoor temperature: **60°**
Festival location: **Six private Victorians**

*Up-to-date festival information is available from:*
*Petaluma Chamber of Commerce*
*(707) 762-2785*

- [ ] Wine tasting/beer for sale
- [x] Food booths
- [ ] Arts/crafts for sale
- [x] Live music
- [ ] Clowns
- [ ] Face painters
- [ ] Childrens games
- [ ] Animal exhibits/petting zoo
- [ ] Dogs allowed on leash
- [ ] Lost and found
- [ ] Bicycle racks
- [ ] First aid area available
- [ ] Self-brought picnics allowed
- [ ] Self-brought alcohol allowed
- [ ] Stroller/wheelchair rentals available

- [ ] Parade
- [ ] Parking fee
- [x] Entrance fee: $7
- [x] Camping facilities: 5 miles
- [x] Boating facilities: River, lake, and bay
- [x] RV facilities w/ hookups: 5 miles
- [x] Accomodations in town
  Best Western, Quality Inn, Motel 6, Cavanagh Cottage B&B, 7th St. Inn B&B
- [x] Restaurants in town
  Petrucci's, Tempura House, Steamer Gold, Cattlemen's, Fino's, Original Marvin's

# Country Christmas Holiday

DEDICATED TO CHILDREN OF all ages, the **Country Christmas Holiday** promises big fun! You'll discover strolling musicians, choirs, Santa's workshop, gaily decorated shops and streets, wine tasting, holiday snacks, ciders, and other festive potables! The tall Christmas tree, erected and decorated by the (hunka- hunka) firefighters, is lit at 7:00 PM to usher in the holiday season!

## Diamond Springs, California

First Saturday in December
Noon - 9:00 PM

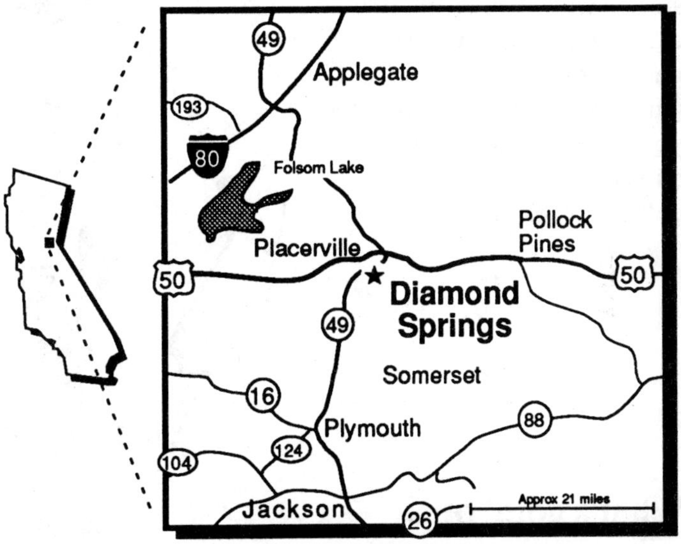


*Up-to-date festival information is available from:*
*Diamond Springs Community Assn.*
*(916) 621-1766*

## What's goin' on...

Town population: **2,000**
Last year's attendance: **500**
Average outdoor temperature: **60°**
Festival location: **Main St./Downtown**

| | |
|---|---|
| X | Wine tasting/beer for sale |
| X | Food booths |
| X | Arts/crafts for sale |
| X | Live music |
| X | Clowns |
| | Face painters |
| X | Childrens games |
| | Animal exhibits/petting zoo |
| X | Dogs allowed on leash |
| | Lost and found |
| | Bicycle racks |
| X | First aid area available |
| X | Self-brought picnics allowed |
| | Self-brought alcohol allowed |
| | Stroller/wheelchair rentals available |

| | |
|---|---|
| | Parade |
| X | Parking fee: (prices not avbl.) |
| X | Entrance fee: (prices not avbl.) |
| X | Camping facilities: 5 miles |
| X | Boating facilities: Lake |
| X | RV facilities w/ hookups: 10 miles |
| X | Accomodations in town<br>Placerville Inn |
| X | Restaurants in town<br>Diamond Motel, The Diggins, The Vineyard House |

CENTRAL

# *Christmas Wine Trails*

INSTEAD OF "HAPPY TRAILS to you," how 'bout **Christmas Wine Trails** to you? Carollers will ring in your holiday season while you spend time inspecting the art, Christmas decorations, crafts, wine, and gift baskets for sale (shop till you drop!). Hors d'oeuvres and other goodies are available for snacking.

## Livermore, California

First weekend in December
Daily 11:00 AM - 4:00 PM

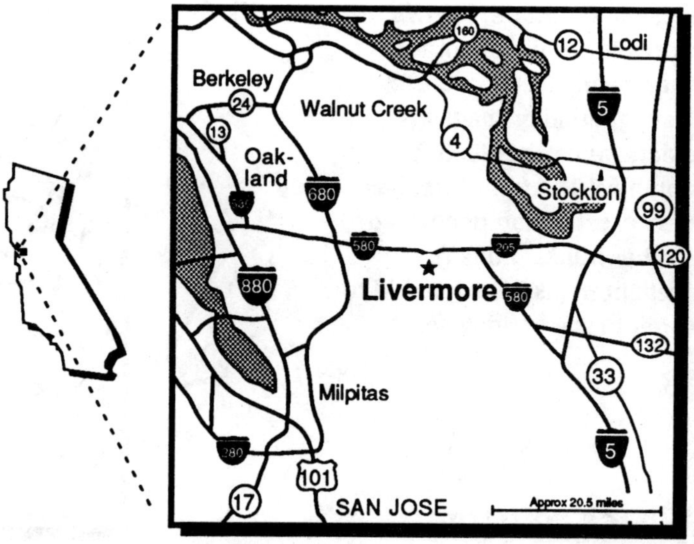


## What's goin' on...

Town population: **56,445**
Last year's attendance: **3,000**
Average outdoor temperature: **50°**
Festival location: **Wente Brothers Winery**

*Up-to-date festival information is available from:*
*Livermore Chamber of Commerce*
*(415) 447-1606*

| | |
|---|---|
| X | Wine tasting/beer for sale |
| X | Food booths |
| X | Arts/crafts for sale |
| X | Live music |
| | Clowns |
| | Face painters |
| | Childrens games |
| | Animal exhibits/petting zoo |
| | Dogs allowed on leash |
| | Lost and found |
| X | Bicycle racks |
| | First aid area available |
| X | Self-brought picnics allowed |
| | Self-brought alcohol allowed |
| | Stroller/wheelchair rentals available |

| | |
|---|---|
| | Parade |
| | Parking fee |
| | Entrance fee |
| X | Camping facilities: 11 miles |
| X | Boating facilities: Del Valle Res. |
| X | RV facilities w/ hookups: 11 miles |
| X | Accomodations in town<br>Townhouse Motel, Residence Inn, Holiday Inn |
| X | Restaurants in town<br>El Lorito, Le Coquelicot, Cruiser's, Beeb's Bar & Grill, Wente Sparkling Cellars Restaurant |

# *Children's Christmas & Holiday Parade*

A FULL TWO HOUR PARADE is the highlight of the **Children's Christmas & Holiday Parade** in Los Gatos. A tradition in this charming town since 1956, it's a scream to see these adorable little ones dressed in their costumes, walking so proudly—and carefully, to stay in step! While in town take a drive through the hills to see the magnificently decorated homes in this area...many are breathtaking!

## Los Gatos, California

First Saturday in December
11:00 AM - 4:00 PM

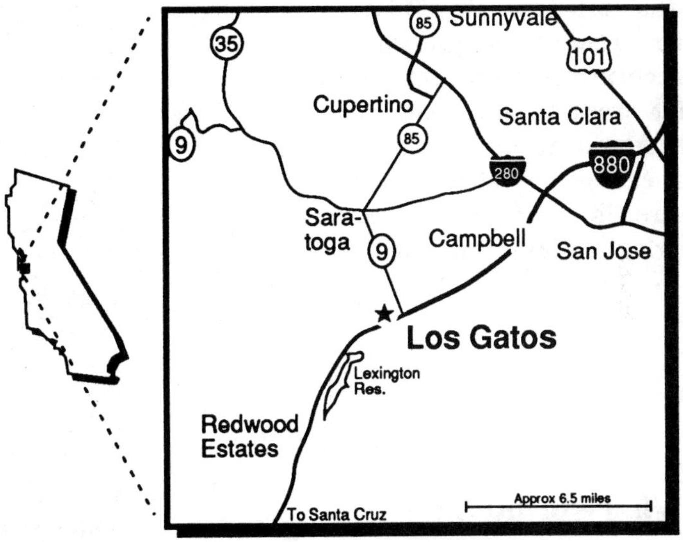


*Up-to-date festival information is available from:*
*Los Gatos Chamber of Commerce*
*(408) 354-9300*

## What's goin' on...

Town population: **28,500**
Last year's attendance: **50,000**
Average outdoor temperature: **50°**
Festival location: **Downtown**

- Wine tasting/beer for sale
- ✗ Food booths
- ✗ Arts/crafts for sale
- ✗ Live music
- ✗ Clowns
- Face painters
- ✗ Childrens games
- Animal exhibits/petting zoo
- Dogs allowed on leash
- Lost and found
- Bicycle racks
- First aid area available
- ✗ Self-brought picnics allowed
- Self-brought alcohol allowed
- Stroller/wheelchair rentals available

- ✗ Parade: 11:00 AM on N. Santa Cruz Ave.
- Parking fee
- Entrance fee
- ✗ Camping facilities: 20 miles
- ✗ Boating facilities
- ✗ RV facilities w/ hookups: 3 miles
- ✗ Accomodations in town
  Toll House, Los Gatos Lodge, La Hacienda Inn, Lodge at Villa Felice, Los Gatos Garden Inn
- ✗ Restaurants in town
  The Chart House, C.B. Hannegan's, Fiorillo's, Mabel's Lantern House, Pedro's, The Diner

# *Ravenswood Victorian Christmas Faire*

THE ELEGANT AND UNIQUE Ravenswood Historical Landmark mansion is the site for the **Ravenswood Victorian Christmas Faire**. This young faire of four years has become a Christmas tradition for Livermore folks. Only handmade crafts, art, and sweets are available. Music by carolers, a harpist and a string quartet is featured.

## Livermore, California

Second weekend in December

Sat. 10:00 AM - 7:00 PM; Sun. 10:00 AM - 4:00 PM

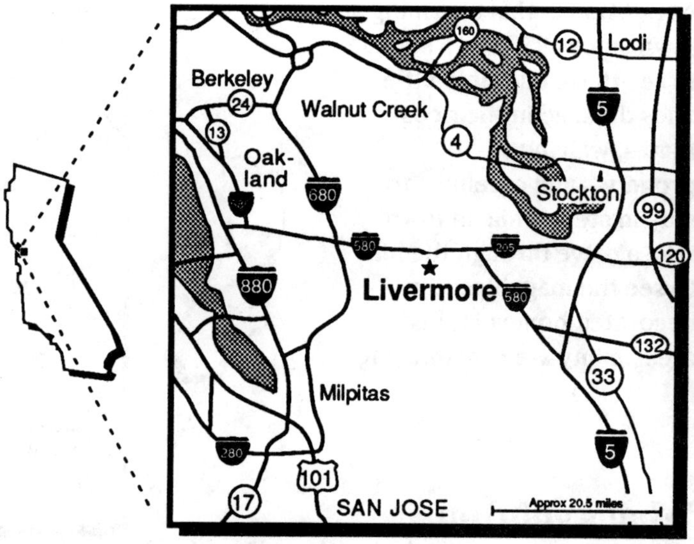


## What's goin' on...

Town population: **56,445**

Last year's attendance: **4,000**

Average outdoor temperature: **80°**

Festival location: **Ravenswood Landmark**

*Up-to-date festival information is available from:*
*Livermore Chamber of Commerce*
*(415) 447-1606*

| | |
|---|---|
| | Wine tasting/beer for sale |
| ✗ | Food booths |
| ✗ | Arts/crafts for sale |
| ✗ | Live music |
| | Clowns |
| | Face painters |
| | Childrens games |
| | Animal exhibits/petting zoo |
| | Dogs allowed on leash |
| ✗ | Lost and found |
| ✗ | Bicycle racks |
| ✗ | First aid area available |
| ✗ | Self-brought picnics allowed |
| | Self-brought alcohol allowed |
| | Stroller/wheelchair rentals available |

| | |
|---|---|
| | Parade |
| | Parking fee |
| | Entrance fee |
| ✗ | Camping facilities, 11 miles |
| ✗ | Boating facilities: Del Valle Res. |
| ✗ | RV facilities w/ hookups: 11 miles |
| ✗ | Accomodations in town<br>Townhouse Motel, Residence Inn, Holiday Inn |
| ✗ | Restaurants in town<br>El Lorito, Le Coquelicot, Cruiser's, Beeb's Bar & Grill, Wente Sparkling Cellars Restaurant |

# *Candyland*

THIS FESTIVAL IS A DREAM come true for children under 10! **Candyland** is a giant replica of the Candyland board game. Upon admittance, children enter Candyland by following the colored trail the number of spaces prescribed by the giant dice. By landing upon a particular space, a child may be entitled to play a carnival game or receive a candy or treat. Santa Claus is at the back door, too!

## Rocklin, California

Second Saturday in December
1:00 PM - 4:00 PM

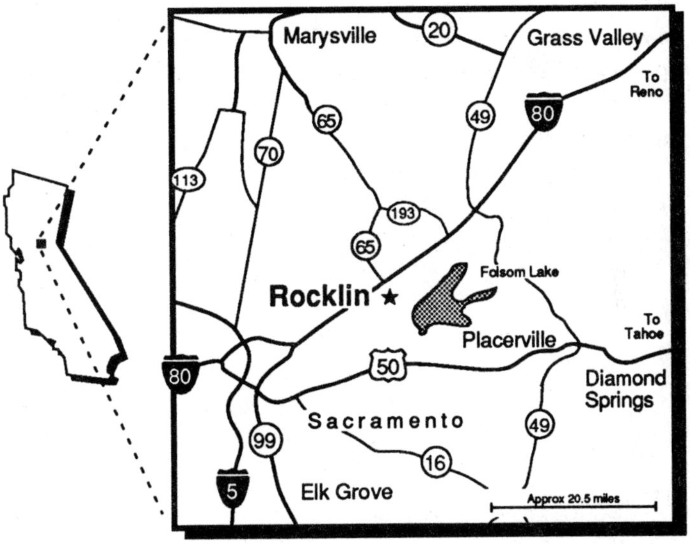


*Up-to-date festival information is available from:*
*Rocklin Chamber of Commerce*
*(916) 624-3391*

## What's goin' on...

Town population: **7,400**
Last year's attendance: **N/A**
Average outdoor temperature: **70°**
Festival location: **Community Center**

| | |
|---|---|
| | Wine tasting/beer for sale |
| X | Food booths |
| | Arts/crafts for sale |
| | Live music |
| | Clowns |
| | Face painters |
| X | Childrens games |
| | Animal exhibits/petting zoo |
| | Dogs allowed on leash |
| | Lost and found |
| | Bicycle racks |
| | First aid area available |
| | Self-brought picnics allowed |
| | Self-brought alcohol allowed |
| | Stroller/wheelchair rentals available |

| | |
|---|---|
| | Parade |
| | Parking fee |
| | Entrance fee |
| X | Camping facilities: 7 miles |
| X | Boating facilities: Folsom Lake |
| X | RV facilities w/ hookups: 7 miles |
| X | Accomodations in town |
| X | Restaurants in town |

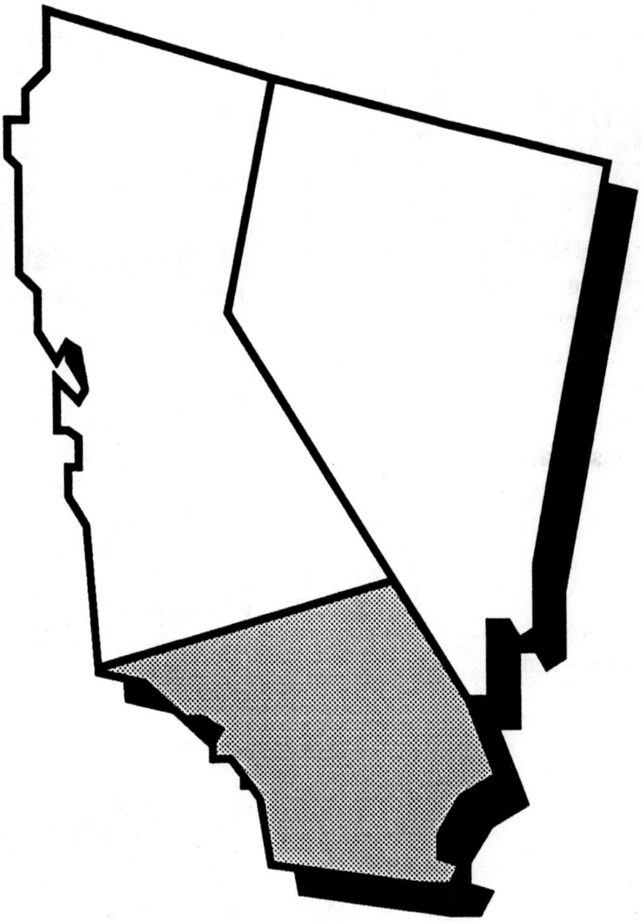

# Southern California

# *Carrot Festival*

THOSE SILLY WABBITS WILL be out in full force for the 44th annual **Carrot Festival** in Holtville! This is a perfect way to enjoy the sunshine of the desert in the middle of the winter. A children's carnival, a carrot-recipe cooking contest, a tractor pull, a 4-H and FFA livestock show, arts and crafts, a fine-arts show, and a parade are all in store for you at this nine-day long event.

## Holtville, California

Nine days—beginning third Saturday in January
Hours vary

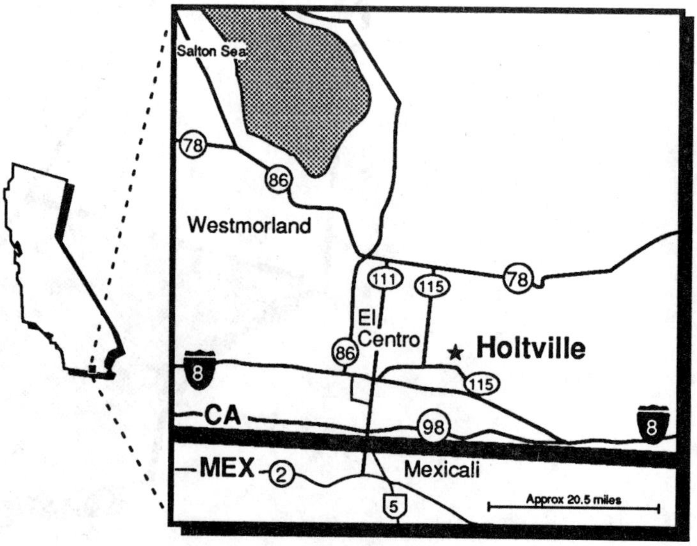


*Up-to-date festival information is available from:*
*Holtville Chamber of Commerce*
*(619) 356-2923*

## What's goin' on...

Town population: **5,108**
Last year's attendance: **N/A**
Average outdoor temperature: **76°**
Festival location: **Holt Park**

| | |
|---|---|
| | Wine tasting/beer for sale |
| X | Food booths |
| X | Arts/crafts for sale |
| X | Live music |
| | Clowns |
| | Face painters |
| X | Childrens games |
| X | Animal exhibits/petting zoo |
| X | Dogs allowed on leash |
| | Lost and found |
| | Bicycle racks |
| X | First aid area available |
| X | Self-brought picnics allowed |
| | Self-brought alcohol allowed |
| | Stroller/wheelchair rentals available |

| | |
|---|---|
| X | Parade: First Sat. 10:00 AM downtown |
| | Parking fee |
| | Entrance fee |
| X | Camping facilities: 7 miles |
| | Boating facilities |
| X | RV facilities w/ hookups: 7 miles |
| X | Accomodations in town<br>Barbara Worth Country Club Hotel, Park Manor Motel |
| X | Restaurants in town<br>Barbara Worth Country Club, J & M Cafe, China Buffalo, Elvira's Fine Food |

# *Southwest Art Festival*

DON'T LET THE DATE SCARE you...remember...this is *California*! The colorful desert flowers are spectacular in the deserts winter climate. You'll have time to take a drive through this area on your way to the **Southwest Art Festival**. This is a wonderful showcase of unique wood carvings, clay work, weavings, watercolors, oils, and traditional south-western art.

## Indio, California

**Third weekend in January**
**Daily 9:00 AM - dusk**

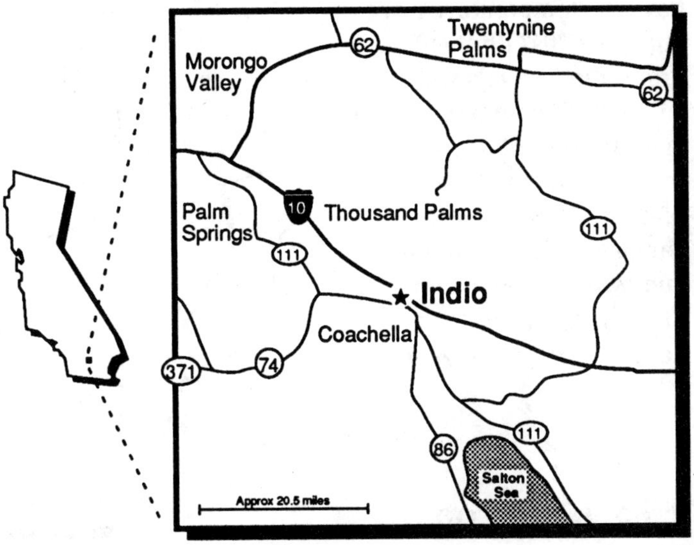


## What's goin' on...

Town population: **36,000**
Last year's attendance: **3,000**
Average outdoor temperature: **70°**
Festival location: **Fairgrounds**

*Up-to-date festival information is available from:*
*Indio Chamber of Commerce*
*(619) 347-0676*

| | |
|---|---|
| | Wine tasting/beer for sale |
| X | Food booths |
| X | Arts/crafts for sale |
| X | Live music |
| | Clowns |
| | Face painters |
| | Childrens games |
| | Animal exhibits/petting zoo |
| | Dogs allowed on leash |
| X | Lost and found |
| | Bicycle racks |
| | First aid area available |
| | Self-brought picnics allowed |
| | Self-brought alcohol allowed |
| | Stroller/wheelchair rentals available |

| | |
|---|---|
| | Parade |
| | Parking fee |
| X | Entrance fee: (prices not avbl.) |
| X | Camping facilities: 10 miles |
| X | Boating facilities: Lake Chauilla |
| X | RV facilities w/ hookups: In town |
| X | Accomodations in town<br>Comfort Inn, Scottish Inn, TraveLodge, Royal Plaza Inn, Super 8 Motel |
| X | Restaurants in town<br>Out to Lunch, Palm Royale, Carrillo's, Cactus Jack's, Elmer's of Indio, La Piñata |

SOUTHERN

# *Colorado River Country Music Festival*

WHERE BUT IN CALIFORNIA can you go to the annual **Colorado River Country Music Festival** in January and have the temperature hovering in the 70s? Blythe! The first three festivals were such a hit that Wayne Barrett and gang are rounding up new entertainment for the third one! The fairgrounds have camping facilities, and the auditorium is open most nights for jam sessions. Three days of pure country fun!

## Blythe, California

Fourth weekend in January (begins Fri.)
Daily 8:45 AM - 5:30 PM

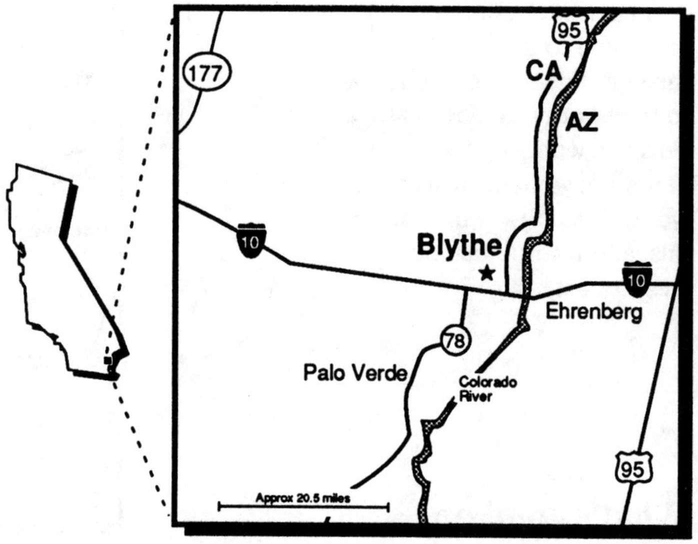


*Up-to-date festival information is available from:*
*Blythe Chamber of Commerce*
*(619) 922-8166*

## What's goin' on...

Town population: **8,300**
Last year's attendance: **4,000**
Average outdoor temperature: **70°**
Festival location: **Fairgrounds**

| | |
|---|---|
| X | Wine tasting/beer for sale |
| X | Food booths |
| X | Arts/crafts for sale |
| X | Live music |
| X | Clowns |
| X | Face painters |
| X | Childrens games |
| X | Animal exhibits/petting zoo |
| X | Dogs allowed on leash |
| X | Lost and found |
| | Bicycle racks |
| X | First aid area available |
| X | Self-brought picnics allowed |
| X | Self-brought alcohol allowed |
| | Stroller/wheelchair rentals available |

| | |
|---|---|
| | Parade |
| | Parking fee |
| X | Entrance fee: (prices not avbl.) |
| X | Camping facilities: On site |
| X | Boating facilities: Colorado River |
| X | RV facilities w/ hookups: 3 miles |
| X | Accomodations in town |
| X | Restaurants in town<br>Mac's Steakhouse, Silly Al's Pizza, Jimmy'z Grill |

# *Carrot Festival*

IF IT'S YOUR SIGHT THAT'S going, you'd better mosey on down to the **Carrot Festival** in Bakersfield for a hearty dose of Vitamin A! Bakersfield really rolls out the orange carpet for this community get together ...and the carrot cake is to die for! Enjoy learning about how this bountiful crop is raised and harvested while you listen to a few home-grown country sounds.

## Bakersfield, California

Last weekend in January through the first weekend in February

Hours vary

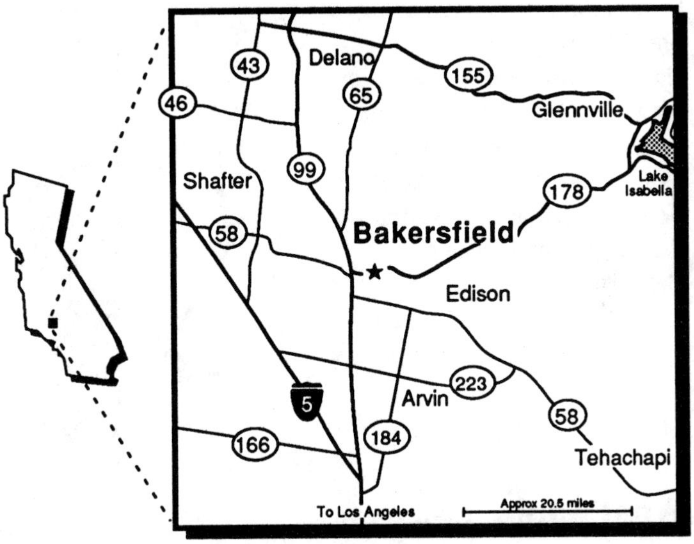


## What's goin' on...

Town population: **222,000**
Last year's attendance: **N/A**
Average outdoor temperature: **75°**
Festival location: **F & 30th Streets**

*Up-to-date festival information is available from:*
*Bakersfield Chamber of Commerce*
*(805) 327-4421*

- [ ] Wine tasting/beer for sale
- X Food booths
- X Arts/crafts for sale
- X Live music
- X Clowns
- [ ] Face painters
- X Childrens games
- X Animal exhibits/petting zoo
- X Dogs allowed on leash
- [ ] Lost and found
- [ ] Bicycle racks
- [ ] First aid area available
- [ ] Self-brought picnics allowed
- [ ] Self-brought alcohol allowed
- [ ] Stroller/wheelchair rentals available

- [ ] Parade
- [ ] Parking fee
- [ ] Entrance fee
- X Camping facilities: 10 miles
- X Boating facilities: Lake Buena Vista
- X RV facilities w/ hookups: 10 miles
- X Accomodations in town
  Red Lion Hotel, Bakersfield Inn
- X Restaurants in town
  Maitia's Basque, Maison Jaussard, Reuben's, The Garden Spot, J.C. Scotts

SOUTHERN

# *International Festival*

LOCATED JUST TWENTY miles from Lopez Lake, Santa Maria celebrates its universal culture with the **International Festival** in February. Taking place at the Veteran's Memorial Cultural Center, Santa Maria's celebration features crafts and edibles from all over the world. Point Sal State Beach is just another attraction in this lush area of California.

## Santa Maria, California

First Saturday in February
10:00 AM - 4:00 PM

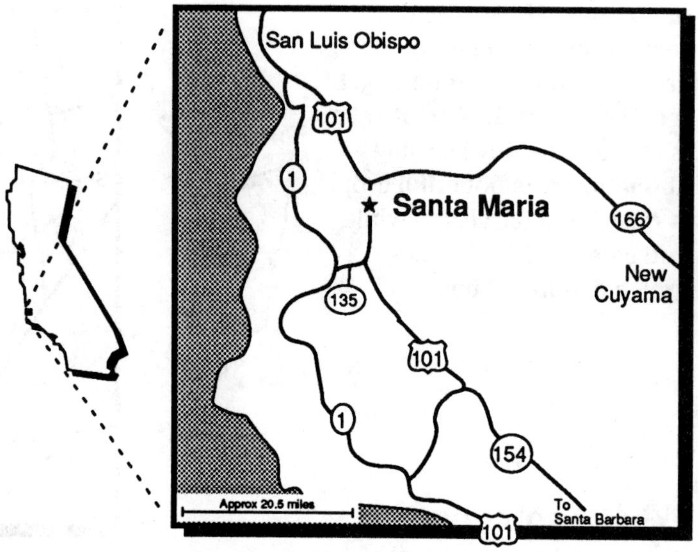


*Up-to-date festival information is available from:*
*Santa Maria Visitor Center*
*(805) 925-2403*

## What's goin' on...

Town population: **47,635**
Last year's attendance: **2,000**
Average outdoor temperature: **69°**
Festival location: **Veteran's Center**

| | |
|---|---|
| | Wine tasting/beer for sale |
| X | Food booths |
| X | Arts/crafts for sale |
| X | Live music |
| X | Clowns |
| X | Face painters |
| X | Childrens games |
| X | Animal exhibits/petting zoo |
| X | Dogs allowed on leash |
| X | Lost and found |
| X | Bicycle racks |
| | First aid area available |
| X | Self-brought picnics allowed |
| X | Self-brought alcohol allowed |
| | Stroller/wheelchair rentals available |

| | |
|---|---|
| | Parade |
| | Parking fee |
| | Entrance fee |
| X | Camping facilities: 1 mile |
| X | Boating facilities: Lopez Lake |
| X | RV facilities w/ hookups: 1 mile |
| X | Accomodations in town<br>Hunters Inn, The Big America, Raffles |
| X | Restaurants in town<br>Landmark, Jocko's, Hitching Post |

# *A Taste of Huntington Beach*

HOW 'BOUT A LITTLE ROAST duck smothered in raspberry dressing? At **A Taste of Huntington Beach** you'll get that plus a whole lot more from the local restauranteers. The festival of feasts is a favorite of locals. Check out Dana Point for the migration of over 12,000 California gray whales at the Spirit of the Whales celebration.

## Huntington Beach, California

Valentine's Day
(call Chamber)

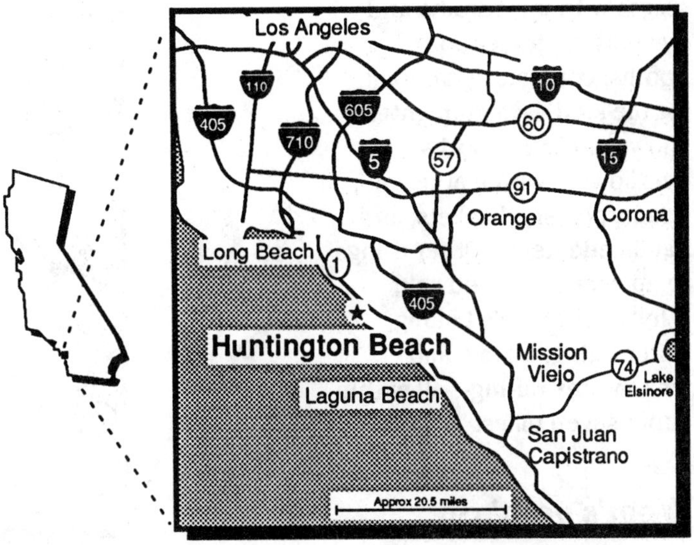


## What's goin' on...

Town population: **185,000**
Last year's attendance: **N/A**
Average outdoor temperature: **68°**
Festival location: **Central Park**

*Up-to-date festival information is available from:*
*Huntington Beach Chamber of Commerce*
*(714) 536-8888*

- X Wine tasting/beer for sale
- X Food booths
- Arts/crafts for sale
- X Live music
- X Clowns
- Face painters
- Childrens games
- Animal exhibits/petting zoo
- Dogs allowed on leash
- Lost and found
- Bicycle racks
- First aid area available
- Self-brought picnics allowed
- Self-brought alcohol allowed
- Stroller/wheelchair rentals available

- Parade
- Parking fee
- Entrance fee
- X Camping facilities: 1 mile
- X Boating facilities: Ocean
- X RV facilities w/ hookups: 1 mile
- X Accomodations in town
  House Guest U.S.A, Hilton, Best Western, Ocean View, Huntington Shores Motel
- X Restaurants in town
  Maxwell's, Charley Brown's, J.C. McLins, Bukhara, Tijuana Willies, Tibbies, Pero's

# *Whiskey Flat Days*

COME ON DOWN AND KICK up yer heels at the street dance at the Kernville **Whiskey Flat Days**! You'll find stages with melodrama and live music; ethnic-food booths; contests; a carnival for the kiddies; a gunfighters' show; and craft booths overflowing with leather goods, pottery, baskets, and handmade items. Other things to do near town, you ask? Why sure! There's fishing, water skiing, hiking, and white-water rafting—all within about seven miles.

## Kernville, California

President's Day weekend (beginning Friday)
Daily 10:00 AM - 7:00 PM

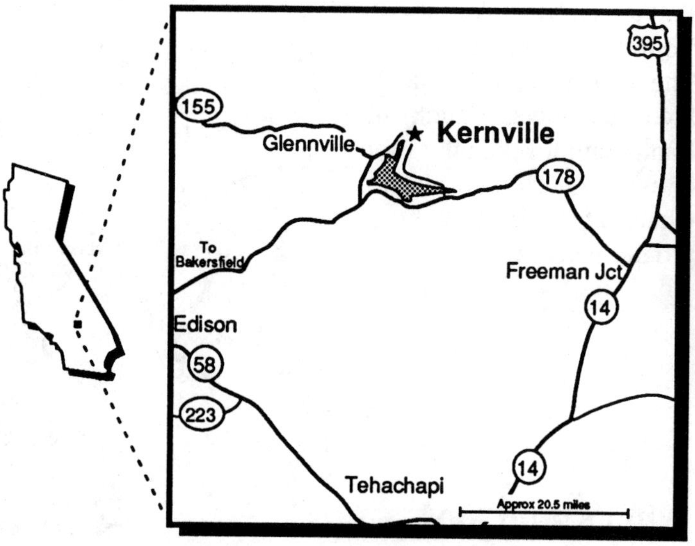


☞ *Up-to-date festival information is available from:*
*Kernville Chamber of Commerce*
*(619) 376-2629*

## What's goin' on...

Town population: **2,500**
Last year's attendance: **20,000**
Average outdoor temperature: **70°**
Festival location: **Citywide**

| | |
|---|---|
| X | Wine tasting/beer for sale |
| X | Food booths |
| X | Arts/crafts for sale |
| X | Live music |
| | Clowns |
| X | Face painters |
| X | Childrens games |
| | Animal exhibits/petting zoo |
| X | Dogs allowed on leash |
| | Lost and found |
| | Bicycle racks |
| X | First aid area available |
| X | Self-brought picnics allowed |
| X | Self-brought alcohol allowed |
| | Stroller/wheelchair rentals available |

| | |
|---|---|
| X | Parade: Sat. 11:00 AM downtown |
| | Parking fee |
| X | Entrance fee: Some, not all, events |
| X | Camping facilities: [illegible] miles |
| X | Boating facilities: Kern River |
| X | RV facilities w/ hookups: In town |
| X | Accomodations in town<br>Lazy River Lodge, Kern Lodge Motel, Hi-Ho Resort Motel, Whispering Pines |
| X | Restaurants in town<br>Cheryl's, Cowboys, McNallys, Roads End, El Sombrero |

# *Date Festival*

NEED A DATE? THEN SHOOT on down to Indio for the National **Date Festival**...and just when you thought it'd be another boring weekend in front of the boob-tube! What a country! Dates in Indio! The talented cooks in the area have conjured up some really tasty recipes— come try 'em out! You'll also find handcrafted items for sale, and some local merchants will have booths as well. So, come to Indio for a *real* date!

## Indio, California

President's Weekend through following weekend in February
Hours vary

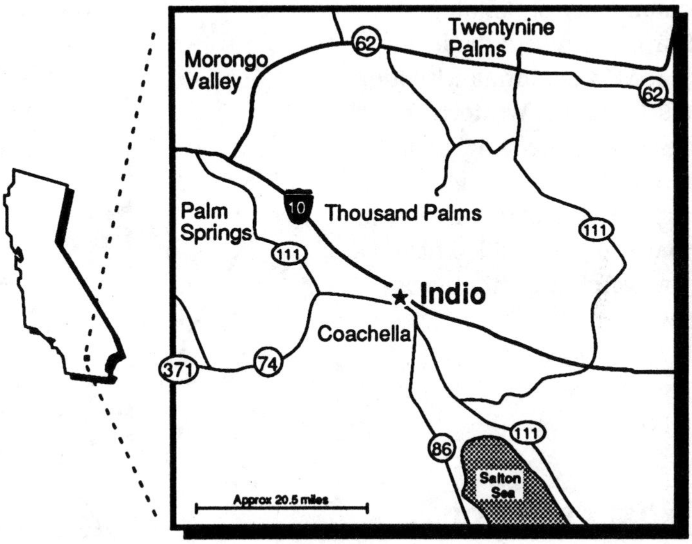


## What's goin' on...

Town population: **36,000**
Last year's attendance: **N/A**
Average outdoor temperature: **73°**
Festival location: **Citywide**

*Up-to-date festival information is available from:*
*Indio Chamber of Commerce*
*(619) 347-0676*

- ✗ Wine tasting/beer for sale
- ✗ Food booths
- ✗ Arts/crafts for sale
- ✗ Live music
- ✗ Clowns
- ✗ Face painters
- ✗ Childrens games
- ✗ Animal exhibits/petting zoo
- Dogs allowed on leash
- ✗ Lost and found
- ✗ Bicycle racks
- ✗ First aid area available
- ✗ Self-brought picnics allowed
- Self-brought alcohol allowed
- ✗ Stroller/wheelchair rentals available

- ✗ Parade: Mon. 10:00 AM downtown
- ✗ Parking fee: $2
- ✗ Entrance fee: S $3.50; A $4; K $2
- ✗ Camping facilities: 10 miles
- ✗ Boating facilities: Lake Chauilla
- ✗ RV facilities w/ hookups: In town
- ✗ Accomodations in town
  Comfort Inn, Scottish Inn, TraveLodge, Royal Plaza Inn, Super 8 Motel
- ✗ Restaurants in town
  Out to Lunch, Palm Royale, Carrillo's, Cactus Jack's, Elmer's of Indio, La Piñata

# *Winterfest*

THIS IS THE PLACE THE anthem "America" refers to in the line "God shed his grace on thee." The small, beautiful community of Running Springs is one of the few places in California with four true seasons. **Winterfest** celebrates the snow on the mountains and the nip in the air! Hot chocolate's available to warm your chilled hands as you watch the parade pass by.

## Running Springs, California

President's Day (three-day) weekend
Hours vary

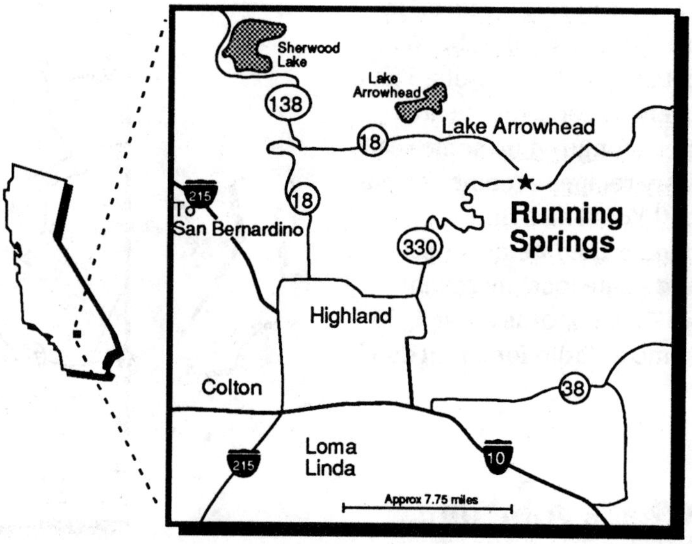


*Up-to-date festival information is available from:*
*Running Springs Chamber of Commerce*
*(714) 867-3775*

## What's goin' on...

Town population: **5,000**
Last year's attendance: **N/A**
Average outdoor temperature: **50°**
Festival location: **Citywide**

- Wine tasting/beer for sale
- ✗ Food booths
- ✗ Arts/crafts for sale
- ✗ Live music
- ✗ Clowns
- ✗ Face painters
- ✗ Childrens games
- ✗ Animal exhibits/petting zoo
- ✗ Dogs allowed on leash
- Lost and found
- Bicycle racks
- First aid area available
- ✗ Self-brought picnics allowed
- Self-brought alcohol allowed
- Stroller/wheelchair rentals available

- ✗ Parade: Sat. 12:00 PM on Hilltop Blvd.
- Parking fee
- ✗ Entrance fee: Some, not all, events
- Camping facilities
- Boating facilities
- RV facilities w/ hookups
- ✗ Accomodations in town
- ✗ Restaurants in town

# *Camellia Festival*

OOOOOH! AAAAAAH! YOU won't believe your eyes and nose at the Temple City **Camellia Festival** and Parade! Youngsters ranging from 6 to 18 years old decorate, design, build, and push their floats made exclusively of camellia blossoms and their foliage! What *spectacular* sights and smells! Known as Home of the Camellias, this little town has been heartily welcoming festival hoppers since 1946!

## Temple City, California

Last weekend in February

Fri.: 4:00 - 10:00 PM; Sat.: Noon - 10:00 PM; Sun.: Noon - 9:00 PM

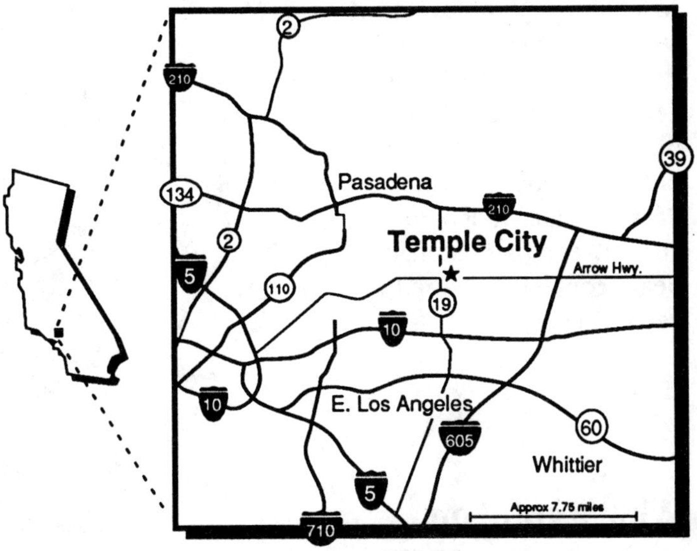


*Up-to-date festival information is available from:*
*Temple City Chamber of Commerce*
*(818) 286-3101*

## What's goin' on...

Town population: **30,000**
Last year's attendance: **5,000**
Average outdoor temperature: **58°**
Festival location: **Temple City Park**

| | |
|---|---|
| | Wine tasting/beer for sale |
| X | Food booths |
| | Arts/crafts for sale |
| | Live music |
| | Clowns |
| | Face painters |
| X | Childrens games |
| | Animal exhibits/petting zoo |
| | Dogs allowed on leash |
| | Lost and found |
| X | Bicycle racks |
| | First aid area available |
| | Self-brought picnics allowed |
| | Self-brought alcohol allowed |
| | Stroller/wheelchair rentals available |

| | |
|---|---|
| X | Parade Sat. 10:00 AM on Las Tunas Blvd. |
| | Parking fee |
| | Entrance fee |
| | Camping facilities |
| X | Boating facilities: Puddingstone Dam |
| X | RV facilities w/ hookups: 10 miles |
| | Accomodations in town |
| | Restaurants in town |

SOUTHERN

# *Heritage Festival*

WHEN THE SWALLOWS return to the majestic Mission San Juan in San Juan Capistrano on March 19th (St. Joseph's Day), thousands of festival hoppers turn out for the **Heritage Festival!** The celebration actually takes place during the entire month of March, mostly at Cook's Park. The fair, rodeo, hat contest, and hairiest-man beard contest, are sure to keep you very busy!

## San Juan Capistrano, California

Month of March
Hours vary

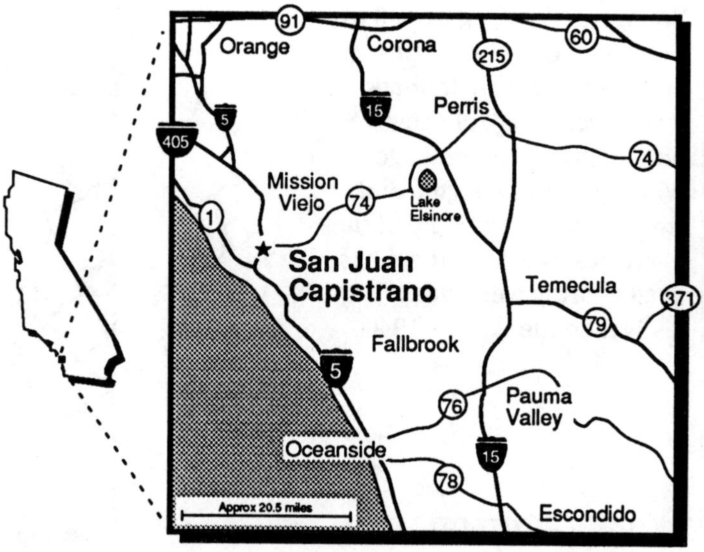


☞ *Up-to-date festival information is available from: San Juan Capistrano Chamber of Commerce (714) 493-4700*

## What's goin' on...

Town population: **27,237**
Last year's attendance: **30,000**
Average outdoor temperature: **75°**
Festival location: **Cooks Park & downtown**

| | |
|---|---|
| | Wine tasting/beer for sale |
| X | Food booths |
| X | Arts/crafts for sale |
| X | Live music |
| X | Clowns |
| X | Face painters |
| X | Childrens games |
| X | Animal exhibits/petting zoo |
| X | Dogs allowed on leash |
| X | Lost and found |
| X | Bicycle racks |
| X | First aid area available |
| X | Self-brought picnics allowed |
| | Self-brought alcohol allowed |
| | Stroller/wheelchair rentals available |

| | |
|---|---|
| X | Parade: 4th Sat. 11:00 AM in town |
| | Parking fee |
| | Entrance fee |
| X | Camping facilities: 5 miles |
| X | Boating facilities: Ocean |
| X | RV facilities w/ hookups: 5 miles |
| X | Accomodations in town: Mission Inn, Dana Point Resort, Capistrano Edgewater Inn |
| X | Restaurants in town: Harry's, Sarducci's, L'Hirondelle French Cuisine, Walnut Grove Restaurant |

# *International Film Festival*

FILM BUFFS UNITE! AT THE **International Film Festival** in Santa Barbara. This 10-day event is jam-packed with fascinating films, critics, workshops, and seminars—not to mention the fabulous film viewing you'll do! Sign-language interpretation for the hearing-impaired is available at some of the events. You can purchase a 10-day pass or pay as you go! Cut...that's a wrap!

## Santa Barbara, California

Second Friday through third Sunday in March
Hours vary

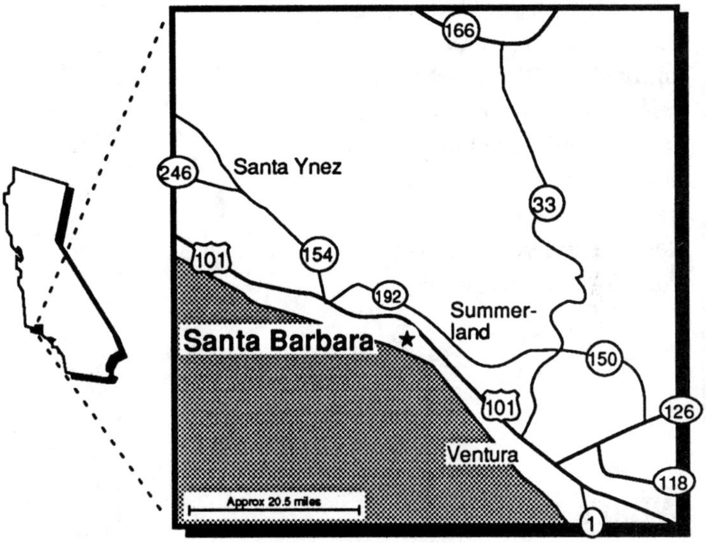


*Up-to-date festival information is available from:*
*Santa Barbara Int'l Film Festival*
*(805) 963-0023*

## What's goin' on...

Town population: **350,000**
Last year's attendance: **13,000**
Average outdoor temperature: **80°**
Festival location: **Four local theaters**

| | |
|---|---|
| ✗ | Wine tasting/beer for sale |
| ✗ | Food booths |
| | Arts/crafts for sale |
| ✗ | Live music |
| | Clowns |
| ✗ | Face painters |
| | Childrens games |
| | Animal exhibits/petting zoo |
| | Dogs allowed on leash |
| ✗ | Lost and found |
| ✗ | Bicycle racks |
| ✗ | First aid area available |
| ✗ | Self-brought picnics allowed |
| | Self-brought alcohol allowed |
| | Stroller/wheelchair rentals available |

| | |
|---|---|
| | Parade |
| | Parking fee |
| ✗ | Entrance fee: $6.50-$150. |
| ✗ | Camping facilities: 3 miles |
| ✗ | Boating facilities: Lake Casitas |
| ✗ | RV facilities w/ hookups: 10 miles |
| ✗ | Accomodations in town |
| ✗ | Restaurants in town<br>Maxim's, The Chart House, Wine Cask, Paradise Cafe |

# *Orchids & Art Festival*

DID YOU KNOW THAT there's such a thing as an orchidologist? It's a horticulturist who deals with orchids...and you'll find more than one at Santa Maria's annual **Orchids & Art Festival!** This colorful and fragrant meeting of flowers and art is a heavenly event at the Veteran's Memorial Cultural Center each year and is a must for orchid lovers!

## Santa Maria, California

Second weekend in March
Daily 10:00 AM - 4:00 PM

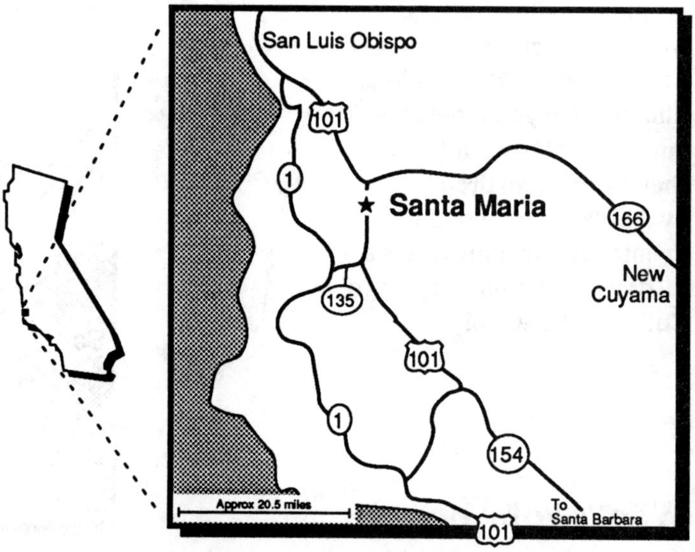


## What's goin' on...

Town population: **47,635**
Last year's attendance: **4,000**
Average outdoor temperature: **69°**
Festival location: **Veteran's Center**

*Up-to-date festival information is available from:*
*Santa Maria Visitor Center*
*(805) 925-2403*

| | |
|---|---|
| | Wine tasting/beer for sale |
| X | Food booths |
| X | Arts/crafts for sale |
| X | Live music |
| X | Clowns |
| X | Face painters |
| X | Childrens games |
| X | Animal exhibits/petting zoo |
| X | Dogs allowed on leash |
| X | Lost and found |
| X | Bicycle racks |
| | First aid area available |
| X | Self-brought picnics allowed |
| | Self-brought alcohol allowed |
| | Stroller/wheelchair rentals available |

| | |
|---|---|
| | Parade |
| | Parking fee |
| | Entrance fee |
| X | Camping facilities: 1 miles |
| X | Boating facilities: Lopez Lake |
| X | RV facilities w/ hookups: 1 mile |
| X | Accomodations in town<br>Hunters Inn, The Big America, Raffles |
| X | Restaurants in town<br>Landmark, Jocko's, Hitching Post |

# *St. Patrick's Day Celebration*

TOP O' THE MORNIN' TO ya...and to all the folks who celebrate from noon till the late hours of the night in Rancho Mirage on **St. Patty's Day!** You'll find sing-alongs, Dixieland jazz bands, and Irish jiggers at the Rancho Las Palmas Shopping Center. Of course, there's lots of green you-know-what being dispensed, as well as all sorts of arts and crafts being sold. Don't forget to wear green...

## Rancho Mirage, California

St. Patrick's Day
11:30 AM - 5:30 PM

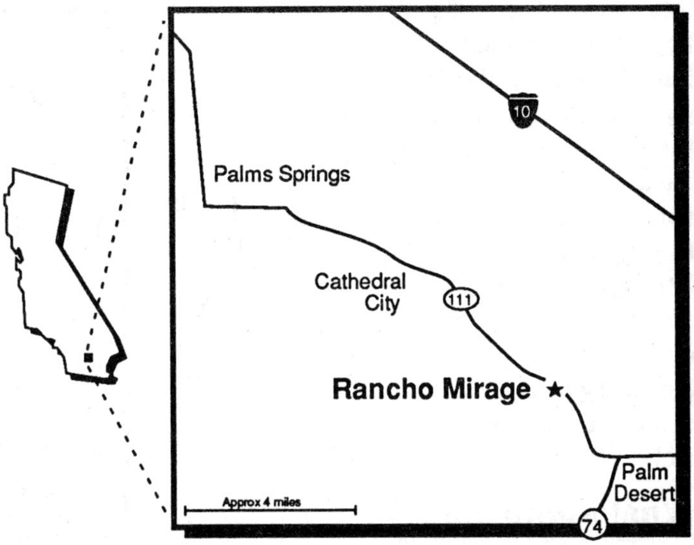


*Up-to-date festival information is available from:*
*Rancho Mirage Chamber of Commerce*
*(619) 568-9351*

## What's goin' on...

Town population: **8,150**
Last year's attendance: **600**
Average outdoor temperature: **85°**
Festival location: **Shopping Ctr.**

| | |
|---|---|
| X | Wine tasting/beer for sale |
| X | Food booths |
| X | Arts/crafts for sale |
| X | Live music |
| X | Clowns |
| | Face painters |
| | Childrens games |
| | Animal exhibits/petting zoo |
| X | Dogs allowed on leash |
| | Lost and found |
| X | Bicycle racks |
| | First aid area available |
| | Self-brought picnics allowed |
| | Self-brought alcohol allowed |
| | Stroller/wheelchair rentals available |

| | |
|---|---|
| | Parade |
| | Parking fee |
| | Entrance fee |
| X | Camping facilities: 10 miles |
| X | Boating facilities: Lake Perris |
| X | RV facilities w/ hookups: 3 miles |
| X | Accomodations in town<br>The Ritz-Carlton Hotel, Rancho Las Palma Resort |
| X | Restaurants in town<br>The Beach House Inn, Garcia's, Scoma's, Pirate & Bull, Mario's |

# *Peg Leg Liars Contest*

NOW HERE'S ONE *TALL* TALE! The **Peg Leg's Liars Contest** is a ritual in Borrego Springs, and it goes something like this: Back in the 1800s, ol' Peg Leg Smith stumbled onto a butte covered with blackened gold nuggets but couldn't find the exact place when he went back with mining tools. Or something like that! Anyway, bring a thermos of hot chocolate, a picnic, and a blanket and get settled in for an evening of *tall* tales about the legendary prospecto! The art of storytelling is alive and kicking in Borrego Springs!

## Borrego Springs, California

Last Saturday in March
Dusk till very dark

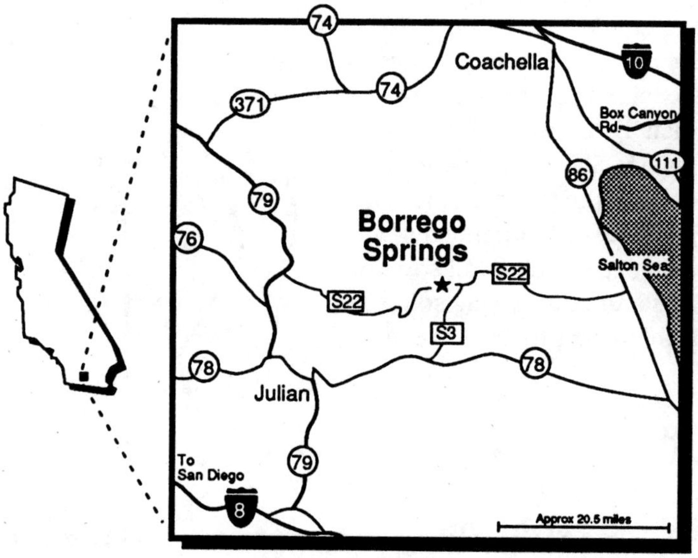


*Up-to-date festival information is available from:*
*Borrego Springs Chamber of Commerce*
*(619) 344-5555*

## What's goin' on...

Town population: **2,712**
Last year's attendance: **300**
Average outdoor temperature: **53°**
Festival location: **Peg Leg Monument**

- [ ] Wine tasting/beer for sale
- [ ] Food booths
- [ ] Arts/crafts for sale
- [ ] Live music
- [ ] Clowns
- [ ] Face painters
- [ ] Childrens games
- [ ] Animal exhibits/petting zoo
- [x] Dogs allowed on leash
- [ ] Lost and found
- [ ] Bicycle racks
- [x] First aid area available
- [x] Self-brought picnics allowed
- [x] Self-brought alcohol allowed
- [ ] Stroller/wheelchair rentals available

- [ ] Parade
- [ ] Parking fee
- [ ] Entrance fee
- [x] Camping facilities: On site
- [x] Boating facilities: Salton Sea
- [x] RV facilities w/ hookups: 7 miles
- [x] Accomodations in town
  Desert Ironwood, Whispering Sands, Oasis Motel, La Casa del Zorro, Stanlund's Motel
- [x] Restaurants in town
  La Casa del Zorro, Rams Hill Country Club, Overland Jct.

# *Grapefruit Festival*

THE BEST GRAPEFRUIT IN the world is grown in Borrego Springs, California, home to year 'round sunshine! The **Grapefruit Festival** may give you some new ideas about how to include these citrus rubies in your daily diet. The food booths have a distinctive slant towards citrus, but there's also barbecues and sweets! Located in the center of Anza Borrego State Park, this is a pretty town!

## Borrego Springs, California

First through the third weekend in April
Hours vary

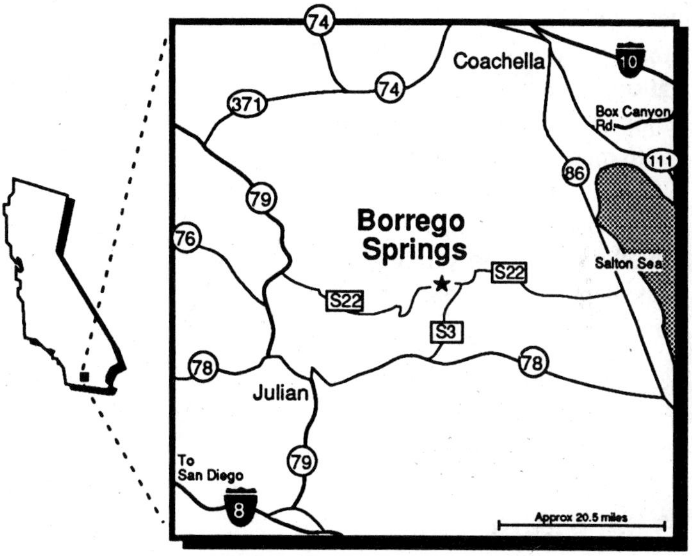


## What's goin' on...

Town population: **1,400**
Last year's attendance: **3,500**
Average outdoor temperature: **82°**
Festival location: **Citywide**

*Up-to-date festival information is available from:*
*Borrego Springs Chamber of Commerce*
*(619) 344-5555*

- [x] Wine tasting/beer for sale
- [x] Food booths
- [x] Arts/crafts for sale
- [x] Live music
- [ ] Clowns
- [ ] Face painters
- [ ] Childrens games
- [ ] Animal exhibits/petting zoo
- [x] Dogs allowed on leash
- [ ] Lost and found
- [x] Bicycle racks
- [ ] First aid area available
- [x] Self-brought picnics allowed
- [ ] Self-brought alcohol allowed
- [ ] Stroller/wheelchair rentals available

- [ ] Parade
- [ ] Parking fee
- [ ] Entrance fee
- [x] Camping facilities: 1 mile
- [x] Boating facilities: 15 miles
- [x] RV facilities w/ hookups: 1 mile
- [x] Accomodations in town
  Desert Ironwood, Whispering Sands, Oasis Motel, La Casa del Zorro, Stanlund's Motel
- [x] Restaurants in town
  La Casa Del Zorro, Rams Hill Country Club

# *Horseweek*

**HORSEWEEK** IS A WEEK OF community involvement! Each and every night there is something for your family to get involved in. A parade starts the week off in a brisk gallop! Then take time to enjoy the beard contest, swap-meet, chili cook-off, weiner roast, horseshoe pitch contest, bingo, gymkhana (for the kiddies), pancake breakfast, and on Easter morning—a sunrise service!

## Norco, California

First Saturday through the second Sunday in April

Hours vary

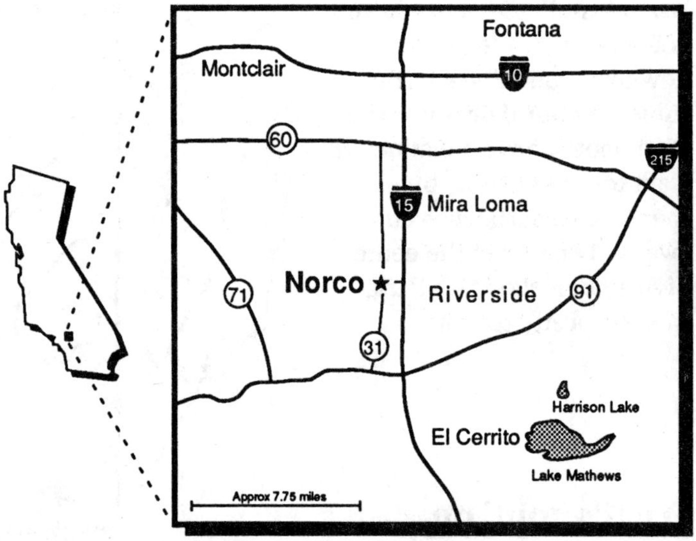


*Up-to-date festival information is available from:*
*Norco Chamber of Commerce*
*(208) 743-2531*

## What's goin' on...

Town population: **50,000**
Last year's attendance: **35,000**
Average outdoor temperature: **70°**
Festival location: **Fairgrounds**

- X Wine tasting/beer for sale
- X Food booths
- Arts/crafts for sale
- X Live music
- Clowns
- Face painters
- X Childrens games
- Animal exhibits/petting zoo
- X Dogs allowed on leash
- Lost and found
- X Bicycle racks
- First aid area available
- Self-brought picnics allowed
- Self-brought alcohol allowed
- Stroller/wheelchair rentals available

- X Parade: 1st Sat. 9:00 AM on Sixth St.
- Parking fee
- Entrance fee
- X Camping facilities: 10 miles
- X Boating facilities: Lake Perris
- X RV facilities w/ hookups: 10 miles
- X Accomodations in town
  Ecoho Lodge
- X Restaurants in town
  Pat's Kitchen, Rapberry's, Sizzler, Country Junction

# *Easter Carnival*

YOUR EASTER BONNETS will be right in style at the **Easter Carnival** in Sunland Park! The rural, country-like towns of Sunland and Tujunga combine efforts for this weekend event. Easter-egg hunts and games such as a goldfish toss will entertain even the youngest of kids. While in town, don't miss the Bolton Hall Museum and McGroarty Art Center. Both are worth the trip!

## Tujunga/Sunland, California

Second weekend in April (beginning Friday)
Fri. noon - 10:00 PM; Sat. 11:00 AM - 11:00 PM; Sun. noon - 6:00 PM

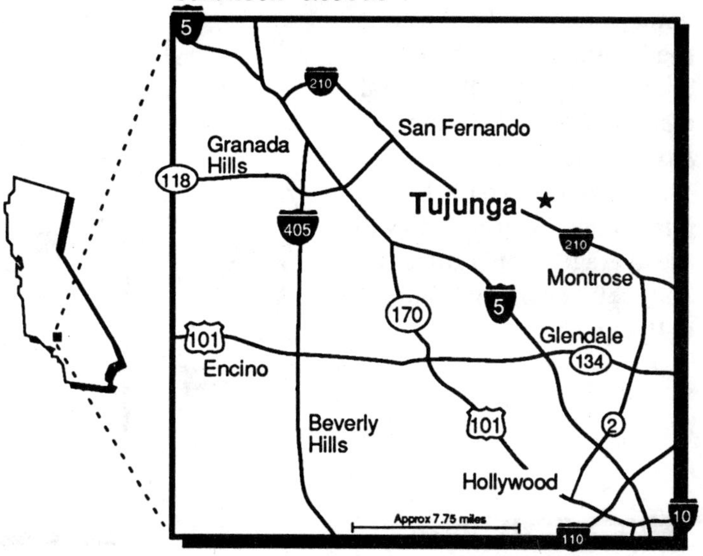


## What's goin' on...

Town population: **62,000**
Last year's attendance: **12,000**
Average outdoor temperature: **80°**
Festival location: **Park**

*Up-to-date festival information is available from: Tujunga/Sunland Chamber of Commerce (818) 352-4433*

| | |
|---|---|
| | Wine tasting/beer for sale |
| X | Food booths |
| X | Arts/crafts for sale |
| X | Live music |
| X | Clowns |
| | Face painters |
| | Childrens games |
| | Animal exhibits/petting zoo |
| X | Dogs allowed on leash |
| X | Lost and found |
| X | Bicycle racks |
| X | First aid area available |
| X | Self-brought picnics allowed |
| | Self-brought alcohol allowed |
| | Stroller/wheelchair rentals available |

| | |
|---|---|
| X | Parade: Sun. noon downtown |
| | Parking fee |
| | Entrance fee |
| X | Camping facilities: 5 miles |
| | Boating facilities |
| X | RV facilities w/ hookups: 10 miles |
| X | Accomodations in town<br>TraveLodge, Harmony Motel, Mt. Gleason Hotel |
| X | Restaurants in town<br>Night Rock Cafe, Sterlings Restaurant |

# *Colorado River Country Fair*

BEFORE THE DRY, HOT weather takes over, Blythe celebrates the **Colorado River Country Fair**. This hometown fun takes place at the fairgrounds in April. It comes complete with animal displays for the kids and *terrific* food and craft booths. The Colorado River is beautiful this time of year...and with the average temperature at about 80°, camping is not out of the question!

## Blythe, California

Third weekend in April
Daily 8:00 AM - 11:00 PM

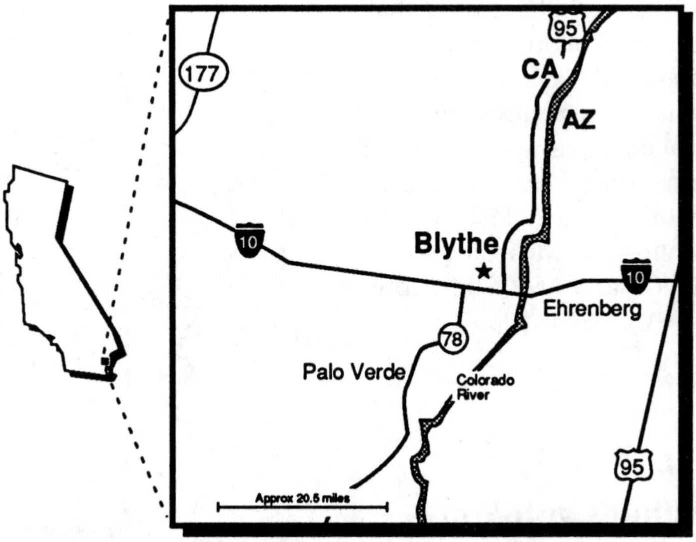


## What's goin' on...

Town population: **8,300**
Last year's attendance: **8,100**
Average outdoor temperature: **80°**
Festival location: **Fairgrounds**

*Up-to-date festival information is available from:*
*Blythe Chamber of Commerce*
*(619) 922-8166*

| | |
|---|---|
| X | Wine tasting/beer for sale |
| X | Food booths |
| X | Arts/crafts for sale |
| X | Live music |
| X | Clowns |
| X | Face painters |
| | Childrens games |
| X | Animal exhibits/petting zoo |
| | Dogs allowed on leash |
| X | Lost and found |
| | Bicycle racks |
| X | First aid area available |
| X | Self-brought picnics allowed |
| | Self-brought alcohol allowed |
| | Stroller/wheelchair rentals available |

| | |
|---|---|
| X | Parade: Sat. 9:00 AM downtown |
| | Parking fee |
| X | Entrance fee: (prices not avbl.) |
| X | Camping facilities: on site |
| X | Boating facilities: Colorado River |
| X | RV facilities w/ hookups: 3 miles |
| X | Accomodations in town |
| X | Restaurants in town<br>Mac's Steakhouse, Silly Al's Pizza, Jimmy'z Grill |

# *Arvin Wildflower Festival*

SPRING HAS SPRUNG IN Arvin—the evidence is in the fields and at the **Arvin Wildflower Festival** at DiGiorgio Park! A 10:00 AM. parade kicks off the day. Then there are food and crafts booths to explore; live bands playing country and popular music; a greased pig catching contest; 5K and 10K runs; a women's softball tournament; and, just before the sun sets, a tri-tip barbecue to complete the day!

## Arvin, California

Third Saturday in April
All day

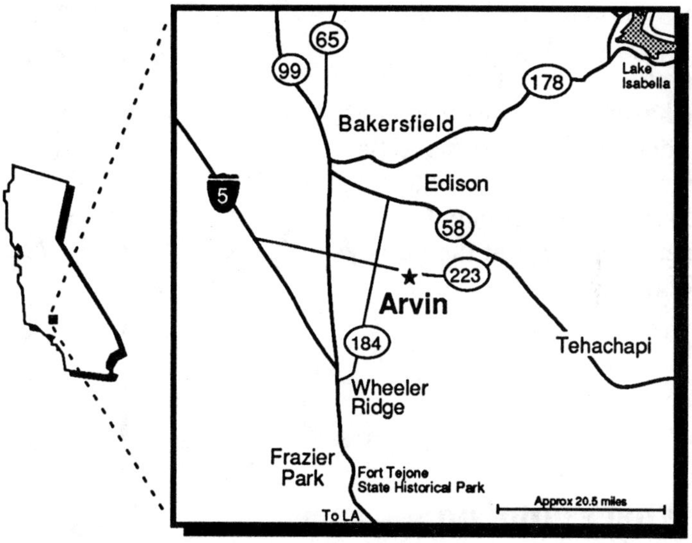


## What's goin' on...

Town population: **26,000**
Last year's attendance: **13,000**
Average outdoor temperature: **75°**
Festival location: **Citywide**

*Up-to-date festival information is available from:*
*Arvin Chamber of Commerce*
*(805) 854-2265*

| | |
|---|---|
| | Wine tasting/beer for sale |
| X | Food booths |
| X | Arts/crafts for sale |
| X | Live music |
| X | Clowns |
| X | Face painters |
| X | Childrens games |
| X | Animal exhibits/petting zoo |
| X | Dogs allowed on leash |
| | Lost and found |
| X | Bicycle racks |
| X | First aid area available |
| X | Self-brought picnics allowed |
| | Self-brought alcohol allowed |
| | Stroller/wheelchair rentals available |

| | |
|---|---|
| X | Parade: 10:00 AM downtown |
| | Parking fee |
| | Entrance fee |
| X | Camping facilities: 5 miles |
| X | Boating facilities: Lake Buena Vista |
| X | RV facilities w/ hookups: 5 miles |
| | Accomodations in town |
| | Restaurants in town |

SOUTHERN

# *Heritage Days*

PIONEER VILLAGE MARKS the spot for the annual **Heritage Days.** Bakersfield, Darrin's hometown, puts on a great spread complete with great food, charming arts-and-crafts, simulated shoot-outs (the kids love 'em!), wagon rides, and lots, lots more. Be sure to take a moment to stop in at the Kern County Museum for a look at the history of the area.

## Bakersfield, California

Third weekend in April
Daily 10:00 AM - 5:00 PM

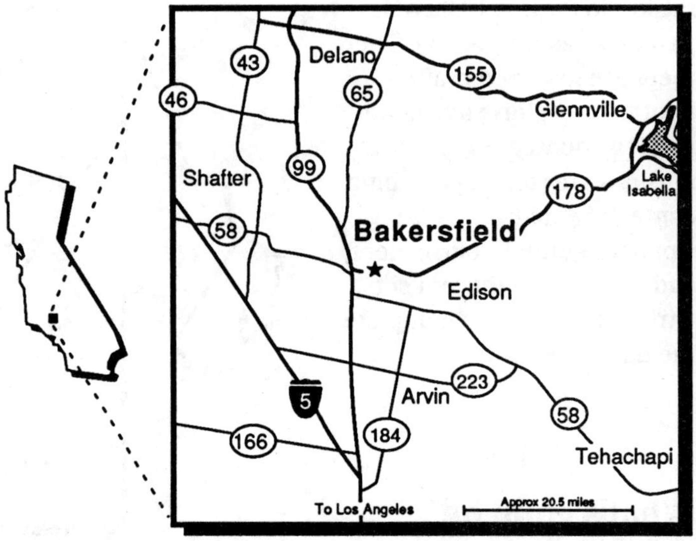


## What's goin' on...

Town population: **222,000**
Last year's attendance: **6,000**
Average outdoor temperature: **75°**
Festival location: **Museum grounds**

*Up-to-date festival information is available from:*
*Bakersfield Chamber of Commerce*
*(805) 327-4421*

| | |
|---|---|
| X | Wine tasting/beer for sale |
| X | Food booths |
| X | Arts/crafts for sale |
| X | Live music |
| | Clowns |
| X | Face painters |
| X | Childrens games |
| | Animal exhibits/petting zoo |
| X | Dogs allowed on leash |
| | Lost and found |
| X | Bicycle racks |
| | First aid area available |
| | Self-brought picnics allowed |
| | Self-brought alcohol allowed |
| | Stroller/wheelchair rentals available |

| | |
|---|---|
| X | Parade: (date & time not avbl.) |
| | Parking fee |
| | Entrance fee |
| X | Camping facilities: 10 miles |
| X | Boating facilities: Lake Buena Vista |
| X | RV facilities w/ hookups: 10 miles |
| X | Accomodations in town<br>Red Lion Hotel, Bakersfield Inn |
| X | Restaurants in town<br>Reuben's, K.C. Steak House, Maitia's Basque, Cash 'n Cleaver |

# *Colorado River Round Up Rodeo*

BEFORE MOTHER NATURE turns up the thermostat in the desert, come on down for the Needles **Colorado River Round Up Rodeo**! The rodeo will keep you entertained during the daylight hours, and you can let the Nevada casinos entertain you during the evening. Laughlin, Nevada, with 11 of them, is just 30 miles north.

## Needles, California

Third weekend in April
Hours vary

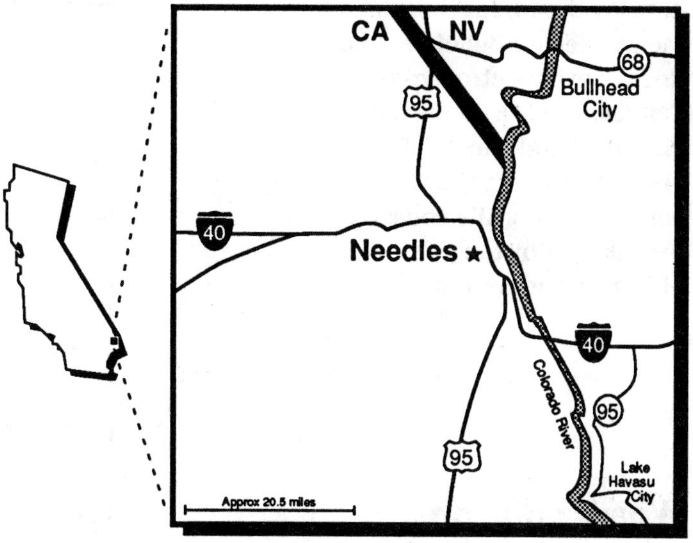


*Up-to-date festival information is available from:*
*Needles Chamber of Commerce*
*(619) 326-2050*

## What's goin' on...

Town population: **6,500**
Last year's attendance: **4,500**
Average outdoor temperature: **78°**
Festival location: **Rodeo Grounds**

| | |
|---|---|
| X | Wine tasting/beer for sale |
| X | Food booths |
| | Arts/crafts for sale |
| X | Live music |
| X | Clowns |
| | Face painters |
| | Childrens games |
| X | Animal exhibits/petting zoo |
| X | Dogs allowed on leash |
| X | Lost and found |
| | Bicycle racks |
| X | First aid area available |
| | Self-brought picnics allowed |
| | Self-brought alcohol allowed |
| | Stroller/wheelchair rentals available |

| | |
|---|---|
| X | Parade: Sat. 10:00 AM downtown |
| | Parking fee |
| X | Entrance fee: Adults $6; Kids $4 |
| X | Camping facilities: 3 miles |
| X | Boating facilities: Colorado River |
| X | RV facilities w/ hookups: 3 miles |
| X | Accomodations in town<br>Motel 6, TraveLodge, Best Western, Allstar Inn |
| X | Restaurants in town<br>Hungry Bear Restaurant |

# *High Desert Natural Wonders Weekend*

LEARN MORE ABOUT THE natural beauty and history of the Ridgecrest area at the **High Desert Natural Wonders Weekend**! Just imagine the wonders to behold at Red Rock Canyon, Petroglyph Canyon, and the Pinnacles! Photo, art and mining displays at the festival will enlighten you while you kick back and enjoy the jazz, bluegrass and rock music.

## Ridgecrest, California

Third weekend in April
Daily: 10:00 AM - 4:00 PM

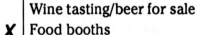

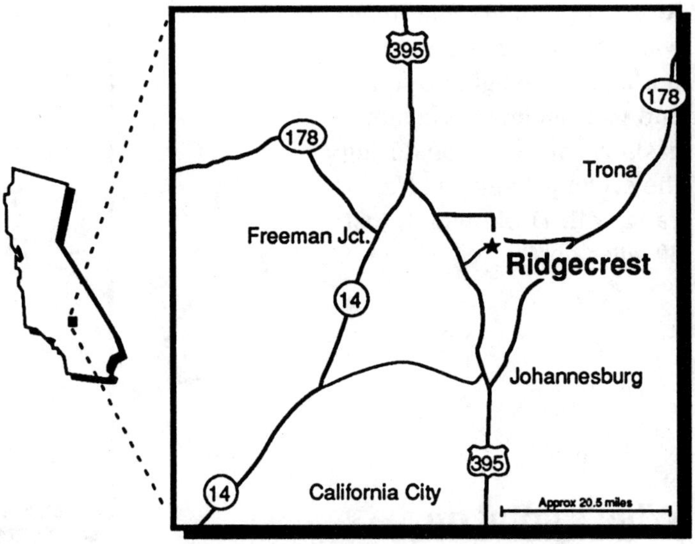


## What's goin' on...

Town population: **28,639**
Last year's attendance: **500**
Average outdoor temperature: **75°**
Festival location: **Community Ctr. & Museum**

*Up-to-date festival information is available from:*
*Ridgecrest Chamber of Commerce*
*(619) 375-8331*

| | |
|---|---|
| | Wine tasting/beer for sale |
| X | Food booths |
| | Arts/crafts for sale |
| X | Live music |
| | Clowns |
| | Face painters |
| | Childrens games |
| | Animal exhibits/petting zoo |
| | Dogs allowed on leash |
| X | Lost and found |
| X | Bicycle racks |
| X | First aid area available |
| X | Self-brought picnics allowed |
| | Self-brought alcohol allowed |
| | Stroller/wheelchair rentals available |

| | |
|---|---|
| | Parade |
| | Parking fee |
| | Entrance fee |
| X | Camping facilities: 5 miles away |
| X | Boating facilities: Lake Isabella |
| X | RV facilities w/ hookups: In town |
| X | Accomodations in town: Pioneer Motel, Heritage House, El Rancho Motel, Econolodge, Carriage Inn |
| X | Restaurants in town: Sandpiper, The Hideaway, White Star Dining Company, Farris' at the Heritage, Schooner Saloon |

# *Renaissance Pleasure Faire*

SIX OUTDOOR STAGES WITH more than 1,000 brilliantly costumed performers portraying people from peasant to queen grace Glen Helen Park for the **Renaissance Pleasure Faire**! This tradition has drawn people from all over the United States since 1962! "Am I in earth, in heaven, or in hell," Shakespeare wrote in The Comedy of Errors. Well, Will, we're in heaven!

## San Bernadino, California

Weekends beginning the third weekend in April through the second weekend in June
Sats. & Suns. 9:00 AM - 6:00 PM

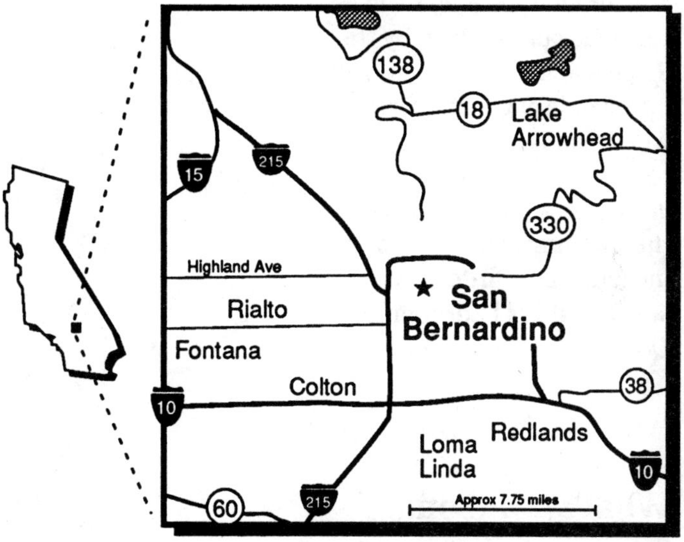


*Up-to-date festival information is available from:*
*San Bernadino Chamber of Commerce*
*(714) 889-3980*

## What's goin' on...

Town population: **160,000**
Last year's attendance: **200,000**
Average outdoor temperature: **80°**
Festival location: **Glen Helen Park**

- ✗ Wine tasting/beer for sale
- ✗ Food booths
- ✗ Arts/crafts for sale
- ✗ Live music
- Clowns
- ✗ Face painters
- Childrens games
- Animal exhibits/petting zoo
- ✗ Dogs allowed on leash
- ✗ Lost and found
- Bicycle racks
- ✗ First aid area available
- ✗ Self-brought picnics allowed
- Self-brought alcohol allowed
- Stroller/wheelchair rentals available

- ✗ Parade: Varies throughout faire
- ✗ Parking fee: $2
- ✗ Entrance fee: S $12; A $15; K $8
- ✗ Camping facilities: 10 miles
- ✗ Boating facilities: Lake Perris
- ✗ RV facilities w/ hookups: In town
- ✗ Accomodations in town
  San Bernadino Hilton, Maruko Hotel, La Quinta, TraveLodge
- ✗ Restaurants in town
  TGI Fridays, Spencers, La Pontinier, Bobby McGees

# *Conejo Valley Days*

CONEJO WALLEY HOLDS ITS **Conejo Valley Days** in April this year! These days are filled with fun and activities and for everyone! While in town, be sure to drop by the Stagecoach Inn Museum, with its legendary ghost, Pierre, who is said to roam the rooms. Pierre, as the story goes, was a guest back when the dwelling actually was an inn and was murdered in a small upstairs bedroom. *Ooooh......*

## Thousand Oaks, California

Fourth weekend in April
Hours vary

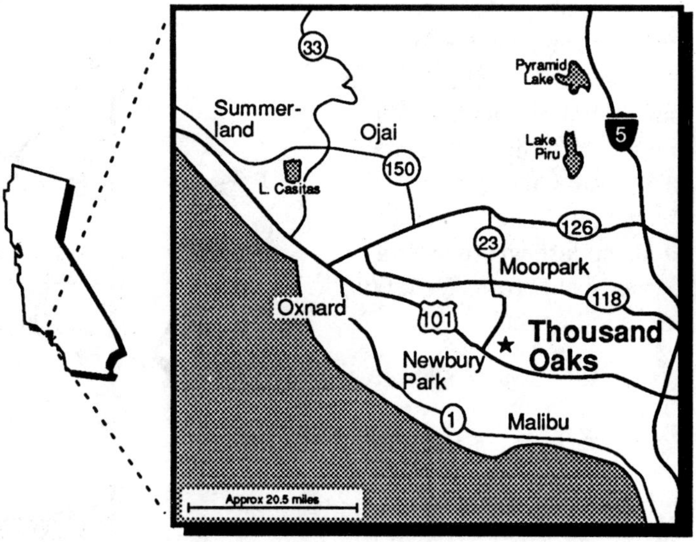


*Up-to-date festival information is available from:*
*Thousand Oaks Chamber of Commerce*
*(805) 499-1993*

## What's goin' on...

Town population: **104,378**
Last year's attendance: **60,000**
Average outdoor temperature: **75°**
Festival location: **Citywide**

- ✗ Wine tasting/beer for sale
- ✗ Food booths
- ✗ Arts/crafts for sale
- ✗ Live music
- ✗ Clowns
- ✗ Face painters
- ✗ Childrens games
- ✗ Animal exhibits/petting zoo
- Dogs allowed on leash
- ✗ Lost and found
- Bicycle racks
- ✗ First aid area available
- ✗ Self-brought picnics allowed
- Self-brought alcohol allowed
- Stroller/wheelchair rentals available

- ✗ Parade: Sat. 9:00 on Thousand Oaks Bl.
- Parking fee
- ✗ Entrance fee: A $2.50; K $2
- Camping facilities
- Boating facilities
- RV facilities w/ hookups
- ✗ Accomodations in town
  Days Inn, Allstar Inn, Hyatt West Lake, Howard Johnson
- ✗ Restaurants in town
  Charlie Brown's, El Torito

# *Springfest*

JUST SOUTH OF THE SAN Gabriel Mission lies the little town of Alhambra—home to **Springfest** in April! This downtown festival cooks up some awfully good eats, such as teriyaki steak-on-a-stick, tacos and nachos, and home-made cookies and ice cream! The craft displays feature beautiful jewelry and unique fabric, clay, and wood items. There's pony rides and game booths, too!

## Alhambra, California

Fourth Saturday in April
10:00 AM - 4:00 PM

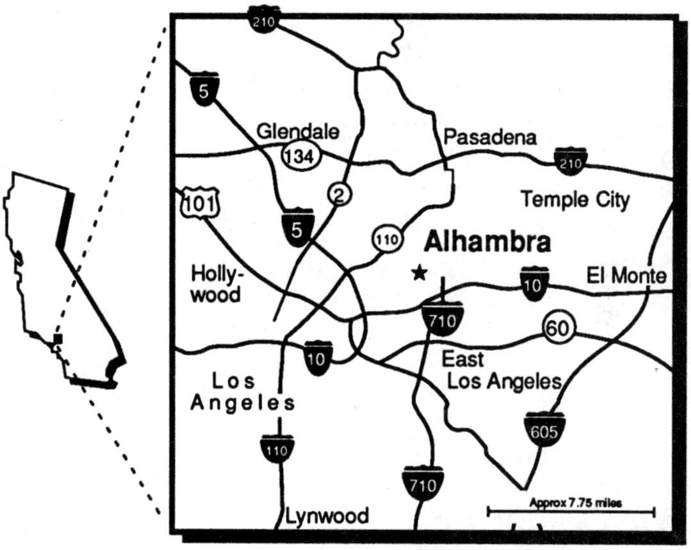


*Up-to-date festival information is available from:*
*Alhambra Central Business Assn.*
*(818) 282-5767*

## What's goin' on...

Town population: **80,00**
Last year's attendance: **8,000**
Average outdoor temperature: **75°**
Festival location: **Downtown**

| | |
|---|---|
| | Wine tasting/beer for sale |
| X | Food booths |
| X | Arts/crafts for sale |
| X | Live music |
| X | Clowns |
| X | Face painters |
| X | Childrens games |
| | Animal exhibits/petting zoo |
| X | Dogs allowed on leash |
| X | Lost and found |
| | Bicycle racks |
| X | First aid area available |
| | Self-brought picnics allowed |
| | Self-brought alcohol allowed |
| | Stroller/wheelchair rentals available |

| | |
|---|---|
| | Parade |
| | Parking fee |
| | Entrance fee |
| | Camping facilities |
| | Boating facilities |
| X | RV facilities w/ hookups: 2 miles |
| X | Accomodations in town<br>Quality Inn, Best Western |
| X | Restaurants in town |

# *Old-Fashioned Days*

THIS SMALL TOWN CELEBRATION—**Old-Fashioned Days** in Altadena—is big on things to do! The parade—complete with local marching bands, floats, baton twirlers, and clowns—starts the day out right! Then mosey down Lake Avenue for the rest of the day and enjoy the homemade goodies cooked up for the occasion.

## Altadena, California

Fourth Saturday in April
9:00 AM - 4:00 PM

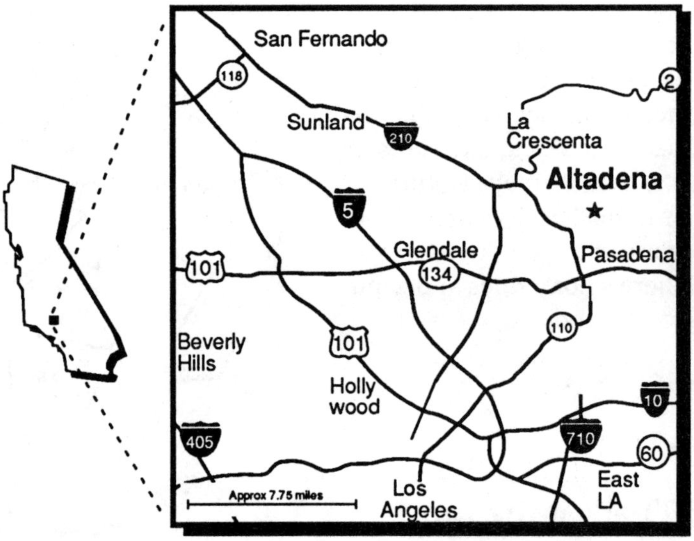


*Up-to-date festival information is available from:*
*Altadena Chamber of Commerce*
*(818) 794-3988*

## What's goin' on...

Town population: **43,000**
Last year's attendance: **3,000**
Average outdoor temperature: **78°**
Festival location: **Lake Ave.**

| | |
|---|---|
| | Wine tasting/beer for sale |
| X | Food booths |
| X | Arts/crafts for sale |
| X | Live music |
| X | Clowns |
| | Face painters |
| | Childrens games |
| X | Animal exhibits/petting zoo |
| X | Dogs allowed on leash |
| | Lost and found |
| | Bicycle racks |
| X | First aid area available |
| X | Self-brought picnics allowed |
| | Self-brought alcohol allowed |
| | Stroller/wheelchair rentals available |

| | |
|---|---|
| X | Parade: Sat. 10:45 AM downtown |
| | Parking fee |
| | Entrance fee |
| | Camping facilities |
| | Boating facilities |
| | RV facilities w/ hookups |
| | Accomodations in town |
| | Restaurants in town |

# *Desert Dixieland Jazz Festival*

JOIN IN THE FOOT STOMPIN', knee-slappin' fun of the annual **Desert Dixieland Jazz Festival** in Cathedral City, California! This three-day event hosts the best in Dixieland music. More than 12 bands will be playing "from the heart" of the fabulous and balmy California Desert. Additional information can be retrieved from the Dixieland Jazz Society of the Desert at (619) 321-JASS (no...that's not a typo!).

## Cathedral City, California

Last weekend in April through the second weekend in May
Hours vary

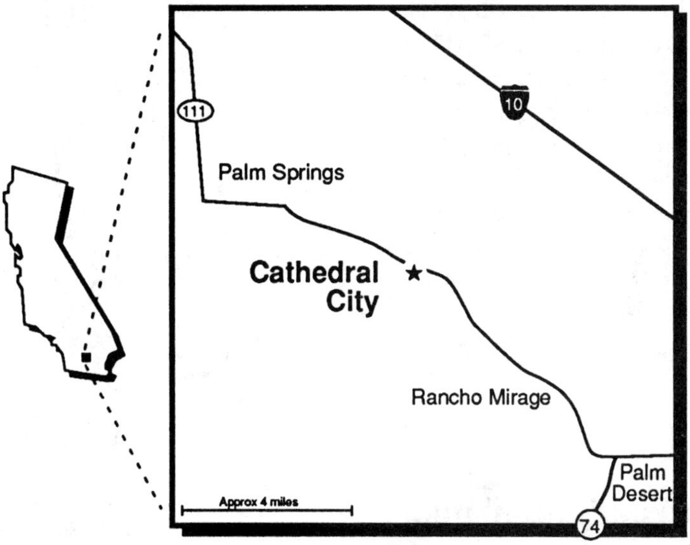


*Up-to-date festival information is available from:*
*Cathedral City Chamber of Commerce*
*(208) 328-1213*

## What's goin' on...

Town population: **28,000**
Last year's attendance: **6,800**
Average outdoor temperature: **90°**
Festival location: **N/A**

| | |
|---|---|
| ✗ | Wine tasting/beer for sale |
| ✗ | Food booths |
| | Arts/crafts for sale |
| ✗ | Live music |
| | Clowns |
| | Face painters |
| | Childrens games |
| | Animal exhibits/petting zoo |
| | Dogs allowed on leash |
| ✗ | Lost and found |
| | Bicycle racks |
| ✗ | First aid area available |
| | Self-brought picnics allowed |
| | Self-brought alcohol allowed |
| | Stroller/wheelchair rentals available |

| | |
|---|---|
| | Parade |
| | Parking fee |
| ✗ | Entrance fee: $30 for 3-day event |
| ✗ | Camping facilities |
| ✗ | Boating facilities |
| ✗ | RV facilities w/ hookups: In town |
| ✗ | Accomodations in town |
| ✗ | Restaurants in town<br>Cattail's, Arthur's |

# *Marine Corps Air Station Air Show*

THE 3RD MARINE AIRCRAFT Wing and **Marine Corps Air Station**-El Toro whole-heartedly welcome you to the Navy Relief **Air Show**! Jim Franklin's "Aero-Fest" Production promises spectacular aeronautical ballets which are sure to provide you with plenty of excitement. Then enjoy the Blue Angels overhead as you look over the historical airplane displays and enjoy the 3rd Marine Aircraft Wing Band!

## Santa Ana, California

Last weekend in April through the second weekend in May

Hours vary

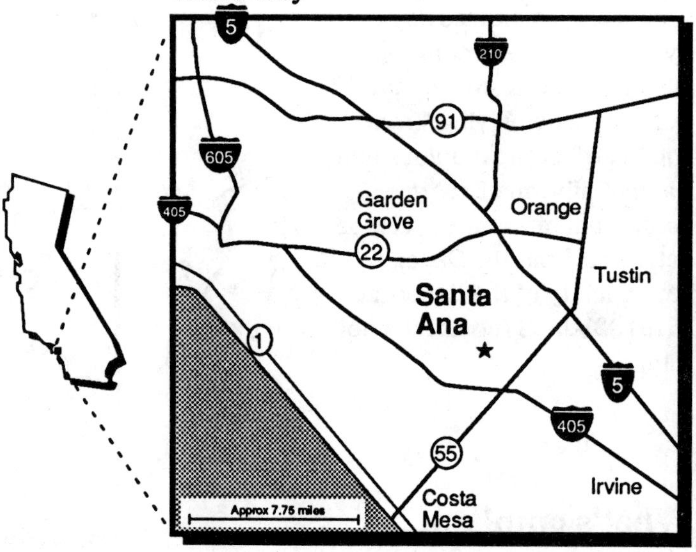


## What's goin' on...

Town population: **20,023**

Last year's attendance: **200,000**

Average outdoor temperature: **88°**

Festival location: **Navy Base**

☞ *Up-to-date festival information is available from:*
*Santa Ana Chamber of Commerce*
*(714) 541-5353*

| | |
|---|---|
| X | Wine tasting/beer for sale |
| X | Food booths |
| X | Arts/crafts for sale |
| X | Live music |
| X | Clowns |
| X | Face painters |
| X | Childrens games |
| | Animal exhibits/petting zoo |
| X | Dogs allowed on leash |
| X | Lost and found |
| | Bicycle racks |
| X | First aid area available |
| X | Self-brought picnics allowed |
| | Self-brought alcohol allowed |
| | Stroller/wheelchair rentals available |

| | |
|---|---|
| | Parade |
| | Parking fee |
| | Entrance fee |
| X | Camping facilities: 10 miles |
| X | Boating facilities: Irvine Lake |
| X | RV facilities w/ hookups: 10 miles |
| X | Accomodations in town |
| X | Restaurants in town |

# *Community Fair*

IN THE HEART OF CALIFORNIA's oil fields lies the bustling little community of Taft—home to the **Community Fair.** Kick up yer heels to the live country western music playing all day, and pig-out at food booths of all kinds abound—barbecue, Mexican, American, Thai, and Cajun. The crafts exhibition include handmade wood carvings, ceramic, dolls, as well as photographs and artwork.

## Taft, California

Fourth weekend in April
Hours vary

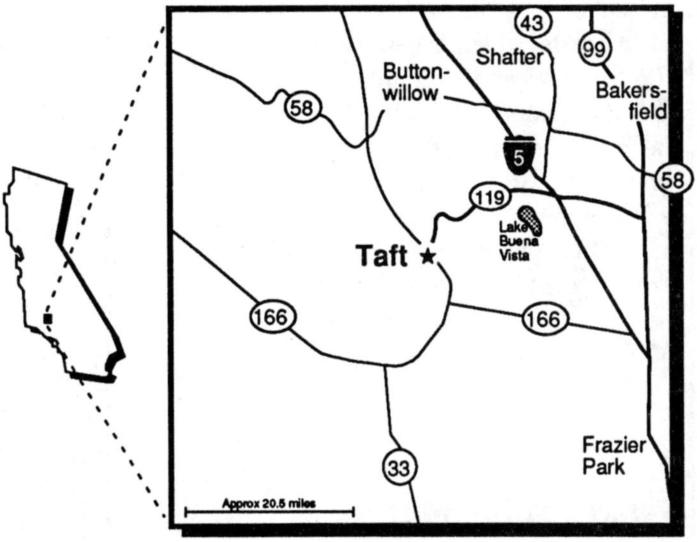


## What's goin' on...

Town population: **25,000**
Last year's attendance: **7,000**
Average outdoor temperature: **85°**
Festival location: **Franklin Field Complex**

*Up-to-date festival information is available from:*
*Taft Chamber of Commerce*
*(805) 765-2165*

| | |
|---|---|
| X | Wine tasting/beer for sale |
| X | Food booths |
| X | Arts/crafts for sale |
| X | Live music |
| X | Clowns |
| X | Face painters |
| X | Childrens games |
| X | Animal exhibits/petting zoo |
| X | Dogs allowed on leash |
| X | Lost and found |
| X | Bicycle racks |
| X | First aid area available |
| X | Self-brought picnics allowed |
| X | Self-brought alcohol allowed |
| | Stroller/wheelchair rentals available |

| | |
|---|---|
| | Parade |
| | Parking fee |
| | Entrance fee |
| X | Camping facilities: 12 miles |
| X | Boating facilities: Lake Buena Vista |
| X | RV facilities w/ hookups: 12 miles |
| X | Accomodations in town<br>Westside Inn, Caprice Motel, Taft Motel, Maricopa Best Western |
| X | Restaurants in town<br>Fric & Frac's, Geno's, Donahoo's, Pizza Factory |

# *California Beach Party*

WHAT WOULD CALIFORNIA be without an authentic **California Beach Party**? Sunny California hosts this annual event at its beach promenade, which is gently tucked between the Emma Wood and McGrath State Beaches. Crafts relating to the great outdoors—beach, sun, wind, water sports—are for sale. This "Annette Funicello/ Frankie Avalon" type beach party features surf music and 50's & 60's rock 'n' roll.

## Ventura, California

Last Saturday in April
10:00 AM - 4:00 PM

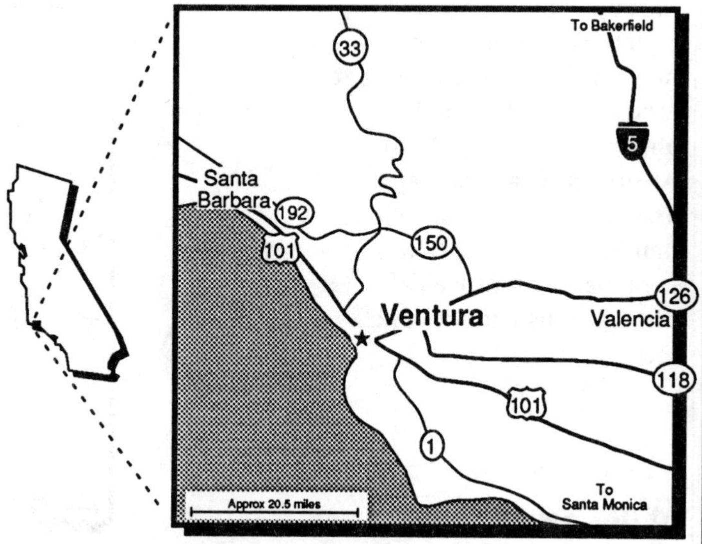


## What's goin' on...

Town population: **92,000**
Last year's attendance: **25,000**
Average outdoor temperature: **74°**
Festival location: **Beach promenade**

*Up-to-date festival information is available from:*
*Ventura Chamber of Commerce*
*(805) 648-2875*

| | |
|---|---|
| | Wine tasting/beer for sale |
| X | Food booths |
| X | Arts/crafts for sale |
| X | Live music |
| X | Clowns |
| X | Face painters |
| X | Childrens games |
| | Animal exhibits/petting zoo |
| | Dogs allowed on leash |
| X | Lost and found |
| X | Bicycle racks |
| X | First aid area available |
| | Self-brought picnics allowed |
| | Self-brought alcohol allowed |
| | Stroller/wheelchair rentals available |

| | |
|---|---|
| | Parade |
| | Parking fee |
| | Entrance fee |
| X | Camping facilities: 3 miles |
| X | Boating facilities: Lake Casitas |
| X | RV facilities w/ hookups: 3 miles |
| X | Accomodations in town |
| X | Restaurants in town |

Tony's Steak/Seafood, Hungry Hunter, Chart House, Eric Ericson's

# *Village Street Faire*

THE CARLSBAD **VILLAGE Street Faire** is such a great time that the Chamber of Commerce decided to hold it twice yearly. The May and November festivals, held downtown in the village, feature international-food booths as well as unique crafts such as handmade dolls and hand-painted clothing. Kids will love the elephant walk, pony rides, and petting zoo. Nearby beaches enhance the ideal California atmosphere.

## Carlsbad, California

First Sunday in May
10:00 AM - 4:30 PM

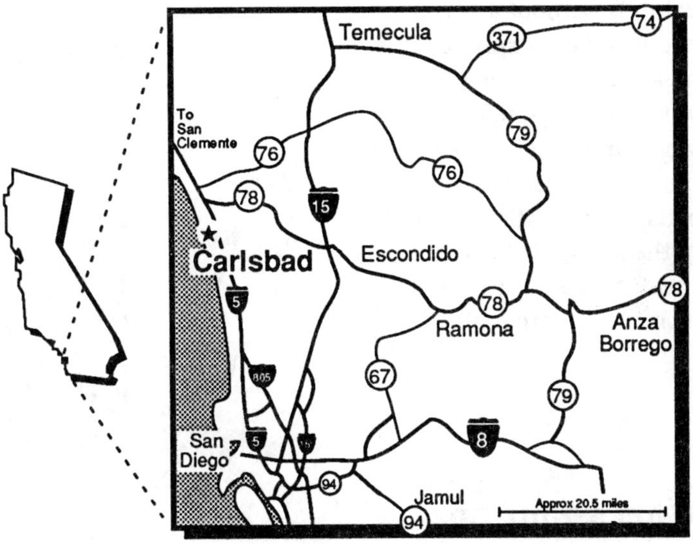


*Up-to-date festival information is available from:*
*Carlsbad Chamber of Commerce*
*(619) 931-8400*

## What's goin' on...

Town population: **62,500**
Last year's attendance: **80,000**
Average outdoor temperature: **70°**
Festival location: **Downtown**

| | |
|---|---|
| X | Wine tasting/beer for sale |
| X | Food booths |
| X | Arts/crafts for sale |
| X | Live music |
| X | Clowns |
| X | Face painters |
| X | Childrens games |
| X | Animal exhibits/petting zoo |
| | Dogs allowed on leash |
| X | Lost and found |
| X | Bicycle racks |
| X | First aid area available |
| | Self-brought picnics allowed |
| | Self-brought alcohol allowed |
| | Stroller/wheelchair rentals available |

| | |
|---|---|
| | Parade |
| | Parking fee |
| | Entrance fee |
| X | Camping facilities: In town |
| X | Boating facilities: Saltwater inlet |
| X | RV facilities w/ hookups: In town |
| X | Accomodations in town<br>Ocean Manor, Beach View Lodge, Carlsbad Inn, Carlsbad Lodge, Motel 6, Surf Motel |
| X | Restaurants in town<br>The Village Grill, Hennessey's Tavern, Cliff's Pantry, The Cove, Dooley McCluskey's |

# *Arts & Crafts Show*

THE **ARTS & CRAFTS SHOW** in Chula Vista has strict requirements for hand- made goods—guaranteeing quality exhibits without a mass-produced atmosphere! This makes the featured paintings, wood carvings, toys, stained glass, and other one-of-a-kind items from more than 100 artists very distinctive. Held in the new Third Avenue area, the show also features grub from local merchants.

## Chula Vista, California

First weekend in May
9:00 AM - 3:00 PM

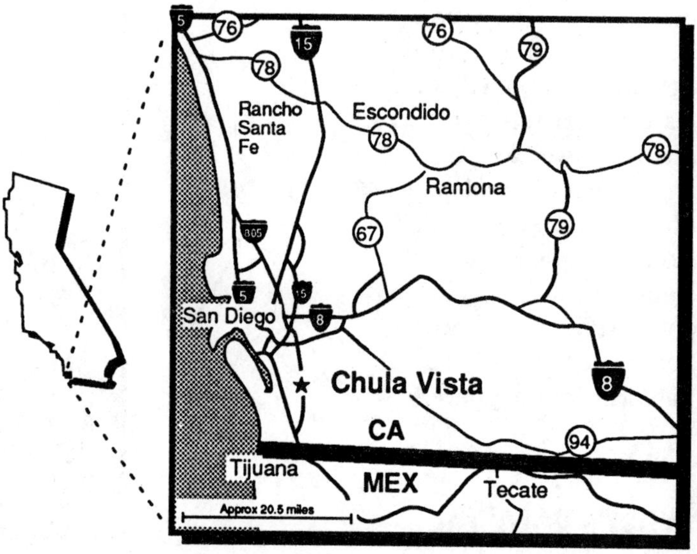


*Up-to-date festival information is available from:*
*Chula Vista Chamber of Commerce*
*(619) 420-6602*

## What's goin' on...

Town population: **131,455**
Last year's attendance: **7,000**
Average outdoor temperature: **75°**
Festival location: **Third Ave.**

- ✗ Wine tasting/beer for sale
- ✗ Food booths
- ✗ Arts/crafts for sale
- ✗ Live music
- Clowns
- ✗ Face painters
- ✗ Childrens games
- Animal exhibits/petting zoo
- ✗ Dogs allowed on leash
- Lost and found
- ✗ Bicycle racks
- ✗ First aid area available
- Self-brought picnics allowed
- Self-brought alcohol allowed
- ✗ Stroller/wheelchair rentals available

- Parade
- Parking fee
- Entrance fee
- ✗ Camping facilities: 3 miles
- ✗ Boating facilities: Otay Res.
- ✗ RV facilities w/ hookups: 3 miles
- ✗ Accomodations in town
  Days Inn, All Seasons, Ramada Inn, Vagabond
- ✗ Restaurants in town
  Sea Food Broiler, La Bella's, House of Nine Dragons

# *Cinco de Mayo*

ENCHILADAS, FAJITAS, burritos, flautas, tamales, sangria, homemade tortillas—everyone loves Mexican food! **Cinco de Mayo** in Borrego Springs is where you'll find it all! Come out in your colorful sarape and sombrero, and swing at the piñatas, and enjoy the Mexican mariachi bands. ¡Olé!

## Borrego Springs, California

Fifth of May
11:00 AM - 7:00 PM

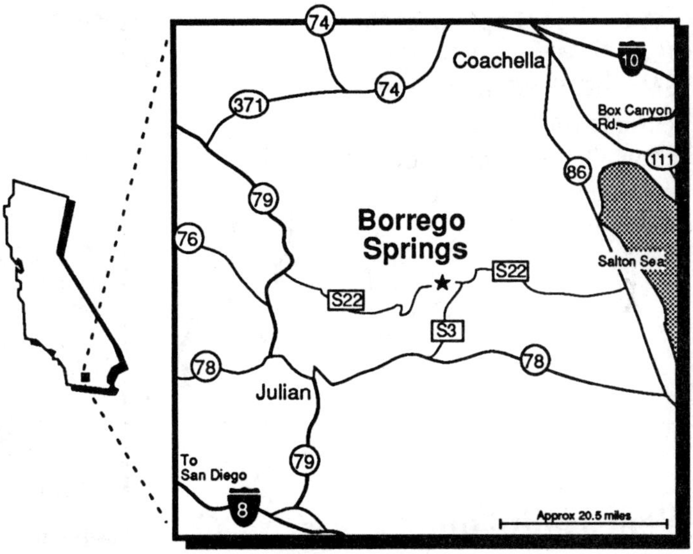


*Up-to-date festival information is available from:*
*Borrego Springs Chamber of Commerce*
*(619) 344-5555*

## What's goin' on...

Town population: **2,712**
Last year's attendance: **2,000**
Average outdoor temperature: **91°**
Festival location: **Park**

| | |
|---|---|
| X | Wine tasting/beer for sale |
| X | Food booths |
| X | Arts/crafts for sale |
| X | Live music |
| | Clowns |
| | Face painters |
| | Childrens games |
| | Animal exhibits/petting zoo |
| X | Dogs allowed on leash |
| X | Lost and found |
| | Bicycle racks |
| X | First aid area available |
| X | Self-brought picnics allowed |
| | Self-brought alcohol allowed |
| | Stroller/wheelchair rentals available |

| | |
|---|---|
| | Parade |
| | Parking fee |
| | Entrance fee |
| X | Camping facilities: On-site |
| X | Boating facilities: Salton Sea |
| X | RV facilities w/ hookups: 7 miles |
| X | Accomodations in town<br>Desert Ironwood, Whispering Sands, Oasis Motel, La Casa del Zorro, Stanlund's Motel |
| X | Restaurants in town<br>La Casa del Zorro, Rams Hill Country Club, Overland Jct. |

# Cinco de Mayo

HOT, HOMEMADE TORTILLAS and fresh tamales...yum! You'll find both of those and lots more Mexican food to tantalize your appetite at the **Cinco de Mayo** celebration in El Monte! The Community Center is the hub of the action all day long, as several mariachi bands, dancers, and piñatas entertain you.

## El Monte, California

Fifth of May
10:00 AM - 6:00 PM

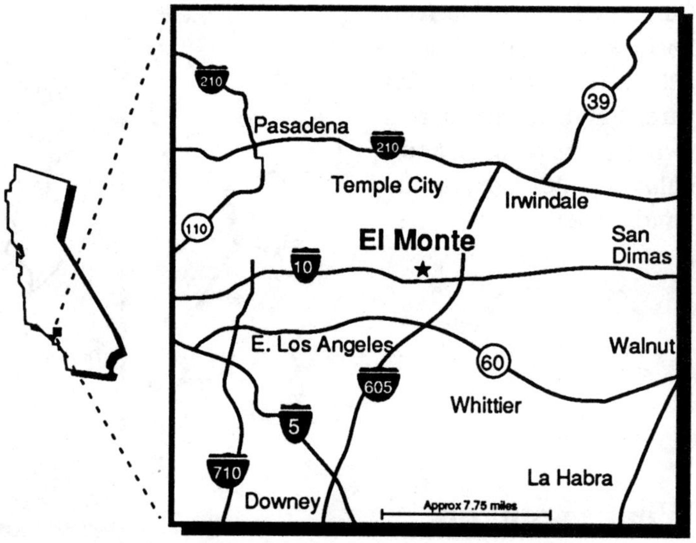


## What's goin' on...

Town population: **19,000**
Last year's attendance: **600**
Average outdoor temperature: **80°**
Festival location: **Community Ctr.**

*Up-to-date festival information is available from:*
*El Monte Chamber of Commerce*
*(818) 433-0180*

| | |
|---|---|
| ✗ | Wine tasting/beer for sale |
| ✗ | Food booths |
| | Arts/crafts for sale |
| ✗ | Live music |
| | Clowns |
| | Face painters |
| ✗ | Childrens games |
| | Animal exhibits/petting zoo |
| ✗ | Dogs allowed on leash |
| ✗ | Lost and found |
| ✗ | Bicycle racks |
| ✗ | First aid area available |
| ✗ | Self-brought picnics allowed |
| | Self-brought alcohol allowed |
| | Stroller/wheelchair rentals available |

| | |
|---|---|
| | Parade |
| | Parking fee |
| | Entrance fee |
| | Camping facilities |
| | Boating facilities |
| | RV facilities w/ hookups |
| | Accomodations in town |
| | Restaurants in town |

# *Wine Expo*

RE-DOE-DOE BEACH, JUST A hop-skip-and-a-jump from Man-happenin' Beach, is host to the annual **Wine Expo**. So if you're into legs, bouquets, Reislings, Chards, Cabs, Noirs, and Zins...then this is definitely your kinda place! Some of California's top wineries will be on hand—serving their finest years. Remember life it too short to drink *cheap* wine!

## Redondo Beach, California

First Sunday in May
(Call Chamber for hours)

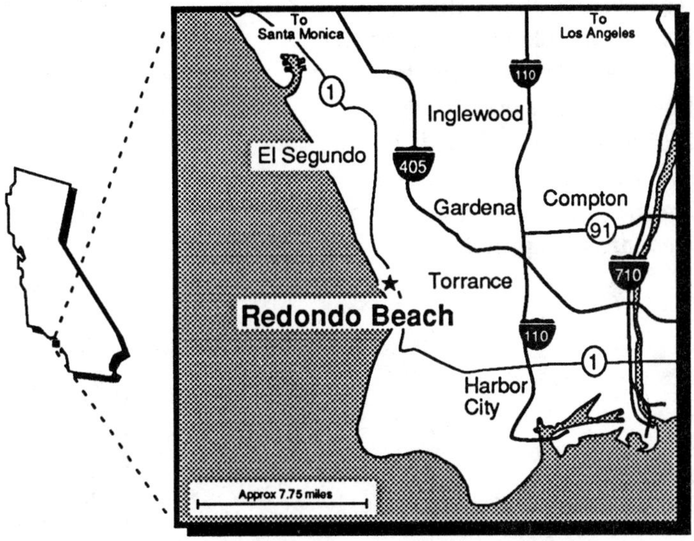


*Up-to-date festival information is available from:*
*Redondo Beach Chamber of Commerce*
*(213) 376-6911*

## What's goin' on...

Town population: **62,400**
Last year's attendance: **1,200**
Average outdoor temperature: **80°**
Festival location: **Seaside Lagoon**

| | |
|---|---|
| X | Wine tasting/beer for sale |
| X | Food booths |
| X | Arts/crafts for sale |
| X | Live music |
| X | Clowns |
| X | Face painters |
| X | Childrens games |
| X | Animal exhibits/petting zoo |
| | Dogs allowed on leash |
| X | Lost and found |
| X | Bicycle racks |
| X | First aid area available |
| X | Self-brought picnics allowed |
| | Self-brought alcohol allowed |
| | Stroller/wheelchair rentals available |

| | |
|---|---|
| | Parade |
| | Parking fee |
| | Entrance fee |
| | Camping facilities |
| X | Boating facilities: Pacific Ocean |
| | RV facilities w/ hookups |
| X | Accomodations in town |
| X | Restaurants in town |

# *Desert Empire Spring Fair*

THE **DESERT EMPIRE Spring Fair** in Ridgecrest has it all—from clowns, jugglers, and a petting zoo for the kids, to food, arts and crafts booths of all kinds, and live music all day till midnight. Located in the northern Mojave Desert, this little town of Ridgecrest does an outstanding job welcoming the freshness of spring!

## Ridgecrest, California

Second Thurs. - Sun. in May
Hours vary

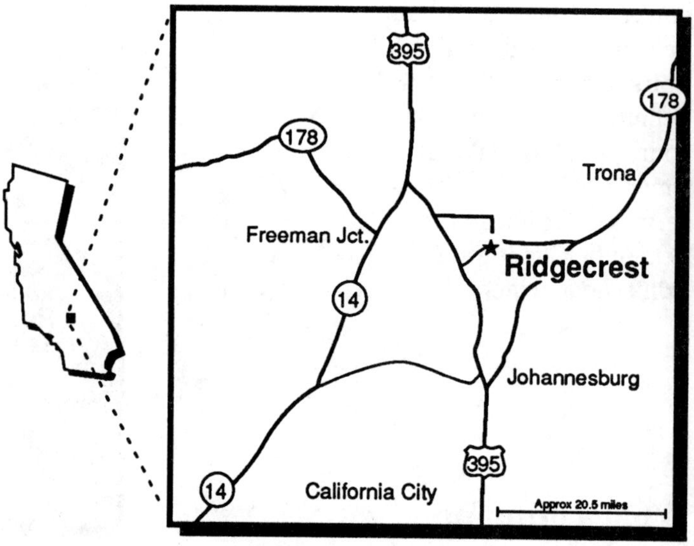


## What's goin' on...

Town population: **28,639**
Last year's attendance: **N/A**
Average outdoor temperature: **95°**
Festival location: **Fairgrounds**

*Up-to-date festival information is available from:*
*Ridgecrest Desert Empire Fairgrounds*
*(619) 375-8000*

- ✗ Wine tasting/beer for sale
- ✗ Food booths
- ✗ Arts/crafts for sale
- ✗ Live music
- ✗ Clowns
- ✗ Face painters
- Childrens games
- ✗ Animal exhibits/petting zoo
- ✗ Dogs allowed on leash
- ✗ Lost and found
- ✗ Bicycle racks
- First aid area available
- Self-brought picnics allowed
- Self-brought alcohol allowed
- Stroller/wheelchair rentals available

- Parade
- Parking fee
- ✗ Entrance fee: (prices not avbl.)
- ✗ Camping facilities: [illegible] miles away
- ✗ Boating facilities: Lake Isabella
- ✗ RV facilities w/ hookups: In town
- ✗ Accomodations in town
  Pioneer Motel, Heritage House, El Rancho Motel, Econolodge, Carriage Inn
- ✗ Restaurants in town
  Sandpiper, The Hideaway, White Star Dining Company, Farris' at the Heritage, Schooner Saloon

# *National Orange Show*

LIVESTOCK SHOWS, TOP name entertainment, carnival rides, games, rodeos, rock and country music, wine tasting, citrus exhibits, and lots and lots of sweet-smelling oranges headline the **National Orange Show** in southern California! This revelry is scads of fun! And you won't go hungry either...plenty of hot dogs, hamburgers, and ethnic food booths *filled* with Thai, Chinese, Greek, and Italian goodies!

## San Bernadino, California

Second Thursday through the third Sunday in May

Hours vary

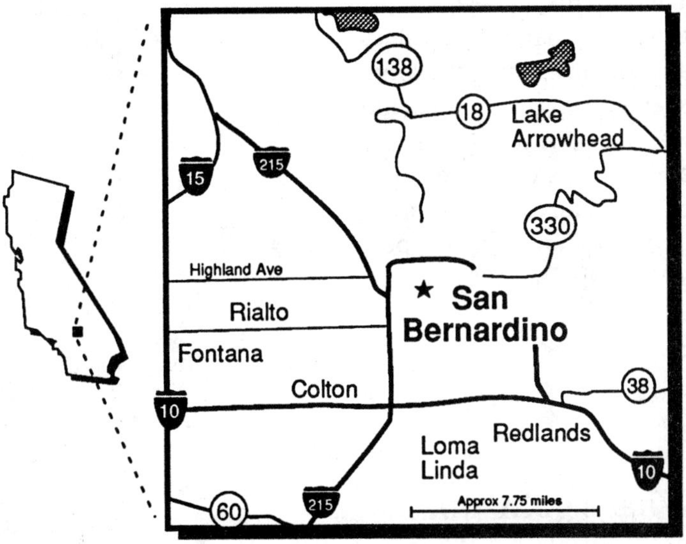


*Up-to-date festival information is available from:*
*San Bernadino Chamber of Commerce*
*(714) 889-3980*

## What's goin' on...

Town population: **160,000**
Last year's attendance: **107,446**
Average outdoor temperature: **78°**
Festival location: **Orange Show Ground**

| | |
|---|---|
| X | Wine tasting/beer for sale |
| X | Food booths |
| X | Arts/crafts for sale |
| X | Live music |
| | Clowns |
| X | Face painters |
| | Childrens games |
| X | Animal exhibits/petting zoo |
| | Dogs allowed on leash |
| X | Lost and found |
| X | Bicycle racks |
| X | First aid area available |
| | Self-brought picnics allowed |
| | Self-brought alcohol allowed |
| | Stroller/wheelchair rentals available |

| | |
|---|---|
| X | Parade: Every day |
| X | Parking fee: $4 |
| X | Entrance fee: $5 |
| X | Camping facilities: 10 miles |
| X | Boating facilities: Lake Perris |
| X | RV facilities w/ hookups: In town |
| X | Accomodations in town<br>San Bernadino Hilton, Maruko Hotel, La Quinta, TraveLodge |
| X | Restaurants in town<br>TGI Fridays, Spencers, La Pontinier, Bobby McGees |

SOUTHERN

# *Sunset Beach Art Festival*

THE SMELL OF SALTY AIR and the screech of seagulls keep 'em coming to the **Sunset Beach Art Festival!** There's an art show, sculpture, hand-painted clothing, and leather goods; the food scene spotlights homemade ice cream, cakes, and pies; and the kids will have a *blast* at the children's craft-making booths! What a way to spend a Mother's Day at the beach.

## Sunset Beach, California

Mother's Day weekend
Daily 10:00 AM - 5:00 PM

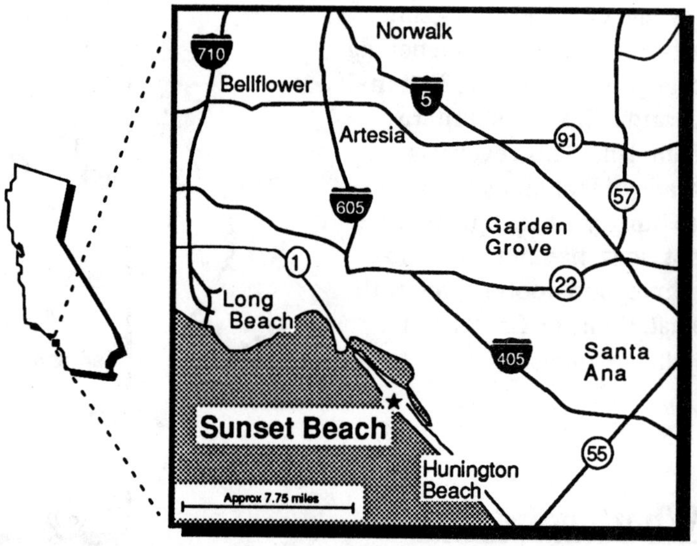


*Up-to-date festival information is available from:*
*Sunset Beach Chamber of Commerce*
*(213) 592-1777*

## What's goin' on...

Town population: **2,300**
Last year's attendance: **3,000**
Average outdoor temperature: **75°**
Festival location: **Community Ctr.**

| | |
|---|---|
| | Wine tasting/beer for sale |
| ✗ | Food booths |
| ✗ | Arts/crafts for sale |
| ✗ | Live music |
| | Clowns |
| | Face painters |
| | Childrens games |
| | Animal exhibits/petting zoo |
| ✗ | Dogs allowed on leash |
| ✗ | Lost and found |
| ✗ | Bicycle racks |
| ✗ | First aid area available |
| ✗ | Self-brought picnics allowed |
| | Self-brought alcohol allowed |
| | Stroller/wheelchair rentals available |

| | |
|---|---|
| | Parade |
| | Parking fee |
| | Entrance fee |
| ✗ | Camping facilities: [illegible] miles |
| ✗ | Boating facilities: Anaheim Bay |
| ✗ | RV facilities w/ hookups: 20 miles |
| ✗ | Accomodations in town<br>Sunset B&B, Islander, Lighthouse Motel, Huntington Beach Best Western |
| ✗ | Restaurants in town<br>Harpoon Harry's, Captain Jacks, Daimon, Red Onion |

# *Wildflower Show & Art Mart*

THE JULIAN TOWN HALL IS where the Julian Women's Club hosts the annual **Wildflower Show & Art Mart**. This week-long celebration in May spotlights the wildflowers of California and highlights arts and crafts relating to these little beauties. The Menghini Winery is on hand to offer a taste of the grapes, and there are wonderful little antique stores in town to explore.

## Julian, California

Third week in May
Daily 9:00 AM - 5:00 PM

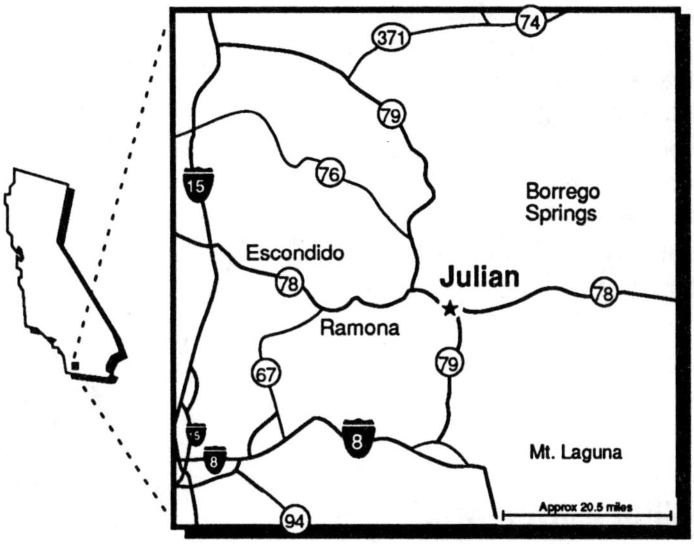


*Up-to-date festival information is available from:*
*Julian Chamber of Commerce*
*(619) 765-1857*

## What's goin' on...

Town population: **2,500**
Last year's attendance: **4,000**
Average outdoor temperature: **70°**
Festival location: **Town Hall**

| | |
|---|---|
| X | Wine tasting/beer for sale |
| | Food booths |
| X | Arts/crafts for sale |
| X | Live music |
| | Clowns |
| | Face painters |
| | Childrens games |
| | Animal exhibits/petting zoo |
| X | Dogs allowed on leash |
| X | Lost and found |
| | Bicycle racks |
| | First aid area available |
| X | Self-brought picnics allowed |
| X | Self-brought alcohol allowed |
| | Stroller/wheelchair rentals available |

| | |
|---|---|
| | Parade |
| | Parking fee |
| | Entrance fee |
| X | Camping facilities: 5 miles |
| X | Boating facilities: 10 miles |
| X | RV facilities w/ hookups: 5 miles |
| X | Accomodations in town |
| X | Restaurants in town |

# *Spring Festival of Arts*

THE STUDIO CITY **SPRING Festival of Arts** displays watercolor and oil paintings from some of the area's elite talent. Along with the exceptional handcrafted items available—such as hand-decorated stationery, household items, and needlework—all of the art is for sale. Adjacent to Studio City is Universal City, with its remarkable Universal Studio Tours.

## Studio City, California

Mother's Day weekend
Daily 10:00 AM - 5:00 PM

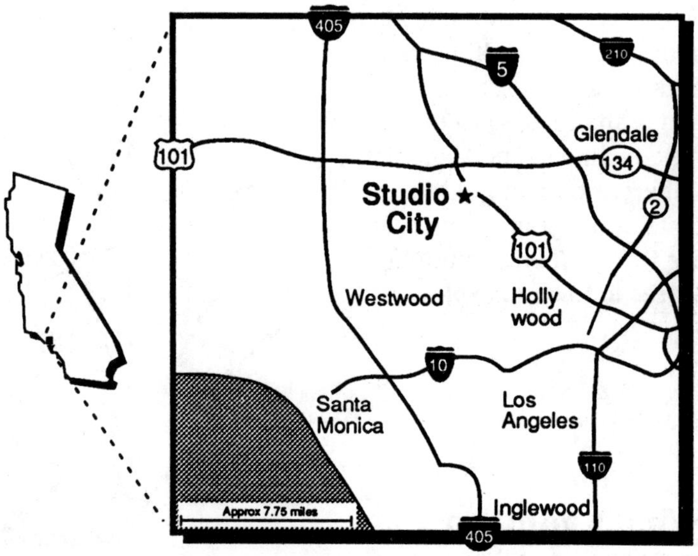


*Up-to-date festival information is available from:*
*Studio City Rotary Club*
*(818) 990-2628*

## What's goin' on...

Town population: **35,000**
Last year's attendance: **5,000**
Average outdoor temperature: **80°**
Festival location: **Park**

- [ ] Wine tasting/beer for sale
- [ ] Food booths
- [X] Arts/crafts for sale
- [ ] Live music
- [ ] Clowns
- [ ] Face painters
- [ ] Childrens games
- [ ] Animal exhibits/petting zoo
- [X] Dogs allowed on leash
- [X] Lost and found
- [X] Bicycle racks
- [ ] First aid area available
- [X] Self-brought picnics allowed
- [ ] Self-brought alcohol allowed
- [ ] Stroller/wheelchair rentals available

- [ ] Parade
- [ ] Parking fee
- [ ] Entrance fee
- [ ] Camping facilities
- [ ] Boating facilities
- [ ] RV facilities w/ hookups
- [X] Accomodations in town
  Valley Hilton, Sportsmen's Lodge
- [X] Restaurants in town
  Art's Deli, Jerry's Famous Deli, St. Moritz, Sportsmen's

# *California Strawberry Festival*

DRESS IN YOUR "BERRY" best for the Friday-night black-tie event that launches the **California Strawberry Festival**! This festival finds the honored fruit dipped in chocolate, whipped into shakes, smothered between layers of chocolate cake, whipped-cream-topped, and stark naked! The Strawberry Shortcake Eating and Strawberry Recipe Contests are two events not to miss! It's ***berry*** good!

## Oxnard, California

Third weekend in May (beginning Friday)
Hours vary

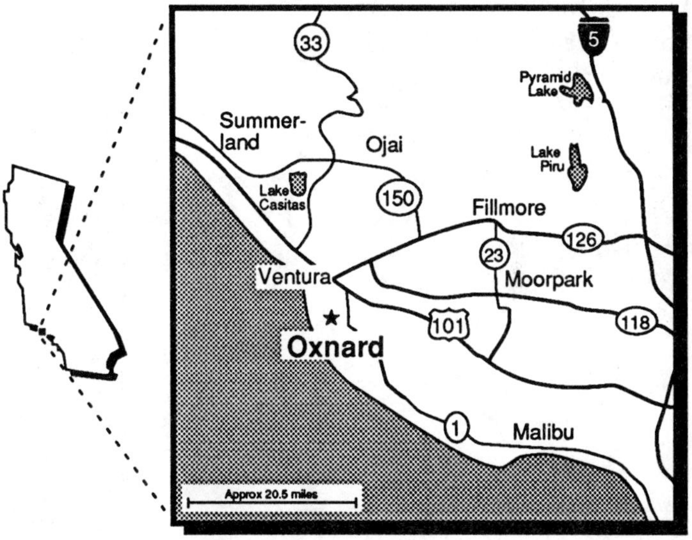


## What's goin' on...

Town population: **25,000**
Last year's attendance: **80,000**
Average outdoor temperature: **78°**
Festival location: **Oxnard State Beach Park**

*Up-to-date festival information is available from:*
*Oxnard Chamber of Commerce*
*(805) 487-6305*

| | |
|---|---|
| X | Wine tasting/beer for sale |
| X | Food booths |
| X | Arts/crafts for sale |
| X | Live music |
| X | Clowns |
| X | Face painters |
| X | Childrens games |
| X | Animal exhibits/petting zoo |
| X | Dogs allowed on leash |
| X | Lost and found |
| X | Bicycle racks |
| X | First aid area available |
| | Self-brought picnics allowed |
| | Self-brought alcohol allowed |
| | Stroller/wheelchair rentals available |

| | |
|---|---|
| | Parade |
| | Parking fee |
| X | Entrance fee: S $2; A $3; K $1 |
| X | Camping facilities: 1 mile |
| X | Boating facilities: Channel Is. Harbor |
| X | RV facilities w/ hookups: 4 miles |
| X | Accomodations in town<br>Embassy Suites, Casa Sirena, Crystal Lodge, Vagabond, Surfside Motel, Angle Motel |
| X | Restaurants in town<br>Filomena's, Siam BBQ |

# *Richmond Street Fair*

IT NEVER RAINS IN SOUTHern California—or so they say! Come and see for yourself at the **Richmond Street Faire** in El Segundo! This annual event attracts people from all over the L.A. area, who come to the coast for fresh seafood and to see what the local artists have been crafting and painting over the past year. Located just south of LAX airport, El Segundo is a tad north of "Manhappenin" Beach.

## El Segundo, California

Third Saturday in May
10:00 AM - 5:00 PM

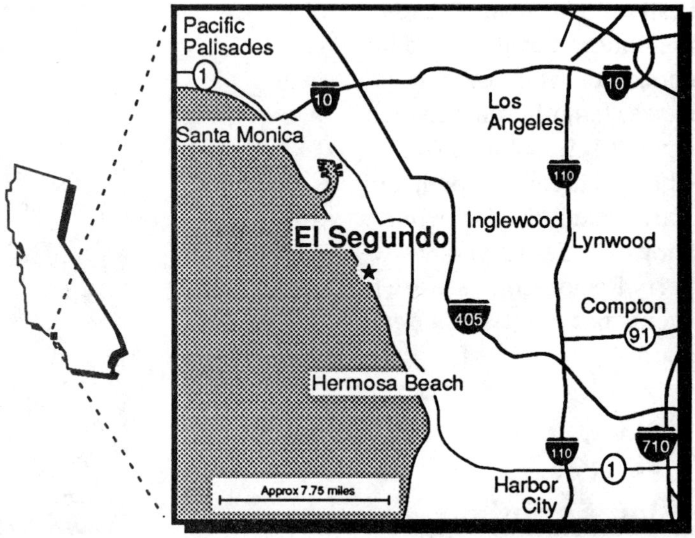


*Up-to-date festival information is available from:*
*El Segundo Chamber of Commerce*
*(213) 322-1220*

## What's goin' on...

Town population: **15,500**
Last year's attendance: **4,000**
Average outdoor temperature: **75°**
Festival location: **Richmond St.**

| | |
|---|---|
| | Wine tasting/beer for sale |
| X | Food booths |
| X | Arts/crafts for sale |
| X | Live music |
| X | Clowns |
| X | Face painters |
| X | Childrens games |
| | Animal exhibits/petting zoo |
| X | Dogs allowed on leash |
| X | Lost and found |
| X | Bicycle racks |
| X | First aid area available |
| | Self-brought picnics allowed |
| | Self-brought alcohol allowed |
| | Stroller/wheelchair rentals available |

| | |
|---|---|
| | Parade |
| | Parking fee |
| | Entrance fee |
| X | Camping facilities: 20 miles |
| X | Boating facilities: Pacific Ocean |
| X | RV facilities w/ hookups: 20 miles |
| X | Accomodations in town |
| X | Restaurants in town |

# *Rancho California Balloon & Wine Festival*

## Temecula, California

Third weekend in May

Sat. 1:00 PM - 8:00 PM; Sun. 7:00 AM - 6:00 PM

BOUQUETS OF FINE WINE, A kaleidoscope of brilliant colors, the laughter of children: All fill the air during the **Rancho California Balloon & Wine Festival!** The festivities begin with a 7:00 a.m. lift-off of more than 60 hot-air balloons racing for prizes (rides, $150, include champagne, Festival pin, and souvenir wine glass). The Kids Faire begins at 10:00 with puppet shows, magicians, clowns, and more! This is great fun! (Kids under 6 will be admitted free!)

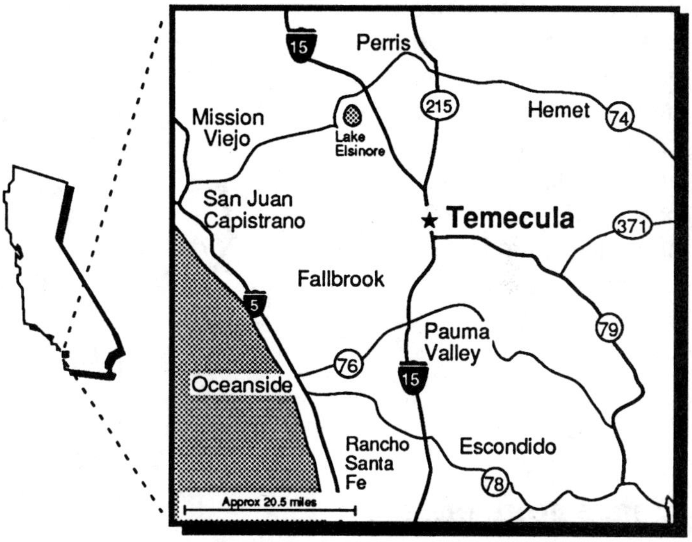


*Up-to-date festival information is available from:*
*Temecula Chamber of Commerce*
*(714) 676-5090*

## What's goin' on...

Town population: **35,000**
Last year's attendance: **100,000**
Average outdoor temperature: **70°**
Festival location: **Lake Skinner**

| | |
|---|---|
| X | Wine tasting/beer for sale |
| X | Food booths |
| X | Arts/crafts for sale |
| X | Live music |
| X | Clowns |
| X | Face painters |
| | Childrens games |
| X | Animal exhibits/petting zoo |
| | Dogs allowed on leash |
| X | Lost and found |
| | Bicycle racks |
| X | First aid area available |
| X | Self-brought picnics allowed |
| X | Self-brought alcohol allowed |
| | Stroller/wheelchair rentals available |

| | |
|---|---|
| | Parade |
| | Parking fee |
| X | Entrance fee: A $5; K $2.50 |
| X | Camping facilities: On-site |
| X | Boating facilities: Lake Skinner |
| X | RV facilities w/ hookups: On-site |
| X | Accomodations in town<br>Loma Linda, Las Brisas |
| X | Restaurants in town<br>Cafe Champagne, Temecula Creek Inn, Guenther's |

SOUTHERN

# *Pioneer Day*

THIS OLD-TIME COUNTRY fair, **Pioneer Day**, celebrates the founding of Whittier in 1887. An entertaining, old-fashioned parade sets the tone. You can watch bread making, butter churning, and quilting and weaving demonstrations—or gnaw on a rib or two. The high school and local bands will be featured on the bandstand!

## Whittier, California

Third Saturday in May
10:00 AM - 4:00 PM

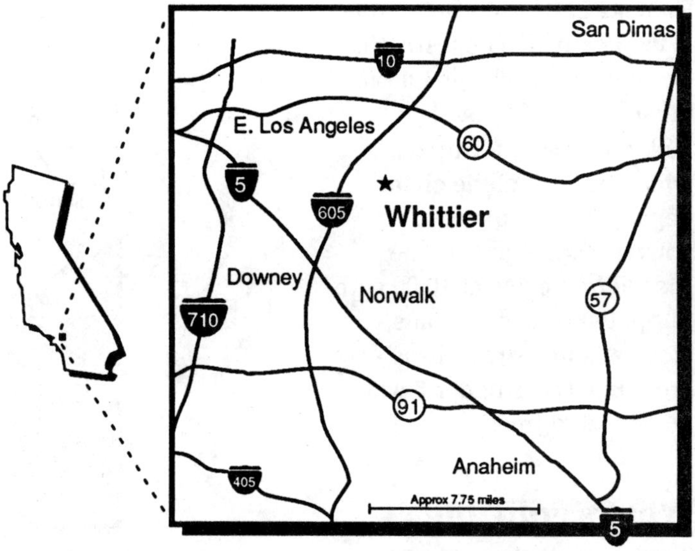


*Up-to-date festival information is available from:*
*Whittier Chamber of Commerce*
*(213) 698-9554*

## What's goin' on...

Town population: **70,000**
Last year's attendance: **1,000**
Average outdoor temperature: **70°**
Festival location: **Central Park**

| | |
|---|---|
| | Wine tasting/beer for sale |
| ✗ | Food booths |
| | Arts/crafts for sale |
| ✗ | Live music |
| | Clowns |
| | Face painters |
| ✗ | Childrens games |
| ✗ | Animal exhibits/petting zoo |
| | Dogs allowed on leash |
| ✗ | Lost and found |
| ✗ | Bicycle racks |
| ✗ | First aid area available |
| ✗ | Self-brought picnics allowed |
| | Self-brought alcohol allowed |
| | Stroller/wheelchair rentals available |

| | |
|---|---|
| ✗ | Parade: Sat. 10:00 AM at City Hall |
| | Parking fee |
| | Entrance fee |
| ✗ | Camping facilities: 4 miles |
| | Boating facilities |
| ✗ | RV facilities w/ hookups: 4 miles |
| ✗ | Accomodations in town<br>Whittier Hilton, Vagabond |
| ✗ | Restaurants in town<br>El Patio, Cafe Rene, Datilo, Village Garden<br>Steak House, New Canton, Los Portales |

# Band in the Park

PACK A PICNIC, GRAB YOUR sunglasses, scoop up a deck chair, and head out to the **Band in the Park**. Now, we understand that the title of the festival says it all: BAND IN THE PARK...but, don't you want to know which band? Well, the headliner is the Long Beach Community Band, and local bands open the shin-dig. If you're not in the mood for your own cooking ...have one of the non-profit groups serve you up a burger!

## Los Alamitos, California

Third Sunday in May
2:00 PM - 6:00 PM

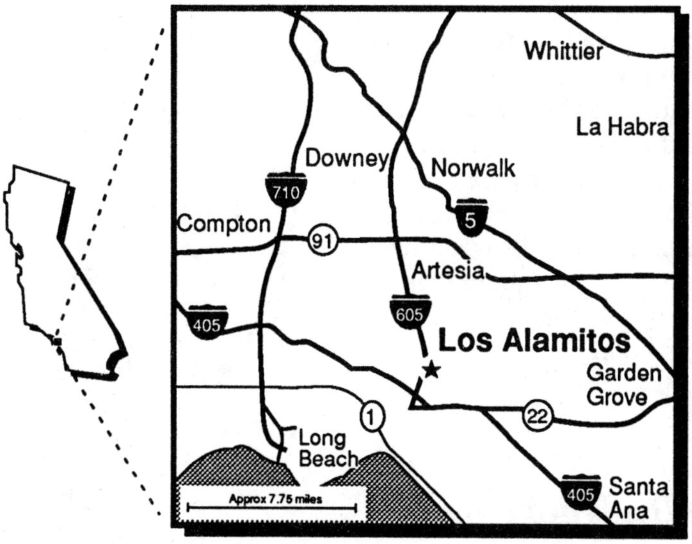


*Up-to-date festival information is available from:*
*Los Alamitos Chamber of Commerce*
*(213) 598-6659*

## What's goin' on...

Town population: **12,200**
Last year's attendance: **900**
Average outdoor temperature: **70°**
Festival location: **Laurel Park**

| | |
|---|---|
| | Wine tasting/beer for sale |
| ✗ | Food booths |
| ✗ | Arts/crafts for sale |
| ✗ | Live music |
| ✗ | Clowns |
| ✗ | Face painters |
| ✗ | Childrens games |
| ✗ | Animal exhibits/petting zoo |
| | Dogs allowed on leash |
| ✗ | Lost and found |
| ✗ | Bicycle racks |
| ✗ | First aid area available |
| ✗ | Self-brought picnics allowed |
| | Self-brought alcohol allowed |
| | Stroller/wheelchair rentals available |

| | |
|---|---|
| | Parade |
| | Parking fee |
| | Entrance fee |
| | Camping facilities |
| | Boating facilities |
| | RV facilities w/ hookups |
| ✗ | Accomodations in town<br>Raddison Inn, Los Alamitos Inn, Don's Turf Motel |
| ✗ | Restaurants in town |

SOUTHERN

# *Strawberry Festival*

GRADEN GROVE GROWS beans, peppers, and corn, but it's famous for its **Strawberry Festival**, which Tom Hoxie started in 1959! It all starts out with a parade, over which Miss Garden Grove reigns, and more than $2,000 worth of trophies are presented to award-winning parade entries. Settlers moved into this beautiful area between 1868 and 1874...and more than 100 years later, it's even more beautiful!

## Garden Grove, California

Memorial Day weekend (beginning Friday)
Daily 10:00 AM - 11:00 PM

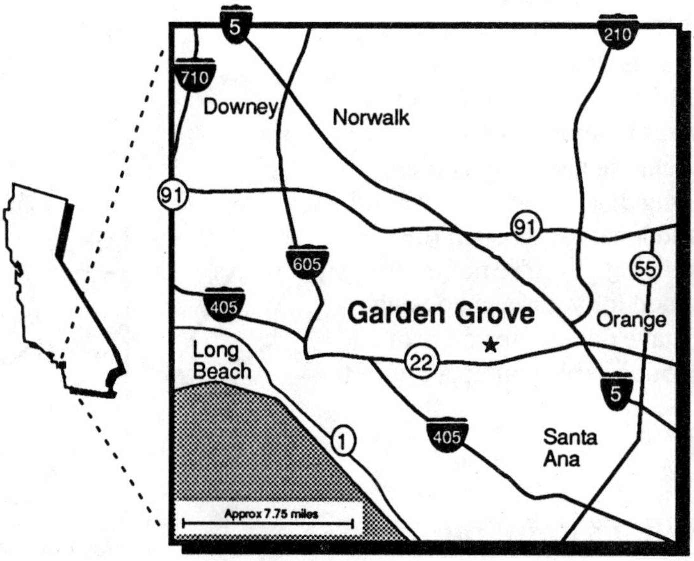


*Up-to-date festival information is available from:*
*Garden Grove Chamber of Commerce*
*(714) 638-7950*

## What's goin' on...

Town population: **123,307**
Last year's attendance: **200,000**
Average outdoor temperature: **70°**
Festival location: **Downtown**

- [ ] Wine tasting/beer for sale
- [X] Food booths
- [X] Arts/crafts for sale
- [X] Live music
- [X] Clowns
- [X] Face painters
- [X] Childrens games
- [ ] Animal exhibits/petting zoo
- [ ] Dogs allowed on leash
- [ ] Lost and found
- [ ] Bicycle racks
- [ ] First aid area available
- [ ] Self-brought picnics allowed
- [ ] Self-brought alcohol allowed
- [ ] Stroller/wheelchair rentals available

- [X] Parade: Sat. 10:30 AM downtown
- [ ] Parking fee
- [X] Entrance fee: (prices not avbl.)
- [ ] Camping facilities
- [X] Boating facilities: Long Beach Marina
- [X] RV facilities w/ hookups: In town
- [X] Accomodations in town
- [X] Restaurants in town
  Red Lobster, Peppers, Lafayette, Black Angus

# Redlands Bicycle Classic

COME ON BABY AND RIDE, ride, ride on down to **Redlands Bicycle Classic!** Lots to see and do! And while in Redlands, take time to visit the Assistencia Mission and the San Bernadino County Museum; or ride around for a look at the Victorian homes.

## Redlands, California

Memorial Day weekend
Sat. 10:00 AM - midnight; Sun. 10:00 AM - 4:00 PM

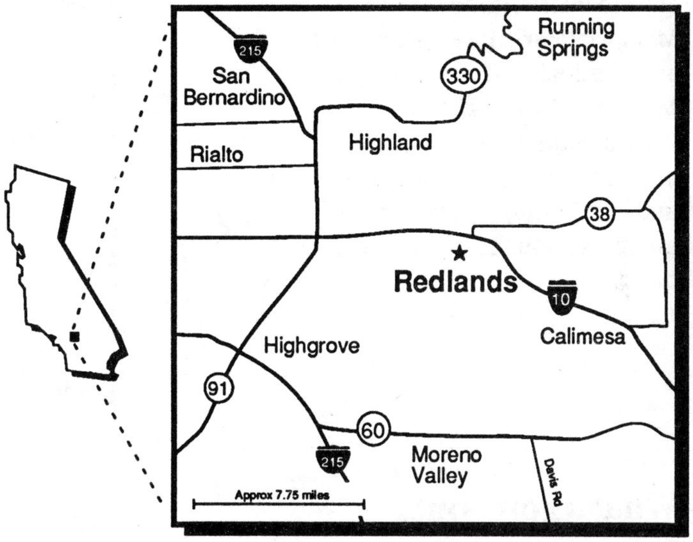


*Up-to-date festival information is available from:*
*Redlands Chamber of Commerce*
*(714) 793-2546*

## What's goin' on...

Town population: **62,000**
Last year's attendance: **20,000**
Average outdoor temperature: **80°**
Festival location: **Downtown (Citrus Ave.)**

| | |
|---|---|
| X | Wine tasting/beer for sale |
| X | Food booths |
| | Arts/crafts for sale |
| X | Live music |
| | Clowns |
| | Face painters |
| | Childrens games |
| | Animal exhibits/petting zoo |
| X | Dogs allowed on leash |
| X | Lost and found |
| X | Bicycle racks |
| X | First aid area available |
| X | Self-brought picnics allowed |
| | Self-brought alcohol allowed |
| | Stroller/wheelchair rentals available |

| | |
|---|---|
| | Parade |
| | Parking fee |
| | Entrance fee |
| | Camping facilities |
| | Boating facilities |
| | RV facilities w/ hookups |
| X | Accomodations in town<br>Goodnite Inn, Redlands Motor Lodge, Geargianna B&B |
| X | Restaurants in town<br>Vesuvio's, Joe Greensleeves |

# *Grubstake Days Celebration & Rodeo*

**GRUBSTAKE DAYS** IN YUCCA Valley is a fun-filled weekend for *all* involved! While you're there for the festivities, be sure to visit Antone Martin Memorial Park, Pioneertown, and the Joshua Tree National Monument. Back at the festival, you can enjoy dancing till midnight to live music and, on Sunday, enjoy the bluegrass sounds of live local bands.

## Yucca Valley, California

Memorial Day weekend
Daily 10:00 AM - midnight

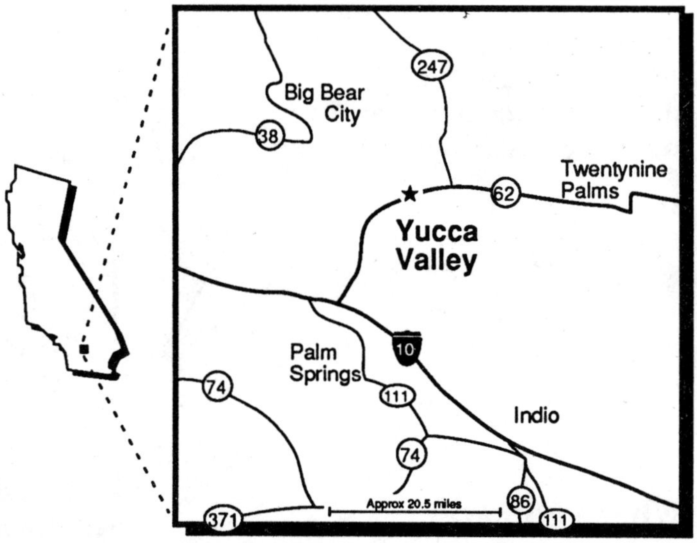


## What's goin' on...

Town population: **28,000**
Last year's attendance: **30,000**
Average outdoor temperature: **80°**
Festival location: **Downtown**

*Up-to-date festival information is available from:*
*Yucca Valley Chamber of Commerce*
*(619) 365-6323*

| | |
|---|---|
| ✗ | Wine tasting/beer for sale |
| ✗ | Food booths |
| ✗ | Arts/crafts for sale |
| ✗ | [illegible] |
| ✗ | Clowns |
| ✗ | Face painters |
| ✗ | Childrens games |
| ✗ | Animal exhibits/petting zoo |
| ✗ | Dogs allowed on leash |
| ✗ | Lost and found |
| ✗ | Bicycle racks |
| ✗ | First aid area available |
| ✗ | Self-brought picnics allowed |
| | Self-brought alcohol allowed |
| | Stroller/wheelchair rentals available |

| | |
|---|---|
| ✗ | Parade: Sat. 10:00 AM on Main St. |
| ✗ | Parking fee: $1 |
| ✗ | Entrance fee: Rodeo only |
| ✗ | Camping facilities: 20 miles |
| | Boating facilities |
| ✗ | RV facilities w/ hookups: 2 miles |
| ✗ | Accomodations in town<br>Super 8, Yucca Inn, Oasis of Eden, Desert View |
| ✗ | Restaurants in town<br>Stefano's Italian, Mandarin Chinese, Edchada's Mexican |

# *Fiesta de las Artes*

THE **FIESTA DE LAS ARTES** is such a fantastic bash...that it happens *twice* a year! Yessiree! There's a May celebration and a September Fiesta in the fall. With more than 100,000 festival hoppers attending last year, the 400 or so artists and craftspersons are kept very busy during the Beach's winter months. The International Food Pavilion boasts more than 30 delicious food booths not to be missed...

## Hermosa Beach, California

Memorial Day weekend
Daily 10:00 AM - 6:00 PM

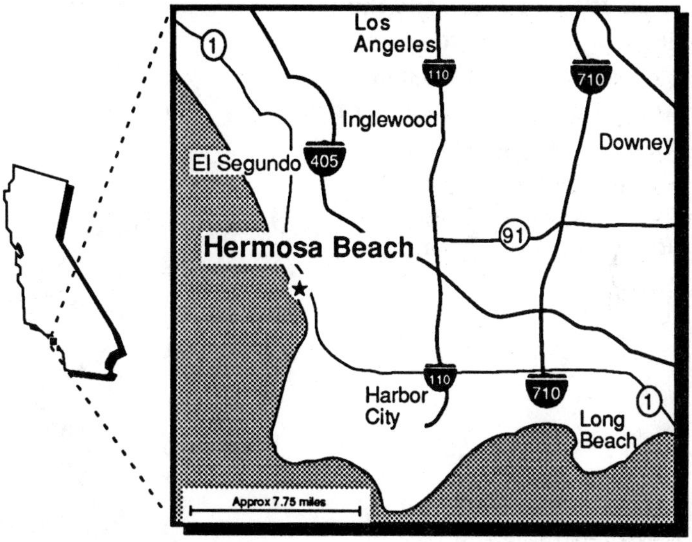


## What's goin' on...

Town population: **19,000**
Last year's attendance: **100,000**
Average outdoor temperature: **76°**
Festival location: **Downtown**

*Up-to-date festival information is available from:*
*Hermosa Beach Chamber of Commerce*
*(213) 376-0951*

| | |
|---|---|
| | Wine tasting/beer for sale |
| X | Food booths |
| X | Arts/crafts for sale |
| X | Live music |
| X | Clowns |
| X | Face painters |
| X | Childrens games |
| X | Animal exhibits/petting zoo |
| X | Dogs allowed on leash |
| X | Lost and found |
| | Bicycle racks |
| X | First aid area available |
| X | Self-brought picnics allowed |
| | Self-brought alcohol allowed |
| | Stroller/wheelchair rentals available |

| | |
|---|---|
| | Parade |
| X | Parking fee: $2 |
| | Entrance fee |
| | Camping facilities |
| X | Boating facilities: Pacific Ocean |
| X | RV facilities w/ hookups: In town |
| X | Accomodations in town |
| X | Restaurants in town<br>Ajetis, Cantina Real, Cafe Christopher, Good Stuff, Mermaid's |

# *A Day in the Country*

**A DAY IN THE COUNTRY** IS just what you need after a tough week of the same ol' grind! Tara, the elephant, will be on hand for rides, and the kids will also enjoy the cart and pony rides. Adults may prefer the full-scale auction of art, crafts, services, and travel. There's lots to do in the Ojai area, and Magic Mountain is just 45 minutes away.

## Ojai, California

Fourth Saturday in May
10:00 AM - 5:00 PM

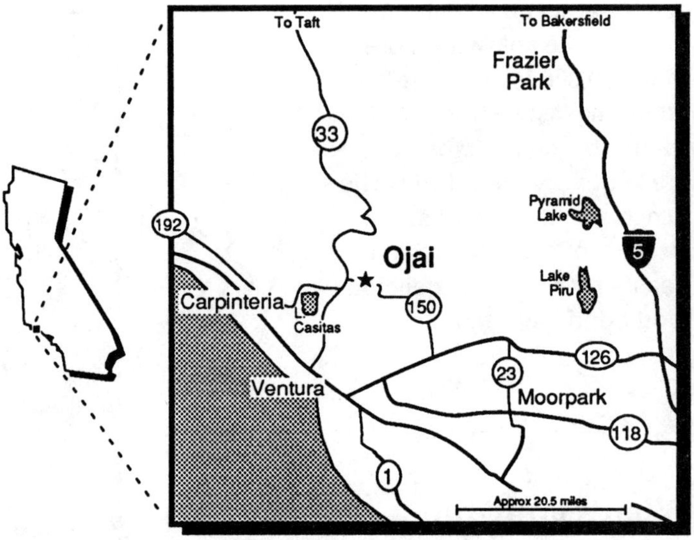


*Up-to-date festival information is available from:*
*Ojai Chamber of Commerce*
*(805) 646-8126*

## What's goin' on...

Town population: **7,000**
Last year's attendance: **500**
Average outdoor temperature: **85°**
Festival location: **N/A**

| | |
|---|---|
| | Wine tasting/beer for sale |
| X | Food booths |
| X | Arts/crafts for sale |
| X | Live music |
| | Clowns |
| | Face painters |
| X | Childrens games |
| X | Animal exhibits/petting zoo |
| | Dogs allowed on leash |
| X | Lost and found |
| | Bicycle racks |
| X | First aid area available |
| X | Self-brought picnics allowed |
| | Self-brought alcohol allowed |
| | Stroller/wheelchair rentals available |

| | |
|---|---|
| | Parade |
| | Parking fee |
| | Entrance fee |
| X | Camping facilities: 5 miles |
| X | Boating facilities: Lake Casitas |
| X | RV facilities w/ hookups: 15 miles |
| X | Accomodations in town: Ojai Valley Inn, Best Western, Capri Motel, Oakridge Inn, Los Padres Inn, Casa Ojai |
| | Restaurants in town: L'Auberge, Roger Keller's Restaurant, The Nest, The Ranch House, Ojai Valley Inn |

# *I MADINNARI Italian Street Painting Festival*

THE **I MADINNARI ITALIAN Street Painting Festival** in Santa Barbara is fabuloso! The piazza of the Old Mission is transformed into the 16th-century tradition of street painting with colored chalk! The International Street Painting Festival is held each year in the village of Grazie di Curtatone, Italy, and The Children's Creative Project is proud to bring this romantic art form to California.

## Santa Barbara, California

Memorial Day (three-day) weekend
Daily 11:00 AM - 6:00 PM

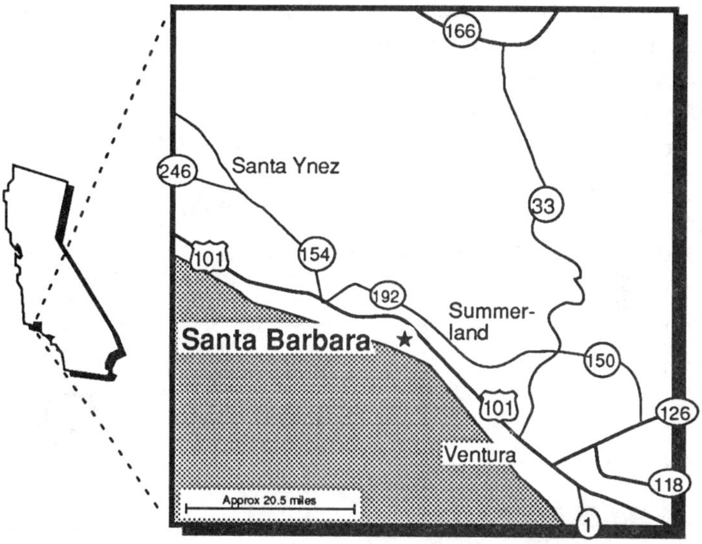


*Up-to-date festival information is available from:*
*Santa Barbara Visitors Bureau*
*(805) 965-3021*

## What's goin' on...

Town population: **350,000**
Last year's attendance: **15,000**
Average outdoor temperature: **80°**
Festival location: **Old Mission**

| | |
|---|---|
| | Wine tasting/beer for sale |
| X | Food booths |
| X | Arts/crafts for sale |
| X | Live music |
| X | Clowns |
| X | Face painters |
| X | Childrens games |
| | Animal exhibits/petting zoo |
| | Dogs allowed on leash |
| X | Lost and found |
| X | Bicycle racks |
| X | First aid area available |
| X | Self-brought picnics allowed |
| | Self-brought alcohol allowed |
| | Stroller/wheelchair rentals available |

| | |
|---|---|
| | Parade |
| | Parking fee |
| | Entrance fee |
| X | Camping facilities: 3 miles |
| X | Boating facilities: Pacific Ocean |
| X | RV facilities w/ hookups: 10 miles |
| X | Accomodations in town |
| X | Restaurants in town<br>Wine Cask, Paradise Cafe, Papagaillos |

# *Western Days*

**WESTERN DAYS** IN VALLEY Center is a perfect example of a rural community's turning out for a day filled with cowboys and a western theme. There are food and craft booths to take in and live music all day long. Be sure to visit the Mt. Palomar Observatory just 19 miles from here and the San Diego Wild Animal Park just 15 short miles away.

## Valley Center, California

Memorial Day
10:00 AM - 8:00 PM

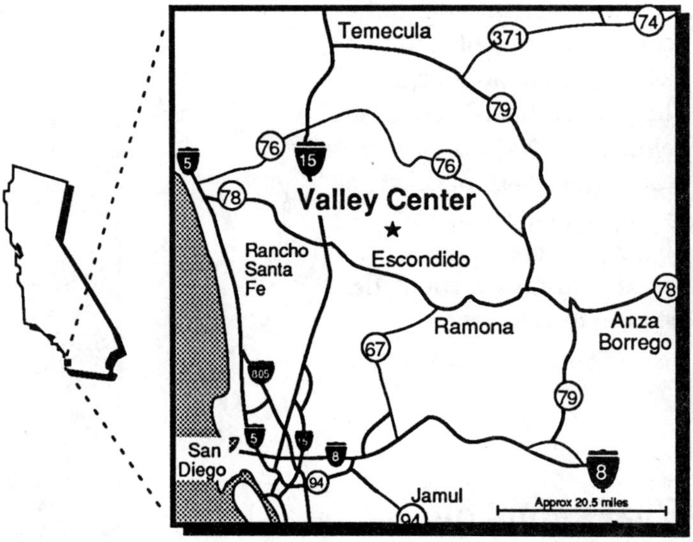


*Up-to-date festival information is available from:*
*Valley Center Chamber of Commerce*
*(619) 749-8472*

### What's goin' on...

Town population: **1,242**
Last year's attendance: **N/A**
Average outdoor temperature: **80°**
Festival location: **N/A**

| | |
|---|---|
| X | Wine tasting/beer for sale |
| X | Food booths |
| X | Arts/crafts for sale |
| X | Live music |
| X | Clowns |
| | Face painters |
| | Childrens games |
| | Animal exhibits/petting zoo |
| | Dogs allowed on leash |
| | Lost and found |
| | Bicycle racks |
| | First aid area available |
| | Self-brought picnics allowed |
| | Self-brought alcohol allowed |
| | Stroller/wheelchair rentals available |

| | |
|---|---|
| X | Parade: 10:00 AM at Matix Field |
| X | Parking fee: $1 |
| | Entrance fee |
| X | Camping facilities: 3 miles |
| X | Boating facilities: Dixon Lake |
| X | RV facilities w/ hookups: 3 miles |
| | Accomodations in town |
| X | Restaurants in town<br>Papa Bear's, Fat Ivors, Grouchy Gaucho's |

# *Ojai Music Festival*

FOR 45 YEARS THE **OJAI Music Festival** has offered a feast of rare old and challenging new music, in informal ease under the oaks and sycamores of the concert bowl. The Festival is noted for the presence of the most distinguished composers of our age—from Stravinsky at the outset, to Pierre Boulez and Elliott Carter at the end of the 80's. In 1991, Sir Peter Maxwell Davies will be among the featured composers.

## Ojai, California

Weekend following Memorial Day
Afternoon and evening performances

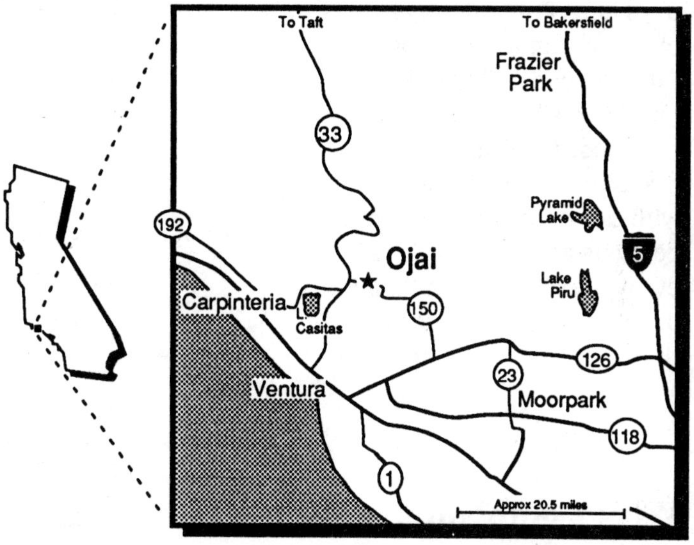


## What's goin' on...

Town population: **7,500**
Last year's attendance: **6,240**
Average outdoor temperature: **72°**
Festival location: **Libbey Park Ampitheater**

*Up-to-date festival information is available from:*
*Ojai Chamber of Commerce*
*(805) 646-8126*

| | |
|---|---|
| | Wine tasting/beer for sale |
| ✗ | Food booths |
| ✗ | Arts/crafts for sale |
| ✗ | Live music |
| | Clowns |
| | Face painters |
| | Childrens games |
| | Animal exhibits/petting zoo |
| | Dogs allowed on leash |
| ✗ | Lost and found |
| ✗ | Bicycle racks |
| ✗ | First aid area available |
| ✗ | Self-brought picnics allowed |
| | Self-brought alcohol allowed |
| | Stroller/wheelchair rentals available |

| | |
|---|---|
| | Parade |
| | Parking fee |
| ✗ | Entrance fee: (prices not avbl.) |
| ✗ | Camping facilities: 1 mile |
| ✗ | Boating facilities: Lake Casitas |
| ✗ | RV facilities w/ hookups: 1 mile |
| ✗ | Accomodations in town<br>Ojai Valley Inn, Best Western, Capri Motel, Oakridge Inn, Los Padres Inn, Casa Ojai |
| ✗ | Restaurants in town<br>L'Auberge, Roger Keller's Restaurant, The Nest, The Ranch House, Ojai Valley Inn |

# *Fontana Days*

NOW HERE'S ONE FESTIVAL that just keeps getting better and better! Seventy-eight years young and now four days long, **Fontana Days** promises fun for everyone! There's scads of good entertainment, plenty of barbecues to choose from, arts-and-crafts booths overflowing with one-of-a-kind items, and contests and competitions everywhere! Veterans Park is definitely the *happening* place to be!

## Fontana, California

First weekend in June
All day

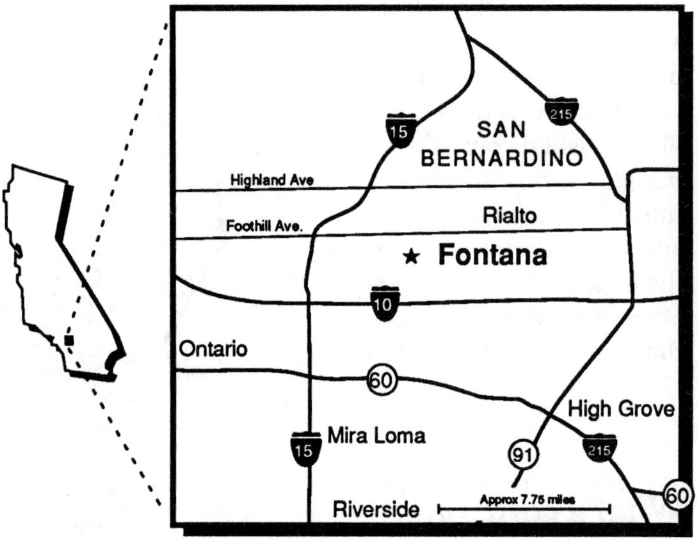


*Up-to-date festival information is available from:*
*Fontana Chamber of Commerce*
*(714) 822-4433*

## What's goin' on...

Town population: **76,000**
Last year's attendance: **35,000**
Average outdoor temperature: **85°**
Festival location: **Veterans Park**

- X Wine tasting/beer for sale
- X Food booths
- X Arts/crafts for sale
- X Live music
- X Clowns
- Face painters
- X Childrens games
- Animal exhibits/petting zoo
- Dogs allowed on leash
- X Lost and found
- Bicycle racks
- X First aid area available
- Self-brought picnics allowed
- Self-brought alcohol allowed
- Stroller/wheelchair rentals available

- X Parade: (time & date not avbl.)
- Parking fee
- Entrance fee
- X Camping facilities 8 miles
- X Boating facilities: Big Bear Lake
- X RV facilities w/ hookups: 8 miles
- X Accomodations in town
- X Restaurants in town

# Glennville Roundup

GIT 'CHER HAT AND PULL your boots on for the annual **Glennville Roundup** at the rodeo grounds. You'll witness wild-cow milking; taste savory deep-pit barbecued chicken, ribs, and beef; and dance, dance, dance till the clock strikes midnight. The rodeo lasts all day on Sunday, right after the morning parade.

## Glennville, California

First weekend in June
Hours vary

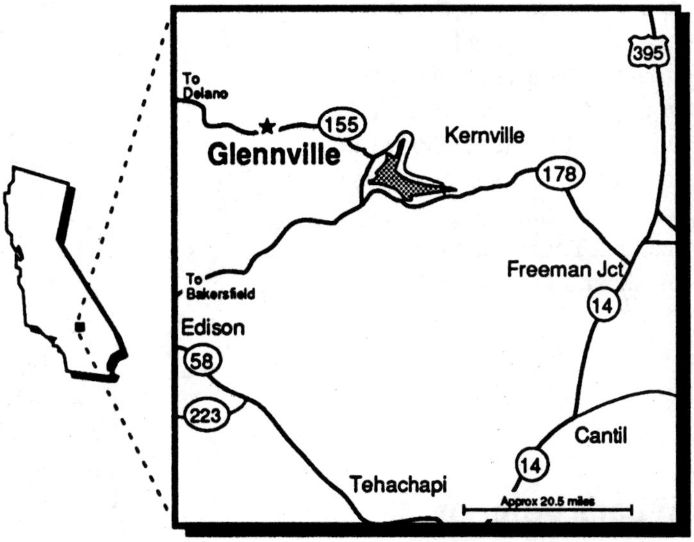


*Up-to-date festival information is available from:*
*Glennville Chamber of Commerce*
*(805) 861-2367*

## What's goin' on...

Town population: **2,000**
Last year's attendance: **N/A**
Average outdoor temperature: **78°**
Festival location: **Rodeo grounds**

X Wine tasting/beer for sale
X Food booths
X Arts/crafts for sale
X Live music
X Clowns
X Face painters
X Childrens games
X Animal exhibits/petting zoo
Dogs allowed on leash
X Lost and found
Bicycle racks
X First aid area available
X Self-brought picnics allowed
Self-brought alcohol allowed
Stroller/wheelchair rentals available

X Parade: Sun.
Parking fee
X Entrance fee: (prices not avbl.)
X Camping facilities: 25 miles
X Boating facilities: Lake Isabella
X RV facilities w/ hookups: 25 miles
Accomodations in town
Restaurants in town

# *San Marcos Chili Cook-Off*

THE FOLKS OF SAN MARCOS are serious about their annual **Chili Cook-Off!** You'll find booth decorators, cooks, and devotees up at the crack of dawn preparing for the two-day event. If chili leaves you cold, then go ahead and fill up on the other good stuff such as corn dogs, churros, ice cream, hamburgers, and nachos! There's also live music and games for the kids.

## San Marcos, California

First weekend in June
Daily: 10:00 AM - 6:00 PM

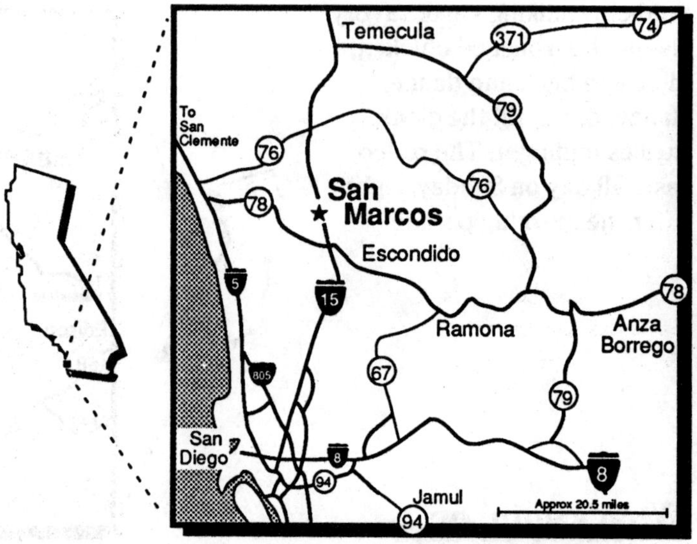


*Up-to-date festival information is available from:*
*San Marcos Chamber of Commerce*
*(619) 744-1270*

## What's goin' on...

Town population: **37,000**
Last year's attendance: **7,500**
Average outdoor temperature: **75°**
Festival location: **Walnut Grove Park**

- ✗ Wine tasting/beer for sale
- ✗ Food booths
- ✗ Arts/crafts for sale
- ✗ Live music
- Clowns
- ✗ Face painters
- ✗ Childrens games
- Animal exhibits/petting zoo
- Dogs allowed on leash
- ✗ Lost and found
- ✗ Bicycle racks
- ✗ First aid area available
- ✗ Self-brought picnics allowed
- Self-brought alcohol allowed
- Stroller/wheelchair rentals available

- ✗ Parade: (time & date not avbl.)
- Parking fee
- ✗ Entrance fee: Adults $5; Kids $3
- ✗ Camping facilities: 5 miles
- ✗ Boating facilities
- ✗ RV facilities w/ hookups: 5 miles
- ✗ Accomodations in town
  San Marcos TraveLodge, La Quinta Inn, San Marcos Motel
- ✗ Restaurants in town
  Bruno's, Jerry Dale's Texas, Katsu, Grecian Gardens, J.K.'s Stage Stop

# *Fiesta del Sol*

TAKE A CALIFORNIA DAY, add an extra dash of sunshine and heaping dose of fun...and what do you have? **Fiesta del Sol!** The young city of Solana Beach really knows how to throw a party—you'll find games for the adults that the kids will find hysterical—and vice-versa!—food booths of every ethnic variety imaginable, and an extensive arts-and-crafts fair! So come on down to where the sun shines all the time!

## Solana Beach, California

First weekend in June
Daily 8:00 AM - 8:00 PM

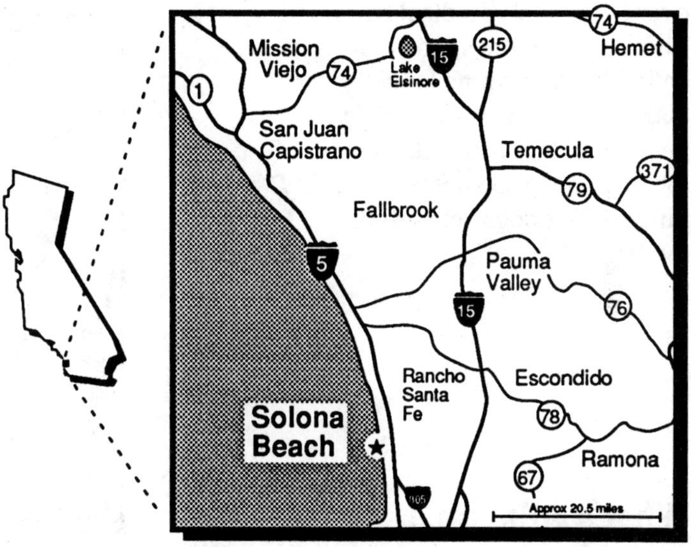


*Up-to-date festival information is available from:*
*Solana Beach Chamber of Commerce*
*(619) 755-4775*

## What's goin' on...

Town population: **15,000**
Last year's attendance: **10,000**
Average outdoor temperature: **70°**
Festival location: **Beach parking lot**

| | |
|---|---|
| X | Wine tasting/beer for sale |
| X | Food booths |
| X | Arts/crafts for sale |
| X | Live music |
| X | Clowns |
| X | Face painters |
| X | Childrens games |
| | Animal exhibits/petting zoo |
| | Dogs allowed on leash |
| X | Lost and found |
| | Bicycle racks |
| X | First aid area available |
| X | Self-brought picnics allowed |
| | Self-brought alcohol allowed |
| | Stroller/wheelchair rentals available |

| | |
|---|---|
| X | Parade: Sat. 11:00 AM on Hwy. 101 |
| | Parking fee |
| | Entrance fee |
| X | Camping facilities: 3 miles |
| X | Boating facilities: Pacific Ocean |
| X | RV facilities w/ hookups: 10 miles |
| X | Accomodations in town |
| X | Restaurants in town |

# *Compton Air Fair*

FOR ALL YOU AIRPLANE buff and buffettes out there—the **Compton Air Fair** is for you! Talk to the pilots, and look over the models on display. There are paintings, posters, shirts, hats, and pins for sale, and a children's entertainment area. You'll also find lots of good grub such as burgers, hot dogs, and ethnic foods.

## Compton, California

Second Saturday in June
10:00 AM - 6:00 PM

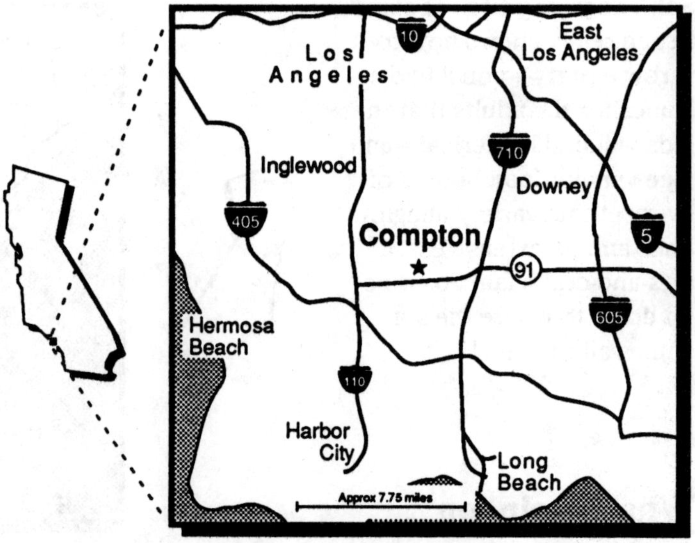


*Up-to-date festival information is available from:*
*Compton Chamber of Commerce*
*(213) 631-8611*

## What's goin' on...

Town population: **100,000**
Last year's attendance: **6,000**
Average outdoor temperature: **78°**
Festival location: **Compton Airport**

| | |
|---|---|
| | Wine tasting/beer for sale |
| ✗ | Food booths |
| ✗ | Arts/crafts for sale |
| | Live music |
| | Clowns |
| | Face painters |
| ✗ | Childrens games |
| | Animal exhibits/petting zoo |
| ✗ | Dogs allowed on leash |
| ✗ | Lost and found |
| ✗ | Bicycle racks |
| ✗ | First aid area available |
| ✗ | Self-brought picnics allowed |
| | Self-brought alcohol allowed |
| ✗ | Stroller/wheelchair rentals available |

| | |
|---|---|
| | Parade |
| | Parking fee |
| | Entrance fee |
| ✗ | Camping facilities: 15 miles |
| ✗ | Boating facilities: Pacific Ocean |
| ✗ | RV facilities w/ hookups: 15 miles |
| ✗ | Accomodations in town |
| ✗ | Restaurants in town |

# *Harbor City Community Fair*

AMONG THE MULTITUDE OF beach communities in Southern California lies Harbor City, with its annual **Community Fair**. The young children will be entertained by clowns and games while you browse through the booths filled with Victorian and modern-day crafts and art items. Greek, Mexican, Thai, and American foods fill the menu for the day!

## Harbor City/Torrance, California

Second Saturday in June
10:00 AM - 5:00 PM

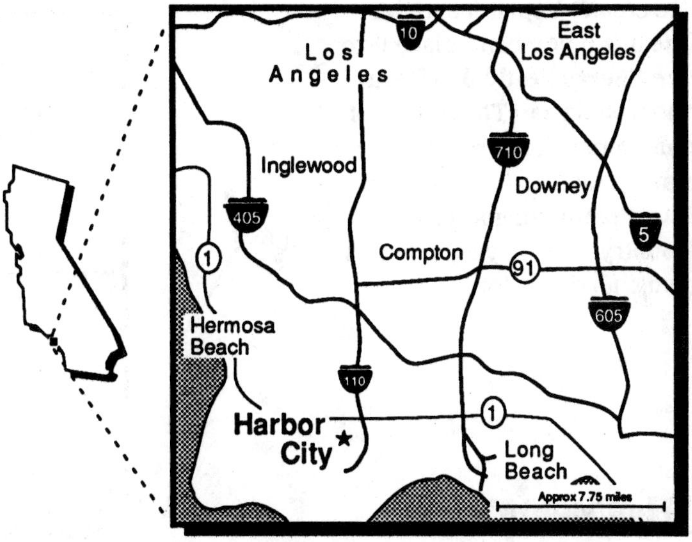


## What's goin' on...

Town population: **36,000**
Last year's attendance: **N/A**
Average outdoor temperature: **80°**
Festival location: **Harbor Park**

*Up-to-date festival information is available from:*
*Harbor City/Torrance Chamber of Commerce*
*(213) 212-6300*

| | |
|---|---|
| | Wine tasting/beer for sale |
| X | Food booths |
| X | Arts/crafts for sale |
| X | Live music |
| X | Clowns |
| X | Face painters |
| X | Childrens games |
| | Animal exhibits/petting zoo |
| | Dogs allowed on leash |
| X | Lost and found |
| X | Bicycle racks |
| X | First aid area available |
| X | Self-brought picnics allowed |
| | Self-brought alcohol allowed |
| | Stroller/wheelchair rentals available |

| | |
|---|---|
| | Parade |
| | Parking fee |
| | Entrance fee |
| X | Camping facilities: 3 miles |
| X | Boating facilities: Long Beach Harbor |
| X | RV facilities w/ hookups: 2 miles |
| X | Accomodations in town<br>Holiday Inn, Quality Inn, TraveLodge |
| X | Restaurants in town<br>Ports O' Call, Papadakis, Nizetich's |

# *Cherry Festival*

OOH, JUST IMAGINE THE wonderful smells...hot cherry pie, homemade cherry jam, cherry tarts, and fresh cherry ice cream! Yep, it'll sure be the pits if you can't make it to the **Cherry Festival** in Beaumont this year! This is lots of fun—a pancake breakfast, parade, games for the youngsters, plenty of good food, country music by local bands, and cherries galore!

## Beaumont, California

Second Wednesday through Sunday in June
Hours vary

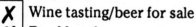

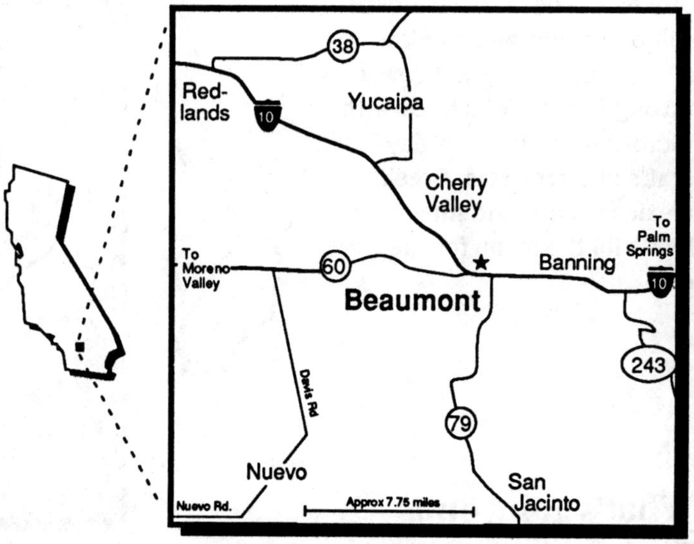


*Up-to-date festival information is available from:*
*Beaumont Chamber of Commerce*
*(714) 845-9541*

## What's goin' on...

Town population: **9,150**
Last year's attendance: **10,000**
Average outdoor temperature: **72°**
Festival location: **Park**

- ✗ Wine tasting/beer for sale
- ✗ Food booths
- ✗ Arts/crafts for sale
- ✗ Live music
- ✗ Clowns
- ✗ Face painters
- ✗ Childrens games
- Animal exhibits/petting zoo
- Dogs allowed on leash
- ✗ Lost and found
- Bicycle racks
- ✗ First aid area available
- ✗ Self-brought picnics allowed
- Self-brought alcohol allowed
- Stroller/wheelchair rentals available

- ✗ Parade: (date & time not avbl.)
- Parking fee
- ✗ Entrance fee: (prices not avbl.)
- ✗ Camping facilities: 5 miles
- ✗ Boating facilities: Lake Perris
- ✗ RV facilities w/ hookups: 5 miles
- ✗ Accomodations in town
  Golden West, Windsor Motel
- ✗ Restaurants in town
  Jimmy's Casa Figuora, Pizza Chalet, Romona's, Rusty Lantern, Roaring 20's Family Pizza

# *Grand Slam Chili Cook-off & Merchant Fair*

GEE, I WONDER WHO'LL BE crowned Mr. Hot Stuff and Miss Chili Pepper at the **Grand Slam Chili Cook-Off and Merchant Fair**!?!? Now, don't be fooled by all the *fun* goin' on...this is a serious competition—the winner goes on to the western regional cook-off! There are all sorts of contests: best hat, best booth, ugliest boot, and the ol' shoot 'n' holler! Come vote for your favorites!

## Granada Hills, California

Third Sunday in June
11:00 AM - 5:00 PM

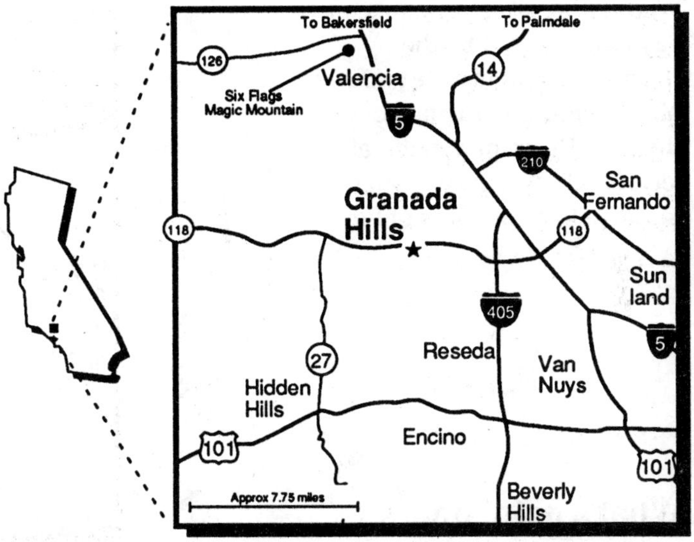


### What's goin' on...

Town population: **70,000**
Last year's attendance: **5,000**
Average outdoor temperature: **80°**
Festival location: **Jenson Filtration Plant**

*Up-to-date festival information is available from:*
*Granada Hills Chamber of Commerce*
*(818) 368-3235*

- X Wine tasting/beer for sale
- X Food booths
- X Arts/crafts for sale
- X Live music
- X Clowns
- Face painters
- X Childrens games
- Animal exhibits/petting zoo
- X Dogs allowed on leash
- X Lost and found
- Bicycle racks
- X First aid area available
- Self-brought picnics allowed
- Self-brought alcohol allowed
- Stroller/wheelchair rentals available

- Parade
- Parking fee
- X Entrance fee: Adults $2; Under 16 free
- X Camping facilities: 10 miles
- X Boating facilities: Lake
- X RV facilities w/ hookups: 10 miles
- X Accomodations in town
  Granada Motel
- X Restaurants in town
  The Odyssey Restaurant

SOUTHERN

# *Whitewater Wednesday*

IN KERNVILLE, THERE'S A certain Wednesday when an awful lot of people call in sick to work! It's **Whitewater Wednesday**! This very special day is sponsored by the Chamber of Commerce and offers white-water trips down the Kern River for a nominal fee. All rafting trips are open to the public...and lots of fun!

## Kernville, California

Third Wednesday in June
9:00 AM - 4:00 PM

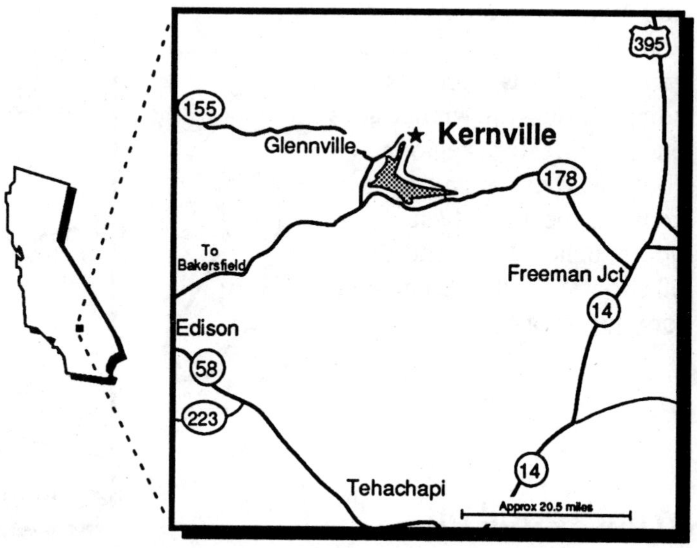


*Up-to-date festival information is available from:*
*Kernville Chamber of Commerce*
*(619) 376-2629*

## What's goin' on...

Town population: **2,500**
Last year's attendance: **200**
Average outdoor temperature: **90°**
Festival location: **Kern River**

| | |
|---|---|
| | Wine tasting/beer for sale |
| | Food booths |
| | Arts/crafts for sale |
| | Live music |
| | Clowns |
| | Face painters |
| | Childrens games |
| | Animal exhibits/petting zoo |
| ✗ | Dogs allowed on leash |
| ✗ | Lost and found |
| | Bicycle racks |
| ✗ | First aid area available |
| ✗ | Self-brought picnics allowed |
| | Self-brought alcohol allowed |
| | Stroller/wheelchair rentals available |

| | |
|---|---|
| | Parade |
| | Parking fee |
| ✗ | Entrance fee: $15 |
| ✗ | Camping facilities, 2 miles |
| ✗ | Boating facilities: Lake Isabella |
| ✗ | RV facilities w/ hookups: In town |
| ✗ | Accomodations in town<br>Lazy River Lodge, Kern Lodge Motel, Hi-Ho Resort Motel, Whispering Pines |
| ✗ | Restaurants in town<br>Cheryl's, Roade End, Chilly Willie's, McNallys, Ewings, El Sombrero |

# *Lompoc Flower Festival*

THE FLOWER SEED CAPITAL of the world will again be ready for one of the best little festivals in the west— the **Lompoc Flower Festival!** Every June since 1952, this valley turns a myriad of color for this festival of flowers, amusement rides, bingo games, a floral parade, great ethnic food dishes, crafts, and colorful entertainment ranging from country to rock! This years theme is "Let's have a Party"...no problem! Lets!

## Lompoc, California

Fourth weekend in June
Hours vary

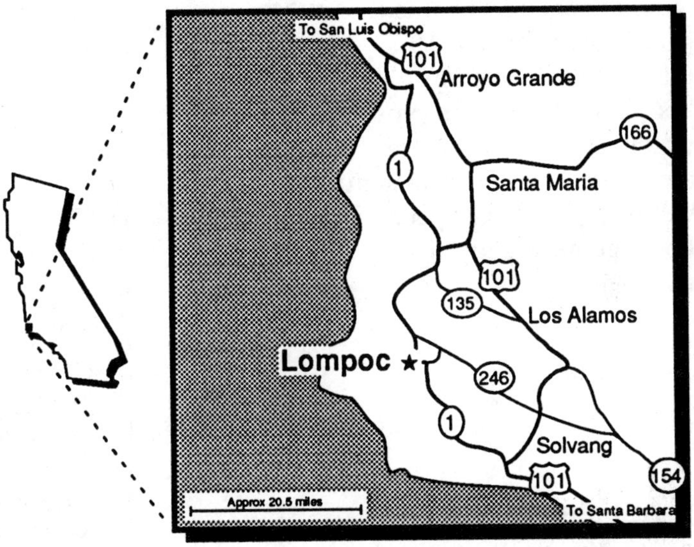


## What's goin' on...

Town population: **33,000**
Last year's attendance: **80,000**
Average outdoor temperature: **70°**
Festival location: **Ryon Park**

*Up-to-date festival information is available from:*
*Lompoc Valley Festival Assn.*
*(805) 736-4567*

| | |
|---|---|
| X | Wine tasting/beer for sale |
| X | Food booths |
| X | Arts/crafts for sale |
| X | Live music |
| X | Clowns |
| X | Face painters |
| X | Childrens games |
| | Animal exhibits/petting zoo |
| | Dogs allowed on leash |
| X | Lost and found |
| | Bicycle racks |
| X | First aid area available |
| X | Self-brought picnics allowed |
| X | Self-brought alcohol allowed |
| X | Stroller/wheelchair rentals available |

| | |
|---|---|
| X | Parade: Sat. 10:00 AM on North H St. |
| X | Parking fee: $2 per car |
| | Entrance fee |
| X | Camping facilities: 2 miles |
| X | Boating facilities: Lake Cachuma |
| X | RV facilities w/ hookups: 2 miles |
| X | Accomodations in town<br>Motel 6, Embassy Suites |
| X | Restaurants in town<br>Dollar Bill, Village Oaks, J.B. McGees |

SOUTHERN

# *Orange County Fiesta*

JUST A FEW MILES INLAND lies Fountain Valley—home to the **Orange County Fiesta** at Mile Square Park. With international food booths galore and more than 60 different arts-and-crafts booths to choose from, you won't be wanting for more anywhere! Live entertainment will keep you shakin' your booty in the streets till midnight!

## Fountain Valley, California

Last Friday in June through the Fourth of July
Hours vary

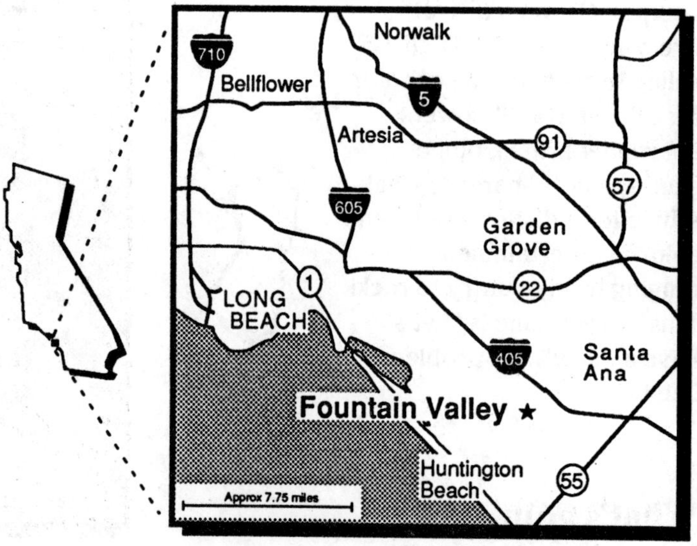


*Up-to-date festival information is available from:*
*Fountain Valley Chamber of Commerce*
*(714) 962-4441*

## What's goin' on...

Town population: **57,000**
Last year's attendance: **55,000**
Average outdoor temperature: **75°**
Festival location: **Mile Square Park**

- X Wine tasting/beer for sale
- X Food booths
- X Arts/crafts for sale
- X Live music
- Clowns
- X Face painters
- X Childrens games
- Animal exhibits/petting zoo
- Dogs allowed on leash
- X Lost and found
- X Bicycle racks
- X First aid area available
- X Self-brought picnics allowed
- Self-brought alcohol allowed
- Stroller/wheelchair rentals available

- Parade
- X Parking fee: $2
- X Entrance fee: Adults $3; Kids $1
- X Camping facilities: 4 miles
- X Boating facilities: Pacific Ocean
- X RV facilities w/ hookups: 2 miles
- X Accomodations in town
- X Restaurants in town
  Clam Jumper, Silky Sullivan's

# *Heritage Quilt Show*

JULIAN'S WOMENS CLUB invites you to come view the spectacular quilts and crafts on display at the **Heritage Quilt Show.** A very friendly town, and the apple capitol of San Diego County, Julian's where "the roads are good, the weather is fine. Drive carefully, come and see us any old time!" So, what 'cha waitin' for?

## Julian, California

First week in July
Daily 9:00 AM - 5:00 PM

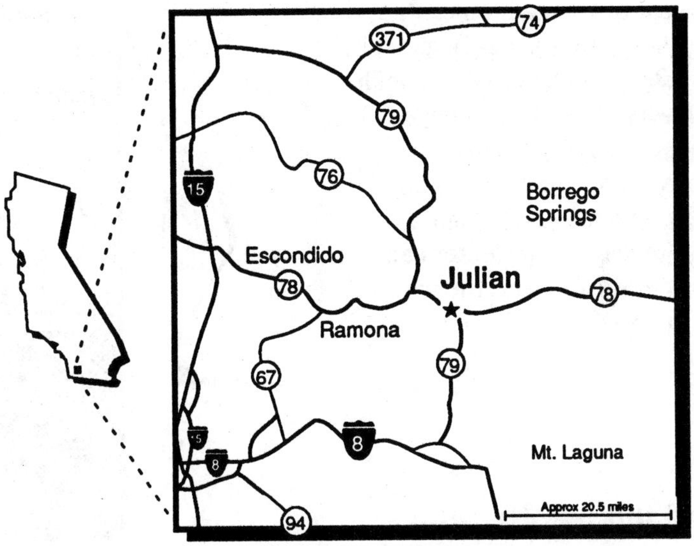


## What's goin' on...

Town population: **2,500**
Last year's attendance: **4,000**
Average outdoor temperature: **80°**
Festival location: **Town Hall**

*Up-to-date festival information is available from:*
*Julian Chamber of Commerce*
*(619) 765-1857*

- X Wine tasting/beer for sale
- Food booths
- X Arts/crafts for sale
- Live music
- Clowns
- Face painters
- Childrens games
- Animal exhibits/petting zoo
- Dogs allowed on leash
- Lost and found
- Bicycle racks
- First aid area available
- X Self-brought picnics allowed
- Self-brought alcohol allowed
- Stroller/wheelchair rentals available

- Parade
- Parking fee
- Entrance fee
- X Camping facilities: 5 miles
- X Boating facilities: 10 miles
- X RV facilities w/ hookups: 5 miles
- X Accomodations in town
- X Restaurants in town

# *Santa Monica Pier Twilight Dance Series*

DANCE, DANCE, DANCE THE summer away during the **Twilight Dance Series**, Thursday evenings on the 75-year-old Santa Monica Pier. These free dances begin at 7:30 and offer music to tickle every fancy: Latin, reggae, 50s rock 'n' roll, Dixieland, calypso, country, and big-band sounds. The Santa Monica Visitor Center can provide you with the who-plays-when.

## Santa Monica, California

Thursdays in July and August
7:30 PM - 9:30 PM

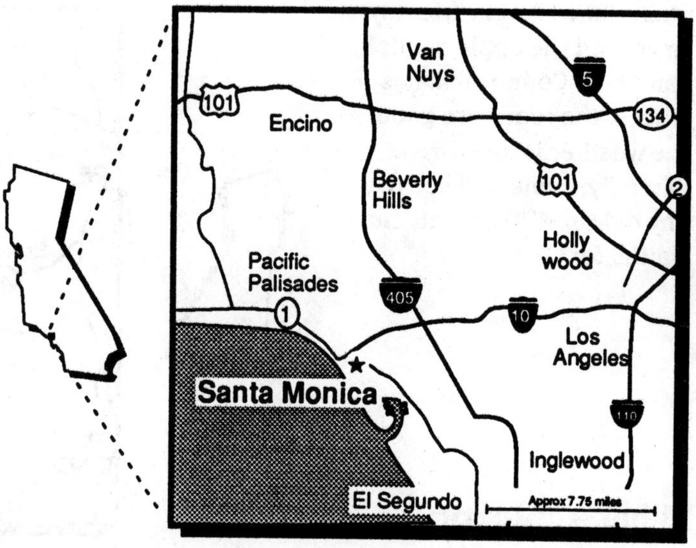


### What's goin' on...

Town population: **94,000**
Last year's attendance: **150,000**
Average outdoor temperature: **72°**
Festival location: **Santa Monica Pier**

*Up-to-date festival information is available from:*
*Santa Monica Visitor Center*
*(805) 925-2403*

| | |
|---|---|
| X | Wine tasting/beer for sale |
| X | Food booths |
| | Arts/crafts for sale |
| X | Live music |
| | Clowns |
| | Face painters |
| X | Childrens games |
| | Animal exhibits/petting zoo |
| | Dogs allowed on leash |
| X | Lost and found |
| X | Bicycle racks |
| X | First aid area available |
| X | Self-brought picnics allowed |
| | Self-brought alcohol allowed |
| | Stroller/wheelchair rentals available |

| | |
|---|---|
| | Parade |
| X | Parking fee: $5 |
| | Entrance fee |
| X | Camping facilities: 10 miles |
| X | Boating facilities: Bay |
| X | RV facilities w/ hookups: 30 miles |
| X | Accomodations in town<br>Econolodge, Belle Bleu Inn, Park Hyatt, Oceana Hotel, Hotel Santa Monica |
| X | Restaurants in town<br>Michael's, 3rd St. Bar & Grill, Ponteueccio, Madame Wu's, Belleview |

# *Fourth of July*

BRIDGEPORT CELEBRATES the **Fourth of July** in a big way! This traditional observance has been happening since 1862...so you can imagine the fun the townspeople have on this gigantic birthday! There's mud volleyball for the big folks (now does that sound like fun or what?), softball tournaments all weekend, arm wrestling, a chili cook-off, dancing, and a fireworks display to top the day off right!

## Bridgeport, California

Fourth of July through the following weekend
Hours vary

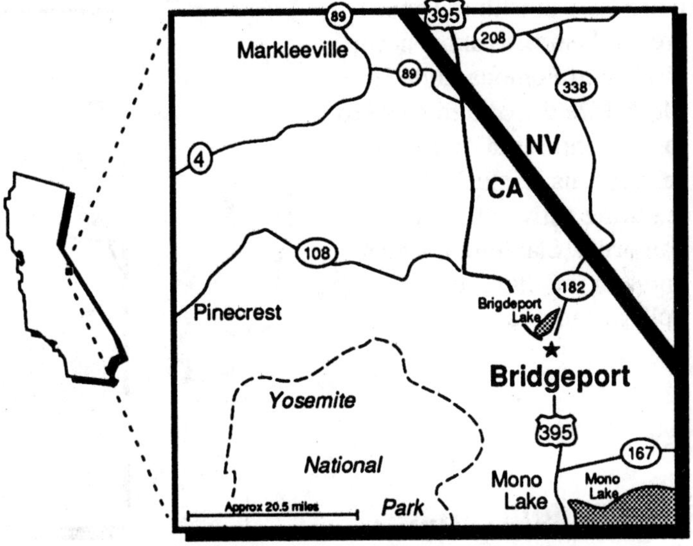


☞ *Up-to-date festival information is available from:*
*Bridgeport Chamber of Commerce*
*(619) 932-7500*

## What's goin' on...

Town population: **600**
Last year's attendance: **5,000**
Average outdoor temperature: **75°**
Festival location: **Citywide**

| | |
|---|---|
| X | Wine tasting/beer for sale |
| X | Food booths |
| X | Arts/crafts for sale |
| X | Live music |
| X | Clowns |
| X | Face painters |
| X | Childrens games |
| | Animal exhibits/petting zoo |
| X | Dogs allowed on leash |
| X | Lost and found |
| | Bicycle racks |
| X | First aid area available |
| X | Self-brought picnics allowed |
| X | Self-brought alcohol allowed |
| | Stroller/wheelchair rentals available |

| | |
|---|---|
| X | Parade: Sat. 10:00 AM downtown |
| | Parking fee |
| | Entrance fee |
| X | Camping facilities: 1 mile |
| X | Boating facilities: Bridgeport Res. |
| X | RV facilities w/ hookups: 1 mile |
| X | Accomodations in town |
| X | Restaurants in town<br>Bridgeport Inn |

SOUTHERN

# *Fourth of July Celebration*

STOP BY THE **FOURTH OF July Celebration** for a day of sampling traditional foods and hanging out with the family! End it with the spectacular fireworks show in the evening at Pomona College Alumni Field. Located close to the Rancho Santa Ana Botanical Gardens, exclusively featuring native plants of California, Claremont is also home to the Claremont College campus.

## Claremont, California

Fourth of July
9:00 AM - 10:00 PM

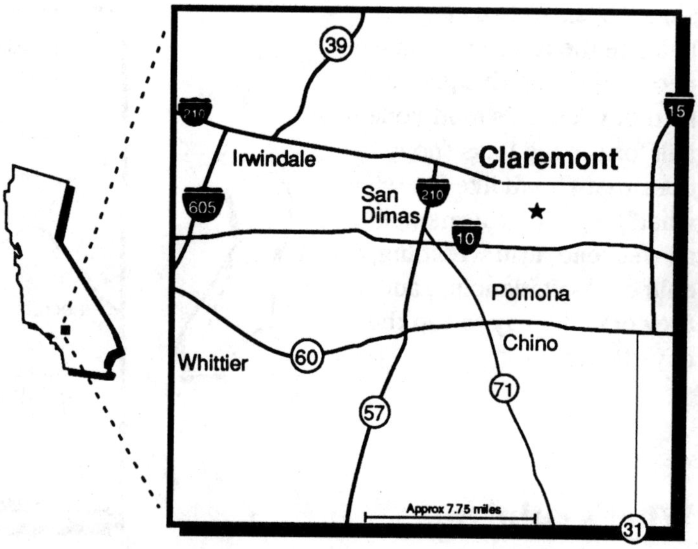


## What's goin' on...

Town population: **36,500**
Last year's attendance: **N/A**
Average outdoor temperature: **75°**
Festival location: **Memorial Park**

*Up-to-date festival information is available from:*
*Claremont Chamber of Commerce*
*(714) 624-4681*

| | |
|---|---|
| X | Wine tasting/beer for sale |
| X | Food booths |
| X | Arts/crafts for sale |
| X | Live music |
| X | Clowns |
| | Face painters |
| X | Childrens games |
| | Animal exhibits/petting zoo |
| X | Dogs allowed on leash |
| | Lost and found |
| X | Bicycle racks |
| | First aid area available |
| X | Self-brought picnics allowed |
| | Self-brought alcohol allowed |
| | Stroller/wheelchair rentals available |

| | |
|---|---|
| X | Parade: (time not avbl.) |
| | Parking fee |
| | Entrance fee |
| X | Camping facilities: 7 miles |
| X | Boating facilities: Lake |
| X | RV facilities w/ hookups: 7 miles |
| X | Accomodations in town: Griswold's Inn, Claremont Motel Inn, Howard Johnson, Ramada Inn |
| X | Restaurants in town: The Danson, Original Shrimp House, Village Grille, 3 C's Cafe, Blue Moon Cafe, Chili's |

# *Independence Day Parade & Fireworks Show*

CELEBRATE THE FOURTH OF July at the **Independence Day Parade & Fireworks Show** in Huntington Beach! There's fun for the whole family from dawn to dusk—with the day's events concluding with a *giant* fireworks extravaganza! Tthe Shipley Nature Center inside Huntington Central Park offers more than 18 acres of natural wonders to stroll through.

## Huntington Beach, California

Fourth of July
8:00 AM - 7:00 PM

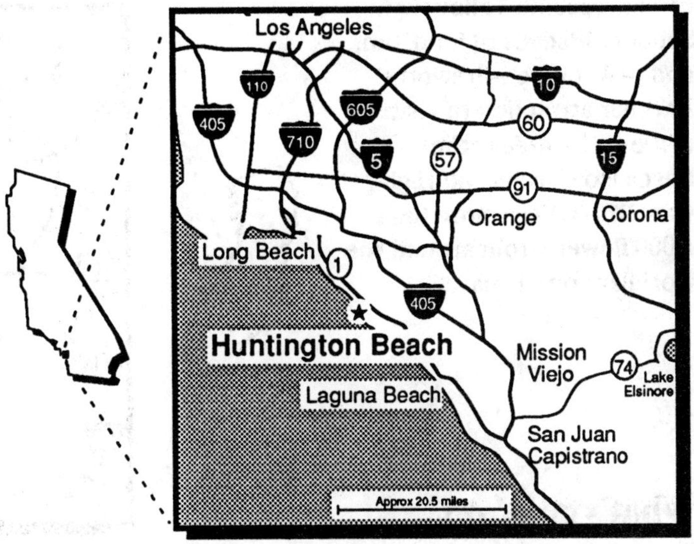


## What's goin' on...

Town population: **185,000**
Last year's attendance: **N/A**
Average outdoor temperature: **80°**
Festival location: **Downtown**

*Up-to-date festival information is available from:*
*Huntington Beach Chamber of Commerce*
*(714) 536-8888*

| | |
|---|---|
| | Wine tasting/beer for sale |
| X | Food booths |
| X | Arts/crafts for sale |
| X | Live music |
| X | Clowns |
| | Face painters |
| X | Childrens games |
| | Animal exhibits/petting zoo |
| X | Dogs allowed on leash |
| | Lost and found |
| | Bicycle racks |
| | First aid area available |
| X | Self-brought picnics allowed |
| | Self-brought alcohol allowed |
| | Stroller/wheelchair rentals available |

| | |
|---|---|
| X | Parade 10:00 AM on Main St. |
| | Parking fee |
| | Entrance fee |
| X | Camping facilities: 1 mile |
| X | Boating facilities: Ocean |
| X | RV facilities w/ hookups: 1 mile |
| X | Accomodations in town<br>House Guest U.S.A, Hilton, Best Western, Ocean View, Huntington Shores Motel |
| X | Restaurants in town<br>Maxwell's, Charley Brown's, J.C. McLins, Bukhara, Tijuana Willies, Tibbies, Pero's |

SOUTHERN

# *Family Festival of Fun*

THEY'LL BE SERVING UP more than burgers and dogs at the **Family Festival of Fun** in La Crescenta! The place to be is Crescenta Valley High School for scads of food, fun, and—of course—fireworks! Another attraction to visit while in the area is the Descanso Gardens off Highway 210—where more than 1,000 flowers from around the world are on display.

## La Crescenta, California

Fourth of July
2:00 PM - 11:00 PM

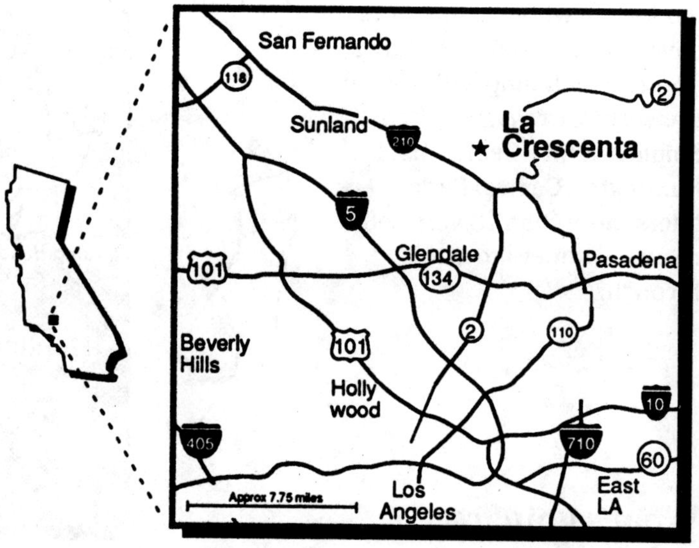


*Up-to-date festival information is available from:*
*La Crescenta Chamber of Commerce*
*(818) 248-4957*

## What's goin' on...

Town population: **45,000**
Last year's attendance: **7,500**
Average outdoor temperature: **85°**
Festival location: **High School**

| | |
|---|---|
| | Wine tasting/beer for sale |
| X | Food booths |
| X | Arts/crafts for sale |
| X | Live music |
| X | Clowns |
| X | Face painters |
| X | Childrens games |
| | Animal exhibits/petting zoo |
| X | Dogs allowed on leash |
| X | Lost and found |
| X | Bicycle racks |
| X | First aid area available |
| X | Self-brought picnics allowed |
| | Self-brought alcohol allowed |
| | Stroller/wheelchair rentals available |

| | |
|---|---|
| | Parade |
| | Parking fee |
| X | Entrance fee: Adults $3; Kids free |
| | Camping facilities |
| | Boating facilities |
| | RV facilities w/ hookups |
| X | Accomodations in town<br>Travel Inn, Mary Lane Motel |
| X | Restaurants in town<br>Reflections, Dominick's Italian |

# *Fourth of July Jamboree*

WHAT DO A THREE-LEGGED race, egg toss, and relay race have in common? Besides being the kind of old-fashioned fun our grandparents enjoyed, they're all part of Norco's **Fourth of July Jamboree**! Bring your own picnic, or polish off a few barbecued burgers—cooked up by local service organizations. Celebrating is a favorite pastime for years in Norco...and guess what happens after dark?!

## Norco, California

Fourth of July
10:00 AM - 10:00 PM

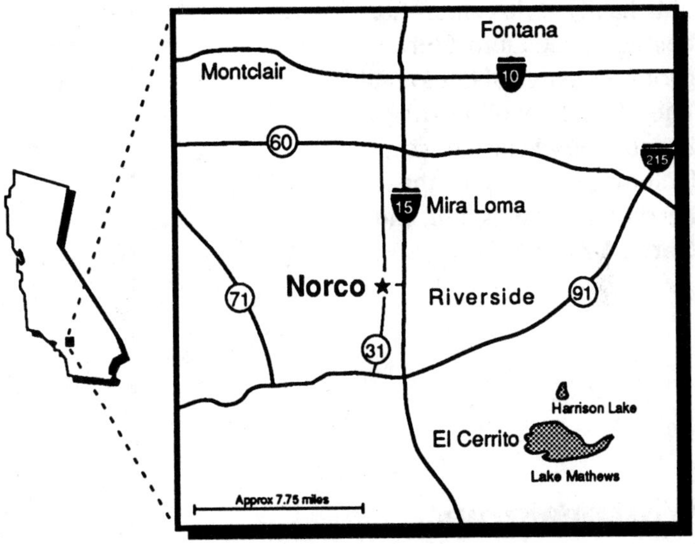


## What's goin' on...

Town population: **25,000**
Last year's attendance: **10,000**
Average outdoor temperature: **93°**
Festival location: **Community Ctr.**

*Up-to-date festival information is available from:*
*Norco Chamber of Commerce*
*(208) 743-2531*

- X Wine tasting/beer for sale
- X Food booths
- X Arts/crafts for sale
- Live music
- X Clowns
- Face painters
- X Childrens games
- X Animal exhibits/petting zoo
- Dogs allowed on leash
- X Lost and found
- X Bicycle racks
- X First aid area available
- X Self-brought picnics allowed
- X Self-brought alcohol allowed
- Stroller/wheelchair rentals available

- Parade
- Parking fee
- Entrance fee
- X Camping facilities: 10 miles
- X Boating facilities: Lake Perris
- X RV facilities w/ hookups: 10 miles
- X Accomodations in town
  Econo Lodge
- X Restaurants in town
  Country Juntion, Pat's Kitchen, Sizzler, Raspberry's

SOUTHERN

# *Fourth of July Parade & Fiesta*

AT THE BASE OF MT. RUdolph sits Nuevo, a town that celebrates the **Fourth of July Parade & Fiesta** in regal style! This family-style celebration, hosted by the Lions Club, promises skads of fun for all! There're lots of other things in and around town to see, including Lake Perris, the Perris Trolley Museum, and March Air Force Base.

## Nuevo, California

Fourth of July
10:00 AM - 4:00 PM

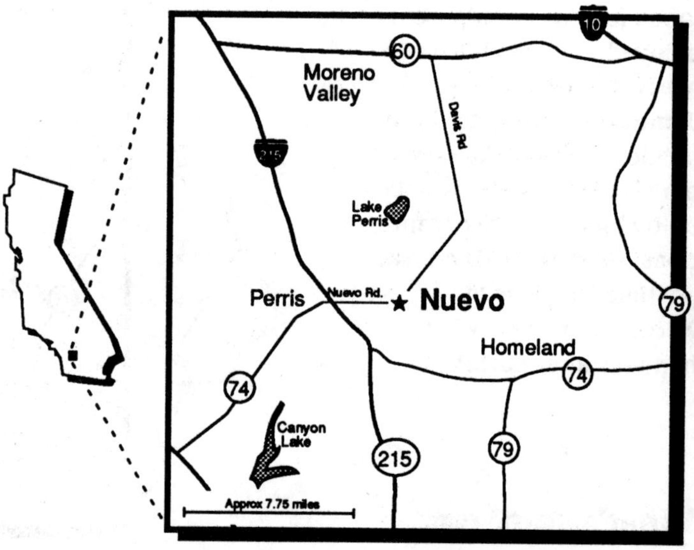


*Up-to-date festival information is available from:*
*Nuevo Auto Parts*
*(714) 928-0202*

## What's goin' on...

Town population: **4,700**
Last year's attendance: **8,000**
Average outdoor temperature: **100°**
Festival location: **Senior Citizens Ctr.**

| | |
|---|---|
| | Wine tasting/beer for sale |
| X | Food booths |
| X | Arts/crafts for sale |
| X | Live music |
| | Clowns |
| X | Face painters |
| X | Childrens games |
| | Animal exhibits/petting zoo |
| X | Dogs allowed on leash |
| X | Lost and found |
| X | Bicycle racks |
| X | First aid area available |
| X | Self-brought picnics allowed |
| | Self-brought alcohol allowed |
| | Stroller/wheelchair rentals available |

| | |
|---|---|
| X | Parade 10:00 on Lakeview Ave. |
| | Parking fee |
| | Entrance fee |
| X | Camping facilities: 1 miles |
| X | Boating facilities: Paris Lake |
| X | RV facilities w/ hookups: 4 miles |
| | Accomodations in town |
| X | Restaurants in town<br>T.P.'s Restaurant |

# *Fourth of July Art Festival*

THE OLD SANTA BARBARA Mission is the site of a bang-up **Fourth of July Art Festival**! Over 150 artists have been screened for quality and invited to show their magnificent handiwork. All media will be represented her—print, photography, water and oil paints, wood, clay, and cloth. Mimes and jugglers will entertain you as you stroll around the mission's grounds.

## Santa Barbara, California

Fourth of July
9:30 AM - 5:00 PM

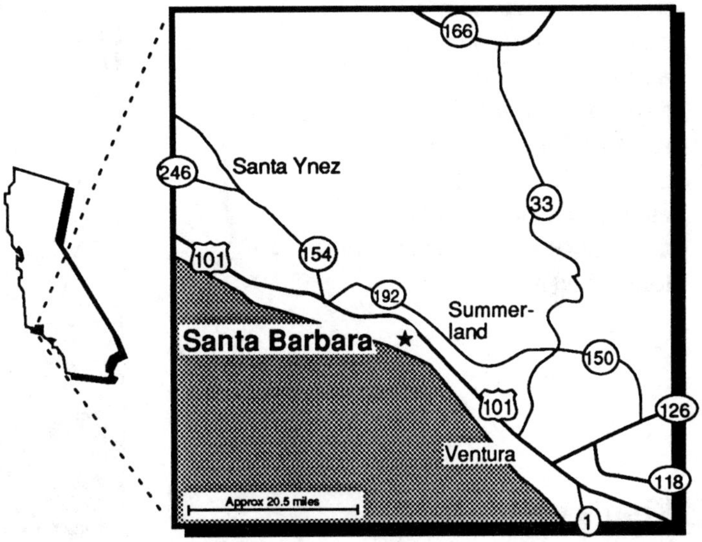


*Up-to-date festival information is available from:*
*Santa Barbara Visitors Bureau*
*(805) 965-3021*

## What's goin' on...

Town population: **350,000**
Last year's attendance: **10,000**
Average outdoor temperature: **70°**
Festival location: **Old Mission**

| | |
|---|---|
| | Wine tasting/beer for sale |
| X | Food booths |
| X | Arts/crafts for sale |
| X | Live music |
| X | Clowns |
| X | Face painters |
| X | Childrens games |
| | Animal exhibits/petting zoo |
| | Dogs allowed on leash |
| X | Lost and found |
| | Bicycle racks |
| X | First aid area available |
| | Self-brought picnics allowed |
| | Self-brought alcohol allowed |
| | Stroller/wheelchair rentals available |

| | |
|---|---|
| | Parade |
| | Parking fee |
| | Entrance fee |
| X | Camping facilities: 3 miles |
| X | Boating facilities: Lake Cachuma |
| X | RV facilities w/ hookups: 10 miles |
| X | Accomodations in town |
| X | Restaurants in town<br>San Ysidro Ranch, The Epicurean, Mousse Odille, Presidio Cafe |

# *Independence Arts Festival*

CASUAL AND COMFORTABLE is the style around beautiful Santa Monica. The **Independence Arts Festival** features fine art from well known California artists, jazz and big band sounds from local clubs as well as dancing—compliments of the neighboring high school drill team! Loll on the beach. Fly a kite. Stroll the shops. Lively and warm Santa Monica has it all!

## Santa Monica, California

Weekend after July Fourth
Daily 10:00 AM - dusk

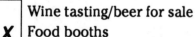

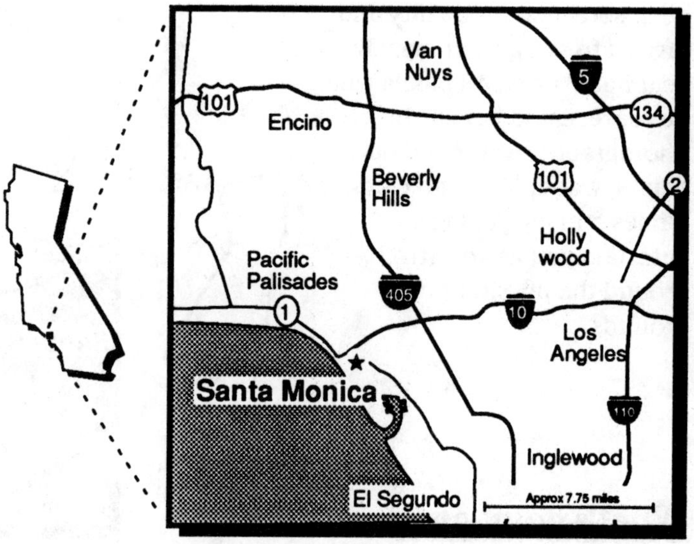


## What's goin' on...

Town population: **94,000**
Last year's attendance: **40,000**
Average outdoor temperature: **70°**
Festival location: **Third St. Promenade**

☞ *Up-to-date festival information is available from:*
*Santa Monica Visitor Center*
*(805) 925-2403*

| | |
|---|---|
| | Wine tasting/beer for sale |
| X | Food booths |
| X | Arts/crafts for sale |
| X | Live music |
| X | Clowns |
| X | Face painters |
| | Childrens games |
| | Animal exhibits/petting zoo |
| X | Dogs allowed on leash |
| X | Lost and found |
| X | Bicycle racks |
| X | First aid area available |
| X | Self-brought picnics allowed |
| | Self-brought alcohol allowed |
| X | Stroller/wheelchair rentals available |

| | |
|---|---|
| | Parade |
| X | Parking fee: free & meters |
| | Entrance fee |
| X | Camping facilities: 10 miles |
| X | Boating facilities: Bay |
| X | RV facilities w/ hookups: 30 miles |
| X | Accomodations in town: Econolodge, Belle Bleu Inn, Park Hyatt, Oceana Hotel, Hotel Santa Monica |
| X | Restaurants in town: Michael's, 3rd St. Bar & Grill, Ponteueccio, Madame Wu's, Belleview |

# *Fourth of July Parade & Festivities*

THE COMMUNITIES OF Sunland and Tujunga combine their energetic spirits every July at the **Fourth of July Parade & Festivities** held in Sunland Park. Sponsored by the local Rotary Clubs, in cooperation with the City Police, Fire Department, and Department of Recreation and Parks, this all-day adventure has the flavor of a small town but is actually in the City of Los Angeles.

## Tujunga/Sunland, California

Fourth of July
10:00 AM - 7:00 PM

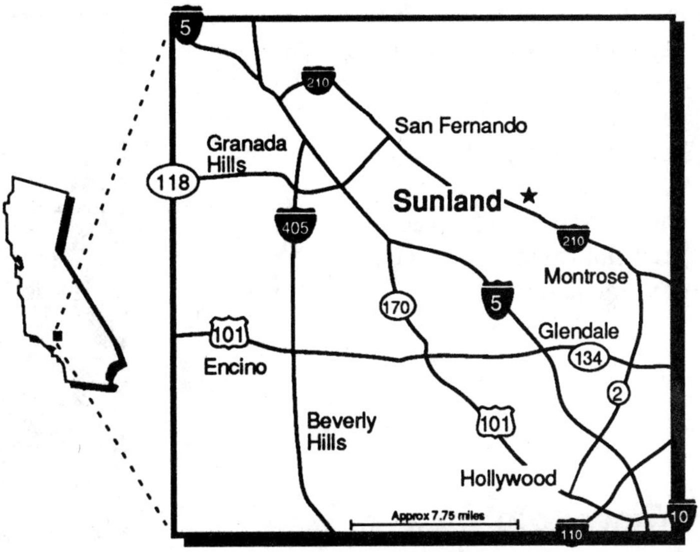


## What's goin' on...

Town population: **45,000**
Last year's attendance: **10,000**
Average outdoor temperature: **80°**
Festival location: **Sunland Park**

*Up-to-date festival information is available from: Tujunga/Sunland Chamber of Commerce (818) 352-4422*

| | |
|---|---|
| | Wine tasting/beer for sale |
| X | Food booths |
| X | Arts/crafts for sale |
| X | Live music |
| X | Clowns |
| | Face painters |
| | Childrens games |
| | Animal exhibits/petting zoo |
| X | Dogs allowed on leash |
| X | Lost and found |
| X | Bicycle racks |
| X | First aid area available |
| X | Self-brought picnics allowed |
| | Self-brought alcohol allowed |
| | Stroller/wheelchair rentals available |

| | |
|---|---|
| X | Parade: 10:00 AM downtown |
| | Parking fee |
| | Entrance fee |
| X | Camping facilities: 5 miles |
| | Boating facilities |
| X | RV facilities w/ hookups: 10 miles |
| X | Accomodations in town<br>Mt. Gleason Lodge, Travel Inn, Harmony Hotel |
| X | Restaurants in town<br>Night Rock Cafe, Sterling's Restaurant |

# *Fourth of July Festival*

DOWNTOWN MAIN STREET IS where you'll find Venturians celebrating our great Fourth! More than 400 artists appear for this **Fourth of July Festival**, with their arts and crafts for sale. Ventura, situated due east of Santa Cruz Island, hosts this holiday in red, white, and blue style! The entertainment varies each year, but there's always lots of music and dancing.

## Ventura, California

Fourth of July
11:00 AM - 5:00 PM

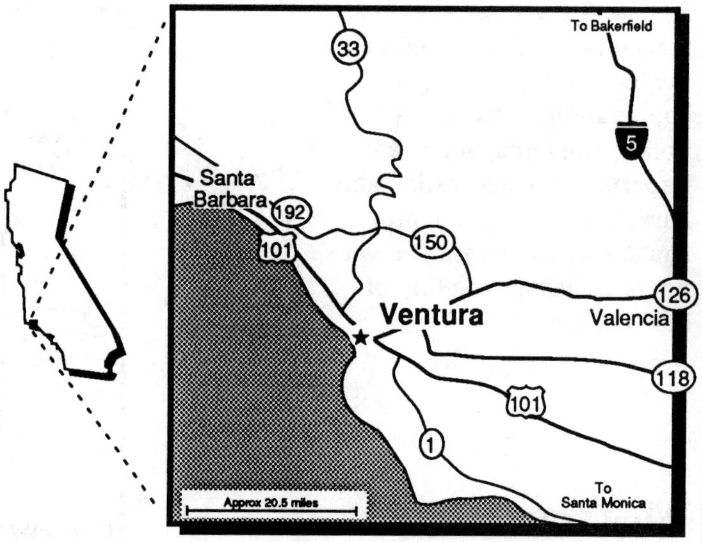


## What's goin' on...

Town population: **92,000**
Last year's attendance: **50,000**
Average outdoor temperature: **70°**
Festival location: **Downtown**

*Up-to-date festival information is available from:*
*Ventura Chamber of Commerce*
*(805) 648-2875*

| | |
|---|---|
| | Wine tasting/beer for sale |
| X | Food booths |
| X | Arts/crafts for sale |
| X | Live music |
| X | Clowns |
| X | Face painters |
| X | Childrens games |
| X | Animal exhibits/petting zoo |
| | Dogs allowed on leash |
| X | Lost and found |
| X | Bicycle racks |
| X | First aid area available |
| X | Self-brought picnics allowed |
| | Self-brought alcohol allowed |
| | Stroller/wheelchair rentals available |

| | |
|---|---|
| X | Parade: 10:00 AM downtown |
| | Parking fee |
| | Entrance fee |
| X | Camping facilities: 3 miles |
| X | Boating facilities: Lake Casitas |
| X | RV facilities w/ hookups: 3 miles |
| X | Accomodations in town |
| X | Restaurants in town<br>Tony's Steak & Seafood |

# *Grand Summer Nights*

HAPPENING AT THE SANTA Monica College campus during July and August in Santa Monica...it's **Grand Summer Nights**! This is not just a young people's concert series—this year will be hot Latin jazz, Doc Severinson and his Tonight Show Band, the L.A. Mandolin Orchestra, Big Daddy (contemporary hits time-warped into 50s style), and many more. For "whos" and "whens," contact the Visitor's Bureau.

## Santa Monica, California

Saturday eves during July and August
8:00 PM

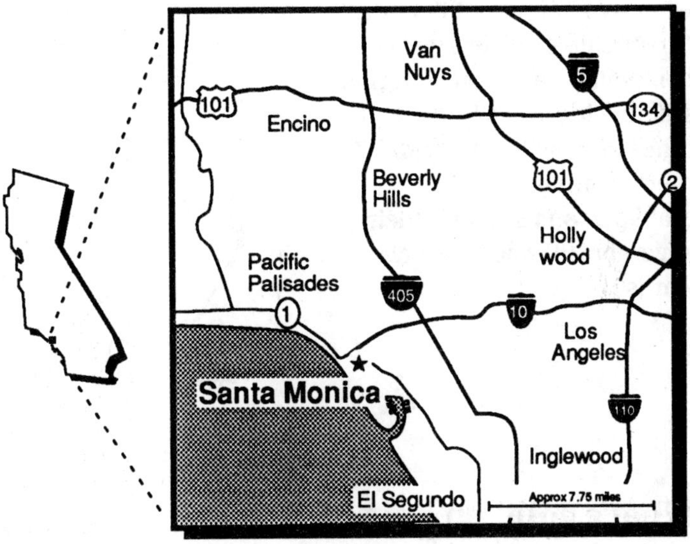


## What's goin' on...

Town population: **90,000**
Last year's attendance: **N/A**
Average outdoor temperature: **72°**
Festival location: **College Campus**

☞ *Up-to-date festival information is available from:*
*Santa Monica Visitor Center*
*(805) 925-2403*

| | |
|---|---|
| | Wine tasting/beer for sale |
| ✗ | Food booths |
| | Arts/crafts for sale |
| ✗ | Live music |
| | Clowns |
| | Face painters |
| ✗ | Childrens games |
| | Animal exhibits/petting zoo |
| | Dogs allowed on leash |
| ✗ | Lost and found |
| ✗ | Bicycle racks |
| ✗ | First aid area available |
| ✗ | Self-brought picnics allowed |
| | Self-brought alcohol allowed |
| | Stroller/wheelchair rentals available |

| | |
|---|---|
| | Parade |
| | Parking fee |
| | Entrance fee |
| ✗ | Camping facilities |
| ✗ | Boating facilities: Bay |
| ✗ | RV facilities w/ hookups |
| ✗ | Accomodations in town<br>Miramar Sheraton, Oceana Hotel, Comfort Inn, Pacific Shore Hotel |
| ✗ | Restaurants in town<br>La Patisserie, La Strada, 3rd Street Pub & Grill, Skorpio's II, Teasers, Taka Sushi, Chanpen |

# *Pioneer Fair & Chili Cookoff*

SUN CITY, SITE OF THE **Pioneer Fair & Chili Cook-Off**, is a peaceful community of retired folks...but from what we hear, the Chili Cook-Off stirs up some energetic competition and some pretty stiff judging! Alma Burke and other local artists will exhibit their paintings—while craftspersons show off their silver, brass, wood, and clay wares.

## Sun City, California

Second weekend in July (beginning Thursday)
All day

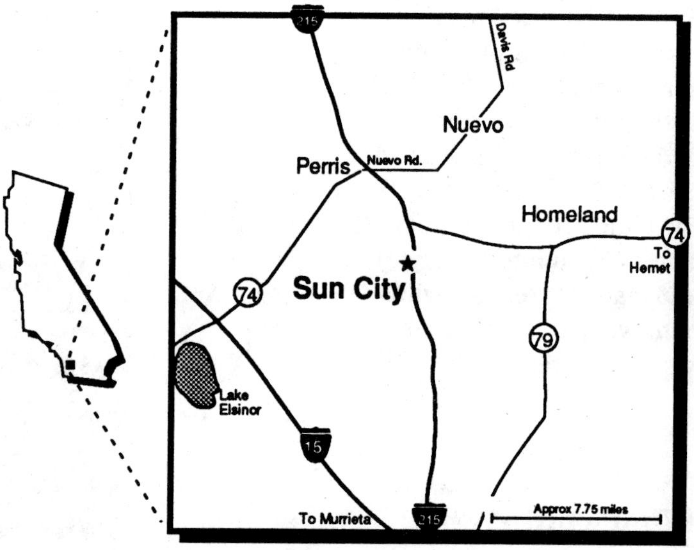


*Up-to-date festival information is available from:*
*Sun City Chamber of Commerce*
*(714) 672-1991*

## What's goin' on...

Town population: **8,460**
Last year's attendance: **2,000**
Average outdoor temperature: **70°**
Festival location: **Downtown**

| | |
|---|---|
| X | Wine tasting/beer for sale |
| X | Food booths |
| X | Arts/crafts for sale |
| X | Live music |
| X | Clowns |
| X | Face painters |
| X | Childrens games |
| | Animal exhibits/petting zoo |
| X | Dogs allowed on leash |
| X | Lost and found |
| X | Bicycle racks |
| X | First aid area available |
| | Self-brought picnics allowed |
| | Self-brought alcohol allowed |
| | Stroller/wheelchair rentals available |

| | |
|---|---|
| X | Parade: Sat. 10:00 AM downtown |
| | Parking fee |
| X | Entrance fee: (prices not avbl.) |
| X | Camping facilities: 10 miles |
| X | Boating facilities: Lake Elsinore |
| X | RV facilities w/ hookups: 15 miles |
| X | Accomodations in town<br>Sun City Motel |
| | Restaurants in town |

# *Uptown Festival*

ENSCONCED IN THE HEART of Angeles County sits the town of Whittier, featuring the **Uptown Festival**. Just four short miles from Pio Pico State Historical Park, this suburb offers a glorious celebration in its uptown streets. With food booths offering Hungarian, Greek, Cajun, Asian, and Mexican food to choose from, you'll hardly go hungry! Enjoy the crafts booths and merry-go-round and donkey rides too.

## Whittier, California

Second weekend in July
Sat. 10:00 AM - 10:00 PM; Sun. Noon - 7:30

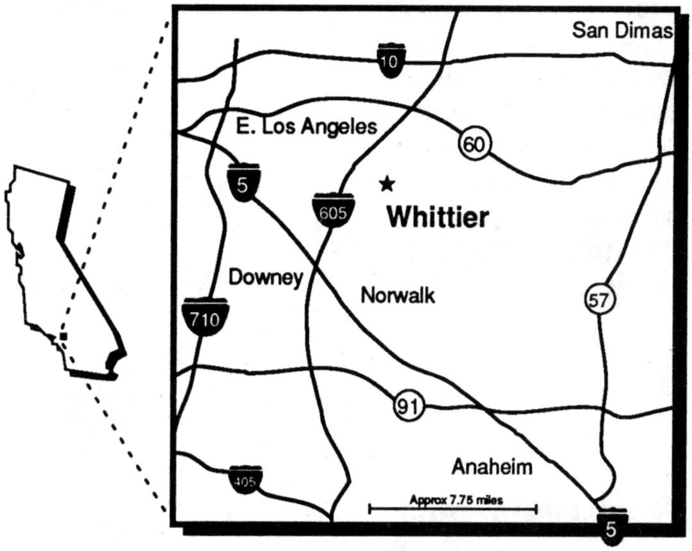


*Up-to-date festival information is available from:*
*Whittier Chamber of Commerce*
*(213) 698-9554*

## What's goin' on...

Town population: **70,000**
Last year's attendance: **100,000**
Average outdoor temperature: **75°**
Festival location: **Uptown**

| | |
|---|---|
| | Wine tasting/beer for sale |
| X | Food booths |
| X | Arts/crafts for sale |
| X | Live music |
| X | Clowns |
| X | Face painters |
| X | Childrens games |
| X | Animal exhibits/petting zoo |
| | Dogs allowed on leash |
| X | Lost and found |
| X | Bicycle racks |
| X | First aid area available |
| X | Self-brought picnics allowed |
| | Self-brought alcohol allowed |
| | Stroller/wheelchair rentals available |

| | |
|---|---|
| | Parade |
| | Parking fee |
| | Entrance fee |
| X | Camping facilities: 4 miles |
| | Boating facilities |
| X | RV facilities w/ hookups: 4 miles |
| X | Accomodations in town<br>Whittier Hilton, Vagabond |
| X | Restaurants in town<br>El Patio, Cafe Rene, Datilo, Village Garden Steak House, New Canton, Los Portales |

# *Custom Car & Hot Rod Show*

CALLING ALL CAR BUFFS! The seventh annual **Custom Car & Hot Rod Show** is designed to entertain the whole family—participants and spectators alike! More than 200 trophies will be given away at Lynwood Citypark. Added attractions are the radio-controlled-car races, slow-drag contest, children's carnival, and raffles galore!

## Lynwood, California

Second Sunday in July
Daily 8:00 AM - 5:00 PM

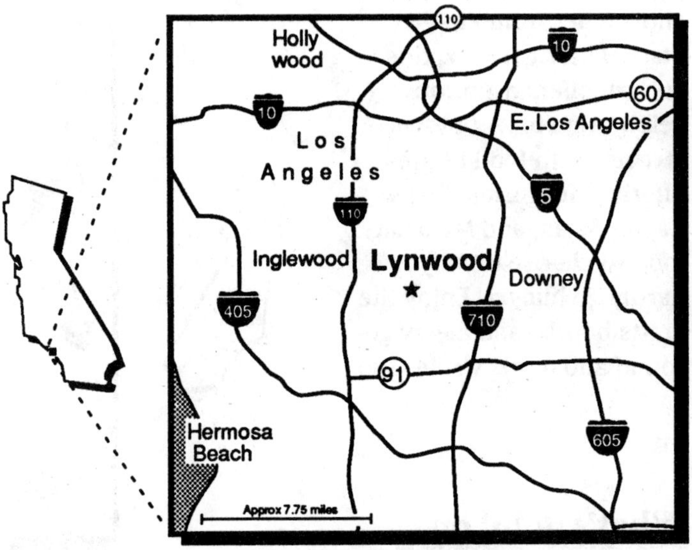


## What's goin' on...

Town population: **55,844**
Last year's attendance: **10,000**
Average outdoor temperature: **80°**
Festival location: **Dymally Park**

*Up-to-date festival information is available from:*
*Lynwood Chamber of Commerce*
*(213) 537-6484*

| | |
|---|---|
| | Wine tasting/beer for sale |
| X | Food booths |
| | Arts/crafts for sale |
| X | Live music |
| | Clowns |
| | Face painters |
| X | Childrens games |
| | Animal exhibits/petting zoo |
| X | Dogs allowed on leash |
| X | Lost and found |
| | Bicycle racks |
| X | First aid area available |
| X | Self-brought picnics allowed |
| | Self-brought alcohol allowed |
| | Stroller/wheelchair rentals available |

| | |
|---|---|
| | Parade |
| | Parking fee |
| | Entrance fee |
| X | Camping facilities: 10 miles |
| X | Boating facilities: Long Beach Harbor |
| X | RV facilities w/ hookups: 10 miles |
| X | Accomodations in town |
| X | Restaurants in town<br>Vasilio's |

# *Tapioca Festival*

WE TOLD YOU ABOUT THE **Tapioca Festival** in first and second editions—and it's ba-a-a-ck! Newcomers who can stand the (whew!) 122° weather are promised a whole lot of fun out at Lake Tamarisk! Come down and vote for the Tapioca Queen (reigning queen is Sheila Ragsdale)! Desert Center, a little town located in the Mojave Desert, is southwest of the Joshua Tree National Monument and Eagle Mountain.

## Desert Center, California

Third Saturday in July
3:00 PM - 2:00 AM

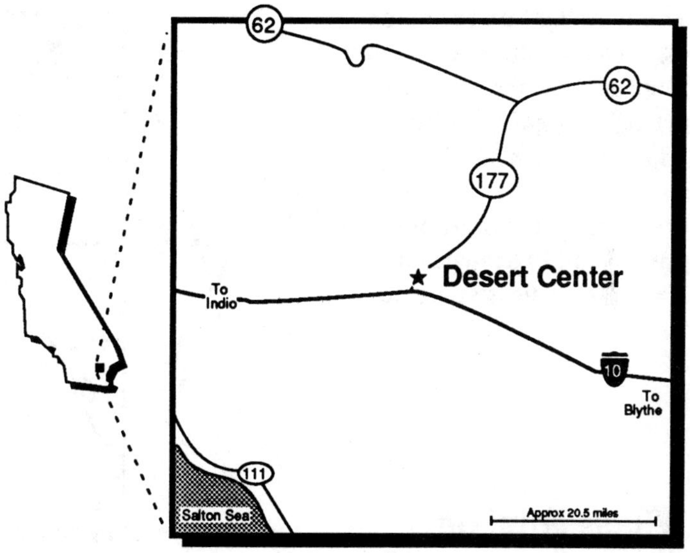


*Up-to-date festival information is available from:*
*Desert Center McGoo's*
*(619) 227-3155*

## What's goin' on...

Town population: **800**
Last year's attendance: **1,200**
Average outdoor temperature: **122°**
Festival location: **Lake Tamarisk**

| | |
|---|---|
| X | Wine tasting/beer for sale |
| X | Food booths |
| | Arts/crafts for sale |
| X | Live music |
| | Clowns |
| | Face painters |
| | Childrens games |
| | Animal exhibits/petting zoo |
| X | Dogs allowed on leash |
| | Lost and found |
| | Bicycle racks |
| X | First aid area available |
| X | Self-brought picnics allowed |
| | Self-brought alcohol allowed |
| | Stroller/wheelchair rentals available |

| | |
|---|---|
| | Parade |
| | Parking fee |
| | Entrance fee |
| X | Camping facilities: 1 mile |
| | Boating facilities |
| | RV facilities w/ hookups |
| | Accomodations in town |
| X | Restaurants in town<br>McGoo's |

S O U T H E R N

# *Redlands Chili Cook-Off/Fireman's Muster*

AHHH, SMELL THAT HEAVENly aroma? It's chili cooking at dawn for the **Redlands Chili Cook-Off/Fireman's Muster**! These firefighters are in top physical condition and raring to go as they participate in fire-fighting games with apparatus from nearly a zillion years ago! There're hotcakes on the morning griddle and live music all afternoon. This is some old-fashioned fun!

## Redlands, California

Third weekend in July

Sat. 10:00 AM - midnight; Sun. 10:00 AM - 4:00 PM

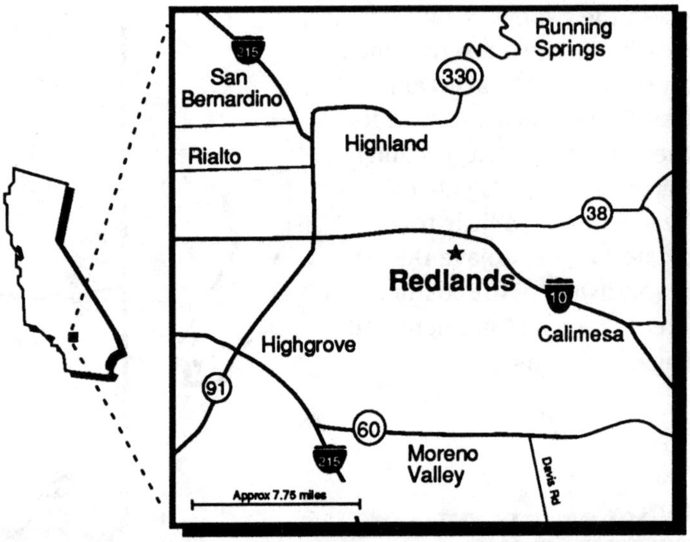


## What's goin' on...

Town population: **62,000**

Last year's attendance: **20,000**

Average outdoor temperature: **95°**

Festival location: **Univ. of Redlands**

*Up-to-date festival information is available from:*
*Redlands Chamber of Commerce*
*(714) 793-2546*

- X Wine tasting/beer for sale
- X Food booths
- X Arts/crafts for sale
- X Live music
- Clowns
- Face painters
- X Childrens games
- Animal exhibits/petting zoo
- X Dogs allowed on leash
- X Lost and found
- Bicycle racks
- X First aid area available
- X Self-brought picnics allowed
- Self-brought alcohol allowed
- Stroller/wheelchair rentals available

- X Parade: Sat. 9:00 AM downtown
- Parking fee
- Entrance fee
- Camping facilities
- Boating facilities
- RV facilities w/ hookups
- X Accomodations in town
  Goodnite Inn, Redlands Motor Lodge, Geargianna B&B
- X Restaurants in town:
  Vesuvio's, Joe Greensleeves

# *International Surf Festival*

HELD ON THE BEACHES OF Hermosa, Redondo, and Torrance, the Daily Breeze **International Surf Festival** draws thousands of spectators and contestants each summer. From sand castle designing to a world-class volleyball tournament to swimsuit gazing, this festival has something for everyone!

## Torrance, California

Last Friday through Tuesday in July
Hours vary

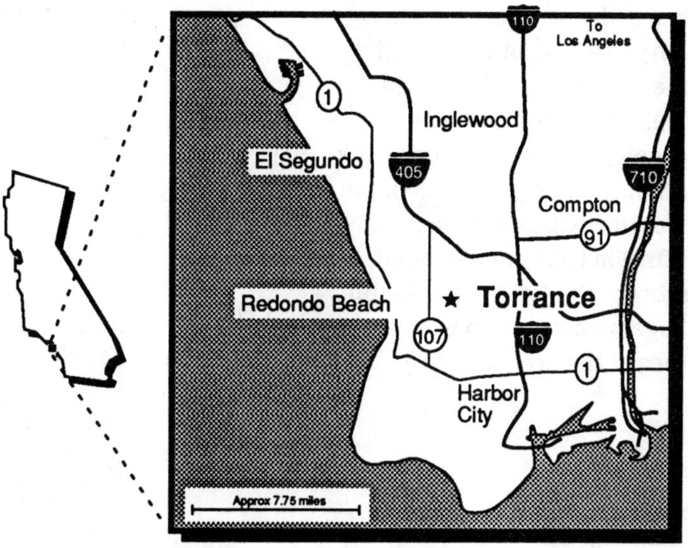


*Up-to-date festival information is available from:*
*Torrance Chamber of Commerce*
*(213) 540-5858*

## What's goin' on...

Town population: **130,000**
Last year's attendance: **N/A**
Average outdoor temperature: **80°**
Festival location: **Beaches**

| | |
|---|---|
| | Wine tasting/beer for sale |
| X | Food booths |
| X | Arts/crafts for sale |
| X | Live music |
| | Clowns |
| | Face painters |
| | Childrens games |
| | Animal exhibits/petting zoo |
| X | Dogs allowed on leash |
| | Lost and found |
| X | Bicycle racks |
| X | First aid area available |
| X | Self-brought picnics allowed |
| | Self-brought alcohol allowed |
| | Stroller/wheelchair rentals available |

| | |
|---|---|
| | Parade |
| | Parking fee |
| | Entrance fee |
| X | Camping facilities: 20 miles |
| X | Boating facilities: Pacific Ocean |
| X | RV facilities w/ hookups: 10 miles |
| X | Accomodations in town<br>Del Arno Inn, Residence Inn, Holiday Inn, Marriott |
| X | Restaurants in town:<br>Alpine Village, Golden Goose, El Paso Cantina, Curry House, Blue Cactus |

# Malibu Arts Festival

THE CALIBER OF THE **Malibu Arts Festival** is high because of the unusually prominent settlement of artists living in or near this lofty beachfront community! Stained glass, unique weaving, ceramics, one-of-a-kind jewelry, quilts, and woodwork are just some examples of the workmanship on display. While in the neighborhood, stop by the Getty and Malibu Lagoon Museum to get an idea of the area's history.

## Malibu, California

Last weekend in July
Daily 9:00 AM - 5:00 PM

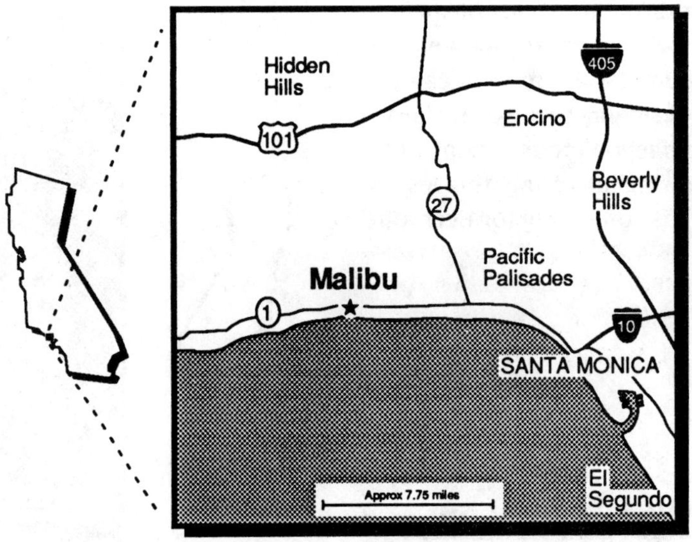


*Up-to-date festival information is available from:*
*Malibu Chamber of Commerce*
*(213) 456-9025*

## What's goin' on...

Town population: **20,000**
Last year's attendance: **6,000**
Average outdoor temperature: **78°**
Festival location: **Colonnade & parking lot**

| | |
|---|---|
| | Wine tasting/beer for sale |
| X | Food booths |
| X | Arts/crafts for sale |
| X | Live music |
| | Clowns |
| X | Face painters |
| | Childrens games |
| | Animal exhibits/petting zoo |
| | Dogs allowed on leash |
| | Lost and found |
| | Bicycle racks |
| | First aid area available |
| | Self-brought picnics allowed |
| | Self-brought alcohol allowed |
| | Stroller/wheelchair rentals available |

| | |
|---|---|
| | Parade |
| | Parking fee |
| | Entrance fee |
| X | Camping facilities: 15 miles |
| X | Boating facilities: Ocean |
| | RV facilities w/ hookups |
| X | Accomodations in town: Malibu Beach Inn, Casa Malibu, Topanga Ranch Motel, Malibu Surfer |
| X | Restaurants in town: Beaurivage, Geoffrey's, LaScala, Alice's, Saddlepeak Lodge |

# *Old Spanish Days Fiesta*

SANTA BARBARA'S OLD **Spanish Days Fiesta** began in 1924! The Fiesta grew out of a prior tradition of infor- mally organized family parties. During Fiesta, the community celebrates its colonial history of different nationalities—Native Amer- ican, Spanish, Mexi- can, American Yankee—with singing, dancing, a mile-long arts-and-crafts show, and great food! The Variety Show is one thing *not* to miss—Saturday at 5:00 PM.

## Santa Barbara, California

First weekend in August (beginning Thursday)
Daily 10:00 AM - midnight

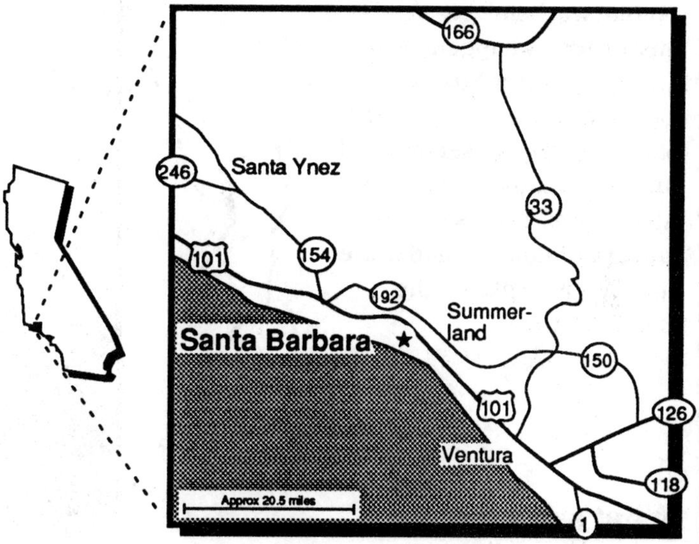


## What's goin' on...

Town population: **350,000**
Last year's attendance: **10,000**
Average outdoor temperature: **78°**
Festival location: **Citywide**

*Up-to-date festival information is available from:*
*Santa Barbara Visitors Bureau*
*(805) 965-3021*

| | |
|---|---|
| X | Wine tasting/beer for sale |
| X | Food booths |
| X | Arts/crafts for sale |
| X | Live music |
| | Clowns |
| | Face painters |
| X | Childrens games |
| | Animal exhibits/petting zoo |
| X | Dogs allowed on leash |
| X | Lost and found |
| X | Bicycle racks |
| X | First aid area available |
| X | Self-brought picnics allowed |
| | Self-brought alcohol allowed |
| | Stroller/wheelchair rentals available |

| | |
|---|---|
| X | Parade: * |
| X | Parking fee |
| X | Entrance fee |
| X | Camping facilities: 3 miles |
| X | Boating facilities: Cachuma Lake |
| X | RV facilities w/ hookups: 10 miles |
| X | Accomodations in town |
| X | Restaurants in town: Wine Cask, Paradise Cafe, Papagaillos |

* HISTORIC PARADE: Thurs. 1:00 PM Cabrillo to State St.; CHILDRENS PARADE: Sat. 10:00 AM on State St.

# *Sports & Smarts Festival*

SANTA MONICA SPARES nothing in August at the **Sports & Smarts Festival!** The Fine Art Show takes place the second weekend, big band pier concerts happen on Thursday and Saturday nights, and discover A Taste of L.A. during the second and third weekends at the Civic Auditorium. Tennis tournaments and dancing under the stars are also part of the excitement!

## Santa Monica, California

Entire month of August
Hours vary

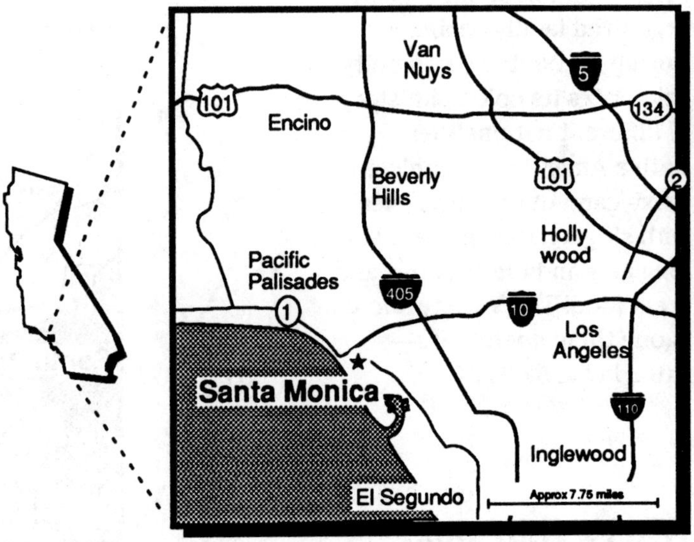


## What's goin' on...

Town population: **94,000**
Last year's attendance: **250,000**
Average outdoor temperature: **75°**
Festival location: **Citywide**

*Up-to-date festival information is available from:*
*Santa Monica Visitor Center*
*(805) 925-2403*

| | |
|---|---|
| | Wine tasting/beer for sale |
| X | Food booths |
| X | Arts/crafts for sale |
| X | Live music |
| | Clowns |
| | Face painters |
| | Childrens games |
| | Animal exhibits/petting zoo |
| | Dogs allowed on leash |
| | Lost and found |
| | Bicycle racks |
| | First aid area available |
| | Self-brought picnics allowed |
| | Self-brought alcohol allowed |
| | Stroller/wheelchair rentals available |

| | |
|---|---|
| | Parade |
| | Parking fee |
| | Entrance fee |
| X | Camping facilities: 10 miles |
| X | Boating facilities: Bay |
| X | RV facilities w/ hookups: 30 miles |
| X | Accomodations in town<br>Hotel Shangri-la, Guest Quarters Suite Hotel, Stardust Motel, Cal Mar Hotel, Comfort Inn |
| X | Restaurants in town:<br>Michael's, 3rd St. Bar & Grill, Ponteueccio, Madame Wu's, Belleview |

# *La Habra Corn Festival*

WAY BACK IN 1951, THE town of La Habra began what's become an annual affair—the **La Habra Corn Festival**! And just what do you suppose they serve at a Corn Festival? Lots and lots of sweet yellow and white corn—barbecued in the husks, ground into tamale casings, and baked into honey-laden cornbread (Marie Callendar, eat your heart out)! There's raffles, contests, a gigantic parade, and a Battle of the Bands!

## La Habra, California

First Fri. & Sat. in August
Fri. 5:00 PM - 11:00 PM; Sat. 11:00 AM - midnight

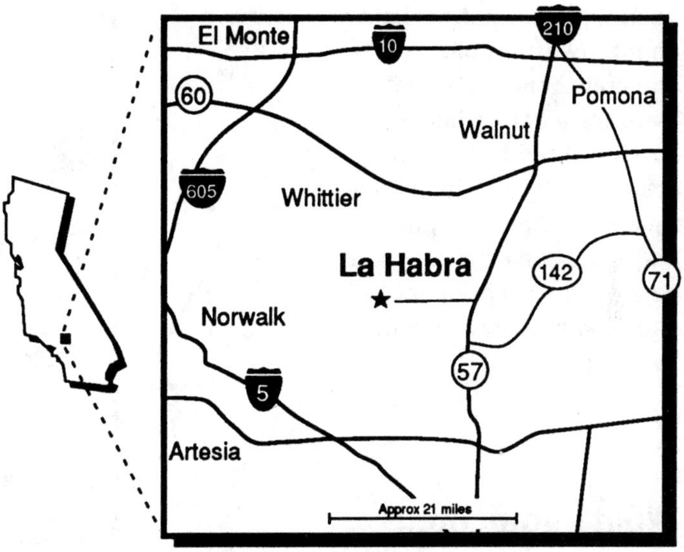


*Up-to-date festival information is available from:*
*La Habra Chamber of Commerce*
*(213) 697-1704*

## What's goin' on...

Town population: **49,000**
Last year's attendance: **60,000**
Average outdoor temperature: **80°**
Festival location: **El Centro Park**

| | |
|---|---|
| ✗ | Wine tasting/beer for sale |
| ✗ | Food booths |
| ✗ | Arts/crafts for sale |
| ✗ | Live music |
| | Clowns |
| | Face painters |
| ✗ | Childrens games |
| ✗ | Animal exhibits/petting zoo |
| | Dogs allowed on leash |
| ✗ | Lost and found |
| ✗ | Bicycle racks |
| | First aid area available |
| ✗ | Self-brought picnics allowed |
| | Self-brought alcohol allowed |
| | Stroller/wheelchair rentals available |

| | |
|---|---|
| ✗ | Parade: Sat. 9:00 AM downtown |
| | Parking fee |
| | Entrance fee |
| | Camping facilities |
| | Boating facilities |
| ✗ | RV facilities w/ hookups: 10 miles |
| ✗ | Accomodations in town<br>Best Western |
| ✗ | Restaurants in town: |

SOUTHERN

# *Dust Bowl Days Festival*

WELL, LAMONT HAD SUCH A good time at their 1990 premiere **Dust Bowl Days Festival**, that it's going to continue the tradition! Lots of country/western music; arts and crafts; and food booths featuring a barbeque sponsored by the Chamber and other food booths including American, Mexican, Indian, and Thai. Come on out , you veteran festival hoppers and show Lamont how to really live it up!

## Lamont, California

Second weekend in August
Daily 11:00 AM - 7:00 PM

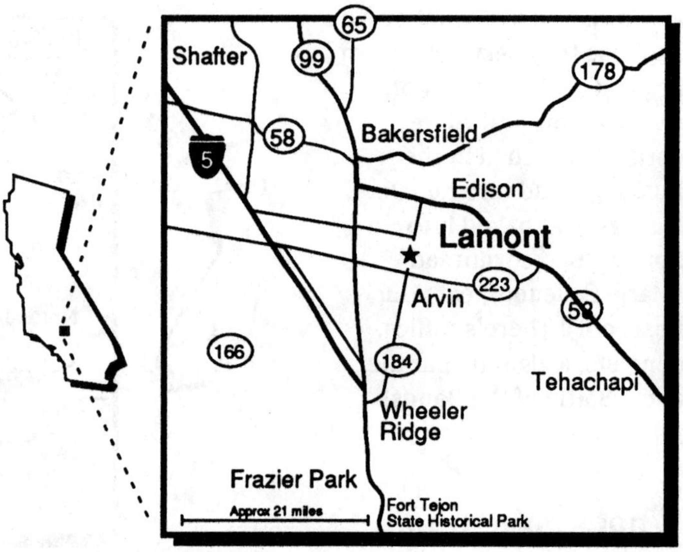


*Up-to-date festival information is available from:*
*Lamont Chamber of Commerce*
*(805) 845-2986*

## What's goin' on...

Town population: **11,000**
Last year's attendance: **1,500**
Average outdoor temperature: **98°**
Festival location: **Lamont Park**

| | |
|---|---|
| ✗ | Wine tasting/beer for sale |
| ✗ | Food booths |
| ✗ | Arts/crafts for sale |
| ✗ | Live music |
| | Clowns |
| | Face painters |
| ✗ | Childrens games |
| | Animal exhibits/petting zoo |
| | Dogs allowed on leash |
| ✗ | Lost and found |
| ✗ | Bicycle racks |
| ✗ | First aid area available |
| ✗ | Self-brought picnics allowed |
| | Self-brought alcohol allowed |
| | Stroller/wheelchair rentals available |

| | |
|---|---|
| | Parade |
| | Parking fee |
| | Entrance fee |
| | Camping facilities |
| | Boating facilities |
| | RV facilities w/ hookups |
| | Accomodations in town |
| ✗ | Restaurants in town: Casa Lopez, El Jacalito |

# *Lake Arrowhead Summer Faire & Swap Meet*

SUMMERTIME, SUMMERTIME, sum...sum...summertime is the perfect time to visit Lake Arrowhead. So check it out just in time for the **Lake Arrowhead Summer Faire & Swap Meet.** You'll find food booths bursting with goodies such as ribs, Chinese food, steak-on-a-stick, sausage samos, nachos, beer, fresh fruit drinks, and lots more! Besides the swap meet, there are handmade-crafts booths too!

## Lake Arrowhead, California

Second Saturday in August

10:00 AM - 5:00 PM

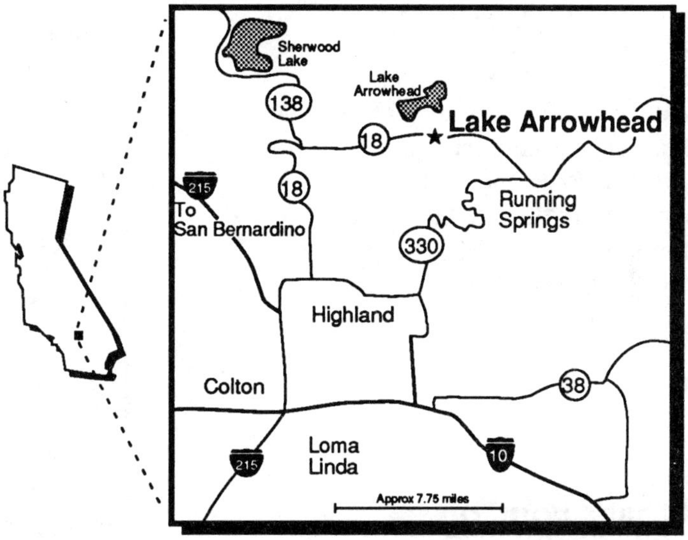


## What's goin' on...

Town population: **22,500**

Last year's attendance: **2,000**

Average outdoor temperature: **80°**

Festival location: **Santas Village Theme Park**

*Up-to-date festival information is available from:*
*Lake Arrowhead Chamber of Commerce*
*(714) 337-3715*

- ✗ Wine tasting/beer for sale
- ✗ Food booths
- ✗ Arts/crafts for sale
- ✗ Live music
- ✗ Clowns
- ✗ Face painters
- ✗ Childrens games
- ✗ Animal exhibits/petting zoo
- ✗ Dogs allowed on leash
- ✗ Lost and found
- ✗ Bicycle racks
- ✗ First aid area available
- Self-brought picnics allowed
- Self-brought alcohol allowed
- Stroller/wheelchair rentals available

- Parade
- Parking fee
- ✗ Entrance fee: 50¢
- ✗ Camping facilities: Lake Arrowhead
- ✗ Boating facilities: 3 miles
- ✗ RV facilities w/ hookups: 3 miles
- ✗ Accomodations in town
  Hilton Lodge, Saddleback Inn
- ✗ Restaurants in town:
  Tudor House, McAffee's, Hilton Lobby Cafe, Saddleback Inn

# *Lake Arrowhead Summer Music Festival*

THE SNOW VALLEY SKI Resort doubles as the site for the **Lake Arrowhead Summer Music Festival**! Set in the ideal atmosphere of San Bernardino Forest, the entertainment for this second annual event will be along the lines of jazz, country and western, R&B, and rock 'n' roll. During the daytime, visit the Summer Faire and Swap Meet at Santas Village Theme Park (see page 413).

## Lake Arrowhead, California

Second Saturday in August
6:00 PM - midnight

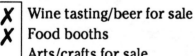

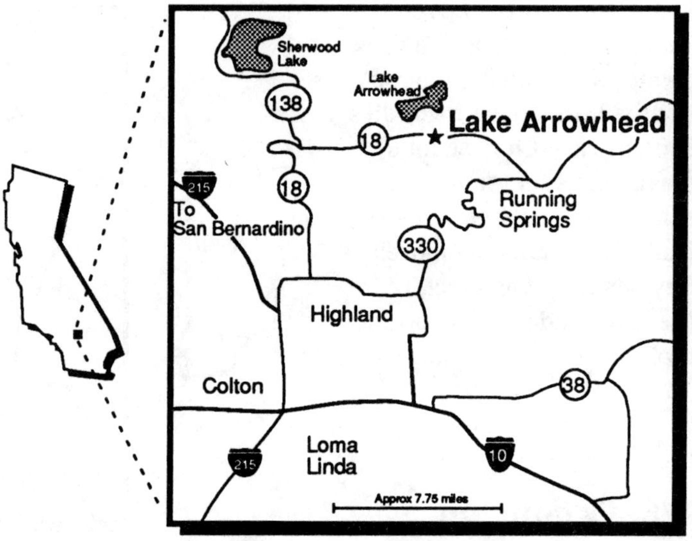


*Up-to-date festival information is available from:*
*Lake Arrowhead Chamber of Commerce*
*(714) 337-3715*

## What's goin' on...

Town population: **22,500**
Last year's attendance: **N/A**
Average outdoor temperature: **80°**
Festival location: **Snow Valley Ski Resort**

| | |
|---|---|
| ✗ | Wine tasting/beer for sale |
| ✗ | Food booths |
| | Arts/crafts for sale |
| | Live music |
| | Clowns |
| | Face painters |
| | Childrens games |
| | Animal exhibits/petting zoo |
| | Dogs allowed on leash |
| ✗ | Lost and found |
| | Bicycle racks |
| ✗ | First aid area available |
| | Self-brought picnics allowed |
| | Self-brought alcohol allowed |
| ✗ | Stroller/wheelchair rentals available |

| | |
|---|---|
| | Parade |
| ✗ | Parking fee: $3 |
| ✗ | Entrance fee: $20 |
| ✗ | Camping facilities: 1 mile |
| ✗ | Boating facilities: 1 mile |
| ✗ | RV facilities w/ hookups: 3 miles |
| ✗ | Accomodations in town<br>Hilton Lodge, Saddleback Inn |
| ✗ | Restaurants in town:<br>Tudor House, McAffee's, Hilton Lobby Cafe, Saddleback Inn |

# A Taste of L.A.

EAT, DRINK, & BE MERRY AT **A Taste of L.A.** The scrumptious food on hand is well worth the $6 entry fee! Complement the cuisine of fine Santa Monica and L.A. restaurants with a glass of full-bodied cabernet, and your taste buds will be rejoicing! Live bands of popular and jazz music will serenade you while you sample the goodies. These are some *great* eats!

## Santa Monica, California

Second and third weekends in August
Hours vary

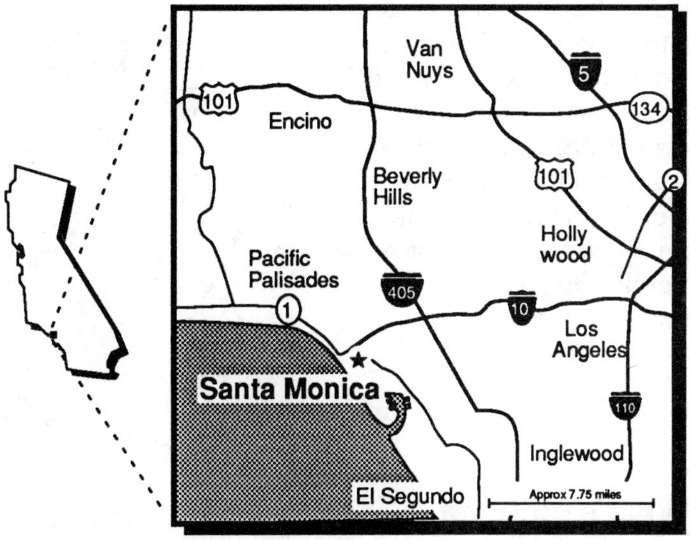


☞ *Up-to-date festival information is available from:*
*Santa Monica Visitor Center*
*(805) 925-2403*

## What's goin' on...

Town population: **90,000**
Last year's attendance: **N/A**
Average outdoor temperature: **72°**
Festival location: **Civic Auditorium**

| | |
|---|---|
| X | Wine tasting/beer for sale |
| X | Food booths |
| X | Arts/crafts for sale |
| X | Live music |
| X | Clowns |
| X | Face painters |
| X | Childrens games |
| X | Animal exhibits/petting zoo |
| X | Dogs allowed on leash |
| X | Lost and found |
| X | Bicycle racks |
| X | First aid area available |
| X | Self-brought picnics allowed |
| X | Self-brought alcohol allowed |
| X | Stroller/wheelchair rentals available |

| | |
|---|---|
| | Parade |
| | Parking fee |
| X | Entrance fee: (prices not avbl.) |
| X | Camping facilities: 4 miles |
| X | Boating facilities: Pacific Ocean |
| X | RV facilities w/ hookups: 2 miles |
| X | Accomodations in town<br>Miramar Sheraton, Oceana Hotel, Comfort Inn, Pacific Shore Hotel |
| X | Restaurants in town:<br>La Patisserie, La Strada, 3rd Street Pub & Grill, Skorpio's II, Teasers, Taka Sushi, The American Diner, Chanpen |

# *Wine Fest*

THE TORRANCE **WINE FEST** is a special event— featuring dozens of a varietal wines for tasting. This is a delightful way to spend a lazy August afternoon in Southern California. While in the area, Knott's Berry Farm, Disneyland, universal Studios, Catalina Island, Hollywood, and Magic Mountain may vie for your time! There's always something fun happening in this part of the world!

## Torrance, California

Second Saturday in August
10:00 AM - 6:00 PM

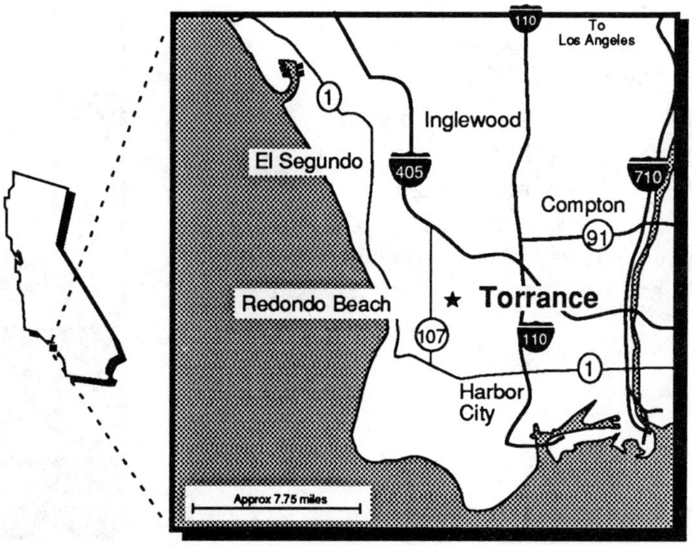


## What's goin' on...

Town population: **130,000**
Last year's attendance: **N/A**
Average outdoor temperature: **80°**
Festival location: **N/A**

*Up-to-date festival information is available from:*
*Torrance Chamber of Commerce*
*(213) 540-5858*

- ✗ Wine tasting/beer for sale
- ✗ Food booths
- ✗ Arts/crafts for sale
- ✗ Live music
- Clowns
- Face painters
- Childrens games
- Animal exhibits/petting zoo
- Dogs allowed on leash
- Lost and found
- Bicycle racks
- First aid area available
- Self-brought picnics allowed
- Self-brought alcohol allowed
- Stroller/wheelchair rentals available

- Parade
- Parking fee
- Entrance fee
- ✗ Camping facilities: 20 miles
- ✗ Boating facilities: Pacific Ocean
- ✗ RV facilities w/ hookups: 10 miles
- ✗ Accomodations in town
  Del Amo Inn, Residence Inn, Holiday Inn, Marriott
- ✗ Restaurants in town
  Alpine Village, Golden Goose, El Paso Cantina, Curry House, Blue Cactus

# *Venice Summer Arts & Crafts Festival*

THE FRIENDLY, RELAXED setting of Venice is ideal for the **Venice Summer Arts & Crafts Festival**—and geez, 50 thousand people can't be all wrong! This festival is overflowing with nearly 350 booths of everything you can possible think of! And as for food and drink, this celebration features oriental, American, Italian, and lots of sweet treats! Take a gondola charter ride or a stroll along the Boardwalk, too!

## Venice, California

Second Sunday in August
10:00 AM - 6:00 PM

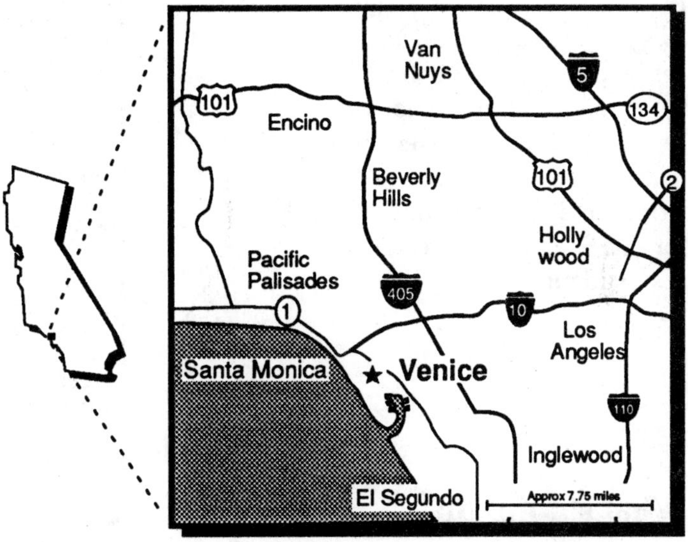


## What's goin' on...

Town population: **39,200**
Last year's attendance: **50,000**
Average outdoor temperature: **90°**
Festival location: **Abbot Kinney Blvd.**

☞ *Up-to-date festival information is available from:*
*Venice Chamber of Commerce*
*(213) 827-2366*

| | |
|---|---|
| | Wine tasting/beer for sale |
| X | Food booths |
| X | Arts/crafts for sale |
| X | Live music |
| X | Clowns |
| X | Face painters |
| X | Childrens games |
| X | Animal exhibits/petting zoo |
| X | Dogs allowed on leash |
| X | Lost and found |
| X | Bicycle racks |
| X | First aid area available |
| | Self-brought picnics allowed |
| | Self-brought alcohol allowed |
| | Stroller/wheelchair rentals available |

| | |
|---|---|
| | Parade |
| X | Parking fee: $3.00 |
| | Entrance fee |
| | Camping facilities |
| X | Boating facilities |
| | RV facilities w/ hookups |
| X | Accomodations in town<br>Marina Pacific Hotel, Jolly Roger, Sea Lodge Hotel, Casa Isabella |
| X | Restaurants in town<br>Benny's BBQ, Dandelion Cafe, Hal's Bar & Grill, Casablanca, Land's End Restaurant, Red Onion |

SOUTHERN

# *Arrowhead Arts Annual Music Festival*

THE SOUNDS OF BACH, Chopin, and Mozart drifting through the air at the **Arrowhead Arts Annual Music Festival** will take your breath away! If you've gone once to this event, you'll probably never miss it again! Besides the music festival, this event features well-known artists' works on display and offered for sale. Please call ahead for reservations.

## Lake Arrowhead, California

Third weekend in August (beginning Friday)
Hours vary

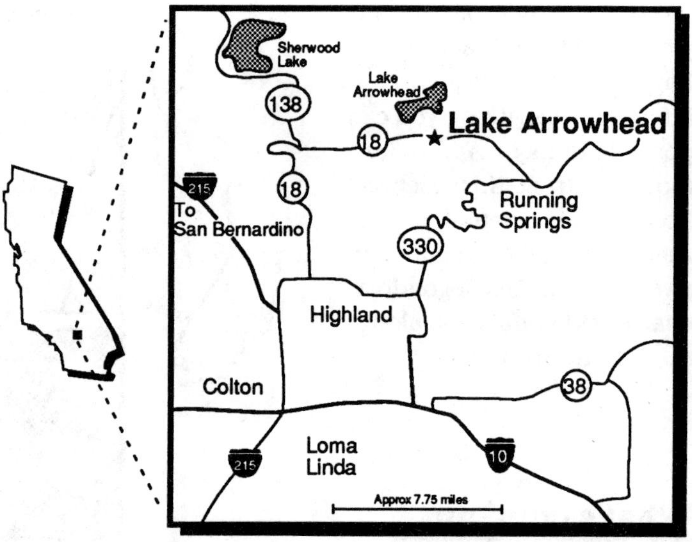


## What's goin' on...

Town population: **22,500**
Last year's attendance: **1,100**
Average outdoor temperature: **75°**
Festival location: **Catholic Church**

☞ *Up-to-date festival information is available from:*
*Lake Arrowhead Chamber of Commerce*
*(714) 337-3715*

| | |
|---|---|
| | Wine tasting/beer for sale |
| X | Food booths |
| X | Arts/crafts for sale |
| X | Live music |
| | Clowns |
| | Face painters |
| | Childrens games |
| | Animal exhibits/petting zoo |
| | Dogs allowed on leash |
| | Lost and found |
| | Bicycle racks |
| | First aid area available |
| | Self-brought picnics allowed |
| | Self-brought alcohol allowed |
| | Stroller/wheelchair rentals available |

| | |
|---|---|
| | Parade |
| | Parking fee |
| X | Entrance fee: $15 - $35 |
| X | Camping facilities: 1 mile |
| X | Boating facilities: Lake Arrowhead |
| X | RV facilities w/ hookups: 3 miles |
| X | Accomodations in town<br>Hilton Lodge, Saddleback Inn |
| X | Restaurants in town<br>Tudor House, McAffee's, Hilton Lobby Cafe, Saddleback Inn |

# *Celebrity Starscene*

LOOSEN UP YOUR ELBOWS for a little star-rubbing at the **Celebrity Starscene**! Taking place near the famous Universal Studios, this festival promises all the enchantment of the Hollywood scene. Lest we forget all the fun this area offers: Disneyland, Knott's Berry Farm, Universal Studio tours, Rodeo Drive, and countless museums and parks to visit.

## No. Hollywood, California

Third weekend in August (beginning Friday)
Fri. 4:00 PM - midnight; Sat. noon - midnight; Sun. noon - 9:00 PM

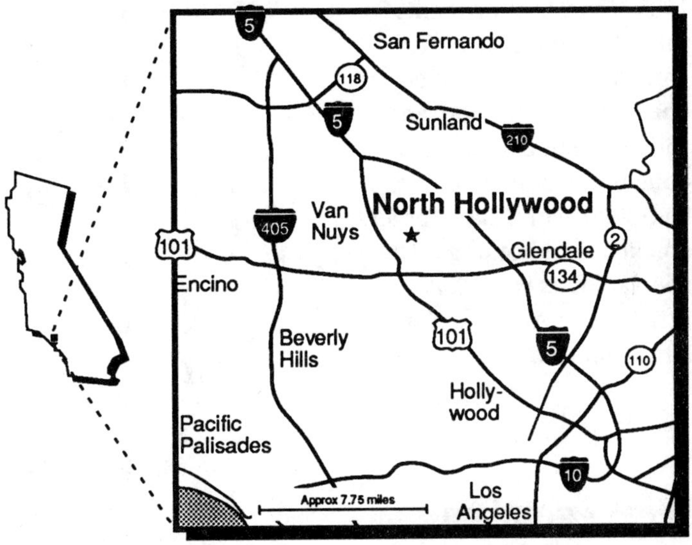


## What's goin' on...

Town population: **15,000**
Last year's attendance: **40,000**
Average outdoor temperature: **90°**
Festival location: **No. Hollywood Park**

*Up-to-date festival information is available from:*
*No. Hollywood Chamber of Commerce*
*(818) 761-6594*

| | |
|---|---|
| X | Wine tasting/beer for sale |
| X | Food booths |
| X | Arts/crafts for sale |
| X | Live music |
| X | Clowns |
| X | Face painters |
| X | Childrens games |
| X | Animal exhibits/petting zoo |
| | Dogs allowed on leash |
| X | Lost and found |
| | Bicycle racks |
| X | First aid area available |
| X | Self-brought picnics allowed |
| | Self-brought alcohol allowed |
| | Stroller/wheelchair rentals available |

| | |
|---|---|
| | Parade |
| X | Parking fee: $2 |
| X | Entrance fee: S $4; A $5; K $2 |
| | Camping facilities |
| | Boating facilities |
| | RV facilities w/ hookups |
| X | Accomodations in town<br>Burbank Hilton, Sportsman Lodge, Sheraton Universal |
| X | Restaurants in town<br>Chez Nous, Beaux Tie Grill, Victoria Station |

SOUTHERN

# *Mountain Festival*

THE TEHACHAPI **MOUNTAIN Festival** began in 1963; it was so successful that PCRA rodeo was added back in 1985. There's a "cow chip" throwing con- test, square dancing, west- ern dance, children's pet parade, and rodeo-queen contest. The concession stands feature a tri-tip barbecue, hamburgers, chicken, and hot dogs. The special focus is on *talented* artists from Arizona, Nevada, and California.

## Tehachapi, California

Third weekend in August
Daily: 10:00 AM - 5:00 PM

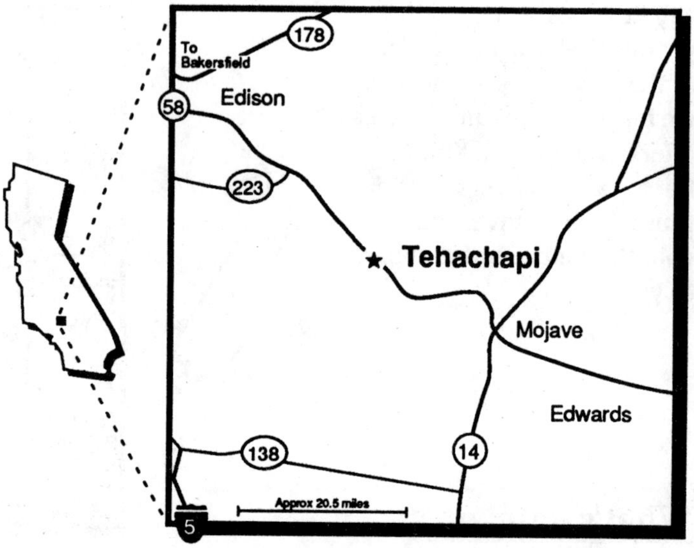


*Up-to-date festival information is available from:*
*Tehachapi Chamber of Commerce*
*(805) 822-4180*

## What's goin' on...

Town population: **20,000**
Last year's attendance: **30,000**
Average outdoor temperature: **82°**
Festival location: **City Park & Rodeo**

| | |
|---|---|
| ✗ | Wine tasting/beer for sale |
| ✗ | Food booths |
| ✗ | Arts/crafts for sale |
| ✗ | Live music |
| | Clowns |
| ✗ | Face painters |
| ✗ | Childrens games |
| | Animal exhibits/petting zoo |
| | Dogs allowed on leash |
| | Lost and found |
| | Bicycle racks |
| | First aid area available |
| | Self-brought picnics allowed |
| | Self-brought alcohol allowed |
| ✗ | Stroller/wheelchair rentals available |

| | |
|---|---|
| ✗ | Parade: Sat. 10:00 on F St. |
| ✗ | Parking fee: $2 |
| ✗ | Entrance fee: Rodeo only |
| ✗ | Camping facilities: [illegible] miles |
| | Boating facilities |
| ✗ | RV facilities w/ hookups: 2 miles |
| ✗ | Accomodations in town<br>Tehachapi Mountain Lodge, Mountain Inn, Best Western |
| ✗ | Restaurants in town<br>Stallion Springs, Flour Mills |

# *Weed Show & Art Mart*

THERE ARE GOLD MINES TO tour in the little town of Julian—but only after you've enjoyed the 31st annual **Weed Show and Art Mart**, happening in late August. Now, we can assure you that even we're not quite sure what's to see at a "weed" show, but if it's their 31st annual...there must be something to it! You can also climb onto the carriage and buckboards they have available for rides.

## Julian, California

Third and fourth week in August
Daily 9:00 AM - 5:00 PM

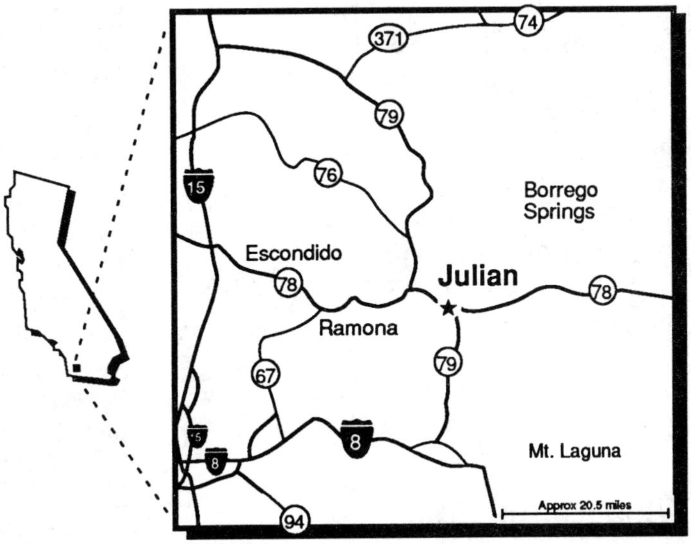


*Up-to-date festival information is available from:*
*Julian Chamber of Commerce*
*(619) 765-1857*

## What's goin' on...

Town population: **2,500**
Last year's attendance: **3,000**
Average outdoor temperature: **80°**
Festival location: **Town Hall**

| | |
|---|---|
| ✗ | Wine tasting/beer for sale |
| | Food booths |
| ✗ | Arts/crafts for sale |
| | Live music |
| ✗ | Clowns |
| ✗ | Face painters |
| ✗ | Childrens games |
| | Animal exhibits/petting zoo |
| ✗ | Dogs allowed on leash |
| ✗ | Lost and found |
| | Bicycle racks |
| ✗ | First aid area available |
| ✗ | Self-brought picnics allowed |
| | Self-brought alcohol allowed |
| | Stroller/wheelchair rentals available |

| | |
|---|---|
| | Parade |
| | Parking fee |
| | Entrance fee |
| ✗ | Camping facilities: 5 miles |
| ✗ | Boating facilities: 10 miles |
| ✗ | RV facilities w/ hookups: 5 miles |
| ✗ | Accomodations in town |
| ✗ | Restaurants in town |

# *Harvest Arts Festival*

LET THE STROLLING MUSICIANS entertain you as you browse through the many, many art and craft booths set up in Ryon Park for the **Harvest Arts Festival**. You'll also enjoy the smell of the barbecues cooking up chicken, tri-tips, and burgers! Take a tour through the La Purisiam Mission too. It's California's most perfectly restored of all the California missions.

## Lompoc, California

Third weekend in September
Daily 10:00 AM - 7:00 PM

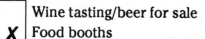

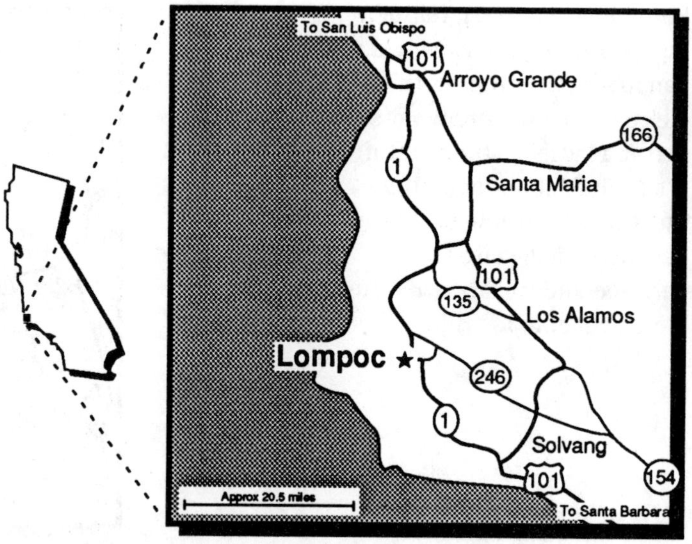


*Up-to-date festival information is available from:*
*Lompoc Valley Festival Assn.*
*(805) 736-4567*

## What's goin' on...

Town population: **33,000**
Last year's attendance: **5,000**
Average outdoor temperature: **72°**
Festival location: **Ryon Park & downtown**

| | |
|---|---|
| | Wine tasting/beer for sale |
| X | Food booths |
| X | Arts/crafts for sale |
| X | Live music |
| X | Clowns |
| X | Face painters |
| X | Childrens games |
| | Animal exhibits/petting zoo |
| | Dogs allowed on leash |
| X | Lost and found |
| X | Bicycle racks |
| | First aid area available |
| X | Self-brought picnics allowed |
| | Self-brought alcohol allowed |
| | Stroller/wheelchair rentals available |

| | |
|---|---|
| | Parade |
| | Parking fee |
| | Entrance fee |
| X | Camping facilities, 2 miles |
| X | Boating facilities: Lake Cachuma |
| X | RV facilities w/ hookups: 2 miles |
| X | Accomodations in town<br>Embassy Suites, Motel 6 |
| X | Restaurants in town<br>Dollar Bill, Village Oaks, J.B. McGees |

# Antelope Valley Fair

YEP! IT'S A SMALL TOWN, all right...but Lancaster sure packs 'em in for the big, ten-day **Antelope Valley Fair!** The townsfolk tell us that this fair is more than 30 years old! Jam-packed with entertaining things to do—this fair offers games, lots of great food, contests, a dynamite parade, livestock shows, amusement rides, and a classic-car show! Sounds like you'll find something to do, right?

## Lancaster, California

Fourth weekend in August through Labor Day
Weekdays 4:00 PM - 11:30 PM; weekends Noon - midnight

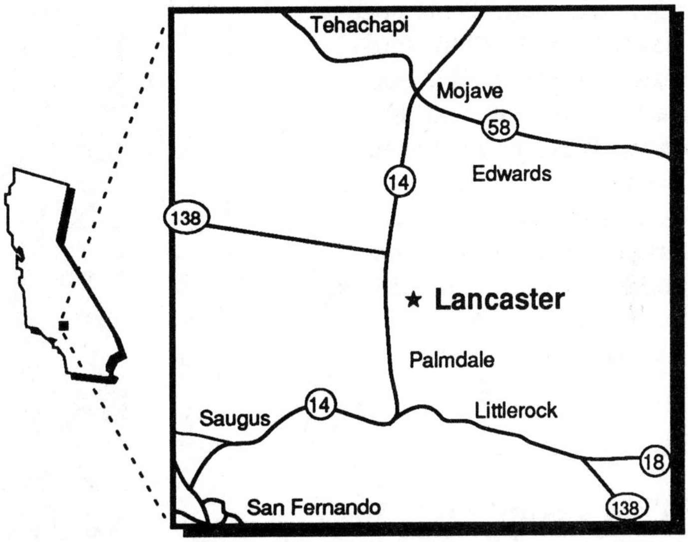


*Up-to-date festival information is available from:*
*Lancaster Chamber of Commerce*
*(805) 948-4518*

## What's goin' on...

Town population: **82,100**
Last year's attendance: **200,000**
Average outdoor temperature: **100°**
Festival location: **Fairgrounds**

- X Wine tasting/beer for sale
- X Food booths
- X Arts/crafts for sale
- X Live music
- X Clowns
- X Face painters
- X Childrens games
- X Animal exhibits/petting zoo
- Dogs allowed on leash
- X Lost and found
- X Bicycle racks
- X First aid area available
- X Self-brought picnics allowed
- Self-brought alcohol allowed
- X Stroller/wheelchair rentals available

- X Parade: Fri. 5:00 PM in town
- X Parking fee: $2
- X Entrance fee: S $1.50; A $3.50; K $2
- X Camping facilities: 10 miles
- X Boating facilities: Castaic Lake
- X RV facilities w/ hookups: 10 miles
- X Accomodations in town
- X Restaurants in town

# *Fiesta de las Artes*

THE **FIESTA DE LAS ARTES** is such a fantastic bash...that it happens twice a year! Yessiree! There's a May celebration and a September Fiesta in the fall. With more than 100,000 festival hoppers attending last year, the 400 or so artists and craftspersons are kept very busy during the Beach's winter months. The International Food Pavilion boasts more than 30 delicious food booths not to be missed...

## Hermosa Beach, California

Labor Day weekend
Daily 10:00 AM - 6:00 PM

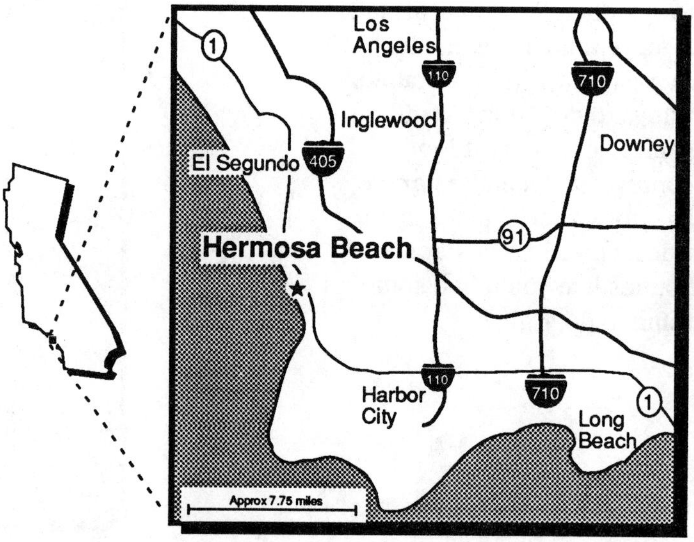


## What's goin' on...

Town population: **19,000**
Last year's attendance: **100,000**
Average outdoor temperature: **76°**
Festival location: **Downtown**

*Up-to-date festival information is available from:*
*Hermosa Beach Chamber of Commerce*
*(213) 376-0951*

- ✗ Wine tasting/beer for sale
- ✗ Food booths
- ✗ Arts/crafts for sale
- ✗ Live music
- ✗ Clowns
- ✗ Face painters
- ✗ Childrens games
- ✗ Animal exhibits/petting zoo
- ✗ Dogs allowed on leash
- ✗ Lost and found
- ✗ Bicycle racks
- ✗ First aid area available
- ✗ Self-brought picnics allowed
- ✗ Self-brought alcohol allowed
- ✗ Stroller/wheelchair rentals available

- ✗ Parade
- ✗ Parking fee: $2
- Entrance fee
- ✗ Camping facilities
- ✗ Boating facilities: Pacific Ocean
- ✗ RV facilities w/ hookups: In town
- ✗ Accomodations in town
- ✗ Restaurants in town

Ajetis, Cantina Real, Cafe Christopher, Good Stuff, Mermaid's

# *Oxnard Air Show*

THRILLING AEROBATIC stunts, parachutists, and wing walking can all be witnessed with jaw-dropping "ahhhhh's" at the **Oxnard Air Show.** During the day, you can enjoy the celebrity air race and jet demonstration, and the aviation-related crafts and art for sale. After-hours, kick up your heels at the black-tie hangar-party dinner and dance. This is one weekend you'll never forget!

## Oxnard, California

Weekend prior to Labor Day
Sat. 10:00 AM - midnight; Sun. 10:00 AM - 5:00 PM

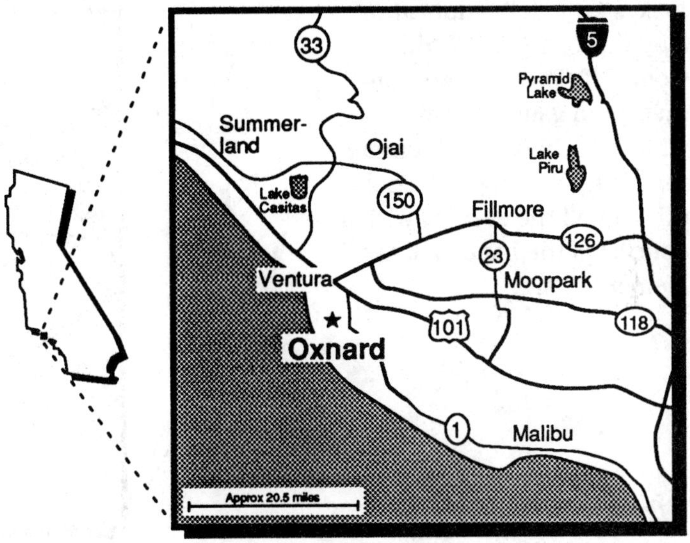


*Up-to-date festival information is available from:*
*Oxnard Chamber of Commerce*
*(805) 487-6305*

## What's goin' on...

Town population: **150,000**
Last year's attendance: **20,000**
Average outdoor temperature: **70°**
Festival location: **Oxnard Airport**

| | |
|---|---|
| X | Wine tasting/beer for sale |
| X | Food booths |
| X | Arts/crafts for sale |
| | Live music |
| X | Clowns |
| X | Face painters |
| | Childrens games |
| | Animal exhibits/petting zoo |
| | Dogs allowed on leash |
| X | Lost and found |
| | Bicycle racks |
| X | First aid area available |
| X | Self-brought picnics allowed |
| | Self-brought alcohol allowed |
| | Stroller/wheelchair rentals available |

| | |
|---|---|
| | Parade |
| X | Parking fee: Prices vary |
| X | Entrance fee: Adults $5; Kids $3 |
| X | Camping facilities: 3 miles |
| X | Boating facilities: Channel Is. Harbor |
| X | RV facilities w/ hookups: 5 miles |
| X | Accomodations in town: Casa Sirena, Embassy Suites, Channel Island Motel, Crystal Lodge, Surfside Motel |
| X | Restaurants in town: Siam BBQ, Filomena's |

SOUTHERN

# *Labor Day Celebration & Chili Cook-Off*

CLAREMONT IS A SUBTLE blend of New England charm and Southern California beauty. And that package makes for a delightful **Labor Day Celebration & Chili Cook-Off!** There's entertainment, and games to enjoy while the chefs are preparing for the rip-roaring chili cook-off. Top off the evening with a concert in the bandshell at Memorial Park.

## Claremont, California

Labor Day
10:00 AM - 9:00 PM

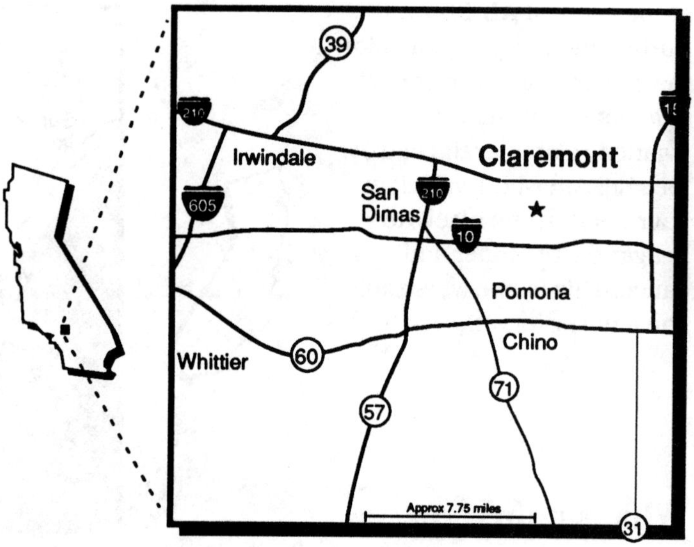


*Up-to-date festival information is available from:*
*Claremont Chamber of Commerce*
*(714) 624-4681*

## What's goin' on...

Town population: **36,500**
Last year's attendance: **N/A**
Average outdoor temperature: **75°**
Festival location: **Memorial Park**

| | |
|---|---|
| ✗ | Wine tasting/beer for sale |
| ✗ | Food booths |
| ✗ | Arts/crafts for sale |
| ✗ | Live music |
| | Clowns |
| | Face painters |
| ✗ | Childrens games |
| | Animal exhibits/petting zoo |
| ✗ | Dogs allowed on leash |
| | Lost and found |
| ✗ | Bicycle racks |
| | First aid area available |
| ✗ | Self-brought picnics allowed |
| | Self-brought alcohol allowed |
| | Stroller/wheelchair rentals available |

| | |
|---|---|
| | Parade |
| | Parking fee |
| | Entrance fee |
| ✗ | Camping facilities: 7 miles |
| ✗ | Boating facilities: Lake |
| ✗ | RV facilities w/ hookups: 7 miles |
| ✗ | Accomodations in town: Griswold's Inn, Claremont Motel Inn, Howard Johnson, Ramada Inn |
| ✗ | Restaurants in town: The Danson, Original Shrimp House, Village Grille, 3 C's Cafe, Blue Moon Cafe, Chili's |

# *Community Fair*

MISSION HILLS HAS BEEN entertaining visitors for years at its annual **Community Fair**. Set in the heart of Southern California, this friendly town serves up eight days of enjoyment—a parade, arts and crafts faire, carnival games, and lots of great entertainment. While there, stop over at Mission San Fernando Rey de España—a beautifully restored and reconstructed 1796 mission.

## Mission Hills, California

First Saturday to the second Sunday in September
Hours vary

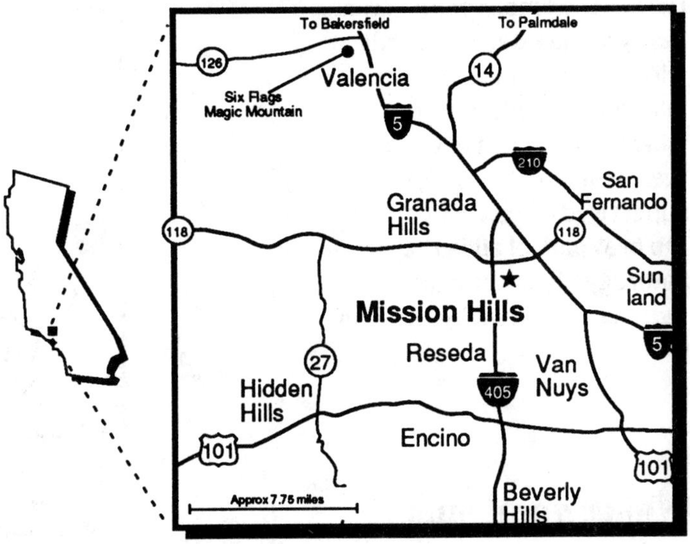


## What's goin' on...

Town population: **50,000**
Last year's attendance: **1,000**
Average outdoor temperature: **80°**
Festival location: **Park**

*Up-to-date festival information is available from:*
*Mission Hills Chamber of Commerce*
*(818) 361-8888*

| | |
|---|---|
| | Wine tasting/beer for sale |
| ✗ | Food booths |
| ✗ | Arts/crafts for sale |
| ✗ | Live music |
| ✗ | Clowns |
| ✗ | Face painters |
| ✗ | Childrens games |
| ✗ | Animal exhibits/petting zoo |
| | Dogs allowed on leash |
| ✗ | Lost and found |
| | Bicycle racks |
| ✗ | First aid area available |
| ✗ | Self-brought picnics allowed |
| | Self-brought alcohol allowed |
| | Stroller/wheelchair rentals available |

| | |
|---|---|
| ✗ | Parade: (time & date not avbl.) |
| | Parking fee |
| | Entrance fee |
| ✗ | Camping facilities: 10 miles |
| | Boating facilities |
| ✗ | RV facilities w/ hookups: 10 miles |
| ✗ | Accomodations in town<br>Best Western |
| ✗ | Restaurants in town<br>Odyssey Restaurant |

# *Wasco Festival of Roses*

WELL, IT'S JUST ABOUT TIME you wake up and smell the **Wasco Festival of Roses**! There's a fun run through the roses—the smells are so great that you may decide to walk with the rest of us! The art faire has a children's area where you can leave the kids (yes, you read right!) for supervised art activities. But the best part of all is the Saturday night buffet and barn dance put on by the Elks Club!

## Wasco, California

Saturday and Sunday following Labor Day
Hours vary

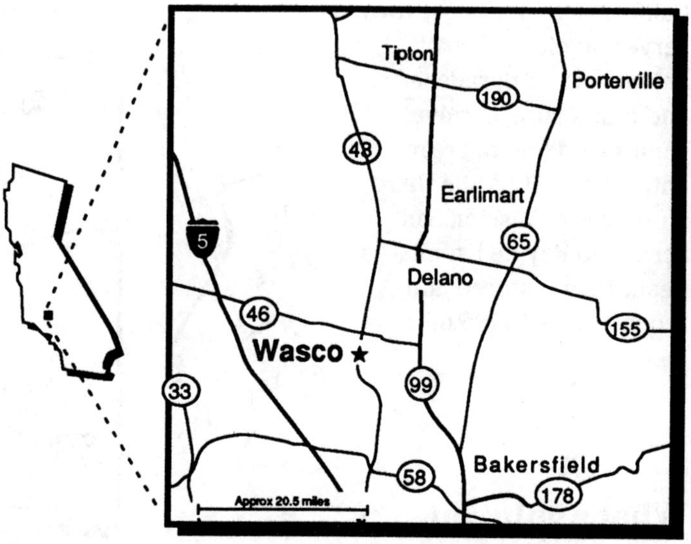


*Up-to-date festival information is available from:*
*Wasco Chamber of Commerce*
*(805) 758-2746*

## What's goin' on...

Town population: **11,240**
Last year's attendance: **15,000**
Average outdoor temperature: **89°**
Festival location: **Park**

| | |
|---|---|
| | Wine tasting/beer for sale |
| X | Food booths |
| X | Arts/crafts for sale |
| X | Live music |
| | Clowns |
| X | Face painters |
| X | Childrens games |
| | Animal exhibits/petting zoo |
| X | Dogs allowed on leash |
| X | Lost and found |
| X | Bicycle racks |
| X | First aid area available |
| X | Self-brought picnics allowed |
| | Self-brought alcohol allowed |
| | Stroller/wheelchair rentals available |

| | |
|---|---|
| X | Parade: Sat. 10:00 AM downtown |
| | Parking fee |
| | Entrance fee |
| X | Camping facilities: [illegible] miles |
| X | Boating facilities: Lake Isabella |
| X | RV facilities w/ hookups: 15 miles |
| X | Accomodations in town<br>Cinderella Motel, Wasco Inn Motel |
| X | Restaurants in town<br>Mings, Victory Cafe, Tom's, Pagoda Inn |

# *Japanese Festival*

THE **JAPANESE FESTIVAL** IN Santa Barbara takes place on the temple grounds. Featuring delicacies such as chicken teriyacki, won tons, and sushi, you will enjoy looking over the Japanese goods and handicrafts to buy. If you aren't familiar with the Japanese culture, this will be a fun and educational experience for your whole family.

## Santa Barbara, California

First Saturday in September
2:00 PM - 8:00 PM

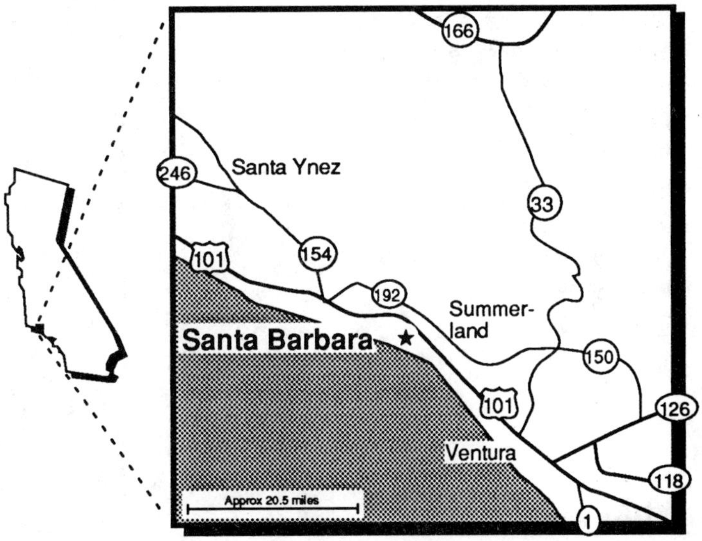


*Up-to-date festival information is available from:*
*Santa Barbara Visitors Bureau*
*(805) 965-3021*

## What's goin' on...

Town population: **350,000**
Last year's attendance: **2,500**
Average outdoor temperature: **75°**
Festival location: **Temple**

| | |
|---|---|
| ✗ | Wine tasting/beer for sale |
| ✗ | Food booths |
| ✗ | Arts/crafts for sale |
| | Live music |
| | Clowns |
| | Face painters |
| | Childrens games |
| | Animal exhibits/petting zoo |
| | Dogs allowed on leash |
| ✗ | Lost and found |
| | Bicycle racks |
| | First aid area available |
| ✗ | Self-brought picnics allowed |
| | Self-brought alcohol allowed |
| | Stroller/wheelchair rentals available |

| | |
|---|---|
| | Parade |
| | Parking fee |
| | Entrance fee |
| ✗ | Camping facilities: 3 miles |
| ✗ | Boating facilities: Lake Casitas |
| ✗ | RV facilities w/ hookups: 10 miles |
| ✗ | Accomodations in town |
| ✗ | Restaurants in town<br>Maxim's, The Chart House |

# *Danish Days*

THERE'S NOTHING QUITE like the smell of æbleskives in the morning! Come find out for yourself at one of California's finest festivals, **Danish Days** in delightful Solvang! You'll see Danish folk dancing and roving entertainers, taste medisterpølse (sausage) and Carlsberg Beer, try out the smørgåsbord, and witness a whole lot of hospitality in this Danish community!

## Solvang, California

Second weekend in September (beginning Thursday)
Hours vary

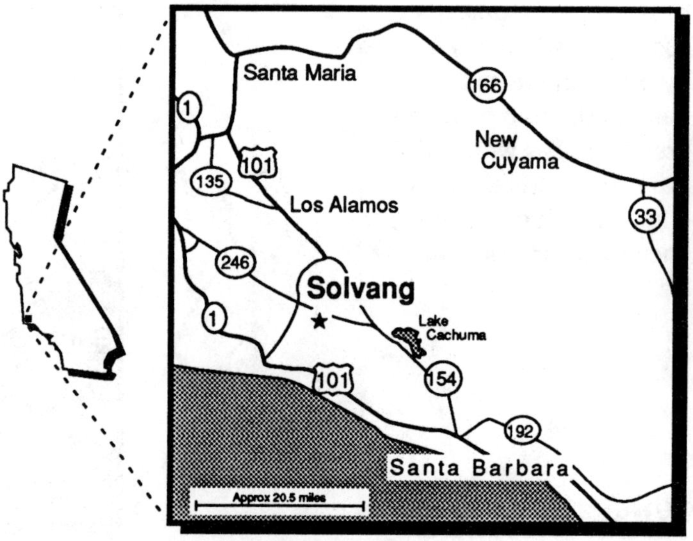


*Up-to-date festival information is available from:*
*Solvang Chamber of Commerce*
*(805) 699-3317*

## What's goin' on...

Town population: **4,000**
Last year's attendance: **20,000**
Average outdoor temperature: **83°**
Festival location: **Villagewide**

- X Wine tasting/beer for sale
- X Food booths
- Arts/crafts for sale
- X Live music
- X Clowns
- X Face painters
- X Childrens games
- Animal exhibits/petting zoo
- X Dogs allowed on leash
- X Lost and found
- X Bicycle racks
- X First aid area available
- X Self-brought picnics allowed
- Self-brought alcohol allowed
- X Stroller/wheelchair rentals available

- X Parade: Sat. & Sun. 3:00 PM in village
- Parking fee
- Entrance fee
- X Camping facilities: 3-12 miles
- X Boating facilities: Lake Cachuma
- X RV facilities w/ hookups: 3-12 miles
- X Accomodations in town
  Svendsgaar's Lodge, Solvang Gaard Lodge, Danish Country Inn, Tivoli Inn, Kronborg Inn
- X Restaurants in town
  Royal Scandia, Bit O'Denmark, Little Mermaid, Møllekroen, Mustard Seed, Viking Garden

# *Gold Rush Days*

MOJAVE, HOME TO THAT big, beautiful hunk of steel—the Voyager Space Shuttle—is also home to **Gold Rush Days**! This two-and-a-half-day event highlights Mojave artists and craftspeople who show and sell—and hold a "best stuff" competition. The music includes 50s, R&B, jazz, country, and a little bit of rock 'n' roll. And the food? Barbecued dogs, ribs, burgers, and chicken.

## Mojave, California

Second weekend in September (beginning Friday)
Hours vary

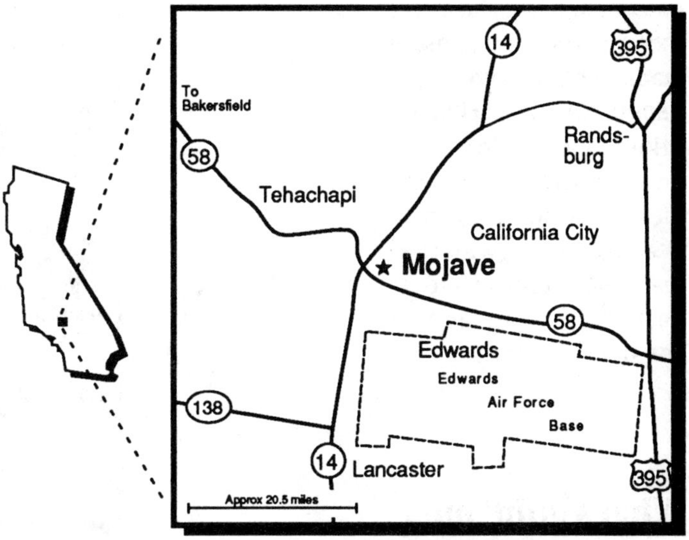


☞ *Up-to-date festival information is available from:*
*Mojave Chamber of Commerce*
*(805) 824-2481*

## What's goin' on...

Town population: **4,500**
Last year's attendance: **35,000**
Average outdoor temperature: **70°**
Festival location: **Downtown**

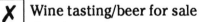

| | |
|---|---|
| X | Wine tasting/beer for sale |
| X | Food booths |
| X | Arts/crafts for sale |
| X | Live music |
| X | Clowns |
| X | Face painters |
| X | Childrens games |
| | Animal exhibits/petting zoo |
| X | Dogs allowed on leash |
| | Lost and found |
| X | Bicycle racks |
| | First aid area available |
| X | Self-brought picnics allowed |
| X | Self-brought alcohol allowed |
| | Stroller/wheelchair rentals available |

| | |
|---|---|
| X | Parade: Sat. 10:00 AM K Street |
| | Parking fee |
| | Entrance fee |
| | Camping facilities |
| | Boating facilities |
| X | RV facilities w/ hookups: 12 blocks |
| X | Accomodations in town<br>Imperial Inns, Mojave TraveLodge |
| X | Restaurants in town<br>Reno's, French's, White's |

# *Newport Seafest*

TEN DAYS OF EXCITING events! **Newport's Seafest** promises a wide variety of events! From kayak races, a macho-men's regatta, log races, surfing contests, and luaus to a little-old-lady regatta, a wind-surfing competition, sand-castle contests, milk-carton–boat racing, and pier-swimming competitions! Team all of that with the marine art festival and A Taste of Newport, and you've got some fun here!

## Newport Beach, California

Second Friday through the third Sunday in September

Hours vary

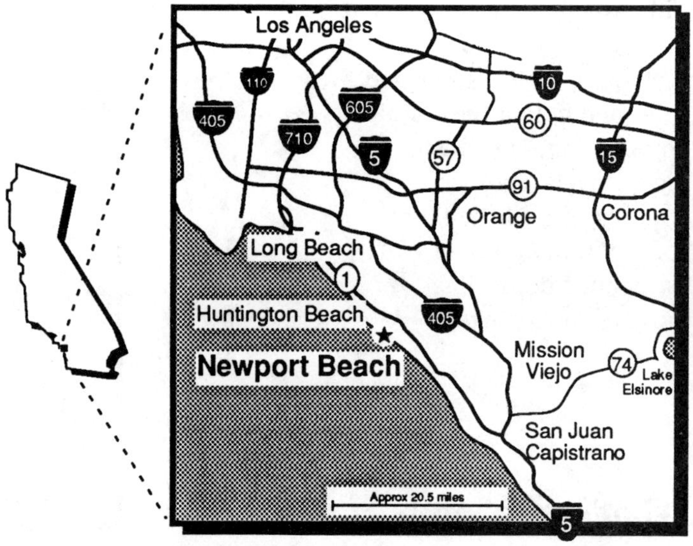


*Up-to-date festival information is available from:*
*Newport Beach Chamber of Commerce*
*(714) 644-8211*

## What's goin' on...

Town population: **71,074**
Last year's attendance: **100,000**
Average outdoor temperature: **74°**
Festival location: **Citywide**

| | |
|---|---|
| X | Wine tasting/beer for sale |
| X | Food booths |
| X | Arts/crafts for sale |
| X | Live music |
| | Clowns |
| | Face painters |
| X | Childrens games |
| | Animal exhibits/petting zoo |
| X | Dogs allowed on leash |
| | Lost and found |
| X | Bicycle racks |
| | First aid area available |
| X | Self-brought picnics allowed |
| | Self-brought alcohol allowed |
| | Stroller/wheelchair rentals available |

| | |
|---|---|
| | Parade |
| | Parking fee |
| | Entrance fee |
| X | Camping facilities: On-site |
| X | Boating facilities: Newport Bay |
| X | RV facilities w/ hookups: On-site |
| X | Accomodations in town<br>Country Side Inn, Four Seasons Hotel, Embassy Suites Hotel, Balboa Inn |
| X | Restaurants in town<br>Tale of the Whale, Five Crowns, Bob Burns, The Cannery, The Red Onion, Chili's, Alfredo's |

# *Avocado & Wine Festival*

ONLY IN CALIFORNIA! THE **Avocado & Wine Festival!** This delectable little fruit has become a favorite of Californians and can be found at this festival fixed in numerous ways—in a salad, mashed and spiced up as "guac", halved and filled with marinated shrimp, or just out of its skin! Wash 'em down with one of the 40 wines available, and you'll have found a wonderful way to spend a Saturday!

## Fallbrook, California

Second Saturday in September
7:30 AM - 3:30 PM

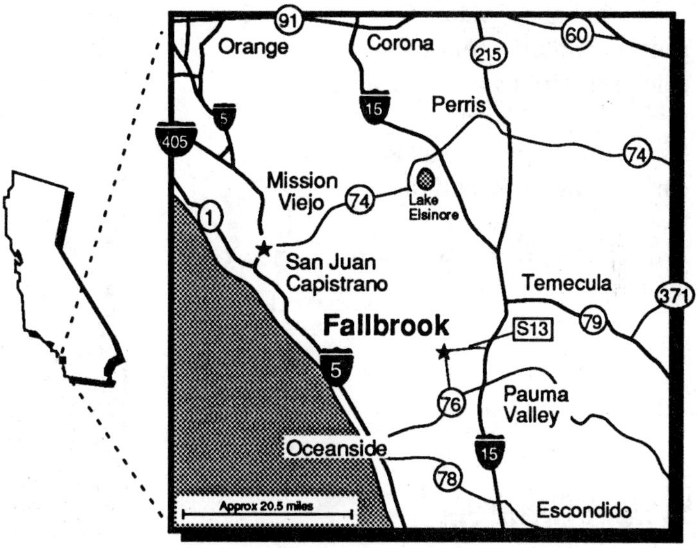


*Up-to-date festival information is available from:*
*Fallbrook Chamber of Commerce*
*(619) 728-5845*

## What's goin' on...

Town population: **30,000**
Last year's attendance: **25,000**
Average outdoor temperature: **85°**
Festival location: **Downtown**

| | |
|---|---|
| X | Wine tasting/beer for sale |
| X | Food booths |
| X | Arts/crafts for sale |
| X | Live music |
| | Clowns |
| X | Face painters |
| | Childrens games |
| X | Animal exhibits/petting zoo |
| | Dogs allowed on leash |
| X | Lost and found |
| | Bicycle racks |
| | First aid area available |
| | Self-brought picnics allowed |
| | Self-brought alcohol allowed |
| | Stroller/wheelchair rentals available |

| | |
|---|---|
| | Parade |
| | Parking fee |
| X | Entrance fee: Adults $2 |
| X | Camping facilities: 10 miles |
| | Boating facilities |
| X | RV facilities w/ hookups: 10 miles |
| X | Accomodations in town<br>Village Inn, Franciscan Inn, Best Western, La Estancia Inn |
| X | Restaurants in town<br>The Packing House, Texas Lil's, Valley Fort Bayou Inn, Le Bistro, Sau Hy's Chinese |

# *Ojai Mexican Fiesta*

¡OLÉ! THE **OJAI MEXICAN Fiesta** has tons of fun for the whole family! There's a music festival, a tennis tournament, mariachi bands, piñatas, pottery and other curios for sale, a children's carnival, and plenty of good Mexican food—homemade tortillas, carnitas, tamales, and the like. Las Casitas Recreation Area is a fine place to explore while visiting the area.

## Ojai, California

Third Sunday in September
Noon - 5:00 PM

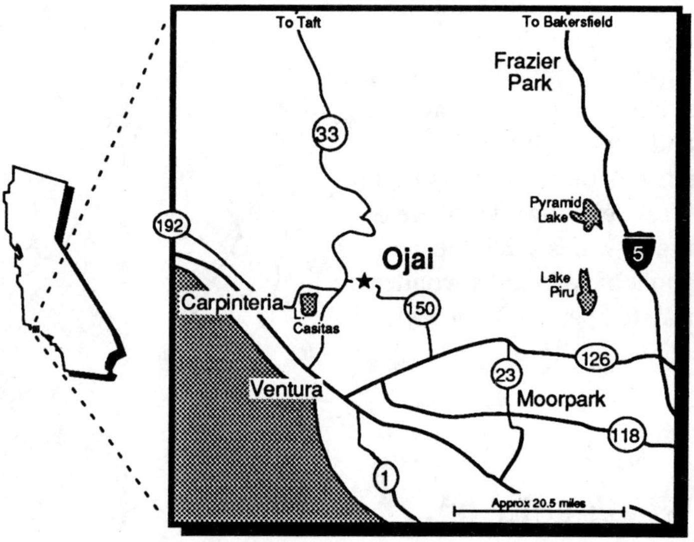


*Up-to-date festival information is available from:*
*Ojai Chamber of Commerce*
*(805) 646-8126*

## What's goin' on...

Town population: **7,000**
Last year's attendance: **800**
Average outdoor temperature: **85°**
Festival location: **N/A**

| | |
|---|---|
| | Wine tasting/beer for sale |
| X | Food booths |
| X | Arts/crafts for sale |
| X | Live music |
| | Clowns |
| | Face painters |
| X | Childrens games |
| | Animal exhibits/petting zoo |
| | Dogs allowed on leash |
| | Lost and found |
| | Bicycle racks |
| | First aid area available |
| | Self-brought picnics allowed |
| | Self-brought alcohol allowed |
| | Stroller/wheelchair rentals available |

| | |
|---|---|
| | Parade |
| | Parking fee |
| X | Entrance fee: (prices not avbl.) |
| X | Camping facilities: 5 miles |
| X | Boating facilities: Lake Casitas |
| X | RV facilities w/ hookups: 15 miles |
| X | Accomodations in town: Ojai Valley Inn, Best Western, Capri Motel, Oakridge Inn, Los Padres Inn, Casa Ojai |
| X | Restaurants in town: L'Auberge, Roger Keller's Restaurant, The Nest, The Ranch House, Ojai Valley Inn |

# *Christopher Street West Gay & Lesbian Pride Celebration*

THE **CHRISTOPHER STREET West Gay & Lesbian Pride Celebration** in West Hollywood is the largest celebration of its kind in Southern California—the 12:30 PM parade is even televised via satellite! Exceptional food, booths, brilliant art, and hand made craft items attract gay and straight people from all over California. Entertainment and live music happens till late on Saturday and Sunday.

## West Hollywood, California

Mid September (call chamber)
Hours vary

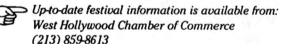

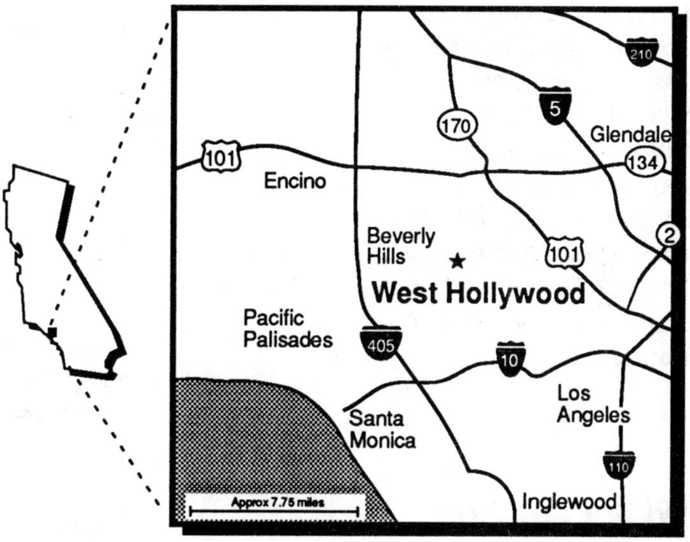


## What's goin' on...

Town population: **35,703**
Last year's attendance: **200,000**
Average outdoor temperature: **80°**
Festival location: **Downtown W. Hollywood**

*Up-to-date festival information is available from:*
*West Hollywood Chamber of Commerce*
*(213) 859-8613*

| | |
|---|---|
| X | Wine tasting/beer for sale |
| X | Food booths |
| X | Arts/crafts for sale |
| X | Live music |
| | Clowns |
| | Face painters |
| | Childrens games |
| | Animal exhibits/petting zoo |
| | Dogs allowed on leash |
| X | Lost and found |
| | Bicycle racks |
| X | First aid area available |
| | Self-brought picnics allowed |
| | Self-brought alcohol allowed |
| | Stroller/wheelchair rentals available |

| | |
|---|---|
| X | Parade: Sun. 12:30 on Santa Monica Bl. |
| X | Parking fee: $1.50 |
| X | Entrance fee: $10 |
| | Camping facilities |
| | Boating facilities |
| | RV facilities w/ hookups |
| X | Accomodations in town |
| X | Restaurants in town<br>Spago's, Trump's, Carlos & Cahrlie's, La Masia, The Melting Pot, La Fabula |

# *Mexican Independence Day*

## Calexico, California

September 16th
5:00 PM - 11:00 PM

LOCATED ON THE MEXICO/ California border, Calexico celebrates **Mexican Independence Day**. As you can imagine, the food is authentic and delicious! As the designated gateway into the wilderness of Baja, California, this little town celebrates the day with folkloric dances and singers, choral groups, Latin rock groups, and mariachi bands. A *huge* fireworks display caps off the day's excitement.

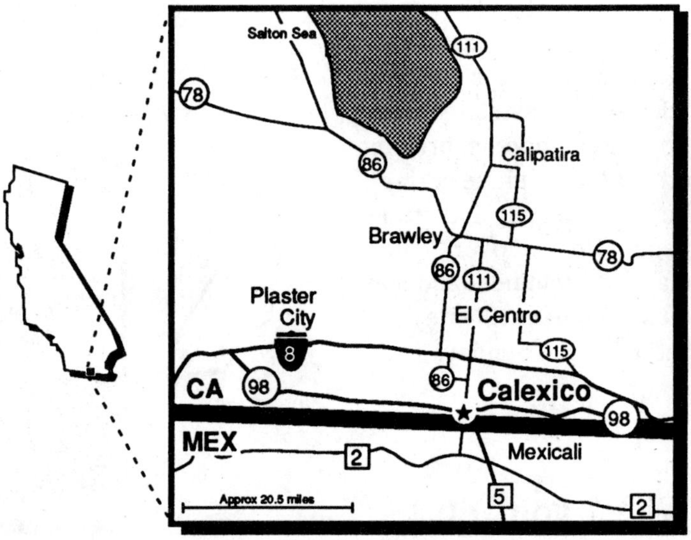


*Up-to-date festival information is available from:*
*Calexico Chamber of Commerce*
*(619) 357-1166*

## What's goin' on...

Town population: **20,000**
Last year's attendance: **12,000**
Average outdoor temperature: **85°**
Festival location: **Crummet Park**

| | |
|---|---|
| X | Wine tasting/beer for sale |
| X | Food booths |
| | Arts/crafts for sale |
| X | Live music |
| X | Clowns |
| X | Face painters |
| X | Childrens games |
| | Animal exhibits/petting zoo |
| X | Dogs allowed on leash |
| X | Lost and found |
| | Bicycle racks |
| X | First aid area available |
| X | Self-brought picnics allowed |
| X | Self-brought alcohol allowed |
| | Stroller/wheelchair rentals available |

| | |
|---|---|
| | Parade |
| | Parking fee |
| | Entrance fee |
| X | Camping facilities: 5 miles |
| | Boating facilities |
| X | RV facilities w/ hookups: 2 miles |
| X | Accomodations in town<br>Hollies Fiesta Motel |
| X | Restaurants in town<br>Alicia's Supper Room & Lounge, Hotel De Anza |

# *Catalina Festival of Art*

CATALINA ISLAND'S AVALON is the site of the annual **Catalina Festival of Art**. This weekend of fun begins with a Friday night dinner, in the world famous Casino Ballroom and an exhibit of former festival art winners. On Saturday and Sunday you can bask in the warm sun and soft breezes of the Pacific while you meander along Crescent Avenue enjoying a variety of fine art.

## Avalon, California

Third full weekend in September
Daily 8:00 AM - 4:00 PM

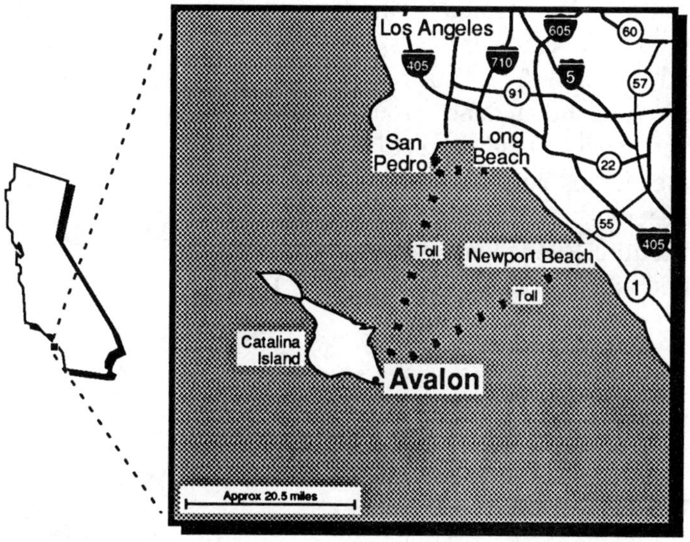


*Up-to-date festival information is available from:*
*Avalon Chamber of Commerce*
*(213) 510-1520*

## What's goin' on...

Town population: **2,022**
Last year's attendance: **11,000**
Average outdoor temperature: **75°**
Festival location: **Citywide**

| | |
|---|---|
| | Wine tasting/beer for sale |
| | Food booths |
| ✗ | Arts/crafts for sale |
| ✗ | Live music |
| ✗ | Clowns |
| ✗ | Face painters |
| ✗ | Childrens games |
| | Animal exhibits/petting zoo |
| ✗ | Dogs allowed on leash |
| ✗ | Lost and found |
| ✗ | Bicycle racks |
| ✗ | First aid area available |
| | Self-brought picnics allowed |
| ✗ | Self-brought alcohol allowed |
| ✗ | Stroller/wheelchair rentals available |

| | |
|---|---|
| | Parade |
| | Parking fee |
| | Entrance fee |
| ✗ | Camping facilities: 26 miles |
| ✗ | Boating facilities: Ocean |
| | RV facilities w/ hookups |
| ✗ | Accomodations in town<br>Garden House Inn, Hotel Monterey, The Old Turner Inn, Cloud "7" Inn, Hotel Vista del Mar |
| ✗ | Restaurants in town<br>The Channel House, Solomon's Landing |

# *Cotton Harvest Festival*

IT'S ONLY APPROPRIATE that a town growing 160,000 bales of cotton per year have a **Cotton Harvest Festival!** Buttonwillow, named for its registered -landmark Buttonwillow Tree, was once a Yokuts Indian dance ground and is only 10 miles east of the famous Tule Elk State Reserve and 16 miles from the beautiful Buena Vista Aquatic Recreation Area.

## Buttonwillow, California

Third Saturday in September
2:00 PM - 11:00 PM

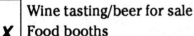

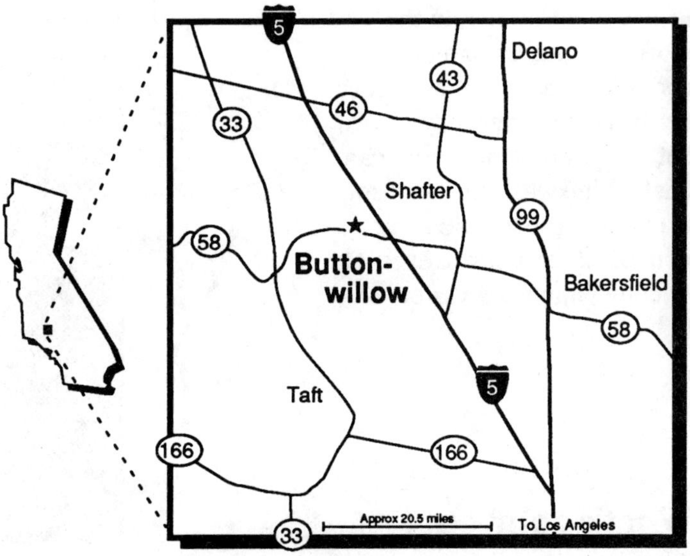


## What's goin' on...

Town population: **1,800**
Last year's attendance: **1,000**
Average outdoor temperature: **80°**
Festival location: **Buttonwillow County Park**

*Up-to-date festival information is available from:*
*Buttonwillow Chamber of Commerce*
*(805) 764-5406*

| | |
|---|---|
| | Wine tasting/beer for sale |
| X | Food booths |
| X | Arts/crafts for sale |
| X | Live music |
| X | Clowns |
| X | Face painters |
| X | Childrens games |
| | Animal exhibits/petting zoo |
| X | Dogs allowed on leash |
| | Lost and found |
| | Bicycle racks |
| | First aid area available |
| X | Self-brought picnics allowed |
| | Self-brought alcohol allowed |
| | Stroller/wheelchair rentals available |

| | |
|---|---|
| X | Parade: Sat. 2:00 PM Buttonwilow School |
| | Parking fee |
| | Entrance fee |
| X | Camping facilities: 20 miles |
| X | Boating facilities: Buena Vista Lake |
| X | RV facilities w/ hookups: 20 miles |
| X | Accomodations in town<br>All Star Inn, Motel 6, Good Night Inn |
| X | Restaurants in town<br>Buttonwillow Lumber Yard Restaurant, Dominique's Basque Restaurant |

# *Arts on the Green*

SINCE 1983 FOLKS HAVE been enjoying **Arts on the Green** in Costa Mesa. The entertainment throughout the weekend is varied and always lively, ranging from storytellers, and dancing exhibitions, to live music and melodramas! You'll be tempted by the great smells wafting through air near the food booths while you enjoy southern California's sunshine.

## Costa Mesa, California

Third weekend in September
11:00 AM - 6:00 PM

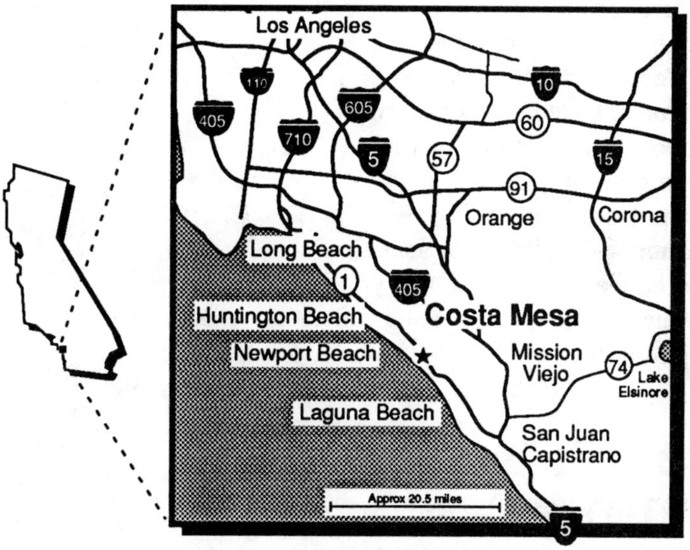


*Up-to-date festival information is available from:*
*Costa Mesa Chamber of Commerce*
*(714) 650-1490*

## What's goin' on...

Town population: **800,000**
Last year's attendance: **24,000**
Average outdoor temperature: **78°**
Festival location: **Town Center Park**

| | |
|---|---|
| | Wine tasting/beer for sale |
| ✗ | Food booths |
| ✗ | Arts/crafts for sale |
| ✗ | Live music |
| ✗ | Clowns |
| ✗ | Face painters |
| | Childrens games |
| | Animal exhibits/petting zoo |
| ✗ | Dogs allowed on leash |
| ✗ | Lost and found |
| ✗ | Bicycle racks |
| ✗ | First aid area available |
| ✗ | Self-brought picnics allowed |
| ✗ | Self-brought alcohol allowed |
| ✗ | Stroller/wheelchair rentals available |

| | |
|---|---|
| | Parade |
| ✗ | Parking fee: $4 |
| | Entrance fee |
| ✗ | Camping facilities: 2 miles |
| ✗ | Boating facilities: Pacific Ocean |
| ✗ | RV facilities w/ hookups: 2 miles |
| ✗ | Accomodations in town<br>Red Lion, Westin, Marriott, Holiday Inn, Beverly Heritage |
| ✗ | Restaurants in town |

SOUTHERN

# *Oceanside Harbor Days*

THE NAME OF THIS TOWN gives away its prized festival of 14 glorious years—**Oceanside Harbor Days!** Perched on Oceanside Pier—the longest pier in the West—this festival offers stuffed baked potatoes, Thai food, *fresh* seafood (natch!), Chinese and Mexican dishes, and ice-cold beer. The handcrafted items for sale are creative works of art, and you can also buy photographs and paintings.

## Oceanside, California

Third weekend in September
Daily 9:00 AM - 6:00 PM

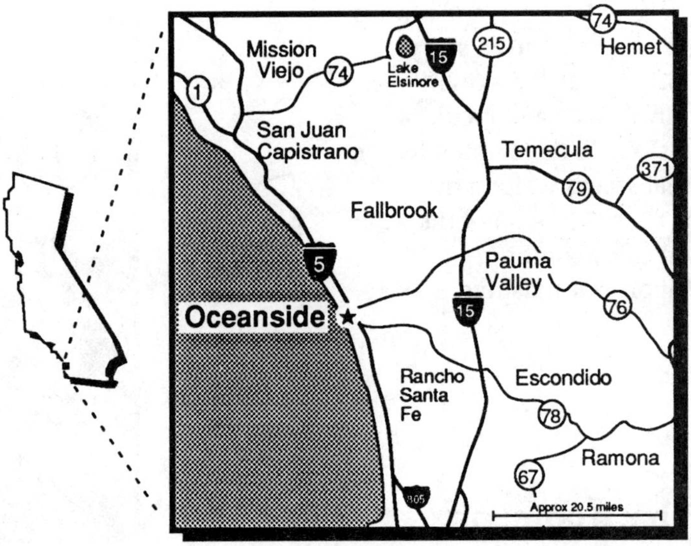


*Up-to-date festival information is available from:*
*Oceanside Chamber of Commerce*
*(619) 721-1101*

## What's goin' on...

Town population: **110,000**
Last year's attendance: **80,000**
Average outdoor temperature: **78°**
Festival location: **Small Craft Harbor**

| | |
|---|---|
| X | Wine tasting/beer for sale |
| X | Food booths |
| X | Arts/crafts for sale |
| X | Live music |
| X | Clowns |
| X | Face painters |
| X | Childrens games |
| X | Animal exhibits/petting zoo |
| X | Dogs allowed on leash |
| X | Lost and found |
| X | Bicycle racks |
| X | First aid area available |
| X | Self-brought picnics allowed |
| | Self-brought alcohol allowed |
| | Stroller/wheelchair rentals available |

| | |
|---|---|
| X | Parade: Sun.10:00 AM boat parade |
| | Parking fee |
| | Entrance fee |
| X | Camping facilities: 5 miles |
| X | Boating facilities: Harbor |
| X | RV facilities w/ hookups: 5 miles |
| X | Accomodations in town |
| X | Restaurants in town<br>Chart House, Fishermans, Jolly Roger, Monterey Bay Cannery |

# *Route 66 Rendezvous*

AH, THE FAMED ROUTE 66! Come down and enjoy the mystique and excitement that surrounds the **Route 66 Rendezvous**! Bobby socks, pony tails, white t-shirts, and slicked back hair are the norm for this two-day festival! Vintage autos show their attention-getting power at the parade on Saturday night and enjoy the sock hop later on!

## San Bernadino, California

Third weekend in September
Daily 7:00 AM - dusk

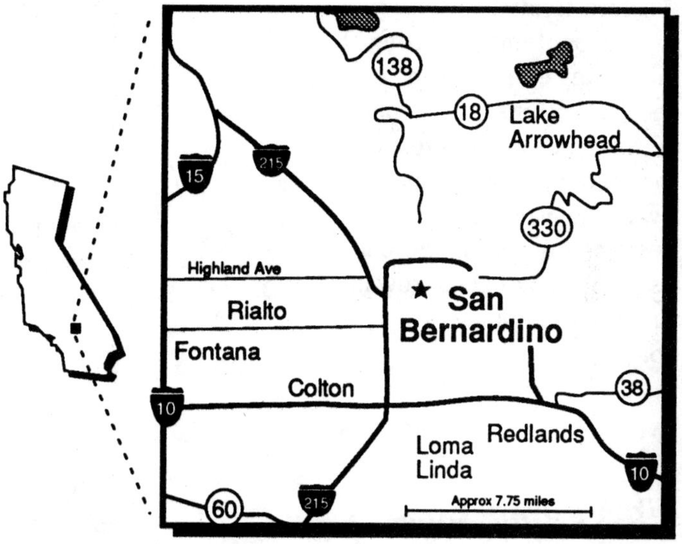


## What's goin' on...

Town population: **160,000**
Last year's attendance: **3,000**
Average outdoor temperature: **88°**
Festival location: **Glen Helen Regional Park**

*Up-to-date festival information is available from:*
*San Bernadino Chamber of Commerce*
*(714) 889-3980*

| | |
|---|---|
| | Wine tasting/beer for sale |
| X | Food booths |
| X | Arts/crafts for sale |
| X | Live music |
| | Clowns |
| | Face painters |
| | Childrens games |
| | Animal exhibits/petting zoo |
| X | Dogs allowed on leash |
| | Lost and found |
| | Bicycle racks |
| | First aid area available |
| X | Self-brought picnics allowed |
| | Self-brought alcohol allowed |
| | Stroller/wheelchair rentals available |

| | |
|---|---|
| X | Parade: Sat. 6:00 PM cruising "E" St. |
| X | Parking fee: $3 |
| X | Entrance fee: $3 - $5; Under 12 free |
| X | Camping facilities: 10 miles |
| | Boating facilities: Lake Perris |
| X | RV facilities w/ hookups: In town |
| X | Accomodations in town<br>San Bernadino Hilton, Maruko Hotel, La Quinta, TraveLodge |
| X | Restaurants in town<br>TGI Fridays, Spencers, La Pontinier, Bobby McGees |

SOUTHERN

# *Western Heritage Mining Days*

RIDGECREST AND THE SURrounding area are rich in mining history. Join in the rip-roarin' days of old at the **Western Heritage Mining Days** in September. Gazing at the mining exhibits and demonstrations, partic- pating in the games and contests, and gold-panning are just a few of the ways to spend this weekend outdoors. There will also be tours of ghost towns and modern mining operations.

## Ridgecrest, California

Last weekend in September
Hours vary

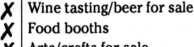

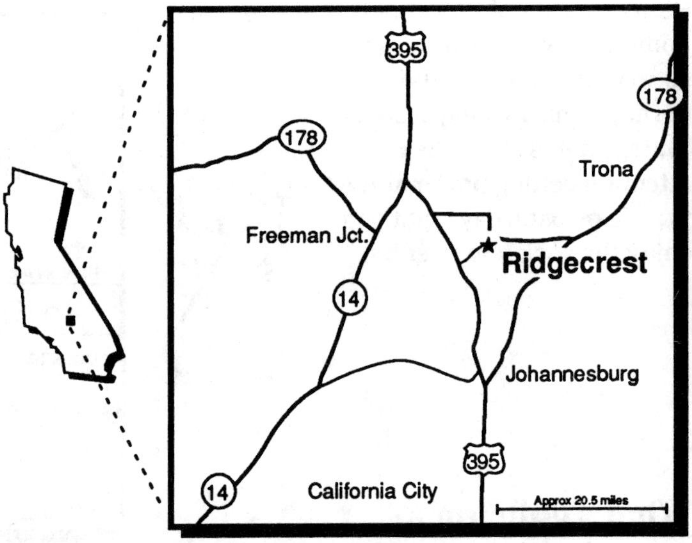


## What's goin' on...

Town population: **28,639**
Last year's attendance: **N/A**
Average outdoor temperature: **80°**
Festival location: **Desert Regional Park**

*Up-to-date festival information is available from:*
*Ridgecrest Chamber of Commerce*
*(619) 375-8331*

- ✗ Wine tasting/beer for sale
- ✗ Food booths
- ✗ Arts/crafts for sale
- ✗ Live music
- ✗ Clowns
- ✗ Face painters
- ✗ Childrens games
- ✗ Animal exhibits/petting zoo
- ✗ Dogs allowed on leash
- Lost and found
- ✗ Bicycle racks
- First aid area available
- ✗ Self-brought picnics allowed
- Self-brought alcohol allowed
- Stroller/wheelchair rentals available

- Parade
- Parking fee
- Entrance fee
- ✗ Camping facilities: 5 miles away
- ✗ Boating facilities: Kern River
- ✗ RV facilities w/ hookups: In town
- ✗ Accomodations in town
  Pioneer Motel, Heritage House, El Rancho Motel, Econolodge, Carriage Inn
- ✗ Restaurants in town
  Sandpiper, The Hideaway, White Star Dining Company, Farris' at the Heritage, Schooner Saloon

# *Cabazon Jamboree & Barbecue*

SMOKEY THE BEAR WILL BE on hand for the **Cabazon Jamboree & Barbecue.** Medieval knights in full costumes will battle and McGruff, the local crime dog are two of the main attractions! Home to the famous Claude Bell dinosaurs and the Wheel Inns fabulous home-made pies, the rural community of Cabazon is surrounded by *beautiful* desert and mountain scenery.

## Cabazon, California

Last Saturday in September
9:00 AM - dusk

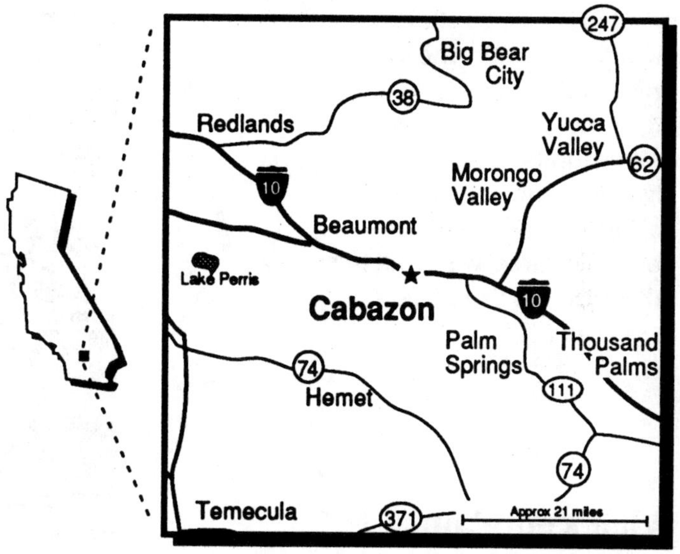


## What's goin' on...

Town population: **1,400**
Last year's attendance: **1,500**
Average outdoor temperature: **76°**
Festival location: **Cabazon's Park**

*Up-to-date festival information is available from:*
*Cabazon Chamber of Commerce*
*(714) 845-6905*

| | |
|---|---|
| | Wine tasting/beer for sale |
| X | Food booths |
| X | Arts/crafts for sale |
| X | Live music |
| X | Clowns |
| | Face painters |
| X | Childrens games |
| X | Animal exhibits/petting zoo |
| X | Dogs allowed on leash |
| X | Lost and found |
| X | Bicycle racks |
| X | First aid area available |
| X | Self-brought picnics allowed |
| | Self-brought alcohol allowed |
| | Stroller/wheelchair rentals available |

| | |
|---|---|
| | Parade |
| X | Parking fee: $1 |
| | Entrance fee |
| X | Camping facilities: 5 miles |
| | Boating facilities |
| X | RV facilities w/ hookups: 5 miles |
| | Accomodations in town |
| X | Restaurants in town<br>Wheel Inn |

SOUTHERN

# *Bonita-Fest*

THE FINAL WEEKEND IN September culminates the month-long **Bonita-Fest** in Chula Vista. This old-fashioned event (in its 18th year) includes a parade, theatrical presentations, square dancing, games, entertainment, craft exhibits, food, and a gigantic community pit barbecue. Not far from the downtown area, where all this takes place, is San Diego's Seaworld.

## Chula Vista, California

Last weekend in September
Hours vary

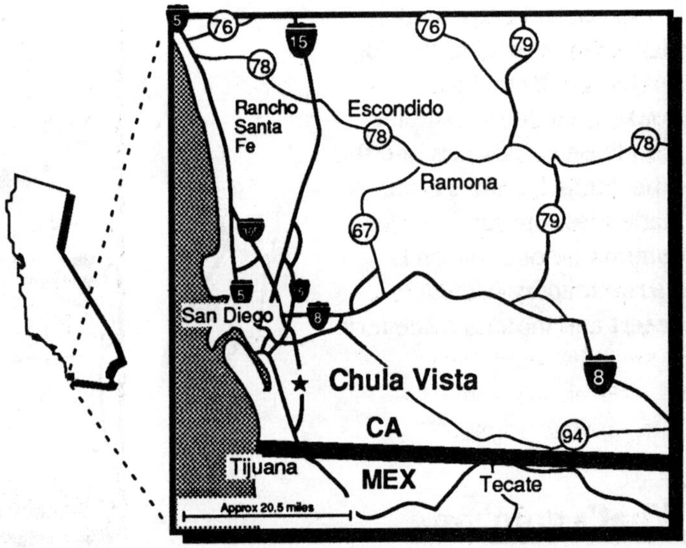


*Up-to-date festival information is available from:*
*Chula Vista Chamber of Commerce*
*(619) 420-6602*

## What's goin' on...

Town population: **131,455**
Last year's attendance: **7,000**
Average outdoor temperature: **75°**
Festival location: **Downtown**

| | |
|---|---|
| X | Wine tasting/beer for sale |
| X | Food booths |
| X | Arts/crafts for sale |
| X | Live music |
| | Clowns |
| X | Face painters |
| X | Childrens games |
| | Animal exhibits/petting zoo |
| X | Dogs allowed on leash |
| | Lost and found |
| X | Bicycle racks |
| X | First aid area available |
| | Self-brought picnics allowed |
| | Self-brought alcohol allowed |
| X | Stroller/wheelchair rentals available |

| | |
|---|---|
| | Parade |
| | Parking fee |
| | Entrance fee |
| X | Camping facilities: 3 miles |
| X | Boating facilities: Otay Res. & Bay |
| X | RV facilities w/ hookups: 3 miles |
| X | Accomodations in town: Day's Inn, All Season, Ramada Inn, Traveler, Vagabond |
| X | Restaurants in town: Sea Food Broiler, La Bella's, House of Nine Dragons |

# *Old World's Oktoberfest*

VISITORS TO THE **OLD World's Oktoberfest** can enjoy a beergarden overflowing with ice cold beers from around the world, and sample the barbecue kitchen's offerings of Bratwurst, roast chicken, sauerkraut, and potato salad. Top it all off with "Apflestrudel" and gigantic pretzels. Then dance he Chicken Dance to the Lustigen Vilstaler Musikanitel oompah pah band! YEOWZA! (Hours: Wednesdays & Thursdays 7:00 PM - 11:00 PM; Fridays, Saturdays and Sundays 2:00 PM - 9:00 PM.)

## Huntington Beach, California

Begins last weekend in September—all through October
(see paragraph for hours)

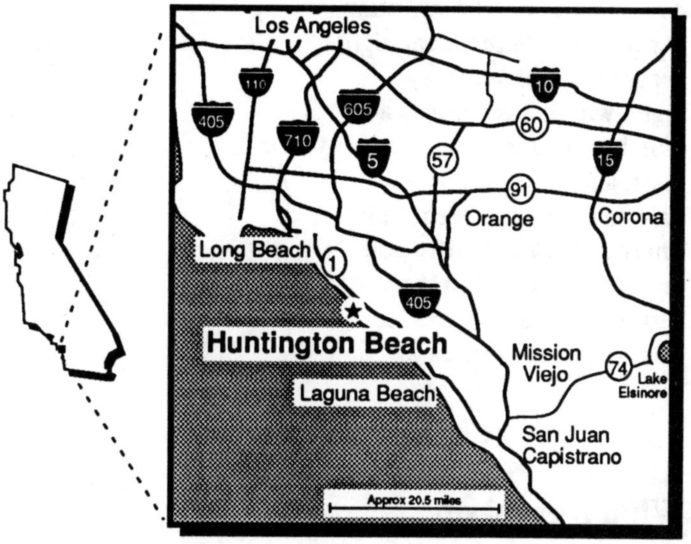


## What's goin' on...

Town population: **185,000**
Last year's attendance: **N/A**
Average outdoor temperature: **75°**
Festival location: **Old World Village**

*Up-to-date festival information is available from: Huntington Beach Chamber of Commerce (714) 536-8888*

- ✗ Wine tasting/beer for sale
- ✗ Food booths
- Arts/crafts for sale
- ✗ Live music
- Clowns
- Face painters
- Childrens games
- Animal exhibits/petting zoo
- Dogs allowed on leash
- Lost and found
- Bicycle racks
- First aid area available
- Self-brought picnics allowed
- Self-brought alcohol allowed
- Stroller/wheelchair rentals available

- Parade
- Parking fee
- Entrance fee
- ✗ Camping facilities: 1 mile
- ✗ Boating facilities: Ocean
- ✗ RV facilities w/ hookups: 1 mile
- ✗ Accomodations in town
  Hilton, Best Western, Ocean View, Huntington Shores Motel, Sunset Beach Inn
- ✗ Restaurants in town
  Maxwell's, Charley Brown's, J.C. McLins, Bukhara, Tijuana Willies, Tibbies, Pero's

# *Lake Arrowhead Fifties Festival*

ONE-TWO-THREE-O'CLOCK four-o'clock rock—down at **Lake Arrowhead's 50's Festival** Weekend! Frankie Avalon and The Platters star "At-the-Hop" in the local high school gym on Saturday night, where 50s dress is a must! There are dance contests, a 50s car parade, and hair-do contests—great fun! There's also a celebrity golf tournament, a walk-a-thon, and rubber-ducky races in this gorgeous area SoCal.

## Lake Arrowhead, California

Last weekend in September
Hours vary

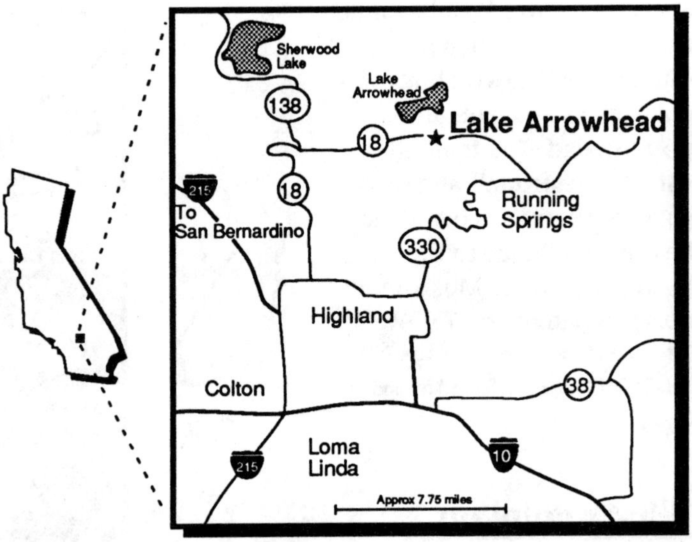


*Up-to-date festival information is available from:*
*Lake Arrowhead Chamber of Commerce*
*(714) 337-3715*

## What's goin' on...

Town population: **22,000**
Last year's attendance: **3,000**
Average outdoor temperature: **75°**
Festival location: **Rim High School Gym**

- [ ] Wine tasting/beer for sale
- [X] Food booths
- [ ] Arts/crafts for sale
- [X] Live music
- [ ] Clowns
- [ ] Face painters
- [ ] Childrens games
- [ ] Animal exhibits/petting zoo
- [X] Dogs allowed on leash
- [X] Lost and found
- [ ] Bicycle racks
- [X] First aid area available
- [ ] Self-brought picnics allowed
- [ ] Self-brought alcohol allowed
- [ ] Stroller/wheelchair rentals available

- [X] Parade: Sun. 5:00 PM Blue Jay Village
- [ ] Parking fee
- [X] Entrance fee: Adults $16.50
- [X] Camping facilities: 2 miles
- [X] Boating facilities: Lake Arrowhead
- [X] RV facilities w/ hookups: 3 miles
- [X] Accomodations in town
  Lake Arrowhead Hilton Lodge, Saddleback Inn, Lakeview Lodge
- [X] Restaurants in town
  Lobby Cafe, McAffees, Heidi's, Beau Rivage, Royal Oak

# *Maturango Junction & Chili Cook-Off*

THE **MATURANGO JUNCtion & Chili Cook-Off** in Ridgecrest is one ***hot*** event! The Ridgecrestians hold this event in October to ensure a less-than-100° day—even though some of the bewitching chili that gets stirred up may raise your temperature! Of course, there's beer, wine and sodas to cool you off, as well as non-chili types of food.

## Ridgecrest, California

Fourth Saturday in September
8:00 AM - 5:00 PM

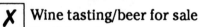

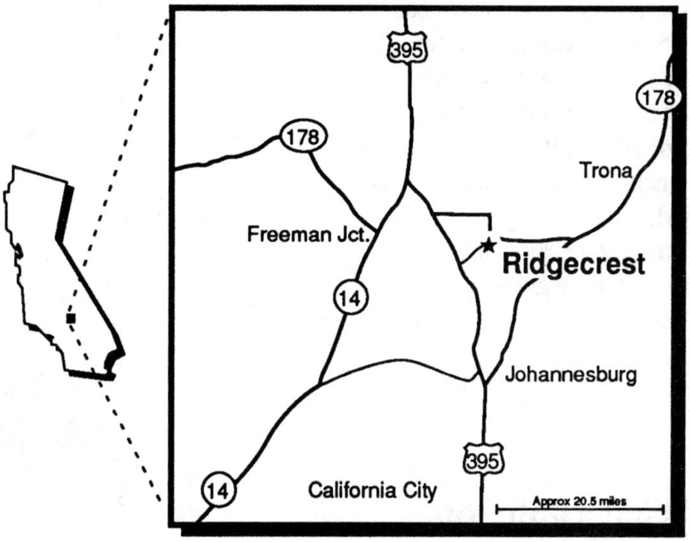


## What's goin' on...

Town population: **28,639**
Last year's attendance: **4,000**
Average outdoor temperature: **70°**
Festival location: **Desert Regional Park**

*Up-to-date festival information is available from:*
*Ridgecrest Chamber of Commerce*
*(619) 375-8331*

| | |
|---|---|
| X | Wine tasting/beer for sale |
| X | Food booths |
| X | Arts/crafts for sale |
| X | Live music |
| | Clowns |
| X | Face painters |
| X | Childrens games |
| | Animal exhibits/petting zoo |
| X | Dogs allowed on leash |
| | Lost and found |
| | Bicycle racks |
| | First aid area available |
| X | Self-brought picnics allowed |
| X | Self-brought alcohol allowed |
| | Stroller/wheelchair rentals available |

| | |
|---|---|
| | Parade |
| | Parking fee |
| | Entrance fee |
| X | Camping facilities: 5 miles away |
| X | Boating facilities: Kern River |
| X | RV facilities w/ hookups: In town |
| X | Accomodations in town<br>Pioneer Motel, Heritage House, El Rancho Motel, Econolodge, Carriage Inn |
| X | Restaurants in town<br>Sandpiper, The Hideaway, White Star Dining Company, Farris' at the Heritage, Schooner Saloon |

# *Fall Festival of Arts*

THE STUDIO CITY **FALL Festival of Arts** displays watercolor and oil paintings from some of the area's elite talent. Along with the exceptional handcrafted items available—such as hand-decorated stationery, household items, and needlework—all of the art is for sale. Adjacent to Studio City is Universal City, with its remarkable Universal Studio Tours.

## Studio City, California

Last weekend in September
Daily 10:00 AM - 5:00

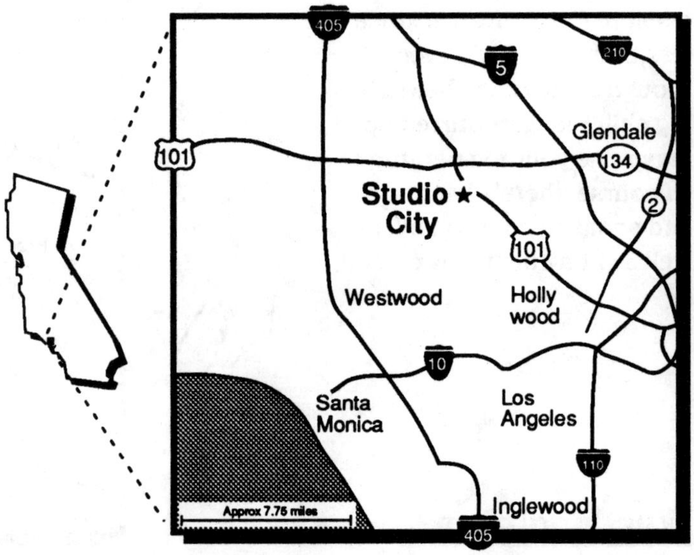


*Up-to-date festival information is available from:*
*Studio City Studio City Rotary Club*
*(818) 990-2628*

## What's goin' on...

Town population: **35,000**
Last year's attendance: **5,000**
Average outdoor temperature: **80°**
Festival location: **Park**

- ✗ Wine tasting/beer for sale
- ✗ Food booths
- ✗ Arts/crafts for sale
- ✗ Live music
- ✗ Clowns
- ✗ Face painters
- ✗ Childrens games
- ✗ Animal exhibits/petting zoo
- ✗ Dogs allowed on leash
- ✗ Lost and found
- ✗ Bicycle racks
- ✗ First aid area available
- ✗ Self-brought picnics allowed
- ✗ Self-brought alcohol allowed
- ✗ Stroller/wheelchair rentals available

- ✗ Parade
- Parking fee
- Entrance fee
- ✗ Camping facilities
- ✗ Boating facilities
- ✗ RV facilities w/ hookups
- ✗ Accomodations in town
  Valley Hilton, Sportsmen's Lodge
- ✗ Restaurants in town
  Art's Deli, Jerry's Famous Deli, St. Moritz, Sportsmen's

# *Stagecoach Days*

**STAGECOACH DAYS** COMmemorates Banning's beginnings as a chief stagecoach stop. The *entire* town participates, as local businesses decorate their shops and residents dress in early-American attire. To keep you busy, there's a PRCA rodeo, a carnival, a "whiskerino" contest, and a grandmothers' contest—not to mention the spaghetti dinner and pancake breakfast. This is a *terrific* tribute to Banning!

## Banning, California

Week that includes first full weekend in October
Hours vary

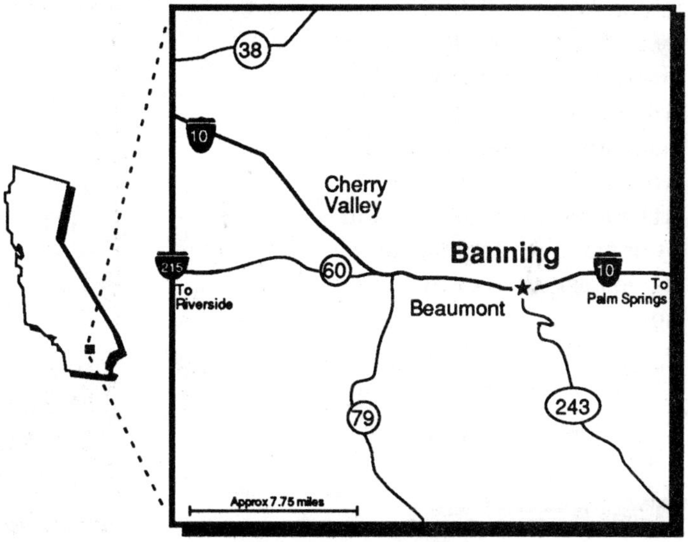


## What's goin' on...

Town population: **21,000**
Last year's attendance: **10,000**
Average outdoor temperature: **85°**
Festival location: **A.C. Dysart Equest. Park**

☞ *Up-to-date festival information is available from:*
*Banning Chamber of Commerce*
*(714) 849-4695*

| | |
|---|---|
| X | Wine tasting/beer for sale |
| X | Food booths |
| X | Arts/crafts for sale |
| | Live music |
| X | Clowns |
| X | Face painters |
| | Childrens games |
| | Animal exhibits/petting zoo |
| | Dogs allowed on leash |
| X | Lost and found |
| | Bicycle racks |
| X | First aid area available |
| X | Self-brought picnics allowed |
| | Self-brought alcohol allowed |
| | Stroller/wheelchair rentals available |

| | |
|---|---|
| X | Parade: Saturday 10:00 AM on Ramsey |
| X | Parking fee: $1 |
| | Entrance fee |
| X | Camping facilities: 3 miles |
| | Boating facilities |
| X | RV facilities w/ hookups: 3 miles |
| X | Accomodations in town<br>Super 8, Peach Tree, Hacienda Inn, Banning Motel |
| X | Restaurants in town<br>Apple Annie's, San Gorgonio Inn |

SOUTHERN

# *La Mesa Oktoberfest*

"OOM-PAH-PAH" IS THE only way to describe the live music that plays during **La Mesa's Oktoberfest**! This rabble-rousing affair serves up authentic German bratwurst, sauerkraut, and potato salad the old-fashioned way...homemade! There are more than 200 booths of arts and crafts to peruse, and a German beer garden featuring domestic *and* German lagers!

## La Mesa, California

First weekend in October (beginning Thursday)
Hours vary

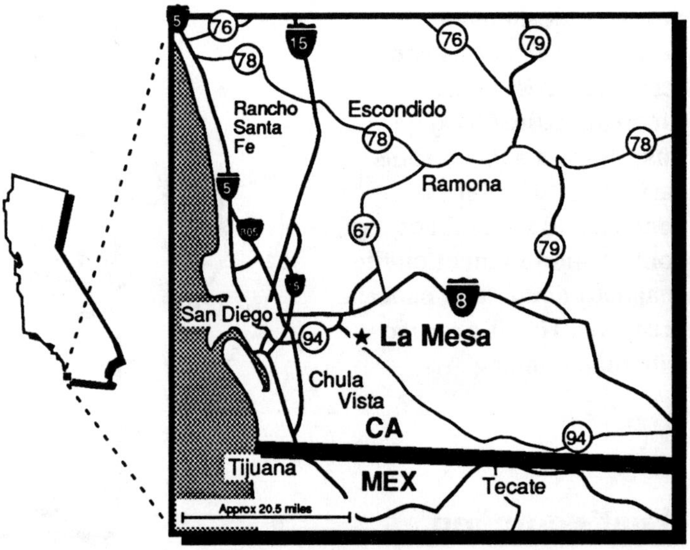


## What's goin' on...

Town population: **50,000**
Last year's attendance: **100,000**
Average outdoor temperature: **75°**
Festival location: **Downtown Village Area**

*Up-to-date festival information is available from:*
*La Mesa Chamber of Commerce*
*(619) 456-7700*

- ✗ Wine tasting/beer for sale
- ✗ Food booths
- ✗ Arts/crafts for sale
- ✗ Live music
- Clowns
- Face painters
- Childrens games
- Animal exhibits/petting zoo
- Dogs allowed on leash
- ✗ Lost and found
- Bicycle racks
- ✗ First aid area available
- Self-brought picnics allowed
- Self-brought alcohol allowed
- Stroller/wheelchair rentals available

- Parade
- Parking fee
- Entrance fee
- Camping facilities
- Boating facilities
- RV facilities w/ hookups
- ✗ Accomodations in town
- ✗ Restaurants in town

# *Grape Harvest Festival*

TAKE YOUR SHOES OFF AND let the little purple squish-balls pop beneath your feet! Well...some people think it sounds like grape fun at the **Grape Harvest Festival** in Rancho Cucamonga! The first vines were planted in these valleys 150 years ago...so these folks have some serious celebrating to do! A carnival, game booths, yummy food and drinks, and name-brand entertainment! This is one we don't miss!

## Rancho Cucamonga, California

First weekend in October (beginning Thursday)
Hours vary

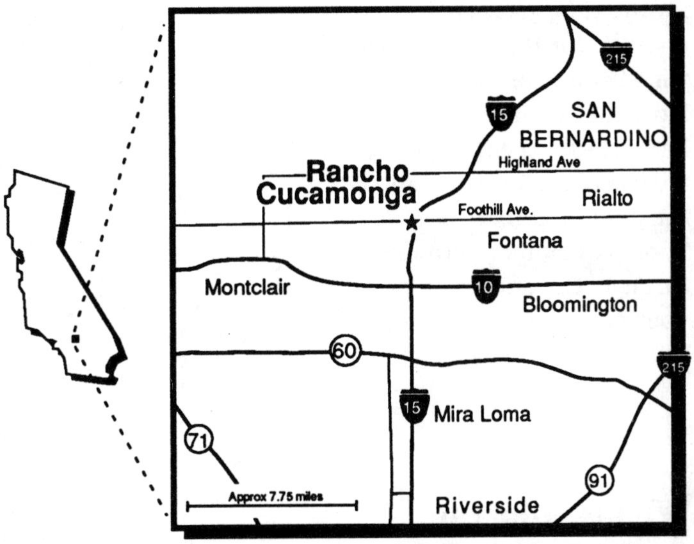


☞ *Up-to-date festival information is available from:*
*Rancho Cucamonga Chamber of Commerce*
*(714) 987-1012*

## What's goin' on...

Town population: **104,700**
Last year's attendance: **30,000**
Average outdoor temperature: **75°**
Festival location: **Regional Park**

| | |
|---|---|
| X | Wine tasting/beer for sale |
| X | Food booths |
| X | Arts/crafts for sale |
| X | Live music |
| X | Clowns |
| X | Face painters |
| X | Childrens games |
| | Animal exhibits/petting zoo |
| | Dogs allowed on leash |
| X | Lost and found |
| | Bicycle racks |
| X | First aid area available |
| | Self-brought picnics allowed |
| | Self-brought alcohol allowed |
| | Stroller/wheelchair rentals available |

| | |
|---|---|
| | Parade |
| | Parking fee |
| X | Entrance fee: S $3; A $5; K free |
| | Camping facilities |
| | Boating facilities |
| | RV facilities w/ hookups |
| X | Accomodations in town<br>Red Lion Inn, Clarion, TraveLodge, Hilton |
| X | Restaurants in town |

SOUTHERN

# *Diamond Bar Ranch Festival*

A NEW ADDITION TO OUR California & Nevada book is the **Diamond Bar Ranch Festival!** At it you'll find rides for the kids, games and contests for the big kids, and wine tasting for the big, big kids! The smoke of the barbecues will entice you to try one of the many meats on the grills, and there are booths of crafts to browse through. Oh, and don't for get your dancin' shoes for both Friday and Saturday nights!

## Diamond Bar, California

First weekend in October

Fri. 4:00 PM - midnight; Sat. 10:00 AM - midnight; Sun. 11:00 AM - 4:00 PM

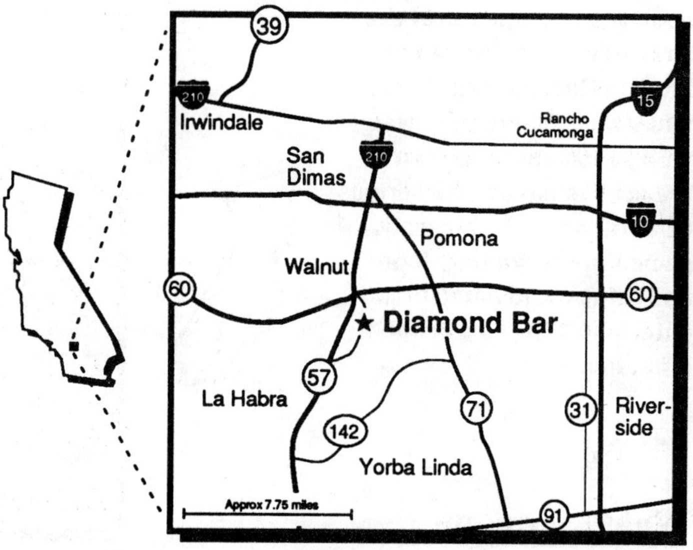


### What's goin' on...

Town population: **72,000**
Last year's attendance: **N/A**
Average outdoor temperature: **75°**
Festival location: **Gateway Center**

☞ *Up-to-date festival information is available from: Diamond Bar Chamber of Commerce (714) 861-2121*

- ✗ Wine tasting/beer for sale
- ✗ Food booths
- ✗ Arts/crafts for sale
- ✗ Live music
- Clowns
- Face painters
- ✗ Childrens games
- Animal exhibits/petting zoo
- Dogs allowed on leash
- ✗ Lost and found
- ✗ Bicycle racks
- ✗ First aid area available
- Self-brought picnics allowed
- Self-brought alcohol allowed
- Stroller/wheelchair rentals available

- ✗ Parade: (time & date not avbl.)
- Parking fee
- ✗ Entrance fee: $4
- ✗ Camping facilities 10 miles
- ✗ Boating facilities: San Dimas Res.
- ✗ RV facilities w/ hookups: 10 miles
- ✗ Accomodations in town Days Inn, Ramada
- ✗ Restaurants in town

# *Maritime Days Festival*

SPORTING YOUR NAUTICAL attire, see and be seen at Oxnard's **Maritime Days Festival!** The Shipwreck Party on Friday night kicks off the three-day affair, and Saturday starts with a hearty pancake breakfast and a stroll through the arts-and-crafts outdoor marketplace. You'll find a chowder cook-off, Mr. & Mrs. Crab Leg, and sand-sculpturing competitions—all this and live music all weekend long!

## Oxnard, California

First weekend in October (beginning Friday)
Hours vary

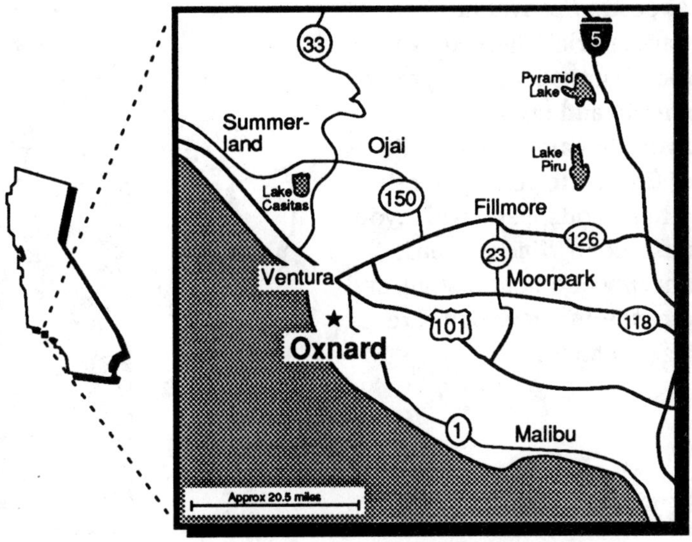


### What's goin' on...

Town population: **125,000**
Last year's attendance: **70,000**
Average outdoor temperature: **75°**
Festival location: **Channel Islands Harbor**

*Up-to-date festival information is available from:*
*Oxnard Chamber of Commerce*
*(805) 487-6305*

- X Wine tasting/beer for sale
- X Food booths
- X Arts/crafts for sale
- X Live music
- X Clowns
- X Face painters
- X Childrens games
- X Animal exhibits/petting zoo
- X Dogs allowed on leash
- X Lost and found
- X Bicycle racks
- X First aid area available
- X Self-brought picnics allowed
- X Self-brought alcohol allowed
- Stroller/wheelchair rentals available

- Parade
- Parking fee
- Entrance fee
- X Camping facilities: 3 miles
- X Boating facilities: Harbor
- X RV facilities w/ hookups: On-site
- X Accomodations in town
  Channel Island Motel, Vagabond Inn, Crystal Lodge, Angle Hotel, Surfside Motel
- X Restaurants in town
  Filomena's, Siam B.B.Q.

# California Avocado Festival

¡HOLY GUACAMOLE! Avocadoice cream? An all-night fishing derby? Yep, and lots, lots more at the **California Avocado Festival** in Carpenteria! There are 25 food booths featuring saucy shrimp and crab on the avocado half shell, and plenty of Greek, Mexican, and other ethnic foods made with...you guessed it! Wine gardens, nonavocado beer tasting, and meandering musicians are also on hand.

## Carpinteria, California

First weekend in October
Sat. 10:00 AM - 7:00 PM; Sun. 10:00 AM - 5:00 PM

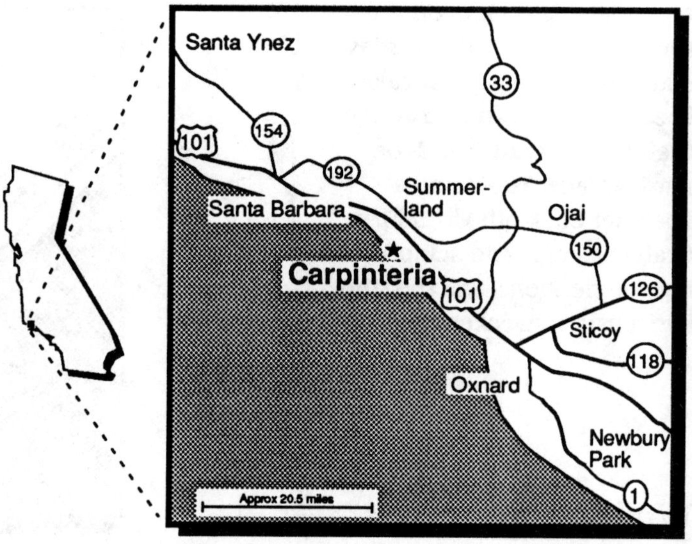


*Up-to-date festival information is available from:*
*Carpinteria Chamber of Commerce*
*(805) 684-5479*

## What's goin' on...

Town population: **13,000**
Last year's attendance: **40,000**
Average outdoor temperature: **63°**
Festival location: **Linden Avenue**

X Wine tasting/beer for sale
X Food booths
X Arts/crafts for sale
X Live music
X Clowns
X Face painters
X Childrens games
Animal exhibits/petting zoo
X Dogs allowed on leash
X Lost and found
X Bicycle racks
X First aid area available
X Self-brought picnics allowed
Self-brought alcohol allowed
Stroller/wheelchair rentals available

Parade
X Parking fee: (prices not avbl.)
Entrance fee
X Camping facilities: In town
X Boating facilities: Ocean
X RV facilities w/ hookups: In town
X Accomodations in town
Fess Parker's Red Lion Resort, Reef Motel, Summerland Inn B&B, Carpinteria Inn

X Restaurants in town
Fish Barrel, Budd's Eggception, The Palm's, Nine Dragons, Clementine's Steak House, Chuy's

# *Golden City Days*

NOT TOO FAR FROM DISNEYland and Knott's Berry Farm lies the town of Santa Ana, host of Santa Ana's **Golden City Days** Festival. With continuous entertainment on three stages in the heart of town (Fourth Street), this festival also features youth safety procedures, sports celebrities, and art activities, in addition to the customary children's games. Food, arts, and crafts booths boast one-of-a-kind items.

## Santa Ana, California

Second weekend in October (beginning Friday)
Hours vary

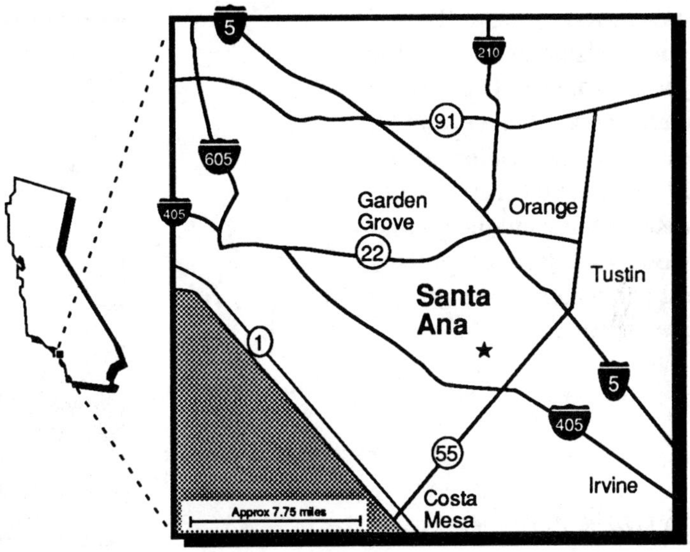


*Up-to-date festival information is available from:*
*Santa Ana Chamber of Commerce*
*(714) 541-5353*

## What's goin' on...

Town population: **20,023**
Last year's attendance: **200,000**
Average outdoor temperature: **75°**
Festival location: **4th Street**

| | |
|---|---|
| X | Wine tasting/beer for sale |
| X | Food booths |
| X | Arts/crafts for sale |
| X | Live music |
| X | Clowns |
| X | Face painters |
| X | Childrens games |
| X | Animal exhibits/petting zoo |
| X | Dogs allowed on leash |
| X | Lost and found |
| X | Bicycle racks |
| X | First aid area available |
| | Self-brought picnics allowed |
| | Self-brought alcohol allowed |
| | Stroller/wheelchair rentals available |

| | |
|---|---|
| | Parade |
| | Parking fee |
| | Entrance fee |
| X | Camping facilities: 10 miles |
| X | Boating facilities: Irvine Lake |
| X | RV facilities w/ hookups: 10 miles |
| X | Accomodations in town |
| X | Restaurants in town |

# *Tustin Tiller Days*

PONY AND ELEPHANT RIDES seem to be the main attraction for the kids at **Tustin Tiller Days**! The tikes will also have a good time at the children's games area while you sample the Thai, Mexican, Greek, Chinese, and plain ol' American edibles at hand! More than 100 craftspeople display their unique goods—woodwork, jewelry, pottery, oil and watercolor paintings, and hand-painted fabric.

## Tustin, California

Second weekend in October (beginning Friday)
Hours vary

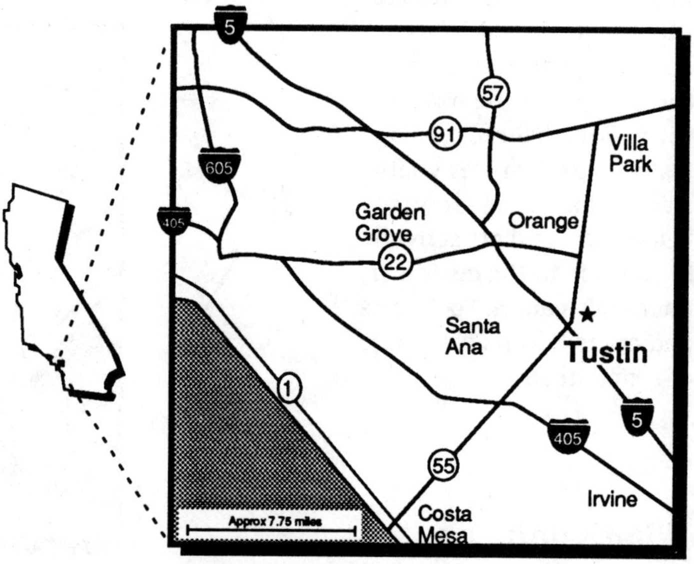


*Up-to-date festival information is available from:*
*Tustin Chamber of Commerce*
*(714) 544-2083*

## What's goin' on...

Town population: **43,000**
Last year's attendance: **45,000**
Average outdoor temperature: **65°**
Festival location: **N/A**

| | |
|---|---|
| X | Wine tasting/beer for sale |
| X | Food booths |
| X | Arts/crafts for sale |
| X | Live music |
| | Clowns |
| X | Face painters |
| X | Childrens games |
| X | Animal exhibits/petting zoo |
| | Dogs allowed on leash |
| X | Lost and found |
| X | Bicycle racks |
| X | First aid area available |
| | Self-brought picnics allowed |
| X | Self-brought alcohol allowed |
| | Stroller/wheelchair rentals available |

| | |
|---|---|
| X | Parade: Sat. 10:00 AM downtown |
| X | Parking fee: $1 |
| | Entrance fee |
| | Camping facilities |
| | Boating facilities |
| | RV facilities w/ hookups |
| X | Accomodations in town |
| X | Restaurants in town |

# *Pioneer Day*

IT'S A HAPPENIN' THANG FOR this Southern California town! **Pioneer Day**, taking place at Artesia Park, promises big fun for your entire family! Food booths stuffed with barbecued meats, sweet treats, and delicious ethnic eats line the park! For the part of you that wants to be entertained, there are colorful dances, lots of live music, an auction, and crafts and art booths to explore.

## Artesia, California

Second Saturday in October
All day

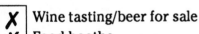

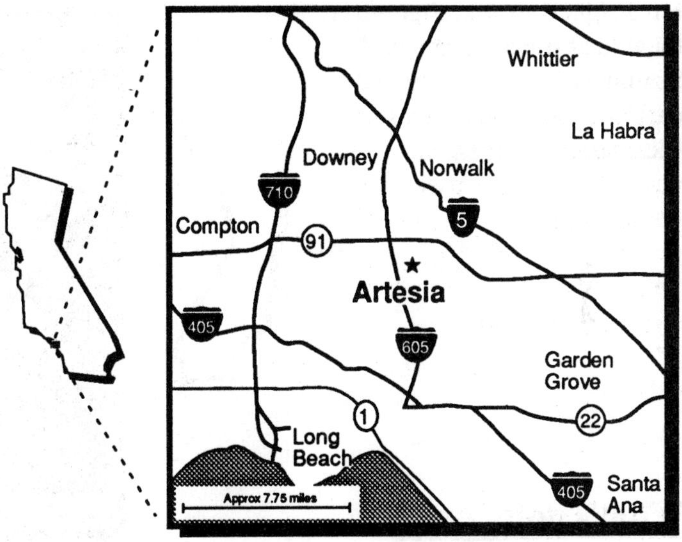


*Up-to-date festival information is available from:*
*Artesia Chamber of Commerce*
*(213) 924-6397*

## What's goin' on...

Town population: **14,301**
Last year's attendance: **N/A**
Average outdoor temperature: **70°**
Festival location: **Artesia Park**

| | |
|---|---|
| X | Wine tasting/beer for sale |
| X | Food booths |
| X | Arts/crafts for sale |
| X | Live music |
| | Clowns |
| | Face painters |
| X | Childrens games |
| | Animal exhibits/petting zoo |
| | Dogs allowed on leash |
| X | Lost and found |
| | Bicycle racks |
| X | First aid area available |
| | Self-brought picnics allowed |
| | Self-brought alcohol allowed |
| | Stroller/wheelchair rentals available |

| | |
|---|---|
| | Parade |
| X | Parking fee: (prices not avbl.) |
| X | Entrance fee: (prices not avbl.) |
| | Camping facilities |
| | Boating facilities |
| | RV facilities w/ hookups |
| X | Accomodations in town |
| X | Restaurants in town |

# *Octoberfest*

EVERY YEAR IN OCTOBER, Nipomo's Regional Park turns into an **Oktoberfest**! German dancers take to the stage as music fills the park. Nipomo is located at the southern end of San Luis Obispo County and east of Pismo Beach. This Oktoberfest happens in authentic German style!

## Nipomo, California

Second Saturday in October
10:00 AM - 4:00 PM

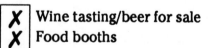

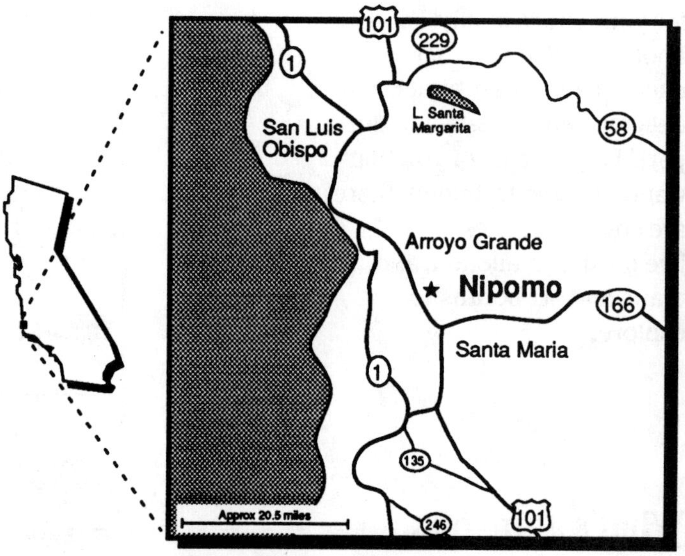


## What's goin' on...

Town population: **20,000**
Last year's attendance: **3,900**
Average outdoor temperature: **75°**
Festival location: **Nipomo Regional Park**

*Up-to-date festival information is available from:*
*Nipomo Chamber of Commerce*
*(805) 929-1593*

- X Wine tasting/beer for sale
- X Food booths
- X Arts/crafts for sale
- X Live music
- X Clowns
- X Face painters
- X Childrens games
- X Animal exhibits/petting zoo
- X Dogs allowed on leash
- X Lost and found
- X Bicycle racks
- X First aid area available
- X Self-brought picnics allowed
- X Self-brought alcohol allowed
- Stroller/wheelchair rentals available

- Parade
- Parking fee
- Entrance fee
- X Camping facilities: 15 miles
- X Boating facilities: Lake Lopez
- X RV facilities w/ hookups
- X Accomodations in town
- X Restaurants in town
  Jockos, Omelets & More, The Bosses

# *Palmdale Fall Festival*

MAGICIANS, BALLOON artists, jugglers, puppets, and mimes demonstrate their specialty at the **Palmdale Fall Festival**. Seven entertainment stages feature 40s, 50s, 60s, folk, big band and country music. Winner of the 1990 California Parks and Recreation Society/ARCO award, there are 28 working artists on display and nearly 200 art and craft booths! A *must* for the true-blue festival hopper!

## Palmdale, California

Second weekend in October
Daily 9:00 AM - 5:00 PM

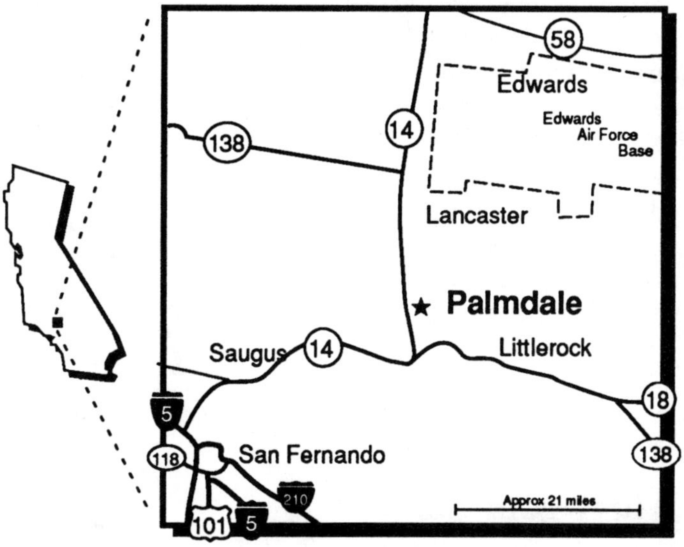


*Up-to-date festival information is available from:*
*Palmdale Chamber of Commerce*
*(805) 273-3232*

## What's goin' on...

Town population: **56,000**
Last year's attendance: **42,000**
Average outdoor temperature: **80°**
Festival location: **McAdam Park**

| | |
|---|---|
| | Wine tasting/beer for sale |
| X | Food booths |
| X | Arts/crafts for sale |
| X | Live music |
| X | Clowns |
| X | Face painters |
| X | Childrens games |
| | Animal exhibits/petting zoo |
| | Dogs allowed on leash |
| X | Lost and found |
| X | Bicycle racks |
| X | First aid area available |
| X | Self-brought picnics allowed |
| | Self-brought alcohol allowed |
| | Stroller/wheelchair rentals available |

| | |
|---|---|
| | Parade |
| | Parking fee |
| | Entrance fee |
| X | Camping facilities |
| | Boating facilities |
| | RV facilities w/ hookups |
| X | Accomodations in town<br>Ramada, Days Inn, Vagabond |
| X | Restaurants in town<br>Chili's, Eduardo's, Le Chene, Dolce Vita |

# *Western Daze*

SAN DIMAS, HOME OF **WESTern Daze**, is a unique town with wooden sidewalks and a western motif. Even though it's only 35 miles west of Los Angeles, it has retained its quaintness—priding itself on its historical sites and renovated old homes. There are more than 130 craft, and ethnic foods booths. Saturday night's festivities sneak well toward the midnight hour with live music and dancing.

## San Dimas, California

Second weekend in October

Sat. 8:00 AM - midnight; Sun. 9:00 AM - 5:00 PM

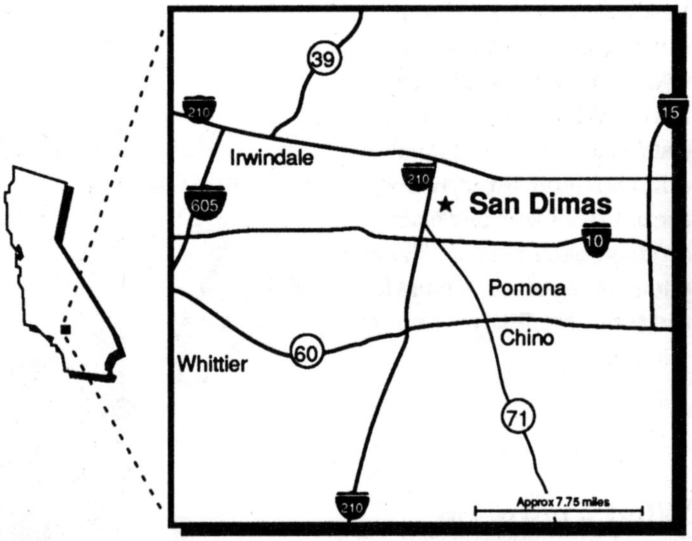


## What's goin' on...

Town population: **24,014**
Last year's attendance: **N/A**
Average outdoor temperature: **75°**
Festival location: **Frontier Village**

*Up-to-date festival information is available from:*
*San Dimas Chamber of Commerce*
*(714) 592-3818*

| | |
|---|---|
| X | Wine tasting/beer for sale |
| X | Food booths |
| X | Arts/crafts for sale |
| X | Live music |
| X | Clowns |
| X | Face painters |
| X | Childrens games |
| | Animal exhibits/petting zoo |
| | Dogs allowed on leash |
| X | Lost and found |
| | Bicycle racks |
| X | First aid area available |
| | Self-brought picnics allowed |
| | Self-brought alcohol allowed |
| | Stroller/wheelchair rentals available |

| | |
|---|---|
| X | Parade: Sat. 9:00 AM on San Dimas Av. |
| | Parking fee |
| | Entrance fee |
| X | Camping facilities: 2 miles |
| X | Boating facilities: Puddingstone Res. |
| X | RV facilities w/ hookups: 1 mile |
| X | Accomodations in town<br>San Dimas Inn, Best Western, Sixpence Inn |
| X | Restaurants in town<br>Ratania's, San Dimas Mansion |

# *San Marcos Chamber Renaissance Faire*

"FETCH ME MY ALE AND A turkey leg, wench!" Well, you don't actually hear that at **San Marcos Chamber Renaissance Faire** in San Marcos, but you *can* have a turkey drumstick for lunch! This entire community works extra hard, so with amazing splendor, the16th century comes alive! Clever and talented craftspersons display their wares, while entertainers seem to pop up out of nowhere!

## San Marcos, California

Second weekend in October
Daily: 10:00 AM - 6:00 PM

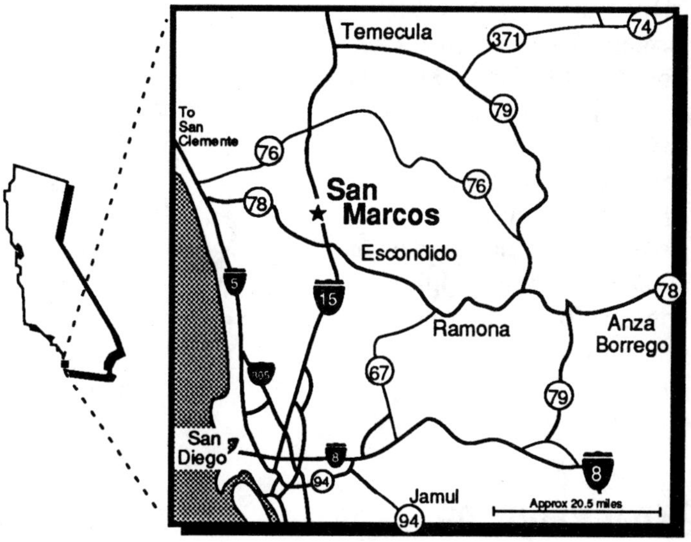


*Up-to-date festival information is available from:*
*San Marcos Chamber of Commerce*
*(619) 744-1270*

## What's goin' on...

Town population: **37,000**
Last year's attendance: **30,000**
Average outdoor temperature: **75°**
Festival location: **Citywide**

| | |
|---|---|
| X | Wine tasting/beer for sale |
| X | Food booths |
| X | Arts/crafts for sale |
| X | Live music |
| | Clowns |
| X | Face painters |
| X | Childrens games |
| | Animal exhibits/petting zoo |
| | Dogs allowed on leash |
| X | Lost and found |
| | Bicycle racks |
| X | First aid area available |
| X | Self-brought picnics allowed |
| | Self-brought alcohol allowed |
| | Stroller/wheelchair rentals available |

| | |
|---|---|
| | Parade |
| | Parking fee |
| X | Entrance fee: Adults $7; Kids $3 |
| X | Camping facilities: 5 miles |
| X | Boating facilities |
| X | RV facilities w/ hookups: 5 miles |
| X | Accomodations in town<br>San Marcos TravaLodge, La Quinta Inn, San Marcos Motel |
| X | Restaurants in town<br>Bruno's, Jerry Dale's Texas, Katsu, Grecian Gardens, J.K.'s Stage Stop |

# *October Applefest*

YOU CAN PICK YOUR APPLES, and you can pick your friends, but you can't pick your friends apples...unless your friends are one of the local farmers of Tehachapi—"Pick Your Own" orchards line this historical valley. But, if you're not into picking your own, come to the **October Applefest** featuring already picked apples and fixed up in apple pie, candied apples, apple crisp, and zillions of other ways! Yummy!

## Tehachapi, California

Second weekend in October
Daily: 10:00 AM - 5:00 PM

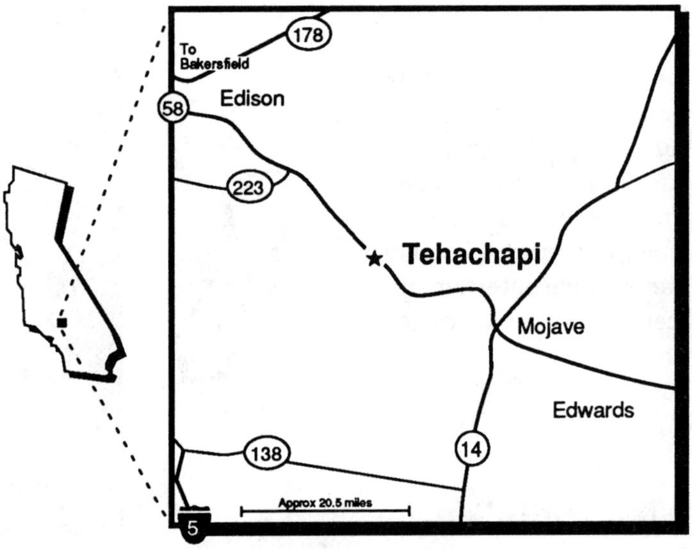


*Up-to-date festival information is available from:*
*Tehachapi Chamber of Commerce*
*(805) 822-4180*

## What's goin' on...

Town population: **20,000**
Last year's attendance: **11,000**
Average outdoor temperature: **72°**
Festival location: **City Park**

| | |
|---|---|
| ✗ | Wine tasting/beer for sale |
| ✗ | Food booths |
| ✗ | Arts/crafts for sale |
| | Live music |
| | Clowns |
| ✗ | Face painters |
| ✗ | Childrens games |
| | Animal exhibits/petting zoo |
| | Dogs allowed on leash |
| ✗ | Lost and found |
| ✗ | Bicycle racks |
| ✗ | First aid area available |
| ✗ | Self-brought picnics allowed |
| ✗ | Self-brought alcohol allowed |
| | Stroller/wheelchair rentals available |

| | |
|---|---|
| | Parade |
| | Parking fee |
| | Entrance fee |
| ✗ | Camping facilities: 2 miles |
| ✗ | Boating facilities |
| ✗ | RV facilities w/ hookups: 2 miles |
| ✗ | Accomodations in town<br>Tehachapi Mountain Lodge, Mountain Inn, Best Western |
| ✗ | Restaurants in town<br>Stallion Springs, Flour Mills, Southfork Inn |

# *Founder's Day— Fiesta de la Luna*

IN COMMEMORATION OF Chula Vista's incorporation, the city has its annual **Founder's Day and Fiesta de la Luna** celebration in October. Part of the festivities for this gigantic party include a birthday cake, entertainment, sidewalk sales, and raffles. This community, located just east of the scenic San Diego Bay, is only miles from the famous San Diego Zoo.

## Chula Vista, California

Second Saturday in October
9:00 AM - 6:00 PM

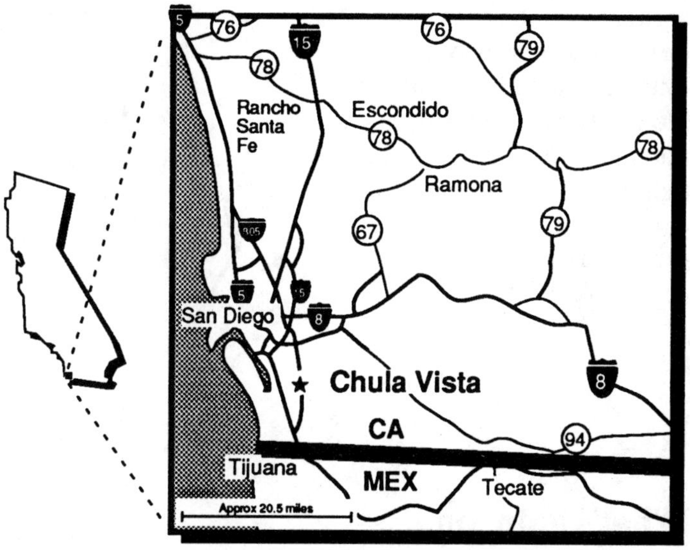


### What's goin' on...

Town population: **131,455**
Last year's attendance: **7,000**
Average outdoor temperature: **75°**
Festival location: **N/A**

*Up-to-date festival information is available from:*
*Chula Vista Chamber of Commerce*
*(619) 420-6602*

| | |
|---|---|
| X | Wine tasting/beer for sale |
| X | Food booths |
| X | Arts/crafts for sale |
| X | Live music |
| | Clowns |
| | Face painters |
| X | Childrens games |
| | Animal exhibits/petting zoo |
| X | Dogs allowed on leash |
| | Lost and found |
| X | Bicycle racks |
| X | First aid area available |
| | Self-brought picnics allowed |
| X | Self-brought alcohol allowed |
| X | Stroller/wheelchair rentals available |

| | |
|---|---|
| X | Parade: Sat. 9:00 AM downtown |
| | Parking fee |
| | Entrance fee |
| X | Camping facilities: 3 miles |
| X | Boating facilities: San Diego Bay |
| X | RV facilities w/ hookups: 3 miles |
| X | Accomodations in town<br>Day's Inn, All Seasons, Ramada Inn, Traveler, Vagabond |
| X | Restaurants in town<br>Anthony's Fish Grotto, Casa Salsa, House of Munich |

# *Desert Empire Fair*

THE **DESERT EMPIRE FAIR** IN Ridgecrest has it all—carnival rides and a Little Miss DEF pageant for the kids—and an agriculture exhibit and destruction derby for the folks! Located in the northern Mojave Desert, this growing community of Ridgecrest has held this festival since 1950!

## Ridgecrest, California

Third Wednesday through Sunday in October
Hours vary

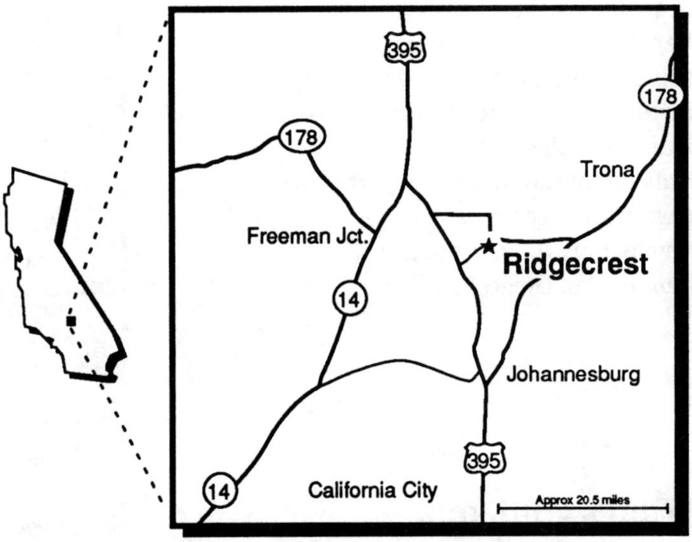


### What's goin' on...

Town population: **30,350**
Last year's attendance: **N/A**
Average outdoor temperature: **75°**
Festival location: **Fairgrounds**

*Up-to-date festival information is available from:*
*Ridgecrest Desert Empire Fairgrounds*
*(619) 375-8000*

- ✗ Wine tasting/beer for sale
- ✗ Food booths
- ✗ Arts/crafts for sale
- ✗ Live music
- ✗ Clowns
- ✗ Face painters
- ✗ Childrens games
- ✗ Animal exhibits/petting zoo
- ✗ Dogs allowed on leash
- ✗ Lost and found
- ✗ Bicycle racks
- ✗ First aid area available
- ✗ Self-brought picnics allowed
- ✗ Self-brought alcohol allowed
- ✗ Stroller/wheelchair rentals available

- ✗ Parade: Sat. 10:00 AM downtown
- Parking fee
- ✗ Entrance fee: (prices not avbl.)
- ✗ Camping facilities: 5 miles away
- ✗ Boating facilities: Lake Isabella
- ✗ RV facilities w/ hookups: In town
- ✗ Accomodations in town
  Pioneer Motel, Heritage House, El Rancho Motel, Econolodge, Carriage Inn
- ✗ Restaurants in town
  Sandpiper, The Hideaway, White Star Dining Company, Farris' at the Heritage, Schooner Saloon

# *Pioneer Days Celebration*

JUST TO THE EAST OF THE Copper Mountains is the town of Twenty-nine Palms with its **Pioneer Days Celebration** in October. It features an outhouse race, men's leg contest, PRCA rodeo, parades, food booths of all kinds, computer portraits, body deco, western wear, and dancing till midnight Friday, Saturday (rock 'n roll), and Sunday (country).

## Twentynine Palms, California

Third weekend in October
Hours vary

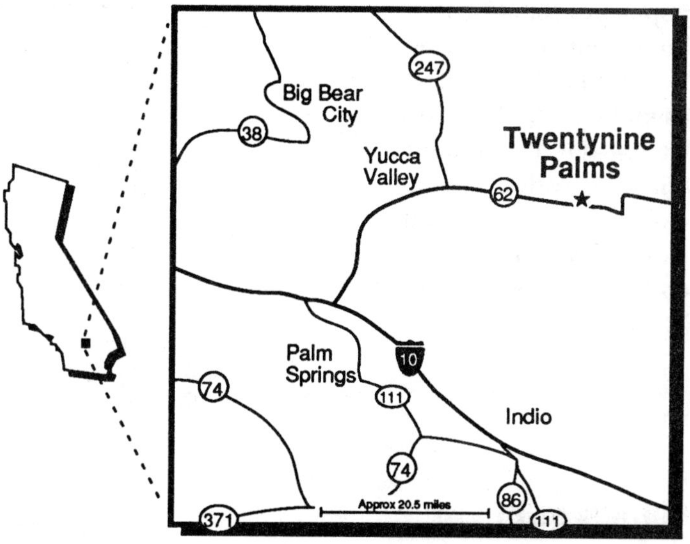


*Up-to-date festival information is available from:*
*Twentynine Palms Chamber of Commerce*
*(619) 367-3445*

## What's goin' on...

Town population: **13,000**
Last year's attendance: **N/A**
Average outdoor temperature: **83°**
Festival location: **Fairgrounds**

- X Wine tasting/beer for sale
- X Food booths
- X Arts/crafts for sale
- X Live music
- X Clowns
- Face painters
- Childrens games
- Animal exhibits/petting zoo
- Dogs allowed on leash
- X Lost and found
- Bicycle racks
- X First aid area available
- Self-brought picnics allowed
- Self-brought alcohol allowed
- Stroller/wheelchair rentals available

- X Parade: (time & date not avbl.)
- X Parking fee: $1
- X Entrance fee: Rodeo only
- X Camping facilities: 2 miles
- Boating facilities
- X RV facilities w/ hookups: 2 miles
- X Accomodations in town
  Best Western Gardens, El Rancho Dolores, The Desert Inn, Civic Center Motel, 29 Palms Inn
- X Restaurants in town
  29 Palms Inn, Pepper's, The Sandtrap, Hwy. 62 Grill, Barnett's Trading Post, Ring's

SOUTHERN

# *Kernville Stampede Rodeo*

THE RODEO ROLLS INTO town every October for the **Kernville Stampede Rodeo**. The two-day rodeo has the popular events—bronc riding, bull riding, barrel racing, trick riding, and kids events such as mutton busting and calf riding—not to mention the chance to watch playful clowns. The lunch menu looks like burgers, hot dogs, and chili. This is some big Kern Valley fun!

## Kernville, California

Third weekend in October

Daily 1:00 PM - 4:00 PM

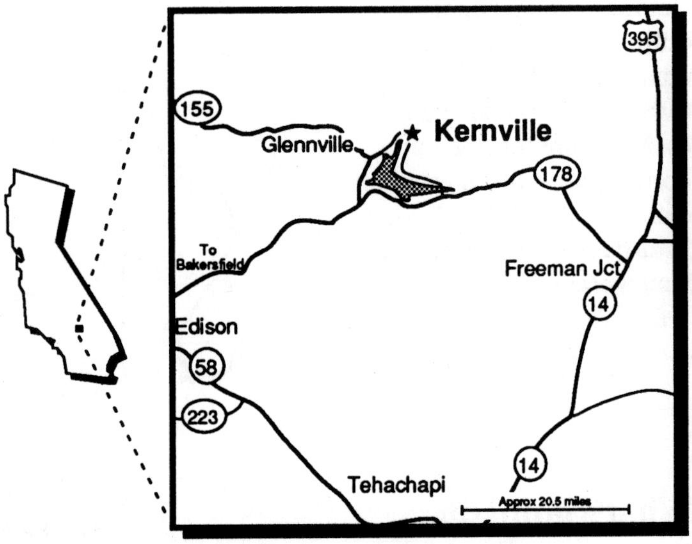


*Up-to-date festival information is available from:*
*Kernville Chamber of Commerce*
*(208) 743-3531*

## What's goin' on...

Town population: **2,500**

Last year's attendance: **2,000**

Average outdoor temperature: **65°**

Festival location: **Rodeo Grounds**

- X Wine tasting/beer for sale
- X Food booths
- Arts/crafts for sale
- Live music
- X Clowns
- Face painters
- Childrens games
- Animal exhibits/petting zoo
- Dogs allowed on leash
- X Lost and found
- Bicycle racks
- X First aid area available
- Self-brought picnics allowed
- Self-brought alcohol allowed
- Stroller/wheelchair rentals available

- Parade
- Parking fee
- X Entrance fee: (prices not avbl.)
- X Camping facilities: 5 miles
- X Boating facilities: Lake Isabella
- X RV facilities w/ hookups: 5 miles
- X Accomodations in town
  Kern Country Motel, Lazy River Lodge, Pine Cone Inn, Road's End Lodge, Western Mote
- X Restaurants in town
  Cheryl's, Roade End, Chilly Willie's, McNallys, Ewings, El Sombrero

# *Apple Valley Days*

HOME TO ROY ROGERS AND Dale Evans, Apple Valley has annually hosted **Apple Valley Days** for over 30 years now—even though the town was incorporated just two short years ago! You won't find the traditional arts-and-crafts booths, but you will find a carnival for the younguns, an unforgettable parade, and a wild-West rodeo to entertain you! While in town, stop and take a look at the Roy Rogers Museum.

## Apple Valley, California

Third Saturday in October
All day

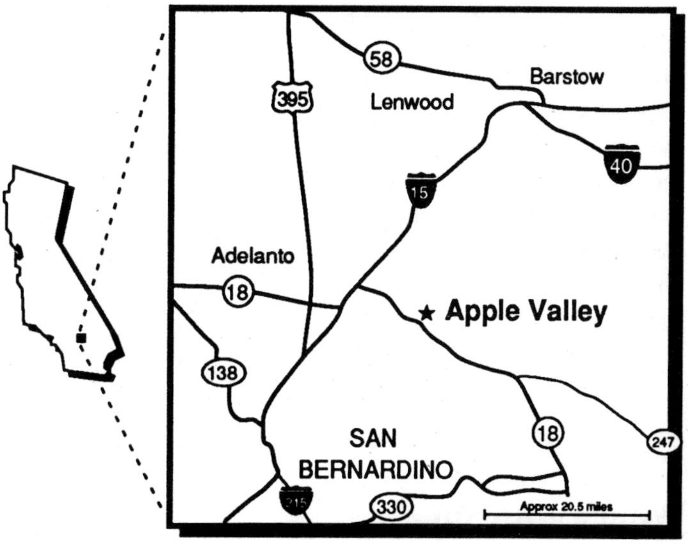


## What's goin' on...

Town population: **60,000**
Last year's attendance: **10,000**
Average outdoor temperature: **87°**
Festival location: **Citywide**

☞ *Up-to-date festival information is available from:*
*Apple Valley Chamber of Commerce*
*(619) 247-3202*

| | |
|---|---|
| | Wine tasting/beer for sale |
| X | Food booths |
| | Arts/crafts for sale |
| | Live music |
| X | Clowns |
| X | Face painters |
| X | Childrens games |
| | Animal exhibits/petting zoo |
| | Dogs allowed on leash |
| X | Lost and found |
| | Bicycle racks |
| X | First aid area available |
| | Self-brought picnics allowed |
| | Self-brought alcohol allowed |
| | Stroller/wheelchair rentals available |

| | |
|---|---|
| X | Parade: (date & time not avbl.) |
| | Parking fee |
| | Entrance fee |
| X | Camping facilities: 20 miles |
| | Boating facilities |
| | RV facilities w/ hookups |
| X | Accomodations in town<br>Apple Valley Lodge |
| | Restaurants in town |

S O U T H E R N

# *Pumpkinfest*

## Westchester, California

Third Sunday in October
9:00 AM - 5:00 PM

PETER, PETER, PUMPKIN - Eater was just a little chauvinistic for us, but nevertheless, he did do some pretty fancy pumpkin carving, no? The **Pumpkinfest** in Westchester guarantees you'll witness some of the best carvers in town! Team that fun with chili, ribs, home-made pumpkin pie, and a little country-and-western music—and you're headed for a wallop of a good time!

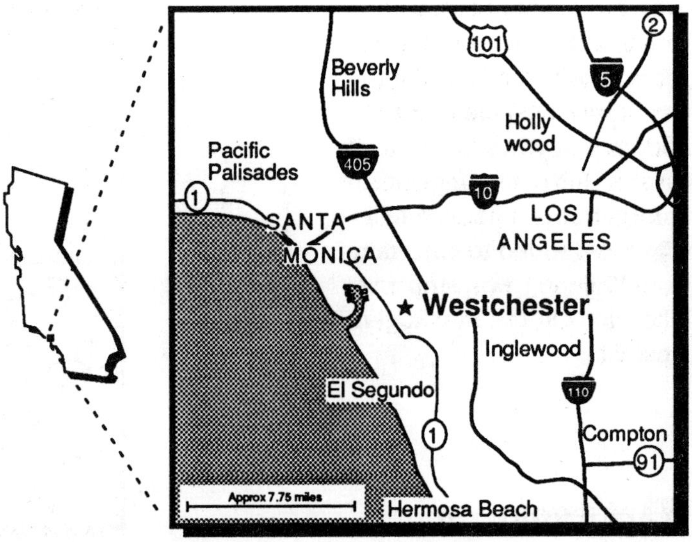


*Up-to-date festival information is available from:*
*Westchester Chamber of Commerce*
*(213) 645-5151*

## What's goin' on...

Town population: **50,000**
Last year's attendance: **400**
Average outdoor temperature: **70°**
Festival location: **N/A**

| | |
|---|---|
| X | Wine tasting/beer for sale |
| X | Food booths |
| X | Arts/crafts for sale |
| X | Live music |
| X | Clowns |
| | Face painters |
| X | Childrens games |
| X | Animal exhibits/petting zoo |
| | Dogs allowed on leash |
| | Lost and found |
| | Bicycle racks |
| | First aid area available |
| | Self-brought picnics allowed |
| | Self-brought alcohol allowed |
| | Stroller/wheelchair rentals available |

| | |
|---|---|
| | Parade |
| | Parking fee |
| | Entrance fee |
| | Camping facilities |
| | Boating facilities |
| | RV facilities w/ hookups |
| X | Accomodations in town |
| X | Restaurants in town |

# *Borrego Days— A Desert Festival*

WHAT A LINE-UP OF EVENTS at **Borrego Days—A Desert Festival!** Activities are all over town—beginning Friday with an arts- and-crafts show at 8:00 AM—and continuing all weekend. On Saturday, you'll be entertained at the VIP breakfast, chile cook- off (that's right—as in pepper), Desert Festival parade, Miss Chile Pepper contest, and variety show in the evening. Sunday's chock full of action as well!

## Borrego Springs, California

Last weekend in October (beginning Friday)
Hours vary

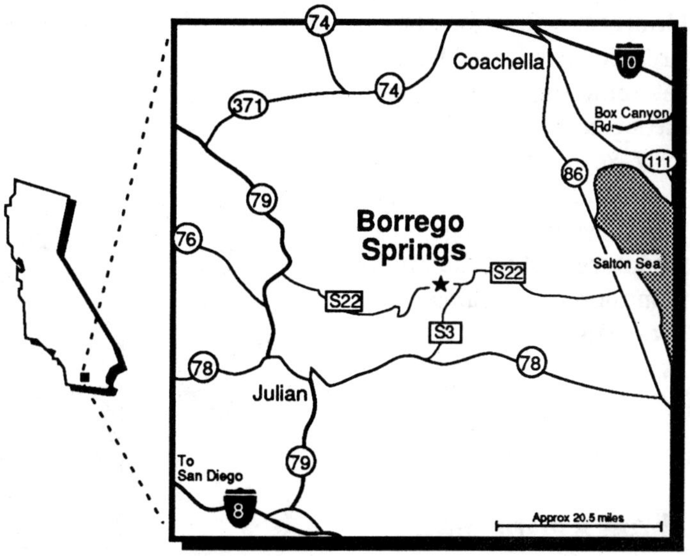


*Up-to-date festival information is available from:*
*Borrego Springs Chamber of Commerce*
*(619) 344-5555*

## What's goin' on...

Town population: **1,400**
Last year's attendance: **3,000**
Average outdoor temperature: **90°**
Festival location: **Citywide**

| | |
|---|---|
| X | Wine tasting/beer for sale |
| X | Food booths |
| X | Arts/crafts for sale |
| X | Live music |
| X | Clowns |
| X | Face painters |
| X | Childrens games |
| | Animal exhibits/petting zoo |
| X | Dogs allowed on leash |
| X | Lost and found |
| X | Bicycle racks |
| X | First aid area available |
| X | Self-brought picnics allowed |
| X | Self-brought alcohol allowed |
| | Stroller/wheelchair rentals available |

| | |
|---|---|
| X | Parade: (date & time not avbl.) |
| | Parking fee |
| | Entrance fee |
| X | Camping facilities: 1 mile |
| X | Boating facilities: 15 miles |
| X | RV facilities w/ hookups: 1 mile |
| X | Accomodations in town<br>Desert Ironwood, Whispering Sands, Oasis Motel, La Casa del Zorro, Stanlund's Motel |
| X | Restaurants in town<br>La Casa Del Zorro, Rams Hill Country Club |

SOUTHERN

# *Liberty Week*

IN A JUNGLE OF VILLAGES, towns, and cities of Los Angeles County lies the town of Bellflower with its annual **Liberty Week**. When you're tired of life in the fast lane, retreat to this festival which has been in the works since 1967. Featuring booths filled with handmade floral arrangements, wood carvings, sculpture, watercolor and oil paintings, there's also lots of good eats for your tummies, as well!

## Bellflower, California

Last Saturday in October to the first Saturday in November
Hours vary

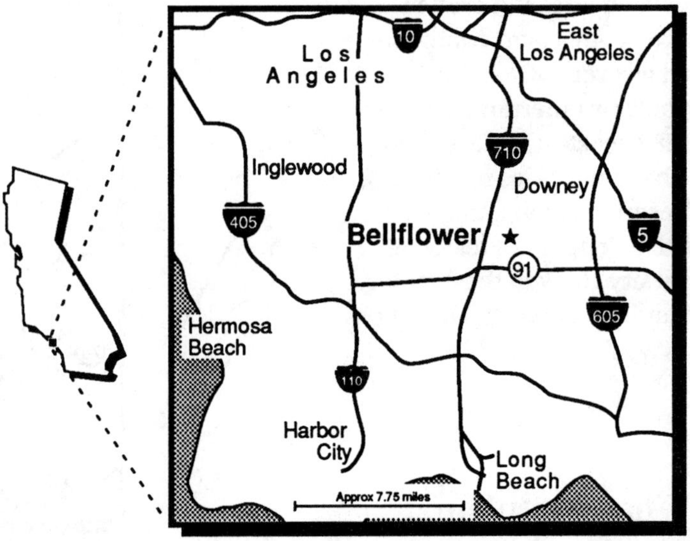


## What's goin' on...

Town population: **60,000**
Last year's attendance: **10,000**
Average outdoor temperature: **70°**
Festival location: **Downtown & park**

*Up-to-date festival information is available from:*
*Bellflower Chamber of Commerce*
*(213) 867-1744*

- X Wine tasting/beer for sale
- X Food booths
- X Arts/crafts for sale
- X Live music
- X Clowns
- X Face painters
- Childrens games
- X Animal exhibits/petting zoo
- Dogs allowed on leash
- X Lost and found
- X Bicycle racks
- X First aid area available
- X Self-brought picnics allowed
- Self-brought alcohol allowed
- Stroller/wheelchair rentals available

- X Parade: 2nd Sat. 11:00 AM downtown
- Parking fee
- Entrance fee
- Camping facilities
- Boating facilities
- RV facilities w/ hookups
- X Accomodations in town
  Motel 6, Rodeway Inn
- X Restaurants in town
  Marino's, Magdalena's, Moffett's, Cafe Camellia

# *Village Venture Street Faire*

**VILLAGE VENTURE STREET Faire** is located in the charming, pedestrian- oriented area of Claremont known as "The Village." More than 75 specialty, and retail, and services businesses share this section of the city along with some very fine restaurants. Annually, craftspeople, artists, and entertainers share their unique talents in the quaint atmosphere during this special day in October.

## Claremont, California

Last Saturday in October
10:00 AM - 4:00 PM

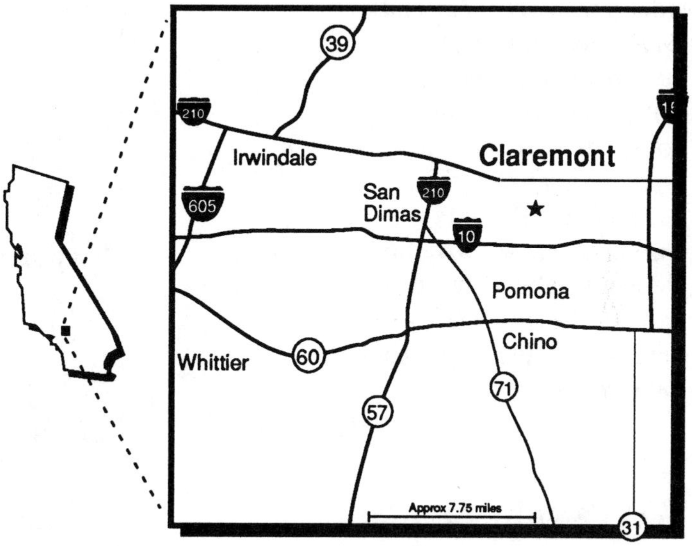


## What's goin' on...

Town population: **36,500**
Last year's attendance: **20,000**
Average outdoor temperature: **75°**
Festival location: **In the village**

*Up-to-date festival information is available from: Claremont Chamber of Commerce (714) 624-4681*

| | |
|---|---|
| | Wine tasting/beer for sale |
| X | Food booths |
| X | Arts/crafts for sale |
| X | Live music |
| X | Clowns |
| X | Face painters |
| X | Childrens games |
| | Animal exhibits/petting zoo |
| X | Dogs allowed on leash |
| X | Lost and found |
| X | Bicycle racks |
| X | First aid area available |
| X | Self-brought picnics allowed |
| | Self-brought alcohol allowed |
| | Stroller/wheelchair rentals available |

| | |
|---|---|
| X | Parade: 10:30 AM at the Street Faire |
| | Parking fee |
| | Entrance fee |
| X | Camping facilities: 7 miles |
| X | Boating facilities: Lake |
| X | RV facilities w/ hookups: 7 miles |
| X | Accomodations in town<br>Griswold's Inn, Claremont Motel Inn, Howard Johnson, Ramada Inn |
| X | Restaurants in town<br>The Danson, Original Shrimp House, Village Grille, 3 C's Cafe, Blue Moon Cafe, Chili's |

# *Village Street Faire*

THE **CARLSBAD VILLAGE Street Faire** is such a great time that the Chamber of Commerce decided to hold it twice yearly. The May and November festivals, held downtown in the village, feature international-food booths as well as unique crafts such as handmade dolls and hand-painted clothing. Kids will love the elephant walk, pony rides, and petting zoo. Nearby beaches enhance the ideal California atmosphere.

## Carlsbad, California

First Sunday in November
10:00 AM - 4:30 PM

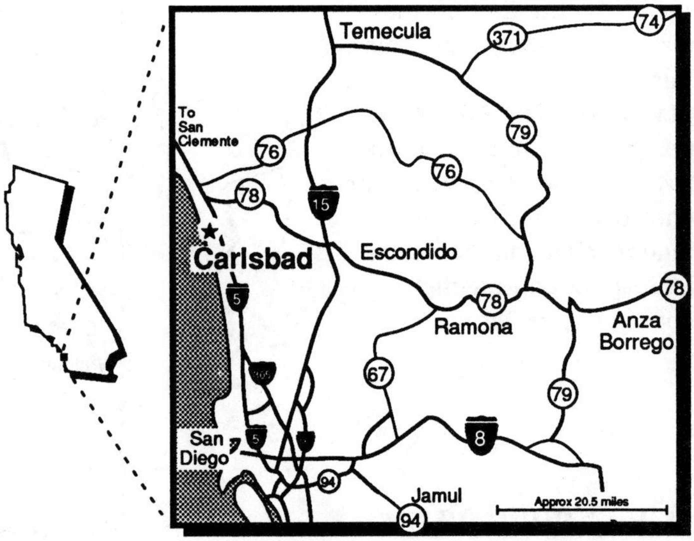


*Up-to-date festival information is available from:*
*Carlsbad Chamber of Commerce*
*(619) 931-8400*

## What's goin' on...

Town population: **62,500**
Last year's attendance: **80,000**
Average outdoor temperature: **70°**
Festival location: **Downtown**

| | |
|---|---|
| X | Wine tasting/beer for sale |
| X | Food booths |
| X | Arts/crafts for sale |
| X | Live music |
| X | Clowns |
| X | Face painters |
| X | Childrens games |
| X | Animal exhibits/petting zoo |
| | Dogs allowed on leash |
| X | Lost and found |
| X | Bicycle racks |
| X | First aid area available |
| | Self-brought picnics allowed |
| | Self-brought alcohol allowed |
| | Stroller/wheelchair rentals available |

| | |
|---|---|
| | Parade |
| | Parking fee |
| | Entrance fee |
| X | Camping facilities: In town |
| X | Boating facilities: Saltwater inlet |
| X | RV facilities w/ hookups: In town |
| X | Accomodations in town<br>Ocean Manor, Beach View Lodge, Carlsbad Inn, Carlsbad Lodge, Motel 6, Surf Motel |
| X | Restaurants in town<br>The Village Grill, Hennessey's Tavern, Cliff's Pantry, The Cove, Dooley McCluskey's |

# *Golf Cart Parade*

WE'VE SEEN A LOT OF ZANY festivals in our time...and we've raised our eyebrows at some pretty remarkable ideas...but the **Golf Cart Parade** just might take the cake! There are *millions* of prizes for *millions* of catagories for the *millions* of golf carts in this town! Come down for the weekend for a few rounds of golf and have a look at this crazy parade!

## Palm Desert, California

First Sunday in November
All day

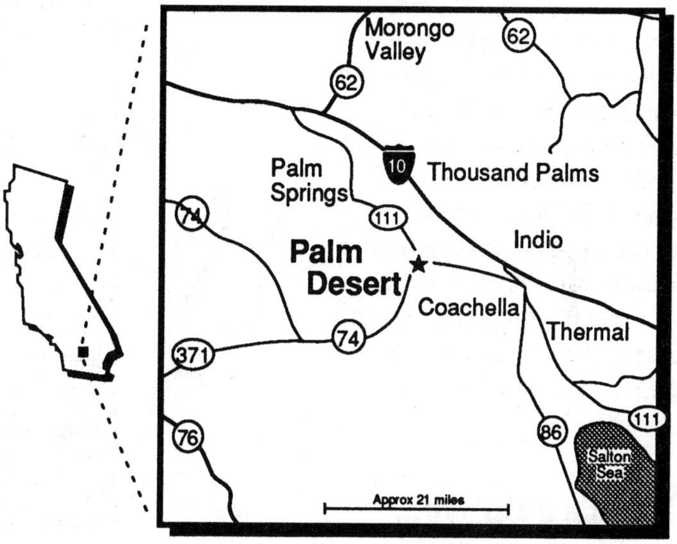


## What's goin' on...

Town population: **22,000**
Last year's attendance: **N/A**
Average outdoor temperature: **80°**
Festival location: **Downtown on El Paseo**

*Up-to-date festival information is available from:*
*Palm Desert Chamber of Commerce*
*(619) 346-6111*

| | |
|---|---|
| | Wine tasting/beer for sale |
| X | Food booths |
| | Arts/crafts for sale |
| X | Live music |
| X | Clowns |
| | Face painters |
| | Childrens games |
| | Animal exhibits/petting zoo |
| | Dogs allowed on leash |
| | Lost and found |
| | Bicycle racks |
| | First aid area available |
| X | Self-brought picnics allowed |
| | Self-brought alcohol allowed |
| | Stroller/wheelchair rentals available |

| | |
|---|---|
| X | Parade: (time & date not avbl.) |
| | Parking fee |
| | Entrance fee |
| | Camping facilities |
| | Boating facilities |
| X | RV facilities w/ hookups: In town |
| X | Accomodations in town |
| X | Restaurants in town |

SOUTHERN

# Brawley Cattle Call

WHAT'S MORE FUN THAN A barrel of monkeys? How 'bout a corral of cattle? You'll find that and a whole lot more at **the Brawley Cattle Call!** All you urban, and even you authentic, cowboys will enjoy the chuckwagon breakfast (it's more like a feast!), PRCA rodeo, blue grass tunes, parade, and plenty of good grub being cooked up on the outdoor barbecues. So git 'cher boots on and come on down!

## Brawley, California

Second weekend in November
Hours vary

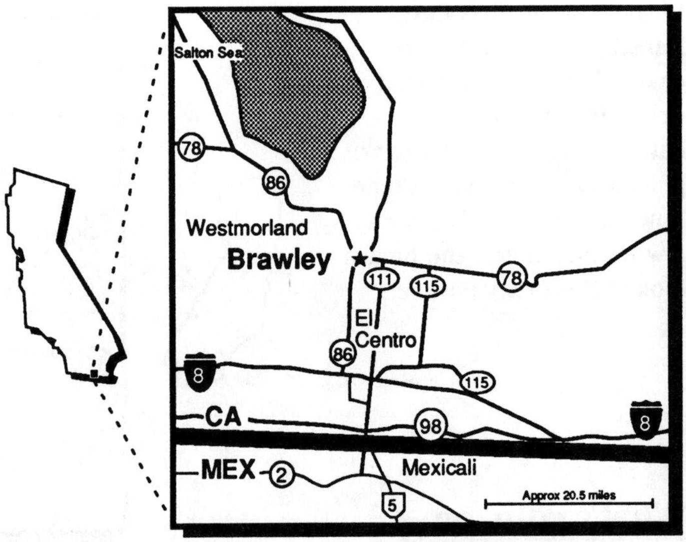


## What's goin' on...

Town population: **19,500**
Last year's attendance: **40,000**
Average outdoor temperature: **80°**
Festival location: **Rodeo grounds**

☞ *Up-to-date festival information is available from:*
*Brawley Chamber of Commerce*
*(619) 344-3160*

| | |
|---|---|
| | Wine tasting/beer for sale |
| ✗ | Food booths |
| ✗ | Arts/crafts for sale |
| ✗ | Live music |
| ✗ | Clowns |
| | Face painters |
| | Childrens games |
| ✗ | Animal exhibits/petting zoo |
| | Dogs allowed on leash |
| | Lost and found |
| | Bicycle racks |
| ✗ | First aid area available |
| ✗ | Self-brought picnics allowed |
| | Self-brought alcohol allowed |
| | Stroller/wheelchair rentals available |

| | |
|---|---|
| ✗ | Parade: Sat. 9:45 AM on Mail St. |
| | Parking fee |
| ✗ | Entrance fee: (prices not avbl.) |
| ✗ | Camping facilities: 7 miles |
| ✗ | Boating facilities: Lake |
| ✗ | RV facilities w/ hookups: 7 miles |
| | Accomodations in town |
| ✗ | Restaurants in town<br>Adobe |

# *Hollywood Bandfest*

MAESTRO, A DRUM ROLL please! The talented youngsters of the Hollywood area, and there are many of them, are pitted against one another at the **Hollywood Bandfest!** This is an exciting competition and will bring you many goosebumps, hoots, and hollers! And of course, while you're in the area, there's always lots to do and see...

## Hollywood, California

Saturday following Thanksgiving
10:00 AM - 2:00 PM

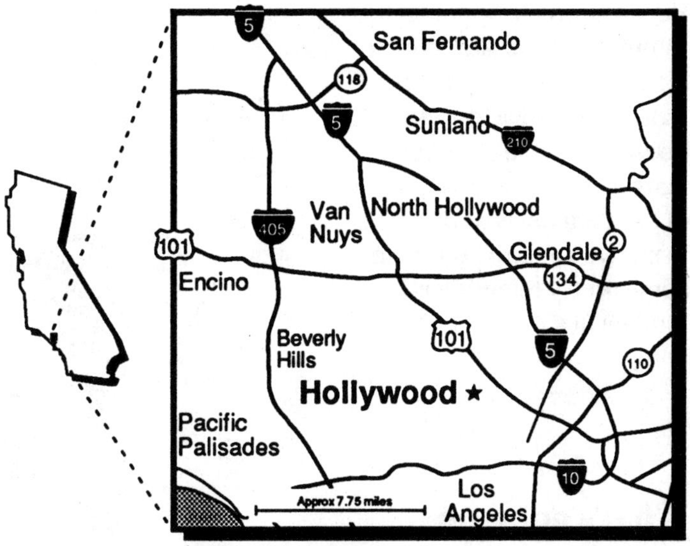


## What's goin' on...

Town population: **250,000**
Last year's attendance: **N/A**
Average outdoor temperature: **70°**
Festival location: **Birmingham High Stadium**

*Up-to-date festival information is available from:*
*Hollywood Chamber of Commerce*
*(213) 469-8311*

| | |
|---|---|
| | Wine tasting/beer for sale |
| | Food booths |
| | Arts/crafts for sale |
| X | Live music |
| | Clowns |
| | Face painters |
| | Childrens games |
| | Animal exhibits/petting zoo |
| | Dogs allowed on leash |
| | Lost and found |
| X | Bicycle racks |
| | First aid area available |
| | Self-brought picnics allowed |
| | Self-brought alcohol allowed |
| | Stroller/wheelchair rentals available |

| | |
|---|---|
| X | Parade: Sun. 6:00 PM on Sunset Blvd. |
| | Parking fee |
| X | Entrance fee: $3. |
| | Camping facilities |
| | Boating facilities |
| | RV facilities w/ hookups |
| X | Accomodations in town: Sheraton Universal, Hollywood Roosevelt, Hollywood Holiday Inn |
| X | Restaurants in town: Musso and Frank, Columbia Bar and Grill, Off Vine |

SOUTHERN

# *Holiday Street Festival*

THERE'S VERY LITTLE CHILL in the Southern California air of Ventura when the **Holiday Street Festival** rolls around. Here's a terrific opportunity to purchase Christmas gifts for the entire family from more than 600 arts-and- crafts booths that line downtown Main Street. This town, home of the Channel Islands Monument, also goes all out with some pretty tempting ethnic food dishes.

## Ventura, California

First Sunday in December
11:00 AM - 4:00 PM

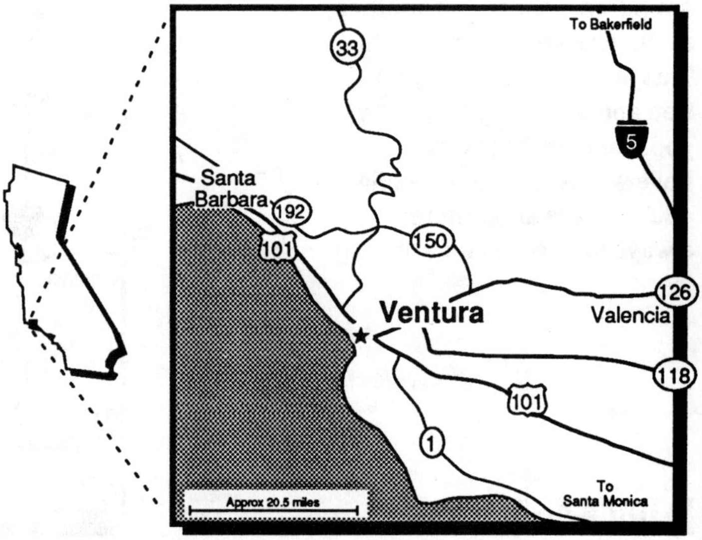


## What's goin' on...

Town population: **566,300**
Last year's attendance: **50,000**
Average outdoor temperature: **75°**
Festival location: **Main Street**

*Up-to-date festival information is available from:*
*Ventura Chamber of Commerce*
*(805) 648-2875*

| | |
|---|---|
| | Wine tasting/beer for sale |
| X | Food booths |
| X | Arts/crafts for sale |
| X | Live music |
| X | Clowns |
| X | Face painters |
| X | Childrens games |
| | Animal exhibits/petting zoo |
| X | Dogs allowed on leash |
| X | Lost and found |
| X | Bicycle racks |
| X | First aid area available |
| X | Self-brought picnics allowed |
| | Self-brought alcohol allowed |
| | Stroller/wheelchair rentals available |

| | |
|---|---|
| | Parade |
| | Parking fee |
| | Entrance fee |
| X | Camping facilities: 2 miles |
| X | Boating facilities: Ocean Marina |
| X | RV facilities w/ hookups: 2 miles |
| X | Accomodations in town |
| X | Restaurants in town<br>Pierpoint, The Chart House, Eric Ericson's |

# *Country Christmas*

FREE MULE RIDES AND pictures with Santa will delight the youngsters at Buttonwillow's **Country Christmas**! Homemade jellies, holiday decorations, hand-made ornaments, and other seasonal crafts will be on display and for sale. It's attending festivals like this during the holiday season that *really* get you into the spirit!

## Buttonwillow, California

First Saturday in December
11:00 AM - 3:00 PM

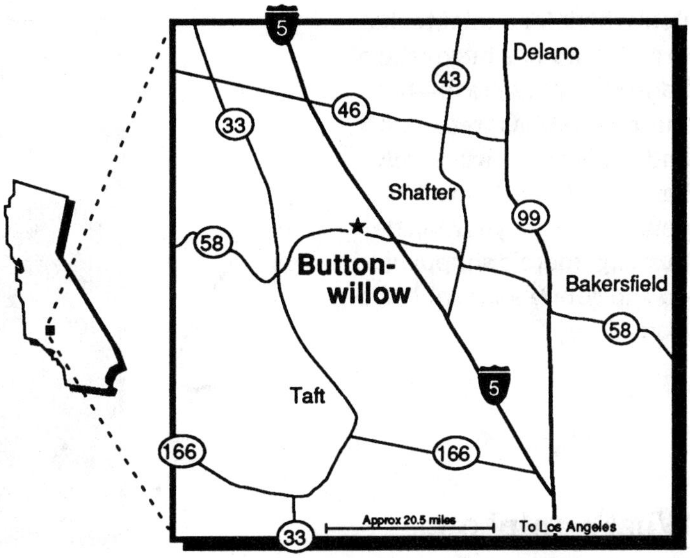


## What's goin' on...

Town population: **1,800**
Last year's attendance: **300**
Average outdoor temperature: **62°**
Festival location: **Buttonwillow County Park**

*Up-to-date festival information is available from:*
*Buttonwillow Chamber of Commerce*
*(805) 764-5406*

| | |
|---|---|
| | Wine tasting/beer for sale |
| X | Food booths |
| X | Arts/crafts for sale |
| | Live music |
| | Clowns |
| X | Face painters |
| X | Childrens games |
| X | Animal exhibits/petting zoo |
| X | Dogs allowed on leash |
| | Lost and found |
| X | Bicycle racks |
| | First aid area available |
| X | Self-brought picnics allowed |
| | Self-brought alcohol allowed |
| | Stroller/wheelchair rentals available |

| | |
|---|---|
| | Parade |
| | Parking fee |
| | Entrance fee |
| X | Camping facilities: 20 miles |
| X | Boating facilities: Buena Vista Lake |
| X | RV facilities w/ hookups: 20 miles |
| X | Accomodations in town<br>All Star Inn, Motel 6, Good Night Inn |
| X | Restaurants in town<br>Buttonwillow Lumber Yard Restaurant, Dominique's Basque Restaurant |

# *Mission Christmas Faire*

CALIFORNIA'S LARGEST mission annually hosts the **Mission Christmas Faire**—for the umpteenth time! And don't think for a minute that dressing up this huge relic of adobe is an easy task—but these Christmas trees, lights, and decorations will surely ignite the holiday spirit in you! And to get your bustle bustling, there's shopping to do and goodies to nibble on! *Merry Merry!*

## Oceanside, California

First weekend in December
Daily 9:00 AM - 6:00 PM

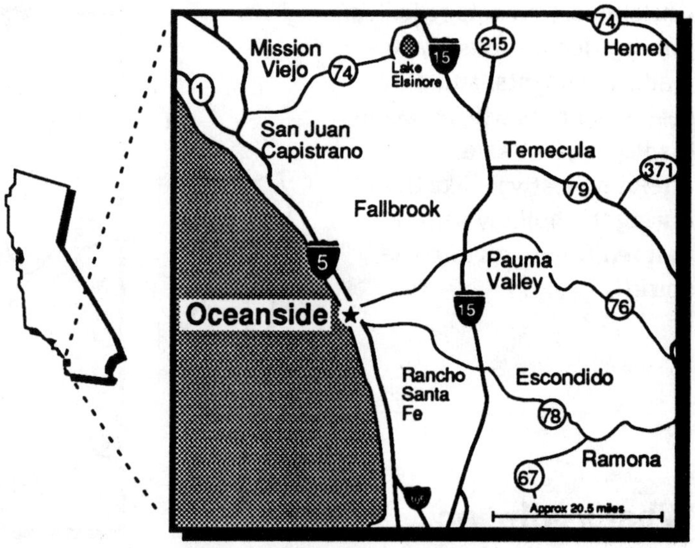


## What's goin' on...

Town population: **110,000**
Last year's attendance: **30,000**
Average outdoor temperature: **78°**
Festival location: **San Luis Rey Mission**

*Up-to-date festival information is available from:*
*Oceanside Chamber of Commerce*
*(619) 721-1101*

| | |
|---|---|
| X | Wine tasting/beer for sale |
| X | Food booths |
| X | Arts/crafts for sale |
| X | Live music |
| X | Clowns |
| X | Face painters |
| X | Childrens games |
| X | Animal exhibits/petting zoo |
| X | Dogs allowed on leash |
| X | Lost and found |
| | Bicycle racks |
| X | First aid area available |
| X | Self-brought picnics allowed |
| | Self-brought alcohol allowed |
| | Stroller/wheelchair rentals available |

| | |
|---|---|
| X | Parade: (date & time not avbl.) |
| | Parking fee |
| | Entrance fee |
| X | Camping facilities: 5 miles |
| X | Boating facilities: On-site |
| X | RV facilities w/ hookups: 5 miles |
| X | Accomodations in town |
| X | Restaurants in town<br>Chart House, Fishermans, Jolly Roger, Monterey Bay Cannery |

# *Christmas Crafts Festival*

DECK THE HALLS WITH crafts galore at the **Christmas Crafts Festival** in Ojai! Now, don't expect bionic, electronic toys here ...because the local crafts- people have been hard at work to fill their booths with handmade items that are one-of-a-kind sorts. Baskets, leather goods, hand-painted clothing, ceramics, and jewelry will tickle your fancy! And to fill your tummies? Lots of good homemade treats!

## Ojai, California

First weekend in December
Daily 10:00 AM - 5:00 PM

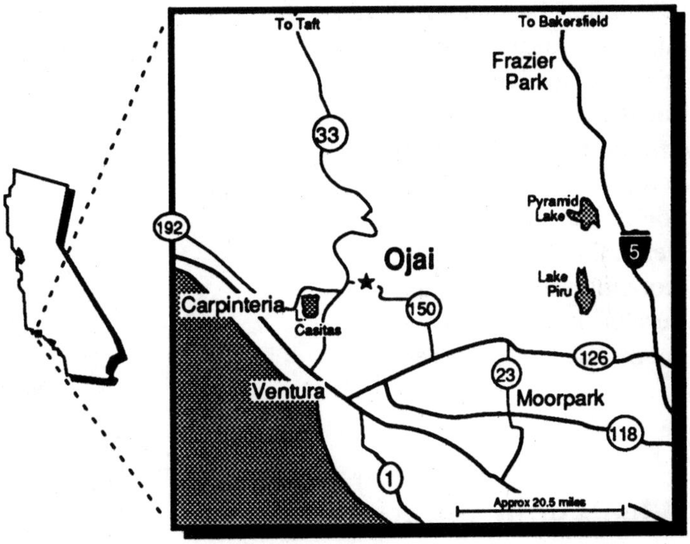


## What's goin' on...

Town population: **7,000**
Last year's attendance: **N/A**
Average outdoor temperature: **73°**
Festival location: **Downtown**

*Up-to-date festival information is available from:*
*Ojai Ojai Art Center*
*(805) 646-8126*

- [ ] Wine tasting/beer for sale
- [x] Food booths
- [x] Arts/crafts for sale
- [x] Live music
- [ ] Clowns
- [ ] Face painters
- [ ] Childrens games
- [ ] Animal exhibits/petting zoo
- [ ] Dogs allowed on leash
- [ ] Lost and found
- [ ] Bicycle racks
- [ ] First aid area available
- [ ] Self-brought picnics allowed
- [ ] Self-brought alcohol allowed
- [ ] Stroller/wheelchair rentals available

- [ ] Parade
- [ ] Parking fee
- [ ] Entrance fee
- [x] Camping facilities: 3 miles
- [x] Boating facilities: Lake
- [x] RV facilities w/ hookups: 3 miles
- [x] Accomodations in town
  Ojai Valley Inn, Best Western, Capri Motel, Oakridge Inn, Los Padres Inn, Casa Ojai
- [x] Restaurants in town
  L'Auberge, Roger Keller's Restaurant, The Nest, The Ranch House, Ojai Valley Inn

# *Cruise of Lights*

THE **CRUISE OF LIGHTS** IN Huntington Harbor is a pure delight! Cruise dates: December 12th - 21st; cruise times: 5:30, 6:30, 7:30, and 8:30. Then sit back and enjoy the 45-minute boat ride through the channels of Huntington Harbor, filled with decorated boats and reflections of homes shimmering on the water. Call the Chamber for more information about purchasing tickets in advance—which is advised.

## Huntington Beach, California

Second Saturday to the third Saturday in December

Daily 5:30, 6:30, 7:30, and 8:30 PM

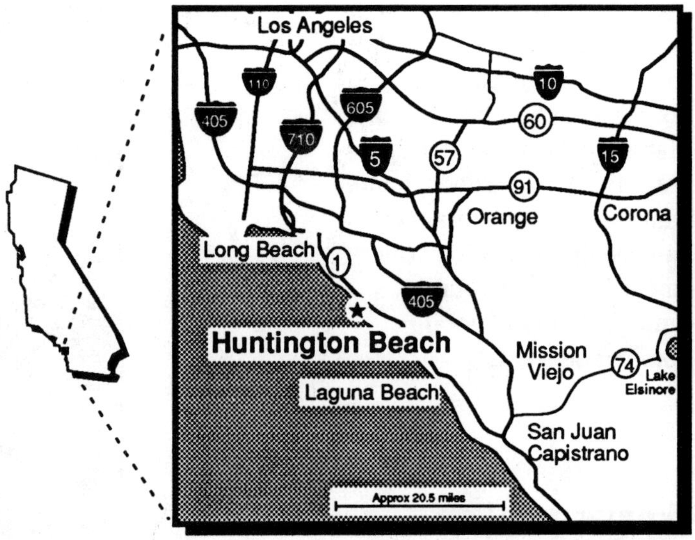


*Up-to-date festival information is available from:*
*Huntington Beach Chamber of Commerce*
*(714) 536-8888*

## What's goin' on...

Town population: **185,000**
Last year's attendance: **24,000**
Average outdoor temperature: **55°**
Festival location: **Huntington Harbor**

| | |
|---|---|
| | Wine tasting/beer for sale |
| | Food booths |
| | Arts/crafts for sale |
| X | Live music |
| | Clowns |
| | Face painters |
| | Childrens games |
| | Animal exhibits/petting zoo |
| | Dogs allowed on leash |
| | Lost and found |
| | Bicycle racks |
| | First aid area available |
| | Self-brought picnics allowed |
| | Self-brought alcohol allowed |
| | Stroller/wheelchair rentals available |

| | |
|---|---|
| | Parade |
| | Parking fee |
| X | Entrance fee: Adults $7; Kids $4 |
| X | Camping facilities: 1 mile |
| X | Boating facilities: Ocean |
| X | RV facilities w/ hookups: 1 mile |
| X | Accomodations in town<br>Hilton, Best Western, Ocean View, Huntington Shores Motel, Sunset Beach Inn |
| X | Restaurants in town<br>Maxwell's, Charley Brown's, J.C. McLins, Bukhara, Tijuana Willies, Tibbies, Pero's |

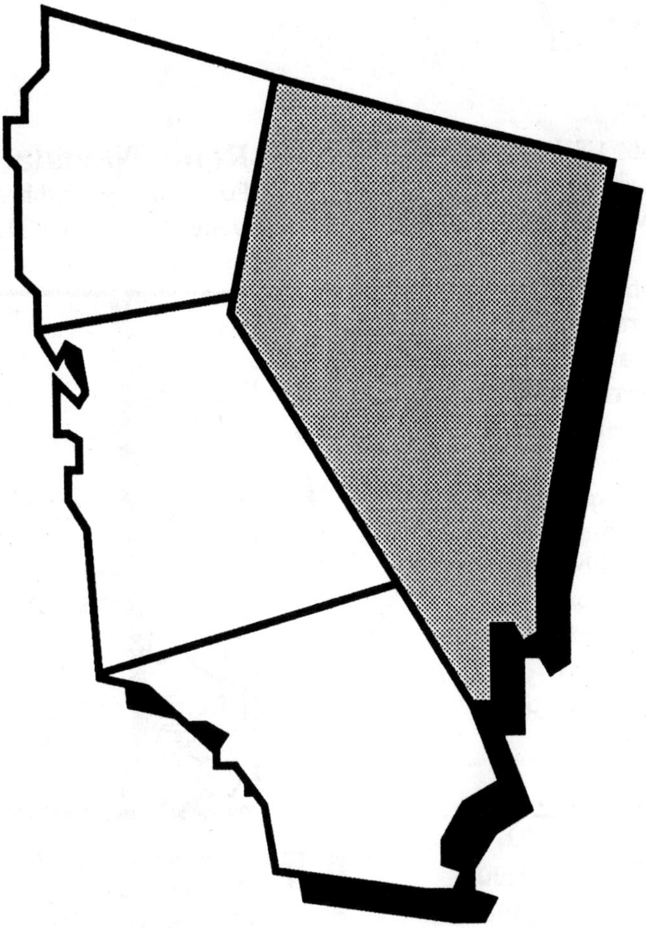

# Nevada

# *Kite Festival*

## Reno, Nevada

First full weekend in April
Daily 10:00 AM - 4:00 PM

"A LIGHT FRAME, USUALLY of wood, covered with paper or cloth, to be flown in the wind at the end of a string" is how Webster describes a kite. If you think it's a rather bland description, we agree! The only way to describe a kite is to see one...at the **Kite Festival**! You'll see kites of all colors, shapes, sizes, comic book characters, heros, and heroines! The food booths take on an international theme as you make time to gobble up tacos, pizza, nachos, hot dogs, and Polish sausage sammies!

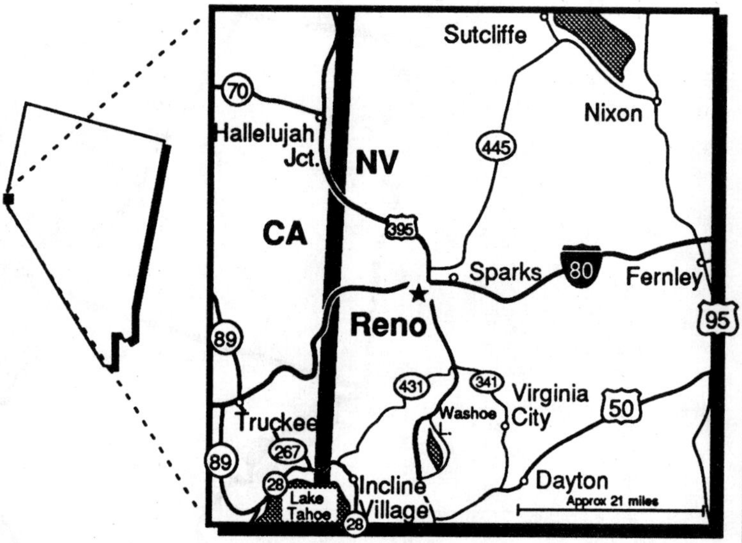


*Up-to-date festival information is available from:*
*Reno Visitors Center*
*(702) 348-7788*

## What's goin' on...

Town population: **250,000**
Last year's attendance: **25,000**
Average outdoor temperature: **62°**
Festival location: **Rancho San Rafael Park**

| | |
|---|---|
| ✗ | Wine tasting/beer for sale |
| ✗ | Food booths |
| ✗ | Arts/crafts for sale |
| | Live music |
| | Clowns |
| ✗ | Face painters |
| ✗ | Childrens games |
| | Animal exhibits/petting zoo |
| ✗ | Dogs allowed on leash |
| ✗ | Lost and found |
| ✗ | Bicycle racks |
| ✗ | First aid area available |
| ✗ | Self-brought picnics allowed |
| | Self-brought alcohol allowed |
| | Stroller/wheelchair rentals available |

| | |
|---|---|
| | Parade |
| | Parking fee |
| | Entrance fee |
| ✗ | Camping facilities: 3 miles |
| ✗ | Boating facilities: Washoe Lake |
| ✗ | RV facilities w/ hookups: In town |
| ✗ | Hotels in town<br>Hilton, Carson Valley Inn, Harrah's, Nugget |
| ✗ | Restaurants in town<br>Rivoli, Seafare, John's Oyster Bar, The Vintage, Pancho and Willie's, Asian Garden |

# *Clark County Fair*

SINCE 1981 FOLKS HAVE enjoyed the **Clark County Fair**! You won't go hungry...there's Mexican, barbecue, Indian, Thai, American, and lots of sweet treats! There's carnival rides and games, crafts and jewelry, and rock and roll! Take a sidetrip to Overton to see the Lost City Museum and another to the Valley of Fire State Park. At the end of a busy day, unwind with a romantic night out!

## Logandale, Nevada

Second weekend in April (beginning Thursday)
Thurs. & Fri. 4:00 PM - midnight; Sat. 10: 00 AM - midnight; Sun. 10:00 AM - 6:00 PM

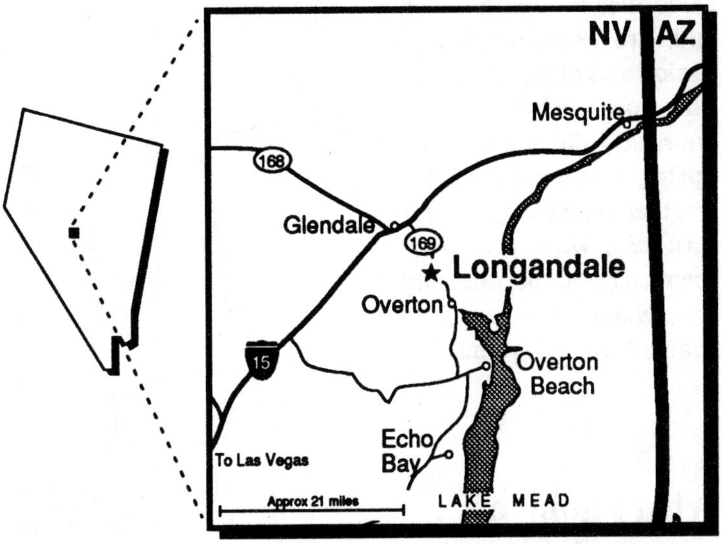


## What's goin' on...

Town population: **7,000**
Last year's attendance: **25,000**
Average outdoor temperature: **74°**
Festival location: **Fairgrounds**

☞ *Up-to-date festival information is available from:*
*Logandale Chamber of Commerce*
*(702) 397-2193*

| | |
|---|---|
| X | Wine tasting/beer for sale |
| X | Food booths |
| X | Arts/crafts for sale |
| X | Live music |
| X | Clowns |
| X | Face painters |
| X | Childrens games |
| X | Animal exhibits/petting zoo |
| | Dogs allowed on leash |
| X | Lost and found |
| | Bicycle racks |
| X | First aid area available |
| X | Self-brought picnics allowed |
| X | Self-brought alcohol allowed |
| | Stroller/wheelchair rentals available |

| | |
|---|---|
| | Parade |
| X | Parking fee: $1 |
| X | Entrance fee: S & K $3; A $5; Under 5 free |
| X | Camping facilities: 10 miles |
| X | Boating facilities: Lake Mead |
| X | RV facilities w/ hookups: 10 miles |
| X | Hotels in town<br>Glendale Motel, Overton Motel, Echo Bay Resort, Plaza Motel |
| X | Restaurants in town<br>Maria's, La Mesa, Herns Cafe, El Burrito, Echo Bay Resort |

# *Spring Jamboree*

SHORTLY AFTER THE Hoover Dam was completed, the Boulder Dam Hotel was erected and was host to celebrities like Clark Gable and Carol Lombard, Boris Karloff and many others! Check out the Hotel for yourself while you attend the **Spring Jamboree** in May! The weather is just beginning to turn warm while you stroll by the many craft booths! And have lunch and a beer at the Brauts N Beer Garden!

## Boulder City, Nevada

First Saturday in May
9:00 AM - 4:00 PM

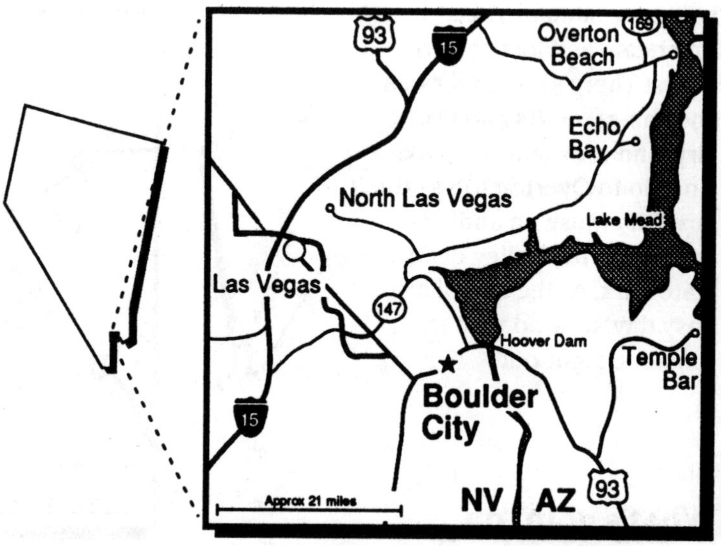


*Up-to-date festival information is available from:*
*Boulder City Chamber of Commerce*
*(702) 293-2034*

## What's goin' on...

Town population: **13,000**
Last year's attendance: **10,000**
Average outdoor temperature: **85°**
Festival location: **Downtown park**

- ✗ Wine tasting/beer for sale
- ✗ Food booths
- ✗ Arts/crafts for sale
- ✗ Live music
- Clowns
- Face painters
- ✗ Childrens games
- Animal exhibits/petting zoo
- Dogs allowed on leash
- Lost and found
- Bicycle racks
- First aid area available
- Self-brought picnics allowed
- Self-brought alcohol allowed
- Stroller/wheelchair rentals available

- Parade
- Parking fee
- Entrance fee
- ✗ Camping facilities: 0 miles
- ✗ Boating facilities: Lake Mead
- ✗ RV facilities w/ hookups: 3 miles
- ✗ Hotels in town
- ✗ Restaurants in town
  Golden Strike Steak House

# *Cinco de Mayo*

MEXICAN INDEPENDENCE Day is celebrated in many cities throughout the west. And the most recent addition to Sparks' list of festivals in the **Cinco de Mayo** celebration in May! This atmosphere spells F-I-E-S-T-A! Traditional dress and dances, crafts for sale, mariachi bands, piñatas, and great Mexican food are all on the agenda! ¡Olé!

## Sparks, Nevada

Fifth of May
11:00 AM - 6:00 PM

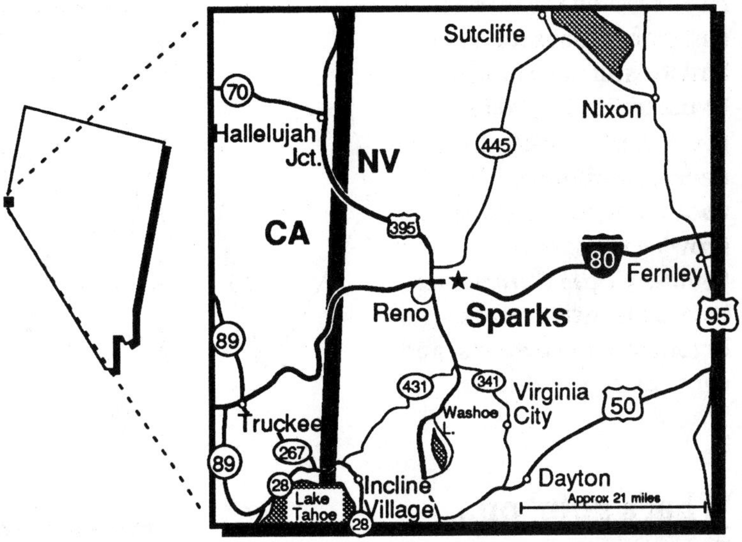


*Up-to-date festival information is available from:*
*Sparks Visitors Center*
*(702) 348-7788*

## What's goin' on...

Town population: **56,000**
Last year's attendance: **N/A**
Average outdoor temperature: **60°**
Festival location: **Downtown**

| | | | |
|---|---|---|---|
| X | Wine tasting/beer for sale | | Parade |
| X | Food booths | | Parking fee |
| X | Arts/crafts for sale | | Entrance fee |
| X | Live music | X | Camping facilities: 3 miles |
| | Clowns | X | Boating facilities: Washoe Lake |
| | Face painters | X | RV facilities w/ hookups: In town |
| X | Childrens games | X | Hotels in town |
| | Animal exhibits/petting zoo | | |
| | Dogs allowed on leash | | |
| X | Lost and found | | |
| X | Bicycle racks | X | Restaurants in town |
| X | First aid area available | | |
| | Self-brought picnics allowed | | |
| | Self-brought alcohol allowed | | |
| | Stroller/wheelchair rentals available | | |

# *Las Vegas Helldorado Days*

THIS HERE CELEBRATION began way back in 1934—the **Las Vegas Helldorado Days**! It's back to its original name (it was called the Elks Helldorado Days for a spell) and it's still packed with lots to do: trail rides; golf tournament; chili cook-off; street dance; art auction; PRCA rodeo; Whiskerino beard-growing contest; "Bulla-A-Poppin"; Wrangler bull fights, wild horse races, entertainment, exhibits, and a carnical for the kiddies! Whew!

## Las Vegas, Nevada

Second Friday in May through Memorial Day
Hours vary

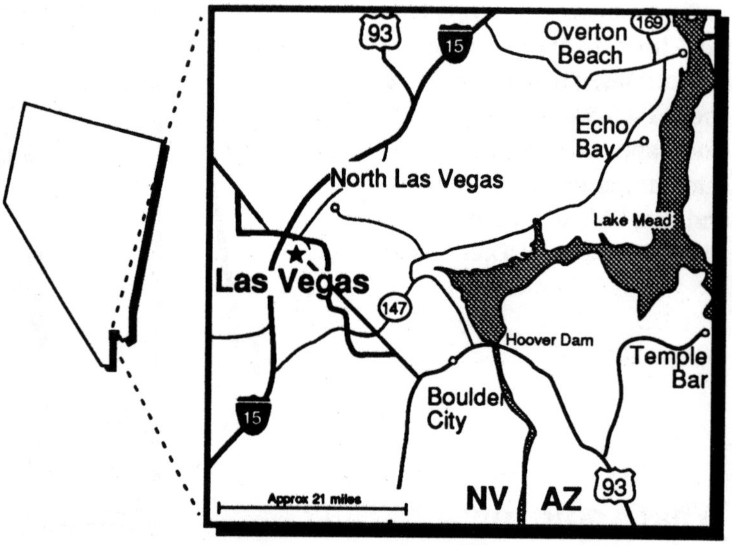


*Up-to-date festival information is available from:*
*Las Vegas Heldorado office*
*(702) 870-1221*

## What's goin' on...

Town population: **730,000**
Last year's attendance: **N/A**
Average outdoor temperature: **80°**
Festival location: **Citywide**

| | |
|---|---|
| X | Wine tasting/beer for sale |
| X | Food booths |
| X | Arts/crafts for sale |
| X | Live music |
| X | Clowns |
| X | Face painters |
| X | Childrens games |
| X | Animal exhibits/petting zoo |
| X | Dogs allowed on leash |
| X | Lost and found |
| X | Bicycle racks |
| X | First aid area available |
| X | Self-brought picnics allowed |
| | Self-brought alcohol allowed |
| | Stroller/wheelchair rentals available |

| | |
|---|---|
| X | Parade: (time & date not avbl.) |
| | Parking fee |
| | Entrance fee |
| X | Camping facilities: In town |
| X | Boating facilities: Lake Mead |
| X | RV facilities w/ hookups: In town |
| X | Hotels in town<br>Flamingo Hilton, Dunes, Tropicana, Circus Circus, Caesars Palace |
| X | Restaurants in town<br>Mary's Diner, Joe's Bayou, The Bootlegger Ristorante, Primavera, Willy & Jose's Cantina |

# *Armed Forces Day Celebration*

## Hawthorne, Nevada

May 13th and weekend prior
Hours vary

WALKER LAKE NEAR Hawthorne, Nevada, is a ominous sight! The intensity of the blue water against the florid mountains is spectacular! This community has been celebrating **Armed Forces Day Celebration** since 1950! There's dancing, rock and country music and lots of beer, pop, and good food! If you're going to camp...let me tell you first hand that the facilities at Walter Lake are desert-like—not forest-like!

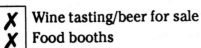

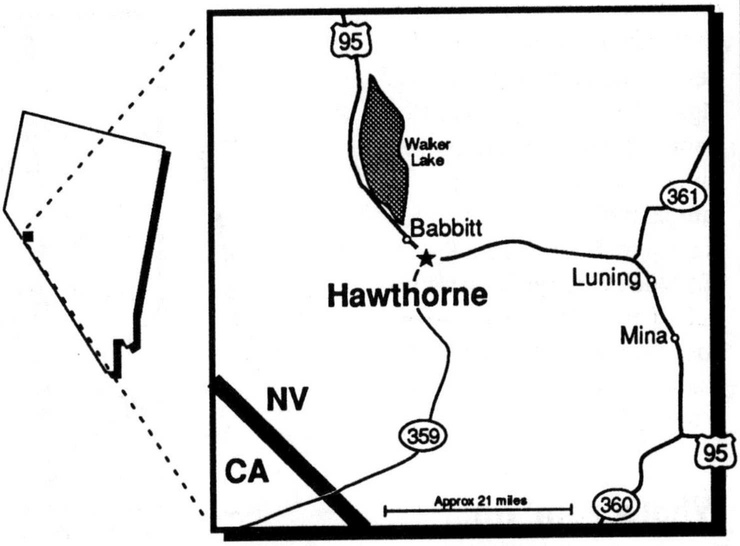


## What's goin' on...

Town population: **5,700**
Last year's attendance: **10,000**
Average outdoor temperature: **85°**
Festival location: **Downtown & fairgrounds**

*Up-to-date festival information is available from:*
*Hawthorne Chamber of Commerce*
*(702) 945-5896*

| | |
|---|---|
| X | Wine tasting/beer for sale |
| X | Food booths |
| X | Arts/crafts for sale |
| X | Live music |
| X | Clowns |
| X | Face painters |
| X | Childrens games |
| | Animal exhibits/petting zoo |
| | Dogs allowed on leash |
| X | Lost and found |
| X | Bicycle racks |
| | First aid area available |
| X | Self-brought picnics allowed |
| X | Self-brought alcohol allowed |
| | Stroller/wheelchair rentals available |

| | |
|---|---|
| X | Parade: On the 13th at noon downtown |
| | Parking fee |
| | Entrance fee |
| X | Camping facilities: 10 miles |
| X | Boating facilities: Walker Lake |
| X | RV facilities w/ hookups: 10 miles |
| X | Hotels in town<br>El Capitan Lodge, Anchor Motel |
| X | Restaurants in town<br>Cliff House, Happy Buddah, El Capitan Casino & Lodge |

# *West Coast Wine Festival*

NEVERMIND THAT IT'S A little peculiar that Reno is host to the **West Coast Wine Tasting**...after all we're Californians! It's a great way to spend a May evening before you head out for a night of gaming and slots! Reno's finest restaurants are on hand with their most tantalizing creations—then wash 'em down with a fine Zinfindel! A string quartet will relax you while you vote for your favorite wines.

## Reno, Nevada

Last Friday in May
6:00 PM - 9:00 PM

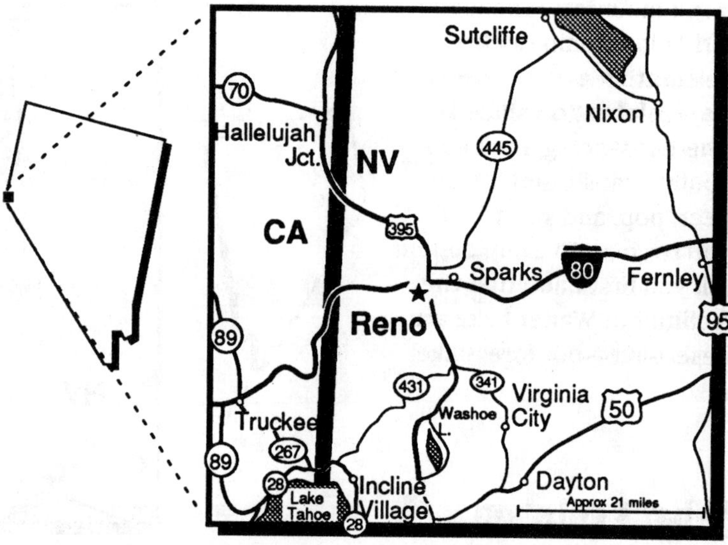


## What's goin' on...

Town population: **250,000**
Last year's attendance: **N/A**
Average outdoor temperature: **70°**
Festival location: **Downtown**

☞ *Up-to-date festival information is available from:*
*Reno Visitors Center*
*(702) 348-7788*

- ✗ Wine tasting/beer for sale
- ✗ Food booths
- Arts/crafts for sale
- ✗ Live music
- Clowns
- Face painters
- Childrens games
- Animal exhibits/petting zoo
- Dogs allowed on leash
- ✗ Lost and found
- Bicycle racks
- ✗ First aid area available
- Self-brought picnics allowed
- Self-brought alcohol allowed
- Stroller/wheelchair rentals available

- Parade
- Parking fee
- ✗ Entrance fee: (prices not avbl.)
- ✗ Camping facilities: 6 miles
- ✗ Boating facilities: Washoe Lake
- ✗ RV facilities w/ hookups: In town
- ✗ Hotels in town
  Hilton, Carson Valley Inn, Harrah's, Nugget
- ✗ Restaurants in town
  Rivoli, Seafare, John's Oyster Bar, The Vintage, Pancho and Willie's, Asian Garden

# *Kit Carson Rendezvous*

NOW THIS WE GOTTA SEE! A mountain man ballet? Yes, folks, you read it here! At the **Kit Carson Rendezvous** you'll see this "ballet" and lots of other interesting stuff—horseshoe tourney, farrier's contest, Traders' Row Gun Slingers, great food, arts and crafts fair, mountain man encampment and Indian village, and the Northern Nevada Amatuer Boxing Championship! Wow...that makes for a busy weekend!

## Carson City, Nevada

Second weekend in June (beginning Friday)
Hours vary

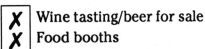

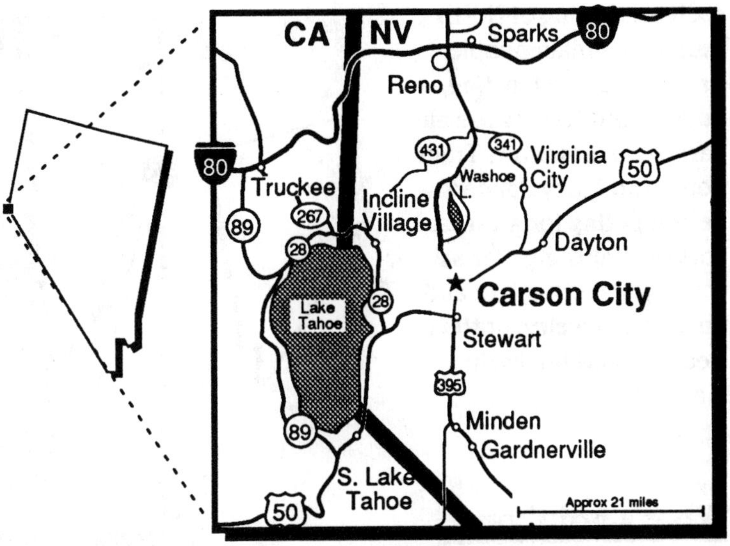


## What's goin' on...

Town population: **37,950**
Last year's attendance: **N/A**
Average outdoor temperature: **87°**
Festival location: **Mills Park**

*Up-to-date festival information is available from:*
*Carson City Chamber of Commerce*
*(702) 782-1844*

- X Wine tasting/beer for sale
- X Food booths
- X Arts/crafts for sale
- X Live music
- Clowns
- X Face painters
- X Childrens games
- X Animal exhibits/petting zoo
- Dogs allowed on leash
- X Lost and found
- X Bicycle racks
- X First aid area available
- X Self-brought picnics allowed
- Self-brought alcohol allowed
- Stroller/wheelchair rentals available

- Parade
- Parking fee
- Entrance fee
- X Camping facilities: In town
- X Boating facilities: Washoe Lake
- X RV facilities w/ hookups: In town
- X Hotels in town
- X Restaurants in town

# *Stewart Indian Museum Arts & Crafts Fair & PowWow*

JOIN IN THE FUN AT THE **Stewart Indian Museum Arts & Crafts Fair & PowWow!** The powwow celebration is a social gathering of North American Indian people. Gaming, dancing, eating, buying, and trading are all part of the powwow. Traditional and fancy dancers will be competing for awards. Lots of neat things for sale or trade—baskets, silver and turquoise jewelry, pottery, weaving, and buckskin moccasins!

## Carson City, Nevada

Third weekend in June
Daily 9:00 AM - 4:00 PM

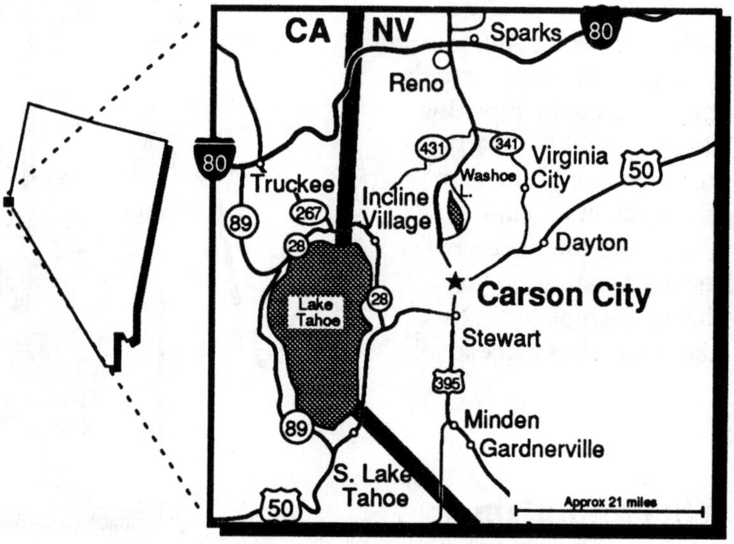


## What's goin' on...

Town population: **37,950**
Last year's attendance: **N/A**
Average outdoor temperature: **90°**
Festival location: **Old School Campus**

☞ *Up-to-date festival information is available from: Carson City Stewart Indian Museum (702) 882-1565*

| | |
|---|---|
| X | Wine tasting/beer for sale |
| X | Food booths |
| X | Arts/crafts for sale |
| X | Live music |
| | Clowns |
| X | Face painters |
| X | Childrens games |
| | Animal exhibits/petting zoo |
| | Dogs allowed on leash |
| X | Lost and found |
| X | Bicycle racks |
| X | First aid area available |
| X | Self-brought picnics allowed |
| | Self-brought alcohol allowed |
| | Stroller/wheelchair rentals available |

| | |
|---|---|
| | Parade |
| | Parking fee |
| | Entrance fee |
| X | Camping facilities: In town |
| X | Boating facilities: Washoe Lake |
| X | RV facilities w/ hookups: In town |
| X | Hotels in town |
| X | Restaurants in town |

# *Hot August Nights*

NEIL DIAMOND RECORDED the album, but Reno lives **Hot August Nights**! This 4-day streak of 50's and 60's nostalgia and entertainment is non-stop! And while you're in town, have a look at the National Automobile Museum, there's nothing quite like it anywhere. It's a comprehensive, unique display of antique, vintage, classic, and special interest cars.

## Reno, Nevada

First weekend in August (beginning Thursday)
Twenty fours hours a day!

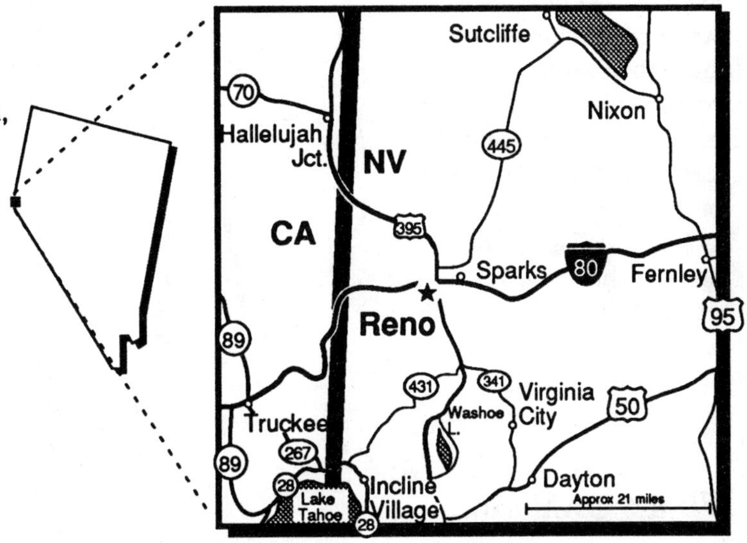


*Up-to-date festival information is available from:*
*Reno Visitors Center*
*(702) 348-7788*

## What's goin' on...

Town population: **56,000**
Last year's attendance: **N/A**
Average outdoor temperature: **88°**
Festival location: **Citywide**

| | |
|---|---|
| X | Wine tasting/beer for sale |
| X | Food booths |
| X | Arts/crafts for sale |
| X | Live music |
| | Clowns |
| | Face painters |
| | Childrens games |
| | Animal exhibits/petting zoo |
| | Dogs allowed on leash |
| X | Lost and found |
| X | Bicycle racks |
| X | First aid area available |
| X | Self-brought picnics allowed |
| | Self-brought alcohol allowed |
| | Stroller/wheelchair rentals available |

| | |
|---|---|
| X | Parade: Sun. 9:00 AM downtown |
| | Parking fee |
| X | Entrance fee: prices vary |
| X | Camping facilities: 3 miles |
| X | Boating facilities: Washoe Lake |
| X | RV facilities w/ hookups: In town |
| X | Hotels in town<br>Hilton, Carson Valley Inn, Harrah's, Nugget |
| X | Restaurants in town<br>Rivoli, Seafare, John's Oyster Bar, The Vintage, Pancho and Willie's, Asian Garden |

# *Reno's Best in the West Nuggett Rib Cook-Off*

COME FOR THE RIBBIES, but stay for the fun at **Reno's Best in the West Nuggett Rib Cook-Off!** Wow, now here's one we won't miss! The cooks here have been bustling about their kitchens for weeks perfecting their marinades and sauces...and perfect they are! Come see for yourself. Rock and country bands will keep your toes tapping while your bellies are getting full!

## Sparks, Nevada

Labor Day weekend (beginning Friday night)
Daily 11:00 AM - 10:00 PM

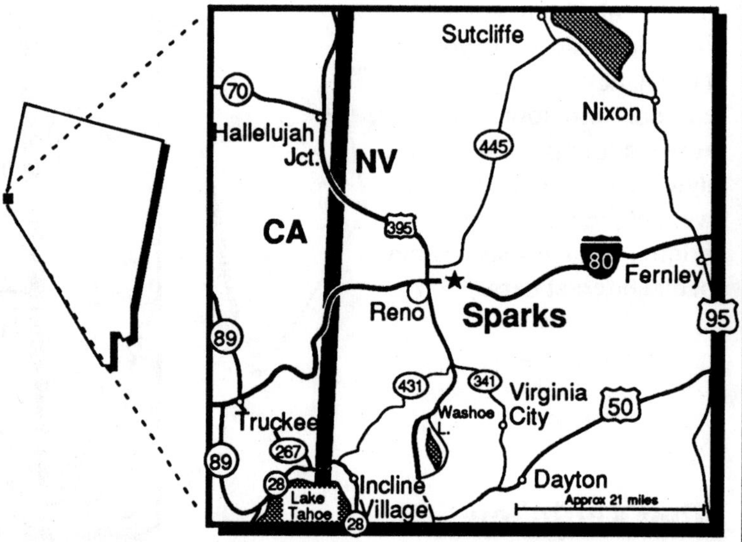


## What's goin' on...

Town population: **56,000**
Last year's attendance: **60,000**
Average outdoor temperature: **42°**
Festival location: **Victorian Square**

☞ *Up-to-date festival information is available from:*
*Sparks Visitors Center*
*(702) 348-7788*

| | |
|---|---|
| X | Wine tasting/beer for sale |
| X | Food booths |
| X | Arts/crafts for sale |
| X | Live music |
| | Clowns |
| X | Face painters |
| X | Childrens games |
| X | Animal exhibits/petting zoo |
| | Dogs allowed on leash |
| X | Lost and found |
| X | Bicycle racks |
| X | First aid area available |
| | Self-brought picnics allowed |
| | Self-brought alcohol allowed |
| | Stroller/wheelchair rentals available |

| | |
|---|---|
| | Parade |
| | Parking fee |
| | Entrance fee |
| X | Camping facilities: 3 miles |
| X | Boating facilities: Washoe Lake |
| X | RV facilities w/ hookups: In town |
| X | Hotels in town |
| X | Restaurants in town |

# Great Reno Balloon Races

WHEN MOST PEOPLE THINK about Reno they think about the state's world famous gaming casinos. But we're here to tell you that there's a whole lot more! Take the **Great Reno Balloon Races** for instance...fabulous food, unique crafts, a wide variety of music, and, of course, rides! If you have never ridden in a giant of the sky—now's your chance! And if you're afraid of heights...well, just come and enjoy the view! Don't forget your camera.

## Reno, Nevada

First full weekend in September (beginning Friday)
Daily 6:00 AM - noon

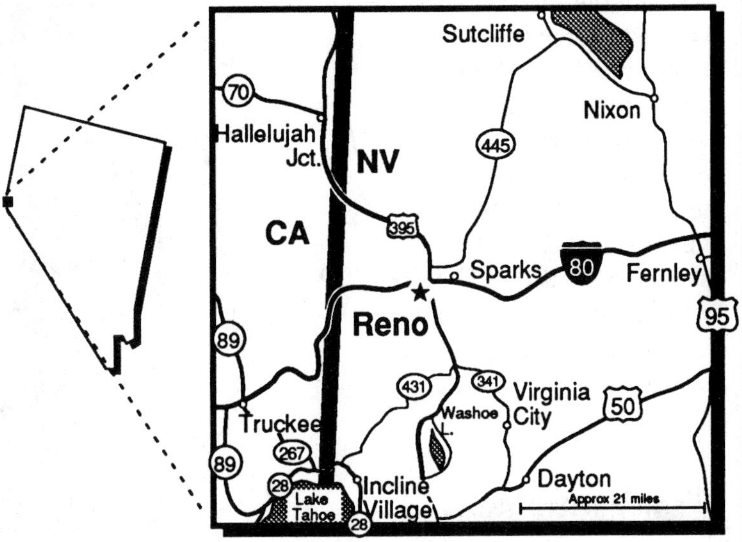


## What's goin' on...

Town population: **250,000**
Last year's attendance: **125,000**
Average outdoor temperature: **70°**
Festival location: **Rancho San Rafael Park**

*Up-to-date festival information is available from:*
*Reno Visitors Center*
*(702) 348-7788*

| | |
|---|---|
| X | Wine tasting/beer for sale |
| X | Food booths |
| X | Arts/crafts for sale |
| X | Live music |
| X | Clowns |
| | Face painters |
| | Childrens games |
| | Animal exhibits/petting zoo |
| | Dogs allowed on leash |
| X | Lost and found |
| X | Bicycle racks |
| X | First aid area available |
| X | Self-brought picnics allowed |
| | Self-brought alcohol allowed |
| | Stroller/wheelchair rentals available |

| | |
|---|---|
| | Parade |
| | Parking fee |
| | Entrance fee |
| X | Camping facilities: 3 miles |
| X | Boating facilities: Washoe Lake |
| X | RV facilities w/ hookups: In town |
| X | Hotels in town<br>Hilton, Carson Valley Inn, Harrah's, Nugget |
| X | Restaurants in town<br>Rivoli, Seafare, John's Oyster Bar, The Vintage, Pancho and Willie's, Asian Garden |

# *Virginia City International Camel Races*

CAMELS? IN NEVADA? YOU bet! At the **Virginia City International Camel Races**! Kids and adults can enjoy the rides and the races, the food and the country music! There's nothing quite like it...to see wooly, galloping, two-humped giants neck-in-neck recklessly speeding to the finish line is quite a sight to behold—and there's ostriches racing too! The Not-To-Miss Gala Costume Ball (what a riot!) is Friday night at 7:00 PM

## Virginia City, Nevada

Weekend following Labor Day (beginning Friday)
Fri. 11:00 AM - 4:00 PM; Sat. 10:00 AM - 5:00 PM; Sun. noon - 4:00 PM

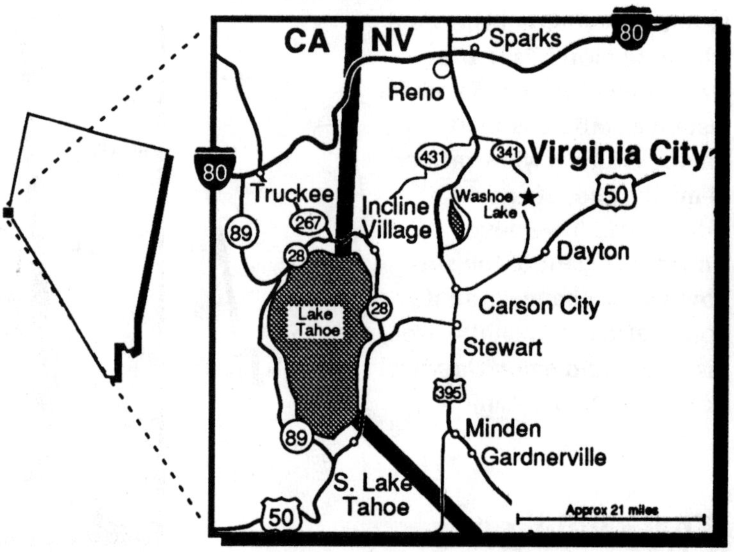


## What's goin' on...

Town population: **800**
Last year's attendance: **25,000**
Average outdoor temperature: **80°**
Festival location: **Citywide**

*Up-to-date festival information is available from:*
*Virginia City Chamber of Commerce*
*(702) 847-RACE*

- X Wine tasting/beer for sale
- X Food booths
- Arts/crafts for sale
- X Live music
- Clowns
- Face painters
- Childrens games
- X Animal exhibits/petting zoo
- X Dogs allowed on leash
- X Lost and found
- Bicycle racks
- X First aid area available
- Self-brought picnics allowed
- Self-brought alcohol allowed
- Stroller/wheelchair rentals available

- X Parade: Sat. 10:0 AM downtown
- X Parking fee: $6
- X Entrance fee: $2
- X Camping facilities: In town
- Boating facilities
- X RV facilities w/ hookups: In town
- X Hotels in town
- X Restaurants in town

# *Dayton Valley Days*

DAYTON IS ONE OF THE oldest mining (alive) ghosttowns in Nevada. It was a popular "passing through" place for immigrants on their way to the California gold country! But Dayton had gold of its own in the Carson River! And **Dayton Valley Days** is a good time to visit this historic town and re-live the days-gone-by! There's over 60 booths of crafts, lots of good food, and plenty of country music to keep you busy!

## Dayton, Nevada

**Third weekend in September**
**Sat. 10:00 AM - midnight; Sun. 10:00 AM - 5:00 PM**

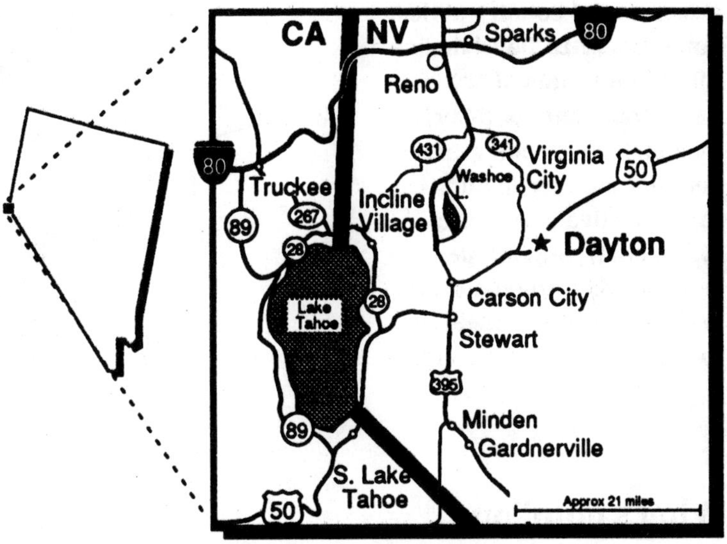


## What's goin' on...

Town population: **3,700**
Last year's attendance: **3,000**
Average outdoor temperature: **78°**
Festival location: **Downtown Pike St.**

*Up-to-date festival information is available from:*
*Dayton Pink Lady Florist*
*(702) 246-0525*

- X Wine tasting/beer for sale
- X Food booths
- X Arts/crafts for sale
- X Live music
- X Clowns
- X Face painters
- X Childrens games
- X Animal exhibits/petting zoo
- X Dogs allowed on leash
- X Lost and found
- X Bicycle racks
- X First aid area available
- X Self-brought picnics allowed
- Self-brought alcohol allowed
- Stroller/wheelchair rentals available

- Parade
- Parking fee
- Entrance fee
- X Camping facilities: 11 miles
- X Boating facilities: Carson River
- X RV facilities w/ hookups: In town
- X Hotels in town
  Motel Carson, Motel Virginia
- X Restaurants in town
  End of Trail, Mia's Swiss Restaurant, Erick's & Jimmy "D's"

# *Bonanza Days*

NEVADA'S MOST BEAUTIFUL treasures lies on the border of California and Nevada—Lake Tahoe! Join the locals for a weekend of country-style fun at **Bonanza Days**! Incline Village hosts lots of activities—crafts and food fair, dancing, music, and great people-watching! In addition to this festival, there are bikes, boats, and mo-peds to rent; or hike and picnic among this sweet-smelling forest.

## Incline Village, Nevada

First weekend in October (beginning Friday)
Hours vary

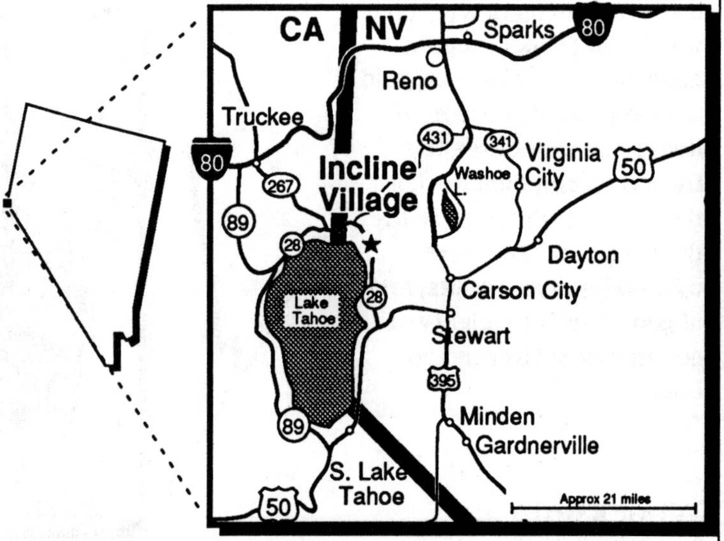


## What's goin' on...

Town population: **9143**
Last year's attendance: **N/A**
Average outdoor temperature: **65°**
Festival location: **Villagewide**

*Up-to-date festival information is available from:*
*Incline Village Chamber of Commerce*
*(702) 831-4440*

| | |
|---|---|
| | Wine tasting/beer for sale |
| ✗ | Food booths |
| ✗ | Arts/crafts for sale |
| ✗ | Live music |
| | Clowns |
| | Face painters |
| | Childrens games |
| | Animal exhibits/petting zoo |
| | Dogs allowed on leash |
| | Lost and found |
| | Bicycle racks |
| | First aid area available |
| | Self-brought picnics allowed |
| | Self-brought alcohol allowed |
| | Stroller/wheelchair rentals available |

| | |
|---|---|
| | Parade |
| | Parking fee |
| ✗ | Entrance fee: To some, not all, events |
| ✗ | Camping facilities: 15 miles |
| ✗ | Boating facilities: Lake Tahoe |
| ✗ | RV facilities w/ hookups: 15 miles |
| ✗ | Hotels in town |
| ✗ | Restaurants in town |

# *Art in the Park*

HOOVER DAM, TRULY A man-made wonder, helped to put Boulder City on the map! And **Art in the Park** has helped to keep it on the map! Well, not really...but this has been a favorite fes- tival since 1961! The local Hospital Auxiliary annual- ly hosts this celebration of art and food (definitely two of our favorites!). Definitely visit the Dam and watch the free movie on just how this 726' monster was consructed in 1938!

## Boulder City, Nevada

First week in October
Daily 10:00 AM - 5:00 PM

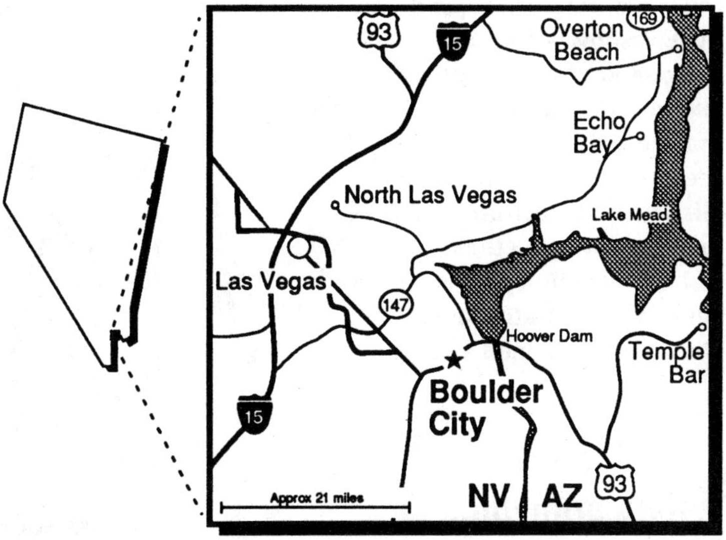


☞ *Up-to-date festival information is available from:*
*Boulder City Chamber of Commerce*
*(702) 293-2034*

## What's goin' on...

Town population: **13,000**
Last year's attendance: **90,000**
Average outdoor temperature: **79°**
Festival location: **Downtown park**

| | |
|---|---|
| X | Wine tasting/beer for sale |
| X | Food booths |
| X | Arts/crafts for sale |
| | Live music |
| | Clowns |
| | Face painters |
| | Childrens games |
| | Animal exhibits/petting zoo |
| X | Dogs allowed on leash |
| X | Lost and found |
| | Bicycle racks |
| X | First aid area available |
| | Self-brought picnics allowed |
| | Self-brought alcohol allowed |
| | Stroller/wheelchair rentals available |

| | |
|---|---|
| | Parade |
| | Parking fee |
| | Entrance fee |
| X | Camping facilities: 3 miles |
| X | Boating facilities: Lake Mead |
| X | RV facilities w/ hookups: 3 miles |
| X | Hotels in town |
| X | Restaurants in town<br>Golden Strike Steak House |

# *Fairshow— Hot Air Balloon Races*

## North Las Vegas, Nevada

Fourth weekend in October (beginning Friday)
Daily 7:00 AM - 6:00 PM

THE TOWN OF NORTH LAS Vegas has many things its big sister does not...like the only night lighted golf course in the state, water slides, and the **Fairshow— Hot Air Balloon Races**! This festival always has a big turn out—that's cuz there's so much to see and do! Over 200 booths filled with handicrafts and 15 food booths with ethnic dishes! Eagle Vineyard is on hand for wine tasting and you'll be entertained all day!

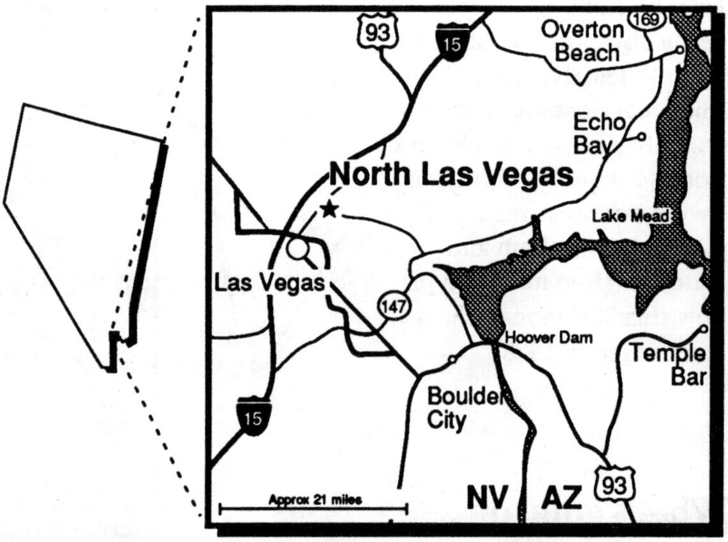


*Up-to-date festival information is available from:*
*North Las Vegas Chamber of Commerce*
*(702) 642-9595*

## What's goin' on...

Town population: **60,000**
Last year's attendance: **65,000**
Average outdoor temperature: **82°**
Festival location: **Clark County College**

- X Wine tasting/beer for sale
- X Food booths
- X Arts/crafts for sale
- X Live music
- X Clowns
- X Face painters
- X Childrens games
- Animal exhibits/petting zoo
- X Dogs allowed on leash
- X Lost and found
- X Bicycle racks
- X First aid area available
- X Self-brought picnics allowed
- Self-brought alcohol allowed
- Stroller/wheelchair rentals available

- X Parade: Sat. 9:00 AM at the College
- Parking fee
- Entrance fee
- X Camping facilities: 30 miles
- X Boating facilities: Lake Mead
- X RV facilities w/ hookups: 1 mile
- Hotels in town
- X Restaurants in town
  Jerry Nugget, Hilda's, Opera House, Poker Palace, BBQ Pit, Silver Nugget

# *Sparks Hometown Christmas*

THE SNOW MAY BE FALLING outside, but bundle up and join us at the **Sparks Hometown Christmas**. This is a great place to do a little Christmas shopping—and pick up a little something special for yourself, too! Music, Santa, carolers, hot cider, and a lot of hustle-bustle make for an enjoyable day!

## Sparks, Nevada

First Saturday in December
Daily 11:00 AM - 5:00 PM

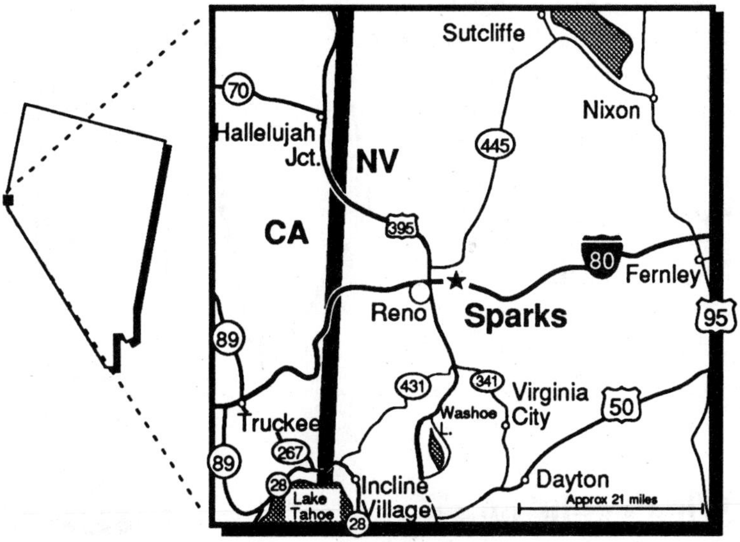


## What's goin' on...

Town population: **56,000**
Last year's attendance: **20,000**
Average outdoor temperature: **42°**
Festival location: **Victorian Square**

*Up-to-date festival information is available from:*
*Sparks Visitors Center*
*(702) 348-7788*

- ✗ Wine tasting/beer for sale
- ✗ Food booths
- ✗ Arts/crafts for sale
- ✗ Live music
- ✗ Clowns
- ✗ Face painters
- Childrens games
- Animal exhibits/petting zoo
- Dogs allowed on leash
- ✗ Lost and found
- ✗ Bicycle racks
- ✗ First aid area available
- ✗ Self-brought picnics allowed
- Self-brought alcohol allowed
- Stroller/wheelchair rentals available

- ✗ Parade: (time & date not avbl.)
- Parking fee
- Entrance fee
- ✗ Camping facilities: 3 miles
- ✗ Boating facilities: Washoe Lake
- ✗ RV facilities w/ hookups: In town
- ✗ Hotels in town
- ✗ Restaurants in town

# *Festival of Trees*

IT'S A BRIGHT TOWN allright, but just wait till all the Christmas trees are lit up at the **Festival of Trees**! Bring a thermos of hot chocolate and kick off your holiday celebrating by watching the parade down Virginia St. Carolers and Santa will help you get in the mood. Bundle up...it's nippy outside!

## Reno, Nevada

Second Saturday in December
5:00 PM - 7:00 PM

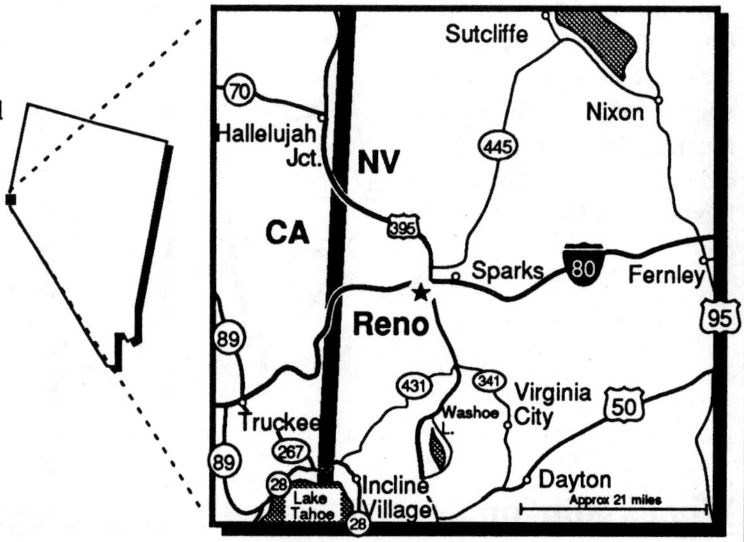


## What's goin' on...

Town population: **250,000**
Last year's attendance: **N/A**
Average outdoor temperature: **35°**
Festival location: **Downtown**

*Up-to-date festival information is available from:*
*Reno Visitors Center*
*(702) 348-7788*

- Wine tasting/beer for sale
- Food booths
- Arts/crafts for sale
- X Live music
- Clowns
- Face painters
- Childrens games
- Animal exhibits/petting zoo
- Dogs allowed on leash
- X Lost and found
- Bicycle racks
- X First aid area available
- Self-brought picnics allowed
- Self-brought alcohol allowed
- Stroller/wheelchair rentals available

- X Parade: 5:00 PM on Virginia St.
- Parking fee
- Entrance fee
- X Camping facilities: [illegible] miles
- X Boating facilities: Washoe Lake
- X RV facilities w/ hookups: In town
- X Hotels in town
  Hilton, Carson Valley Inn, Harrah's, Nugget
- X Restaurants in town
  Rivoli, Seafare, John's Oyster Bar, The Vintage, Pancho and Willie's, Asian Garden

# Index by City
## CALIFORNIA

# *Index by City*
## CALIFORNIA




# *Index by City*
## CALIFORNIA

# *Index by City*
## CALIFORNIA




# *Index by City*
## CALIFORNIA

# *Index by City*
## CALIFORNIA



# *Index by City*
## CALIFORNIA

# Index by City
## CALIFORNIA




# Index by City
## CALIFORNIA


# Index by City
## NEVADA

# *Index by Festival*
## CALIFORNIA




# *Index by Festival*
## CALIFORNIA

# *Index by Festival*
## CALIFORNIA



# *Index by Festival*
## CALIFORNIA

# *Index by Festival*
## CALIFORNIA

# *Index by Festival*
## CALIFORNIA

# *Index by Festival*

## CALIFORNIA



# *Index by Festival*

## CALIFORNIA



# *Index by Festival*

## NEVADA

# *Festival Coordinators/Vendor Information*

Atascadero Colony Days
Atascadero
Atascadero Colony Days Committee, P.O.B. 1913, Atascadero, CA 93423

Eastern Sierra Tri-County Fair
Bishop
Ned Londo, Manager Eastern Sierra Tri-County Fair, P.O.B. 608, Bishop, CA 93515; (619) 873-3588

Mule Days
Bishop
Stephanie Fritz c/o Bishop Chamber of Commerce, 690 N. Main St., Bishop, CA 93514; (619) 873-8405

Wild West Rodeo Weekend
Bishop
Dan Scarbrough c/o Bishop Chamber of Commerce, 690 N. Main St., Bishop, CA 93514; (619) 873-8405

Colorado River Country Fair
Blythe
River Country Fair/Chamber of Comm. Festival Coordinator 201 So. Broadway Blythe, CA 92225; (619) 922-8166

Colorado River Country Music Festival
Blythe
F. Wayne Barrett/Chamber of Comm. Festival Coordinator, 201 So. Broadway, Blythe, CA 92225; (619) 922-8166

Fishermen's Festival & Kite Fly
Bodega Bay
Roma Robbins, P.O.B. 8, Bodega Bay, CA 94923; (707) 875-3777

Boulder Creek Art & Wine Festival
Boulder Creek
Diane Aldisfirenzi, 13136 Hiway 9, Boulder Creek, CA 95007; (408) 338-6910

Brownsville Mountain Fair
Brownsville
Joann Ercolini Health Center, 1611 Willow Glenn Rd., Brownsville, CA 95919; (916) 675-2831

Cabazon Jamboree & Barbeque
Cabazon
Linda Harrelson & Steven Thomas, P.O.B. 782, Cabazon, CA 92230

Apple Hill Festival
Camino
Misty diVittorio, Apple Hill Growers Assn., P.O.B. 494 Camino, CA 95709; (916) 622-9595

Begonia Festival & Parade
Capitola
Nels Wesman 410 Capitola Ave., Capitola, CA 95010; (408) 476-3566

Village Street Faire
Carlsbad
Keith Kennedy Chamber of Commerce, P.O.B. 1605, Carlsbad, CA 92008

Artichoke Festival
Castroville
Joe Micheli, P.O.B. 1041, Castroville, CA 95012; (408) 633-2465

Village Venture Street Faire
Claremont
Village Venture Street Faire Claremont Chamber of Commerce, 205 Yale Ave., Claremont, CA 91711; Application due: September 1

Halloween Ghost Walk
Clayton
Richard Taylor; (415) 672-6171
Coyote Howl
Coulterville
Coyote Howling Committee, P.O.B. 463, Coulterville, CA 95311

Gunfighter's Rendezvous
Coulterville
Coyote Howling Committee, P.O.B. 463, Coulterville, CA 95311

Fiddle Contest
Crescent City
Crescent City Soroptimist Club, P.O.B. 991 Crescent City, CA 95531

Fourth of July Celebration
Crescent City
Crescent City Chamber of Commerce, 1001 Front St., Crescent City, CA 95531; (707) 464-3174

Seafood Festival
Crescent City
Commercial Fishermen's Wives, P.O.B. 674 Crescent City, CA 95531; (707) 464-4502

Teddy Bear Picnic
Crescent City
Rural Human Services 811 "G" St., Crescent City, CA 95531; (707) 464-7441

World Championship Crab Races
Crescent City
Crescent City Chamber of Commerce, 1001 Front St., Crescent City, CA 95531; (707) 464-3174

Tapioca Festival
Desert Center
Kenneth Statler, P.O.B. 159 Desert Center, CA 92239; (619) 227-3212

Diamond Bar Ranch Festival
Diamond Bar
Lois Vihlen Chamber of Commerce, 1081 Grand Ave., Diamond Bar, CA 91765

Country Christmas Holiday
Diamond Springs
Diamond Spr. Community Assn., P.O.B. 1930 Diamond Springs, CA 95619

Labor Day Country Bazaar
Diamond Springs
Diamond Spr./El Dorado Firefighters, P.O.B. 741 Diamond Springs, CA 95619

Lambtown U.S.A. Festival
Dixon
Sam Crawford Chamber of Commerce, 201 South First St., Dixon, CA 95620; (916) 678-2650

# *Festival Coordinators/Vendor Information*

Railroad Days
Dunsmuir
Alison Maartensen 5860 Shasta Ace. Dunsmuir, CA 96025; (916) 235-4678; Application due: 9/10/91

Fair Oaks Fiesta
Fair Oaks
Marsha Karley Fair Oaks Chamber of Commerce, P.O.B. 352 Fair Oaks, CA 95629; (916) 967-2903

Galt Craft Faire
Galt
Karol Messersmith, P.O.B. 442 Galt, CA 95632

Garlic Festival
Gilroy
Dick Nicholls, Executive Mgr., P.O.B. 2311 Gilroy, CA 95021; (408) 842-1625

Gilroy Hispanic Cultural Festival
Gilroy
Ken Noonan, P.O.B. 1221 Gilroy, CA 95021; (408) 848-5780

Wine Country Film Festival
Glen Ellen
Wine Country Film Festival, P.O.B. 303 Glen Ellen, CA 95442; (707) 935-FILM

Christmas Crafts Faire
Guerneville
Brenda Adelman, P.O.B. 501 Guerneville, CA 95446; (707) 869-0054

Renaissance of Kings Faire
Hanford
City Recreation Dept.. 400 North Douty Hanford, CA 93230; (209) 585-2525

Beer & Sausage Fest
Healdsburg
Susan Matheny Soroptimist Int'l. of Healdsburg, P.O.B. 124, Healdsburg, CA 95448; (717) 433-4175/433-3806

Russian River Wine Festival
Healdsburg
Chamber of Commerce, 217 Healdsburg Ave., Healdsburg, CA 95448; (707) 433-6935

Hilmar Dairy Festival
Hilmar
Hilmar Dairy Festival Coordinator, 19664 Crane Ave., Hilmar, CA 95324; (209) 668-2855

Carrot Festival
Holtville
Chamber of Commerce, P.O.B. 185, Holtville, CA 92250; (619) 356-2923

20th Century Crafts Faire
Hughson
20th Century Club, P.O.B. 205 Hughson, CA 95326; (209) 883-0631

20th Century Crafts Faire
Hughson
20th Century Club, P.O.B. 205, Hughson, CA 95326; (209) 883-0631

Jenner Whale of a Gala
Jenner
Michael Ecton, P.O.B. 2893, Santa Rosa, CA 95405; (707) 539-6887

Heritage Quilt Show
Julian
Betty Donlan Julian, CA 92036; (619) 765-1944

Weed Show & Art Mart
Julian
Willmeta H. Rasmussen Chamber of Commerce, P.O. Box 413 Julian, CA 92036; (619) 765-1857

Wildflower Show & Art Mart
Julian
Willmeta H. Rasmussen Chamber of Commerce, P.O. Box, 413 Julian, CA 92036; (619) 765-1857

Kenwood Fourth of July Celebration
Kenwood
Just Call Marla, 1410 Neotomas Ave., Suite 104 ,Santa Rosa, CA 95405; (707) 571-8071

La Habra Corn Festival
La Habra
La Habra Lions Club Chuck Overby, P.O.B. 248, La Habra, CA 90631; (213) 691-3482

Sunny Hills Grape Festival
Larkspur
Miriam Hall/Dorothy Burton Sunny Hills Children's Services 300 Sunny Hills Dr. San Anselmo, CA 94960; (415) 457-3200

Classical-to-Jazz Under the Stars Concert
Lemoore
Father David McDonald Christ Episcopal Church, P.O.B. 215 Lemoore, CA 93245; (209) 924-5067

Art in the Vineyard
Livermore
Mike Perry Wente Brothers Winery, 5565 Telsa, Livermore, CA 94550; (415) 447-3603

Christmas Wine Trails
Livermore
Mike Perry Wente Brothers Winery, 5565 Telsa, Livermore, CA 94550; (415) 447-3603

Old Fashioned Fourth of July
Livermore
City of Livermore, Dave Adams, 1052 S. Livermore Ave., Livermore, CA 94550; (415) 373-5100

Ravenswood Victorian Christmas Faire
Livermore
Ranger Mike Nicholson LARPD, 71 Trevarno Rd. Livermore, CA 94550; (415) 373-5770

Wings of Charity Airshow
Livermore
Michal Dittrich, 6640 Sierra Lane, Dublin, CA 94568; (415) 828-8520

# Festival Coordinators/Vendor Information

World's Fastest Rodeo
Livermore
Rodeo Association, P.O.B. 180 ,Livermore, CA 94551; (415) 447-3008

Lompoc Flower Festival
Lompoc
Lompoc Valley Festival Assn., P.O.B. 505, Lompoc, CA 93438; (805) 735-8511

Mayfest
Los Altos
Kathy Tuttle, 132 Belvue Dr. Los Gatos, CA 95032; (408) 358-3373

Children's Christmas & Holiday Parade
Los Gatos
Los Gatos Chamber; (408) 354-9300; Application due: October 10
Fiesta de Artes
Los Gatos
Helen Mendel 50 University Ave., Los Gatos, CA 95030; (408) 354-6596

Strawberry Festival
Los Gatos
Eastfield Ming Quong, 251 Llewellyn Ave., Campbell, CA 95008

Summerfest
Los Gatos
Helen Mendel, 50 University Ave., Los Gatos, CA 95030; (408) 354-6596

Beckwourth Western Days Festival
Marysville
Leela Rai ,Yuba-Sutter Chamber of Commerce, P.O.B. 1429, Marysville, CA 95901; (916) 743-6501

Obon Festival
Marysville
Matysville Buddhist Church, 125 B Street, Marysville, CA 95901

Mill Valley Mountain Plays
Mill Valley
Mountain Paly Association, P.O.B. 2025 ,Mill Valley, CA 94942; (415) 472-7470

Millbrae Art & Wine Festival
Millbrae
Millbrae Festival Coordinator, Festival Productions, 2323 Poplar Oakland, CA 94607; (415) 268-8463

Milpitas Art & Wine Fetival
Milpitas
Nancie Allie California Artists, P.O.B. 1963, Burlingame, CA 94011; (415) 348-7699

Modesto á la Carte
Modesto
Gamut Promotions, 3158 Auto Center Circle, #A Stockton, CA 95212; (209) 477-8103

Octoberfest
Nipomo
Richard K. Theriot, 385 Tejas Place, Nipomo, CA 93444; (805) 929-6486

Ruby Jubilee
North Highlands
Chamber of Commerce, 3651 Elkhorn Blvd., North Highlands, CA 95660; (916) 334-2214

Novato Art, Wine & Music Festival
Novato
E. Marie Dávalos Novato Chamber of Commerce, 807 DeLong Ave., Novato, CA 94945; (415) 897-1164

Fourth of July Parade & Fiesta
Nuevo
Paul R. Jones, Nuview Lions Club, P.O.B. 172, Nuevo, CA 92367; (714) 928-0202

1890's Days
Oakdale
Oakdale Museum; (209) 847-9229

Christmas Crafts Festival
Ojai
Teri Mettala, Ojai Art Center, 113 S. Montgomery St., Ojai, CA 93023; (805) 646-0117

Ojai Music Festival
Ojai
Sarah Digel Asst., Director, Ojai Festivals Ltd., P.O.B. 185, Ojai, CA 93024

Olivehurst Spring Festival
Olivehurst
Al Mazon; (916) 743-8784

Golf Cart Parade
Palm Desert
Palm Desert Chamber of Commerce, 72-990 Hiway 111, Palm Desert, CA 92260; (619) 346-6111; ( include 50¢ postage pls.)

Palmdale Fall Festival
Palmdale
Steve Buffalo City of Palmdale,708 E. Palmdale Blvd., Palmdale, CA 93550; (805) 273-3162

California Mid-State Fair
Paso Robles
California Mid-State Fair, P.O.B. 8 Paso Robles, CA 93447; (805) 239-0655

Paso Robles Wine Festival
Paso Robles
Paso Robles Chamber 548 Spring St., Paso Robles, CA 93446; (805) 238-0506

Pioneer Day
Paso Robles
Paso Robles Chamber, 548 Spring St., Paso Robles, CA 93446; (805) 238-0506

Beaujolais Nouveau Festival
Pebble Beach
Sandra Kasky, P.O.B. 567, Pebble Beach, CA 93953; (408) 649-2723

Butter & Egg Days Parade
Petaluma
Petaluma Main Street Assn., Alice Forsyth, 149 Kentucky St., Suite 2 Petaluma, CA 94952; (707) 762-9348

# *Festival Coordinators/Vendor Information*

Heritage Homes Christmas Parlour Tour
Petaluma
Heritage Homes Assn., Debi Riddle 416 G St., Petaluma, CA 94952; (707) 763-9219

Old Adobe Fiesta
Petaluma
Joel Swartz Old Adobe Assn., P.O.B. 631 Petaluma, CA 94953; (707) 778-0263

Petaluma Antique Street Faire
Petaluma
Pat Easley, Petaluma Antique Dealers Assn., 148 Petaluma Blvd., N Petaluma, CA 94952; (707) 763-7686

Petaluma River Festival
Petaluma
Pennylee Christensen Petaluma River Festival Assn., P.O.B. 2031, Petaluma, CA 94953

Petaluma Summermusic Festival
Petaluma
Marvin Klebe ,Cinnabar Theater, 333 Petaluma Blvd., N Petaluma, CA 94952; (707) 763-8920

Sonoma Marin Fair
Petaluma
Sonoma-Marin Fair Coordinator, P.O.B. 182, Petaluma, CA 94953; (707) 763-0931

Western Weekend & 4-H Livestock Show
Point Reyes Station
Ed Vacha, P.O.B. 305, Pt. Reyes Station, CA 94956; (415) 663-1504

Porterville Stagecoach Stampede
Porterville
Montie Montana, Jr., P.O.B. 1060, Springville, CA 93265; (209) 539-3500; Application due: 9/1/91

Shasta Dixieland Jazz Festival
Redding
Tom Riley, Shasta Dixieland Jazz Festival, P.O.B. 520, Redding, CA 96099; (916) 244-5870

Redlands Bicycle Classic
Redlands
Peter Brandt; (714) 793-3368
Desert Empire Fair
Ridgecrest
Desert Empire Fair, 520 S. Richmond Rd., Ridgecrest, CA 93555; (619) 375-8000

Desert Empire Spring Fair
Ridgecrest
Desert Empire Fair 520, S. Richmond Rd., Ridgecrest, CA 93555; (619) 375-8000

High Desert Natural Wonders Weekend
Ridgecrest
Ridgecrest Tourism Manager, 100 W. California St., Ridgecrest, CA 93555; (619) 371-3771

Maturango Junction & Chili Cook-Off
Ridgecrest
Maturango Museum of Ridgecrest, 100 E. Las Flores, Rigdecrest, CA 93555; (619) 375-6900

Western Heritage Mining Days
Ridgecrest
Ridgecrest Chamber of Commerce, P.O.B. 771, Ridgecrest, CA 93556; (619) 375-8331

Riverbank Cheese & Wine Expo
Riverbank
Wanda Haycraft, 3237 Santa Fe St., Rivervank, CA 95367; (209) 869-4541; (209) 847-7922

Spring Festival
Riverdale
Spring Festival, P.O.B. 77, Riverdale, CA 93656; (209) 867-3310

Outdoor Antiques Faire
San Anselmo
Pat Newsom Creekside Antiques, 241 Sir Frances Drake, San Anselmo, CA 94960; (415) 457-1266

A Taste of San Mateo
San Mateo
Anne LeClair Chamber of Commerce, 1730 S. El Camino Real, San Mateo, CA 94408; (415) 341-5679

Farmers Market Festival
San Rafael
Brigitte Moran/Patti Reeves, 18 Mary St., San Rafael, CA 94901; (415) 457-2266

Shakespeare Under the Stars
San Rafael
Lesley Currier Marin Shakespeare Company, 33 Meadow Dr., San Rafael, CA 94901; (415) 499-1108

Grape Bowl Festival
Sanger
Sanger Chamber of Commerce, 1348 Church St., Sanger, CA 93657

Brussels Sprout Festival
Santa Cruz
Ann Parker, Santa Cruz Beach Boardwalk, 400 Beach St., Santa Cruz, CA 95060

Calamari Festival
Santa Cruz
Tom Ellison, 1001 Center St., Santa Cruz, CA 95060; (408) 427-3554

Migration Festival
Santa Cruz
Monterey Bay Natural Historical Assn., 101 Madeline Dr., Aptos, CA 95003; (408) 423-4609

Santa Cruz County Vinter's Festival
Santa Cruz
Pamela Storrs, 303 Potrero St., Santa Cruz, CA 95060; (408) 458-5030

Shakespeare Santa Cruz
Santa Cruz
Shakespeare Santa Cruz Performing Arts Complex, Univ. Calif. Santa Cruz Santa Cruz, CA 95064

Santa Monica Pier Twilight Dance Series
Santa Monica
Elaine G. Mutchnik, 200 Santa Monica Pier, Suite A, Santa Monica, CA 90401; (213) 458-8900

# *Festival Coordinators/Vendor Information*

Health & Harmony Music & Arts Festival
Santa Rosa
Debra Guisti ,Wishing Well Productions, P.O.B. 484, Graton, CA 95444; (707) 823-4989

Sonoma County Folk Festival
Santa Rosa
Betty Nudelman, Pres. Sonoma County Folk Society, P.O.B. 1018, Windsor, CA 95492

Spirit of Christmas Crafts Faire & Celebration
Santa Rosa
Debra Guisti Wishing Well Productions, P.O.B. 484 Graton, CA 95444; (707) 823-4989

Mustard Festival
Saratoga
Barbara Jonsson Congress Springs Winery, 23600 Congress Springs Rd.,Saratoga, CA 95070

Saratoga Blossom Festival
Saratoga
Marilyn White, 20811 Canyon View Dr. ,Saratoga, CA 95070

Scotts Valley Living History Faire
Scotts Valley
Jack Boone, 552 Bean Creek Rd., Scotts Valley, CA 95067; (408) 438-1352

Sonoma Valley Wine Festival & Liberty 100K Bicycle Race
Sonoma
Cindi Williams, P.O.B. 1493, Eldridge, CA; (707) 938-6791

Art & Wine Festival
Sunnyvale
(Artists only!) California Artists, P.O.B. 1963, Burlingame, CA 94010; (415) 348-7699

Sunset Beach Art Festival
Sunset Beach
Las Damas, P.O.B. 197 Sunset Beach, CA 90742; (213) 592-1777

President's Doll Show
Tehama
Margaret C. Bauer 25101 Second St., Los Molinos, CA 96055; (916) 384-2420

Tehama County Museum Jubilee
Tehama
Margaret C. Bauer, 25101 Second St., Los Molinos, CA 96055; (916) 384-2420

Camellia Festival
Temple City
Temple City, Camellia Festival, 5827 Temple City Blvd., Temple City, CA 91780; (818) 287-9150

California Dry Bean Festival
Tracy
Tom Hawkins Chamber of Commerce, P.O.B. 891 Tracy, CA 95378; (209) 835-2131

Dairy Festival
Tulare
Libby Boghosian, Chamber of Commerce, 260 N. "L" St., Tulare, CA 93274; (209) 686-1547

Dairy & Poultry Festival
Turlock
Sherry Meyers, Chamber of Commerce, 1156 Golden State Blvd. ,Turlock, CA 95380; (209) 632-2221

Onion Festival
Vacaville
Onion Festival Coordinator, Chamber of Commerce, 400 East Monte Vista Ave., Vacaville, CA 95688

Venice Summer Arts & Crafts Festival
Venice
Marjorie Alatorre Chamber of Commerce, 13470 Washington Blvd., Suite 302-C, P.O.B. 202 Venice, CA 90291

SEER— Solar Energy Expo & Rally
Willits
Keith Rutledge SEER, 733 So. Main, Suite 204 Ukiah, CA 95490

Sonoma County Hot Air Balloon Classic
Windsor
Jerry Mead Special Event Productions, 9504 Jessica Dr., Windsor, CA 95492; (707) 838-9697

# 1991

### January

| S | M | T | W | T | F | S |
|---|---|---|---|---|---|---|
| | | 1 | 2 | 3 | 4 | 5 |
| 6 | 7 | 8 | 9 | 10 | 11 | 12 |
| 13 | 14 | 15 | 16 | 17 | 18 | 19 |
| 20 | 21 | 22 | 23 | 24 | 25 | 26 |
| 27 | 28 | 29 | 30 | 31 | | |

### February

| S | M | T | W | T | F | S |
|---|---|---|---|---|---|---|
| | | | | | 1 | 2 |
| 3 | 4 | 5 | 6 | 7 | 8 | 9 |
| 10 | 11 | 12 | 13 | 14 | 15 | 16 |
| 17 | 18 | 19 | 20 | 21 | 22 | 23 |
| 24 | 25 | 26 | 27 | 28 | | |

### March

| S | M | T | W | T | F | S |
|---|---|---|---|---|---|---|
| | | | | | 1 | 2 |
| 3 | 4 | 5 | 6 | 7 | 8 | 9 |
| 10 | 11 | 12 | 13 | 14 | 15 | 16 |
| 17 | 18 | 19 | 20 | 21 | 22 | 23 |
| 24 | 25 | 26 | 27 | 28 | 29 | 30 |
| 31 | | | | | | |

### April

| S | M | T | W | T | F | S |
|---|---|---|---|---|---|---|
| | 1 | 2 | 3 | 4 | 5 | 6 |
| 7 | 8 | 9 | 10 | 11 | 12 | 13 |
| 14 | 15 | 16 | 17 | 18 | 19 | 20 |
| 21 | 22 | 23 | 24 | 25 | 26 | 27 |
| 28 | 29 | 30 | | | | |

### May

| S | M | T | W | T | F | S |
|---|---|---|---|---|---|---|
| | | | 1 | 2 | 3 | 4 |
| 5 | 6 | 7 | 8 | 9 | 10 | 11 |
| 12 | 13 | 14 | 15 | 16 | 17 | 18 |
| 19 | 20 | 21 | 22 | 23 | 24 | 25 |
| 26 | 27 | 28 | 29 | 30 | 31 | |

### June

| S | M | T | W | T | F | S |
|---|---|---|---|---|---|---|
| | | | | | | 1 |
| 2 | 3 | 4 | 5 | 6 | 7 | 8 |
| 9 | 10 | 11 | 12 | 13 | 14 | 15 |
| 16 | 17 | 18 | 19 | 20 | 21 | 22 |
| 23 | 24 | 25 | 26 | 27 | 28 | 29 |
| 30 | | | | | | |

### July

| S | M | T | W | T | F | S |
|---|---|---|---|---|---|---|
| | 1 | 2 | 3 | 4 | 5 | 6 |
| 7 | 8 | 9 | 10 | 11 | 12 | 13 |
| 14 | 15 | 16 | 17 | 18 | 19 | 20 |
| 21 | 22 | 23 | 24 | 25 | 26 | 27 |
| 28 | 29 | 30 | 31 | | | |

### August

| S | M | T | W | T | F | S |
|---|---|---|---|---|---|---|
| | | | | 1 | 2 | 3 |
| 4 | 5 | 6 | 7 | 8 | 9 | 10 |
| 11 | 12 | 13 | 14 | 15 | 16 | 17 |
| 18 | 19 | 20 | 21 | 22 | 23 | 24 |
| 25 | 26 | 27 | 28 | 29 | 30 | 31 |

### September

| S | M | T | W | T | F | S |
|---|---|---|---|---|---|---|
| 1 | 2 | 3 | 4 | 5 | 6 | 7 |
| 8 | 9 | 10 | 11 | 12 | 13 | 14 |
| 15 | 16 | 17 | 18 | 19 | 20 | 21 |
| 22 | 23 | 24 | 25 | 26 | 27 | 28 |
| 29 | 30 | | | | | |

### October

| S | M | T | W | T | F | S |
|---|---|---|---|---|---|---|
| | | 1 | 2 | 3 | 4 | 5 |
| 6 | 7 | 8 | 9 | 10 | 11 | 12 |
| 13 | 14 | 15 | 16 | 17 | 18 | 19 |
| 20 | 21 | 22 | 23 | 24 | 25 | 26 |
| 27 | 28 | 29 | 30 | 31 | | |

### November

| S | M | T | W | T | F | S |
|---|---|---|---|---|---|---|
| | | | | | 1 | 2 |
| 3 | 4 | 5 | 6 | 7 | 8 | 9 |
| 10 | 11 | 12 | 13 | 14 | 15 | 16 |
| 17 | 18 | 19 | 20 | 21 | 22 | 23 |
| 24 | 25 | 26 | 27 | 28 | 29 | 30 |

### December

| S | M | T | W | T | F | S |
|---|---|---|---|---|---|---|
| 1 | 2 | 3 | 4 | 5 | 6 | 7 |
| 8 | 9 | 10 | 11 | 12 | 13 | 14 |
| 15 | 16 | 17 | 18 | 19 | 20 | 21 |
| 22 | 23 | 24 | 25 | 26 | 27 | 28 |
| 29 | 30 | 31 | | | | |

# 1992

**January**

| S | M | T | W | T | F | S |
|---|---|---|---|---|---|---|
| | | | 1 | 2 | 3 | 4 |
| 5 | 6 | 7 | 8 | 9 | 10 | 11 |
| 12 | 13 | 14 | 15 | 16 | 17 | 18 |
| 19 | 20 | 21 | 22 | 23 | 24 | 25 |
| 26 | 27 | 28 | 29 | 30 | 31 | |

**February**

| S | M | T | W | T | F | S |
|---|---|---|---|---|---|---|
| | | | | | | 1 |
| 2 | 3 | 4 | 5 | 6 | 7 | 8 |
| 9 | 10 | 11 | 12 | 13 | 14 | 15 |
| 16 | 17 | 18 | 19 | 20 | 21 | 22 |
| 23 | 24 | 25 | 26 | 27 | 28 | 29 |

**March**

| S | M | T | W | T | F | S |
|---|---|---|---|---|---|---|
| 1 | 2 | 3 | 4 | 5 | 6 | 7 |
| 8 | 9 | 10 | 11 | 12 | 13 | 14 |
| 15 | 16 | 17 | 18 | 19 | 20 | 21 |
| 22 | 23 | 24 | 25 | 26 | 27 | 28 |
| 29 | 30 | 31 | | | | |

**April**

| S | M | T | W | T | F | S |
|---|---|---|---|---|---|---|
| | | | 1 | 2 | 3 | 4 |
| 5 | 6 | 7 | 8 | 9 | 10 | 11 |
| 12 | 13 | 14 | 15 | 16 | 17 | 18 |
| 19 | 20 | 21 | 22 | 23 | 24 | 25 |
| 26 | 27 | 28 | 29 | 30 | | |

**May**

| S | M | T | W | T | F | S |
|---|---|---|---|---|---|---|
| | | | | | 1 | 2 |
| 3 | 4 | 5 | 6 | 7 | 8 | 9 |
| 10 | 11 | 12 | 13 | 14 | 15 | 16 |
| 17 | 18 | 19 | 20 | 21 | 22 | 23 |
| 24 | 25 | 26 | 27 | 28 | 29 | 30 |
| 31 | | | | | | |

**June**

| S | M | T | W | T | F | S |
|---|---|---|---|---|---|---|
| | 1 | 2 | 3 | 4 | 5 | 6 |
| 7 | 8 | 9 | 10 | 11 | 12 | 13 |
| 14 | 15 | 16 | 17 | 18 | 19 | 20 |
| 21 | 22 | 23 | 24 | 25 | 26 | 27 |
| 28 | 29 | 30 | | | | |

**July**

| S | M | T | W | T | F | S |
|---|---|---|---|---|---|---|
| | | | 1 | 2 | 3 | 4 |
| 5 | 6 | 7 | 8 | 9 | 10 | 11 |
| 12 | 13 | 14 | 15 | 16 | 17 | 18 |
| 19 | 20 | 21 | 22 | 23 | 24 | 25 |
| 26 | 27 | 28 | 29 | 30 | 31 | |

**August**

| S | M | T | W | T | F | S |
|---|---|---|---|---|---|---|
| | | | | | | 1 |
| 2 | 3 | 4 | 5 | 6 | 7 | 8 |
| 9 | 10 | 11 | 12 | 13 | 14 | 15 |
| 16 | 17 | 18 | 19 | 20 | 21 | 22 |
| 23 | 24 | 25 | 26 | 27 | 28 | 29 |
| 30 | 31 | | | | | |

**September**

| S | M | T | W | T | F | S |
|---|---|---|---|---|---|---|
| | | 1 | 2 | 3 | 4 | 5 |
| 6 | 7 | 8 | 9 | 10 | 11 | 12 |
| 13 | 14 | 15 | 16 | 17 | 18 | 19 |
| 20 | 21 | 22 | 23 | 24 | 25 | 26 |
| 27 | 28 | 29 | 30 | | | |

**October**

| S | M | T | W | T | F | S |
|---|---|---|---|---|---|---|
| | | | | 1 | 2 | 3 |
| 4 | 5 | 6 | 7 | 8 | 9 | 10 |
| 11 | 12 | 13 | 14 | 15 | 16 | 17 |
| 18 | 19 | 20 | 21 | 22 | 23 | 24 |
| 25 | 26 | 27 | 28 | 29 | 30 | 31 |

**November**

| S | M | T | W | T | F | S |
|---|---|---|---|---|---|---|
| 1 | 2 | 3 | 4 | 5 | 6 | 7 |
| 8 | 9 | 10 | 11 | 12 | 13 | 14 |
| 15 | 16 | 17 | 18 | 19 | 20 | 21 |
| 22 | 23 | 24 | 25 | 26 | 27 | 28 |
| 29 | 30 | | | | | |

**December**

| S | M | T | W | T | F | S |
|---|---|---|---|---|---|---|
| | | 1 | 2 | 3 | 4 | 5 |
| 6 | 7 | 8 | 9 | 10 | 11 | 12 |
| 13 | 14 | 15 | 16 | 17 | 18 | 19 |
| 20 | 21 | 22 | 23 | 24 | 25 | 26 |
| 27 | 28 | 29 | 30 | 31 | | |

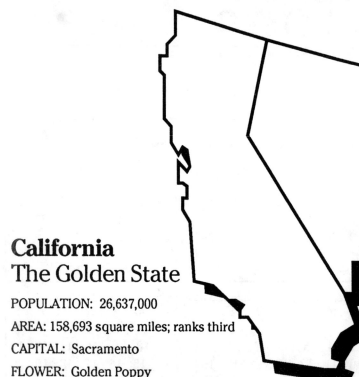

## California
### The Golden State

POPULATION: 26,637,000

AREA: 158,693 square miles; ranks third

CAPITAL: Sacramento

FLOWER: Golden Poppy

STATE TREE: California redwoods (Sequoia sempervirens & Sequoia gigantea)

STATE BIRD: California valley quail

STATE ANIMAL: California grizzley bear

STATE FISH: California golden trout

STATE COLORS: Blue and gold

STATE SONG: "I Love You, California"

MOTTO: Eureka (I Have Found It)

ENTERED UNION: September 9, 1850 (31st)

California Commission of Tourism
1121 L Street, Suite 600
Sacramento, CA 95814
(916) 322-1397

California State Park System
Dept. of Parks an Recreation
P.O.B. 942896
Sacramento, CA 94296-0001
(916) 445-6477

National Park Service Information
Fort Mason, Bldg. 201
Bay and Franklin Streets
San Francisco, CA 94123
(415) 556-0560

Fishing and Hunting Regulations
Dept. of Fish and Gme
1416 9th St.
Sacramento, CA 95814
(916) 445-3531

## Nevada
### The Silver State

POPULATION: 910,800

AREA: 109,540; ranks seventh

CAPITAL: Carson City

FLOWER: Sagebrush

STATE TREE: Single-leaf pinon and Bristle-cone Pine

STATE BIRD: Mountain bluebird

STATE ANIMAL: Desert bighorn sheep

STATE COLORS: Silver and blue

STATE SONG: "Home Means Nevada"

MOTTO: All For Our Country

ENTERED UNION: Oct. 31, 1864 (36th)

Nevada Commission of Tourism
5151 S. Carson St.
Carson City, NV 89710
(702) 687-4322

Nevada Division of State Parks
Capitol Complex
Carson City, NV 89710
(7102) 885-4384

National Forest Information
Intermountain Region
324 25th St.
Ogden, UT 84401
(801) 625-5182

Fishing and Hunting Regulations
Nevada Dept. of Wildlife
State Headquarters
1100 Valley Rd.
Reno, NV 89512
(702) 789-0500

# ORDER FORM

***FESTIVAL HOPPER*** ______________________________

***ADDRESS*** ______________________________

***CITY, STATE, ZIP*** ____________________ ***PHONE*** __________

**QUANITY** **PRICE**

_____ The Festival Hopper's Guide to California & Nevada $12.95 _____

_____ The Festival Hopper's Guide to the Great Northwest $11.95 _____
(Alaska, Idaho, Montana, Oregon, & Washington)

_____ The Festival Hopper's Guide to the Rocky West $11.95 _____
(Arizona, Colorado, New Mexico, Utah, and Wyoming)

Shipping charges: $1.75 for first book and
.75¢ for each additional book

SHIPPING CHARGES: _____

Make checks payable to Creative Chaos. Or use your VISA
or MASTERCARD:

***TOTAL:*** _____

Card #____________________ Exp. ______

Signature____________________

**California residents, please add 7% sales tax for each book**

Creative Chaos
3108 Acorn Ct.
San Jose, CA 95117
(408) 249-0657


# ORDER FORM

***FESTIVAL HOPPER*** ______________________________

***ADDRESS*** ______________________________

***CITY, STATE, ZIP*** ____________________ ***PHONE*** __________

**QUANITY** **PRICE**

_____ The Festival Hopper's Guide to California & Nevada $12.95 _____

_____ The Festival Hopper's Guide to the Great Northwest $11.95 _____
(Alaska, Idaho, Montana, Oregon, & Washington)

_____ The Festival Hopper's Guide to the Rocky West $11.95 _____
(Arizona, Colorado, New Mexico, Utah, and Wyoming)

Shipping charges: $1.75 for first book and
.75¢ for each additional book

SHIPPING CHARGES: _____

Make checks payable to Creative Chaos. Or use your VISA
or MASTERCARD:

***TOTAL:*** _____

Card #____________________ Exp. ______

Signature____________________

**California residents, please add 7% sales tax for each book**

Creative Chaos
3108 Acorn Ct.
San Jose, CA 95117
(408) 249-0657

How many festivals did you attend in 1990? in 1991?

Has this book been helpful? If so, what specifically?

Is there other stuff you'd like to see in the book—information that we aren't currently providing? Have we missed any of your favorite festivals? *All comments are welcomed!*

CA & NV

How many festivals did you attend in 1990? in 1991?

Has this book been helpful? If so, what specifically?

Is there other stuff you'd like to see in the book—information that we aren't currently providing? Have we missed any of your favorite festivals? *All comments are welcomed!*

CA & NV